WRITINGS OF
HUGH SWINTON LEGARÉ

Volume II

WRITINGS OF
HUGH SWINTON LEGARÉ

Volume II

DA CAPO PRESS · NEW YORK · 1970

A Da Capo Press Reprint Edition

This Da Capo Press edition of the
Writings of Hugh Swinton Legaré
is an unabridged republication of the first edition
published in Charleston, South Carolina, in 1846.

Library of Congress Catalog Card Number 70-107413

SBN 306-71885-5

Published by Da Capo Press
A Division of Plenum Publishing Corporation
227 West 17th Street, New York, N. Y. 10011
All Rights Reserved

Manufactured in the United States of America

WRITINGS OF
HUGH SWINTON LEGARÉ

Volume II

WRITINGS

OF

HUGH SWINTON LEGARÉ,

LATE ATTORNEY GENERAL

AND ACTING SECRETARY OF STATE OF THE UNITED STATES :

CONSISTING OF

A DIARY OF BRUSSELS, AND JOURNAL OF THE RHINE;

EXTRACTS FROM HIS

PRIVATE AND DIPLOMATIC CORRESPONDENCE;

ORATIONS AND SPEECHES;

AND CONTRIBUTIONS TO THE

NEW-YORK AND SOUTHERN REVIEWS.

PREFACED BY A

MEMOIR OF HIS LIFE.

EMBELLISHED WITH A PORTRAIT.

———

EDITED BY HIS SISTER.

———

IN TWO VOLUMES.
VOL. II.

———

CHARLESTON, S. C.:
BURGES & JAMES, 6 BROAD-STREET.
PHILADELPHIA: THOMAS, COWPERTHWAIT & CO.
NEW-YORK: D. APPLETON & CO.
BOSTON: JAMES MUNROE & CO.
1845.

CHARLESTON:
BURGES AND JAMES, PRINTERS,
6 BROAD-STREET.

TABLE OF CONTENTS.

VOLUME II.

CONTRIBUTIONS TO SOUTHERN REVIEW.

WRITINGS

OF

HUGH SWINTON LEGARÉ.

CLASSICAL LEARNING.*

1. An Address on the Character and Objects of Science, and especially on the influence of the Reformation on the Science and Literature, past, present and future, of Protestant Nations; delivered in the First Presbyterian Church, on Wednesday, the 9th of May, being the Anniversary of the Literary and Philosophical Society of South-Carolina. By THOMAS S. GRIMKE. 8vo. *Charleston. Miller.* 1827.

2. An Address, delivered before the South-Carolina Society, on the occasion of opening their Male Academy, on the 2d July, 1827. By WM. GEO. READ, Principal of the same. 8vo. *Charleston. Miller.* 1827.

3. Inaugural Discourse, delivered in Trinity Church, Geneva, New-York, August 1st, 1827. By the Rev. JASPER ADAMS, President of Geneva College. *Geneva.* 1827.

WE Americans take nothing for granted—except, indeed, as it would appear from the tone of some recent publications—the immeasurable superiority of those who have lived to see this "Age of Reason," over all that have not been so fortunate. With this exception, however, (since we must needs consider it as such,) all postulates are rigorously excluded from our most approved systems of logic—and when, in the fulness of time, those mathematicians shall rise up amongst us, who, according to a cheering prophecy of Mr. Grimké, are to throw into the shade, as intellectual beings, the Newtons and the La Places, no less than the

---

* [The reprint of this and the following articles, from the "Southern Review," is made from a bound copy of that work, which belonged to Mr. Legaré, and which was revised by him, as indicated by frequent notes, penned or pencilled by him, on the margin or at the foot of the several numbers. We shall indi-

Euclids and the Apollonius,' we shall scarcely be satisfied with their improvements in geometry, unless they begin by demonstrating its axioms.* We take up all questions *de novo*, and treat every subject of general speculation and philosophy, no matter how frequently and fully discussed, or how solemnly decided elsewhere, as what is called at the bar *res integra*, that is to say, as fair game for criticism and controversy. Besides this, we may be permitted to observe, while we are upon this topic, that the pleasant exhortation, *mon ami, commence par le commencement*, seems to have been made expressly for our use. We are for coming out on all occasions, not only with the truth, but the whole truth, and seem utterly unable to comprehend the reason of that peevish rule,

> Nec reditum Diomedis ab interitu Meleagri,
> Nec gemino bellum Trojanum orditur ab ovo.

For instance, it would not surprise us much if a member of Congress from one of the more enlightened, because less *ancient* and prejudiced States, should introduce a speech upon the Colonial Trade by a "brief" account of Columbus and his discoveries, as it is every day's experience to see even our leading politicians lay hold of the most casual and ordinary questions of commerce and finance, to spout whole volumes of the merest rudiments and generalities of political economy. There are some people, we dare say, in this censorious world, who would be apt to consider all this as *outrageously* rational ; but, perhaps, after all, it will not do in so new a country to adopt old ideas and assume established truths—and no one, we humbly conceive, can address the American public with effect, who is not himself patient enough to begin at the very beginning, and to accommodate his mode of discussion to this decided national predilection for elementary inquiry, and regular and exact demonstration according to the utmost rigour of the logical forms.

We have thought it advisable to premise thus much, at the very outset of our critical labors, by way of preventive apology,

---

cate these marginal notes by enclosing them in brackets. On a blank leaf of the first volume are the following remarks and quotations in pencil :

["As this volume has many typographical errors, the reader must let *Martial* speak for us all:

> ' Si qua videbuntur chartis tibi, lector, in istis,
> Sive obscura nimis, sive latina parum ;
> Non meus est error ; nocuit librarius illis,
> Dum properat versus annumerare tibi.'—*l.* 2. *Epig.* 8.

But if *we* complain, what must it have been before printing was invented. 'De latinis' vero, says Cicero, 'quo me vertam, nescio; ita mendose et scribuntur et veneunt.' Epist. ad Quintum Frat. l. 3. b. Epist. 5. Cf. Aul. Gell. l. 11. c. 14., et passim. Strabo. l. 13. A. Gell. l. 20. c. 6."]

[* * Nondum tritis nostrorum hominum auribus nec eruditâ civitate tolerabiles (loci inanes). Cic. de Orat.]

so to speak, for the manner in which we shall find ourselves constrained to examine many matters that are considered in other countries as quite settled. For instance, a formal discussion at this time of day, of the comparative merits of the ancients and moderns, and the advantages of a classical education, would be set down in England by the side of that notable argument to prove, that a general can do nothing without troops, of which Cicero,* if we mistake not, has somewhere made such honorable mention. But what might there very properly be rejected as supererogation, or even quizzed as downright *twaddling*, (to borrow a phrase from an English magazine) may be imperiously called for by the state of public opinion on this side of the Atlantic. The Edinburgh Review, in an able and elaborate article on Cobbett's writings, despatched *his* opinions upon the subject now before us in a summary and sweeping denunciation, as "his trash about the learned languages." But what shall we say, when in the midst of a society, once distinguished above all others in this country by these very attainments,† a gentleman having so many and such high claims to our respect, as Mr. Grimké, declares it to be his solemn conviction—and that too, founded, as he assures us, upon the fullest and fairest experiment—that they are absolutely good for nothing. Nor does that gentleman stand alone. We have frequently heard the same opinions expressed by persons of scarcely less authority and influence in the southern states, to say nothing of occasional essays in the newspapers and periodicals, and discourses before the philosophical and literary societies of other cities. It is quite impossible, therefore, we apprehend, however strongly inclined we might be to do

---

* [II. Off. 5. Panætius, of whom Cicero says, "utitur, in re non dubia, testibus non necessariis."]

† Before and just after the Revolution, many, perhaps it would be more accurate to say most, of our youth of opulent families, were educated at English schools and universities. There can be no doubt their attainments in polite literature were very far superior to those of their contemporaries at the north, and the standard of scholarship, in Charleston was, consequently, much higher than in any other city on the continent. We have still amongst us a venerable relic of that cultivated and heroic age, whom we may single out without an invidious distinction, and to whom we gladly avail ourselves of this opportunity to offer a tribute justly due to such a union, in one accomplished character, of the patriot, the gentleman, and the scholar—of the loftiest virtue, exercised in all the important offices and trying conflicts of life, with whatever is most amiable and winning in social habitudes, in polished manners and elegant taste. To add that he is now crowning the honors of his useful and blameless life, with a blessed and venerated old age, is only to say, that he has received the sure reward *purè et eleganter actæ ætatis.* But there is something melancholy in the reflection, that the race of such men is passing away, and that our youth are now taught to form themselves upon other models. These improvements, with so many more, are beginning to spring up and blossom with great freshness and luxuriance about the favoured city of Boston—our Western Florence, in which industry has been the willing tributary of letters and the arts, and which is, throughout all its institutions, its character and its pursuits, one great monument of what commerce has done to civilize and adorn life.

so, to consider the instance before us as a mere *sporadic* case, deserving, indeed, on account of its peculiarly aggravated symptoms, to be remarked and recorded as a striking phenomenon in its kind, but not calculated to excite any alarm from its supposed connexion with the state of the atmosphere, or its probable effects upon the general health of the vicinage. We do believe, on the contrary, that this grievous malady is rapidly becoming epidemical, and that it behoves all, who, with us, think it a matter of serious public concernment, that its progress should be arrested, to apply the most efficacious remedies, and adopt all necessary precautions with the least possible delay.

As our observations will be chiefly confined to such parts only of the three discourses named at the head of this article, as relate to the study of the classics, it will, of course, be unnecessary to enter into any thing like a detailed analysis of them. We will briefly state, that the first in the order of time was Mr. Grimké's, which was delivered at the last anniversary of the Literary and Philosophical Society of this city ; and that its principal object seems to be, to make out, by a comprehensive survey of the history of the human mind, the two following propositions :— First, "that more has been done in three centuries by the Protestants, in the profound and comprehensive, the exact, rational and liberal development, culture and application of every valuable department of knowledge, both theoretical and practical, than has been done by all the rest of the world, both ancient and modern, since the days of Lycurgus," (page 50) ; and, secondly, "that in every department of knowledge, whether theoretical or practical, where thinking and reasoning are the means and the criterion of excellence, our country must, if there be truth and power in the principles of the Reformation, (and that there is, no man entertains so little doubt as Mr. Grimké) surpass every people that ever existed," (page 65). To establish and illustrate these propositions, our author has certainly spared no pains. Beginning at a period not more recent than the creation itself, he pries into the secret recesses of the garden of Eden, and speculates about the branches of science, with which it were most reasonable to suppose that its happy inmates were particularly conversant. He has not, therefore, gone quite so far as the Rabbins, who ascribe to the first man the perfection of all knowledge and wisdom; and among whom, "as learned as Adam," is a proverbial saying. We will just remark in passing, that his notions of these primitive and paradisiacal accomplishments reminded us, a good deal, of a grave disquisition in Dante's *Tractate de Vulgari Eloquio ;* in which the Father of modern poetry has endeavoured to shew, that Adam spoke, or must have spoken, or should have spoken before Eve—that his first word was Eli or Eloi—and his mother tongue (if it is not a catachresis to call it so) the Hebrew. From this remote period Mr. Grimké rapidly descends to the æra of the Reformation, distinguishing the intermediate space of about 5523 years (to imitate his own precision) by such epochs as the building of the Tower of Babel and its disastrous results—a gigantic enterprise, he observes, "to be undertaken by the new world when only 115 years old"—the call of Abraham, the exodus of the Jews, the age of Thales, &c. Looking back from the last mentioned æra to take a survey of what the human race had done to better its condition, or to elevate its character, Mr. Grimké affirms that "the moral improvement of man, and the cultivation of those sciences, which relate to his political and moral welfare, were totally neglected ;" and adds, with great emphasis, "THE PEOPLE were as yet unnoticed and unknown in the history of science." We call the particular attention of our readers to these passages, and especially to the last, because we shall have occasion, in the sequel, to expose what appears to us, to be a singular confusion of ideas that runs through them all ; and, indeed, through the whole discourse from which they are extracted.

But it is upon the second proposition that our author enlarges with the greatest fondness and triumph. He is evidently one of those that indulge in the pleasing day-dreams of perfectibility. He seems persuaded that the world, or at least this part of it, is to end, as other parts of it are fabled to have begun, with a race of (intellectual) Titans. In his visions of the future glories of his country, his imagination is wrought up to the highest pitch of rapture, and he pours out prediction after prediction, with all a patriot's enthusiasm and a prophet's fire. "I fear not," he says, "the great names of Archimides, Aristotle and Plato, of Demosthenes and Cicero, of Tacitus and Thucydides. I *know* that we must excel them. I fear not the greater names of Bacon and Newton, of Locke, Butler, Hume and Robertson, Chatham, Burke and Pitt. I *know* that we shall surpass *them* also." (p. 66.) These immortal men, it seems, did but lay the foundations upon which *we* shall build up far more lofty and enduring monuments of genius and wisdom;—they were only allowed to point out the career which is to be run by *us*, and to enjoy a faint antepast and distant prospect of that glorious perfection, with which the efforts and aspirations of the human mind are destined to be crowned in this new land of promise. "Even in this autumnal age of the world (we continue to quote our author's words) at the going down of the sun, a nation has arisen, European in language and descent, which has laid the foundations of literature broader and deeper than ever nation did before,—in the nature of man, in the character of universal society, in the principles of social order, in popular rights and popular government, in the welfare and education of the people." Now we do not deny that all this is exceedingly brilliant and encouraging, and that it is impossible to read such passages as these (and they are a fair specimen of the spirit in which the whole discourse is written) without conceiving the highest esteem for the character of the author, and even kindling, in some measure with a zeal, apparently so cordial, in the holiest of all causes, that, namely, of the moral and intellectual improvement of mankind. But it is our very painful and prosaic duty to request Mr. Grimké, in his own language, "to curb this patriot feeling which hurries him on from flight to flight," and return for a few moments, to what in this aerial excursion he has more than once lost sight of,—the true state of the question between himself and the venerable names of antiquity. We shall resume the subject as soon as we shall have paid our respects to Mr. Read and Mr. Adams.

The former of these gentlemen, upon being inducted into the office which he now so honorably fills, of principal of the South-Carolina Academy, was requested by the committee of trustees or managers, to deliver a discourse explanatory of their views and anticipations, in making the changes that have been recently introduced into that important foundation. In performing this task, he very naturally adverted to the opinions of Mr. Grimké, which had been just before published, and in his examination of them, though very little time was allowed him for preparation, acquitted himself to the entire satisfaction of a most numerous and respectable auditory. The style of this address, although occasionally too florid and ambitious, is in general, however, very good. We were particularly pleased with those idiomatic turns of expression with which it abounds, and a certain air of colloquial ease and freedom so rare in our American writing, and so essential to all true grace and elegance in composition. But we were still more pleased with Mr. Read's style of thinking. This brief and hasty production shews him to be deeply imbued with an enlightened spirit of improvement, and to combine, in rather an uncommon degree, for so young a man, the refined taste of a scholar, with more enlarged and philosophical views, than have always directed the studies of philologists and grammarians. We have very little doubt about the success of the experiment, of which the results depend so much upon his zeal and ability; and we need scarcely add with what heartfelt satisfaction we anticipate a complete revolution, or at least a visible and decided improvement, in our hitherto defective system of elementary education. We would not be understood as denying all merit to the primary schools established in this city within a few years past, some of which, we are well aware, deserve the thanks of the community for the progress they have already made in the great work of reformation.* But much—very much remains yet to be

* It is nothing but justice to state that these improvements received their first impulse from the Rt. Rev. Bishop England.

done before the system will be good for any thing, and the establishment of a rival institution of such promise as the Academy of the South-Carolina Society, under the conduct of a gentleman so zealous and accomplished as Mr. Read, can scarcely fail to inspire a new ardor, and lead to more vigorous and persevering efforts than have hitherto been made to perfect those improvements, and to secure the benefits of them to a future generation.

And, here, we will take the liberty of addressing ourselves more particularly to a class of men who occupy amongst us a post, which is, in our opinion, beyond all comparison or controversy, the most important of any in the whole circle of social avocations, especially in a country where the national character is, in a great measure, yet to be formed. It is vain to talk of having good schools until we get truly learned teachers, or of becoming a literary and refined *people*, until the education of youth shall be committed to accomplished and elegant, and we will add, enthusiastic scholars. From time to time, indeed, a few of our young men, by visiting foreign institutions at a very great expense, or by devoting themselves to these studies with a zealous and determined assiduity, scarcely to be expected at that early age, and by keeping out of the arena of professional or political ambition longer than is usual, or than may, perhaps, be quite expedient, will, probably, attain to a high degree of excellence in this kind. But such examples make no impression whatever upon the great mass of society, at least they produce no useful or meliorating effects. "They shed," to borrow a fine thought of Mr. Grimké's, "their unheeded beams on the moral desert around, and remind us of scattered stars, diffusing unnatural light amidst the gloom of an eclipse." Besides, the young scholar, after all his labor and vigils, may, perchance, find himself in any thing but an enviable situation, and learn by his own painful—happy, if not worse than painful!—experience, the wisdom of that profound sentence of Tacitus, *ignotæ* (Parthis) *virtutes, nova vitia.** It is, indeed, the unfortunate results which occasionally take place in isolated instances of this kind, that have given most colour to the speculations of those innovators in literature and education amongst us, who are urging us to forsake the fountains of living waters, and to hew out for ourselves, after some rude and uncouth model in their great patent-office of untried projects and infallible quackery, broken cisterns that will hold no water. But where are we to find these erudite and accomplished teachers? Are we to fold our arms in indolent and supine imbecility, until "the march of mind" shall bring about these changes in due season; or shall we send a

*The scholar will be reminded of poor Ovid's lamentation—
Barbarus hic ego sum quia non intelligor ullis,
Et rident stolidi verba latina Getæ.

solemn embassy across the Atlantic, to tempt by offers of extravagant emolument and honor, a small colony of adventurous
scholars to come over and propagate literature in these parts?
We answer, no such thing.   We have the means of improvement within ourselves.   Let our young schoolmasters begin by
teaching themselves profoundly, thoroughly—as it is undoubtedly in their power to do.   There is no earthly reason, except a
most inglorious, and to us unaccountable, apathy and sloth, why
our primary schools should not become, in the course of a few
years, certainly in less than a generation, quite equal, for all
practical purposes, to any in the world.   We know that there
are those who will set this down for a paradox, and a very extravagant one.   There are some scholars, especially the English,
and those bred at English schools, who lay infinite stress upon
the advantage of having what is called a proper foundation laid
in the regular discipline of the boy and the youth, without
which, they conceive it to be quite impossible, even for the most
shining parts, aided by the greatest assiduity and perseverance,
to attain to anything like refined and perfect scholarship.   All
that is meant by this, we presume, is, that bearded men are not,
in general, likely to acquire any great proficiency in capping and
making nonsense verses, or to become so deeply versed in the
endless varieties of the Trochaic, and Choriambic, and Antispas-
tic, and Dactylic metres of the Greek tragedies, as Porson or
Burney.*   This may or may not be so for aught that concerns
the present inquiry ; but if it is pretended that such refinements
are *essentials* of a scholarship, profitable both for use and for ornament, (the scholarship, for instance, of Gibbon and Burke)
we take leave to say, that we consider such notions as rank pedantry.   We are far from denying that prosody ought to be cultivated, and cultivated with all possible care and assiduity, for
no species of illiteracy is at once so obtrusive and so disagreeable as a vicious pronunciation ; we only maintain that that exquisite degree of proficiency in it, which is not attainable by the
enlightened studies and persevering industry of manhood, must
be set down to the account of what—

> Is vanity or dress,
> Or learning's luxury or idleness.

So it is next to impossible for an Englishman or American,

---

*Perhaps nothing more is meant than the repetition of certain "old saws"—e. g.,
the following from Quinctilian, (l. i. c. 12) which are full of the good sense for
which he is remarkable, though they seem to be pushed too far.   Magis scias si
quem jam robustum instituere literis cœperis, non sine causâ dici, παιδομαϑεῖς
eos qui in suâ quidque arte optime faciant.   Et patientior est laboris natura pueris
quàm juvenibus.   ****** Abest illis (pueris) laboris judicium.—*Ibid.*

Sed ne temporis quidem unquam plus erit : quia his ætatibus omnis in audiendo
profectus est.   Cum ad stylum secedet, cum generabit ipse aliquid atque componet,
tum inchoare hæc studia, vel non vacabit, vel non libebit.—*Ibid.*

after a certain age, to learn to speak French with a perfectly pure accent, yet will it be pretended that he may not be critically versed in its literature, and derive from his knowledge of it all the advantage which one can promise himself, as a mere *scholar*, from a foreign tongue? Nay, how few, even of those who write their own language with the greatest accuracy and elegance, have pushed their researches into the mere minutiæ and curiosities of its philology as far as many great critics have gone into those of the Latin and Greek.

Admitting, however, as we readily do, that it is a great advantage, inasmuch as it saves a world of pains at a period of life when time becomes more precious, to have been regularly bred under accomplished teachers; still we repeat, that this advantage is prodigiously overrated when it is considered as an indispensable condition of excellence. As to the doctrine of those who think that there is something magical in the very name of Eton or Westminster, who regard the learned languages as a sort of Mysteries into which an aspirant can be initiated no where else but in the sacred temple, and by none but hierophants of a privileged race, we need scarcely say, that no superstition was ever more extravagant. Latin and Greek are learned just as all other languages are, by long practice and critical observation in reading, writing and speaking them, and by these alone. We incline to the opinion, indeed, that a self-taught student would, in these days, be more sure of acquiring a profound and exact knowledge of them than of the modern tongues; such are the facilities that are afforded by the best grammars, dictionaries, thesaurus', gradus', clavis', &c. Add to this, what is still more important than all, the excellent editions that have been published of the classical authors, with references and annotations adapted to every variety of capacity and of proficiency in this branch of knowledge, and affording the most satisfactory explanation of every difficulty that can possibly present itself to a scholar in the progress of his inquiries, so as very nearly to supersede the necessity of a *viva voce* instruction. Considering these things, it becomes, we confess, altogether inconceivable to us, how so many schools should have existed for the last half century, in the more populous parts of the United States, without, long ere this, filling the country with a race of accomplished scholars, not only sufficient to supply the places of the instructors and the ranks of the learned professions, but to diffuse an elegant taste, and the love of letters and of liberal pursuits throughout all classes of the community. Let any one who possesses a competent knowledge of the Latin grammar (and the same thing may be said of Greek, *mutatis mutandis*) and who has read the authors commonly taught at our academies, as imperfectly as they are commonly taught there, sit down with a determination to go through Livy's History, in one of the best editions, (Crevier's for instance) twice, faithfully and laboriously, referring to the notes for an explanation of whatever might be obscure in the text, and reserving for future investigation and comparison those passages which he is unable immediately to understand, and we undertake to say, that by the time he shall have accomplished his task, all the difficulties that embarrassed and discouraged his early progress will have insensibly vanished from before him. Let him then proceed to read in the same manner all the writings of Cicero, but especially the Epistles, the Rhetorical works, and the more familiar treatises on philosophical subjects, devoting an hour every day to the drudgery of double translation, and he will find, when he comes to extend his studies to other authors—Tacitus, Sallust, the Plinies, &c. that those passages which are obscure to him will generally prove to have been the subject of dispute, even among veteran philologists. We are aware that this course requires great resolution and perseverance. No one, who has not experienced them himself, can have any adequate idea of the difficulties and discouragements that crowd about the threshold of these unaided studies. But labor is the price of all excellence,* and it is fit that it should be so. It is by this discipline, and by this alone, that a thorough knowledge of any language, ancient or modern, or indeed of any thing else, can be acquired. Hac arte Pollux et vagus Hercules, &c. It was by such means that some of the most learned men of past times, Erasmus and Cujas for instance, self-taught scholars—the former in an age comparatively barbarous, the latter without the smallest assistance from any teacher—raised themselves to such a height of reputation, not only in divinity or the civil law, or in profound erudition generally, but also in the humbler capacity of linguists and philologers. It is vain to say that these are rare instances, and that it is unphilosophical to reason from exceptions. We deny the fact. The literary history of the last three centuries, and indeed of all ages, abounds with such examples, and even if it did not, no young man of a generous and aspiring mind ought to deem any thing impossible that has ever been accomplished by mortal man, especially if it be what is obviously due, not to the supposed inspirations of genius, but to mere dint of toil and perseverance.†

---

*————————πῶν πόνων,
Πωλοῦσιν ἡμιν πάντα τ' ἀγαθὰ θεοί.
Epicharmus apud Xenophon: Memorab. l. ii. c. 1

† The text is paraphrase of a favorite maxim from Macchiavelli. Non sia pertanto nessuno che si sbigotisca di non potere conseguire quello che é stato conseguito da altri; perché gli uomini (come nella prefazione nostra si disse) nacquero vissero e morirono sempre con un medisimo ordine.—*Discorsi.*

We are not satisfied, therefore, with the manner in which Mr. Read accounts for the miserable defectiveness of our school-education. It is not sufficient to say, that "the task of element-ary instruction, offering but limited returns of dignity or emolu-ment, has been suffered to devolve from its legitimate function-aries on the adventurers of learning; who, feeling the sting of genius, have wrested some slender opportunities from niggard fortune, and seek an honorable barter of their limited acquire-ments for present support while pressing on in the paths of pro-fessional ambition." It is, indeed, a melancholy truth, that the education of our southern youth has been of late too often com-mitted to these great men *in transitu;* but making all reason-able allowances for such cases, it still remains to be explained, how it has happened that so many professors of Greek and Latin in our numerous American colleges, in possession of comfort-able livings, and discharged from all other duties and engage-ments, have dozed over their sealed volumes in such stupid un-aspiring ignorance—how so many shoolmasters, in New-Eng-land, for instance, looking to nothing beyond success as teachers in this elementary department, have been satisfied to "barter" (how "honorably" is none of our concern) for competent fees and a precious period of their pupils' lives, such a wretched, vulgar, and worthless smattering of classical literature—how *all,* emphatically *all,* the attainments of a young man *liberally,* that is, expensively educated from his seventh or eighth to his fourteenth or fifteenth year, have been, with very few, if any, exceptions, limited to what is ironically called translating the ancient authors: in other words, rendering into uncouth or non-sensical English, the most exquisite beauties of poetry and elo-quence, without so much as the remotest idea, of what it is that has recommended to the admiration of all ages, those "Del-phic lines," whose unspeakable harmony he utterly destroys by a barbarous pronunciation*—above all, how the most frugal, money-making, managing, practical people in the world, have quietly sat down under such enormous abuses, and borne, for no solitary good purpose that we are able to discover, a bur-then of taxation that could only have been supportable because it was self imposed.† Now we freely admit that Mr. Grimké

* We mean, of course, the attainments for which he is indebted to the school-master and the school. In addition to the New-England authorities, cited in the next note, we beg leave to refer our readers to the 7th No. of the (Boston) Jour-nal of Education, p. 409, where the writer, after presenting a view of the exercises exacted at the public examinations of the English universities, adds, "at the period when we were at *our own* Cambridge, the very idea of performing such exercises, would have *petrified* both student and preceptor." As well it might! We add for ourselves, "*experto crede Ruperto.*"

† This last notion may be found in an article of Blackwood's Magazine for Feb-ruary or March, 1819, which was written by a New-England scholar, a gentleman who is now endeavoring to improve the wretched system which he then censured

is in the right, if he means, as we are more than half inclined
to suspect that he does, *this* system of classical studies, and
we scruple not to say, that we should most heartily co-operate
with him in his efforts to explode it as soon as possible, as a
criminal waste of a period of life, every moment of which ought
to be sacred to improvement, if we did not think that we could
even now descry above the verge of our horizon, the first flush
of a kindling zeal and the dawn of a brighter hope.

The extent of our subject, and the limits within which we are
constrained to circumscribe the present discussion of it, make it
impossible for us to say more of the very sensible and well written discourse of our late fellow-townsman, Mr. Adams, than that
it exhibits an outline of the course of studies to be pursued at
Geneva college, in the state of New-York, together with a concise and comprehensive sketch of the recent improvements and
present state of mathematical and physical science. As his
opinions upon the subjects of classical learning agree with our
own, we hope he will be successful at once in making proselytes
to his theory, (what will be still better) living examples of
its beneficial effects. One circumstance we cannot help remarking by the way, and that is, the great demand which from
the case of this gentleman and from some others of a similar kind,
we infer to exist in all parts of the United States, for the talents
of able instuctors of youth—to which, we may add, the evidence
which such instances afford, amidst all the glaring imperfections
of our system of elementary education, that the love—or as it
would be more forcibly as well as accurately expressed in
French, the *besoin*—of knowledge, is an essential element of the
national character, and one of the "canon laws of our foundation." Mr. Adams was called from the Charleston college, of
which he was the principal, to preside over an institution of a
similar, or even a still more important character, in the flourishing town of Geneva—a town, which is itself but a creation of
yesterday, and in a country which has burst upon our sight,
with all its rapidly increasing prosperity, and population, and
improvements, with an unparalleled and almost magical sud-
denness.

It is now time to proceed to the subject of our controversy
with Mr. Grimké. Two distinct questions are involved in it:—
first what are the merits of the Greek and Roman classics, considered merely as works of art, and as models for imitation; and,
secondly, how far it is worth while, under existing circumstances, to study them, and more especially, to make them an

---

with such just severity. As exception may be taken in *certain quarters* to what we
have said of New-England schoolmasters, whom we mention because they might be
expected to be the best, we refer, further, to Professor Ticknor, who will be allowed
we presume, to speak *en connaissance de cause*. *See his Remarks, &c.*, 1825.

essential part of a regular academic education. It is obviously impossible to do any thing like justice to the former question (or indeed to either of them) in a single dissertation, that shall not run out to the size of a bulky volume. We purpose, accordingly, to illustrate and enforce our opinion upon the various subjects which it embraces, in a series of articles that shall appear, as occasion serves, in our future numbers. In the present instance, we shall confine ourselves, principally, to the business of refutation. We shall accept the issues which Mr. Grimké and other writers have recently tendered to the advocates of classical literature, and endeavor to shew that if this good cause *is* (quod Deus avertat omen) destined to be defeated before the enlightened tribunal of public opinion in this country, it will, at least, not be owing to the unanswerable force of these *new* arguments. We will fearlessly say of it, what has been said (if we recollect right) of the fifth book of Euclid's Elements, that "it has weathered the vicissitudes of opinion for 2000 years, and notwithstanding this new attack, we still conclude, as Barrow did more than one hundred years ago, *nisi machinis validioribus impulsa, in æternum durabit*".*

But we must take the liberty of entering a preliminary *caveat* against any use, on the part of Mr. Grimké, of the authority of great names. As we are well aware that we shall have to do, through him, with a sort of illuminati, that consider all those by whose opinions we should, otherwise, be most desirous of fortifying our own, as inadmissible, because interested witnesses; and moreover, as men grievously abused by the delusions of a superstition altogether unworthy of this enlightened and philosophic age; we have no objection to dispense, on this occasion, with the services of our natural auxiliaries, but we must insist, at least, upon meeting our adversaries upon equal terms. In the forum of letters, whatever it may be in a court of law, we see no reason why ignorance should not be just as fatal to the competency of evidence, to say the least of it, as a very slight or rather perfectly ideal interest; and if we are fastidious enough to except to the only persons that know any thing about the matter, under the idea that their knowledge itself infers some bias, we fear we shall scarcely be consistent with ourselves, unless we exclude those also who are, most probably, so little acquainted with the subject of the controversy that their testimony must necessarily be made up of vague hearsay and wild conjecture. We do, therefore, in the first place, solemnly protest against all and singular, the sentences in a certain note of Mr. Grimké's, begining with "Dr. Dwight *was wont* to say;" or, "the author of the British spy hath said"; or, even, the younger Lord Lyttle-

* Edinburgh Review.

ton (in Letters, by the bye, which he did not write) has not hesitated to say," &c. Dr. Timothy Dwight we have always been taught to consider as a very able man, *especially* in theology—and we have not the least doubt, that the present Attorney General of the United States is quite a formidable antagonist at the bar. But, really, when we are sitting in judgment in the exercise of a self-constituted jurisdiction, upon Homer and Sopocles, or Demosthenes and Tully, it is too much to expect that we should receive exactly, as the responses of an oracle, the *dicta* of such a poet as the author of Greenfield Hill, or of such a writer as the biographer of Patrick Henry. We beg to be understood; we mean no personal disrespect to Mr. Wirt, nor would we cast a slur upon the memory of so respectable a person as Dr. Dwight, but we humbly conceive, that in giving up the authority of all great men, without an exception, that Europe has ever produced, we have a right to expect that we shall not be required to defer very implicitly to the opinion of an individual or two of a new school, or even of ten times as many scores of individuals who—whatever may be their pretensions or their merits in other respects—cannot reasonably bo supposed to be the best of all possible judges in such a case. For what W. Schlegel, whom Mr. Grimké has, to our infinite surprise, attempted to press into the service of his anti-classical "root and branch" reformation, says of the antique in sculpture, is true also of the remains of Greek eloquence and poetry; viz.—that there is but one voice throughout the whole of civilized Europe respecting its matchless excellence; and if ever it was called in question, it was when the taste of the moderns was fallen into a miserable state of mannerism and depravity. At least, if the merits of the latter have not been so universally and uniformly placed above all competition as those of the great masters in the plastic art, who have not even had a follower worthy of them but Canova, yet even in those branches of literature in which their modern rivals have sometimes been preferred to them, they have met with the fortune of Themistocles, and may seem fairly entitled to the first place, because each of their competitors, in his turn, concedes to them the second. For instance, Homer, in the opinion of some British critics, may be inferior to Milton, but the same critics would be scandalized by any camparison between the Jerusalem Delivered, or the Lusiad, and the Iliad or the Odyssey ; and although in France, since the earlier part of the last century, when all sound learning began to decline there, and in its stead, the crude speculations of sophisters, economists, encyclopœdists and atheists came into vogue, the tragedies of Sophocles are considered as having been immeasurably surpassed by Corneille and Racine; yet it would be set down at Paris, as a most extravagant absurdity, to speak of Shakspeare and Calderon as rivals of the Greeks.* In Germany however, whose learned men, whatever may be thought of the accuracy or refinement of their scholarship, are the most impartial, precisely because they are most conversant with universal literature, and with what has been very expressively called its comparative anatomy, ample justice has been done to *all* the remains of ancient genius. If we were called upon to exemplify the difference between sound criticism and the petulant and presumptuous dogmatism of prejudice and ignorance, we should refer to W. Schlegel's course of dramatic literature for the one, and Voltaire's strictures upon the Greek tragedies, in his various prefaces, commentaries, &c., for the other.†

Another preliminary, but with a view to the issue of the controversy, a far more important matter to be adjusted between Mr. Grimké and ourselves, concerns the *ground* of his hostility to the classics, and the *extent* to which he would be understood as pushing his principles. We are not quite sure that we perceive the true scope of his reasonings. At one time he speaks as if his objection to the study of the ancient models were founded upon the supposed unprofitableness of it, by reason of the vast superiority of modern genius in every department of philosophy and letters. He puts the question, and predicts with a precision quite characteristic, that 'it will be reconsidered and decided by the educated men who shall *close* the *present* century'—"Whether the languages and authors of Greece and Rome are not to be. regarded as institutions, once indispensable, invaluable; but having answered their end, shall they not yield, especially in our country, to a higher order of institutions, viz : the science and literature of modern nations ?" But, at other times, he would seem to concede the superiority of the ancients, so far at least as style and execution are concerned, in poetry, in eloquence, in the narrative part of history, &c., while he objects to them a want of practical usefulness and of adaptation to the condition and characteristics of society in modern times, and especially in these United States. Thus, at page 61, we find the following admission—"Grant that Hume, Robertson, and Gibbon are not the rivals in style of Thucydides and Herodotus, of Livy and Sal-

---

* *Apropos of France.* Classical learning which had long been on the decline, perished entirely during the storm of the Revolution—what has become of her literature and her elegance ? Where are the successors of Boileau and Racine, of Fenelon and La Bruyère.

† See Racine's preface to Iphigénie, which does as much honor to the judgment and candor of the author, as the tragedy itself does to his genius.

We have said, since the beginning of the last century, for it is a remarkable fact, that in the famous controversy about the ancients and moderns, during the reign of Louis XIV. Boileau and Racine took the compliments of La Motte and Perrault, (who asserted the equality of those two poets with any of the great names of antiquity) as so many outrages upon common sense, and disguised sarcasms upon themselves.

lust, &c." However, from the general spirit of his speculations, from the eternal recurrence of certain favorite phrases, such as "practical," "the people," &c.; and from some single passages in which he has expressed himself to the same effect with peculiar emphasis and distinctness, we find it difficult to resist the conclusion, that his theory of education is such as would prove, in the long run, just as fatal to Milton and Shakspeare, or to Jeremy Taylor and Burke, as to the orators and poets of antiquity. We are persuaded, for instance, that if Mr. Grimké were to sit down to give us, as it was once the fashion for every philosopher to do, his scheme of an imaginary commonwealth, he would not only, after the example of Plato, expel from his ideal territory, the whole inspired tribe *en masse,* (except perhaps the inoffensive race of Didactic versifiers, with the "English Lucretius"* at their head) but would exterminate along with them every thing that had in it the smallest particle of the divine spirit.† He would thus prepare his citizens for their place in his perfect polity as Lucian's ghosts are fitted by Charon and Mercury for their residence on the other side of the Styx, by stripping them entirely of all the form and comeliness of life, and leaving nothing but the shade or the skeleton of a man to pine away, in those dreary regions, an existence, without joy or hope, and anything but vital. Thus, at page 70, our author reasons as follows :—

"What, though my country should never produce a Homer or a Virgil, a Phidias or an Apelles! What, though Michael Angelo and Raphael, Tasso and Shakspeare, may never have a rival in our land; yet have we already brought forth men, greater and better, wiser and more *valuable,* than the poet, the painter, the statuary, and the architect. Even at this day, have we done more for the solid, permanent, rational happiness of man, than all the artists that ever lived One citizen, the fruit and example of *institutions virtuous,* benevolent and peaceful, wise and free is *worth more* to his family, his social circle, his country, than the Clouds of Aristophanes, the Group of the Rhodian sculptors, or the Transfiguration of Raphael. If the sons of Cornelia were her jewels, each citizen free, educated and happy, is to America, a pearl above price.

" The time is fast coming [prophecy again] when the wide-spread influence of moral wisdom and of instructed common sense shall assign, to poetry and the fine arts, a rank far below that which they have held, from a *singular concurrence of circumstances,* in the judgment of the world. *When* this consummation shall have been fulfilled [aye, but not till then], the poet and the artist, however eminent, shall be classed far below the statesman and orator, the philosopher and historian. But let me curb the patriot feeling," &c.

We have only to repeat, here, what we have already said, that these sentiments are in the highest degree honorable to Mr. Grimké's heart, but we do not think that the occasion called

* So Mr. Grimké is pleased to entitled Akenside. Plato made a similar exception.
† Divinæ particulam auræ.—*Hor.*

for the expression of them. We readily admit, that if the stern alternative implied in the above extract were really presented to us in the nature of things; if the only condition, on which we could possess the refined enjoyments of poetry and its kindred arts, were the sacrifice of all those substantial virtues and accomplishments that form the character and ensure the happiness of the man and the citizen, no rational mind could hesitate a moment to adopt the old Roman choice—

Excudant *alii*, spirantia mollius æra, &c.

But fortunately for mankind this is very far from being the case. The harsh and crabbed philosophy which would thus proscribe the purest pleasures, as well as the most elegant and ennobling pursuits of the human mind, is as false and superficial in theory as it is disagreeable in its effects and repulsive in its aspect. Indeed, if Mr. Grimké will pardon us for expressing ourselves with so much freedom, we will confess to him that we are at a loss to conceive how such an opinion could have escaped him in any other way than that of ingenious and sportive paradox. These principles have, in truth, a plausible air about them at first sight. They seem to rest upon the solid basis of utility, and to address themselves to a severe reason, in contradistinction to such as depend for their influence upon the illusions of feeling and an excited imagination. But push them a little farther and they lead to consequences so extravagant, as to reduce the whole argument, at once, to a manifest absurdity. They naturally, nay, almost inevitably engender that war of extermination, which illiterate and vulgar fanatics, of all names and nations, have waged against the highest graces and embellishments of society. It is owing to precisely such notions as these, that the verses of Menander and Alcæus were effaced in the dark age, to make way for monkish legends and barbarous homilies; and that, in later times, and under a change of opinions, the venerable monuments of Gothic architecture, and the gorgeous ornaments of the cathedral and the monastery, provoked the gloomy and unsparing rage of the Covenanters. Their full force was seen in the destruction of the Alexandrian library, because, said the Caliph, its numerous volumes have been superseded or condemned by the Koran—and in the conduct of those frantic ribalds who disgraced the character and impeded the early progress of the Reformation by their crimes and their follies, and who, in setting up their kingdom of the New Jerusalem, under Bernard Knipperdolling and Gerard Kippenbroch, began by burning all the books they could find except the Bible.*

---

* See Jortin's Erasmus, v. i. p. 328. This account of the Anabaptists is taken from Perizonius' Hist. sec. xvi. p. 194.

L'avarice, says La Rochefoucault, est plus opposée à l'écono-
mie qua la libéralité. We have the same answer to make to
those, who, in the matter of education, would sacrifice what is
really useful to their own narrow or perverse *theory* of utility,
and, out of sheer abhorrence of the luxuries and prodigality of
learning, would indulge the neophyte in a very scanty allowance
of its bare necessaries. They who apply to literature this radical levelling, degrading *cui bono* test—who estimate genius and
taste, by their value in exchange, and weigh the results of science
in the scales of the money-changer, may be wiser in their generation than the disinterested votaries of knowledge—but they
have, assuredly, made no provision in their system for the noblest
purposes of our being.† The same thing may be said of those
who, like Mr. Grimké, are for sacrificing what are rather am-
biguously called the ornamental to what are just as absurdly
considered as *par excellence* the useful parts of education.   According to this theory, a boy should be taught mathematics,
chemistry, mineralogy, metaphysics, and the metaphysical part
of moral philosophy, and be allowed, from his most tender years
we suppose, to dabble *ad libitum* in politics, speculative and
practical—in other words, he is to be brought up in studies,
which, although they lead to far more important results, are, as
a mere discipline for youth with a view to future usefulness in
life, we really think, not a great deal better than the dry thorny
dialectics of the schoolmen,—while no object should be suffered
to approach him that may speak to his taste, his imagination, or
his heart.   Our youth are to be trained up as if they were all
destined to be druggists and apothecaries, or navigators and
mechanists—or, if it sounds better, they are to be deeply versed
in the economy of the universe, and the most recondite and
shadowy subtleties of transcendental geometry, or transcendent
psychology—but what, after all, ought to be the capital object of
education, to form the *moral* character, not by teaching what to
think but persuading to act well; not by loading the memory
with cold and barren precepts, but forming the sensibility by the
habitual, fervid and rapturous contemplation of high and heroical models of excellence; not by definitions of virtue and speculations about the principle of obligation, but by making us *love*
the one and *feel* the sacredness of the other—would, in such a
system of discipline, be sadly neglected.   This is a radical and
an incurable defect in the *cui bono* theory.   If we compare different æras of history with each other, and inquire what it is that
distinguishes the flourishing and pure from the degenerate and
declining state of commonwealths, we shall seldom find that
it is any falling off in mere speculative knowledge, or even

† Romani pueri longis rationibus assem,
  Discunt in partes centum diducere, &c. *Hor. Ars. Poet.* 325.

in the mass of talent and ability displayed at any one time.—
The softest Sybarites of Juvenal's day provoked his indignant
satire by talking of morality with the sternness of Cato—courage
was, no doubt, as well understood and defined by the Sophists who lectured to the slavish and cowardly successors of
the Scipios, as it had been in the wars against Pyrrhus and
Hannibal—and legislation became more ingenious just in proportion as it was less efficacious, according to the pointed saying
of the great historian *corruptissimâ republicâ plurimœ leges.*[*]
But what a difference was there, and how essential is that
difference in the eyes of posterity, between the age of Cicero
and that of Domitian (to go no further) in genius, in taste and in
moral character!

Now if Mr. Grimké seriously means to associate himself with
these levellers and fifth monarchy men of the commonwealth
of letters of whom we have been speaking, we are afraid that
we must fairly give up the controversy, and with it, all hope of
ever reclaiming him from the error of his ways. We really
cannot, with a clear conscience, undertake to promise, that
Greek and Latin will make better artisans and manufacturers,
or more thrifty economists; or, in short, more useful and skilful
men in the ordinary routine of life, or its mere mechanical offices
and avocations. We should still refer a young student of law,
aspiring to an insight into the mere craft and mystery of special
pleading, to Saunders' Reports, rather than to Cicero's Topics;
the itinerant field-preacher, would, doubtless, find abundantly
greater edification, and for *his* purposes, more profitable doctrine, in honest John Bunyan, than in all the speculations of the
lyceum and the academics; and we do conscientiously believe,
that not a single case, more or less, of yellow fever, would be
cured by the faculty in this city, for all that Hippocrates and
Celsus have said, or that has been ever said (or sung) of Chiron
and Æsculapius. It is true, their peculiar studies would not be
hurt, and might, occasionally even be very much helped and
facilitated, by a familiar acquaintance with these languages; and
what would they not gain as enlightened and accomplished men!
But it is not fair to consider the subject in that light only. It is
from this false state of the controversy, that the argument of Mr.
Grimké derives all its plausibility.[†] We on the contrary, take
it for granted in our reasonings, that the American people are to
aim at doing something more than "to draw existence, propagate and rot." We suppose it to be our common ambition to
become a cultivated and a literary nation. Upon this assump-

* Tacit. Ann. l. iii.

[† Τὸ δε ζητεῖν πανταχοῦ το χρήσιμον ἥκιστα ἁρμόττει τοις μεγαλοψύχοις
καὶ τοῖς ἐλευθέροις. Arist., Pol. Lib. 8, c. 3.]

tion, what we contend for, is, that the study of the classics is and ought to be, an essential part of a *liberal* education—that education of which the object is to make accomplished, elegant and learned men—to chasten and to discipline genius, to refine the taste, to quicken the perceptions of decorum and propriety,* to purify and exalt the moral sentiments, to fill the soul with a deep love of the beautiful both in moral and material nature, to lift up the aspirations of man to objects that are worthy of his noble faculties and his immortal destiny—in a word, to raise him as far as possible above those selfish and sensual propensities, and those grovelling pursuits, and that mental blindness and coarseness and apathy, which degrade the savage and the boor to a condition but a little higher than that of the brutes that perish. We refer to that education and to those improvements, which draw the broad line between civilized and barbarous nations, which have crowned some chosen spots with glory and immortality, and covered them all over with a magnificence, that, even in its mutilated and mouldering remains, draws together pilgrims of every tongue and of every clime, and which have caused their names to fall like a 'breathed spell' upon the ear of the generations that come into existence, long after the tides of conquest and violence have swept over them, and left them desolate and fallen. It is such studies we mean, as make that vast difference in the eyes of a scholar between Athens, their seat and shrine, and even Sparta with all her civil wisdom and military renown, and have (hitherto at least) fixed the gaze and the thoughts of all men with curiosity and wonder, upon the barren little peninsula between Mount Cithæron and Cape Sunium, and the islands and the shores around it, as they stand out in lonely brightness and dazzling relief, amidst the barbarism of the west on the one hand, and the dark and silent and lifeless wastes of oriental despotism on the other. Certainly we do not mean to say, that, in any system of intellectual discipline, poetry ought to be preferred to the severe sciences. On the contrary, we consider every scheme of merely *elementary* education as defective, unless it develope and bring out all the faculties of the mind as far as possible into equal and harmonious action. But, surely, we may be allowed to argue from the analogy of things, and the goodness that has clothed all nature in beauty, and filled it with music and with fragrance, and that has at the same time bestowed upon us such vast and refined capacities of enjoyment, that nothing can be more extravagant than this notion of a day of philosophical illumination and didactic soberness being at hand, when men shall be thoroughly disabused of their silly love for poetry and the arts. Indeed we know nothing that at all

---

* Nihil est difficilius quam quid deceat videre.—*Cic.*

comes up to this idea, but a tirade of one of Molière's comic heroe's (Sganarelle we believe) against the pernicious charms of women—who, however, winds up his invectives, as might have been expected, by the bitter avowal—

Cependant on fait tout pour ces animaux là.

So it is, has been, and ever will be (it is more than probable,) as long as man is constituted as he is. And the same thing may be said of poetry and the arts which are only another form of it. For what is poetry? It is but an abridged name for the sublime and beautiful, and for high wrought pathos. It is, as Coleridge quaintly, yet, we think, felicitously expresses it, "the blossom and the fragrance of all human knowledge." It appears not only in those combinations of creative genius of which the *beau idéal* is the professed object, but in others that might seem at first sight but little allied to it. It is spread over the whole face of nature—it is in the glories of the heavens and in the wonders of the great deep, in the voice of the cataract and of the coming storm, in Alpine precipices and solitudes, in the balmy gales and sweet bloom and freshness of spring. It is in every heroic achievement, in every lofty sentiment, in every deep passion, in every bright vision of fancy, in every vehement affection of gladness or of grief, of pleasure or of pain. It is, in short, the feeling— the deep, the strictly *moral* feeling, which, when it is affected by chance or change in human life, as at a tragedy, we call sympathy—but as it appears in the still more mysterious connection between the heart of man and the forms and beauties of inanimate nature, as if they were instinct with a soul and a sensibility like our own, has no appropriate appellation in our language, but is not the less real or the less familiar to our experience on that account. It is these feelings, whether utterance be given to them, or they be only nursed in the smitten bosom—whether they be couched in metre, or poured out with wild disorder and irrepressible rapture, that constitute the true spirit and essence of poetry, which is, therefore, necessarily connected with the grandest conceptions and the most touching and intense emotions, with the fondest aspirations and the most awful concerns of mankind. For instance, religion has been in all ages and countries the great fountain of poetical inspiration, and no harps have been more musical than those of the Prophets. What would Mr. Grimké say of him whose lips were touched by one of the Seraphim with a live coal from off the altar ; or does he expect the day to come when "the wide spread influence of moral wisdom and instructed common sense" shall assign to the Psalms or the Book of Job, in the library of a cultivated mind, a lower place than to Robertson and Hume? Milton pronounces "our sage and serious poet, Spenser," a better teacher than Scotus and Aquinas*—and in another place, has expressed himself to the same effect so admirably; and, for our present purpose, so appositly, that we cannot refrain from citing the whole passage: "To which (viz. logic) poetry should be made subsequent—or, indeed, rather precedent, as being less subtile and fine, and more simple, sensuous and passionate, I mean not here the prosody of a verse, which they could not but have hit on before, among the rudiments of grammar, but that sublime art which in Aristotle's Poetics, in Horace, and the Italian commentaries of Castlevetro, Tasso, Mazzoni, and others, teaches what the laws are of a true Epic Poem, what of a dramatic, what of a lyric, what *decorum* is, which is the great masterpiece to observe. This would make them soon perceive what despicable creatures our common rhymers and play-writers be, and shew them what religious, what glorious and magnificent use might be made of poetry both in divine and human things."— (*Tract: on Education.*†)

We have enlarged the more upon this head, because we have uniformly observed, that those who question the utility of classical learning, are at bottom, equally unfavourable to all elegant studies. They set out, it is true, in a high-flown strain, and talk largely about the superiority of modern genius. But the secret is sure to be out at last. When they have been dislodged, one by one, from all their *literary* positions, they never fail to take refuge in this cold and desolate region of utility. They begin by discoursing magnificently of orators, poets and philosophers, and the best discipline for forming them ; and end by citing the examples of A, the broker, or B, the attorney, or C, and D, members of congress, and what not, who have all got along in the world without the least assistance from Latin and Greek. Just as if every body did not know that, as that sage moralist Figaro has it, *pour avoir du bien le savoir faire vaut mieux que le savoir;* and just as if our supposed great men had troubled

---

* Areopagitica—So Hor. Epist. i. 2. says of Homer,

    ——quid sit pulchrum, quid turpe, quid utile, quid non
    Plenius ac melius Chrysippo et Crantore dicit.

† See Bishop Lowth's first and eighteenth Lectures on Hebrew poetry. He cites, among other things, a famous passage on the same subject from the Nov. Organon, l. ii. c .13, with which we regret that our limits do not permit us to favour the reader. In addition to the instances adduced by that learned and elegant scholar to shew that poets were generally ranked, among the Greeks, with the sophists or philosophers as instructors of mankind, see Isocrates Παραινεσις—*passim*—or Οἱ παλαιοὶ φιλοσοφιαν τινὰ λέγουσιν πρώτην τὴν ποιητικήν, εἰσάγουσαν εἰς τον βίον ἡμας ἐκ νέων κ᾽ διδάσκουσαν ηδη κ᾽ πάθη κ᾽ πραξεις μεθ᾽ ἡδονῆς. Strabo, l. i, c. 1. Erastosthenes, who, it seems, thought like Mr. Grimké, had pronounced poetry γραωδης μυθολογια. [ἢ δὲ ἐτράπημεν, δοχεῖ μοι χρῆναι ἰέναι, σκοποῦντα (τὰ) κατὰ τοὺς ποιητάς. ὁυτοι γὰρ ἡμῖν ὥσπερ πατέρες τῆς σοφίας εισι και ἡγεμόνες. Plat. Lysis. 213.]

their heads any more about the exact sciences and modern literature, than about the classics, or were not quite as little indebted to Newton, to Milton, or to Tasso, as Virgil and Tully, and
just as if an argument, which proves so much, were good for any
thing at all!

Assuming it, therefore, that our systems of education are to
be founded on more liberal principles, and to aim at loftier objects, we proceed to point out a few other defects in the reasonings of Mr. Grimké. We have already had occasion to observe,
in citing some passages from the Discourse, that there prevails
throughout the whole of it a singular confusion of ideas, which
those quotations were intended to exemplify. This confusion
appears to be twofold, and consists, first in not distinguishing
between the *diffusion* of knowledge, and its *absolute* state or
condition; and, secondly, in mistaking the progress of those sciences which are capable of being extended (as metaphysics and
moral philosophy are *not*) by a mere accumulation of details, and
an accession of new facts and principles, for a positive improvement
or enlargement, rather, of the capacity and powers of the understanding itself.

Examples of the former occur perpetually throughout the
whole discourse, but we will content ourselves with the following citations:

"It is not customary to consider the history of science as connected
with the history of society. In tracing the development of its principles
or their progressive application to *practical* matters, most authors have
instituted no inquiry into their effects, beyond the immediate science itself,
or the arts and other sciences connected with or dependent upon it. But
what is the value of human learning if it do not bless as well as adorn society; if it enlighten its professors only *and not the people?* Is it only a
matter of speculation for the intellectual powers of man, or of entertainment for his taste? Can its sublimity and beauty be objects of just admiration, unless it improve the condition of the ignorant and oppressed; while
it enlightens and corrects, refines and elevates those, on whom the progress
and future character of society depend? No. The true glory and excellency of science consist in its aptitude to meliorate the condition of man,
and to promote substantial, *practical,* permanent improvement, in the education and government of the people," &c. p. 11.

"Take the whole body of Grecian philosophy, natural, political, moral,
and social, and we must acknowledge that it exerted scarcely any salutary
influence on the mass of the community—that their education was no
part of its theory or practice; that it lived and moved, and had its being,
almost independently of the very society which it adorned; and left behind no monument, save the writings of its devotees." p. 20.

"It is a melancholy and humiliating reflection, that the genius and learning, the eloquence and taste of Greece and Rome, did so little in the
cause of truth, moral, political and philosophical." p. 21.

Then follows the grand inference—

"If the opinion expressed above as to their *usefulness in their own day,*
with a view to the people on whom they conferred dazzling honours, but

not *practical* blessings, be correct, it becomes a momentous question for those who devote so many precious years to the classics," &c. p. 22.

Now, we find no fault with the great leading idea in these passages when stated in the abstract. We, of course, agree with our author, that the light of knowledge ought to be diffused as widely as possible, and that it is the great distinguishing privilege of modern times, and the surest pledge of the future improvement and happiness of mankind, that, by means of the press, it *has* been diffused within the last three centuries and a half, and especially in our own day, to an extent altogether unparalleled at any previous period. It is also, we admit, very conceivable that a philosophic mind, of a certain turn, should dwell as Mr. Grimké does, with more complacency and interest, upon these beneficial effects of literature, than upon the beauties of its most perfect works considered merely as objects of curiosity or of taste. But how does this concession benefit the argument against the study of the classics ? What does the prodigious diffusion of knowledge in modern times prove, except what nobody ever doubted, that the invention of the art of printing was a great blessing, and that books, nowadays, especially of the coarser stereotype editions, cost a great deal less money, and may be multiplied a great deal more easily than MMS. upon parchment ? But what sort of connection is there between the premises and the conclusion in the following proposition—Cicero's writings were not read by as many of his contemporaries as, on account of their extraordinary excellencies, it was desirable they should have been, *therefore* they ought not to be read at all by us ! We would venture to back such an enthymeme against any thing that can be found among the logical exploits of the irrefragable Doctors. Or are we to understand, that the style of the classical authors, which is so remarkable for clearness and simplicity now, was originally cabalistic or esoterical on purpose that "the people" should not understand and profit by them, in imitation of what has been said of the hieroglyphics of the Egyptian priests. Or what are we to understand by it ?

With respect to the other notion of our author, that the human understanding is, at some future period (he has not precisely said when, but we presume it will be soon after we shall have thrown off the bondage of classical learning,) to attain to a sort of Patagonian stature, and that too, as we infer, by the natural and inevitable progress of scientific discovery—we confess that it appears to us quite original. According to this new rule, the true measure or exponent of the *strength and capacity* of the human mind, at any given period, is the bulk of the Encyclopædia for the time being ; and of two men, he will be, in point of intellect, the greater, who knows one fact more than the other, however inferior to him in more important points. According to this notion, the last will always be first, and the disciple necessarily equal, at least, with a good chance of being superior to his master. The honors that have been absurdly paid to Lavoisier and to Newton—to the men whose philosophical and creative minds bring order out of chaos, lay the foundation, discover the principles, and project the great outlines of a system—are due, it seems, to those humble followers, who by an isolated, perhaps, an accidental discovery, add another truth to the general stock. This confusion of two things, so perfectly distinct as extent of knowledge and vigour and originality of genius, needs no comment.*

A late writer,† addressing himself to this very subject, remarks, that it is this diffusion of knowledge through the press, "and not the height to which individual genius had soared, that forms the grand distinction between ancient and modern literature. The triumph of modern literature consists not in the point of elevation to which it has attained, but in the extent of its conquests—the extent to which it has refined and quickened the mass of mankind. It would be difficult to adjust the intellectual precedence of Newton and Archimides, of Bacon and Aristotle, of Shakspeare and Homer, of Thucydides and Hume ; but it may be declared with certainty, that the people of modern nations, in consequence of literature becoming more widely diffused, are become more civilized and enlightened." These remarks are perfectly just, and it is amazing that the speculations of Mr. Grimké did not lead him to the same conclusions. The question, whether the ancient models ought to be studied, has immediate reference to the "intellectual precedence" of the great masters, but it has no connection whatever with the general condition of mankind at that time. Nobody, we believe, ever pretended‡ that Homer lived in a very advanced state of society ; yet we never heard that urged as a reason why his poems should

---

* Hæc nostra (ut sæpe diximus) felicitatis cujusdam sunt potius quàm facultatis, et potius temporis partus quàm ingenii, as Bacon expresses it with admirable precision.—*Nov. Organ.* l. i. c. 23.

It is curious to observe the revolutions in opinion. It was quite fashionable about 200 years ago, to compare the moderns, in their intellectual relation to the ancients, to a dwarf mounted upon the back of a giant—seeing further, indeed, from the advantage of position, but no more to be compared with the mighty being under him, than any other dependant, with him on whose bounty he subsists. In these times the picture is exactly reversed. The giant is mounted upon the dwarf, and is to go on, it seems, increasing in dimensions, until his stature shall reach the skies. The *superstition* of Europe believed too much of the past—the *enthusiasm* of America expects too much from the future.

† Dunlop's Hist. Rom. Literature. Pref.

‡ We beg pardon of the ingenious and elegant writer; in a late number of the Quarterly Review, who, in reviewing Milton's Works, endeavors to make out, that the age of Homer was far from barbarous.

not be read, though we think it is a very good one why they should be.

Before we quit this point, we beg leave to make one other remark. The superiority of the moderns, from the causes just adverted to, is not confined to the mass of mankind—the *people* only. Great men, also, have been more completely enlightened. Their genius has not been (for it could not be) increased, but it has been purged of many errors and superstitions. Nothing could be more exquisite than the judgment of the Greeks, yet their successors listen with a smile of increduility, or of pity, to many of their opinions. In short, the influence of an enlightened *communis sensus*, in Quinctilian's use of that phrase*—meaning not our common sense, (for in that, nothing could excel antiquity) but the general conclusions or results of inquiry and reasoning about such subjects as are most universally interesting to mankind—upon the speculations of great and ruling minds, has been very visible. The importance of this restraint upon the caprices and the infirmities of genius will be obvious on a moment's reflection. There is no folly that may not be united to the most splendid talents ; and the foremost men of all the world are always more or less affected by the spirit of the age in which they live. Thus, Melancthon was a believer in judicial astrology and a caster of nativities,† and Bacon himself was not exempt from many superstitions of those times.

Hitherto, we think we are safe, in affirming, that the reasonings of Mr. Grimké have utterly failed. We would gladly pursue him through all his paradoxes, but we are alarmed at the length to which our remarks are already run out, and we must be as brief as possible in what is to follow. Our author, as we have seen, denies the ancients all merit "in moral, political and social philosophy," to which he has elsewhere added what he calls the "philosophy of history." We will reserve all these for future occasions, except the first, touching which, we will here submit a few remarks.

Mr. Grimké's assertion that the ancients did nothing in ethics, struck us as one of the boldest (and that is saying much) in his whole discourse. We have been always accustomed to think, that if those refined ages have left us anything, in any department of knowledge, of which the excellence is beyond all dispute, it is (after the Greek geometry, perhaps,) their moral philosophy. We presume it will not be considered as derogating from their merit in this particular, that they did not by mere dint of reasoning, *a priori*, make themselves partakers in the benefits of the Christian Revelation. Neither do we conceive ourselves

---

* Institut. Orator. l. i. c. 2.—*Communis sensus* may there be very well rendered "public, or general opinion."
† Jortin's Erasmus, I. 146.

responsible for certain strange customs and heathenish practices, into which they occasionally fell, in their conduct and way of living. We must repeat, once more, that the question here, is not what the mass of mankind, in those ages, *were* or *did*, but what the *élite* wrote and spoke, and not whether we should follow the example of the former, but whether we ought to study the literary works of the latter. We concede, therefore, to save trouble, that their morality—that for instance of Rome in the time of the first Punic war—would not be good enough to stand the *severe* censure of London, of Paris, or of New-York. Let us now see how it fares in other respects with Mr. Grimké's propositions.

The science of morals has very properly been divided into two distinct kinds. The one contemplates man as an active being, having duties to perform and obligations to fulfil, approving good and disapproving evil, pursuing happiness and avoiding misery and pain. The other regards this moral constitution itself, as a subject of inquiry and analysis, and aims at explaining its phenomena (with how much success Mr. Grimké may, perhaps, be able to inform our readers,) in the same way as Natural Philosophy arranges and accounts for those of the material world. The former is obviously practical—the latter altogether speculative and metaphysical. Under the discipline of the first, we are taught to love virtue, to feel what is so beautifully called, in the language of the Scriptures, "the beauty of holiness,"* to abstain from false and deceptive pleasures, and pursue only rational and solid good, to resist the temptations and to encounter with fortitude and patience the conflicts and sufferings of life—and, above all things, "to hate the cowardice of doing wrong." In one word, it is the great object of this part of a "generous education" to fit a man, as Milton expresses it, for performing, justly and magnanimously, all the offices, both public and private, of peace and war. The end of the second is nothing more—its fruit, at least, has been and can be nothing more, than the gratification of a liberal—certainly, but still an unprofitable curiosity, by shewing *why* it is we love virtue, what is the principle of obligation, whether it is utility or a moral sense or sympathy, or what else that causes us to approve or to blame, &c. Now, in the former kind, the ancients not only attained to a high degree of excellence, but there is nothing in all that the copious literature of modern times has to boast of—with the exception, *perhaps*, of Telemachus, and the finest compositions of Addison—that will bear a moment's comparison with the Dialogues of Plato and Tully, to say nothing of the numerous other remains of the portico, the lyceum and the academy, that have come down to us. This position is quite incontro-

* το καλον.

vertible, and has been, if we are not very much mistaken, stated
in so many words by the author of one of the most ingenious,
and by far the most eloquent work on the other, or metaphysical branch of moral philosophy, that has ever been published.*
It is impossible, indeed, to imagine any thing more sublime and
consoling, more sweet, more touching, more persuasive than the
Apology for Socrates, the Crito and the Phædo of his great disciple, or the Somnium Scipionis, the whole Treatise de Senectute, but especially the close of it, the Tusculan Questions, nay
all that remains in this kind of the Roman orator. As for the
metaphysical part of this science of human nature, we would express ourselves with a becoming diffidence†—but we must be
allowed to say, that until Mr. Grimké shall have put his finger
upon any one thing, in the whole compass of it, that is perfectly
settled and has been recognized as a profitable, and, as he would
call it, *practical* addition to the stock of human knowledge, we
shall continue to think it, as we now do, very immaterial, whether
the ancients or the moderns have had the best of it in this noc-
turnal, and what is worse, far from decisive, conflict of wits.
Nothing is more possible than that we are ignorant of the understanding of these writers, instead of understanding their
ignorance, according to the distinction of an ingenious admirer
of the philosophy of Kant.‡ Be it so. We do, however, for
our own part, cheerfully resign these thorny and unprofitable
studies to those who profess to comprehend and to read with edification such things as the Theætetus of Plato or the cloudy
transcendentalism of the German school. In the mean time,
without denying, as we do not deny, that a young man ought,
about his seventeenth or eighteenth year, to study metaphysics,
for several good reasons, we fearlessly appeal to our readers to
decide whether he ought not to be deeply imbued with the spirit
and the precepts of ancient ethics, conveyed as they are in a
style, of which the faultless execution is the best discipline of
taste, whilst its glowing eloquence fills every generous bosom
with the most elevated and ennobling moral enthusiasm.§

* Adam Smith's Theory of Moral Sentiments.
† We really debated with ourselves a long time whether we should venture to
encounter those awful personages, the Metaphysicians.
    Dii, quibus *imperium* est *animarum*, umbræque silentes;
    Et Chaos et Phlegethon, loca nocte silentia late,
    Sit mihi fas audita loqui. Æn. vi. 264.
‡ Coleridge's Biographia Literaria.
§ We will indulge in the freedom of a note, so far as to repeat that we are at a
loss to understand how any discoveries—above all, any important and available
discoveries for the purposes of education or discipline can be made in "the subjects of our consciousness," (to use Dugald Stewart's phrase for what is vulgarly
called, the mind,) or what there *can* be in ontology, pneumatology, psychology, or
any other metaphysic-ology, except, indeed, a great deal of neology, and mere
verbal refinements and distinctions of that notable kind that surprised Monsieur
Jourdain so much, *videlicit*, that what one speaks so naturally and without know-

In discussing the comparative merits of the ancients and moderns, we have sometimes seen it roundly asserted by those who come to their knowledge of the former by inspiration or instinct—that the literature, but especially the poetry of the latter, is more various, profound and passionate than that of Greece and Rome. The origin of this notion, we dare say, may be traced to certain speculations of the German critics, who maintain that there is a fundamental difference between the *beau ideal* of modern poetry and art, and that of the antique; giving to the one the name of the Romantic, to the other, its old title of the Classical Style. This distinction would form the subject of a very interesting inquiry, but we have not time to enter into it here. It may be as well, however, to expose the fallacy of one inference which we have known to be drawn from this, or something like this, view of the subject.

Thus, we have seen a remark of Dr. Johnson cited with great triumph by those who thought it time lost to study the ancient models, viz. that the Greek and Roman poets draw all their figures of speech from external or material objects. This notable discovery is considered as decisive of the superiority of modern genius, which is hence inferred to be more conversant with the depths of the heart and its passions, with abstract ideas and the operations of the world of spirits. The fact, we shall, for the sake of argument, admit, yet we really cannot perceive how such a sweeping conclusion is deduced from it. We suppose that if there is any body of poetry in the world, about the unrivalled sublimity of which, all the modern, *i. e.* Romantic critics are agreed, without a dissenting voice, it is the sacred

---

ing why or wherefore, is actually prose. "All a rhetorician's rules," &c. Rhetoric, once so important, however, is never talked of nowadays out of the grammar school, and we think it probable, metaphysics will share (as it deserves) the same fate. We quote the following sentence from the old (and now obsolete) philosopher of Malmesbury—one of the most ingenious and original thinkers of any age or country, and from whome even Locke, Hume and Burke have successively condescended to borrow more than they have chosen to acknowledge. He was, as every body knows, the successor of Bacon, in England, and a contemporary of Des Cartes and Gassendi.

"On the other side, those men who write concerning the faculties, passions and manners of man, that is to say of moral philosophy and of policy, government and laws, whereof there be infinite volumes, have been so far from removing doubt and controversy in the questions they have handled, that they have very much multiplied the same. Nor does any man at this day so much as *pretend* to know more than hath been delivered more than two thousand years ago by Aristotle." *Hum. Nat.* c. 13. This thesis, with some slight modification, we are ready to maintain against all comers—with the exception of what philosophers "*pretend to*," each of whom, in these enlightened times, is a *tanto promissor hiatu.* Thus we may see how the world wags. Hobbes had his day, and a brighter one than any has had since, and is forgotten—then Locke followed—then Berkely and Hume—then Drs. Reid and Beattie—then Dugald Stewart (who is still at it)—and now we think that Kant is likely to take possession of all who will not be prevailed on to abandon the inside for the outside of the skull, and to study the *organic* philosophy, of which we say something in another article.

poetry of the Hebrews. Now, not only may the same thing be predicated of it, but it is this very feature in the style of the Old Testament that the elegant Lowth extols as its distinguishing excellence.* Nay,. he further remarks, and that most justly, that some of the sublimest images of the prophetic writings are taken from the more familiar and humble, not to say vulgar occupations of life, from the barn, the threshing-floor, and the wine-press. Even Milton, who has drawn together his materials from a greater variety of sources than any other writer, and whose mighty genius is for nothing more remarkable than the apparent ease with which it appropriates and applies, and melts and moulds into new and original combinations, the most multifarious learning that ever fell to a poet's lot, is still distinguished by an antique and severe simplicity, even in his boldest and vastest conceptions. We do not remember, in any of his works, rich even to gorgeousness and redundancy, in all sorts of imagery, any tropes or figures, that, in their external form and character merely, give the least countenance to this notion of a romantic, or spiritual, or mystical poetry, essentially distinct from the classical (not in its subjects or spirit, for that is certainly true, but) in its rules and proportions, its lineaments and contour. The same thing may be said of Shakspeare, and of all our great English classics. The poets of our day, indeed, have, in quest of—novelty—a pursuit which has ever led to the corruption of taste, deviated from this primitive simplicity.† Byron, especially, is remarkable for farfetched allusions and quaint conceits, that are more worthy of Cowley than of himself, and this straining after effect is precisely the besetting sin of his muse. However, as Johnson has somewhere else observed, it is surprising after all how continually the same images are occurring in all literature—in new combinations, to be sure, and if properly introduced, always with the same effect of elevating, enlivening, or beautifying style; and it is one of the most curious and not the least instructive parts of criticism, to trace out the use and application that have been made of the same stock of figurative language in different ages and nations.‡ For

* Lectures on Sacred Poetry, &c. Lect. 6; cf. Lect. 12, (p. 252) in which he extends his observations to Homer and Virgil.

[† ''Απαντα μὲν τοι, τὰ ὅντως ἄσεμνα, διὰ μίαν ἐμφύεται τοῖς λόγοις αἰτίαν, διὰ τὸ περι τας νοήσεις καινόσπουδον, (περι ὅ δη μάλιστα κορυβαντιῶσιν ὁι νῦν.) Longin. 5.]

‡ For instance, there is a simile in the Paradise Lost, l. ii, 486, beginning ''Thus they their consultations dark,''&c, which is uncommonly beautiful and striking, and which has an air of perfect originality about it—but we have found one not materially differing from it in the Iliad, Π, 301— Ὡς Δαναοὶ νηων μὲν απωσάμενοι δήιον πυρ.

the rest, it is, we think, rather puerile to lay so much stress upon mere imagery, which is far from being of the *essence* of a good style either in poetry or prose. High wrought metaphors and such like are seldom admissible in the pathetic,* and the noblest eloquence which the lips of man ever uttered—that of Demosthenes—is almost entirely free from them.

There is an argument to prove the superiority of the moderns, which is, in some degree, connected with the last, and "is like unto it." It goes to shew, not only that they are, but that they must necessarily be in possession of a richer, more various and more lofty literature, because they have more "materials of thought." This, to be sure, is taking "the high *priori* road" to some purpose, and the demonstration would be perfect were it only as conclusive as it is brief and simple. But in the first place, it is on the very face of it a gross *non sequitur*, for we *have* heard of such a thing as *materiam superabat opus*. But what in fact are those materials of thought of which the stock may be accumulated and handed down, with continual accessions from one generation to another? In short, in what departments of thought and of knowledge have the moderns decidedly gone farther than their predecessors? The reader will find them extremely well summed up by Mr. Adams, and by Mr. Grimké (who, however, claims for his favourites, much more than they have any right to) in the following enumeration:—

"The compass, gunpowder, paper, printing, engraving and oil-painting; the whole department of navigation, including ship-building; the system of modern tactics by land and sea, of modern commerce, political economy and banking; algebra, fluxions and the sublime works of Newton and La Place; anatomy and surgery; chemistry, electricity, magnetism and botany; the telescope and microscope; the time-piece, the air-pump, the steam-engine and galvanism; the *true* theory and practice of government; the *division and subordination of power;* the principles of evidence and trial; diplomacy, the balance of power and the law of nations; the *history of man*, of arts and sciences, and of literature; *philology*, and the *philosophy of history;* and lastly, a nobler and better scheme of morals, and *a profound, rational and comprehensive theology*—all these and numberless other *inventions, discoveries* and improvements, are the work of the *modern* world. Wherever that world shall judge boldly," &c. pp. 61-62.

Now here are materials of thought enough, in all conscience, but we should really be glad to know what there is in this interesting catalogue, striking 'out of it such particulars (philology for instance) as are the common property of the ancients and the moderns, that *quà* "materials of thought" have had such a wonderful effect on *literature*, as to supersede entirely the study of the historians, moralists, orators and poets of antiquity. Every body perceives that *science* has been enlarged, and that the com-

* Tragicus plerumque dolet sermone pedestri.—*Hor.* Ars Poetica, 95.

forts and accommodations of society have been wonderfully increased by them—but is it seriously pretended, that such things
are calculated to make men more eloquent than the Greek language, a stormy democracy, and an attic audience? Are the
reasoning powers improved, merely by having more to reason
about, and has the invention of the modern analysis and the
application of mathematics to mechanical philosophy made the
Greek geometry less a model of simple and elegant demonstration?* Are our future statesmen and jurists—our Cannings
and D'Aguesseaus—to be formed in the chemist's laboratory,
and to be armed for the forum and the deliberative assembly,
with a retort and a crucible, or a supply of alkalis and acids?
Could such a history as that of Thucydides be bettered in the
least by the mariner's compass or gunpowder, the telescope and
microscope, the steam-engine and the time-piece? Is there any
thing either sublime or beautiful in the convulsions of a frog's
leg under the operation of galvanism, (see Mr. Adams) or that
most edifying and instructive spectacle, the death of a mouse,
for want of air, in an exhausted receiver? Besides we do not
exactly perceive how the contemporaneous state of science can be
made to appear in a work of art, either directly or indirectly, without violating the rules of good taste—for instance, by exaggerated
and scarcely intelligible metaphors, or, as in Good's Lucretius,
by smothering a text of ordinary verses, under a load of notes
stuffed with cumbersome pedantry. But if painting is to come
in for her share of "the materials of thought"—as there in no
reason why she should not—we really should like to know how
those, who are heareafter to surpass the Transfiguration, will con-
trive to shew (admitting for a moment such an extravagance)
that their superior excellence has been due, not to greater genius,
but to the "march of mind." Would it be expected, for example,
of Washington Alston, that, by way of letting posterity see that
he lived in this philosophic age, he should fill the back ground
of an historical picture with globes and quadrants, and tele-

---

* We are glad on this part of the subject to be able to vouch such an authority
as the late venerable Professor Playfair—whose prælections came more nearly up
to our idea of the conversations of a Greek sage, than any thing we have ever listened to in that kind. He was the very personification of truth and science, in all
their modesty, simplicity and sanctity.

"In nothing, perhaps, is the inventive and elegant genius of the Greeks, better
exemplified than in geometry. The elementary truths of that science were connected by Euclid, into one great chain, beginning from the axioms and extending to
the properties of the five regular solids; the whole digested into such admirable
order, and explained with such clearness and precision, that no similar work of superior excellence has appeared, even in the present advanced state of mathematical
science."—*Dissertation for the Supplem. Encyclopæd.* p. 9.

We will add to this high authority, what Cicero says, Tusc. Qu, l. i. c. 3.—In
summo apud illos, (Græcos) honore geometria fuit. Itaque nihil mathematicis
illustrius. At *nos* metiendi, ratiocinandique utilitate hujus artis terminavimus
modum. [Cf. an apposite passage in Plato's Republic, l. VII. fol. 525c.]

scopes and electrical machine—or haply, with human sculls, not as a *memento mori*, but for a sign that the mysteries of phrenology had been brought to light? As for poetry, which delights in wonder and prodigies—which seeks out its subjects where it catches its loftiest inspirations, in fabulous periods, in a heroic or feudal age, among argonauts and demi-gods, or pilgrims and crusaders,

> And if aught else great bards beside,
> In sage and solemn tunes have sung,
> Of tourneys and of trophies hung,
> Of forests and enchantments drear:—

What she is to gain by the conquests of her arch enemy truth, is really more than we can divine. In the progress of knowledge, the idols of fancy and the forms of enchantment that once covered the whole earth, have disappeared one by one. Look at the effect of the modern inprovements in geography. Take the discoveries of Columbus and Vasco de Gama for an example; what have they done for the muse? So long, indeed, as a mist still hovered over the shores they had touched upon, so long they afforded scope for the marvellous, and haunts for fiction. Accordingly, the first adventurers of the Portuguese gave us the Lusiad; and some time after the discovery of America, men dreamed of an El Dorado in its unknown climes. But now that the sea and the land have been so thoroughly explored, and such an immense accession of "materials of thought" (not to mention certain materials of a still more substantial kind) made to the stock of the geographer, the statist, the natural historian, the merchant, &c., what is become of the poetry? So far, her stores, at least, seem to have been sorely diminished by these great discoveries. Thus, we have exchanged the Hesperian gardens for the tooth coast, and the gold coast, and the slave coast, and the young ladies themselves, and their dragon, for the emperor of Morocco and the Mandingos, and the Congoes and the Hottentots. The Canary Islands, or the Azores, are scarcely a fit substitute for those fortunate islands of which poets sang, and which a hero sighed for amidst the crimes and troubles of war and conquest;* or, unless we take it to have been a prefiguration of the happiness we enjoy under our government of laws, we should not look with better success in the swamps and pine-barrens of the South, or on the rocky shores of New-England, for the place of that Elysium beyond the ocean, where the spirits of the just made perfect were to live forever amidst fragrance and flowers, and be refreshed by soft vernal airs. These illusions, at least, have been dissipated, as all such illusions necessarily are, by severe science—and those airy and fantastic images, that "played in the plighted clouds" of fiction and popular

---

* Plutarch in Sertorio.

credulity, taking so many pleasing shapes, and so many bright and beautiful and variable hues to the eyes of inventive genius, are utterly melted away in the broad and gairish light that has filled the whole hemisphere.

After all, it is some consolation to reflect, that, if we are mistaken in our notions upon this subject, and if the increase of the "materials of thought" is, indeed, to produce such wonderful effects upon the creative powers of genius, Shakspeare and Milton must, ere long, cease to be talked of as unrivalled, as we own, considering "the march of mind," it is high time they were. The mention of these great names, however, reminds us of what appears to be very much against this new theory, viz. that not only in England, but in all the other nations of Europe, except Germany, and in truth throughout the whole history of letters, the era of literature has preceded, sometimes by a vast interval, that of science. What have our philosophers to say to such a work as the Divina Commedia—on the very threshold of modern learning—three whole centuries before the age of Galileo and Bacon?

We now approach, with more confidence, the second question, how far it is worth our while to study the writings of the ancients as models, and to make them a regular part of an academic course. We shall be obliged to be more brief upon this branch of the subject than we could wish to be, but will endeavor to urge some of the strongest grounds in favor of the established system.

And first, it is, independently of all regard to their excellence, a most important consideration, that our whole literature in every part and parcel of it, has immediate and constant reference to these writings. This is so true, that no one, who is not a scholar can even understand—without the aid of labored scholia, which, after all, can never afford a just, much less a lively idea of the beauties of the text—thousands of the finest passages, both in prose and poetry. Let any one who doubts this, open Milton where he pleases, and read ten pages together, and we think he will confess that our opinion is well founded. Indeed, a knowledge of Latin and Greek is almost as much *presupposed* in our literature, as that of the alphabet, and the facts or the fictions of ancient history and mythology, are as familiarly alluded to in the learned circles of England, as any of the laws or phenomena in nature. They form a sort of conventional world, with which it is as necessary for an educated man to be familiar as with the real. Now, if there is no sort of knowledge which is not desirable, and scarcely any that is not useful—if it is worth the while of a man of leisure to become versed in the Chinese characters, or the Sanscrit, or to be able to decypher the Egyptian hieroglyphics, what shall we say of that branch of learning which was the great fountain of all European literature—which has left its impress upon every part of it, of which we are every moment reminded by its beauties, and without which, much that is most interesting in it is altogether enigmatical? It is vain to say, that good translations are at hand, which supersede the necessity of studying the originals. Works of *taste*, it is impossible to translate; and we do not believe there is any such thing in the world as a faithful version, that approaches to the excellence of the original work.* They are casts, in plaster of Paris, of the Apollo or the Venus—and, indeed, not near so good, inasmuch as eloquence and poetry are far less simple and more difficult of imitation than the forms of sculpture and statuary. There remains nothing but the body—and even that not unfrequently, so altered in its very lineaments, that its author would scarcely recognize it—while all "the vital grace is wanting, the native sweetness is gone, the color of primeval beauty is faded and decayed." It will not be so easily admitted, that the same objection holds in works of which utility, merely, is considered as the object, such as histories, &c. Yet it certainly does. The wonderful, the magical power of certain expressions, cannot by any art of composition be transfused from one language into another. The associations connected with particular works and phrases, must be acquired by long acquaintance with the language as it came warm from the hearts of those who spoke it, or they are frigid and even unmeaning. What translation can give any idea to the English reader of the bitter and contemptuous emphasis, and the powerful effect with which Demosthenes pronounces his Μάκεδων ανηρ, or of the force of that eloquent horror and astonishment with which Cicero exclaims against the *crucifixion* of a Roman citizen?†

In this connection, we would insist upon the stores of knowledge which are sealed up to all who are not conversant with the learned languages. This is a trite topic, but not the less important on that account. By far the most serious and engrossing concern of man—revealed religion—is built upon this foundation. The meaning of the Scriptures, which it is so important to understand, can be explained only by scholars, and the controversies of the present day, turn almost exclusively upon points of biblical criticism, &c. How *can* a divine, whose circumstances allow him any leisure, sit down in ignorance of such things?— How *can* he consent to take the awful information which he imparts to the multitudes committed to his care, at second hand? Surely here, if any where, it may emphatically be said *tardi ingenii est consectari rivulos, fontes rerum non videre.* Indeed,

---

* Pope's *imitations* of Horace are better translations than his Iliad. They are just what Horace would have done in English.
† On this subject we refer once more to the admirable remarks of Bishop Lowth's Lectures on Hebrew Poetry.—*Lect.* 8.

this single consideration is weighty enough to maintain the learned languages in their places, in all the universities of christendom.

But, it is not to theologians only that this branch of study is of great importance. How is the jurist to have access to the *corpus juris civilis*, of which Mr. Grimké expresses so exalted an opinion?—(page 26.) We agree with him in this opinion,* and while we deem with a mysterious reverence of our old and excellent common law—uncodified as it is—still we would have our lawyers to be deeply versed in the juridical wisdom of antiquity. Why? For the very same reason that we think it desirable that a literary man should be master of various languages, viz: to make him distinguish what is essentially, universally and eternally good and true, from what is the result of accident, of local circumstances, or the fleeting opinions of a day. That most invaluable of intellectual qualities—which ought to be the object of all discipline, as it is the perfection of all reason—a sound judgment, can be acquired only by such diversified and comprehensive comparisons. All other systems rear up bigots and pedants, instead of liberal and enlightened philosophers. Besides, every school has its mannerism and its mania, for which there is no cure but intercourse with those who are free from them, and constant access to the models of perfect and immutable excellence, which other ages have produced, and all ages have acknowledged. To point the previous observations, which are of very general application, more particularly to a topic touched upon before; even admiting that modern literature were as widely different from the ancient as the ememies of the latter contend, yet that would be no reason for neglecting the study of the Classics, but just the contrary. Human nature being the same in all ages, we may be sure that men agree in more points than they disagree in, and the best corrective of the extravagancies into which their *peculiarities* betray them, is to contrast them with the opposite peculiarities of others. If the tendency, therefore, of the modern or romantic style is to mysticism, irregularity and exaggeration—and that of the classical, to an excess of precision and severity, he would be least liable

---

* Mr. Grimké subjoins to the remarks, referred to, an extraordinary one, and says, he rejoices in being able to make it, viz: that the excellence of the civil law was owing to Justinian's being a christian. We are sorry to say, this opinion has to encounter the following difficulties,—1st. That the Golden Age of that Jurisprudence was three centuries before Justinian's reign; the age of Papinian, Paullus, Ulpian, &c. 2d. That Ulpian, so far from being a christian, was a most bigoted Pagan, and did all he could to poison the mind of Alexander Severus, with the maxims and the spirit of persecution.—*Gravin. Origin. I. C.* l. i. p. 125. 3d. Julius Cæsar had it in contemplation to "codify" the Roman law.—*Sueton: in Divo Julio.* c. 44. [4. The compiling of the Perpetual Edict. 5. The Gregorian and Hermogenian Codes, compiled under Constantine by two Pagans, to preserve the old Pagan Jurisprudence. Giannone, l. II.]

to fall into the excesses of either, who was equally versed in the excellencies of both. Certainly a critic who has studied both Shakspeare and Sophocles, must have a juster notion of the true excellence of dramatic composition, than he who has only studied one of them. Where they agreed he would be sure they were both right; where they happened, as they frequently do, to differ, he would, at once, be led to reflect much, before he awarded the preference to either, and to have a care lest, in indulging that preference, he should overstep the bounds of propriety and "the modesty of nature." It is thus, we repeat it, and only thus, that sound critics, sound philosophers, sound legislators, and lawyers worthy of their noble profession, can be formed.

There are other kinds of knowledge, besides what is interesting to divines and jurists, locked up in the learned languages. Whole branches of history and miscellaneous literature—of themselves extensive enough to occupy the study of a life. Look into Du Cange, Muratori, Fabricius, &c. In short, we pronounce, without fear of contradiction, that no man can make any pretentions to erudition, who is not versed in Greek and Latin.* He must be forever at a loss, and unable to help himself to what he wants in many departments of knowledge, even supposing him to have the curiosity to cultivate them, which is hardly to be expected of one who will not be at the pains of acquiring the proper means to do so with success. For we have always thought and still think—Mr. Grimké's speculative opinions being outweighed by his own practice—that those, who refuse to study a branch of learning so fundamental and so universally held in veneration as the Classics, have forgotten "the know thy self," when they prattle about profound erudition. In addition to all this, we venture to affirm that the *shortest* way to the knowledge of the history, antiquities, philosophy, &c., of all those ages, whose opinions and doings have been recorded in Greek and Latin, even supposing English writers to have gone over the same ground, is through the originals.† Compare the knowledge which a scholar acquires, not only of the policy and the *res gestæ* of the Roman emperors, but of the minutest shades and inmost recesses of their *character*, and that of the times in which they reigned, from the living pictures of Tacitus and Suetonius, with the cold, general, feeble, and what is worse, far from just and precise idea of the same thing, communicated by modern authors. The difference is incalculable. It is that between the true Homeric Achilles, and the Monsieur or Monseig-

[* Docti a Græcis petere malent, indocti ne a nobis quidem accipient. 2. Acad. Lib. 1. c. 2.]

[† Sin a Græcorum artibus et disciplinis abhorrerent, ne hæc quidem curaturos quæ sine eruditione Græcâ intelligi non possunt—says VARRO, in Cic. 2. Acad. Lib. 1. c. 2.]

neur Achille of the Théatre Français, at the beginning of the
last century, with his bob wig and small sword. When we read
of those times in English, we attach modern meanings to ancient
words, and associate the ideas of our own age and country,
with objects altogether foreign from them. In this point of view
as in every other, the cause of the Classics is that of all sound
learning.

We mention as another important consideration, that the
knowledge of these languages brings us acquainted, familiarly,
minutely and impressively, with a state of society altogether unlike any thing that we see in modern times. When we read a
foreign author of our own day, we occasionally, indeed, remark
differences in taste, in character and customs ; but in general, we
find ourselves *en pays de connaissance.* Modern civilization,
of which one most important element is a common religion, is
pretty uniform. But the moment we open a Greek book, we are
struck with the change. We are in quite a new world, combining all that is wonderful in fiction, with all that is instructive in
truth. Manners and customs, education, religion, national character, every thing is original and peculiar. Consider the priest
and the temple, the altar and the sacrifice, the chorus and the
festal pomp, the gymnastic exercises, and those Olympic games,
whither universal Greece repaired with all her wealth, her
strength, her genius and taste*—where the greatest cities and
kings, and the other first men of their day, partook with an enthusiastic rivalry, scarcely conceivable to us, in the interest of
the occasion, whether it was a race, a boxing match, a contest
of musicians, or an oration, or a noble history to be read *to* the
mingled throng—and where the horse and the rider, the chariot
and the charioteer, were consecrated by the honors of the crown
and the renown of the triumphal ode. Look into the theatres
where "the lofty grave tragedians" contend, in their turn, for
the favor of the same cultivated people, and where Aristophanes,
in verses, which, by the confesssion of all critics, were never
surpassed in energy and spirit, in Attic purity and the most exquisite modulations of harmony, is holding up Socrates—the
wisest of mankind—to the contempt and ridicule of the mob, if
that Athenian Demus, that could only be successfully courted with
such verses, does not disdain the appellation. Next go to the
schools, or rather "the shady spaces" of philosophy—single one
object out of the interesting groupe—let it be the most prominent—he, in short, who for the same reason was made to play
so conspicuous a part in the "Clouds." Consider the habits of
this hero of Greek philosophy, according to Xenophon's account†
of them ; now unlike any thing we have heard among the mo-

* Isocrates, Περι Ζευγους.
† Memorab. 1. A. 10.

derns ; passing his whole life abroad and in public—early in the morning visited the gymnasia and the most frequented walks, and about the time that the market-place was getting full, resorting thither, and all the rest of the day presenting himself wheresoever the greatest concourse of people was to be found, offering to answer any question in philosophy which might be propounded to him by the inquisitive. Above all, contemplate the fierce democracy in the popular assembly, listening to the harangues of orators, at once, with the jealousy of a tyrant and the fastidiousness of the most sensitive critics, and sometimes with the levity, the simplicity, and the wayward passions of childhood. Read their orations—above all, his, whose incredible pains to prepare himself for the perilous post of a *demagogue*, and whose triumphant success in it, every body has heard of—how dramatic, how mighty, how sublime ! Think of the face of the country itself, its monumental art, its cities adorned with whatever is most perfect and most magnificent in architecture—its public places peopled with the forms of ideal beauty—the pure air, the warm and cloudless sky, the whole earth covered with the trophies of genius, and the very atmosphere seeming to shed over all the selectest influences, and to breathe, if we may hazard the expression, of that native Ionian elegance which was in every object it enveloped.

It is impossible to contemplate the annals of Greek literature and art, without being struck with them, as by far the most extraordinary and brilliant phenomenon in the history of the human mind. The very language—even in its primitive simplicity, as it came down from the rhapsodists who celebrated the exploits of Hercules and Theseus, was as great a wonder as any it records. All the other tongues that civilized man have spoken, are poor and feeble, and barbarous, in comparison of it. Its compass and flexibility, its riches and its powers, are altogether unlimited. It not only expresses with precision, all that is thought or known at any given period, but it enlarges itself naturally, with the progress of science, and affords, as if without an effort, a new phrase, or a systematic nomenclature whenever one is called for. It is equally adapted to every variety of style and subject—to the most shadowy subtlety of distinction, and the utmost exactness of definition, as well as to the energy and the pathos of popular eloquence—to the majesty, the elevation, the variety of the epic, and the boldest license of the dithyrambic, no less than to the sweetness of the elegy, the simplicity of the pastoral, or the heedless gaiety and delicate characterization of comedy. Above all, what is an unspeakable charm—a sort of *naiveté* is peculiar to it, which appears in all those various styles, and is quite as becoming and agreeable in a historian or a philosopher—Xenophon for instance—as in the light and jocund numbers of Anacreon. Indeed, were there no other object in learning Greek but to see to what perfection language is capable of being carried, not only as a medium of communication, but as an instrument of thought, we see not why the time of a young man would not be just as well bestowed in acquiring a knowledge of it—for all the purposes, at least, of a liberal or elementary education—as in learning algebra, another specimen of a language or arrangement of signs perfect in its kind. But this wonderful idiom happens to have been spoken, as was hinted in the preceding paragraph, by a race as wonderful. The very first monument of their genius—the most ancient relic of letters in the Western world—stands to this day altogether unrivalled in the exalted class to which it belongs.* What was the history of this immortal poem and of its great fellow? Was it a single individual, and who was he, that composed them? Had he any master or model? What had been his education, and what was the state of society in which he lived? These questions are full of interest to a philosophical inquirer into the intellectual history of the species, but they are especially important with a view to the subject of the present discussion. Whatever causes account for the matchless excellence of these primitive poems, and for that of the language in which they are written, will go far to explain the extraordinary circumstance, that the same favoured people left nothing unattempted in philosophy, in letters and in arts, and attempted nothing without signal, and in some cases, unrivalled success. Winkelmant† undertakes to assign some reasons for this astonishing superiority of the Greeks, and talks very learnedly about a fine climate, delicate organs, exquisite susceptibility, the full developement of the human form by gymnastic exercises, &c. For our own part, we are content to explain the phenomenon after the manner of the Scottish school of metaphysicians, in which we learned the little that we profess to know of that department of philosophy,

---

*Milton is, perhaps, more sublime than Homer, and, indeed, than all other poets, with the exception, as we incline to think, of Dante. But if we adopt his own division of poetry into three great classes, viz. the epic, the dramatic, and the lyrical—the Paradise Lost, like the Divina Commedia, is more remarkable for Lyrical, (and sometimes for dramatic) than for epic beauties—for splendid details, than an interesting whole—for prophetic raptures bursting forth at intervals, than for the animation, the fire, the engrossing and rapid narrative of a metrical Romance. Who cares anything about the story or the plot, or feels any sympathy with the dramatis personæ—not even excepting Adam and Eve, whose insipid faultlessness reminds one of the Italian proverb—tanto buon che val niente. Besides, are not the preposterous vauntings and menaces of the devil against the Omnipotent, like the swaggering insolence of a slave behind his master's back—or his conspiracy like that of Caliban with Trinculo and Stephano, against the magic powers of Prospero? Devoted, as we are proud to avow ourselves, to Milton, we have always felt there was something even savouring of the comic in his Rabbinical plot.

† Historie de l'Art, &c.—Liv. 4.

by resolving it at once in an original law of nature : in other words, by substantially, but decently, confessing it to be inexplicable. But whether it was idiosyncrasy or discipline, or whatever was the cause, it is enough for the purposes of the present discussion, that the *fact* is unquestionable.

In one of Mr. Grimké's notes, (p. 77) we have the following remarks upon the story of Demosthenes' having repeatedly copied the great work of Thucydides with his own hand.

"Were instructors in *our* day to recommend an imitation of this example of the Athenian orator, it would be considered as *downright folly.* If the student of Divinity were told to copy Butler's Analogy, the student of Law, Blackstone's Commentaries, the student of Belles Lettres, *Kames* or *Alison*, and the student of Philosophy, Paley or Locke, it would be pronounced an unpardonable waste of time, and a very unintelligible mode of improvement."

Undoubtedly it would, and by no man sooner than Demosthenes himself, if he had the good fortune to live again "in *our* day." But what earthly analogy is there between the two cases? In that of the Greek orator, we see a young man preparing himself for the very hazardous career of a public speaker, in such an assembly as we have already described—the shrewd, sagacious, cavilling, hypercritical, but most polished and *musical* Athenian Demus—by endeavouring to acquire a perfect command of his language—the great instrument by which he was to accomplish every thing. In order to effect this, he not only attended the schools of Isæus and Plato, but he did what was still better ; he selected the *model* which he thought most perfect, and traced its lineaments over and over again, until he acquired, or rather surpassed, if possible, the excellencies of his great master. Besides, Mr. Grimké does not seem to be aware that the Greek language, admirable as it was in itself—vast and various as its powers had appeared in the older poets—and much as had been done for its prose by Plato, Isocrates, and others, had not yet attained to its utmost perfection—at least, for the purposes of popular declamation ; and that it was actually reserved for Demosthenes, by these very studies which would, it seems, be looked upon as "downright folly" in *our* day, to give it its last finishing—to impart to it,

   ——the full· resounding line,
The long majestic march and energy divine :*

but whoever heard Butler's Analogy or Kames' Elements commended for style, and who could not master their sense and argument without copying them at all ?

* So says Philostratus. βιος Ισοκρατους. In Cicero's time, the Pseudo or soi-disant Attics, who pestered him with their affectations and impertinences, held up Thucydides as the most perfect model of Attic purity and elegance. The orator himself, however, declares for Demosthenes—Quo ne Athenas quidem ipsas magis credo fuisse Atticas.—*Orat. ad Brut.* c. 7.

But our main purpose in quoting these remarks of Mr. Grimké, was to advert to the conclusion he draws from them, which we shall endeavour to turn against his own argument. It is as follows:

"Does not this act of Demosthenes very remarkably illustrate the fundamental difference between the ancients and moderns, that the former regarded *style* as an *end;* the latter as a means: that the former excel CHIEFLY in *style*, the latter PRE-EMINENTLY in *thought*."

We will treat this sentence (which we print just as it stood in the original) as Jupiter, among the poets, so often treats the prayers of unhappy mortals—half of it shall be granted, the other half dispersed in air. We think it undoubtedly true, as a general proposition, that the ancients, especially the Greeks, were more fastidious in regard to style than the moderns, and this is the very reason why they have been, and ought to be, universally preferred as models to form the taste of youth upon. But it is as undoubtedly wrong to affirm, that they were less scrupulous about sense or thought. Of their extreme delicacy and correctness of taste, innumerable proofs might be cited from all the writings of antiquity, but especially from that rich mine of philosophical criticism, both theoretical and practical, the rhetorical writings of Cicero. His manner of expressing himself upon this subject is quite remarkable. He speaks of the niceness and scrupulosity of the Attic ear*—which was so great that a single false quantity or misplaced accent would excite the clamours of a whole theatre,† besides many other instances which our limits forbid us to adduce. An example of the same thing that has always struck us very forcibly, is to be found in the gibes which Æschines, even upon an occasion of such extraordinary interest and importance as the famous accusation of Ctesiphon, so confidently indulges in, with regard to certain expressions that had escaped his great rival in former debates; as if, said Demosthenes, it concerned the well-being of the commonwealth, whether I used this word or that or stretched forth my arm thus or thus. Yet we are willing that the whole cause of Greek literature should depend upon that single controversy, and upon the opinion of any liberal and enlightened critic, as to the merits of those very orations so laboriously prepared, and so unsparingly censured. Indeed, (as has already been remarked with respect to the comedies of Aristophanes) what better proof can be given of the wonderful refinement of an Athenian audience than that this peerless orator felt it *necessary* to take so much pains in preparing his harangues, and met with such tri-

---

* Teretes et religiosas aures Atticorum.—(We quote this and the following from memory.) Brutus c. 9.

† At in his (numeris et modis,) &c. tota theatra reclamant :—*Brutus.* Something like this may be seen in the parterre of the Theatre Français; but Paris is not Athens.

umphant success in delivering them? It is impossible to imagine a work of genius, executed in a more simple and severe taste; and Hume does not, we think, exaggerate their merit when he affirms, that of all human productions, the orations of Demosthenes present us with the models which approach nearest to perfection.* But wherein, principally, did that wonderful excellence consist? In this—that his style, elaborate and admirable as it was, seemed to make no part of his concern, and that he was wrapped up with his whole heart and soul, in the subject—in the occasion—in the measure proposed—in the glory of Athens, and the welfare and liberties of all Greece. So it is with the other Greek classics. This naked simplicity of style, united with the highest degree of refinement, is what strikes a modern reader most, especially before he is become familiar with it. Yet this peculiar people, who would tolerate no expressions but the most chaste and natural†—who would have spurned from the βημα a public speaker that did not know how to sink the rhetorician in the statesman and the man of business‡—to whom any thing like the ambitious ornaments so much admired in this philosophic age, would have been an abomination§—this people it is, that are represented as considering *style* as an *end*, instead of a *means*, and as sacrificing sense to sound!

The conclusion which we draw from Mr. Grimké's premises is, as we have already intimated, that this proposed *defect* of the classical authors, would be alone sufficient to keep them where they are in our schools. We shall now add the last consideration which our limits will permit us to suggest, on this part of the subject.

In discussing the very important question whether boys ought to be made to study the Classics, as a regular part of education—the innovators put the case in the strongest possible manner against the present system, by arguing as if the young pupil, under this discipline, was to learn nothing else but language itself. We admit that this notion has received some sort of countenance from the excessive attention paid in the English schools to prosody, and the fact that their great scholars have been, perhaps, (with many exceptions to be sure) more distinguished by the refinement of their scholarship, than the extent and profoundness of their erudition. But the grand advantage of a classical education consists far less in acquiring a language or two, which, as languages, are to serve for use or for ornament in

---

* Essay xiii. of Eloquence.　　　　† See Longinus, c. 3.

‡ Isocrates Παναθηναικὸς in exordio.

§ Cicero characterizes the Asiatic style—as opimum quoddam et tanquam adipatæ dictionis genus, (Brutus, c. 8,)—(a felicitous and *untranslateable* phrase) which the Rhodians did not relish much, and the Attics could not tolerate at all. We fear the style so much in vogue nowadays—in Scotland especially—is in this category.

future life, than in the things that are learned in making that acquisition, and yet more in the *manner* of learning those things. It is a wild conceit to suppose, that the branches of knowledge, which are most rich and extensive, and most deserve to engage the researches of a mature mind, are, therefore, the best for training a young one. Metaphysics, for instance, as we have already intimated, though in the last degree unprofitable as a science, is a suitable and excellent, perhaps, a necessary part of the intellectual discipline of youth. On the contrary, international law is extremely important to be known by publicists and statesmen, but it would be absurd to put Vattel (as we have ourselves seen it done, in a once celebrated academy, in a certain part of the United States,) into the hands of a lad of fifteen or sixteen. We will admit, therefore, what has been roundly asserted at hazard, and without rhyme or reason, that classical scholars discontinue these studies after they are grown wise enough to know their futility, and only read as much Greek and Latin as is necessary to keep up their knowledge of them, or rather to save appearances, and gull credulous people; yet we maintain that the concession does not affect the result of this controversy in the least. We regard the whole period of childhood and of youth—up to the age of sixteen or seventeen, and perhaps longer—as one allotted by nature to growth and improvement in the strictest sense of those words.* The flexible powers are to be trained rather than tasked—to be carefully and continually practised in the preparatory exercises, but not to be loaded with burthens that may crush them, or be broken down by overstrained efforts of the race. It is in youth, that Montaigne's maxim, always excellent—is especially applicable—that the important question is, not who is most learned, but who has learned the best. Now, we confess we have no faith at all in young prodigies—in your philosophers in teens. We have generally found these precocious smatterers sink in a few years into barrenness and imbecility, and that as they begin by being men when they ought to be boys, so they end in being boys when they ought to be men. If we would have good fruit we must wait until it is in season. Nature herself has pointed out, too clearly to be misunderstood, the proper studies of childhood and youth. The senses are first developed—observation and memory follow—then imagination begins to dream and to create—afterwards ratiocination, or the dialectical propensity and faculty, shoots up with great rankness†—and last of all, the crowning perfection of intellect, sound judgment and solid reason, which, by much experience in life, at length ripen into wisdom.‡ The vicissitudes

---

[* See Plato, Rep. 1. vi. 498.]   [† Plato, Rep. 1. 7. 53. 9 b.]
[‡ Quid est autem non dicam in homine sed in omni cœlo atque terra, ratione divinius? (Quæ, quum adolevit, atque perfecta est, nominatur rite sapientia. Cic. de Leg. Lib. 1. c. 7.]

of the seasons, and the consequent changes in the face of nature, and the cares and occupations of the husbandman, are not more clearly distinguished or more unalterably ordained. To break in upon this harmonious order—to attempt to anticipate these pre-established periods, what is it, as Cicero had it, but, after the manner of the Giants, to war against the laws of the Universe, and the wisdom that created it? And why do so? Is not the space in human life, between the eighth and twentieth year, quite large enough for acquiring *every* branch of liberal knowledge, as well as is needed, or, indeed, can be acquired in youth? For instance, we cite the opinion of Condorcet, repeatedly quoted, with approbation, by Dugald Stewart, and if we mistake not, by Professor Playfair too, (each of them the highest authority on such a subject,) that any one may, under competent teachers, acquire all that Newton or La Place knew, in *two* years. The same observation, of course, applies a *fortiori* to any other branch of science. As for the modern languages, the study of French ought to be begun early for the sake of the pronunciation, and continued through the whole course, as it may be, without the smallest inconvenience. Of German, we say nothing, because we cannot speak of our own knowledge ; but for Italian and Spanish, however difficult they may be, especially their poetry—to a mere English scholar, they are so easy of acquisition to any one who understands Latin, that it is not worth while even to notice them in our scheme. All that we ask then, is, that a boy should be thoroughly taught the ancient languages from his eighth to his sixteenth year, or thereabouts, in which time he will have his taste formed, his love of letters completely, perhaps enthusiastically awakened, his knowledge of the principles of universal grammar perfected, his memory stored with the history, the geography, and the chronology of all antiquity, and with a vast fund of miscellaneous literature besides, and his imagination kindled with the most beautiful and glowing passages of Greek and Roman poetry and eloquence: all the rules of criticism familiar to him—the sayings of sages, and the achievements of heroes, indelibly impressed upon his heart. He will have his curiosity fired for further acquisition, and find himself in possession of the golden keys, which open all the recesses where the stores of knowledge have ever been laid up by civilized man. The consciousness of strength will give him confidence, and he will go to the rich treasures themselves and take what he wants, instead of picking up eleemosynary scraps from those whom, in spite of himself, he will regard as his betters in literature. He will be let into that great communion of scholars throughout all ages and all nations—like that more awful communion of saints in the Holy Church Universal—and feel a sympathy with departed genius, and with the enlightened and the gifted minds of other countries, as they appear before him, in the transports of a sort of Vision Beatific, bowing down at the same shrines and glowing with the same holy love of whatever is most pure and fair, and exalted and divine in human nature. Above all, our American youth will learn, that liberty—which is sweet to all men, but which is the *passion* of proud minds that cannot stoop to less—has been the nurse of all that is sublime in character and genius. They will see her form and feel her influence in every thing that antiquity has left for our admiration—that bards consecrated their harps to her*—that she spoke from the lips of the mighty orators—that she fought and conquered, acted and suffered with the heroes whom she had formed and inspired; and, after ages of glory and virtue, fell with *Him*—her all-accomplished hope—*Him*, the LAST of ROMANS— the self-immolated martyr of Philippi.† Our young student will find his devotion to his country—his free country—become at once more fervid and more enlightened, and think scorn of the wretched creatures who have scoffed at the sublime simplicity of her institutions, and "esteem it," as one expresses it, who learned to be a republican in the schools of antiquity,‡ much better to imitate the old and elegant humanity of Greece, than the barbaric pride of a Norwegian or Hunnish stateliness; and, let us add, will come much more to despise that slavish and nauseating subserviency to rank and title, with which all European literature is steeped through and through. If Americans are to study any foreign literature at all, it ought, undoubtedly, to be the Classical, and especially the Greek.

The very difficulties of these studies, which make it necessary that so many years should be devoted to them—the novelty, the strangeness of the form, are a great recommendation. This topic is a most important one, and we would gladly follow it out; but we have already far exceeded our limits. We will just observe, that the reason, which Quinctilian gives for beginning with the Greek, is of universal application. The mother-tongue is acquired as of course—in the nursery—at the fire-side—at the parental board—in society—every where. It is familiar to us long before we are capable of remarking its peculiarities. This familiarity has its usual effects of diminishing curiosity and interest, and of making us regard, without emotion and even without attention, what, if it came recommended by novelty, would leave the deepest impression. It is so with every thing in nature and in art. "Difficulties increase passions of every kind,

---

* See Lowth's first Lecture before referred to.
† Who can read Appian's account of this ever memorable battle without shedding tears? [Brutus quidem noster, excellens omni genere laudis, &c. Cic. 2. Acad. Post. l. 3. Cf. Plutarch in Brut.]
‡ Milton—Areopagitica.

and by rousing our attention and exciting our active powers, they produce an emotion, which nourishes the prevailing affection."[*] Before his eighth year, a boy should be perfectly well grounded in the rudiments of English—and then if his master be a scholar that deserves the name, he could learn his own language better by having occasion to use it in translations, both prose and metrical, of the ancient languages, than by all the lessons and lectures of a mere English teacher from his birth to his majority. Indeed, it would be difficult, in the present state of our literature to imagine any thing more insipid, spiritless, imperfect, and unprofitable than such a course. But we must break off here.

We were going to appeal to experience, but we know the answer that will be made. It is not sufficient: but this too must be deferred. In the mean time, we earnestly exhort our readers to consider the state of the question as we have put it. Not to have the curiosity to study the learned languages is not to have any vocation at all for literature: it is to be destitute of liberal curiosity and of enthusiasm; to mistake a self-sufficient and superficial dogmatism for. philosophy, and that complacent indolence which is the bane of all improvement for a proof of the highest degree of it. As somebody quoted by Horne Tooke says, *qui alios a literarum et linguarum studio absterrent, non antiquæ sapientiæ, sed novæ stultitiæ doctores sunt habendi.* Mr. Grimké's speculative opinions we think utterly erroneous— his excellent example cannot be too closely imitated—but it is unfortunately easy for all to repeat the one, while few have the industry and perseverance to follow the other.

[*]Hume's Essay XXII. of Tragedy.

ROMAN LITERATURE.

History of Roman Literature, from its earliest period to the Augustan Age. By John Dunlop, Author of the History of Fiction. 2 vols. From the last London Edition. *E. Littell. Philadelphia.* 1827.

Mr. Dunlop is already known to many of our readers by his interesting and popular History of Fiction. By the accomplishment of the present undertaking he will have greatly added to the obligations which he has already imposed upon the public. He is supplying a very important desideratum in English literature. The execution of the work thus far, is, upon the whole, worthy of the design, and few books can be mentioned in which so much useful knowledge is conveyed in so agreeable a style. There is, however, very little novelty either in the views of our author, or in the learning with which he illustrates and enforces them. The numerous subjects that fall within his comprehensive plan, have been long ago 'bolted to the bran' by many erudite men, and nothing remained for the historian but to collect and arrange the abundant materials that had been prepared for him, and to embellish them with the graces of an elegant and attractive style. If we may be allowed moreover to speak our minds with perfect freedom, we will confess that there is something wanting, after all, in Mr. Dunlop's manner of treating his subject. He does not appear to us to write altogether *con amore.* At least, there is not that hearty zeal, that captivating and *contagious* enthusiasm which breathes through the pages of Schlegel and Sismondi, and imparts to them so lively an interest, and such a warm and delightful coloring. In a word, the history of Roman literature, however great an acquisition to the general reader, partakes too much of the character of *mere* compilation, and though, as compilation, uniformly satisfactory, exact and elegant, is occasionally, withal, rather cold and spiritless.

Perhaps, however, we are imputing to the workman what ought to be considered as, in some degree at least, the defects of his materials. Roman literature, especially the earlier Roman literature, which occupies so large a space in the work before us, is far less calculated to inspire enthusiasm, than that of the Greeks, or even that of the South of Europe, especially about the period of the revival of letters. The reason may be given in a single word—it is altogether exotic and imitative. Greek literature, on the contrary, was perfectly original. That wonderful people was, in this respect, at least a primitive race—a nation of αυτοχθονες.* There is no trace in their poetry and eloquence of any foreign influence or heterogeneous admixture. With them every thing was barbarous that was not Greek. Their genius drew its inspiration from the living fountains of nature—from the scenes in which it actually moved—from events which immediately affected its own destinies—from opinions that had laid a strong hold on the popular belief—from the exaggerated traditions of an heroic ancestry—from every thing, in short, that is most fitted to excite the imagination, and to come home to the heart, and all its deep and devoted affections. The theme of their matchless Epic was the war which first united them in a great national object, and proved that they were formed to conquer and to subjugate barbarians.† The calamities of the Labdacidæ and the Pelopidæ furnished the scenes of their "gorgeous tragedy." The animated interest of their Olympic contests inspired the muse of Pindar, and the valor of Harmodius and Aristogiton was celebrated in many a festal hymn, and by many a tuneful lyre. Their elegant and poetical mythology peopled all nature with animated and beautiful forms, and consecrated, ennobled, and adorned the most ordinary objects. A local habitation, a temple, a grove, a grotto—was assigned, amidst the scenes of daily toil and the resorts of busy life, to every divinity in their endless calendar. Their Parnassus was no unmeaning common place—no empty name as it is in our modern poetry. It was "haunted, holy ground"—breathing inspiration from its caves, and covered all over with religious awe.‡ Attica, says Strabo, was a creation and a monument of God and godlike ancestors. Not a part of it but is signalized and celebrated by history or fiction.§ Is it any wonder that objects like these, that scenes so full of religion and poetry should have awakened all the enthusiasm of genius, which, in its turn, was to reflect back on them its own glory, and to hallow them with associations still more awful and affecting? The Ædipus Coloneus and the Eumenides, both of them written professedly to honor Athens and the Athenians, are memorable examples of a poetry, which seems to have been inspired by the event and the place, and to have made both more interesting and impressive.

There is reality in all this. The literature of such a people

---

[* ἡ μεν Αττικὴ μουσα καὶ ἀρχαία καὶ αὐτόχθων.—Dion. Hal. περι ΤΩΝ ΑΡΧ. ΡΗΤ. μπομν. proemium.]

† Isocrates, Ἑλενῆς εγκωμιον.

‡ Ἱεροπρεπὴς δ᾽ ἐςι πᾶς ὁ Παρνασσος ἔχων αντρα τε και αλλα χωρια, τιμωμενα τε και ἀγιστευομένα.—Strabo, B. ix., c. 3.

§ Ibid, c. 1.

is an essential part of their history as a nation. *Its* character stands in intimate relation, both of cause and effect, to *their* character. Springing out of their most touching interests and associations—out of what would be called, by German critics, their "inward life"—it deserves to be classed among their most important social institutions. Instead of being, as classical learning once was all over Europe, the business of mere pedants and book-worms, producing no effect whatever upon the mass of mankind—the mighty multitude who feel and act—it is inwoven into the very frame and constitution of society—pervades, informs, warms, quickens it throughout. Men of genius, indeed, experience its first and its strongest impulses ; but the people too, and even the populace, are very much under its influence. They partake of the enthusiasm that is abroad—they feel, though in a less degree, the same passionate love for that ideal beauty which is the object of the arts, and with somewhat of the same aspirations after excellence, they acquire an instinctive perception, or feeling rather, which enables them to discern and to enjoy it with all the delicacy and the sensibility of refined taste. These are the causes and the characteristics of a *national* literature ; and there is no example in this kind that will bear to be mentioned in comparison with that of Greece.

The early literature of the South of Europe, to which we alluded above, though not so perfectly spontaneous and unmixed, is still distinguished by a striking air of originality. It bears the stamp of the times and the manners. The lay of the Troubadour, full of gallantry and sentimental love, was indebted for none of its charms to the lyrical poetry of antiquity. These simple effusions, the first language, perhaps the first lessons of chivalry, breathed a spirit which had never animated the numbers of Anacreon and Tibullus. It was evident, even from them, that a new order of ages was beginning from a new era. The Divina Comedia, the Decamerone, and the Canzoni of Petrarch, although the productions of men who had read more, and who rank among the most renowned votaries and restorers of classical learning, are certainly not formed upon the ancient models. They exhibit all the freedom, the freshness and originality of a primitive literature. Dante, indeed, avows himself a follower, an humble follower of Virgil, but no two things can be more unlike than the original and the supposed copy. The antique grandeur and simplicity of the Æneid, and the perfect regularity of its proportions are not more strikingly contrasted with the wildness and eccentricities of his fable, than its whole spirit and character with the dark, dismal, and dreadful imaginings of the Inferno, or those dazzling visions of glory and beatitude, which are revealed by Beatrice in the Paradiso. The same thing may be said of Ariosto, and, with all his classic elegance and accuracy, of Tasso too. Their subjects alone are full of poetry. They are such as address themselves most powerfully to the feelings of a modern reader. They are connected with all that we have been taught to consider as most venerable and captivating, and imposing in the history of modern society: with the holy land and the holy cross, with the knight and the priest, with palmers and pilgrims, and paladins and peers, with "the fierce wars and the faithful loves," and the thousand other incidents, and consequences and associations, direct or remote, of chivalry and the crusades. There is something like enchantment in the very names of those who are supposed to have figured in this heroic age of the modern world—the heroes and heroines of Turpin's Chronicle. Nor is this altogether due, as some may think, to the elegant fictions into which these rude materials have been wrought up in later times. The simplest old romaunt or fabliau, has, we confess a secret charm for us as an image, however imperfect, of that interesting state of society, the gentis cunabula nostræ. Imagine Dante and Ariosto to have confined themselves to a bare translation of the celebrated poems of antiquity, or to have attempted the same subjects in a close and studied imitation. With what different feelings would they have been regarded by us! and how much less interest would have been excited by the literary history of that period!

Roman literature, especially in its earliest stages, had, of all others, the least originality. It was five whole centuries after the building of the city, before that nation of sages and warriors could boast of a single author. During this long period, there is no vestige of any thing that can be supposed to have been a regular composition in verse, except a sort of Pythagorean poem of Appius Claudius Cæcus, mentioned by Cicero.* The only history which can be given of their literature during all that interval, as Mr. Dunlop forcibly remarks, consists in the progress and improvement of the Latin language. When, at length, it arose, it was not only not indigenous like that of the Greeks, but it bore the stamp of inferiority, and even of servility upon its brow. Livius Andronicus, who first attempted a regular dramatic fable, was a native of Magna Græcia, where he was taken prisoner, according to Tiraboschi, and became the slave and afterwards the freedman of Livius Salinator. Terence was a slave, and what is still more extraordinary, a Carthaginian. Cæcilius also was a slave, and Plautus, if not in the same degraded condition, was yet in such humble circumstances as to be compelled to labor at a mill for his daily bread. These were among the fathers, (if we do not abuse the word) of Roman literature. Their works were servile copies. It is cu-

* Tuscul. Quæst.—lib. iv. c. 2.

rious to collate the lists, which Mr. Dunlop furnishes, of the lost tragedies of Ennius, Attius, Pacuvius, &c. They are all—to judge from their names and the fragments—upon subjects that had been treated by the Greek tragedians, and were no doubt very coarse and imperfect imitations of those beautiful works. The Paulus of Pacuvius is the first, and one of exceedingly few instances of the Tragedia Prætextata, or tragedy turning upon a domestic story. All the comedies of Plautus and Terence are professed translations of Menander, Philemon, and other Greek writers—how free or literal need not be mentioned here.* In a word, if those heroic ballads or metrical chronicles, in which Niebuhr supposes the principal events of Roman story for the first four centuries to have been versified, ever existed at all, they had not the effect of giving rise to any thing like a *national* poetry at a more advanced period of letters.

The phenomenon, which the early Literary History of Rome thus presents, is easily explained. The nation was essentially *practical.*† Sallust, speaking of the Athenian wits who had extolled the glory of their country to the skies in their writings, expresses himself as follows:—"The Roman people never possessed the same advantage, because, with us, the ambition of men of talents was to excel in the conduct of affairs. No one addicted himself to speculative pursuits. The best men chose rather to act than to speak well—to have their own deeds recorded by others, than to relate what others had done. So that, both at home and abroad, in peace and in war, good morals were the great object of their attention and discipline." These good morals could not exist, according to the true Roman standard, without mortifying and subduing those feelings which are the very soul of poetry and eloquence. Their langauge, as might have been expected, bore the impress of their opinions upon these subjects. The highest and favorite epithets of praise are *vir fortis—vir gravis:* courage and constancy, with a sort of toical gravity and austerity, were, it seems, essential to their idea of virtue. They were predestined to the conquest of the world and the government of mankind, and they seem to have pursued these great objects from the very first, with a single eye and a systematic and inflexible ambition. Almost all politcal power, notwithstanding the veto of the Tribune, and the occasional disorders of the Comitia Tributa, was practically vested in the Patrician order. These haughty and martial descendants of Censors and Consuls—of the Furii, the Junii, the Cornelii,—would

---

* [See them mentioned, Brutus, c. 19.]

† [Quæ omnes artes in veri investigatione versantur, cujus studio a rebus gerendis abduci contra officium est; virtutis enim laus omnis in actione consistit. Cic. de Offic. l. i. c. 6. Et iis *forsitan* concedendum sit rempublicam non capessentibus qui excellenti engenio, &c. Ib. c. 21.]

have thought themselves degraded by literary pursuits. It would have been considered as a proof of degenerate sloth—a despicable effeminacy and poorness of spirit in a young man to exchange the hopes of a triumph, and the glory of adding to the *images* and honors of his family, even for the highest possible distinction in the studies of Greeks and slaves. Their military training and service were alone sufficient to preclude these studies in the earlier and severer ages of the Commonwealth—Ingenium nemo sine corpore exercebat. This aversion from literary pursuits was not the effect of mere ignorance or rudeness, but of system and policy. These ancient Romans were an eminently enlightened people. Their scheme of conquest had been organized with profound wisdom, all the departments of their government were filled with consummate skill and ability, and in every sense of the word, "there was nothing barbarous in the discipline of these barbarians." It ought not to surprise us, therefore, to find the prejudices we are speaking of so deeply rooted and inveterate at Rome. It is plain, from the pains which Cicero* takes, in so many parts of his philosophical writings, to apologise for the composing of them, that he felt the studies of Plato to be somewhat unworthy of himself; Virgil characterises his own pursuits as "studia ignobilis otii," and there is a remarkable passage in the life of Agricola, which shews that, even in his time, the dignity or the duties of "a Roman and a Senator" did not permit him to be very profoundly versed in philosophy and learning.† At Athens, on the contrary, and, indeed, throughout all Greece, the enthusiasm of the people for works of genius and taste, showed itself on all occasions, in the liveliest demonstrations of admiration and homage for those who excelled in them. Sophocles held the rank of General along with Thucydides and Pericles—a matchless combination! We are assured by Aristophanes, the grammarian, in his "Argument" to the Antigone, that the success of that tragedy got its author the command in the Samian expedition, while the verses of Euripides softened even the bitterness of hatred and hostility, and saved from butchery, in a war of extermination, all who were fortunate enough to be able to repeat them.

Certainly nothing could be more unfavourable to literature, especially to its more refined productions, than the state of public opinion at Rome, and the whole spirit and character of her institutions as they are pourtrayed in the preceding observations. Not to speak of the more direct and obvious discourage-

---

[*De Off. II. c. 1 and 2.—N. D. l. 4—Lucull (2 Acad.) c. 2—de Fin.— l. l. c. 1 Orat. c. 41.|

†Memoriâ teneo solitum ipsum (Agricolam) narrare se, in primâ juventâ, studium philosophiæ acrius ultrà quam concessum *Romano et senatori*, hausisse, &c. c. 4. [Cf. Sallust. De B. J., proem.]

ments that have been alluded to, there was something essentially tame and prosaical in such a condition of society. "Ce n'est pas aux lois les plus sages, says M. de Sismondi, aux temps d'ordre et de prosperité, qu' est réservé le plus grand développement del' imagination chez un peuple." This position is strikingly exemplified by the history of France, from the 11th to the 15th century. In the first half of this period, the nation was exclusively under the influence, and received all its impulses from the character and pursuits of the *seigneurs de chateaux*. In the second, the commercial spirit of the towns predominated. The lawless Baron, who held only his sword, and, submitting to no sovereign, scarcely deigned to acknowledge a superior—

Che libito fe' licito in sua legge—

and whose castle was an emblem and epitome of the existence which it protected, with its moat and drawbridge for retreat and seclusion, its turretted battlements for defence, its donjon keep where the captive pined in darkness and chains, its hall resounding with revelry and merriment, with the minstrel's song and the dance of the gay and the fair—if not himself a Troubadour, like Cœur de Lion, or Alfonso I., was at least the natural friend of the Troubadour. This simple, but pleasing and peculiar poetry, accordingly flourished under their favour and cultivation. Under the influence of the commercial spirit, on the contrary, it died away—men at arms yielded to men of business—the useful supplanted the agreeable, and the *ærugo et cura peculi*, of which Horace speaks, produced the same effect in France as at Rome.

The following remarks of Mr. Dunlop deserve to be cited in this connection :—

"Literary history is, *secondly*, of importance, as being the index of the character and condition of a people—as holding up a mirror, which reflects the manners and customs of remote or ancient nations. The less influence, however, which literature exercises, the less valuable will be its picture of life and manners. It must also be admitted that, from a separate cause, the early periods, at least, of Roman literature possess not in this point of view any peculiar attractions. When literature is indigenous, as it was in Greece, where authors were guided by no antecedent system, and their compositions were shaped on no other model than the objects themselves which they were occupied in delineating, or the living passions they pourtrayed, an accurate estimate of the general state of manners and feeling may be drawn from works written at various epochs of the national history. But, at Rome, the pursuit of literature was neither a native nor predominant taste among the people. The Roman territory was always a foreign soil for letters, which was not the produce of national genius, but were naturalized by the assiduous culture of a few individuals reared in the schools of Greece. Indeed, the early Roman authors, particularly the dramatic, who, of all others, best illustrate the prevalent ideas and sentiments of a nation, were mere translators from the Greek. Hence those delineations, which at first view might appear to be characteristic national sketches, are in fact the draught of foreign manners, and the mirror of customs which no Roman adopted, or of sentiments in which, perhaps, no Roman participated.

"Since, then, the literature of Rome exercised but a limited influence on the conduct of its citizens, and as it reciprocally reflects but a partial light on their manners and institutions, its history must, in a great measure, consist of biographical sketches of *authors*—of critical accounts of their *works*—and an examination of the *influence* which these works have exercised on modern literature. The *authors* of Rome were, in their characters, and the events of their lives, more interesting than the writers of any ancient or modern land. The authors who flourished during the existence of the Roman Republic, were Cato, the Censor, Cicero and Cæsar : men who (independently of their literary claims to celebrity) were unrivalled in their own age and country, and have scarcely been surpassed in any other. I need not here anticipate those observations which the *works* of the Roman authors will suggest in the following pages. Though formed on a model which has been shaped by the Greeks, we shall perceive, through that spirit of imitation which marks all their literary productions, a tone of practical utility, derived from the familiar acquaintance which their writers exercised with the business and affairs of life ; and also that air of nationality, which was acquired from the greatness and unity of the Roman Republic, and could not be expected in literary works, produced where there was a subdivision of states in the same country, as in Greece, modern Italy, Germany and Britain. We shall remark a characteristic authority of expression, a gravity, circumspection, solidity of understanding, and dignity of sentiment, produced partly by the moral firmness that distinguished the character of the Romans, their austerity of manners, and tranquillity of temper, but chiefly by their national pride, and the exalted name of Roman citizen, which their authors bore. And finally, we shall recognize that love of rural retirement, which originated in the mode of life of the ancient Italians, and was augmented by the pleasing contrast, which the undisturbed repose and simple enjoyments of rural existence presented to the bustle of an immense and agitated capital. In the last point of view that has been alluded to—the *influence* which these works have exercised on modern letters—it cannot be denied that the literary history of Rome is peculiarly interesting. If the Greeks gave the first impulse to literature, the Romans engraved the traces of its progress deeper on the world."—*Pref.* ix–xi.

Mr. Dunlop remarks that "there are three great ages in the literary history of Rome—that which precedes the era of Augustus—the epoch which is stamped with the name of that emperor, and the interval which commenced immediately after his death, and may be considered as extending to the destruction of Rome." In the present volumes, he has brought down his work only to Cicero, inclusive. Whether he shall extend his researches to the other two periods, will depend, he assures us, on the reception which his first effort may obtain from the public. We are happy to learn that a third volume has recently issued from the press, the contents of which, together with the multifarious remains of the great Roman orator, and the remarks of our author concerning Sallust, and the older historians, may furnish the materials of a future article. For the present, we shall confine ourselves to the following heads : 1. Etruria and

the Latin Language.   2. The Drama, including the Attellane
Fables and the Mimes.   3. Miscellaneous Literature.

1. The origin of the first inhabitants of those Italian States,
which were finally merged in the Roman Republic, is hidden
in the mist of ages—nor are the antiquities of India or of Egypt
more impenetrable than those of Etruria.   Discouraging, however, as a subject wrapped up in so much obscurity, might
be. expected to prove, it has attracted the most persevering
researches, and excited endless controversy both among the
ancients and the moderns.   The situation of Italy—accessible
on all sides but one by sea—afforded facilities, while the fertility
of its soil and the softness of its delicious climate, were a strong
temptation to those wandering tribes whose adventurous emi-
grations so frequently occur in the early history of all nations.
It is very probable, therefore, that this rich and beautiful peninsula received colonies, in a remote age, from many different points in the extensive coast of the Mediterranean, the
Ægean and the Adriatic ; nor ought it to surprise us that Egyptian, Phœnician and Greek customs, and even names, may
be recognised in various parts of it.   Nothing, it is evident
therefore, can be more unsafe than to build up a theory on
such facts and appearances as these, with a view to explain the
first peopling of the country.   What greatly confirms this view
of the subject is, that "there is scarcely an ancient history or
document entitled to credit, and recording the arrival of a colony
in Italy, which does not mention that the new comers found
prior tribes, with whom they waged war or intermixed."

Judging from our own distaste for antiquarian researches, we
suppose our readers to be as little inclined to receive, as we are
to furnish, a detailed account of the various hypotheses, or rather
wild guessing, to which this puzzling question has given rise.
We will content ourselves, therefore, with stating, in a very
summary manner, some of the more prominent opinions that
have been entertained in relation to it, as they are set forth by
our author.   The earliest is that of Herodotus,* who represents
the Etruscans as a colony of Lydians, who were themselves a
tribe of wandering Pelasgi.   In the reign of Atys, son of Menes,
a sore famine made it necessary that half of the Lydian nation
should go abroad in quest of food, under Tyrrhenus, a son of
that monarch.   It was not, however, before they had tried, for
eighteen years together, the singular expedient of fasting every
other day, and inventing all the common games and pastimes,
to forget, if possible, their hunger in their amusement, that they
repaired to Smyrna, where they built vessels and committed
themselves to the mercy of the winds and the fates.   After
touching upon various shores, they at length settled in Umbria,

* Clio, c. 94.

which they called Tyrrhenia, after the name of their leader.
This account of Herodotus is said to be corroborated by certain
resemblances in the religion, language and pastimes of the Lydians and the Etrurians ; and as some of the sailors *may* have
been Phœnicians, Egyptians or Greeks, a mixture of this sort
may account for those appearances which have led antiquarians
to consider the Etruscans as descendants of these latter nations.
Herodotus was followed (with some slight variations) by the
majority of ancient writers, Cicero, Strabo, V. Paterculus, Seneca, Pliny, Plutarch* and Servius, to whom we may add, Catullus
and Horace.   The Etruscans themselves seem to have been of
the same opinion.† Hellanicus of Lesbos,‡ who was almost contemporary with the father of history, believed that people to be a
colony of Pelasgi, direct from Greece.   Dionysius of Halicarnassus, is dissatisfied with both the foregoing opinions, and pronounces them a race of Aborigines. He admits, however, that a
tribe of Pelasgi passed from Thessaly to the mouth of the Po
many years before the Trojan war, and spreading themselves
over Italy, ultimately mingled with the native race.

The opinion of Dionysius has been adopted by several learned
men, and among them Gibbon, who affirms that the story of
Herodotus *ne peut convenir qu' aux poétes.*§ Some recent Italian
writers are for a race of Aborigines, tracing their pedigree to an
Adam and Eve of their own.‖   Gori and Lord Monboddo derive both the Etruscans and the Pelasgi from Egypt and Phœ-
nicia.   Mazzochi adopts, in general, the oriental theory, which
he endeavors to help out by some fanciful etymologies.   Our
readers may be glad to have a specimen of these.   They may
be justly commended as belonging to that perfection of logic, of
which the boast is to deduce *quidlibet ex quolibet*.   Padus (the
Po) is clearly derived from Paddan, the plain of Mesopotamia.
The author is, however, aware of the objection, that the more
ancient name of that river was Eridanus, but this difficulty is
easily and satisfactorily disposed of as follows :   Eraz, it seems,
signifies in Hebrew, a cedar or any resinous tree, and *z* is con-
vertible with *d*.   Now the banks of the Po abound with that
species of trees—nothing can be more evident, therefore, than
that Eraz is the etymon of Eridanus, and the Hebrews, or some
other oriental people, the origin of the Italian races.   If the
reader is satisfied with this account of the matter, it will not
diminish his gratification to be informed, that Mr. Mazzochi
himself most heartily participates in it. "Confesso ingenuamente,
(says he) che questa etimologia della voce Eridano mi é sempre
piaciuta assai."   The reasonings of Maffei are scarcely less cogent.   He supposes these Etruscans to be the race expelled from

[* Qu. Rom.]   † Tacitus Ann lib. iv. c. 55.   ‡ Apud Dionys. Halicar. lib. i.
§ Miscell. W. vol. iv. p. 184.   ‖ Micali, Bossi.

Canaan by the Moabites or children of Lot. Nothing is more probable, as will appear from the following circumstances. The river Arnon (whence obviously Arno) flowed not far from that part of Canaan where Abram and Lot first sojourned, and one of its districts also was called Etroth, which is very nearly Etruria. Moreover, they erected their places of worship on hills or high places—they formed corporeal images of their gods—and what is most conclusive of all, were much addicted to divination and augury. If any one is so very a Pyrrhonist as to withhold his assent from a theory supported by such arguments, we recommend to his consideration the opinion of Guarnacci, who brings the race directly from the East, and represents them as originally a set of stragglers dispersed by the flood, or at furthest, by the confusion of Babel. The Umbri, the Aborigines of the Etrurians, he supposes to have been the same people, who, from their wandering habits, got the name of Pelasgi, and at length emigrated to Greece and to Lydia. So that Signor Guarnacci turns the tables completely upon the last mentioned nations, and accounts for any resemblance in language, religion, manners or arts between them and the Etruscans, by tracing their origin up to this people.

In general, the oriental theory has been supported chiefly upon the ground that the Etruscans wrote from right to left and frequently marked only the consonants, leaving the vowels, as in the Hebrew, to be supplied by the reader. But this system in all its modifications and varieties, has been opposed by other antiquarians, who have declared for a Celtic origin, and who have supported their opinions by reasonings as refined, and analogies as remote and fanciful. The chief of these are Bardetti, Pelloutier, Adelung and Heyne. After all, the most learned and judicious writer upon this subject is Lanzi, who does not pretend formally to discuss and determine the origin of the Etruscans, although he is inclined to think them descendants of the Lydians. But he maintains, that all that they are remarkable for—their religion, learning, language and arts—is to be traced up to Greece as their source. Those beautiful urns and vases so much celebrated in modern times, he maintains, were executed after the reduction of Etruria by the Romans, and when there subsisted a thorough intercourse between Italy and Greece.

But whatever may have been the origin of the Etruscans, they became at one period a powerful and victorious people. They conquered Liguria, made the Latins their tributaries or allies, expelled the Osci from Campania, and founded the famous city of Capua. Their name almost superseded the general denomination of Italians. They enjoyed all the prosperity which good laws, a flourishing commerce, and the successful cultivation of the arts confer. The league or confederacy, however, by which their different states were united, became, in the end, discordant and feeble—their enemies multiplied upon them, and they successively lost all that they had ever acquired. The Samnites expelled them from Campania—the Gauls from the region between the Alps and the Apennines—the Umbrians recovered some of the territories which they had conquered on that side—they were driven from the sea by the Syracusans and Carthaginians—and, at length, a city arose upon the banks of the Tiber, of which the foundations had been laid, in obscurity, by a colony from Alba, or by a band of outlaws from the towns of the Equi, the Volsci, the Marsi, &c., and which was destined not only to assume the entire dominion of Italy, but to "veil earth in her haughty shadow." There appears to have subsisted from the building of the city, a constant and very intimate intercourse in peace and in war, between the Romans and these their politer neighbours. Traces of such an intercourse were visible in many forms and usages at Rome. For instance, it was from the Etruscans that they borrowed the purple vest, the sceptre surmounted by an eagle, the curule chair, the lictor and the fasces—and in common with the same people, and probably, in imitation of them, they celebrated the triumph and the ovation, the gladiatorial combat, and the circensian game. There was a still more important particular, in which we have the best evidence, that they long continued to acknowledge their dependence upon their first instructors. This was divination, which seems to have been taught in Etruria as a regular system or science—a sort of art for the interpretation of natural signs—and of which, the mysteries or occult doctrines and ceremonies were confided only to some privileged families. Their prognostics were taken, according to Bentley, from three things—exta, fulgura and ostenta—the entrails of cattle, thunders and monstrous births. This branch of knowledge was reckoned so important at Rome, that some of the Patrician youth used, in more ancient times to be sent into Etruria, for the purpose of being regularly instructed in its principles.[*]

It is worthy of remark, that the religion of the Etruscans and Latins was very unlike the elegant and voluptuous mythology of Greece. Their divinities were more simple and rustic, but as it generally happens, less licentious than the refined society of Olympus, with whom, however, some of them were, in progress of time, confounded by the Romans. This difference is pointed out by Dionysius of Halicarnassus, in a passage which is thus translated by Mr. Dunlop.[†] "The Romans did not admit into

---

[*] Val. Max. lib. i. c. 1. Cic. de Divin. lib. i. c. 4,
[†] Antiq. Roman—lib. ii. c. 15.

their creed those impious stories told by the Greeks of the cas-
tration of their gods, or of destroying their own children, of
their wars, wounds, bonds and slavery, and such like things as
are not only altogether unworthy of the divine nature, but disgrace even the human. They had no wailing and lamentations
for the sufferings of their gods, nor, like the Greeks, any Bac-
chic orgies or visits of men and women together in the temple.
And if at any time they admitted such foreign pollutions, as
they did with regard to the rites of Cybele and the Idæan
Goddess, the ceremonies were performed under the grave inspection of Roman magistrates: nor even now does any Roman
disguise himself to act the mummeries performed by the priests
of Cybele." Dionysius thinks, however, that this difference was
altogether owing to the reforms introduced by their first lawgiver unto the national religion, which he supposes to have been
originally the same with that of the Greeks. It seems, upon
the whole, to be a better account of the matter, that the religion of the Romans had its origin among a graver and severer
people, and this difference, in so important an element of society, (whether it be considered as a cause or an effect) may
throw great light upon other important phenomena in the character and history of the POPULUS REX.

Of the Etruscan and Latin languages, the origin is traced by
different authors agreeably to their theories concerning the first
peopling of the country. Lord Monboddo, for example, deduces them from the Pelasgic, which, he affirms, was introduced
into Italy by a colony of Arcadians, *only* seventeen generations
before the siege of Troy. The Latin he considers as the most
ancient dialect of the Greek, and as it came off the parent stock
before any other now known to us, we are not to wonder at
its retaining more of the roughness of the Hebrew, from which
he believes the Pelasgic to be derived. Lanzi is also of opinion
that both the Latin and the Etruscan sprang from the Greek,
and accounts for the resemblance between them, by this fact of
a common origin. Horne Tooke thinks that "the bulk and
foundation of the Latin language is Greek; but that great part
of the Latin is the language of our Northen ancestors, grafted
upon the Greek." It is the opinion of Mr. Dunlop that both
these propositions are too broadly stated by that distinguished
philologist. For, in the first place, he does not believe that any
Northern tongue was grafted *immediately* upon the Greek, after
the latter had been introduced into Italy, though he admits that
the Celtic or the Sclavonic, or both, may originally have contributed to form the primitive Italian language, which, from the
oldest monumental inscriptions, appears, at one time, to have
prevailed over the whole peninsula, from the Alps to Calabria.
He considers it, however, as a still greater error, to suppose

that the Greek language is the basis of the Latin. That much of the Augustan Latin is derived from that source, he does not dispute; but he maintains that this copious admixture of Greek may be distinctly traced to a period not more remote than the close of the fifth century of the Roman era, i. e. to the taking of Tarentum, A. U. C. 482. It seems difficult to resist this conclusion, but we think from the specimens by which we shall presently exemplify this change, that our readers will agree with us in pronouncing it one of the most extraordinary revolutions of the kind that have ever taken place in any country. There are many instances, indeed, of nations that have been subjugated and overrun by barbarians, learning, by degrees, to speak the language of their conquerors, or mingling their own with it, so as to form, in process of time, a new one altogether different in structure and pronunciation from either of the primitive tongues. The history of the Teutonic irruptions of the fifth and subsequent centuries is full of these. But the example before us is that of a decided revolution, brought about in an incredibly short space of time, in the language of an ambitious, triumphant, and governing nation, by what would seem to be, after all, a distant and comparatively slight intercourse with a conquered people. There is, to be sure, some weight in the considerations by which it is attempted to explain the phenomenon. Foreigners were admitted, without much difficulty, to the freedom of the city, and all languages not fixed and ascertained by literary composition are liable to great fluctuation. The authority of Polybius* too, is express, that a treaty concluded between the Romans and Carthaginians, in the 245th year of the city, was written in a dialect so perfectly obsolete as to be, at his time, scarcely intelligible, even to the most learned men at Rome. Making every allowance, however, for the operation of such causes, it is still difficult to conceive that we are in possession of all the facts connected with the subject, so as to repose entire confidence in any conclusions to which we may come in relation to it.

Magna Græcia, to the conquest of which this sudden revolution in language and literature is ascribed, was, at the period alluded to above in a very advanced state of improvement in all the arts of civilized life. The Greek colonies, in that part of Italy, had preserved, unimpaired, the manners and institutions of the mother country, with which, indeed, they continued to keep up a constant intercourse, both social and political. "Herodotus, the father of history, says Mr. Dunlop, and Lysias, whose orations are the purest models of the simple attic eloquence, were, in early youth, among the original founders of

* Antiq. Roman.—lib. ii. c. 3.

the colony of Thurium, and the latter held a share in its government until an advanced period of life. The Eleatic school
of philosophy was founded in Magna Græcia, and the impulse
which the wisdom of Pythagoras had given to the mind, promoted also the studies of literature. Plato visited Tarentum
during the consulship of Lucius Camillus and Appius Claudius,
which was in the 406th year of Rome, and Zeuxis was invited
from Greece to paint at Crotona the magnificent temple of
Juno, which had been erected in that city. History and poetry
were cultivated with a success that did not dishonor the Grecian
name. Lycus of Rhegium was the civil, and Glaucus of the
same city was the literary historian of Magna Græcia. Orpheus
of Crotona was the author of a poem on the expedition of
the Argonauts, attributed to an elder Orpheus. The lyric productions of Ibicus of Rhegium rivalled those of Anacreon and
Alcæus. Two hundred and fifty-five comedies, written by Alexis
of Thurium, the titles of which have been collected by Meur-
sius, and a few fragments of them by Stephens, are said to have
been composed in the happiest vein of the middle comedy of
the Greeks, which possessed much of the comic force of Aristophanes and Cratinus, without their malignity, &c." And to
all this it may be added, that the legislation of Zaleucus and
Charondas had laid the foundations of social improvement deep
in a system of wise and salutary laws.*

Some very curious specimens of the primitive Latin language
are come down to us. The hymn of Fratres Arvales is supposed to be as ancient as the time of Romulus. It was inscribed, during the reign of Heliogabalus, on a stone which was discovered in opening the foundations of the Sacristy of St. Peter's,
in 1778. It is as follows:—

"Enos Lases juvate,
Neve luerve Marmar sinis incurrer in pleoris.
Satur fufere Mars; limen sali sta berber:
Semones alternei advocapit cunctos.
Enos Marmor juvate,
Triumpe! triumpe!"

These lines have been variously interpreted by learned men.
Mr. Dunlop adopts Herman's version which is as follows:—
"Nos Lares juvate, neve luem Mamuri sinis incurrere in plures
[fortasse, flores] Satur fueris Mars: limen [i. e. postremum] sali
sta vervex: Semones [semihomines] alterni jam duo capit cunctos. Nos Mamuri juvato—Triumphe! Triumphe!" We do not
pretend to see very clearly, the meaning of *limen sali sta vervex*, or of *Semones alterni jam duo capit cunctos*, and feel
quite sure that these words have not been correctly interpreted
by Herman. But be that as it may, every reader will perceive,

* [Aristot, Polit. 1, 2. c. 10.]

at once, the peculiarities of this old language, when compared with that of the Augustan age.

The following is the fragment of an old law of Numa, as restored by Festus—which, in this age of codification and reform, deserves no less the attention of legislators for its brevity, and the *simplicitas legibus amica*, as Justinian expresses it, than that of the philologist for the strangeness of the language in which it is written. "Sei cuips hemonem lobsum dolo sciens mortei duit pariceidad estod, sei im imprudens se dolo malod occisit pro capited oceisei at nateis eiius endo concioned arietem subicitod,"—which, being interpreted, is as follows :—"Si quis hominem liberum dolo sciens morti dederit, parricida esto : Si eum imprudens, sine dolo malo, occiderit, pro capite occisi et natis ejus in concionem arietem subjicito."

The next specimen of the Latin language which we shall exhibit, and the earliest that is extant after the Leges Regiæ, are the laws of the XII Tables, adopted at the beginning of the fourth century of Rome. Those who have studied the civil law are, of course, aware of Terrasson's laboured and rather ingenious attempt to restore the purity of the old Oscan text,* in which he supposes them to have been originally written. They are, however, even in the shape in which they have been handed down to us quite curious, and puzzling enough. But as they do not seem to have been perfectly understood, even by the ancient writers themselves, and great liberties, as Terrasson observes, were probably taken with them, by the authors to whom we are indebted for the fragments we possess, to accommodate them to the language of their own times, they can scarcely be regarded as fair specimens of what the Latin was at the period of their promulgation. We will mention here, by the way, that we think the evidence derived from all such sources far less conclusive in a philological point of view, than it appears to be considered by Mr. Dunlop, and other writers. The language of law, says Voltaire, is every where barbarous, and we may add, that many circumstances may account for a monumental in-

---

* Historie de la Jurisprud. Romaine. p. 64, where we have an account of his system and means of conjectural emendation, as far as regards the Jus Papyrianum, and a much fuller development of the subject in the text than Mr. Dunlop's book affords. His history of the XII Tab. begins at page 74 cf. 88. As specimens of his labor, we cite the following passages:—L. Iᵉ C'est Cicéron dans son second livre *de legibus* qui nous a transmis le texte, de cette loi en ces termes. S'I N. JUS. VOCAT. ATQUE-EAT. Mais ce texte tel que Cicéron le présente, n'est que le sens de l'ancien texte qui doit être exprimé ainsi dans l' ancienne langue Osque SIN. JOVS. VOC. ATQUEEAT. p 94.

Loi troisiéme. Voici l'ancien texte. SEI. CALVITUR. PEDEMVE. STRVIT. MANUM ENDO. JACITO. Pour rétablir absolument ce texte dans son ancien langage, je crois qu'il suffirait d'ôter l'M qui est à la fin du mot PEDEM. de mettre par abréviation MAN'ENDO au lieu de MANUM ENDO et de mettre un D à la fin de jacito. &c. p. 96.

scription or two, being written in a quaint, affected style, very little approaching to that of ordinary conversation, or even in a dialect comparatively obsolete.

During the next two centuries, there is scarcely any vestige remaining of the Latin language. At the end of that long interval, we have the incription of the celebrated *columna rostrata*, erected in honor of the naval victory of Duillius over the Carthaginians, A. U. C. 492. This column was dug up in the vicinity of the capital, in the year 1565. There are also extant the epitaphs of L. Scipio Barbatus and of his son Lucius Scipio, of which the one is somewhat more ancient, the other a year later than the abovementioned inscription. We shall present our readers with the latter, which certainly forms a very striking contrast with the language of Livius Andronicus, whose earliest dramas were published only twenty years after. It it worthy of remark too, that the epitaph of the son, though the later of the two by a good many years, is written in a more antiquated style than that of the father. As we cannot bring ourselves to believe that a corresponding change had taken place in the spoken language of that period, we must ascribe this difference, as we hinted just now, to some accidental and peculiar cause. The inscription is as follows :—

"Honc oino ploirume consentiunt duonoro optumo fuise viro Lucium Scipione. Filios Barbati Consol Censor Ædilis hec fuit. Hec cepit Corsica Aleriaque urbe: dedit tempestatibus aide mereto ;" which is thus modernised, "Hunc unum plurimı consentiunt Romæ bonorum optimum fuisse virum Lucium Scipionem. Filius Barbati, Consul, Censor, Ædilis hic fuit. Hic cepit Corsicam Aleriamque urbem: dedit tempestatibus ædem merito."

The following observations of Mr. Dunlop are a very good commentary upon the preceding specimens, if we admit with him the conclusiveness of the evidence derived from inscriptions and the like, as to the general state of a language.

"On comparing the fragments of the *Leges Regiæ* with the Duillian and Scipian inscriptions, it does not appear that the Roman language, however greatly it may have varied, had either improved or approached much nearer to modern Latin in the fifth century than in the time of the kings. Short and mutilated as these laws and inscriptions are, they still enable us to draw many important conclusions with regard to the general state of the language during the existence of the monarchy, and the first ages of the republic. It has already been mentioned that the dipthong *ai* was employed where *ae* came to be afterwards substituted, as aide for æde ; *ei* instead of *i*, as castreis for castris ; and *oi* in place of *œ*, as coilum for cœlum. The vowel *e* is often introduced instead of *o*, as hemo for homo, while, on the other hand, *o* is sometimes used instead of *e*, as vostrum for vestrum; and Scipio Africanus is said to have been the first who always wrote the *e* in such words. *U* is frequently changed into *o*, as honc for hunc, sometimes into *ou*, as abdoucit for abducit, and sometimes to *oi*, as oino for uno. On the whole, it appears that the vowels were in a great measure used indiscriminately, and often, especially in inscriptions, they were altogether omitted, as bne for bene, though sometimes, again, an *e* final was added, as face for fac, dice for dic. As to the consonants,—*b* at the beginning of a word was *du*, as duonorum for bonorum, and it was *p* at the middle or end, as opsides for obsides. The letter *g* certainly does not appear in those earliest specimens of the Latin language—the hymn of the *Fratres Arvales*, and *Leges Regiæ*, where *c* is used in its place. Plutarch says, that this letter was utterly unknown at Rome during the space of five centuries, and was first introduced by the grammarian Spurius Carvillius in the year 540. It occurs, however, in the epitaph of Scipio Barbatus, which was written at least half a century before that date; and, what is remarkable, it is there placed in a word where *c* was previously and subsequently employed, Gnaivo being written for Cnæo. The letter *r* was not, as has been asserted, unknown to the ancient Romans, but it was chiefly used in the beginning and end of words—*s* being employed instead of it in the middle, as lases for lares. Frequently the letters *m* and *s* were omitted at the end of words, especially, for the sake of euphony, when the following word began with a consonant—thus we have Aleria cepit, for Aleriam cepit. The ancient Romans were equally careful to avoid a hiatus of vowels, and hence they wrote ein in place of si in. Double consonants were never seen till the time of Ennius; and we accordingly find in the old inscriptions sumas for summas; *er* was added to the infinitive passive, as darier for dari, and *d* was subjoined to words ending with a vowel, as in altod, marid, pucnandod. It likewise appears that the Romans were for a long period unacquainted with the use of aspirates, and were destitute of the *phi* and *chi* sounds of the Greek alphabet. Hence they wrote triumpe for triumphe, and pulcer for pulcher. We also meet with a good many words, particularly substantives, which afterwards became altogether obsolete, and some are applied in a sense different from that in which they were subsequently used. Finally, a difference in the conjugation of the same verb, and a want of inflection in nouns, particularly proper names of countries or cities, where the nominative frequently occurs instead of the accusative, show the unsettled state of the language at that early period.

"It is unnecessary to prosecute farther the history of Roman inscriptions, since, immediately after the erection of the Duillian column in 494, Latin became a written literary language; and although the dipthongs *ai* and *ei* were retained for more than a century longer, most of the other archaisms were totally rejected, and the language was so enriched by a more copious admixture of the Greek, that, while always inferior to that tongue, in ease, precision, perspicuity, and copiousness, it came at length to rival it in dignity of enunciation, and in that lofty accent which harmonized so well with the elevated character of the people by whom it was uttered."—pp. 48–49.

2. A great diversity of opinion seems to have prevailed among the Roman critics of a more recent period, concerning the merits of the earlier comic and tragic writers, but especially the former. Cicero generally expresses himself with regard to them in respectful and even flattering terms*—it was a saying of Varro's, that if the Muses spoke Latin they would use the language of Plautus—Cæsar complimented Terence, as in style, at least, a successful imitator of Menander, and we may judge, from a well known passage of Velleius Paterculus,

---

* [De Off. l. i. c. 29. elegans, urbanum, ingeniosum, facetum.]

that some of the best educated men, even to the last, entertained the same sentiments. Indeed, it might fairly be inferred from the keenness and vehemence with which Horace declaims against the perverse taste of the times in this particular, that they were exceedingly popular in the Augustan age. That elegant satirist seems to be out of all patience with his countrymen for their misplaced, not to say foolish admiration, as he is pleased to express it, of such rude, unfinished works. Nor are we to suppose, as W. Schlegel affirms, that Horace was unable or unwilling to see excellence in any thing but a cold and prosaical accuracy, and the polished littleness of a finical and fastidious age. If we could, by any possibility, be brought to think thus of so enthusiastic an admirer of the Greek models—of a poet who has celebrated the genius of Pindar in a strain not unworthy of his own matchless lyre—we must recollect, that on this occasion, at least, his opinion is confirmed by that of Quinctilian,* of all critics, perhaps, the most enlightened and unerring, as the most dispassionate and impartial. That grammarian speaks of the tragedies of Attius and Pacuvius very much as Horace does in the epistle to Augustus.† He bestows upon them some commendation, but it is quite evident that he considers no Roman tragedy as at all approaching to the excellence of the Greek models, but the Thyestes of Varius, and perhaps the Medea of Ovid, while he condemns the comic writers, *en masse*, and scruples not to throw out a doubt whether the Latin language were susceptible of those nice shades and delicate graces that constitute the perfection of the comic style, as it had been exemplified in the master pieces of Aristophanes and Menander. There is a passage in Aulus Gellius,‡ which deserves, on more accounts than one, to be cited in reference to these Latin imitations, or translations rather of the Greek drama. "We often read, says he, the comedies which our poets have taken from Menander and Posidius, Apollodorus and Alexis, &c. While we are reading them by themselves, we find no fault with them; they even seem to be written with so much elegance and grace, that you would suppose nothing could be better done. When you come, however, to compare them with the Greek originals from which they are taken, and to examine them together verse for verse, with a deliberate and scrupulous criticism, it is surprising how despicable they appear : so entirely are they eclipsed by the inimitable wit and beauty of the Greek compositions. He mentions an instance that had but re-

---

* Inst. Orat. lib. x. c. 1.

† Tentavit quoque rem si digné vertere posset ;
   Et placuit sibi, naturâ sublimis et acer
  • Nam spirat tragicum satis et feliciter audet ;
   Sed turpem putat in scriptis metuitque lituram. p. 164, and seq.

‡ Lib. ii. c. 23.

cently occurred to him, in reading the Plocius of Cæcilius, which he bethought him of subjecting to the test of such an examination with the original, the Plocius of Menander. He declares that it was the exchange of Diomed and Glaucus, and has endeavored, by a comparison of several passages, to point out the disadvantage to which the Greek poet was seen in his Latin dress.

The regular drama at Rome was divided, as to comedy, into Comedia simply, (or Comedia palliata) and Comedia togata—the former treating Greek subjects, and representing Greek characters and manners—the latter, Roman. There was a corresponding division of tragedy into Tragedia palliata, and Tragedia prætextata. As for domestic subjects, they were so seldom handled by the dramatic writers, that the class of Togatæ and Prætextatæ must have been very far from extensive. Afranius is celebrated as having excelled in the former, but Mr. Dunlop thinks with Schlegel that his plays were probably Greek pieces, accommodated to Roman manners, since Afranius lived at a period when Roman literature was altogether imitative.

The first attempt at a regular dramatic fable was made, as we have already had occasion to observe, by Livius Andronicus, who was taken prisoner A. U. C. 482, and brought to Rome as a slave. He began to publish, that is to act his plays about the year 513–514, immediately after the first Punic war. He was for some time the sole performer. By overstraining his voice in declamation, it at length failed him, and he was constrained to resort to a very singular expedient to supply its defects, which was no other than employing a boy to declaim with the flute in the Monologues and other parts requiring extraordinary exertion while he gesticulated in concert, and only used his own voice in the colloquial and easy passages. What is still more remarkable, this whimsical division of labor—calculated, one would suppose, to produce an effect ludicrous in itself, and inconsistent with every idea of good *acting* or scenic illusion—actually grew up into a system, and continued under certain modifications to subsist on the Roman stage during the most refined periods of taste and literature.

Livius Andronicus appears to have written both tragedies and comedies, but scarcely any thing more than their titles are come down to us. The longest passage that remains is a hymn to Diana, recited by the chorus, in the tragedy of Ino. We quote these verses for the purpose of exemplifying that sudden change in the Latin language, of which we have already had occasion to say so much :—

"Et jam purpureo suras include cothurno
Baltheus et revocet volucres in pectore sinus ;
Pressaque jam gravidâ crepitent tibi terga pharetrâ
Dirige odorisequos ad cæca cubilia canes,"

Indeed, we are not surprised—if we are to suppose that the Scipian monuments afford us a fair specimen of what the language was at that time—that the authenticity of these smooth and accurate hexameters, which are not fixed upon Livius Andronicus by the most conclusive evidence in the world, has been called in question by some very able critics.

According to Cicero,* the plays of this ancient writer were not worthy of being read a second time : yet, it appears from Horace's Epistle to Augustus, that even in that cultivated age, they were used as a school book at Rome.

The first imitator of Livius Andronicus in the regular drama, was Nævius, a native of Campania. His early plays were published about A. U. C. 519. Very little more than the titles of his tragedies have been preserved : they are like all the rest of this period, every one of them Greek, such as Alcestis, Dulorestes, Iphigenia, Hector, Protesilaus, &c. He seems to have excelled more, however, in comedy and railing. Some of his sarcasms were levelled at the elder Scipio, who treated them with profound contempt: but an attack of the same kind upon the great family of the Metelli eventuated in his being cast into prison, and ultimately compelled to take refuge at Utica, where he died about the year 550.

Besides his dramatic works, Nævius translated the Cyprian Epic, an old Greek poem, which may be considered as standing in somewhat the same relation to the Iliad, as the Orlando Innamorato to the Orlando Furioso. This ancient Epic was by some ascribed to Homer, but Herodotus† affirms with great confidence, that it was not the work of that poet. The last production of Nævius was a metrical chronicle of the first Punic war, of which Cicero,‡ with his usual partiality for these antiquated writers, expresses a very high opinion, and from which he supposes Ennius to have borrowed much. His chronicle was written in the uncouth, irregular Iambics, called the Saturnian verse—

Versibus quos olim Fauni vatesque canebant—

which was the genuine, primitive Italian measure, before the Latin language had been moulded into poetical form by the rules and models of the Greek. According to Hermann, the regular Saturnian line consisted of two Iambuses, an Amphibrachys, and three Trochees : subject, of course, to the usual metrical liberties.

But a much more prominent name in this early period of Roman literature, presents itself next in order. This was Ennius, who has been universally entitled the Father of Roman Song. He was a native of Rudiœ, a town in Calabria, and died about A. U. C. 585, at the age of seventy. After having been absent

---

* Brutus, c. 18.   † Lib. ii. c. 93.   ‡ Brutus, c. 19.

a long time in the military service, he returned to Rome with Cato the Censor, about the year 550, and setting up a frugal establishment upon the Aventine, devoted himself to literary studies, and endeavoured to gain a livelihood by teaching the Patrician youth the language of his native country. He died very poor—but his great patrons "helped to bury whom they helped to starve." His bust was placed in the family tomb of the Scipios, which is supposed to have been discovered in the year 1780, on a farm between the Via Appia and the Via Latina. The sepulchre, however, was "tenantless of its heroic dwellers," and no memorial or monument of the conqueror of Hannibal was found by the side of that "laurelled bust."

It is impossible to reflect upon the vast space which Ennius fills in the history of Roman literature—on the interesting epoch at which he flourished—on the number and variety of his works, and on the extraordinary popularity which they continued to enjoy for centuries after his death, without most heartily uniting in Scaliger's wish, that he had been preserved to us instead of Lucan, Statius, Silius Italicus, and *tous ces garcons là*. What, indeed, was all the turgid imbecility—the stuffed and painted decrepitude of a superannuated and declining literature, in comparison of those simple and native charms, whatever they were, which recommended the old bard to Virgil's imitation and the praise of Horace, which caused his Annals to be recited amidst the plaudits of the theatres, even in the age of the Antonines,* and Seneca to nickname the whole Roman people, a *populus Ennianus*. Wakefield, in one of his letters to Fox, cited by Mr. Dunlop, (v. i. p. 228) says, that "a very imperfect notion is entertained in general, of the copiousness of the Latin language, by those who confine themselves to what are styled the Augustan writers. The old comedians and tragedians, with Ennius and Lucilius, were the great repositories of learned and vigorous expression. I have ever regarded the loss of the old Roman poets, particularly Ennius and Lucilius, from the light they would have thrown upon the formation of the Latin language, and its derivation from the Æolian Greek, as the severest calamity ever sustained by philological learning." We are persuaded, from the circumstances already adverted to, that our loss has not been confined to the curiosities of philology. Ennius, of all those old writers, was the only one that produced any thing like a *national* work, and this was, doubtless, the true secret of his popularity at Rome. His "Annals" were a metri-

---

* Aul. Gellius, lib. xviii. c. 5. Antoninus Julianus, the rhetorician, heard that a certain reader was reciting Ennius in the Theatre. Eamus, inquit, auditum nescio quem istum *Ennianistam:* hoc enim se ille nomine appellari volebat. Quem cum jam *inter ingentes clamores* legentem invenissemus (legebat autem librum ex Annalibus Ennii septimum, &c.

cal chronicle, similar to that of Nævius mentioned above, but
far more extensive, inasmuch as it comprehended the whole
series of events from the earliest and fabulous periods of Roman
story, down to the Istrian war. Our regret, indeed, for the
supposed loss, would be greatly diminished, if we thought with
Mr. Dunlop, that this work of Ennius was no more than a
gazette in verse—for nothing, of that kind, could aspire to a
comparison with the "pictured page" of Livy, the most animated, eloquent and graphic of historians—but we imagine that
there was a much stronger infusion of poetry and fiction in the
"Annals," than could have been tolerated in any prose composition.   Indeed, such is the necessary inference even from our
author's own account of the matter in the following passage.

"The Annals of Ennius were partly founded on those ancient traditions and old heroic ballads, which Cicero, on the authority of Cato's
Origines, mentions as having been sung at feasts by the guests, many
centuries before the age of Cato, in praise of the heroes of Rome.
Niebuhr has attempted to show, that all the memorable events of Roman
history had been versified in ballads, or metrical chronicles, in the Saturnian measure, before the time of Ennius; who, according to him,
merely expressed in the Greek hexameter, what his predecessors had
delivered in a ruder strain, and then maliciously depreciated these ancient compositions, in order that he himself might be considered as the
founder of Roman poetry. The devotion of the Decii, and death of
the Fabian family—the stories of Scævola, Cocles, and Coriolanus—
Niebuhr believes to have been the subjects of romantic ballads. Even
Fabius Pictor, according to this author, followed one of these old
legends in his narrative concerning Mars and the Wolf, and his whole
history of Romulus. Livy too, in his account of the death of Lucretia,
has actually transcribed from one of these productions; since, what
Sextus says, on entering the chamber of Lucretia, is nearly in the Saturnian measure:—

"Tace, Lucretia, inquit, Sextus Tarquinius sum,
Ferrum in manu est, moriere si emiseris vocem."

But the chief work, according to Niebuhr, from which Ennius borrowed,
was a romantic epopee, or chronicle, made up from these heroic ballads,
about the end of the fourth century of Rome, commencing with the accession of Tarquinius Priscus and ending with the battle of Regillus.
The arrival, says Niebuhr, of that monarch under the name of Lucumo
—his exploits and victories—his death—then the history of Servius Tul-
lius—the outrageous pride of Tullia—the murder of the lawful monarch
—the fall of the last Tarquin, preceded by a supernatural warning—Lucretia—Brutus and the truly Homeric battle of Regillus—compose an epic,
which, in poetical incident, and splendor of fancy, surpasses every thing
produced in the latter ages of Rome. The battle of Regillus, in particular, as described by the annalists, bears evident marks of its poetical
origin. It was not a battle between two hosts, but a struggle of heroes.
As in the fights painted in the Iliad, the champions meet in single combat,
and turn by individual exertions the tide of victory. The dictator Pos-
thumius wounds King Tarquin, whom he had encountered at the first onset. The Roman knight Albutius engages with the Latin chief Mamilius,
but is wounded by him, and is forced to quit the field. Mamilius then

nearly breaks the Roman line, but is slain by the Consul Herminius, which decides the fate of the day. After the battle of Regillus, all the events are not so completely poetical; but in the siege of Veii we have a representation of the ten years war of Troy. The secret introduction of the troops by Camillus into the middle of the city, resembles the story of the wooden horse, and the Etruscan statue of Juno corresponds to the Trojan Palladium.* p. 79.

The tragedies and comedies of Ennius were mere translations from the Greek, as may be inferred from their very names, Medea, Bresphontes, Erestheus, Hecuba, Eumenides, &c. Of his other works, it would be more regular to speak under the head of miscellaneous literature, but it may be as well to dispatch them here. The principal of these were satires *phagetica,* (a sort of culinary digest or *Almanach des Gourmands,*) a poem on the nature of things, entitled *Epicharmus,* and a prose translation of the Ιερα Αναγραφη of Euhemerus. The Phagetica would have been a rare curiosity in these times; to us, who humbly confess ourselves at an immeasurable distance from the transcendental gastronomy of Kitchner and Beauvilliers, a much greater curiosity, than those enlarged and scientific treatises which, in this philosophic age, have so signally enlarged the boundaries of that interesting department of knowledge. His translation of Euhemerus, would have been, if possible, a still more curious relic.

"Euhemerus is generally supposed to have been an inhabitant of Messene, a city of Peloponnesus. Being sent, as he represented, on a voyage of discovery by Cassander, king of Macedon, he came to an island called Panchaia, in the capital of which, Panara, he found a temple of the Tryphilian Jupiter, where stood a column inscribed with a register of the births and deaths of many of the gods. Among these, he specified Uranus, his sons Pan and Saturn, and his daughters Rhea and Ceres; as also Jupiter, Juno, and Neptune, who were the offspring of Saturn. Accordingly, the design of Euhemerus was to show, by investigating their actions, and recording the places of their births and burials, that the my-

---

* As a specimen of the poetry of Ennius, we subjoin the following pretty verses. Ilia is relating to her sister Eurydice the dream, in which her pregnancy by Mars was announced to her.

"Talia commemorat lacrumans, exterrita somno;
"Euridica prognata, pater quam noster amavit,
Vivens vita meum corpus nunc deserit omne.
Nam me visus homo polcer per amœna salicta
Et ripas raptare, locosque novos: ita sola
Post illa, germana soror, errare videbar;
Tardaque vestigare, et quærere, neque posse
Corde capessere: Semita nulla pedem stabilibat.
Exin compellare pater me voce videtur
Heis verbis—O gnata, tibi sunt antegerendæ
Ærumnæ; post ex fluvio fortuna resistet.
Hæc pater ecfatus, germana, repente recessit;
Nec sese dedit in conspectum corde cupitus:
Quamquam multa manus ad cœli cærula Templa
Tendebam lacrumans, et blanda voce vocabam.
Vix ægro tum·corde meo me somnus reliquit."

thological deities were mere mortal men, raised to the rank of gods on
account of the benefits which they had conferred on mankind—a system
which according to Meiners and Warburton, formed the grand secret revealed at the initiation into the Eleusinian mysteries. p. 94.*

The most important remains, however, of this period of Roman literature, are the comedies of Plautus and Terence. The
former was the son of a freedman, and was born at Sarsina, a
town of Umbria, about A. U. C. 525. The latter, as has been
already mentioned, was a Carthaginian slave. The Andria, his
first comedy, was published in the year 587, when the author
was 27 years of age. After he had given to the stage the six
comedies which we now possess, he went to Greece with a view
to improve himself in his art, but he never returned having
died there at the early age of 34.

The works of these writers possess, independently of their
intrinsic merit, the accidental attraction of being the only specimen that has been preserved to us of the new comedy of the
Greeks. The numerous or rather innumerable productions of
Menander,* Diphilus, Philemon, Apollodorus, Epicharmus, &c.,
are, with the exception of a few fragments, all perished, and we
are left to conjecture what they were from the Latin copies of
Plautus and Terence. From the chapter in Aulus Gellius, however, of which we translated a part in a preceding page, it is
certain that these afford us but a very imperfect idea of the
originals. What Terence says in his own justification, in the
prologue to the Adelphi, is additional evidence to the same effect.
It shews that both he and Plautus took such liberties with the
plots of their Greek masters, as to make it sometimes difficult to
judge, from their imitations, what the original fable had been.

What first strikes a modern reader upon a perusal of these
plays, is the eternal recurrence of the same characters, scenes
and catastrophes. In the twenty comedies of Plautus, with the
exception of the Amphytrion, which is a drama of a peculiar
class, or as the author himself calls it, a tragi-comedy, there is
scarcely any variety in his *dramatis personæ*. In this respect,
they bear a striking resemblance to the ancient Italian masques,
which were so contrived as to generalize the usual classes and
professions of society in which the shopkeeper, (Pantalone) the
attorney, (Balanzoni) the intriguer, (Brighella) the stupid valet,
(Harlequin) the braggart captain, (Captain Spaviento) &c., are
always on the scene. What is still worse, very few of those
personages are exactly *comme il faut*. Perhaps, it would be
somewhat extravagant to compare these pictures of Athenian
manners (for such they were) with the scenes exhibited in a cer-

---

* [Cf. Cic. de N D. l. 1 c. 42.]
† Aul. Gellius informs us that Menander wrote 106 Comedies, of which only
eight were crowned.

tain popular farce, which is dignified with the title of "Life in London." But the truth is, that human nature appears to very nearly as great advantage in "Tom and Jerry," as in the comedies of Plautus and Terence. The very names of some of their favourite characters will not bear mentioning in decent company, and there are passages, in which their low manners and practices are painted in such strong colours, as to be quite disgusting. We refer for examples of such pictures, to the first scene of the fourth act, to the third scene of the first act, and to the second scene of the second act of the Asinaria, and to the passage quoted in a subsequent page from the Capteivei.*
"Their plots," says Dryden, "were commonly a little girl, stolen or wandering from her parents, brought back unknown to the city—there got with child by some one, who, by the help of his servant, cheats his father—and, when her time comes to cry Juno Lucina, one or other sees a little box or cabinet which was carried away with her, and so discovers her to her friends— if some god do not prevent it by coming down in a machine, and taking the thanks of it to himself. By the plot, you may guess much of the character of the persons—an old father who would willingly, before he dies, see his son well married; a debauched son, kind in his nature to his mistress, but miserably in want of money; and a servant or slave, who has so much art as to strike in with him, and help him to dupe his father; a braggadocio captain; a parasite; a lady of pleasure. As for the poor honest maid, on whom the story is built, and who ought to be one of the principal actors in the play, she is commonly mute in it. She has the breeding of the old Elizabeth way; which is, for maids to be seen and not heard."

We are to look, for the cause of this singular uniformity, to the manners and customs of the Greeks. These did not admit of that variety of character which presents such an inexhaustible field to modern comedy. In the works of Molière, for example, we see the impress of a cultivated age. It was a period when manners were reduced to a system which was regulated by its own code—and that a most rigorous one—of usages and laws, and were infinitely diversified by the various tastes, pursuits and conditions of a very advanced stage of society. The perpetual intercourse of the *beau monde*—of the opulent, the educated, and the witty—for the sole purposes of pleasure and conversation, made it the study of every individual to approximate as nearly as possible to the approved standard of character and conduct, however arbitrary or artificial, and the exquisite sense of propriety, in reference to that standard, which was thus acquired,

---

*Dum fallax servus, durus pater, improba lena
Vivent, et meretrix blanda, Menandros erit.—*Ovid Amor.*

enabled them to detect the slighest deviation from it, and to expose it to an unsparing, though polished and elegant ridicule. The same state of things has continued ever since. Modern comedy has thus an unlimited range for the choice of its subjects and materials. The minutest peculiarities of character or behavior, eked out with a suitable stock of adventures and intrigues, which it costs very little to invent, furnish the groundwork of an amusing play. Great stress is generally laid upon the artificial distinction of ranks, as if comedy could only exist, in its perfection, under a monarchical or an aristocratic form of government. There is undoubtedly something in that, but far more depends, we conceive, upon the variety of professions with their peculiarities and pedantry, upon the state of manners with reference to rudeness or simplicity and cultivation, and upon the greater or less intercourse of society, than upon the form of the political constitution. For instance, the follies of those who imitate their superiors in accomplishments and education, or in wealth and influence, which are ridiculed in the *Bourgeois Gentilhomme*, prevail more or less, wherever what is called the "ton" is attended to—wherever there are fantastic people to set a fash- ion, and apes to follow one—that is to say, wherever the accumulation of wealth admits of retired leisure and good company. But among the Greeks, there was very little of what is known among us by the name of *society*. They had no home—no family circle with its unreserved intercourse and social discipline, no tea-parties, and tertúlias or soirées, and conversazioni. Your Greek gentleman did not value himself very highly upon the exploits of the drawing room or the amiable frivolities of our modern dandyism. They lived for the public, and in public— in the streets, the promenades, the *agora*, the porticoes, the gymnasia, and the theatres. Their whole existence was a part which they played before the people, as their tragic heroes acted theirs before its representative, the chorus. They were, indeed, a most poetical and inspired race, the development of their taste and genius was perfect, and nothing could be more exquisite or more mature than their whole intellectual discipline and cultivation. But all this is quite consistent with the most perfect simplicity of manners, and a very inconsiderable progress in the great modern accomplishments of quizzing, persiflage, mystification, and all the other shapes and varieties of a refined ridicule. The single fact that their virtuous women were condemned to a sort of oriental seclusion, and exercised scarcely any perceptible influence upon society, is enough to establish the truth of the preceding remarks. The exclusion of females from the society of the other sex, is a decisive proof of a state of manners savoring of rusticity and barbarism. We may judge from our own parties of brawling politicians and professed wine bib-

bers,* from which the charms of female conversation are so rigorously shut out, what such a system leads to, even under the
most favorable circumstances. Accordingly, a Greek festival
was a downright drinking bout; it was called, as Cicero nicely
remarks, a symposium, and not a convivium.† All the delicacies
of a chastened wit and raillery that make French society so delightful, must have been drowned in boisterous merriment and
bacchanalian debauchery, and the very idea of *manners* is inconsistent with the "swilled insolence of such rude wassailers."‡

We may safely affirm, then, that the state of society at Athens
was such as to restrict comedy to a very limited range in the
choice of its subjects. We allude, of course, to comedies of *character*, such as Menander and the rest of that school professed to
furnish. They could only paint the private life of the Athenians as they found it, and we have very little doubt that they
did so faithfully—but their way of living was essentially unfit
for theatrical exhibitions of this kind. We do not mean to say—
for it would be absurd to call in question the judgment of the
ancient critics in such a matter—that these Greek plays were
not written with exquisite elegance, and abundantly seasoned
with Attic salt: although we *will* venture the opinion that their
subjects are such as suit Plautus better than Terence. But a
good comic poem, and a good comedy, are two very distinct
things. We may illustrate the difference by the plays of Aristophanes. We think those critics in the right who consider these
dramas as *sui generis*—as poems in the nature of comedy, (to
borrow a phrase from the bar) rather than as comedies. Aristophanes was not eminently remarkable as a painter of individual character or an observer of private society. He was a man
of extraordinary genius, the first of poets in his own way, and
who might have been the first of orators, as his style has been
pronounced one of the best models for forming them§; but he
is not to be classed in the same category with the writers of the
new comedy. He was a severe satirist of public abuses—a vehement and relentless enemy of great state criminals,‖ whom he
thinks it quite fair to hold up to derision, even by the exaggera-

[* Græco more bibere.]
[† Cf. Cic. in Verr. Act. II. 1. c. 24. c. 26.]
[‡ See Demosthenes' account of the conduct of Æschines to an Olynthian
female. περι παραπρεσϐειας, 359. Æschines, in his reply, speaks, by way
of compliment, of Philip's being δεινος (πινειν) συμπιειν, which is gravely noticed by Δ. Cf. Iliad. Δ 257, et seq.]

§ Quinctil. Inst. Orat. Lib. x., c. 1. [τῶν δε κωμωδῶν μιμεῖσθαι τὰς λεκ-
τικὰς ἀρετὰς ἁπάσασ· εἰσί γὰρ καὶ τοῖς νοήμασι καθαροὶ καὶ σαφεῖς και
ϐραχεῖς καὶ μεγαλοπρεπεῖς καὶ δεινοὶ καὶ ἠθικοί. Dion. Hal. των αρχαιων
κρισις. κεφ. ϛ.]

[‖Cic. frag· apud. D. Augustin. C. D.1. II. c. 9. civitat. improbos in rempublicam.

tions of buffoonery and caricature, and to overwhelm with the most bitter and unmerciful mockery. We consider the old comedy as the genuine, as it was the first and spontaneous production of the Attic soil. It grew up naturally out of their manners and their institutions, and ceased only because another order of things had taken place, and made it necessary to accommodate the style of the imitation to the altered character of the thing imitated.

The following description of two of the parts that so frequently occur in Plautus and Terence, are well executed, though that of the Parasite falls far short of the picture drawn by the strong but coarse pencil of the former ; and that of the courtezan is far more flattering than it ought to be according to the Latin comedies.*

"The parasites of Plautus are almost as deserving a dissertation as Shakspeare's clowns. Parasite, as is well known, was a name originally applied in Greece to persons devoted to the service of the gods, and who were appointed for the purpose of keeping the consecrated provisions of the temples. Diodorus of Sinope, as quoted by Athenæus, after speaking of the dignity of the sacred parasites of Hercules, (who was himself a noted *gourmand*,) mentions that the rich, in emulation of this demigod, chose as followers persons called parasites, who were not selected for their virtues or talents, but were remarkable for extravagant flattery to their superiors, and insolence to those inferiors who approached the persons of their patrons. This was the character which came to be represented on the stage. We learn from Athenæus, that a parasite was introduced in one of his plays by Epicharmus, the founder of the Greek comedy. The parasite of this ancient dramatist lay at the feet of the rich, ate the offals from their tables, and drank the dregs of their cups. He speaks of himself as of a person ever ready to dine abroad when invited, and, when any one is to be married, to go to his house without an invitation—to pay for his good cheer by exciting the merriment of the company, and to retire as soon as he had ate and drunk sufficiently, without caring whether or not he was lighted out by the slaves. In the most ancient comedies, however, this character was not denominated parasite, and was first so called in the plays of Araros, the son of Aristophanes, and one of the earliest authors of the middle comedy. Antiphanes, a dramatist of the same class, has given a very full description of the vocation of a parasite. The part, however, did not become extremely common till the introduction of the new comedy, when Diphilus, whose works were frequently imitated on the Roman stage, particularly distinguished himself by his delineation of the parasitical character. In the Greek theatre, the part was usually represented by young men, dressed in a black or brown garb, and wearing masks expressive of malignant gaiety. They carried a goblet suspended round their waists, probably lest the slaves of their patrons should fill to them in too small cups ; and also a vial of oil to be used at the bath, which was a necessary preparation before sitting down to table, for which the parasite required to be always ready, at a moment's warning.

"It was thus, too, that the character was represented on the Roman stage ; and it would further appear, that the parasites, in the days of Plau-

* Captiv. Act I. sc. 1. Act IV. sc. 3–4.

tus, carried with them a sort of Joe Miller, as a manual of wit, with which they occasionally refreshed their vivacity. Thus the parasite, in the *Stichus*, says,

"Ibo intro ab libros, et discam de dictis melioribus;"

and again—

"Libros inspexi, tam confido, quam potest,
Me meum obtenturum ridiculis meis."

* * * * * * *

"The parasite in the *Captivi*, may be considered as a fair enough representative of his brethren in the other plays of Plautus. He submits patiently to all manner of ignominious treatment—his spirits rise and sink according as his prospects of a feast become bright or clouded—he speaks a great deal in soliloquies, in which he talks much of the jests by which he attempted to recommend himself as a guest at the feasts of the great, but we are not favoured with any of these jests. In such soliloquies, too, he rather expresses what would justly be thought of him by others, than what even a parasite was likely to say of himself." p. 121.

"The Greek courtezan possessed attainments, which the more virtuous of her sex were neither expected nor permitted to acquire. On her the education, which was denied to a spotless woman, was carefully bestowed. To sing, to dance, to play on the lyre and the lute, were accomplishments in which the courtezan was, from her earliest years completely instructed. The habits of private life afforded ample opportunity for the display of such acquirements, as the charm of convivial meetings among the Greeks was thought imperfect, unless the enjoyments were brightened by a display of the talents which belonged exclusively to the wanton. But though these refinements alone were sufficient to excite the highest admiration of the Greek youth, unaccustomed as they were to female society, and often procured a splendid establishment for the accomplished courtezan, some of that class embraced a much wider range of education; and having added, to their attainments in the fine arts, a knowledge of philosophy and the powers of eloquence, they became, thus trained and educated, the companions of orators, statesmen and poets. The arrival of Aspasia at Athens is said to have produced a change in the manners of that city, and to have formed a new and remarkable epoch in the history of society. The class to which she belonged was of more political importance in Athens than in any other state of Greece; and though I scarcely believe that the Peloponnesian war had its origin in the wrongs of Aspasia, the Athenian courtezans, with their various interests, were often alluded to in grave political harrangues, and they were considered as a part of the establishment of the state. Above all, the comic poets were devoted to their charms, were conversant with their manners, and often experienced their rapacity and infidelity; for, being unable to support them in their habits of expense, an opulent old man, or dissolute youth, was in consequence frequently preferred. The passion of Menander for Glycerium is well known, and Diphilus, from whom Plautus borrowed his *Rudens*, consorted with Gnathena, celebrated as one of the most lively and luxurious of Athenian charmers. Accordingly, many of the plays of the new comedy derive their names from celebrated courtezans; but it does not appear from the fragments which remain, that they were generally represented in a favourable light, or in their meridian splendor of beauty and accomplishments. In the Latin plays, the courtezans are not drawn so highly gifted in point of talents, or even beauty, as might be expected; but it was necessary to paint them as elegant, fascinating, and expensive, in order to account for the infatuation and ruin of their lovers. The

Greeks and Romans were alike strangers to the polite gallantry of modern Europe, and to the enthusiastic love which chivalry is said to have inspired in the middle ages. Thus their hearts and senses were left unprotected, to become the prey of such women as the Phronesium of the *Truculentus*, who is a picture of the most rapacious and debauched of her class, and whose vices are neither repented of, nor receive punishment, at the conclusion of the drama. Dinarchus may be regarded as a representation of the most profligate of the Greek or Roman youth, yet he is not held up to any particular censure; and, in the end, he is neither reformed nor adequately punished. The portion, indeed, of the lady whom he had violated, and at last agrees to espouse, is threatened by her father to be diminished, but this seems merely said in a momentary fit of resentment." p. 158.

The comparative merits of Plautus and Terence have been so often stated and canvassed, that very little novelty can be expected in such a parallel at this time of day. The obvious difference between them is, that the one excels in *vis comica*, the other in the portraiture of character, and the purity and elegance of his style. Plautus seems to have been a blunt, downright, hearty lover of fun, and to have written for those who are for the most part equally so—the lowest of the populace. He is always in a good humour, and never misses an occasion for raising a laugh, even by a coarse joke or by low buffoonery. His *dramatis personæ*, like some of those in Shakspeare's comedies, are shrewd cavillers and wordcatchers, always on the watch for a *double-entendre*, and unmercifully given to forced and farfetched conceits, and to all the abominations of professed punning and wit with malice aforethought. His plays, indeed, like those of the great English dramatist—as Mr. Dunlop justly observes in reference to Ennius—abundantly refute the notion that *concetti* are vices of a declining literature. Terence is entirely free from these blemishes. His dialogue is precisely what we may conceive (making allowance for the metre) the conversation of well-bred people to have been at that time in Rome, familiar and unaffected, but extremely polished, correct and elegant. Writers of all ages, from Julius Cæsar downwards, have vied with each other in extolling the merits of his style. Heinsius speaks quite rapturously of his *mira et propé ineffabilis amœnitas*, the incredible charms of which he thinks with Joseph Scaliger that not one in a hundred, even of the most learned men, have eyes to see. It will be reckoned, we suppose, very absurd of us to speak of what is ineffable, and to set ourselves up for competent judges of invisible beauties. Yet we may be allowed to give in our *experience*. It agrees, in some measure, with the opinion of some of the contemporaries of Terence, who, as we learn from the Prologue to the Phormio, maintained that

————————————quas fecit fabulas,
Tenui esse oratione, et scripturâ levi.

For the mere negative merit of purity and propriety of diction, he ought to be put into the hands of every young student of Latin, and may be read with advantage by the most accomplished scholars. But there is a faultlessness that is altogether insipid and spiritless—non peccat nisi eo quod non peccat—and it appears to us that the style of Terence is to a certain extent liable to this objection. He seems to compose always with the fear of Scipio and Lælius before his eyes, and to aim at nothing more than doing a perfectly genteel thing—"content to live in decencies forever." We should be more struck with his elegance if he wrote with a bolder pen—if it accompanied him through all the varieties of an animated, brilliant, and diversified style. It is quite evident that his genius is not above mediocrity, and we do not suppose that without the aid of the Greek originals, his name would ever have been known to posterity. In short, nature intended him for a good translator, and he is so. Plautus has, in every respect, more boldness and originality. There is reason to think that his plays were less exact versions of the Greek comedies, than those of Terence. His own turn of mind as well as the character of his audience, may satisfy us that they were less refined than the originals: his system being, as Heinsius expresses it, *fabulas de Græco petitas argumento, Latinis salibus condire.* But it is impossible to read Plautus without feeling that he was born to write comedy. His coarse jests, his broad humour, his buffoonery, and extravagance—these are no doubt vices, but they are the rank growth of a fertile and generous soil. His very style—excessively given as he is to the use of words that occur nowhere else, and were no doubt coined by him for the occasion—proves him a writer of no ordinary powers. It is vigorous, pointed, and copious, and bears the stamp upon it of adventurous and creative talent. We have seen how highly it was esteemed by Varro. Schlegel, indeed, and after him, Mr. Dunlop, think that that learned Roman spoke merely as a philologist when he bestowed so much praise upon it; but this is only a conjecture, and we think, an unfounded one. From a passage in an author to whom we have often had occasion to refer,* it appears that Varro was very much addicted to the study of Plautus. There were twenty-one of the comedies which had been pronounced genuine by him, and which were, therefore, called "Varronianæ," but there were others which he did not doubt were the work of the same author; because they were written in his manner, and abounded with comic humour.

* Aul. Gell. lib. iii. c. 3—the title of the chapter is De noscendis explorandisque Plauti comœdiis, &c. lib. vii. c. 17.

Of the tragedies of Pacuvius and Attius,* we have already said almost as much as is warranted by our limits, and by the very scanty fragments of those writers which we possess. The former was a nephew of Ennius, born at Brundusium, A. U. C., 534. He died in 624, at the advanced age of 90. Attius lived at a still later period; it is supposed from 584 to 664. Cicero had seen and conversed with him. Their characters as writers, are hit off in a line of the epistle to Augustus.

*   *   *   *   aufert
Pacuvius docti famam senis, Accius alti.

As almost all their tragedies were close imitations or translations of the Greeks, and turned upon the old stories of Thebes' and Pelop's line, we think it impossible they should have had much of the force and fervour of their originals, or have made a deep and living impression upon the hearts of the Roman people. No poets of any nation can expect to handle those subjects with the same effect as Æschylus and Sophocles. Turn from the Œdipus Tyrranus to the Œdipe of Voltaire, which has always been considered by the French critics as one of that anthor's happiest efforts, and by some of them, we believe, as decidedly superior to the original. The difference between the Greek name, and the French mutilation of it, (bad as that is) is not, by any means, so great as between the things themselves. Even Racine, with all his admirable talents for this department of poetry, has fallen far short of the Greeks, whenever he has attempted the same subjects, as we think is clearly made out by Schlegel, in his comparison of Phedre with the Hippolytus of Euripides. The reason is obvious, and has already been hinted at in our introductory remarks. Greek tragedy was essentially and unchangeably Greek. There are associations that hallow and consecrate its subjects and its heroes, which it is impossible to call up by any composition in our modern tongues. We venture to say, that whoever has read the story of Œdipus in a French or Italian tragedy, before he took up Sophocles, will confess that he found it, in some degree, revolting and disgustful, and that it was not before he had made himself familiar with the glorious triology of that poet, that he felt the touching interest and awful grandeur of the theme.

The *Fabulæ Attellanæ* were a favourite and privileged amusement among the Romans. These were a sort of rude improvisatory farces resembling, it is supposed, the *Commedie dell' arte* of the Italians. They were originally derived from the *Osci*, or indigenous inhabitants of Campania. Young men of the most distinguished families of Rome, used to perform them

---

[* See some animated lines of his describing a Shepherd's wonder at his first sight of a ship. Apud Cic. de N. D. l. 1. c. 35.]

without reproach, and even the professed actors who made their livelihood by appearing in them, were exempted from the ignominy and the disabilities which were visited upon other theatrical exhibitions.* Until the 600th year of Rome, the old Oscan language continued to be employed in them, but as this was become by that time scarcely intelligible to the people, Q. Novius introduced into them the use of Latin. In the age of Sylla, Lucius Pomponius was still more distinguished in this kind, which enjoyed the same high degree of reputation and favour, until it was in some measure superseded by the Mimes of Laberius and Publius Syrus. The principal characters seem to have been all cast in the same mould with those heroes of the Carnival and the Fair, Harlequin and Scaramouch.

It is certainly a very curious fact, that the practical and politic, the grave and austere Romans should have been addicted to a species of buffoonery so gross and extravagant as this—and not less surprising, that the taste of the modern Italians should, at the present time, be marked by precisely the same peculiarity— so just is the observation, that the games and pastimes of children and the vulgar, retain the image of antiquity long after it has been effaced from all the other usages and institutions of society ! But, as Schlegel well observes, "how would Harlequin and Pul- cinello be astonished, were they to be told that they descended in a right line from the buffoons of the ancient Romans, and even from the Osci ! With what drollery would they be disposed to requite the labours of the antiquarian who should trace back their glorious pedigree to this root ! We know from the figures on the Greek vases, that a dress, very much resembling theirs, was used even in the grotesque masks of the old comedy—long breeches and a waistcoat with arms, articles of dress which the Greeks as well as the Romans never used except on the stage. Even in the present day, *Zanni* is one of the names of Harle- quin ; and *Sannio*, in the Latin farces, was a buffoon, who, according to the accounts of ancient writers, had a shaved head, and a dress patched together of all colours.† The figure of Pulcinello is said to be an accurate resemblance of one that has been found painted on the walls of Pompeii. If he came origin- ally from Atella, he may still be accounted a citizen of his ancient country."

It is impossible to decide, from any remains we possess of them, what was the precise character of the *Roman Mimes;*‡ and wherein they differed from the Attellane Fable. Some writers

*Valer. Maxim. lib ii. c. 4.
† [Cic. de Orat. l. 2. c. 61.]
‡ [Atque ita est totum hoc ipso genere ridiculum ; ut cautissime tractandum sit. Mimorum est enim ethologorum, si nimia est imitatio, sicut obscœnitas. Cic. de Orat, lib ii. c. 59.]

contend, that they were a sort of *monodrames*—it is more probable, however, that they contained a variety of parts, which it appears, were all taken from the lowest dregs of society— thieves, courtezans, &c. Among, or perhaps above them all, however, appeared the eternal Zany, with his grotesque costume, his absurd blunders, his whimsical gesticulation, and the "ineffable stupidity" of his whole demeanour. There is a certain class in every society that take pleasure in this sort of drollery and buffoonery—but Italy is the true country of Scaramouch. "Les étrangers les traitaient," says M. de Sismondi, in reference to the Commedie dell' arte, "avec un souverain mépris; les Italiens rougissaient et ne savaient comment se défendre et cependant le public ne riait qu'à ces comèdies, de l'art; il y accourut toujours en foule, tandis qu'il laissait deserte la salle ou l'on reprèsentait les comèdies èrudites: le public avait raison. Les reproches,.qu'on faisait.aux comedies del'art étaient fondès cependant elles seules étaient vraiment en harmonie avec l'esprit national; elles seules reprèsentaient la gaîté Italienne dans tout son naturel."

The Mime, however, rose in dignity in the hands of Decimus Laberius and Publius Syrus. These were two contemporaries of Julius Cæsar. The former was a Roman Knight, who at the age of 60, went upon the stage at the request of the Dictator. We still have the prologue to his first piece, in which all the critics from Macrobius down have discovered the high spirit of a Roman citizen, complaining bitterly of his degradation. A degradation it certainly was, but so harsh a measure was not in analogy with the rest of Cæsar's conduct, and we confess that the lamentations of the old knight appear to us to be almost as much for appearing too late upon the stage, as for appearing at all. "It would," indeed, "have been [otherwise] difficult to conceive how, in such a frame of mind, he could assume the jocund and unrestrained gaiety of a Mime, or how the Roman people could have relished such a spectacle." The other celebrated Mime was Publius Syrus—who was brought a slave to Rome from Asia in early youth, and having been well educated, and manumitted by his master, distinguished himself by his wit and humor. He had been a performer in the provincial towns, but came to the capital to contribute his share to the splendor and popularity of Cæsar's despotism. We know nothing of his works except by some hundreds of detached sentences or maxims, which are quite remarkable for beauty and correctness of sentiment, as well as for pointed expression—some of which are in every scholar's mouth.

"The age of Laberius, P. Syrus, and Matius, was the most brilliant epoch in the history of the actors of Mimes. After that period, they relapsed into a race of impudent buffoons: and, in the reign of Augustus, were classed, by Horace, with mountebanks and mendicants. Pantomimic actors, who did not employ their voice, but represented every thing by gesticulation and dancing, became, under Augustus, the idols of the multitude, the minions of the great, and the favorites of the fair. The *Mimi* were then but little patronized on the stage, but were still admitted into convivial parties, and even the court of the emperors, to entertain the guests like the Histrions, Jongleurs, or privilged fools, of the middle ages; and they were also employed at funerals, to mimic the manners of the deceased. Thus, the Archimimus, who represented the character of the avaricious Vespasian, at the splendid celebration of his obsequies, inquired what would be the cost of all this posthumous parade; and on being told that it would amount to ten millions of sesterces, he replied, that if they would give him a hundred thousand, they might throw his body into the river. The audacity of the Mimes was carried still further, as they satirized and insulted the most ferocious emperors during their lives, and in their own presence. An actor, in one of these pieces, which was performed during the reign of Nero, while repeating the words, "*Vale pater, Vale mater*," signified by his gestures, the two modes of drowning and poisoning, in which that sanguinary fiend had attempted to destroy both his parents. The *Mimi* currently bestowed on Commodus, the most approbrious appellation.— One of their number, who performed before the enormous Maximin, reminded the audience, that he, who was too strong for an individual, might be massacred by a multitude, and that thus the elephant, lion and tiger are slain. The tyrant perceived the sensation excited in the theatre, but the suggestion was veiled in a language unknown to that barbarous and gigantic Thracian.

"The Mimes may be traced beyond the age of Constantine, as we find the fathers of the church reprehending the immorality and licentiousness of such exhibitions." p. 335.

Before we quit the subject of the Roman Drama, we will remark that two circumstances in its history appear to us to be very singular. The one is that the first beginnings of Roman literature were almost exclusively in that department; and the other that, after that constellation of dramatic writers was passed away, they had not a single imitator or follower, until Varius and Ovid, each of whom wrote a tragedy. The Roman people were much more addicted to the sports of the circus and the amphitheatre, than to those refined and edifying entertainments which our managers call "the legitimate drama." Terence, in the prologue to the Hecyra, alludes to some sad mishaps that had befallen him in the performance of that comedy. He had brought it out twice without success—the first time, his whole audience was thrown into an uproar by a rope-dancer and a boxing match, which put an end to the play. The second time, it did very well for the first act, but presently a rumor got abroad through the theatre, that a combat of gladiators was about to take place— straightway every thing was in disorder:

——————populus convolat,
Tumultuantur, clamant, pugnant de loco
Ego intereà meum non potui tutari locum

3. The Miscellaneous Literature of the period under conside-

ration, so far as we shall be concerned with it, comprehends satire, the writings of Cato and Varro, and the poems of Lucretius and Catullus.

The controversy about the origin of satire is familiar to every one who has ever looked even into the Delphin edition of Horace, where Dacier's discourse upon the subject is to be found. It is somewhat curious, but principally as a philological speculation, since, whatever may have been the origin of the name or the thing, there is no visible trace either of the satyric drama of the Greeks, or the ribald farce of the Etrurian Histrions in the elegant raillery of Horace, and the lofty invective of Juvenal. The first specimens in this kind, that deserve the name, were the satires of Ennius, which were imitated by Pacuvius. But the writer, to whom it was most indebted, was Lucilius—born A. U. C. 605. Very few fragments of his compositions have been preserved—so that it is impossible for us to determine what their merit was—but we know that it was the subject of much controversy among the Roman critics. Horace sneers at the haste and carelessness of his predecessor, while there were others, who, in a still later age, considered him as the greatest of poets. The judicious Quinctilian* pronounces both these opinions equally extravagant, and leaves us to infer that he entertained, upon the whole, a favorable idea of this old writer's merits. The improvements, which Lucilius introduced into satiric composition, were so great as to make it doubtful whether it was the same thing in his hands that it had been in those of Ennius and Pacuvius. Horace speaks of him as the first that ever wrote in this kind,† by which he means, of course, only that the satires of the older authors were not worthy of being mentioned as specimens of it.

Under this head, learned men usually speak of a work of Varro's called the Menippean Satire‡ This seems to have been a jumble of prose and verse, Greek and Latin, philosophy and facetiousness, grave precept and light burlesque. It is from this work that the epithet Varronian has come to be attached to other medleys of a similar kind. Its style, we must suppose to have been much more exalted than that of the Italian Macoronic poetry, if we are to judge from works which are admitted imitations of it—the Apocolocyntosis of Seneca, the little treatise of Boëthius de Consolatione Philosophiæ, and the Satyricon of Petronius Arbiter. Some of the maxims contained in the following extract, will, we have no doubt, strike our readers as eminently

* Inst. Orat. lib. x. c. 2. † Sat. 1. lib. ii.
[‡ In illis veteribus nostris, quæ Menippum imitati, non interpretati, quadam hilaritate conspersimus, multa admixta et intima philosophia, multa dicta dialecticé; quæ, quo facilius minus docti intelligerent, jucunditate quadam ad legendum invitati. &c. 2. Acad. l. 1. c. 2.]

just, especially his rules for good conversation, and the philosophic reflection for the hen-pecked husband.

"Many fragments of this *Menippean* satire still remain, but they are much broken and corrupted. The heads of the different subjects or chapters contained in it, amounting to near one hundred and fifty, have been given by Fabricius in alphabetic 1 order. Some of them are in Latin, others in Greek. A few chapters have double titles: and though little remains of them but the titles, these show what an infinite variety of subjects was treated by the author.

* * * * * * *

"There is a chapter concerning the duty of a husband, (De officio Mariti,) in which the author observes, that the errors of a wife are either to be cured or endured ; He who extirpates them makes his wife better, but he who bears with them improves himself. Another is inscribed, "You know not what a late evening or supper may bring with it," (Nescis quid vesper serus vehat.) In this chapter he remarks that the number of guests should not be less than that of the Graces, or more than that of the Muses. To render an entertainment perfect, four things must concur—agreeable company, suitable place, convenient time, and careful preparation. The guests should not be loquacious or taciturn. Silence is for the bed-chamber, and eloquence for the Forum, but neither for a feast. The conversation ought not to turn on anxious or difficult subjects, but should be cheerful and inviting, so that utility may be combined with a certain degree of pleasure and allurement. This will be best managed, by discoursing of those things which relate to the ordinary occurrences or affairs of life, concerning which one has not leisure to talk in the Forum, or while transacting business. The master of the feast should rather be neat and clean than splendidly attired ; and if he introduce reading into the entertainment, it should be so selected as to amuse, and to be neither troublesome nor tedious. A third chapter is entitled περι ἐδεσματων; and treats of the rarer delicacies of an entertainment, especially foreign luxuries. Au. Gellius has given us the import of some verses, in which Varro mentioned the different countries which supplied the most exquisite articles of food. Peacocks came from Samos ; cranes from Melos ; kids from Ambrachia ; and the best oysters from Tarentum. Part, of that chapter γνωθι σεαυτον was directed against the Latin tragic poets." Vol. ii. pp. 48–49.

Cato the Censor was as conspicuous among his countrymen for his literary studies and abilities, as for the severity of his manners and his services in war. He is spoken of in the highest terms by Cicero, in many passages of the Rhetorical works, and there is one especially, in which he represents him as wanting nothing but the elegance and polish of a foreign education.* There was one peculiarity of his character, which pre-eminently distinguished him as a writer no less than as a senator and a magistrate, and that is a sturdy, exclusive nationality. It is said to have been from some such motives that he undertook his work, "De Orginibus," in seven books, which he began in his old age, and finished just before his death. It was the object of this inquiry into the history and antiquities of the Roman people, to

---

* Quid enim M. Catoni præter hanc politissimam doctrinam transmarinam atque adventitiam, defuit.—*De Orat.* lib. iii. c. 33.

shew how little they had been indebted to Greece, either for the origin or the improvement of their population, their language, and the arts and virtues of civilized life. It was in this work, also, that he fixed the era of the building of the city, which he determined to have been in the first year of the 7th Olympiad. How much is it to be regretted that this precious book should have perished, and, with it, all the light it would have thrown upon the subject of our second article !

In addition to his numerous orations and the work De Originibus, Cato was the first Roman that wrote any thing upon the subject of medicine. Rome, if we are to believe Pliny the elder, existed 500 years, without the least assistance from the Faculty. The first physician that practised medicine professionally there, was a Greek of the name of Archagatus, who arrived in Italy, A. U. C. 534, and whose system got him the enviable title of *carnifex*, or the executioner. Cato held him and his drugs in great horror. He believed these latter to be a secret poison, by means of which the Greeks had conspired to extirpate all barbarians, and chiefly the Romans, and that they took pay for their pretended services, only to impose the more effectually on the people, and insure the accomplishment of their diabolical purpose.* He defended his simples, therefore, especially colewort or cabbage (which was his favourite) most manfully, and earnestly exhorted his beloved countrymen "to remain steadfast," as Mr. Dunlop pleasantly observes, "not only by their ancient Roman principles and manners, but also by the venerable unguents and salubrious balsams which had come down to them from the wisdom of their grandmothers."

The only production of Cato which is still exant, is his treatise De Re Rustica, and even that seems to have been very much disfigured and mutilated by time. As it now stands, it is a loose, unconnected collection of memoranda or notes, upon the various departments of rural economy, such as any farmer might throw together from the results of his daily experience. Varro's treatise upon the same subject is far more systematic and comprehensive. Agricultural pursuits were, of all others, the most favoured at Rome. When our ancestors, says Cato,† praised any one as a good man, they said of him that he was a good husbandman, a good farmer.‡ Nor was this at all to be wondered at in a nation of soldiers, since, as he goes on to remark, the bravest men and the best troops are to be found among the cultivators of the soil. The consequence of this love of rural life, and the high consideration attached to such pursuits, was a wonderful progress in agricultural riches and im-

* Plin. Hist. Nat. lib. xxix. c. 1.   Pliny seems to side with Cato.

† Cato De Re Rus. c. 1.

‡[But see Sallust, proem. to Bell. Catilin.]

provements. "No country," says Varro,* "can be compared with
Italy in point of cultivation and abundance. What barley is
equal to that of Campania? What wheat to the Appulian?
What wine to the Falernian? What oil to the Venafrian? To
such an extent has cultivation been carried, that the whole
country looks like the suburbs of a great city."

The last mentioned writer flourished somewhat upwards of a
century after Cato, and was a burning and a shining light in
that constellation of talents which, in the age of Cicero, mingled
its mild and unavailing splendors with the departing glories of
the commonwealth. Varro was proclaimed, by his contemporaries, the most learned of the Romans, and their decree has
been ratified by posterity. Although, according to the fashion
of his country, which required every citizen to take a part in
the public concerns, he discharged the duties of a magistrate,
and appeared, on some interesting occasions during the civil
war ,at the head of the republican legions. By far the greater
portion of his long life was passed in rural and literary ease at
his villas, which he furnished with ample libraries, and embellished with all the objects of a cultivated and elegant taste.
At the age of 70, he was included with Cicero and Atticus in
the proscriptions of the second triumvirate, but he was saved
by the courage of a devoted friend, and survived the liberties of
Rome twenty years. His beautiful villas, however, had been
seized by Mark Antony, and it is conjectured, that we owe the
composition of his three books, *De Re Rustica*, to the destruction of his libraries, and his consequent inability to pursue more
recondite and profound studies. His works were extremely
voluminous—indeed, there is scarcely any branch of literature
and philosophy, to which he had not extended his researches—
and all his researches, if we are to believe the learned men of
antiquity, were attended with signal success.

A list of his works is given by Mr. Dunlop, but as they are
all lost, except his treatise on Agriculture, we shall be excused
for omitting any further mention of them. The pains, however,
which he took to enrich his libraries, and the progress of the
Romans in the formation of those institutions, deserve to be
more particularly noticed.

"Nor did Varro merely delight and instruct his fellow-citizens by his
writings. By his careful attention in procuring the most valuable books,
and establishing libraries, he provided, perhaps, still more effectually
than by his own learned compositions, for the progressive improvement
and civilization of his countrymen. The formation of either private or
public libraries was late of taking place at Rome, for the Romans were
late in attending to literary studies. Tiraboschi quotes a number of
writers who have discovered a library in the public records preserved at

* De Re Rus. c. 2.

Rome, and in the books of the Sibyls. But these, he observes, may be classed with the library which Madero found to have existed before the flood, and that belonging to Adam, of which Hilscherus has made out an exact catalogue. From Syracuse and Corinth the Romans brought away the statues and pictures, and other monuments of the fine arts; but we do not learn that they carried to the capital any works of literature or science. Some agricultural books found their way to Rome from Africa, on the destruction of Carthage: but the other treasures of its libraries, though they fell under the power of a conquerer not without pretensions to taste and erudition, were bestowed on the African princes in alliance with the Romans.

Paulus Emilius is said by Plutarch to have allowed his sons to choose some volumes from the library of Perseus, king of Macedon, whom he led captive to Rome in 585. But the honor of first possessing a library in Rome is justly due to Sylla; who on the occupation of Athens, in 667, acquired the library of Apellicon, which he discovered in the temple of Apollo. This collection, which contained, among various other books, the works of Aristotle and Theophrastus, was reserved to himself by Sylla from the plunder; and, having been brought to Rome, was arranged by the grammarian Tyrannio, who also supplied and corrected the mutilated text of Aristotle. Engaged, as he constantly was, in domestic strife and warfares, Sylla could have made little use of this library, and he did not communicate the benefit of it to scholars, by opening it to the public; but the example of the Dictator prompted other commanders not to overlook the libraries, in the plunder of captured cities, and books thus became a fashionable acquisition. Sometimes, indeed, these collections were rather proofs of the power and opulence of the Roman Generals, than of their literary taste or talents. A certain value was now affixed to manuscripts; and these were, in consequence, amassed by them, from a spirit of rapacity, and the principle of leaving nothing behind which could be carried off by force or stratagem. In one remarkable instance, however, the learning of the proprietor fully corresponded to the literary treasures which he had collected. Lucullus, a man of severe study and wonderfully skilled in all the fine arts, after having employed many years in the cultivation of literature, and the civil administration of the republic, was unexpectedly called in consequence of a political intrigue to lead on the Roman army in the perilous contest with Mithridates; and, though previously unacquainted with military affairs, he became the first captain of the age with little farther experience, than his study of the art of war, during the voyage from Rome to Asia. His attempts to introduce a reform in the corrupt administration of the Asiatic provinces procured him enemies, through whose means he was superseded in the command of the army, by one who was not superior to him in talents, and was far inferior in virtue. After his recall from Pontus and retreat to a private station, he offered a new spectacle to his countrymen. He did not retire, like Fabricus and Cincinnatus, to plough his farm, and eat turnips in a cottage—he did not, like Africanus, quit his country in disgust, because it had unworthily treated him; nor did he spend his wealth and leisure, like Sylla, in midnight debauchery with buffoons and parasites. He employed the riches he had acquired during his campaigns, in the construction of delightful villas, situated on the shore of the sea, or hanging on the declivities of hills. Gardens and spacious porticos, which he adorned with all the elegance of painting and sculpture, made the Romans ashamed of their ancient rustic simplicity. These would doubtless be the objects of admiration to his contemporaries; but it was his library, in which so many copies of valuable works were multiplied or preserved, and his distinguished patronage of learning, that claim the gratitude of posterity. "His library," says Plutarch, "had walks, galleries, and cabinets belonging to it, which were open to all visitors; and the ingenious Greeks resorted to this abode of the muses to hold literary converse, in which Lucullus delighted to join them. Other Roman patricians had patronized literature, by extending their protection to a favoured few, as the elder Scipio Africanus to Ennius, and the younger to Terence; but Lucullus was the first who encouraged all the arts and sciences, and promoted learning with princely munificence.

*   *   *   *   *   *

"The library of Varro, however, and all the others which we have mentioned, were private—open, indeed, to literary men, from the general courtesy of the possessors, but the access to them still dependent on their good will and indulgence. Julius Cæsar was the first who formed the design of establishing a great public library; and to Varro he assigned the task of arranging the books which he had procured. This plan, which was rendered abortive by the untimely fate of Cæsar, was carried into effect by Asinius Pollio, who devoted part of the wealth he had acquired from the spoils of war, to the construction of a magnificent gallery, adjacent to the Temple of Liberty, which he filled with books, and the busts of the learned. Varro was the only living author who, in this public library, had the hononur of an image, which was erected to him as a testimony of respect for his universal erudition. He also aided Augustus, with his advice, in the formation of the two libraries which that emperor established, and which was part of his general system for the encouragement of science and learning." Vol. ii. pp. 50-53.

The last writers included within the limits prescribed to the present article, are Catullus and Lucretius.

In reference to the merits of any merely *literary* composition, a foreigner must ever distrust his own opinions when they do not entirely coincide with those of native critics. For this reason, we feel bound to admit that we probably overrate Catullus and Lucretius in considering them (for we profess to have always considered them)—as in point of original genius, the two first poets of ancient Rome. The critics of their own country say nothing that is not in their favour, but it is plain that they do not entertain so exalted an opinion of their excellence as we have ventured to express. When we speak of "the poet," says Justinian, in the beginning of his Institutes, we mean Homer among the Greeks, and Virgil among the Romans—and there are others besides the Mantuan bard, who seem in the same way to take precedence of our favourites in the estimation of ancient writers.

Catullus had, among the poets of his own country, the title of *doctus*, or learned—for what reason, is not quite clear. If we are to suppose, however, with some of the commentators, that it was because of his familiar acquaintance with the Greek language and literature, we must do him the justice to say, that of all imitators he has the most originality—that of all erudite men he retains the greatest share of the playfulness, the buoyancy, and the vigor of natural talent. There is no constraint whatever in his movements—no parade or pedantry in his style. On

94 ROMAN LITERATURE.

the contrary, there never was a poet—we do not even except
Shakspeare—who seemed to write more as the mood happened
to prompt, and whose verses are stamped with such a decided
character of facility and of spontaneity. This, indeed, is the
great, and among the Latin poets, the peculiar charm of Catullus. Of all the Romans, he is most of a Greek, not by study
and imitation, but by nature. His lively wit, his voluptuous
character, his hearty affections, his powerful imagination, seem
naturally to overflow in verse and "voluntary wake harmonious
numbers." Julius Cæsar Scaliger, who finds fault with every
thing, disputed this poet's pretensions to learning, and denounced his works as stuffed with nothing but vulgarity and ribaldry,
but he afterwards sung a palinodia, declaring the Galliambic
ode a most noble composition, and the Epithalamium of Thetis
and Peleus, worthy to be placed by the side of the Eneid.
Other writers have been equally lavish of their praise for other
excellencies ; Martial, for instance, ascribes to him an unrivalled
superiority in the epigram. It is impossible to imagine any
two things from the same pen more entirely unlike each other,
than the ode just mentioned, and the sweet and delicate effusion
upon Lesbia's Sparrow, nor any falling off so sudden as from
either of these to the vulgarity and nastiness of some of the
Hendecasyllables. His amatory poetry is less tender than that
of Tibullus—and less gay and *gallant* than that of Ovid—but it
is more simple, more cordial, more voluptuous than either. A
modern reader would be very much disappointed if he expected
to find in it that delicacy of sentiment—-that *culte des femmes*—
that distant, mysterious, and adoring love which inspired the
muse of Dante and Petrarch, and which has ever since characterized the amorous ditties of our sonnetteers. The passion of
Catullus had not a particle of Platonic abstraction in it—it was
as far as possible from being metaphysical. It is deeply tinged
with sensuality—but it has absolute possession of his whole being—he seems to be smitten to the bottom of his heart with its
power—to be quite intoxicated with its delicious raptures.* It
is that "drunkenness of soul" of which Byron speaks—from an
imagination excited and exalted by visions of bliss and images

* We will exemplify this in one or two extracts—thus in the beautiful Carmen
de Acme and Septimio, (the 45th.)
    At Acme leviter caput reflectens
    Et dulcis pueri ebrios ocellos
    Illo purpureo ore suaviata,
    Sic inquit, mea vita Septimille, &c.
And so in that to Juventius (the 48th.)
    Mellitos oculos tuos Juventi,
    Si quis me sinat usque basiare
    Usque ad millia basiem trecenta, &c.
So Carm. (8th.)
    Quem Basiabis ? quoi labella mordebis, &c.

of beauty—with every feeling absorbed in one devoted passion, and all the senses dissolved in a dream of love.

The sensibility of Catullus, however, is not confined to the subjects of amatory song. There are several of his poems, on various occasions, which are full of tenderness and deep pathos. Quando leggete, says Flaminio, his imitator and almost his rival—"non vi sentite voi liquefare il cuore di dolcezza." Nothing can be more true to nature and more touching than his address to the Peninsula of Sirmio—his home, and perhaps his birthplace. The Carmen Nuptiale has been often imitated, and is committed to memory by every scholar, and the Epithalamium of Julius and Manlius may be regarded as perfect in its kind.* But the noblest specimen, beyond comparison, of poetry and pathos which the works of Catullus present—the most powerful appeal to the sympathies of the human bosom as the liveliest picture of its hidden workings and intensest agonies, is that Galliambic ode to which we have already alluded. The subject is, to be sure, a very affecting one. Under the influence of a frenzied enthusiasm, a young man forsakes his home and his country, for the purpose of dedicating himself to the service of the Idæan Goddess. The vow of chastity which a monk may break, was rendered inviolable to the Gallæ (for so the priests of Cybele were called) by the same means which, in later times, a father of the church adopted to disarm the temptations of the flesh. Atys, in the frenzy of his first excitement, is regularly initiated. He rushes madly forth to mingle in the revelry of the Gallæ, whom he arouses by the trump and the timbrel, and wildly exhorts to follow him to the lofty groves of the goddess. Their frantic demeanor, the Bacchanalian dances, their shrill and piercing howls are painted with a force of coloring which nothing can surpass. The imitative harmony of the versification is perfect—it is abrupt, irregular, disordered. You hear in it the hurried step, the clashing cymbal, the resounding timbrel. To all this commotion and disorder, a moment of repose—of soft but fatal repose succeeds. The Mænades, exhausted by their furious excitement, sink down at the threshold of the temple to sleep. A beautiful morning rises upon them, and Atys wakes—to despair. His lament is affecting beyond the power of language to describe. It seems wrung from a broken heart, and is fraught with all its agony and desolation. All the poetry of all ages may be safely challenged to produce any thing more painfully interesting and pathetic.

* A stanza of this little poem, which has been often quoted, is the following :
  Torquatus, volo, parvulus
  Matris e gremio suæ
  Porrigens teneras manus
  Dulce rideat ad patrem
  Semihiante labello.

We regret that the length, to which we have already extended our remarks, precludes the possibility of our bestowing upon Lucretius as much attention as the excellencies of his great work fairly entitle him to. Indeed, to do anything like justice to him, would require a separate article. Of all Didactic poems, excepting the Georgics of Virgil, his is incomparably the first. There is a very great difference, however, between the characters of these immortal poems. To say of the Georgics that it was the most elaborate and finished composition of its author, in the maturity of faculties, is to pronounce it a master-piece of its kind. It is, accordingly, a model of that high-wrought and studied elegance of which it is scarcely too much to say that no writer was ever so great a master as Virgil; and is full of the most beautiful and lofty poetry. The wonder is how the poet was able to reconcile his genius to his subject—how he could describe a plough for instance, without either sinking down into prose, or elevating his style far above the matter, and how he has contrived to throw a sort of Epic dignity and animation without any air of burlesque, into his pictures of the Bee-hive. Indeed, to say what we think upon the subject in one word—the perfection of the Georgics is unapproachable in Didactic poetry, and were it not that we have that work and Lucretius De Rerum Naturâ before our eyes, we should even doubt whether the very phrase "Didactic poetry" were not somewhat of a contradiction in terms. The brevity and simplicity of Virgil's precepts, indeed, make his poem scarcely an exception. He lays very little emphasis upon them, and is not at all ambitious of being associated with Cato and Varro as a writer *de re rusticâ*. He looks upon the face of nature and upon the labors of the husbandman with the eye of poetical genius. He seizes those features of rural life which paint themselves most strongly upon the imagination and the memory of those who have once tasted of its sweetness and repose. He dwells upon those subjects which have least of the vulgarity of business about them, and embellishes and elevates and colors them with the most interesting and poetical associations. In short, his picture of the country, and a country life, is the Beau Ideal.

The poem De Rerum Naturâ is more strongly didactic and therefore less *uniformly* perpetual than the Georgics. The author seems more concerned about utility than beauty—about the accuracy and perspicuity of his philosophical analysis, than the elegance of his style or the smoothness and harmony of his numbers. It is an attempt to develope in six books, of from twelve to fifteen hundred lines each, the whole system of Epicurus. This philosopher, who does not seeem to have died in odour of sanctity—for he had rather a bad name among the ancients—is now admitted to have laid the foundations, in physics at least, of the true philosophy. The other schools and doctors of Greece,

with a crude and precipitate generalization, had attempted to reduce all things to some one element or principle, or to a very few
elements and principles which they conceived to pervade the
universe, and to enter into all its multifarious combinations. Before experiments had been instituted, and while observation was
superficial and irregular, the absurdity of a theory that did not
agree with the phenomena might easily escape exposure, and,
when guessing was the order of the day, one wild conjecture
stood as good a chance as another. We are not to wonder, therefore, that the philosophers in their conceits rather than systems
about cosmogony, &c., hinted, as it happened, at fire, air, earth or
water, as the possible universal element, or gravely taught such
doctrines in their schools. The atomic system of Epicurus was
quite a distinct thing—it was, with all its errors, a decided step
in the progress of science—and deserved to be expounded by
philosophers, and celebrated in song.

The task of the poet, however, who undertakes to do both,
must be admitted to be one of no ordinary magnitude and difficulty. There would scarcely seem to be an *atom* of poetry floating about in the void of Epicurus. We very much doubt, accordingly, whether any poet but Lucretius could have produced
such a work out of such materials. He seems, as was before
observed, to think only of his philosophy. He proceeds, step by
step, in a regular progress, and brings out the whole doctrine in
all its bearings and consequences with a systematic fulness and
accuracy. His style is admirably adapted to the subject. Like
that of Catullus, it is characterised by the utmost simplicity and
ease. He was withal a true poet, and whenever occasion serves,
he pours out the most beautiful strains of inspiration and harmony without an effort. These delightful passages occur in every
part of his work—when the reader least expects them—in the
midst of a concourse of jagged or polygonal atoms, bringing about
heaven only knows what combinations—they blossom forth like
wild flowers, to regale his wearied senses with their freshness
and perfume. This perfect simplicity, however, united with so
much poetical beauty, makes it next to impossible, to translate
his work into a readable English book. Good's attempt appears to us a wretched failure. It is Lucretius in the last stage
of the dropsy, bloated even to suffocation, and utterly deformed.

In order to give the reader some idea of the plan of the work,
and the difficulties with which the poet had to contend in his
subject and materials, we will furnish a very concise summary
of the first three books.

The first opens with that celebrated invocation to Venus,
who is represented in a strain of wonderful poetry, as the goddess of universal nature, her spirit animating all things, and
her smiles diffusing over the whole face of creation, light and

beauty and joy. For her the earth sends forth her flowers, the floods rejoice at her presence, and the heavens shed around her their selectest influences. The very birds of the air, smitten with her power, pour out their songs of love, and the beasts of the field are warmed with her fires, and agitated by her impulses. The poet beseeches her to stay the car of the Thracian god, that he may enjoy a short interval of peace for the composition of his work, and draws a picture of Mars throwing himself upon her lap, and gazing with insatiable and unutterable love upon her divine beauty, which no description can surpass. After a dedication of his work to his friend Memmius, he declares the motive that induced him to undertake it. This was to relieve the minds of men from the bondage of superstition, whose terrors are not to be dispelled by "the light of the sun or the glittering shafts of day," but by reason alone. He not only repels the charge of impiety, but retorts it upon those who advance it, exemplifying by the sacrifice of Iphigenia, the accursed influence of a false religion. His personification of superstition is exceedingly grand, but too well known to be more than alluded to here. He next enters upon his subject, and begins by proving the truth of the maxim, ex nihilo nihil fieri, and that all things are formed of certain minute corpuscles or atoms, endued with solidity and mobility, which, though not palpable to sense, are easily conceived by the mind—that there is also a vacuum—that nothing exists in nature besides these, all other objects about which we are conversant in life, being mere incidents of varieties, or combinations of them—and that the elementary corpuscles are in consequence of their independent existence and impenetrability, indivisible and so eternal. He confutes the opinion of Heraclitus, who held the first principle of all things to be fire, and of other philosophers who taught the same of air, water and earth. His next sally is against the Homoemery of Anaxagoras, of which he exposes the absurdity. He contends that the universe is infinite—that space is from its very nature, unconfinable—that this attribute of boundlessness, if it may be so expressed, belongs equally to body and to void. Hence, he infers that there can be no central point of gravitation, and concludes the book with a panegyric upon philosophy, by the light of which we are enabled to understand so much that is wonderful in the economy of nature. The whole discussion is interspersed with passages of beautiful poetry, such as that beginning with "Juvat integros accedere fontes, &c."—and the well known simile, "Sed veluti pueris absinthia tetra medentes, &c." His explanations also of the rarity of bodies, of specific gravity, and of time, are accurate and curious, and every point is argued with the closest logic. He apologises in this book for his native tongue, as yet a stranger to the language of science and philosohy.

The second opens with some beautiful verses upon the pleasures which arise from study of philosophy. There is in the famous episode upon the happiness of a rural life in the second Georgic, O fortunatos nimium, &c.—a close imitation of some parts of this passage. The poet then returns to his subject and shews that there is, of necessity, a perpetual motion in atoms, and that this motion is of three kinds, direct, repercussive, and oblique or curvilinear—that they are not all of the same magnitude or shape, some of them being globular, others polygonal, and others again hooked (hamata)—and that though not infinite in variety, they are so in number. The descent of these atoms through the void is described as being more or less accelarated in proportion to the quantity of matter, and not to the superficial contents and a slight eccentricity in their course—"exiguum clinamen principiorum"—preserves, in some unaccountable manner, the freedom of the will which might otherwise seem to be subjected to inflexible and merely mechanical laws and impulses. The formation of compound bodies is then explained, and all their varieties as to hardness, smoothness, grossness, &c., are accounted for by corresponding varieties in the atoms of which they are composed. The prismatic colours are next explained, and we are taught that they do not belong to the atoms themselves, but are mere effects of their combination.* The next matters treated of, are the immensity of creation and the plurality of worlds. But as no compound being can be eternal, all these worlds are destined after certain periods, to decay and dissolution, when their fragments or rather their disengaged atoms, will enter again into other combinations, and grow at length into new worlds. Our earth, Lucretius thought, was even then in a state of exhaustion and decline, and ought, ere this, to have undergone its last change.

In the third book, the poet proceeds to the great object of the Epicurean philosophy, and its proudest boast, which was to relieve its disciples from those terrors and anxieties about death and a state beyond it, that haunt the minds of the unenlightened. The soul (anima) he believes to be material. It was the same in kind as the mind, (animus) but inferior to it in rank, the latter being seated about the heart, which is the source of life, whilst the former is diffused over the whole body, and receives its impulses from its better companion. They were not of a simple nature, but made up of air, (aer) heat (calor)—a certain venti cæca potestas—and a refined, undefinable something which

---

* The poet's notion of colours is worth comparing with those of our modern philosophers.

is the origin of sensibility. Thus, in some passions, such as anger, there is a predominance of *heat*—in others, such as fear, of the cold *aura*—while a tranquil character or state of mind is to be ascribed to the influence of the mild and placid *aer*. The same ingredients, in various proportions, enter into and distinguish the natures of the inferior races of animals. The soul being thus compounded of different elements or ingredients, it followed that it could be dissolved, and so was not immortal, but perished with the body—a proposition which Lucretius takes great pains to establish. The popular opinions of the times are scouted—and the whole story of the infernal regions is explained as an allegorical representation of the errors, delusions and passions of our minds, and the sufferings which they bring upon restless mortals. The stone hanging over the head of Tantalus, and filling him with perpetual apprehension, is figurative of the gloomy terrors of the superstitious. Tityus with his entrails forever renewed, and forever devoured by a ravenous vulture, is a picture of the sleepless anxieties of love and the thousand other troubles and disquietudes of life. The remedy, says the poet, is found in the gardens of Epicurus—in that "sublime oblivion of low-thoughted care," which he alone knew how to teach. Look back upon the time which has passed away before our birth—how still and tranquil, how free from all that can disturb or distress us! It will be even so with the future which we dread so much. And, after all, why shrink back with so much horror at the approach of death? Why be so anxious to add a few moments to this poor, fleeting existence? It will be at most a mere nothing saved from that total annihilation into which we must fall when we shall have ceased to breathe.

It is evident that to treat such a subject with philosophical accuracy and clearness, and, at the same time to write a most interesting and beautiful poem, required a genius of an extraordinary stamp. But the difficulty, which Lucretius had to encounter in the poverty of the Latin language, was almost as great as those arising out of the nature of his materials. While it was his boast, that he was venturing upon an unexplored region of poetry, where no footsteps of a predecessor were to be found he might justly say—

> Nec me animi fallit, Grajorum obscura reperta
> Difficile illustrare Latinis versibus esse
> Multa novis verbis prosertim quom sit agundum
> Propter egestatem linguæ et rerum novitatem.

In this respect, he undertook to do in verse, what Cicero soon after accomplished in prose. Inferior in almost every department of thought and of knowledge to the Greeks, there is none in which the Romans fell far so short of them, as in the different branches of philosophy. Their language which richly deserved the epithet "barbarous," in comparison of that of Athens and Rhodes, seemed formed only for a race of conquerors and of politicians. What Quinctilian, as we have seen, said of it with respect to the delicacies of the comic style, was eminently true in reference to philosophical inquiries; it furnished no names even for some of the first objects and elementary principles of science, and still less was it capable of defining them with precision, or of drawing with a subtile accuracy, the refined distinctions, which it is the great aim of philosophy to establish. Accordingly, there is an awkward, and, as it were, foreign air about the Latin language when applied to such subjects, which not even Cicero's unrivalled skill in composition could altogether change or conceal.* This defect would, of course, be more felt by the poet than by prose writers.

Varro, Catullus, Lucretius—these great names remind us that we are arrived at the most glorious era of Rome. In the midst of victory and conquest in the East and West, on the banks of the Rhine, and the shores of the British channel, as well as on those of the Euphrates and the Euxine, and while the spirit of republican liberty, though contaminated in many of her citizens by licentiousness and corruption, was still as strong and glowing in the second Brutus and his compeers, as it had been in the first—all the elegancies of polished life adorned her manners and pursuits. Greek literature was universally and enthusiastically studied by her scholars, and there were some of them, who, having been bred in the schools of Athens, were as familiar with the use of that language, as with their own. Cicero, already the rival of Demosthenes in the Forum and the Senate, now emulated, in quite another sphere, the genius of Plato, and every thing announced the approach—we ought rather to say the presence—of that perfect civilization and full and dazzling development of literary genius, with which, under the name of the AUGUSTAN AGE, a cruel reverse of fortune has forever identified the fame of a usurper and a despot.

* [Cicero himself, however, does not think so. Quo in genere tantum profecisse videmur, ut a Græcis ne verborom quidem copia vinceremur. De N. D. l. I. c 4.]

KENT'S COMMENTARIES.

Commentaries on American Law. By JAMES KENT. Vol. I. 1826. Vol. II. 1827. 8vo. *O. Halsted. New-York.*

IT is quite a matter of course that "the influence of America upon the mind," (to borrow a convenient, though somewhat pedantic phrase) should become first and chiefly, if not exclusively perceptible, in the department of politics and law. We are not aware that any new and peculiar sources of poetical enthusiasm have been revealed to us, nor have we as yet seen any thing in our history or condition, to justify the belief—so confidently inculcated by many of our prophetic fellow-citizens—that some great revolution in the abstract sciences and in speculative phi-losophy is to be reckoned among the probable consequences of the declaration of independence. The adventurers that first peopled this continent were not a race of barbarians, whose character was yet to be formed or developed. They brought with them the manners, the knowledge, and the modes of thinking, which belong to a highly advanced state of social improvement. All their historical recollections and hereditary feelings—their literary associations and philosopical tenets—nay, even their very religious doctrine and discipline, which were the motive that determined so many of them to quit their homes—were essentially European. Nor was there any thing in their situation here, to sever these strong ties—to give a new impulse to opinion in matters of philosophy and learning, or, in short, to influence, in any material degree, their own intellectual character and pursuits—much less to produce a sensible effect upon the general condition of the human mind. It is, on the contrary, our misfortune, in one sense, to have succeeded, at the very outset of our career, to an over-grown inheritance in the literature of the mother country, and to have stood for a century in that political and social relation towards her, which was of all others most unfavourable to any originality in genius and opinions. Our good fathers piously spoke of England as their *home.* The inferiority—the discouraging and degrading inferiority—implied in a state of colonial dependence, chilled the enthusiasm of talent, and repressed the aspirations of ambition. Our youth were trained in English schools to classical learning and good manners; but no scholar-ship—great as we believe its efficacy to be—can either inspire or supply, the daring originality and noble pride of genius, to which, by some mysterious law of nature, the love of country and a national spirit seem to be absolutely necessary. We imported our opinions ready-made —"by balefuls," if it so pleases the Rev. Sidney Smith. We were taught to read by English schoolmasters—and to reason by English authors—English clergymen filled our pulpits, English lawyers our courts—and above all things, we deferred to and dreaded the dictatorial authority and withering contempt of English criticism. It is difficult to imagine a state of things more fatal to intellectual dignity and enterprise, and the consequences were such as might have been anticipated. What is still more lamentable, although the cause has in a good measure ceased, the effect continues, nor do we see any remedy for the evil until our youth shall be taught to go up to the same original and ever-living fountains of all literature, at which the Miltons, and the Barrows, and the Drydens drank in so much of their enthusiasm and inspiration, and to cast off entirely that slavish dependence upon the opinions of others which they *must* feel, who take their knowledge of what it is either their duty, their interest or their ambition to learn, at second hand.

But in politics and jurisprudence, the American people were compelled by the very novelty of their situation to think for themselves. Nature, which is explained by philosophers and imitated by the artist and the poet, is every where the same, and it is not impossible that our literature and science, to however an exalted a pitch of excellence they may ultimately attain, may never exhibit any strictly national peculiarities. But the case is very different with the civil and juridical institutions of a country. These are, in a great degree, the work of man, and may be moulded, and have been moulded into endless varieties of form to suit his occasions or caprices. In this respect, our founders could not, if they would, be imitators. They could bring with them from the mother country only the general principles of government and jurisprudence—the great outlines of a free constitution, and the invaluable maxims of the common law. But its institutions were more or less inapplicable to their present circumstances, and their civil polity had to be recast and built up anew from the very foundation. Their wisdom was thus tasked from the beginning, in selecting such parts only of the laws of England, as were adapted to their situation,* while they were of course studious to preserve whatever had so pre-eminently distinguished them, among the institutions of modern Europe, as most auspicious to liberty and jus-

---

* Mr. Brougham's bill proposes to do, in England, little more than was universally done in America, from the beginning.

tice. That superstitious veneration for English example and opinion, which, in merely speculative matters, led to servile imitation and implicit acquiescence, was here precluded, or at least corrected by the very nature of things, and the stores of useful information which they acquired in studying the constitution, civil and political, of the mother country, could, in such novel circumstances, serve at most to enlighten speculation and direct experiment. We need scarcely add that those vehement and protracted discussions of all the principles of public law, that preceded the war of the revolution, had a strong tendency still more to disenthrall the minds of our leading politicians from any undue influence which the authority or the reasonings of English jurists and publicists may have exercised over them before.

These observations are, however, more strictly applicable to law than to politics; because the former, as we shall presently attempt to shew, is at once the most exact and the most complicated of all the *moral* sciences, while the latter, in spite of all that has been written and said about it, can, in our opinion, scarcely aspire to the dignity of a science at all. We know that in hazarding this position we shall scandalize many, probably most of our readers. If anything is taken for granted in this country, as a truth better established than all others, it is, that in matters of government we have found out the philosopher's stone—and are now in possession of an infallible secret to make men free and happy, and to keep them so forever, even in spite of themselves. The first lesson we inculcate upon our young politicians, (and most of our politicians are young) is that a true statesman, like a true philosopher, is quite independent of circumstances, and can pull down the whole fabric of a government and put it up again, as easily as Owen of Lanark would lay out a parallelogram, and with the same absolute certainty of improving the condition of the people. Now, we are heterodox enough to think this not only an error, but a most pernicious error. We believe that no constitution in the world is worth a straw but public opinion and national character, and that it is altogether impossible for mortal man to predict what is to be the result of any important change in the distribution of political powers. In a word, that no general principles in politics—except such as are too general to be of much practical utility—can be safely depended upon in the administration of affairs. But we must reserve this topic—which, however, we seriously believe to be one of the most important that can be pressed upon the consideration of the American public—for some future remarks.

To address ourselves more particularly to the causes which affected the condition of jurisprudence in this country, in the manner alluded to above. In all the Provinces, as is well known, the common law of England was adopted, but only so far forth as it was not inconsistent with the genius of their institutions, and the letter and spirit of their own statutes. The latter, as we have seen, were necessarily very numerous and important. The whole law of tenures, once constituting with its various incidents and consequences, so vast a department of English jurisprudence, was omitted entirely. The forms of conveyancing were materially altered and simplified, as were those, also, of judicial proceedings. All that was local and customary—all that, in England, was preserved because antiquity had hallowed it, or prescription turned it into property, was discarded ; and wherever these and such like changes left any chasm in the system, it was filled up by positive legislation, or by judicial decisions, founded upon the analogies of the constitution and the laws. Here, at once, we perceive a vast field opened up for original speculation and reasoning. Every case might present a two-fold difficulty ; first, to decide what was the law in England, and secondly, whether it were applicable here. The latter question it was impossible to answer without going into the true grounds and reasons of the law; and Burke's lawyer, who was at a loss, "whenever the waters were out," and "the file afforded no precedent," would often find himself as much embarrassed in an American court of justice, as in our deliberate assemblies. Indeed, this single circumstance is sufficient to shew that that great man's notions upon the effect of a legal education must be received—if they are to be received at all—with many grains of allowance—so far, at least, as concerns the profession on this side of the Atlantic.

Another important point in the judicial history of this country, is the effect of its separation from England by the war of the revolution. This great event took place at what may be considered, with a view to our jurisprudence, as a very critical juncture. Lord Hardwicke had not many years before resigned the great seal, having greatly amplified and improved the chancery system, begun by Lord Nottingham, without, however, exhausting the complicated subjects that fall within it. Lord Mansfield was, even then, at the head of the King's Bench introducing those innovations (real or supposed) into the law, which alarmed Lord Kenyon and other narrow-minded men so much, but which, by his own account of it, threw Mr. Justice Buller into a perfect extacy of wonder, at the depth, the comprehensiveness, and the acumen of that powerful and ruling understanding. The *jurisprudentia nova*,* which dates about Lord Holt's time, was still in a state of progress and improvement. Many important principles were yet to be settled, many obsolete errors or hasty opinions to

* Gravina Orig. J. C. p. 86.

be exploded, many fundamental statutes to be interpreted, and applied, and the whole law merchant, and the whole law of prize, to be sanctioned by decision and reduced to a system. We need only refer to the vast accessions that have been made to the body of English law—the jurisprudence des arrêts—from the publication of Douglas' Reports to the present day. Our courts have, thus, had an opportunity of reconsidering many matters, after they had been disposed of in England, and, in coming to their conclusions, have had all the benefit of the argument without being bound by the authority of the cases in Westminister Hall.

It was natural, also, that in order to assist them in making up their judgments upon matters of new impression, as they are called, they should not confine themselves to the English Reports and text books, but should have recourse to other systems of cultivated jurisprudence, and especially to the writings of the Civilians. We were very happy to find our own opinions upon this subject expressly sanctioned by the authority of Chancellor Kent, and, indeed, it may be observed that among the benefits, conferred upon his country, by that venerable and learned man, it is not the least that he has exemplified, in his own brilliant success, the use that may be made in our courts of the enlightened equity of the Roman jurisconsults. "It may be observed," says our author, "that a very large proportion of the matter contained in the old reporters, prior to the English revolution, has been superseded, and is now cast into the shade by the improvements of modern times; by the disuse of real actions and of the subtleties of special pleading; by the cultivation of maritime jurisdiction; by the growing value and variety of personal property; by the spirit of commerce and the enlargement of equity jurisdiction; by the introduction of more liberal and enlightened views of justice and public policy; and, in short, by *the study and influence of the civil law*."* The English lawyers, on the other hand, have entertained a strange jealousy of the *corpus juris civilis*, and have studiously disclaimed and deprecated the idea of being under any obligations to it. The answer of their "sturdy ancestors," at Merton, has been always repeated with approbation, and even with triumph, as their example has been faithfully followed (with some distinguished exceptions, however) in all succeeding times. Perhaps it was erring on the safe side in England to discountenance every attempt to interpolate into their own common law the doctrines of a foreign jurisprudence; but, situated as we are in this country, we do not see why the Reports of Westminster Hall, *since* our revolution, should be in such request as to be found in all our libraries, while the works of the Civilians are banished from most of them like a

* Vol. i. pp. 453–454.

contamination. To be sure, as long as feudal tenures subsisted in all their rigor, and land property was the exclusive object of the law, there could be no great intercommunity of principles between systems so opposite in all their essential characteristics. Feuds were altogether of positive institution, and as far as possible removed from the common standard, which we shall presently advert to, of the law of nature.* It is worthy of remark, however, that it is evident from Bracton,† who often uses the very words of the Justinian collection, that the maxims of justice, taught by Proculus and Capito, by Gaius and Papinian, had enlightened the understandings and mingled with the opinions and feelings of mankind even in that age, and thus contributed much to form the *mores*—the common law, which is only the common sense—of the English people.

Independently, however, of any historical connection of that kind, very little reflection will be necessary to convince us of what vast utility the volumes of the Civilians may be to us in our legal inquiries. Widely as systems of positive law may differ, there will always be some—frequently many points of coincidence and similarity between them. Besides this, in the progress of things, there is a tendency to a gradual abolition of merely technical rules and arbitrary institutions, and to the adoption in their stead of such as are more simple and rational, and of more universal application. This tendency is, of course, increased by the progress of commerce and the intercourse of nations. Thus, the *Lex Mercatoria*—the great body of the law merchant, is strictly *juris gentium*—and there would, at the present day, be very little discrepancy between the decisions of a French and English, and an American court, upon any commercial question.

The use of the word *juris gentium*, in this connection, suggests to us an illustration of this topic, from the writings of the Civilians, which deserves, on more accounts than one, to be brought to the notice of our readers

The Roman lawyers, besides their first great division of law into the *jus publicum* and *jus privatum*, analyzed it into three distinct kinds, or rather constituents. 1° *jus naturale*, which they described as being common to the whole animal creation, such, for instance, as the union of the sexes, the procreation and education of offspring, &c. 2° The *jus gentium*, which we must be careful not to confound (as is often done) with what is

---

* LEGES LEGUM ex quibus informatio peti possit, quid in singulis legibus bene aut perperam positum aut constitutum sit.—*Bacon de Fontib. Jur. Aph.* 6.

* Mr. Kent adopts the opinion of Reeve (Hist. English Law, vol. iv. pp. 570-71) that Bracton is the father of the English law, and that what Saunders throws out, arguendo, in Stowel vs. Lord Zouch (Plowd. 367) in disparagement of him and Glanville, is a foul aspersion.

called, in the language of modern jurisprudence, the law of nations.* The jus gentium of the Civilians comes nearer to what
we term the "law of nature," and was by them distinguished
from the *jus naturale*, in that the latter was common to all animals, whereas the former extended only to the human species.
In another place, they have defined it thus—quod naturalis
ratio inter omnes homines constituit, id apud omnes peræque
custoditur, vocaturque jus gentium, quasi quo jure omnes gentes utuntur.—l. 9. in. fin. ff de just. et jur. To this *jus gentium*
they accordingly refer most of the usages and institutions, the
pursuits and relations of civilized men—among which we find the
following particulars enumerated under the same head in the
Pandects. Ex hoc jure introducta bella, discretæ gentes, regna
condita, dominia distincta, agris termini positi, ædificia collo-
cata commercium, emptiones, venditiones, locationes, conduc-
tiones, obligationes institutæ—l. 5. eod. That is to say, they
class together, under this head, those things which are so manifestly reasonable and proper, or so agreeable to the general condition and exigencies of society, as to have found their
way into every system of laws. In by far the majority of cases,
the *jus gentium*, as thus defined, would be found to coincide with
the law of nature, according to the opinion of Cicero who affirms, broadly, that *omni prorsus in re omnium comensus lex
naturæ putanda est*. It may happen, however, that an extraordinary concurrence of circumstances, the barbarism of an age,
or other similar causes, shall lead to the universal adoption of
customs and principles that shall not coincide with the conclusions of right reason, or the feelings of a refined humanity. Pi-
racy was once *juris gentium*, and so was the seizure of property
wrecked. It is in this sense of the word also, that Sir H. Spel-
man speaks of the feudal system as the "law of nations in our
western world"—a system (as has already been observed) as
artificial, as far removed from the natural state of society as it
is possible to imagine. 3° The third kind was the *jus civile*,
which it were inaccurate to translate "municipal law," for the
Civilians mean by *jus civile*, not that law which is contradistinguished from *international*, but only that part of the municipal
law of every country, which arises from arbitrary legislation
and peculiar customs, and which therefore, cannot be classed
either with the *jus naturale* or the *jus gentium*. "Itaque," as it is
elegantly expressed in the Digest, "cum aliquid addimus vel de-
trahimus juri communi, jus proprium id civile efficimus"—l. 6. eod.
    If we adopt this precise and philosophical arrangement of the
Civilians, we shall find that in an advanced state of society, a very

*[Neque vero hoc solum naturâ, et jure gentium. Cic. De Off. l. 3. c. 5. Qua-
rundam enim rerum dominium nancisimur jure naturali, quod (sicut diximus)
appellatur jus gentium. Just. l II. Tit. 1. § 11.]

large, if not the largest portion of every system of jurisprudence is, what is strictly speaking, *juris gentium*. The peculiarities of positive law are gradually effected by the intercourse of nations, and each code approximates more and more to the standard of that—quod naturalis ratio apud omnes gentes constituit. In this respect it will be found to be with the laws as it is with the characters of different peoples; they appear, at first sight, to be infinitely diversified, but very little examination is necessary to convince us that they resemble each other much more in the great, eternal principles of a common nature, than they differ in respect of local or national peculiarities. Thus, by our law, the most solemn contract is in the shape of a sealed writing— by the civil, it was a verbal stipulation. So far there is a wide difference between them; but for one question that arises about the *form* of a covenant, there will be, at least, a hundred involving principles of universal application ; as to the meaning of the parties, the extent to which their responsibility goes, the effect of fraud, mistake or duress, the rights and liability of sureties, &c. In all such matters, the writings of the Civilians are a never-failing source of light and instruction, and we have no hesitation in saying that, in many most important enquiries, we have derived, in the course of our own experience, much greater assistance from Voet and Cujacius, or Domat and Pothier, than from our own books. Indeed, the juridical history of England furnishes illustrious examples of the same fact. The boasted essay of Sir W. Jones, on the law of bailments, contains very little that is not familiar to every student of the *corpus juris civilis*, and if his classification is more complete, and his discussion of the subject more satisfactory than that of Lord Holt in Coggs v. Barnard, it is, no doubt, owing altogether to his familiarity with the works of the Civilians. The same thing may be predicated of the still more boasted improvements of Lord Mansfield. That great judge invented nothing. He was called upon to expound the contracts of merchants, and he did so, with the assistance of special juries at Guildhall, by the lights of the *jus gentium*. He had before him, besides the monuments of the ancient civil law, and the learning of the commentators, the French ordonnance de la marine and the commentary of Valin, and he did no more than sanction by the authority of judicial decision, and accommodate, in some few instances, to the usages of his own country, the principles which he found developed in those great repositories of wisdom and equity.

It is foreign from our present purpose (even if we were prepared) to express any opinion as to the comparative merits of the common and civil law. Each has, no doubt, its peculiar excellencies and defects,—points in which it approximates more nearly to, or deviates more widely from, the common standard of right reason, than the other, and the comparing them together, even in these particulars, affords one of the most profitable exercises that can be imagined for a reflecting mind. We will just remark, by the way, however, that we think the civil law will be found, in general, to study a refined equity more than the policy of society, whereas the common law seldom departs from its stern maxim, that a private injury is better than a public inconvenience. It is very important to keep in mind this point of difference between them. Thus there is something captivating in the equity of the principle, that a sound price implies a warranty of the soundness of the commodity; but it is certain that this rule is productive of great practical inconveniences, and we believe that, in this State, where we have had ample opportunity to witness its operation, there are very few experienced lawyers but would gladly expunge from our books the case which first introduced it here.*

But whatever may be the comparative merits of these two systems of jurisprudence, considered *per se*, it is certain that the civil law has greatly the advantage of ours in the manner in which it has been expounded and illustrated. This, indeed, is a difficulty, for which allowance must be made by the readers of the volumes before us. They are another attempt to arrange and to develope the elements of a branch of knowledge that has never yet been taught as it ought to be. In comparing what the Civilians have written upon any subjects that have been treated of by English text writers, or discussed in the English courts, it is, we think, impossible not to be struck with the superiority of their truly elegant and philosophical style of analysis and exposition. Their whole arrangement and method—the division of the matter into its natural parts, the classification of it under the proper predicaments, the discussion of principles, the deduction of consequences and corollaries—every thing, in short, is more luminous and systematic—every thing savors more of a regular and exact science. Even Blackstone, with all his prepossessions in favour of whatever is English, admits that before his time "the theoretical, elementary parts of the law had received a very moderate share of cultivation," and although his own Commentaries have abridged and facilitated the studies of professional men, and made a certain knowledge of legal principles accessible even to mere amateurs, yet we think, that they have, by no means, superseded the necessity of future labors in the same vineyard. There is, in spite of all the pompous eulogies that have been passed upon that work, a great deal of justness in Horne Tooke's remark, that "it is a good gentleman's law book, clear, but not deep." The truth is, that

*See also Abbott on Shipping, 299.

"the learned commentator" was any thing but an original or philosophical thinker. He has done nothing more than fill up the outline sketched by Sir Matthew Hale, and with all his perspicuity and precision, and comprehensiveness, one is continually tempted to say of it, as D'Arguessau does of the Institutes of Justinian—quoique l'ordre de ce livre ne soit pas vicieux, vous souhaiterez néanmoins plus d'une fois qú'êlle eût pu être tracé par M. Domat au lieu de l'être par M. Tribonien. If Lord Bacon had lived in the reign of George III., and accomplished the great work which he was so desirous of undertaking, even in his own time, his profound and systematic understanding had left us, no doubt, a *novum organon* of jurisprudence, worthy of the science and the age. The other elementary writers of our law—the compilers of institutes, abridgements, &c., even down to the present day, are, with few, if any exceptions, liable to the same criticism. The most that can be said of them is par negotiis, neque suprà. None of them stand upon that "vantage ground," of which Bolingbroke speaks. They are mere *pragmatici*—who treat their subjects in a strictly technical manner, and whose whole system of logic consists of a case in point. They seem to dread nothing more than generalization, or the stating a proposition in the form of a theorem. They string together cases from which it is often difficult to extract any distinct, general principle, and which are determined to be analogous, or otherwise, by circumstances comparatively immaterial. Let any one reflect upon the confusion into which the courts of England were betrayed in their attempts to reconcile the necessity of words of perpetuity to carry the fee in a will, with the rule that the intention shall govern, and the figure which a digest of these decisions makes as part of a scientific system! So of the controversies occasioned by Porter vs. Bradley, and the other cases on that point. Would it be believed that stress has been laid by grave lawyers upon the verbal distinction between "leaving issue" and "leaving issue behind," as if issue could be left any where else.* Compare Chitty on Bills with Pothier's Traité du Contrat de Change, or any other elementary book in our law with a corresponding treatise of that admirable writer, and it will be impossible to dispute the justness of the preceding

* It is such things as these that Hottoman alludes to in a passage which seems to have scandalized Mr. Butler excessively, and which he misinterprets in quite a laughable manner. Stephanus Pasquerius, &c., libellum mihi *Anglicanum* Littletonium dedit, quo Feudorum Anglicorum jura exponuntur, ita inconditè, absurdè et inconcinnè scriptum ut facile appareat, verissimum esse quod Polydorus Virgilius, in Anglicâ Historiâ, de *jure Anglicano* testatus est, stultitiam in eo libro, cum *malitiâ et calumniandi studio*, certare. That is to say, was a mixture of foolishness and cavilling. Upon this, Mr. Butler gravely remarks—"Hottoman, if he had read it, *might* think it (Littleton's Tenures) inelegant and absurd; but he *could not* think it *malicious* or indicative of a *disposition to slander!*—*Pref. to Coke upon Littleton*, 13th edit.

observatiofis. In a word, the remark of a celebrated French jurist,* in reference to the law of his own country as it stood in his day, is entirely applicable to the appearance which our jurisprudence makes in these very inelegant and unphilosophical compilations : It seems to be a mass of irregularities and incoherencies, which consists rather in particular usages and occasional decisions, than in immutable principles, or in consequences deduced immediately from the rules of natural justice.

There *was* a time when the same complaints were made about the civil law. Cicero repeatedly touches upon the subject, and urges the necessity of introducing into it the light and the order of a philosophical arrangement. In his treatise De Legibus, (i. 5,) he exhorts his young friends to elevate their views to loftier objects than were commonly aimed at by men engaged in forensic pursuits. "The science of jurisprudence ought to be drawn," says he, "not from the edict of the Prætor, as is usual nowadays, nor from the Twelve Tables, as was formerly the practice, but out of the very depths of philosophy—*penitus ex intimâ philosophiâ.*" His remarks upon the character of his distinguished contemporary, Servius Sulpicius, also deserve to be cited as very apposite and striking. He does not scruple to prefer that jurisconsult before Mutuis Scævola, who was generally considered as the first lawyer of the age. In accounting for the preference, he admits that Scævola was as thoroughly versed in the laws as a man can become by long practice and assiduous study. And so were other lawyers who made a figure at that time. But he declares that he knew no one besides Sulpicius, who was master of that higher *art*, as he calls it— very distinct from mere technical skill, and not to be acquired by the experience and discipline of the forum—which discovered itself in a lucid order, in precise definition, in sound interpretation, in a systematic development of the whole doctrine in question, and a logical deduction of all its legitimate consequences, at the same time that everything false or irrelevant was rigorously excluded by the analysis. In another passage, which throws great light upon the subject of the preceding observations, he expresses himself still more fully and precisely to the same effect.†

It is evident from these citations, that the excellencies, which

*Œuvres de D'Aguesseau. Tom. 1.ᵉ 395.
† De Orat : lib. i. c. 42. Omnia fere quæ sunt conclusa nunc *artibus*, &c. *Ars* quædam extrinsecus ex aliò genere quodam, quod sibi totum philosophi assumunt, quæ rem dissolutam divulsamque conglutinaret, et ratione quadam constringeret, &c. Si enim aut mihi facere licuerit, *quod jam diù cogito*, aut alius quispiam, aut me impeditq occuparit, aut mortuo effecerit, ut primum omne jus civile in genera digerat quæ perpauca sunt. &c. Perfectam artem juris civilis, habebitis, magis magnam atque uberem, quàm difficilem atque obscuram. [Cf. Plato Phœdrus, Euthrydemus.]

have been alluded to as characteristic of the writings of the Civilians, do not arise out of any thing in the nature of that law, but solely from the preparatory discipline and general intellectual habits of its professors. Philosophical studies had made but little progress at Rome before the time when Cicero and Sulpicius flourished. It was, indeed, principally to the beautiful treatises of the former upon the various questions discussed in the Athenian schools, that the citizens of that martial commonwealth were indebted for their initiation into such pursuits. It was not to be expected, therefore, that men of business, absorbed in the occupations of the Forum, and attached by habit to its forms, should outstrip their own age so far as to incorporate into the doctrines and method of a practical profession, improvements that were not yet familiar even to men of a speculative turn of mind and of learned leisure. But the subsequent fortunes of the civil law were much brighter. Heineccius states it as a fact, acknowledged on all hands, that the greater part of the ancient jurisconsults of a subsequent period, were very much addicted to the study of philosophy, and employed, in expounding and interpreting their own science, those rules and principles which they had learned in the discipline of the Lyceum and the Porch.* Indeed, this fact, especially as regards the latter school, cannot fail to strike every one who looks, however superficially, into the *corpus juris civilis*, many of the reasonings collected there, and even the very maxims and definitions, being strongly tinctured with the characteristic subtlety,† as well as with the severe and elevated ethics of this favourite sect. In modern times, that jurisprudence has enjoyed the same advantage. While, in all the courts of continental Europe, it has been consulted as written reason, or enforced as common law from the time of Irnerius even down to the present day, it has been considered in their universities as a necessary part of a regular academic education. It has thus been taught as a branch of liberal studies, and, indeed, most of the great men who have identified their names with it, were, in the strictest sense of the word, mere scholars and philosophers. Gravina‡ mentions Brissonius as a singular exception to this remark. Cujacius, the great coryphæus of the band, was not only himself a scholastic man, but went so far as to declare that, if he had ever acquired any knowledge of the law by practice, he should strive to forget it—"ne a Romano júre distraheretur." Some of these writers, it is true, have treated questions of jurispru-

* Antiq. Jur. Civ. v. i. 34.
† It is not generally known that the stoics were the most subtle of dialecticians. Cicero says they were so remarkable for this, ut—sintque architecti pæne verborum.—*Brutus*, c. 31. See also Pickett v. Loggon 14 Ves. 229,
‡ Orig J. C. 222.

dence altogether as matters of elegant literature—"flores magis quam fructus attulerant," as the author, just quoted, says of Peter Faber, Vultejus, Pacius, &c.*

There are among the Civilians those who have pushed this love of systematic arrangement and close rigorous logic so far, as to emulate the reasonings of the geometricans. Thus, Puffendorf made his debut in the learned world by a work, entitled "Elements of Natural Law, according to a Mathematical Order." Heineccius also, who has been pronounced by a high authority, the first of elementary writers, adopts the same precise method in his popular commentaries upon the Digest and the Institutes. His way is to begin with a definition, which is made as comprehensive as possible. He then proceeds to deduce from it, what he calls *axiomata*, or clear, indisputable propositions. These he again applies to more complicated questions, and runs them down to all their consequences, with wonderful exactness and logical connections.

It is, no doubt, such examples that suggested to Dugald Stewart some very just and striking observations, which as they are connected with the subject of elementary institution and law, we shall present to our readers. They serve also to illustrate and confirm a position advanced in the course of the preceding remarks, that with the single exception of mathematics, jurisprudence is that department of knowledge, of which the principles are best settled, the reasonings at once the most refined and the most exact, and the conclusions the most safe and satisfactory.

"In those branches of study," says the Scotch philosopher, "which are conversant about moral and political propositions, the nearest approach which I can imagine, to a hypothetical science analogous to mathematics, is to be found in a code of municipal jurisprudence; or rather might be conceived to exist in such a code, if systematically carried into execution, agreeably to certain general or fundamental principles. Whether these principles should or should not be founded in justice and expediency, it is evidently possible, by reasoning from them consequentially, to create an artificial or conventional body of knowledge, more systematical, and, at the same time, more complete in all its parts than, in the present state of our information, *any* science can be rendered, which ultimately appeals to the eternal and immutable standards of truth and falsehood, of right and wrong. This consideration seems to me to throw some light on the following very curious parallel which Leibnitz has drawn (with what justness I presume not to decide) between the works of the Roman Civilians and those of the Greek geometers. Few writers, certainly,

*Ibid. 227. Gravina adds indignantly—quod nostrates *pragmatici* de universo Ic^tm Jurisconsultorum genere insulsè admodum, ne dicam stultè pronunciant.

have been so fully qualified, as he was, to pronounce upon the characteristical merits of both.

"I have often said that, after the writings of the Geometricians, there exists nothing which, in point of force and subtlety, can be compared to the works of the Roman lawyers. And as it would be scarcely possible, from mere intrinsic evidence, to distinguish a demonstration of Euclid from one of Apollonius or Archimedes, (the style of all of them appearing no less uniform than if reason herself were speaking through their organs) so also the Roman lawyers all resemble each other like twin-brothers; insomuch that, from the style alone of any particular opinion or argument, scarcely any conjecture could be formed with respect to the author. Nor are the traces of a refined and deeply meditated system of natural jurisprudence any where to be found more visible or in greater abundance. And even in those cases where its principles are departed from, either in compliance with the language consecrated by technical forms, or in consequence of new statutes, or of ancient traditions, the conclusions, which the assumed hypothesis renders it necessary to incorporate with the eternal dictates of right reason, are deduced with the soundest logic, and with an ingenuity which excites admiration. Nor are these deviations from the law of nature so frequent as is commonly imagined."*

In order fairly to appreciate the justness of the comparison instituted in the preceding remarks, between jurisprudence and the exact sciences, it would be necessary to go at large into Mr. Stewart's theory of mathematical evidence. This our limits will not permit us to do—but it is worth while, with a view to make the illustration of our own remarks, more perfect, to state his general principle.† It is that, in all other sciences, the propositions, which we attempt to establish, express *facts*, real or supposed, whereas in mathematics (and we may add, in jurisprudence also) the propositions which we demonstrate, only assert a connection between certain suppositions and certain consequences. The premises which we proceed upon are altogether arbitrary— we frame our definitions at will and reason from them. Thus all the properties of a circle are deducible from the assumed equality of the radii. Our reasonings, therefore, in mathematics and in law, are directed to objects essentially different from those of the other sciences—not to ascertain *truths* with respect to real existences, but to trace the logical filiation of consequences which follow from an arbitrary hypothesis, and, if, from this hypothesis we reason with precision, the evidence of the result is of course irresistible. The Scotch philosopher, it is true, takes too much

* Philosophy of the Human Mind, v. ii. p. 147.
† Which he took from Hobbes without acknowledging the obligation.

for granted, when he speaks of its being possible to devise a set of arbitrary definitions in jurisprudence that shall be as precise as those of geometry—a notion, by the way, which ought to be particularly acceptable to the reformers of the Jerry Bentham school, but which is unfortunately not quite just. But the fact, that such a degree of accuracy may even be approximated, is sufficient to shew that the logical method of the Civilians, is not mere formal parade and idle affectation.

Blackstone ascribes the neglect of the common law, as a branch of a liberal education, and, therefore, a good share of the defects adverted to in the preceding remarks, to the influence of the Romish clergy, who had an absolute control over the English schools and universities. The discovery of the Pandects at Amalfi, which is *supposed* to have taken place early in the century after the conquest, he adds, had nearly occasioned its total ruin, and, indeed, nothing seems more probable. England was at that time overrun with foreign ecclesiastics who engrossed all the little knowledge of the age, and had an unbounded influence over the opinions of mankind. Being the only persons that had any acquaintance with the Latin language, they alone had access to these long hidden treasures of ancient wisdom and civilization, and to make their devotion for them more exclusive and bigotted, Pope Innocent IV., it seems, forbade them so much as to look into the volumes of the common law. Independently, however, of any undue influence of this kind, it is easy to imagine what an impression the sudden appearance of such a volume as the Pandects must have made in the midst of the darkness and barbarism of the twelfth century, when we consider that, according to the forcible expression of a late writer, it was the very first book which spoke the language of reason to the modern world. All Christendom resounded with its praises—there sprang up among the nations a general emulation to understand and adopt its principles—and, in less than half a century after Irnerius began his lectures at Bologna, a professorship of civil law was established at Oxford, under the patronage of the Norman Archbishop of Canterbury, to which Vacarius, a dependant of that dignitary, was appointed. The common law was, in the mean time, left to barons and barbarians, and, upon the whole, we ought rather to wonder, how, under such disadvantages, that venerable code should have come down to us in so perfect a state as to present, upon the whole, as noble a scheme of practical liberty and justice as the world has ever seen.*

The improvements which have been made in it in this coun-

---

* We have spoken of the discovery of the Pandects at Amalfi, in compliance with Blackstone and custom; though the better opinion is, that no such event ever took place. See Ginguenè, Hist. of Ital. Lit. c. 3; Pfeffel, v. i. p.—.It is certain, however, that the civil law began about that time to be generally studied.

try, and to which we have already had occasion to advert, have almost entirely "depurated it from the dregs and feculence" of feudal times. Many of the decisions, made within the last twenty years, shew that the spirit of these improvements has not been lost on our courts. We venture to say, that no case in the English books, upon the law of corporations, can sustain a comparison with that of the trustees of Dartmouth College vs. Woodward, reported in the 4th Wheaton: and the same decided superiority may be claimed for some other arguments and judgments, not only in the Supreme Court of the United States, but in those of the States. It is true that, owing to something in the state of public opinion here, or the uncertainty of popular elections, the bench in America is not always as ably filled as it might be, and our books of reports, along with much learning and ability, are often encumbered with disgraceful trash—with truisms pompously elaborated, or with exhibitions of deplorable ignorance. We are disposed to think, that our lawyers, although they sometimes excel the English in the discussion of great principles and of new points, are not, however, so *thorough-paced* in their profession, so familiar with "the file," as they. This may, in some degree, be accounted for by the very fact that they are often compelled to look abroad into other systems of jurisprudence and the decisions of foreign tribunals, for assistance and authority, instead of confining themselves, as is the case in Westminster Hall, to their own precedents and analogies. It cannot be disguised, however, that it is also owing in a good measure to their being less exclusively devoted to their profession, and the facility with which popular talent forces itself into reputation, at the expense of less showy, but more useful acquirements. But this evil will be corrected in the progress of things: and, in the mean time, the character, which is already stamped upon the profession in this country, of liberal, and enlarged and philosophical enquiry, holds out to us the most encouraging prospects of future excellence.

Nothing can contribute more to strengthen these good dispositions, than the mode of teaching by lectures, (which we are glad to find becoming so common in different parts of the country) and the publication of works upon the elements of jurisprudence. We have already illustrated this truth by the example of the civil law, but it is sufficiently evident of itself. Under the pressure of business, neither advocates nor judges have time to digest philosophical methods. It is quite as much as can generally be expected of them, that they should apply established principles, and shew that "the principal case" is analogous to others already decided. Extraordinary occasions, indeed, will lead—as in this country they frequently have led—to a more profound investigation of principles in the courts—but this can obviously be done to a much greater advantage by a lecturer who confines himself exclusively to the elements of the science. In the present state of our law, especially, the task of arranging and developing its whole systen, according to the plan alluded to in the foregoing observation, must of necessity, devolve upon speculative men. Accordingly, if we have any fault to find with the excellent work before us, it is, that it is, too much of a mere index or compilation—it is not such a book as Chancellor Kent would have produced, had he been all his life, like Cujas or Pothier, a professor of law, instead of a judge, although the bench would seem to be more favourable to enlarged and systematic thinking than the bar.

Chancellor Kent, however, has rendered an essential service to the profession. The two volumes before us, contain an excellent summary of the general rules of law, as it is practised in this country. Some of the subjects are better treated than they have been by English text-writers, while there is always this advantage in favour of the work, that it presents that view of them which must be taken in American courts of justice. The lecture on alienage, for instance, strikes us as decidedly superior to Wooddeson's, upon the same subject, and as containing an able and just exposition of that very difficult doctrine in reference to the effects of our revolution upon it. The same thing may be said of the lectures upon marriage, and the domestic relations growing out of it. Even in these, however, we discover some of the defects of which we have already complained so much. For instance, there are many questions connected with the disabilities of alienage, which must have presented themselves to every one who has reflected deeply upon that subject, and which we have known to become important in the course of a judicial inquiry, that have not been so much as hinted at by our author. How comes it, that a principle apparently so contradictory and paradoxical, should have been admitted into the law, as that any one might acquire what he was not allowed to hold—that law, of which one of the first maxims is, that it does nothing in vain? Why did the land purchased by an alien go to the king, and not to the lord as it would have done, had the alien been made a denizen *before* he purchased, and then died without leaving any heir but the *ultimus heres* of the tenure? Was this right of the king a royal prerogative— one of the *jura regalia* so familiar to feudal lawyers—analogous for instance, to the emperor's interest in the property of Jews, who were considered in Germany as *servi fisci*?* Did the estate, in such cases, vest in the king by way of escheat or for-

* Pfeffel, v i. p.—, rémarques particulières sur les empereurs de la maison de Franconie. Cf Molloy, v. ii. p. 283. Feudor. lib. ii. Tit. 56.

feiture? a question of great importance with reference to the distinctions taken in Burgess vs. Wheate. Suppose a conveyance from an alien who dies before office found; is the title of the purchaser good as against the king? Chancellor Kent answers this question, in conformity with the English authorities, in the negative. Yet the reason of the law seems scarcely intelligible, unless it be assumed, that aliens were allowed to acquire solely for the benefit of the crown, whose revenue in feudal times, depended very much upon fines and forfeitures. If this be the principle, to hold the title good in the case proposed, would be to defeat the very object of the law, in allowing the alien to take a title at all. Accordingly, it is laid down in Dyer, (26 in margin) that an alien cannot take a copy-hold, and the reason given is, because the king shall not have it—a position which, we have no doubt is good law, some authorities, seemingly, to the contrary notwithstanding.* But whether this conjecture is well founded or not, the omitting all remark upon matters of so much curiosity and importance, appears to us a great defect in an elementary treatise.

The work of Chancellor Kent, as far as it is perfected in these volumes, is divided into five parts. The first, which embraces nine lectures, is devoted to the law of nations. The second presents a view of the government and constitutional jurisprudence of the United States. The third treats of the various sources of American municipal law. The fourth and fifth, which occupy the whole of the second volume, are an exposition of the rights of persons and the law of personal property. We shall devote the rest of this article to some observations suggested by our author's discussion of the subjects under the first and second heads.

1. We are by no means so well satisfied with the execution of the first part of Chancellor Kent's work, as with the rest of it. It is little better than a digest of the cases in prize law, decided in England by Sir W. Scott, and in this country by the Supreme Court of the United States; interspersed with a few general principles from the common elementary treatises. Presenting, therefore, as it does, (and, indeed, as it pretends to do) only a hasty sketch and brief outline of the system of international law, although it may be convenient enough as a book of occasional reference, or a manual for young students, it cannot be considered as forming a very valuable accession to the library of an experienced jurist.

It may still be affirmed that an elementary work, worthy of the present condition of international law, is a desideratum in jurisprudence.

* Molloy, J. M. v. ii. p. 320. Thom. Co. Litt. Citing Styles. 20,

It will have been perceived by our readers, from the brief abstract which has been given of the arrangement of the civil law, according to the system of Justinian, that no separate place is allotted in it to the law of nations; for their *jus gentium* had a far more comprehensive signification. Indeed, when we reflect that the Roman Empire extended over the whole civilized world, (for to be conquered by that people was, in those times, the only means to become civilized) and when we consider, moreover, the cruel maxims of all ancient warfare, we shall be less surprised at this omission. Their system was calculated for perpetual success: they did not contemplate the possibility of their wanting the protection of such a code. As soon as a Roman citizen fell into the hands of an enemy, he was *capitis minor* and dead to the commonwealth. The senate sometimes even refused to ransom their countrymen, when they could do so on easy terms, lest it should impair their military virtue and discipline in future wars. We are aware of the noted passage of the oration of Balbus (c. 6.) in which Cicero commends Pompey for what he calls singularis quædam laus ejus et præstabillis scientia, in fœderibus, pactionibus, conditionibus, populorum, regum, exterarum nationum; in universo denique *belli jure et pacis.* But it would be a gross error to infer from such a rhetorical flourish that the Romans bestowed upon the rights of nations, with regard to each other, any thing like the same pains with which they cultivated their municipal law. Their *jus belli et pacis* was excessively simple—extending no further than to the fair interpretation and religious observance of *treaties,* and to such other obvious and necessary usages as must exist even among barbarians and outlaws, as for example, the immunity of ambassadors and the like: nor, indeed, do the words of Cicero strictly imply any thing further. This accounts more sensibly than some conjectures which we have seen, for Grotius' adopting that title for his great work. He wrote Latin with too much purity to deviate from the best standards, and that language did not express, in any other way, the idea of international law.*

It is to the genius and learning of that extraordinary man, that the world is indebted for the first successful effort to reduce to a system, those principles upon which alone the intercourse of independent nations, in an enlightened state of society, can be carried on. Jeremy Bentham finds fault with this great work, as not being of a sufficiently definite and practical character. "Of what stamp," says Jeremy, "are the works of Grotius, Puf-

---

**Jus Feciale was precisely the same thing. See Cic. de legib. ii. 9. De Offic. i. 11. And cf. the whole 19th chap. of the Vth against Verres, which affords a good illustration of the remarks in the text. Condillac supposes Grotius adopted that title to excite curiosity.

fendorf and Barlamaqui? Are they political or ethical, historical
or juridical, expository or censorial? Sometimes one thing,
sometimes another; they seem scarcely to have settled the matter
among themselves." There is, undoubtedly, much truth in this
criticism—and so far as it applies to Puffendorf and Burlama-
qui—although Sir James M'Intosh speaks of the former in terms
of high praise—we must confess that we are disposed to concede
to it even more, if possible, than its author would demand. We
own with D'Aguesseau, que nous n'avons jamais pu achever la
lecture du gros livre de Puffendorf—but it is impossible to reflect
upon the era at which Grotius wrote, in the midst of the horrors
and atrocities of religious persecution and of civil war—calamities, of whose utmost bitterness he had himself been compelled
to taste—without acknowledging that his treatise De Jure Belli
et Pacis, in which enlightened reason, refined humanity, immense
learning and elegant scholarship, mingle their winning and varied
attractions, and where strong sense and convincing argument are
rendered still more persuasive and venerable by the authority of
great names, was at once a most noble nonument of that day,
and the herald of one yet brighter and more auspicious. In spite
of the "march of mind," we believe no one has ever attentively
studied it without being the wiser for it, and although the author,
had he lived in our times, would, perhaps, have blotted out half
of it, as cumbersome and superfluous—we doubt whether the
public would have been, either in profit or amusement, a gainer
by it. In short, we perfectly concur in the eulogium bestowed
upon it by Sir James M'Intosh, that Grotius "produced a work
which we now, indeed, justly deem imperfect, but which is, perhaps, the most complete that the world has owed, at so early a
stage of any science, to the genius and learning of one man."
    Still there can be no doubt that it has many defects—partly
because so little had been done before it—partly and still more,
because so much has been done since. The *new* law of nations
was, indeed, even then known in practice. The merciful and
benignant spirit of Christianity had made itself visible, amidst
the carnage of Smithfield and St. Bartholemew's, in its effects
upon modern civilization; courage had been refined and softened
by chivalry; and the insolence of victory was subdued, and
the rights of conquest were circumscribed and settled throughout Europe by a controlling public opinion. But the customary
and conventional law of nations was yet in its infancy. Those
intimate relations, commercial and political, which have since
bound up all Christendom in one of great society, and, as it were,
family union, were just beginning to be formed and consolidated.
The idea of the balance of power, which had, of course, been
familiar to mankind in all ages, wherever the many found it necessary to combine against the strong, but which was not acted

on as a standing rule of conduct upon a grand scale, until mighty governments were formed, and distant enterprises became common—gave to treaties the effect of precedence, and clothed them with the authority of law. That of Westphalia, for instance, was considered as the very foundation of the *Jus Publicum* of Germany. Since Grotius wrote, two centuries more fruitful by far of great events, and magnificent improvement than any equal period in the history of mankind, have been continually adding to the number of such principles and confirming and consecrating them as they have been ascertained.

It is to combine in one great work these conventional and customary rules, so far as they have been universally acceded to among nations, with the principles of reason and natural law, to which they ought to approximate as much as possible, that some master hand is now called for. As it is, the student of international law is compelled to have recourse to the reports of adjudicated cases. "Elementary writers," says Mr. Justice Story, in the case of the Nereide,* "rarely explain the principles of public law with that minute accuracy of distinction which legal precision requires. Many of the most important doctrines of the prize courts will not be found to be treated of, or even glanced at in the elaborate treatises of Grotius, Puffendorf and Vattel. A striking illustration is their total silence as to the illegality and penal consequences of a trade with the public enemy. Even Bynkershoëk, who writes professedly on prize law, is deficient in many important doctrines which every day regulate the decree of prize courts. And the complexity of modern commerce has added incalculably to the number, as well as to the intricacy of questions of national law. In what publicists are to be found the doctrines as to the illegality of carrying enemy's despatches: or of engaging in the coasting, fishing, or other privileged trade of the enemy? Where are transfers *in transitu* pronounced illegal? Where are accurately and systematically stated all the circumstances which impress upon the neutral, a general or limited hostile character, either by reason of his domicil, his territorial possessions, or his connection with a house of trade in the enemy's country. The search would be nearly in vain," &c.

No one, we are persuaded, however, will have occasion to regret the necessity of resorting to the volumes of reports in this branch of jurisprudence, since, besides the intrinsic advantages of that mode of study (after all that has been said against it, the surest and the best for those who wish to become profound in the science) they hold out other attractions of no ordinary kind. The judicial eloquence of Lord Stowel, is the very *copiose loquens sapientia* of the great Roman orator, abounding in so

* 9 Cranch, 437.

many charms and graces, that his decrees deserve to be cited as models of style, and will bear a comparison with the most finished compositions of our English classics, at the same time that it is difficult to treat such subjects with greater ability and acumen, or with a more enlarged philosophy. Nor have we any reason to shrink from a comparison with such exalted excellence. The great man who presides over the Supreme Court of the United States (to confine ourselves to him) does not, indeed, display the same exquisite elegance and felicity of diction, but he is second to no judge that ever lived, in some of the most important attributes of the judicial character ; in depth and comprehensiveness of intellect, in luminous arrangement, in clearness of expression, in a logic, which, in general (for alas ! even Judge Marshall has erred) is proof against all sophistry, and against which. no sophistry is proof—in a word, in a large, sound, pervading good sense, which is satisfied only with the fullest and fairest views of a subject, but which, where it is once satisfied, seldom fails to impart its own convictions entirely to others.

2. The constitutional jurisprudence of the United States ! Under this imposing title is presented to us, one of the most striking examples which history furnishes, to illustrate and support an opinion advanced in the course of the preceding remarks. If any one wishes to be convinced how little, even the wisest men, are able to foresee the results of their own political contrivances, let him read the constitution, with the contemporaneous exposition of it contained (even) in the *Federalist ;* and then turn to this part of Chancellor Kent's work, to the inaugural speech of the present Executive of the United States, and to some of the records of Congress, during the memorable session which is just past.

He will find that the government has been fundamentally altered by the progress of opinion—that instead of being any longer one of enumerated powers and a circumscribed sphere, as it was beyond all doubt intended to be, it knows absolutely no bounds but the will of a majority of Congress—that instead of confining itself in time of peace to the diplomatic and commercial relations of the country, it is seeking out employment for itself by interfering in the domestic concerns of society, and threatens in the course of a very few years, to control, in the most offensive and despotic manner, all the pursuits, the interests, the opinions and the conduct of men. He will find that this extraordinary revolution has been brought about, in a good degree by the Supreme Court of the United States, which has applied to the constitution—very innocently, no doubt, and with commanding ability in argument—and thus given authority and currency to, such canons of interpretation, as necessarily lead to these extravagant results. Above all, he will be perfectly satis-

fied that that high tribunal affords, by its own shewing, no barrier whatever against the usurpations of Congress—and that the
rights of the weaker part of this confederacy may, to any extent,
be wantonly and tyrannically violated, under color of law, [the
most grievous shape of oppression] by men neither interested in
its destiny nor subject to its control, without any means of redress being left it, except such as are inconsistent with all idea
of order and government. Perhaps, he will think with us, that
the effect of a written constitution, interpreted by lawyers in a
technical manner, is to enlarge power and to sanctify abuse,
rather than to abridge and restrain them—perhaps, he will conclude that the American people have not been sufficiently careful,
at the beginning of their unprecedented experiment in politics,
what principles they suffered to be established—perhaps, he
may look forward to the future, with anxiety and alarm, as
holding forth a prospect of a rapid accumulation of power in
the hands of those who have already abused it, or, on the contrary, with a strong hope that experience will teach wisdom, and
diversified interests and conflicting pretensions, lead to moderation in conduct—perhaps, (and surely nothing could be more
rational) he might wish to see proper means adopted to bring
back the government to its first principles, and put an end to
the unhappy jealousies and heart-burnings which are beginning
to embitter one part of our people against another—we do not
undertake to anticipate his inferences—but we have no doubt in
the world that he will agree with us as to the *fact*—that he will
confess Congress to be, to all intents and purposes, omnipotent
in theory, and that if, in practice, it prefer moderate counsels and
a just and impartial policy, it will be owing, not to any check
in the constitution, but altogether to the vigilance, the wisdom,
and the firmness of a free people.

We are not, indeed, sure but that this conclusion will, in the
end, be productive of much good, and that we ought rather to
rejoice than complain that, at so early a period of our history, it
has been forced upon the public mind—in one part at least of
this confederacy—by evidence too strong to be resisted, and with
a depth and seriousness of conviction which promise to make
it an active, permanent and universal principle of conduct.
Our political opinions, it appears to us, have been hitherto, in
the last degree, wild and visionary. We have been so much
accustomed to talk in a high-flown strain, of the perfection—
the faultless and unalterable perfection—of our institutions, that
we were begining to think that every thing had been done for
us by our predecessors, and that it were impossible to mar their
work by any errors of doctrine, or any defect in discipline among
ourselves. We do not sufficiently reflect, what a rare and glorious privilege it is to be a free people, (in the only proper sense

of that term) and how difficult it is, even under the most favourable circumstances, to keep so. We have unbounded faith in forms, and look upon a written constitution as a sort of talisman, which gives to the liberties of a nation "a charmed life." In short, no people was ever so much addicted to abstractions. It is really curious to look into the debates of Congress, when measures pregnant with important consequences are the subject of discussion. The University of Paris, in the hey-day of scholastic divinity, never excelled them in the thorny, unprofitable, and unintelligible subtleties of dialectics. Our statesmen are, in general, any thing but practical men—a fact that may be, in some degree, accounted for by the vast predominance of mere professional lawyers, (not of the first order) and the fact, that we have a written constitution to interpret by technical rules. We look in vain for that plain, manly, unsophisticated good sense—that *instinct* of liberty, which characterizes the controversial reasoning of the great farthers of the English constitution—the Seldens, the Sidneys, the Prynnes—and their worthy descendants and disciples, the founders of our own revolution. A measure is proposed, revolting to the moral sense and the common sense of mankind—unequal and oppressive, inconsistent with the cardinal objects and the whole genius of the government. It is opposed by those upon whom it bears hardest as *unconstitutional*—that is to say, as unfit to be adopted by the rulers of a free people, because it is unjust, and is not *bonâ fide* intended to fulfil the purposes of the federal compact. Immediately a metaphysical disputation ensues, and if by such jargon as has immortalized the angelical and seraphic doctors, the constitutionality of the scheme be made to appear *very doubtful*, it is at once assumed by the majority as demonstrated, and, perhaps, acquiesced in by the minority, because the question, if it should be thought sufficiently important, can be tried again before the Supreme Court. The responsibility of those who pass the law is shifted upon those who interpret it; and thus the former venture a great deal farther upon the questionable ground than they would were their decision entirely without appeal. If, again, when the law comes before the Supreme Court, that judicatory, from some defects in its constitution or its administration, will not or cannot pronounce it void—the will of the majority is at once considered as sanctified—its act is of course lawful, is just, is reasonable and proper. The people at large, after a few unheeded murmurs, submit to this imposing authority, and think that their discontents must be unreasonable, because their understandings have been puzzled by sophisters, and awed by the learning of the bench! In short, the constitution is made to have the effect of an *estoppel* (an odious thing in law) upon their just complaints, and they are expected

to suffer, like poor Shylock, any hardship which a subtile interpretation can deduce from their "bond."

We will now proceed to make some remarks upon the total
unfitness of the Supreme Court to act the part of an umpire in
questions of constitutional law, from the very principles of construction which itself has established.

It is obvious, at the very first view of the constitution, that it
confers upon the Government of the United States, in the shape
of distinct, substantive powers, many which would now be considered, and which, indeed, seem to be in the nature of things,
merely subsidiary and instrumental. For instance, to authorize
Congress expressly "to make rules for the government of the
land and naval forces," after charging it with the declaration
of war, the levying of armies, and the maintenance of a navy,
was wholly unnecessary according to the notions of our constitutional lawyers; for such a right would follow of course, and
ex necesitate rei. Nay, it would place this subject in rather a
striking light to draw up the *projet* of a constitution, in conformity with the doctrines of the Supreme Court, in the case of
McCullough vs. Maryland. Such an instrument would be admirable for its pregnant brevity. All that needed to have been
done in the way of express grants of power, was, according to
that opinion, to enable Congress,

1. To declare war (*subaudi* and prosecute it effectually.)
2. To regulate commerce.

To these provisions, the convention might or might not have
added a third, which is nothing more than a maxim of universal
law, "quando lex aliquid alicui concedit, concedere videtur et
id sine quo res ipsa esse non potest"—viz.

3. To make all laws necessary and proper to carry into execution, the foregoing powers.

All the other clauses of the eighth section, with the exception
of three very unimportant ones, are, according to those principles, perfectly superfluous—the most unmeaning and nugatory
verbiage that ever disgraced a set of tyros in law-making. Is
there any power omitted in our project that may not be easily
deduced from the frame and objects of the government, by the
same course of reasoning which is supposed to have demonstrated
the right of Congress to incorporate a bank? Can it be pretended, that the prerogative of investing a body of men with
corporate franchises, is not by the law which the people of the
states lived under, by the language which they spoke, by the
opinions which they universally entertained in '89, as perfectly
well defined and ascertained, as a distinct, substantive power—
one of the admitted *jura regalia*—as any other in the constitution, and much more than some of them?

The Supreme Court, it is true, does endeavour to shew that

it is not; and it does so by a course of reasoning, which, however plausible at first sight, appears to us to be utterly fallacious and unsound. "The power of creating a corporation," says the Chief Justice, "though appertaining to sovereignty, is not like the power of making war, or *levying taxes*, or of regulating commerce, a *great, substantive and independent power*, which cannot be implied as incidental to other powers, or used as *a means of executing them.* It is never the end for which other powers are exercised, but a means by which other objects are accomplished. No contributions are made to charity for the sake of an incorporation, but a corporation is created to administer the charity. The power of creating a corporation is never used for its own sake, but for the purpose of effecting, something else," &c. The power of *"levying taxes"* not used as *a means* to execute the power of *making war!* What is the history of the national debt in England or in this country? Besides, we should like to be informed what power ever was "used for its own sake," and not for the purpose of effecting something else? Who ever declared war for the bare sake of declaring war—except, indeed, that great constitutional lawyer and original thinker, Caligula, who is said to have triumphed over Britain, by merely parading his troops on the opposite shore, and marching off with the shells gathered there, for spoils and for trophies. Nay, the only idea which we are able to conceive of any power, is, as producing effects—it is *ex vi termini*, a means. Yet, according to the metaphysics of the Supreme Court, the fact that it may be a means proves it no power!

We do not know that an attempt has ever been made by any of our constitutional lawyers, either in Congress or in the Courts, to explain what is meant by "sovereign-political powers"—a phrase, however perpetually used in such discussions, as if nothing could be more ascertained and precise. Thus, taking the matter up on principle—why should coining money be a great state prerogative, any more than issuing bank notes and other negotiable paper, which constitute by far the greater part of the circulating medium of this country? Why should the right of war be exclusively confined to the whole society, and not be, as in the baronial times, the privilege of every gentleman of a certain degree? These questions are just as difficult to answer, as that so triumphantly asked in McCullough's case; why should the granting a corporate franchise be regarded as a prerogative of sovereignty? It is obvious to reply that the policy of society requires it—but it is enough for us to say that such powers have, *in fact*, been regarded as state prerogatives or jura regalia—and, especially, that they were so considered by the common law of this land at the adoption of the constitution. If any stress, therefore, is to be laid, (and great stress *is* laid by the Supreme Court) on the idea of "these great, substantive and independent powers," that instrument must be construed in reference to the general understanding of mankind—and if, after granting some of them, it expressly withholds all that have not been enumerated, it is passing strange to say that, under any vague words of course—any mere expressio eorum quæ tacitè insunt—such as the clause authorising Congress to pass all laws necessary, &c.—those which were expressly refused have been implicitly granted.

It only remains to be shewn that the power of instituting a corporation is defined by the common law as an attribute—a distinct and peculiar attribute, if there ever was one—of sovereignty. Indeed, this is admitted by the Chief Justice, and that concession seems to give up the whole controversy—for, if it was a "substantive, independent power" at all, it is clearly a power not granted. But the doctrine on this subject deserves to be more particularly stated.

By the law of England, the king alone—quâ talis, and not as part of the legislature—can grant a charter of incorporation. It is as much his prerogative to do so as it is to confer a title of nobility or to declare war. This doctrine is expressly laid down by Blackstone.* It is true, that in some few cases of extraordinary exigence, the Parliament has undertaken to confer a franchise, and may do so still, but such acts have always been regarded as irregular, although the king, of course, must assent even to them. "The Parliament," says Blackstone, *"by its absolute and transcendant authority,* may perform this, *or any other act whatsoever:* and actually did perform it to a great extent, by Stat. 39, Eliz. c. 5, which incorporated all hospitals and houses of correction founded by charitable persons, without further trouble, and the same has been done in other cases of charitable foundations. But, otherwise, it has not formerly been usual thus to trench upon the prerogative of the crown, and the *king may prevent it when he pleases."†* Now, we ask, if this does not demonstrate beyond a doubt that, by the *common law,* the right of creating a corporate franchise, "is regarded as a transcendant power of sovereignty in the British constitution," the opinion of Mr. Pinkney of Maryland, to the contrary notwithstanding. If this be admitted to be, as it unquestionably is, the true theory of the British constitution, we may save ourselves the trouble of inquiring, what is the doctrine of the civil law upon the subject. The constitution of the United States is not to be construed in reference to that jurisprudence—it is matter of positive institution, of peculiar character, of strict law—Nihil ad edictum Prætoris. Still less, we take it,

* Bl. Comm. p. 273.   † 2 Ibid. p. 474.

ought it to be controlled by the wild imaginings and speculative conceits of men as to what might, could, would or should be law. Surely the sound rule of interpretation is to suppose that the people of this country meant what they said, that they spoke the language of their own day, and acted upon the ascertained and immemorial maxims of their hereditary institutions. Besides, it is not true, as Mr. Pinkney affirms, upon no better authority than Blackstone's Commentaries, that a corporation was, by the civil law, a mere voluntary association of individuals, not particularly controlled by the state. The doctrine of that jurisprudence may be seen upon reference to Domat, who has collected all the texts, and states the principle with his usual clearness and judgment.* Nor is any stress, whatever, to be laid upon a circumstance which, the learned advocate just mentioned, seems to consider as so important, viz., that the king might authorize a subject to institute a corporation. He would have found by going a little beyond the English text books, that the question whether the *jura regalia* may be delegated has been fully discussed and decided, under some qualifications, in the affirmative, by those who are accustomed to look rather more deeply into such subjects than "Doctor Blackstone."†

Instead, therefore, of inferring from the fact that, in England, the authority of Parliament is not necessary to create a corporation, as Mr. Pinkney does in McCullough's case, that the granting of such franchises is no act of soverneigty, we deduce from the same premises, precisely the opposite conclusion. We ask, how it comes to pass, that the reasoning of the Court in that case, never occurred to the great constitutional lawyers of the mother country ? Why should the granting a charter, even by an omnipotent Parliament, be considered "as trenching upon the king's prerogative," if the doing so would be only employing a "means" within the ordinary range of legislative discretion ? Is it not manifest that the argument would apply to that government with the same, and, indeed, with greater force than it does here ? Ought not the British legislature—of which the monarch too is a constituent part—to have as large a discretion as a Congress of few, and those specified and enumerated powers ? If Parliament should undertake, with a view to accomplish some of its legitimate objects, to incorporate a company, the king, says Blackstone, would have a right to say to them, "you have begun at the wrong end, you ought to have requested the crown to exercise its prerogative ;" then, with what sort of colour can it be pretended that such a statute differs in no wise from any other act of legislation, according to the com-

*Public Law, B. I. Tit. 15, sec. 2.
† See the note of Godefroy on Feudor, lib. ii. Tit. 56.

mon law of England, which was, and is the common law of this land.* But we shall presently cite other instances to shew that the federal government, in laying down its principles, has assumed more—has been less scrupulous in its regard for the ancient landmarks and consecrated maxims of law and liberty, according to the faith of our fathers, even than that of England.

Does the Supreme Court mean to say that Congress, under one of its two cardinal powers, that of regulating commerce, would have a right to found and incorporate a city within the limits of a state? Yet, why not; since its acts are the supreme law, and what "laws are necessary and proper," is matter of legislative discretion, not to be passed upon by the courts? In short, there is no end to the consequences that may and will be deduced from the doctrine in M'Cullough's case. The amount of it really is that the enumeration of powers in the constitution was a vain attempt to confine what is necessarily illimitable—that such an instrument never can ascertain its objects with any sort of precision—that it can, at most, hint a vague purpose and sketch a sweeping outline, which is to be filled up at discretion—in short, that it is not the plan of a government formed and settled, and circumscribed from the first, as it is intended to continue forever, but is a mere nucleus, around which a government is *to be* formed, according to the circumstances of the times, and the opinions of mankind. Such a principle being once established, no man can pretend to anticipate what shape the constitution of the United States (not that written by the convention, but the other which is to be built upon it) is destined to take. We are fairly at the mercy of sophisters and metaphysicians, and we shall see fully verified the wise old maxim of the schools *dolus versatur in generalibus.* One usurpation will be a precedent for another—it will be treason to complain in future of abuses, that in point of principle can be no worse than those we have already submitted to. Thus Mr. Pinkney begins his argument in this very case, by declaring that he did not consider the constitutionality of the bank as an open question, because it had been *assumed* by Congress, and acquiesced in for thirty years! We venture to predict that no act of the federal government (supposing it to have common discretion) will ever be pronounced unconstitutional in that court, for the simple reason that the principle of M'Cullough's case covers the whole ground of political sovereignty, and consecrates usurpation in advance.— A regular bred dialectician† shall demonstrate, drop by drop,

* So the pope, though he usurped very great authority never could make a corporation. Com. Dig. Franchise, F. 5. It is astonishing that even the Canonists—subtle and contriving as they were—should have fallen so far short of our constitutional lawyers.

† [The same illustration is used by Aristotle, Pol. l. 5. c. 7. to shew the danger of usurpations παρα μιχρον.

with the most vigorous logic, that a ton of wine will not get a man drunk if his hearer will only consent to surrender his senses to a Sorites. The consequences in such deductions shall be inevitable, and no man be able to say this or that link in the chain of reasoning is bad; on this side is Ionia and not Peloponnesus—here law ends, and usurpation begins. For a man of common sense—indeed, for plain, practical men—it is enough that such reasonings, however ingenious and consequential, lead to manifest absurdity, and so must be radically vicious somewhere. That argument, for instance, cannot be sound which necessarily converts a government of enumerated into one of indefinite powers, and a confederacy of republics into a gigantic and consolidated empire. But such moderation is not to be expected of those who deal in sweeping abstractions and reason about government and the most interesting and practical concerns of mankind, precisely as a scholastic divine—"he that hight irrefragable" would argue upon an unintelligible thesis in ontology or pneumatology. Ought not the maxim of the federal government—from its very end and constitution—from its inevitable tendency to encroachment and usurpation, and the extreme difficulty of defining its jurisdiction with sufficient accuracy—to be *quod dubitas* ne feceris? Can any thing justify those who administer such a government—from first to last, a matter of compromise and concession, of complex organization and discordant materials—in venturing upon measures of such dubious character (to say the least of them) as to require all the ingenuity of the most practised disputants to reconcile the common sense of mankind to them?

M'Cullough's case established a doctrine sufficiently latitudinarian. It gave the government an unbounded discretion in the choice of "means" to effect its constitutional objects. Nor does it confine the exercise of this arbitrary power to cases of absolute necessity. It declares that Congress has the same latitude in matters even of the most doubtful character, by way of *standing policy*—in time of peace, for example, it may do what could only be justified by the pressing exigencies of war, when the urgency of the case creates its own law and supersedes all others. A national bank is, no doubt, in many points of view, an excellent institution, but did any one ever before hear of such an establishment being founded for the purpose of collecting revenue? But whether as a *means*, "it is necessary and proper," it seems, is for the legislature to decide, and the court has no right to look into that question. What is this but to say that Congress may do any thing, provided they declare that it is done with a view to effect something else—it is not material what—that is within their undoubted powers? Add to this the rule laid down in Fletcher vs. Peck that the *motives* of the lawgiver cannot be looked into by the judges, unless he vouchsafe to declare them, and this whole doctrine is as complete as the most ambitious political libertine could wish it to be. Thus the only chance of having the present tariff declared unconstitutional by the Supreme Court was that its authors should call it what it really is—an act, passed to encourage domestic industry, and for no other purpose in the world. A conscientious man would feel himself bound—a high-minded and honourable man would think it at least ungenerous not to avow the motives upon which he acted, and which he believed to be fully sufficiently to justify his conduct. Mr. Drayton's motion to that effect however, at the last session, seems to have been scouted, and this outrageous enactment (for we are unwilling to call it law) comes before the court, and is treated by it as a *bonâ fide* revenue measure; a fraud upon the constitution, which is notorious to every man in the nation, being absolutely invisible to its highest judicatory! Were such a rule of interpretation adopted in the *Jus Privatum,* as has been laid down in the *Jus Publicum* of this confederacy, there is not a statute but might become a dead letter. Let any one only reflect upon the ingenious devices of money-lenders to evade the usury acts—but these have been all foiled, because the courts have looked into *the motives* of the parties, and the emphatic language of Lord Mansfield is literally true, that it is not in the wit of man to reserve, with impunity, more than the lawful interest, on any contract which amounts, substantially, to a loan of money.

Perhaps it may be said that this would be allowing too much discretion to the court—but we do not see that it would exceed the bounds of a sound, legal discretion, such as is absolutely necessary in every part of the administration of justice. Besides, that discretion would have the inestimable advantage of being in *favorem libertatis,* whereas the uncontrolled discretion of Congress is just the contrary. None but the worst consequences can reasonably be anticipated from it. In a country extending over such an immense territory—already comprising a multitude of commonwealths, differing so widely in interests, in character, and in political opinions, and still going on to increase without any assignable limit—it is preposterous to expect that a central government, which shall attempt to meddle with the domestic concerns of society, can be tolerable to its subjects. It will be inevitably *societas mater discordiarum ;* or, if two sections should unite to give the law, it would be the most impracticable, impenetrable and reckless tyranny that ever existed. At all events, whether we have pointed out the true causes of the evil, and whether there be any remedy for it or not, we are satisfied that no purity of character, no rectitude of intentions, no superiority of judgment and capacity in the judges of the Supreme

Court (and we can scarcely expect greater than it is already distinguished by) will ever enable that tribunal to answer its great end, as an umpire between the states and the confederacy. The mischief has already been done—the first step is taken, and the whole *system* is radically wrong.

Another instance in which the Federal Courts seem to have sanctioned principles at variance with the genius and practice of the common law is remarked by Chancellor Kent, whose observations we shall present to our readers. He is addressing himself to the case of the *United States* vs. *La Vengeance*,[*] and others, that have since been decided in conformity to it:

"It may now be considered as the settled law of this country, that all seizures under laws of imposts, navigation and trade, if made upon tide waters navigable from the sea, are civil cases of admiralty jurisdiction, and the successive judgments of the Supreme Court upon this point, are founded upon the judiciary act of 1789. If the act of Congress declares them to be cases of admiralty jurisdiction, it is apprehended that this is an extension of admiralty powers beyond the English practice. Cases of forfeiture for breaches of revenue law are cognizable in England in the exchequer upon informations, though the seizure was made upon navigable waters, and they proceed there to try the fact on which the forfeiture arises by jury. Informations are filed in the Court of Exchequer for forfeiture upon seizure of property, for breach of laws of revenue, impost, navigation, and trade. In the case of the *Attorney General* vs. *Jackson*, the seizure was of a vessel lying in the port of Cowes, for breach of the act of navigation, and the proceeding was by information and trial by jury, according to the course of the common law.—Lord Hale said, that information of that nature lay exclusively in the exchequer. Congress had a right, in their discretion, to make all such seizures and forfeitures cognizable in the district courts, but it may be a question whether they had any right to declare them to be cases of admiralty jurisdiction, if they were not so by the law of the land when the constitution was made. The constitution secures to the citizen trial by jury in all criminal prosecutions, and in all civil suits at common law, where the value in controversy exceeds twenty dollars. These prosecutions for forfeitures of large and valuable portions of property, under revenue and navigation laws, are highly penal in their consequences; and the government and its officers are always parties and deeply concerned in the conviction and forfeiture. And, if, by an act of Congress, or by judicial decisions, the prosecution can be turned over to the admiralty side of the district court, as being neither a criminal prosecution nor a suit at common law, the trial of the cause is then transferred from a jury of the country to the breast of a single judge. It is probable, however, that the judicial act of 1789 did not intend to do more than declare the jurisdiction of the district courts over these cases; and that all prosecutions for penalties and forfeitures upon seizures under laws of impost, navigation and trade, were not to be considered of admiralty jurisdiction, when the case admitted of a prosecution at common law, for the act saves to "suitors, in all cases, the right of a common law remedy, where the common law was competent to give it." We have seen that it is competent to give it, because, under the vigorous system of the English law, such prosecutions *in rem* are in the exchequer according to

* Dall. p. 297.

the course of the common law, and it may be doubted whether the case of *La Vengeance*, on which all the subsequent decisions of the Supreme Court have rested, was sufficiently considered. There is, however, much colonial precedent for this extension of admiralty jurisdiction. The Vice-Admiralty Courts in this country, when we were colonies, and also in the West-Indies, obtained jurisdiction in revenue causes to an extent totally unknown to the jurisdiction of the English admiralty and with powers quite as enlarged as those claimed at the present day. But this extension of the jurisdiction of the American Vice-Admiralty Courts beyond their ancient limits, to revenue cases and penalties, was much discussed and complained of on the part of this country at the commencement of the revolution.

"Whatever admiralty and maritime jurisdiction the district courts possess would seem to be *inclusive*, for the constitution declares that the judicial power of the United States shall extend to *all cases* of admiralty and maritime jurisdiction; and the act of Congress of 1789 says, that the district courts shall have *exclusive* original cognizance of all civil causes of admiralty and maritime jurisdiction. It is certain, however, that the state courts take an extensive and unquestioned cognizance of maritime contracts, and on the ground that they are not cases, strictly and technically speaking, of admiralty and maritime jurisdiction. If, however, the claim of the district courts be well-founded to the cognizance of all maritime contracts, wheresoever the same may be made, or whatever may be the form of the contract, it would seem that the jurisdiction of the state courts over those contracts could not be sustained. But I apprehend it may fairly be doubted whether the constitution of the United States meant by admiralty and maritime jurisdiction, any thing more than that jurisdiction which was settled and in active practice under the English jurisprudence when the constitution was made; and whether it had any retrospective or historical reference to the usages and practice of the admiralty, as it once existed in the middle ages, before the territories of the admiralty had been invaded and partly subdued by the bold and free spirit of the courts of common law, armed with the protecting genius and masculine vigor of trial by jury." Vol. i. pp. 349–352.

The last observations point to the pretensions of the admiralty, as stated and sanctioned in the case of De Lovio vs. Boit.* We confess that we once regarded this sally of the learned judge who decided that case as a notable piece of knight errantry, very ingenious, very romantic, and quite harmless. We regarded, with indulgence, the natural disposition of a mind much addicted to certain studies, to overrate their importance, and make their application as universal as possible—like the musician in Cicero, who explains every thing by the principles of harmony, and the dancing master in Moliere, who considers his own art as the foundation of all the sciences. We even sympathised with what we thought the generous and uncalculating zeal of such an enterprise, and felt all the pathos of the following very touching appeal. "In both these cases, (enforcing the judgments of foreign admiralty courts and proceeding *in rem* upon bottomry bonds executed in foreign parts) the authority of the

*2 Gall, p. 398.

admiralty has been admitted in the most ample manner, and in a recent case of bottomry, triumphantly upheld against every objection. These *melancholy* remains of its former splendour stand upon the ancient foundations of the admiralty before the reign of Richard II. and if they have survived the assaults of *enmity* and time, it is because the principles on which they rest, are solid and immoveable."* But we did not, at that time, think it possible that these notions should be gravely entertained by any minds not possessed with the same *passion.* We think somewhat differently now. It would not surprise us much to see these exploded doctrines of unsettled and barbarous times re-established amongst us, and the flag of "the Admiral" floating triumphantly over the vast field of maritime contracts.

Having already exceeded the limits allotted to this dry article, we shall not enter into a detailed discussion of the subject, but we cannot refrain from making a very few remarks upon it before we lay down our pen.

It would be difficult to support a paradox with greater ingenuity and learning, and, in general, in a more able and persuasive manner, than the very learned judge who decided De Lovio vs. Boit, has displayed in defence of his. He has done all that could be done for the cause. *Si Pergama dextrâ, &c.* If any one could re-edify the crumbled and mouldering fabric of the admiralty, it were he. But it appears to us that the reasoning of Lord Coke, in the 4th Institute,† is as conclusive as it is simple and obvious. In his answer to the sixth objection, he says— "The like answer as to the first. And it is further added, that for the death of a man, and of mayhem (in those two cases only) done in great ships, being and hovering in the maine streame only, beneath the points of the same rivers nigh to the sea, and no other place of the same rivers, nor in other causes, but in those two only, the admiral hath cognisance. But for all contracts, pleas, and querels made or done upon a river, haven or creek, within any county of this realm, the admiral, *without question,* hath not any jurisdiction, for *then he should hold plea of things done within the body of a county, which are triable by verdict of twelve men,* and *merely determinable by the common law,* and not within the court of the admiralty, according to the civil law. For that were *to change and alter the laws of the realm* in those cases, and make those contracts, pleas and querels triable by the common laws of this realm, to be drawn *ad aliud examen,* and to be sentenced by the judge of the admiralty according to the civil laws."

This, statement rather than argument, in our opinion, exhausts the whole subject. All that is necessary to be done by the de-

* 2 Gall, p. 444.   † Chap. xxii.

fenders of the common law and the trial by jury in this matter, is, to explain the text of Coke, and refute the cavils (for they can be nothing more) of his adversaries. But the light in which he puts the controversy is entirely satisfactory to men of plain sense. Suppose, without having regard to precedents, one were asked, whether, from the general spirit of the English law, he thought it probable that such an anomalous and foreign jurisdiction were tolerated by it? Could he possibly doubt about it? Surely he would suppose that the jurisdiction of the common law courts was co-extensive with the realm and all its social concerns, wherever that jurisdiction could be effectual—wherever every right could be protected, and every wrong redressed by it. He could not conceive how a people who have been in all ages so jealous on the subject of their own institutions—especially so stout and heroic in defending the trial by jury, and the principles of *magna charta*—could think of admitting an exception of so important a kind, and that too without the smallest occasion for it. For, as to the notion of its being so advantageous to have maritime cases disposed of *velts levatis*, according to their phrase, that would go too far to be entertained even for a moment. Speedy justice is, doubtless, a very good thing, but pure justice and public liberty are still better—at least, so have thought the people of England in all ages. Why, we repeat it, should there be more than one system of law in a country, where that law is competent to do perfect justice? Why should the authority of a tribunal depend upon the ebbing and flowing of the tide in a river within the body of a county any more than upon the changes of the moon. As to the *divisum imperium* on the sea-shore, there is reason in that, because if the jurisdiction is to stop at the bounds of a territory, as it must somewhere, and if the sea be assumed as the proper boundary, the extent of its waters is a good-enough practical line of demarcation. At all events, being settled, it is not worth while to disturb it for the purpose of establishing another that may not be a jot better. But is there any sense in the pretension of exercising jurisdiction in one river, or one part of a river, and not another, because the tide flows or does not flow there, while there are tribunals open that can do ample justice, whether it flows or not?* The analogy of chancery is *really* against the friends of the admiralty, who so confidently rely upon it. The true theory of our jurisprudence is, that the court entertains jurisdiction only where the complainant is remediless at law. We are, of course, aware that there are cases of concurrent jurisdic-

[* See the just remarks of Barrington on the Statute 13 Rich. II. (1389.) The admiral was only following the example of the Constable and Marshal—whose jurisdiction had been restrained by the 8th Rich. II. (1384,) both being equally in derogation of the Common Law.]

tion, and that even where the common law courts, adopting the principles of equity, have administered the same remedies, the jurisdiction of the latter is not considered as necessarily ousted. But these are mere abuses. Mr. Brougham has, we perceive, in his scheme of reform, declared war against trusts, and we shall, on a future occasion, make some further remarks upon the excesses or superfluities of the Prætorian jurisdiction. As for the case of hypothecation, it comes within our principle, and is a fair exception, because the common law courts do not afford the stipulated remedy. The other exception, of seaman's wages, is, as Lord Holt considers it, a mere indulgence, and a very convenient way of settling such small matters.

Another important consideration, and one that greatly strengthens (if any thing were wanted to strengthen) the decided opinion of Lord Coke, is, that the authorities cited on the other side are mostly taken from barbarous and unsettled times, or from foreign law. Suppose it could be shown that the statutes of Richard II. do not mean what that illustrious lawyer says they do, and that there were, at remote periods, even stronger and more numerous precedents in favour of the admiral's usurpations, than Judge Story's indefatigable researches have yet discovered. How much ought they to weigh, at this time of day, against the reason of the thing, the analogies of the law, the genius of the constitution, and the almost unbroken current of authorities for a century and a half together. Nearly all that has ever been done to make England what she is, and to lift up the common law to its present just supremacy in that realm, over the tyrannical forms and principles of other systems, has been accomplished since Lord Coke's time. His commanding authority, and virtuous efforts and example, eminently contributed to bring about these improvements. When Mr. Justice Buller is quoted to shew that the first of our common lawyers was inimical to the admiralty, it ought to be remembered that he was equally so to every thing else that savored of arbitrary power and of hostility to the liberties of Englishmen. Some indulgence may be extended—perhaps an especial degree of authority conceded— to that incorruptible and undaunted champion of *magna charta*— the author and proposer of the Petition of Rights, and one of the founders of that very freedom which we now enjoy. Those who overthrew the Star Chamber, and the High Commission Court,* would scarcely tolerate the pretension of the admiralty—while on the contrary,—

Qui Bavium non odit, amettua carmina Mævi.

Accordingly, Sir Leoline Jenkins expressly informs us that the famous order in council of 1632 "was punctually observed as

* [4th Inst. 324. Hallam's Constitutional Hist. Vol. 2. 136.]

to the granting and denying of prohibitions, till the *late disorderly times* bore it down, as an *act of prerogative prejudicial* (as was pretended) to the *common law and the liberty of the subject.*"* The wise and the practical men who founded the Commonwealth of England—who breathed into her constitution the breath of life, and whose reforms triumphed even over the prejudices of their wretched successors, and the untoward events that for a moment threatened to have obliterated them all, have, in this, as in other respects, set us an example worthy of our imitation.

The reputation of these Admiralty Courts does not appear to have been very high in the century before Lord Coke published the fourth Institute. Mr. Justice Johnson, in his excellent opinion in Ramsay vs. Allegre, remarks upon it as somewhat surprising, that, from the time of Richard II. down to the beginning of the seventeenth century, this jurisdiction should have attracted so little of the attention of the Common Law Courts. But if it eluded the jealous vigilance of a rival judicatory, it was not fortunate enough to escape the censure of public opinion. We have historical evidence of this fact. In the year 1549, we find the ministers of Charles V. complaining to Paget, ambassador of Edward VI. that foreign merchants could get no justice done them in the English admiralty. Paget defends himself by an *argumentum ad hominem*, retorting the reproach upon its authors. His logic had its effect, and it was cofessed on all hands, that there were great corruptions and abuses in these courts.†

In a word, the principle laid down by Chancellor Kent, in the extract just made from his work, is unquestionably the sound one, that the admiralty jurisdiction is to be taken as it stood at the time the constitution was adopted, and not as it possibly may have been in dark and remote ages. Of the extent of it, according to this rule, there can be very little doubt. The (then recent) English cases are clear—the doctrine of great constitutional lawyers is clear—the reasoning from the principles of a free government and the provisions of *magna charta* is clear—and we have the concurrent authority of two American judges of the highest respectability, and at a distance from each other, expressly upon the point.‡ Every argument that applies in England, is applicable *a multo fortiori* here—where we have not only the law of the land and the trial by jury to look to, but the conflicts of state and federal jurisdiction to prevent or to reconcile.

---

* Argum. before the Lords, p. 71.
† 2 Burnet's Hist. Reform. p. 132.
‡ Judges Hopkinson of Pennsylvania, and Bee of South-Carolina.

In closing these remark upon the constitutional jurisprudence of the United States, we repeat what we said at the beginning of them. We think the course which things are taking in this country must lead to a passive and slavish acquiescence under usurpation and abuse. Liberty is a practical matter—it has nothing to do with metaphysics—with entity and quiddity. It is a thing to be judged of altogether in the *concrete*. Like the point of honor, or the beauties of art, or the highest perfection of virtue, it addresses itself to the common sense and feelings of mankind. There is no defining it with mathematical exactness—no reducing it to precise and inflexible rules. What, for instance, does it signify, that a skilful disputant might possibly prove the tariff law to be within the words of the constitution: would that prevent its being a selfish and oppressive, and, therefore, a tyrannical measure? Is there any practical difference whatever, between the usurpation of a power not granted, and the excessive and perverted exercise of one that is? If a man abuses an authority of law under which he is acting, he becomes a trespasser *ab initio*—and if it be an authority in fact, he is a trespasser for the excess. The master of a ship and other persons in authority, have a right to correct those who are subject to their control—is an act of immoderate severity less a trespass and an offence on that account? What, if the government should suspend the *habeas corpus* act, without such an overruling necessity as could alone excuse the measure, and the courts would not control its discretion, would not the people, with reason, laugh at the man who should talk of such an outrageous abuse of power as constitutional, because the judges did not pronounce it otherwise? Nor does this depend upon the express provision in the constitution. Not at all. In a free country, every act of injustice, every violation of the principles of equality and equity, is, *ex vi termini* a breach of all their fundamental laws and institutions. In the ordinary administration of the law, indeed, the distinction between usurpation and abuse, may sometimes be important, but in great questions of public liberty, in reason, and in good faith, it is wholly immaterial. The moment that this sensibility to its rights and dignity is gone, a people, be its *apparent* or nominal constitution what it may, is no longer free. A quick sense of injustice, with a determination to resist it, in every shape and under every name and pretext, is of the very essence and definition of liberty, political as well as personal. How far, indeed, this resistance is to be carried in any particular instance, is a question of circumstances and discretion. So dreadful are all revolutions in their immediate effects—so uncertain in their ultimate issues—that a wise man would doubt long—that a moderate and virtuous man would bear much—before he could be prevailed upon to give his consent to extreme measures. We would be any thing rather than apostles of discord and dismemberment, sorely as the government to which South-Carolina, and the south in general, have been so loyal and devoted, is beginning to press upon all our dearest interests and sensibilities. But we feel it to be our duty to exhort our fellow-citizens to renewed exertion, and to a jealous and sleepless vigilance upon this subject. The battle must be fought inch by inch—no concession or compromise must be thought of. The courage and constancy of a free people can never fail, when they are exerted in defence of right. It is, indeed, an affecting spectacle, to look around us at the decay and desolation which are invading our pleasant places and the seats of our former industry and opulence—there is something unnatural and shocking in such a state of things. A young country already sinking into decrepitude and exhaustion—a fertile soil encroached upon again by the forests from which it has been so recently conquered—the marts and sea-ports of what might be a rich country, depopulated and in ruins. Contrast with this our actual condition, the hope and the buoyancy, and the vigor and the life that animated the same scenes only twenty-five years ago, and which have now fled away from us to bless other and more favored regions of the land. It is scarcely less discouraging to reflect upon the probable effects which the admission of an indefinite number of new states into the union, with political opinions, perhaps, altogether unsettled and unsafe, will produce. But we are yielding too much to feelings, with which recent events have, we own, made our minds but too familiar,—and we will break off here.

We take our leave of Chancellor Kent, in the hope of soon meeting with him again. We have generally given him, throughout this article, the title which he honored far more than it honored him, and which it is an everlasting disgrace to the greatest state in the union, that he does not still bear. What a mean and miserable policy! Lest it should have to pay their paltry salaries to a few superannuated public servants, to deprive itself of the accumulated learning, the diversified experience, and the ripe wisdom of such a man at the age of sixty! A commonwealth, flourishing beyond example or even imagination, wantoning and rioting in the favors of fortune, which have been poured upon it without stint, chaffering and higgling in, by far, the most important concern of society, like an usurious pawnbroker, for a few thousand dollars. In some of the poorer states, such stupid economy would be more excusable, or rather less unaccountable, for nothing can excuse it. The rarest thing in nature—certainly, the rarest thing in America—is a learned and able judge, at the same time, that he is not only, in the immediate administration of justice, but still more, if possible, by his immense influence over the bar and the community at large, beyond all price. But we Americans do not think so, or rather we act as if we did not. The only means of having a good bench is to adopt the English plan—give liberal salaries to your judges, let them hold their offices during good behaviour, and when they begin to exhibit symptoms of senility and decay, hint to them that their pensions are ready to be paid them. The last is a necessary part of the system—but it is what the American people never can be brought to submit to. They are economical, (God save the mark!) and, therefore, will not spend money without a present and palpable *quid pro quo*—they are metaphysical, and, therefore, they will not violate what is called, we know not why, *principles*. They deem anything preferable. Extinguish the light of a Kent or a Spencer—submit to the drivellings of dotage and imbecility—nay, even resort to the abominations of an elective judiciary system—anything rather than adopt the plain, manly, and only sure means of securing the greatest blessing, but liberty, which civil society can attain to, the able administration of the laws!

In the present instance, the people of New-York alone are the sufferers. The distinguished person before us has laid up abundantly those *miseris viatica canis*, which wisdom and virtue, and they alone, confer upon the chosen few—which the world cannot give, neither take away.

CRAFTS' FUGITIVE WRITINGS.

A selection in Prose and Poetry, from the Miscellaneous Writings of the late WILLIAM CRAFTS. To which is prefixed a Memoir of his life. 8vo. *Charleston. C. C. Sebring and J. S. Burges.* 1828.

WE have read through this little volume with a melancholy interest. Having been intimately acquainted with Mr. Crafts, we can add our testimony to that of his biographer, in favour of the amiableness of his disposition, and the gentleness and suavity of his manners, which were such as to disarm even the hostility which his imprudences occasionally excited, and to awaken in this community a very general feeling of regret, we might almost say, of affectionate sorrow, for his premature death. We remember what he was, and what he was expected to become—under what favourable auspices he entered upon life—admired even to idolatry for his talents and accomplishments—honoured with the confidence of the virtuous, and the attentions of the fashionable and the gay—and seeming to have, at his command, whatever could gratify the fondest ambition of an aspiring young man. It is, at all times, painful to reflect upon the disappointment of such hopes, but there is an air of pensive sadness—a tone of settled, though subdued melancholy, and of meek resignation under misfortune—pervading some of his later essays, which imparts to them a still deeper interest of the same kind, whilst it presents the character of Mr. Crafts to us, we confess, in a new light. We had always given him credit for an irrepressible buoyancy of spirit, and a self-complacency which defeat and disappointment never seriously disturbed—but the essays alluded to are too much "sicklied o'er with the pale cast of thought," to have been the effusions of so light a heart.

These "Miscellaneous Works" are preceded by a well written and interesting biographical memoir of their author, from the hand of a literary friend. It appears from this sketch, that Mr. Crafts was born in January, 1787, and was consequently in his fortieth year, when he died at Lebanon, in September, 1826. After being prepared for college, as boys generally are in this country, he was admitted, in the autumn of 1802, into the Sophomore class of Harvard University. We are told by his biographer, that "he has retained to the present day, within those walls, a sort of traditionary reputation as one of the most brilliant *Belles Lettres* scholars who ever passed through them." His attention, at the same time, to the regular exercises of the institution, entitled him to the highest rank, as (what is called,) a general scholar. We should form rather an exalted idea of his ambition and his assiduity, if we believe with the author of the memoir, that in addition to the ordinary studies of his classes, he became a "tolerable proficient in the Hebrew." But we were not before aware of the fact, and we doubt extremely whether his knowledge of that language ever went beyond a mere smattering. Mr. Crafts' own notion, that the neglect with which the Hebrew was generally treated at Cambridge, was as unjust as "the treatment a Jew receives from a Christian," although it proves him to be free from the prejudice, is not absolutely decisive as to his own *conduct*. We are informed, however, that

"The high collegiate reputation of Mr. Crafts must principally have depended on his *vivâ voce* qualifications—such as his readiness at every exercise of memory, his happy and elegant construction of the languages, and his beautiful declamation. It may appear somewhat remarkable, that his admirable talent at English composition had not yet proportionally developed itself. On inspecting his college themes, and other contemporaneous exercises, we could find not one, of a *precocious* character, not one, from which his subsequent eminence as a writer would have been predicted, or which we could submit to the reader as a worthy and kindred gem in the present crown of his fame. They are all, indeed, correct and respectable, and written with praise-worthy care; nor had William Crafts, the *collegian*, cause to be ashamed of them. But still they never rise above the mark of a good college theme. He even adopted, for his English oration at the Major Exhibition, the ominous subject of Fancy, which he treated, sometimes in a prosaic, and sometimes in a puerile style, that must have owed very much to his fine delivery for whatever enthusiastic reception it met from the audience. It would seem as if the hand of time had not yet stretched to the requisite point, even for some prelusive notes, that particular chord of his forming genius, which, after a very few years, was to throw off sounds that should enchant and instruct every hearer. The sphere, moreover, in which he now moved, was comparatively contracted. His intellect was one of those that rise with circumstances, and perhaps, we may add with regret, that sink with them too. When transferred from the walls of the seminary, when starting on the labors and hopes of a noble and arduous profession, when the eyes of a community, or rather of a country, were directed, or to be drawn towards him, he was still found equal to the highest demand of favouring *circumstances*, in achieving, as he at that time did, some of the splendid productions which open the ensuing selections from his writings.

Much of these inspiring influences his sanguine mind already seems to have caught from without, when he arrived, at the close of his college life, and felt himself approaching the responsibilities, trials and honors that awaited him in the field of public society. His Latin oration, at the taking of his first degree, evidently exhibits a remarkable *move* in the progress of his powers. Happy in the choice and management of his subject, manly in his tone throughout, and nearly ripened in those external graces which were peculiarly his own, he now made an impression on his audience, and through them on the public, sufficient to satisfy any young man at his entrance into life. We should probably have given this oration a place in the selection, much as every educated reader would demur at the thought of having one's commencement exercises thus exposed, and small as might be the number of any readers who would feel interested in a Latin composition; but presuming that many of the author's friends would expect the insertion of his oration for the *second* degree, it seemed advisable to tread no further on questionable ground, than the admission of this last mentioned performance alone." pp. xi–xiii.

We agree with the author of the memoir as to the propriety of omitting one of these orations, and only regret that he ventured so far upon "questionable ground" as to publish the other. We have nothing to say against the translation. The conception of the orator was a very happy one, and all that prevented the execution being quite as good, was his ignorance of Latin, or to express the same thing less harshly, his evident want of practice in Latin composition. His Latinity is execrable, but the substance of the oration as it is conveyed in an English version in the memoir, is so piquant, that we cannot refrain from extracting it for the gratification of our readers. We are not at all surprised at the impression it is said to have made upon the afflicted audience:—

"From time immemorial, the audience at Commencement had listened with meekness to the Latin valedictory, as to a performance, whose lugubrious solemnity, stately march, and arbitrary length, were altogether matters of prescription, and must be borne with, like a fixture of the day, or a decree of fate. When, therefore, our young orator came forward on this occasion, and in an address of three or four minutes, rather bantered his hearers with playfulness, than taxed their resigned attention, there was something so daring in the originality, and so unexpected in the relief, that the company present were thrown unawares into that state of "sudden glory," described by Hobbes, as causing the most grateful of all our convulsions. Every sentence and word, too, were spoken so distinctly, deliberately, and emphatically, and with a grace so peculiarly insinuating, that those who possessed the slightest acquaintance with the Latin, readily comprehended, while even the uninitiated could almost as easily imagine, what was meant. Just as they were expecting a great deal of parade, a great many words, and a tedious detention, he began to this effect:

'Enough of ceremony, and enough of talk. It is full time to retire. This day, O friends, you have listened to a variety of tongues—the Greek, with its rolling accents—the Latin, surpassing in elegance—and the English, more copious than all; and you now turn your wearied ears to me. The Hebrew alone we have missed, that sweet-toned, that heaven-invented language, which was once cherished among us with peculiar honour, but is now, with sorrow be it said, thought worthy of contempt. Yet we have been entertained by youthful orators of happy promise; a throng of fair spectators, and the Muse, have favoured us with their inspiring presence,—so that the air is resounding with varied song. Nothing remains, but that you, whom either the love of science, or a crowd, or noise, or any other cause hath attracted hither, should in due form be dismissed. Brief shall be my harangue. The parting of friends is to be marked by tears rather than by words. Indeed, so agreeable is your presence, so enchanting the proud power of beauty, so delightful the fair countenances which beam down upon me, that I fear lest I should utterly forget mine office, and be incapable of pronouncing farewell in a tone of sadness. Nor will such a tone be demanded of me. Already a large number of you appear to be retiring, and the whole of you seem on the point of saying, Merciful Powers, when will it be over? How can my poor eloquence, how could the wisdom of a Cato, or the matchless rhetoric of a Cicero, or any thing short of manacles and fetters, hope to detain within these sacred precincts, those, who are impatient for their dinner? The renowned Socrates himself, when unveiling the mysteries of philosophy, was almost deserted by the Athenian populace. But neither have I the skill of Socrates in speaking, nor have you the taste of the Athenians in hearing. Should I attempt, therefore, to beguile you longer, I should probably be left alone. And I have not so great a rage for talking, as to discourse before the bare walls.

'I bid you then, all, farewell!'

"He now, after the usual custom, analyzed his audience, uttering short and graceful valedictories, in succession, to the Governor, Lieut. Governor, President of the University, Professors and Tutors, Classmates and Friends. Next followed the peroration, of which the following is the substance, the manner being untranslatable":—

'Farewell, I repeat again and again, a long farewell.
Farewell, my Companions!
Farewell, ye Virgins, dearer than the light!
Farewell, ye Youths, with vigour crowned!
Farewell, grave Seniors, on the verge of Heaven!
Farewell, ye regions, to the Muses dear!
And Good Day to the Multitude!
Enough of ceremony," &c. &c. pp. xvii, xviii.

Mr. Crafts returned to his native city at the age of nineteen. He immediately entered upon the study of law, to which, it seems, he devoted himself with assiduity and success, "though not abandoning his favourite intercourse with the Muses, or the indulgence of his natural taste for the Classics and *Belles-Lettres.*" And, we are further assured, that

'The high expectations formed as to his future celebrity both by his brethren and the public, were justified by his earliest exhibitions. As an advocate before a jury, he was surpassed by none. A classical education gave him an eminent command of language; an acute, logical mind gave clearness and spirit to his reasonings, which he illustrated and adorned by rhetorical aids drawn from ancient and modern literature. Nor in his public harangues, while he was admired for his oratory and pointed reasonings, did he appear to be deficient in the knowledge and application of such parts of the law as were appropriate to the matter in hand. In his occasional arguments on points of law before the judges, he seldom failed to bring out the principles and authorities that were proper to be adduced, and these he always blended with so much of his favourite play of fancy as to make the dryest discussion matter of entertainment to the bench and the bar. In the Court of Sessions, and the defence of the accused, he was remarkably successful. In this court, his aid was often sought; and when the judges had occasion to assign counsel from amongst the bar, for the defence of the accused, he was often called upon by the court, and considered as a favourable selection by the destitute prisoner. His eloquence was popular, and as an advocate he stood high in the public estimation. He had a considerable extent of practice, although his friends often wished that he could have spared more time from the pursuits of literature and cultivation of the Muses, to be devoted to the severe studies of the law.

Those who knew the powers of his mind, were well convinced, that in such case, there was no point of legal erudition, however lofty, which he would not have attained if his life had been spared.' pp. xx, xxi.

In another extract, we are told that Mr. Crafts did not choose to become "a *special pleader*," because the "classic structure of his mind could never relish prolonged investigations, or resort to the common practice of common lawyers, that of exhausting every topic and hackneying every argument that either principally or incidentally belongs to the case."

Now, let us pause a few moments, and consider the justness of the preceding observations, and the truth of the facts to which they refer. We are arrived at the most important period of Mr. Crafts' life—that which decided his fate. He was now of age—had been admitted to the bar—was admired as a popular speaker—was esteemed and beloved even by his political opponents—and, in addition to all this, and what a thorough-paced lawyer would consider as *instar omnium*—"his business increased with a rapidity before unknown at our bar." How is it to be accounted for, that, with all these advantages, natural and subsidiary, Mr. Crafts never attained to any eminence in his profession, and that, even in public life, to which he was more inclined, after enjoying a momentary éclat, he, at an early age, so completely lost his influence and reputation? This interesting question, we think, may be answered in one word,—Mr. Crafts never did make himself a lawyer. Without fortune, he depended absolutely upon his own exertions at the bar, not only for preferment in the world, but for his regular support. Yet, whatever may have been his progress in them at first, he must, in a very short time, have utterly neglected his professional studies, for, at no period, since our acquaintance with him began, could he pass even for an ordinary lawyer, and that belief had already taken a strong hold upon the public mind. Inde prima mali labes.

On this subject, Mr. Crafts labored under a fatal delusion. We have frequently heard him express it, as his deliberate opinion, that a profound knowledge of the laws was quite unnecessary here. Instead, therefore, of sitting down to acquire it by severe and unremitted study—the only price at which it can be had—he ridiculed those who did so, as mere plodders that had forfeited all claim to the reputation of men of genius. There were two characteristics of his, which inclined him especially to entertain such a notion—he had more vanity than pride, and his extraordinary facility in composition and in speaking, made labor unnecessary to him for any occasional display. As soon, therefore, as he began to appear at the bar, his ambition took a wrong turn. Instead of projecting a scheme of study and exertion, requiring the utmost efforts of his industry and talent to accomplish it, but promising him at the end of a few years, a complete and triumphant and permanent success, he aimed always at immediate effect, and the fleeting and delusive applauses of the day. His love of praise, inordinate at best, was thus more and more inflamed until it became an incurable disease. He thought no longer of the future. It was the height of his ambition to pass for a man of genius among the "men of wit and pleasure about town." His fine talents were thus prostituted and perverted. They were talked of by every body, and neglected, by none but him—the *enfant gâté*—upon whom they had been lavished. Man, woman and child, ran after Mr. Crafts' society, repeated his brilliant sallies, and laughed at his witty jokes. He was universally caressed—but his admirers were "hugging him into snares." He contracted a distaste for study—indeed, for all serious occupations. Whatever he was to do was to be done quickly; and he just reversed the maxim, "sat cito, si sat bene." He began to boast less of the merits of his compositions, than of the facility with which he could throw them off, and to write and mémorize an ordinary oration in two or three days, soon appeared to him a greater exploit than to send forth a work worthy of being transmitted to posterity. Meanwhile, he became every day less capable in the management of affairs, whether public or private—business which had long courted, now deserted him—those coruscations of a lively fancy which had delighted and dazzled in the youth, seemed to be out of place in the senator of mature years—his little stock of knowledge, acquired almost exclusively by his early studies, was exhausted—his exertions as an advocate ceased to be called for, because his opinions as a counsellor were not respected, and, at the age of thirty-five, Mr. Crafts had already survived his hopes, his popularity and his reputation.

This is a brief but just account of the signal and melancholy failure of a man from whom so much was expected in his youth. It is a mistake to suppose, that devotion to literary pursuits had any thing to do with it, and that, for the best of all reasons, viz. that Mr. Crafts never was devoted to literary pursuits, at least, after he came to the bar. "His favorite intercourse with the Muses," if by that is meant inditing sonnets for the newspapers, and songs for "festive occasions," may, indeed, have contributed to bring him into disrepute with men of business—but these effusions did him quite as little honor in the opinion of men of letters. The truth is, that so far from suffering by his reputation as a scholar, he was very much, if not mainly indebted to it, for his extraordinary popularity and success at the outset of his career. A felicitous allusion, an apt quotation, the elegance of his diction, and the various other graces of a classical education that adorned his style, were quite peculiar to him among his contemporaries, and contributed very much to secure for him the character, which he ever afterwards enjoyed, of *the* man of genius *par excellence*. In this respect, as in many others, Mr. Crafts was eminently fortunate—for there can be no doubt but that, throughout the Southern States at least, and, perhaps, throughout the whole country, a taste for literary studies (much more any serious or continued application to them) stands very much in the way of a young man in the pursuits of active life. It raises a presumption among worldly people, that he can never become *practical*, and such a notion when it has once taken root in the public mind, is, beyond all comparison, the most formidable obstacle a man of talents can encounter in such a state of society as ours. Still farther is it from being correct that the "classic structure" of Mr. Crafts' mind, was what prevented him from becoming sufficiently conversant with special pleading. A "classic structure of mind," if there is any meaning in the phrase, is precisely the thing that is wanted in that most refined of all intellectual exercises—for we will take it upon us to assure the very respectable author of the "Memoir," that the notions of his correspondent upon this subject, are as far as possible from being just. "Pleading," or as it is vulgarly called, "special pleading," is neither more nor less than the art of stating a case upon paper, with the utmost brevity and precision that its circumstances will admit of. Instead of "exhausting," it teaches a lawyer to *exclude* every topic that is not necessarily connected with the issue to be submitted to the Court ; and, instead of "hackneying every argument," however incidental or unimportant, to select and to set forth the strongest point of his case, and that alone. It has been said a thousand times, and deserves to be repeated a thousand more, that there is nothing out of the exact sciences, that can bear a moment's comparison with the subtle and rigorous logic of our Common Law Pleadings.* "Let none enter here without a knowledge of geometry," was what a Greek philosopher is said to have written over the door of his school. We say the same thing of pleading, in reference to the bar. If a young man finds that he cannot understand the principles, or relish the beauties of this admirable system of reasoning, let him be assured that law is not his vocation. His ignorance may escape detection in the haste and confusion of a Nisi Prius scramble, and he may even be pre-eminently successful in the management of his cases before juries; but his want of that exact and scientific know-

---

* As the Common Law is said to be the perfection of reason, so its system of pleading is the perfection of reasoning. However, in England, not unfrequently

Le raisonnement en bannit la raison:

and some improvements, though, perhaps, they might mar the science, would help justice.

ledge of legal principles, of which good pleading is at once the fruit and the test, must make itself glaringly manifest in every argument before the higher tribunals. We have no manner of doubt, (be it recorded in passing) that much of the confusion and delay attendant upon our judicial proceedings, is owing to the increasing deficiency of the bar in this particular.

We have dwelt the longer upon this part of the subject, because we fear that the unfortunate error which led Mr. Crafts to neglect his professional studies, and proved ultimately fatal to his hopes, still prevails among our young barristers to a most pernicious extent. His example is an impressive one. We are confident, that, had he employed the first four or five years after his admission to the bar, in the assiduous study of law, he would have continued, to the end of his life, to hold the same elevated rank in society, which his talents had commanded for him at first. We are aware that a notion has generally prevailed, that his reasoning powers were irremediably feeble, and that he could never have done much in a mere didactic and practical style of speaking. We are not of this opinion ourselves. The frivolities and crudities with which all his later speeches, whether at the bar or in the legislature, were overrun, furnish no fair criterion of his intellectual character, which had been for a long time sadly on the wane. Nay, for the reasons already given, we do not think that he ever did full justice to his talents for public speaking. The specimen of forensic eloquence, preserved in the present collection, (p. 83) although, perhaps, creditable enough to a young man, is by no means a flattering representation of Mr. Crafts' talents as an orator. It was our good fortune to hear him, in the winter of that very year, deliver, at Columbia, an incomparably better speech—the only one, indeed, which ever gave us an idea of what his powers in debate would have been, had he cultivated them with care, and employed them, seriously and zealously, for the accomplishment of important practical ends, instead of wasting them upon occasions of mere parade and show, and directing them to no other object than the obtaining for himself a little ephemeral applause. The earnest and strenuous advocacy of some real interest—an effort in the orator to impart his own convictions to his audience, and to persuade them to act in conformity with his views—this is an essential element of "true eloquence," which, as Milton* admirably expresses it, "we find to be none but *the serious and hearty love of truth.*" Now, it was precisely this all-important ingredient of "true eloquence" that was wanting in Mr. Crafts' ordinary style of speaking. He sunk the orator in the rhetorician—he forgot the subject in the man-

---

* An apology for Smectymnuus.

ner, and sacrificed the ends to the means. Instead of pushing his point with might and main, with powerful argument, and an honest, hearty zeal, like a man of business, a statesman, an advocate, a patriot intent upon the matter in hand—he thought of nothing but the appearance he was to make before his audience. There was always something in his manner that reminded one of an under-graduate at a college exhibition. His whole air, and demeanor, and diction, were expressive of artifice and study. His passion for producing effect, was perpetually breaking out, and his style was depraved and deformed by every variety of *concetti*—we mean of course, his general style; for there were times when he spoke with more simplicity and singleness of purpose, and, consequently, with much greater eloquence. The occasion alluded to just now, was one of these. He was urging the impeachment of a man who had been guilty of many outrageous acts of injustice and oppression in the exercise of an inferior judicial office. All the leading lawyers of the house opposed him. We shall never forget his manner of delivering that speech, which was, for a young man, truly admirable, and has, in some respects, probably, never been surpassed on that floor. His shrill but musical voice, elevated to a thrilling pitch—his fine countenance animated with the ardor of debate—the perfect grace and *decorum* of his gesticulation, free from all constraint or artifice—the unaffected elegance and manly simplicity of his diction—the clearness of his statements—the closeness and cogency of his reasonings—the apparent disinterestedness of his zeal—his lofty indignation against injustice—the vigor and perseverance with which he maintained his ground in the debate, against a formidable array of talent and influence—all conspired to give earnest of a high degree of excellence at a more advanced period of life.

We do not mean to say, that, by any application to study or business, however serious and intense, Mr. Crafts could have made himself a *first-rate* debater or an orator after the manner of Demosthenes. Nature had not cast him in that mould. His character was more distinguished by the amiable, than by the sterner virtues, and his understanding was not one of the very largest capacity. Even his physical qualities, although all of them exceedingly prepossessing and attractive, were not of a commanding cast. He was more remarkable for the grace than the dignity, for the beauty than the strength of his person, and there was something effeminate in his exquisitely touching and melodious voice. In short, he was not what is called, in a phrase of the day, a man of great calibre, but he had, certainly, marked talent, and nothing but his suicidal indolence and perverse vanity prevented his becoming able in business and debate. He might have made himself a most brilliant and effective orator in any assembly in the world. Perhaps, no public speaker in this country, ever expressed himself with more uniform purity and elegance, and, occasionally, with more felicity and beauty. He had the great merit of never fatiguing his hearer, while he seldom spoke without delighting him with the point and brilliancy of his occasional sallies, and supplying him with excerpts for his common-place book or the next conversation. It was these shining passages, indeed—the *dulcia vitia* of his style—that attracted so much attention from bad judges, and, at last, as we have already observed, took the place, in almost all that he wrote and spoke, of the simple elegance and severe graces which he had emulated in his early studies.

Montesquieu defines talent "un don que le ciel nous á fait en secrèt et que nous revélons sans le savoir." We like this definition, although it is not the most precise that can be imagined, and were we called upon to exemplify it, we should cite the instance of Mr. Crafts. He was not a man of genius—for that is a word not to be profaned;—he never became an able man, as we have seen—yet it is impossible to read these imperfect remains, picked up here and there, out of a heap of ephemeral rubbish, without perceiving that he was highly gifted by nature. It is very remarkable, too, that (so far as our intercourse with him enabled us to judge) he seldom knew when he had done a good thing. His most hasty and careless compositions, often happened to be his best ; while those which he took the most pains with, were sure to be written in his worst taste. He set most value upon such of his compositions as were overrun with metaphor and exaggeration, with antithesis and epigram—while there were simple effusions—spontaneous beauties—which flowed from his pen without his knowing it—which, to borrow a very pretty thought of Sir Walter Scott's, his fancy yielded him with as little effort as a tree resigns its leaves to the gale in autumn, and which he appreciated as men are apt to do, whatever costs them least. But, though their merits escaped him, they were at once perceived and felt by others—by the unlearned as well as the learned—by gentle and simple, by people of taste, and by people of no taste. We were very much struck with the effect which his editorial essays in the *Courier* immediately produced. We have heard him say with a good natured triumph, that, by the end of each month, he regularly got back what he had published, with interest, from all parts of the United States.

We shall, doubtless, be considered by his friends as greatly underrating his poetical talent, when we say that nothing of his that we have seen in verse, would deserve to be published in a separate volume. The author of the "Memoir" entertains a very exalted opinion of some of his minor poems, which he pronounces the best specimens of the Anacreontic style, that are to

be found in our language.   We think this altogether extravagant.   We do not consider these verses as at all better than can
be had, at any time, for the "poetical corner" of a fashionable
newspaper, or monthly magazine.   We have read over all that
are collected in the volume before us, with great attention, but
our previous opinion has only been confirmed by the attempt to
correct it.   The poem entitled the "Raciad," is lively and spirited,
and may be read with interest.   "Sullivan's Island" is equally
commendable—but their merit is not high enough to challenge
honor from gods, or men, or pillars.   However, as they are far
from being bad, and many of our readers may think more highly
of them than we do, we will submit some extracts for their perusal.   There are at least half a dozen bagatelles, in each of
which, the poet tells us of some new exploit of Love.   The first
time we meet with him, he is going to the races, having made
a car for himself out of "a part of the ceiling of the sky," which
happened to fall "when Love was nigh" enough to catch it.   The
whole history of this excursion is as follows :—

"Love went out to see the race ;
I marvel if there be a place
Where Love goes not ; unless it be
Some place unknown to you or me.

Love did not in a sulkey go,
The surly equipage of wo ;
Nor rode he in a coach and four,
By vulgar eyes gazed o'er and o'er.

Nor travelled like the common throng,
Who mutter as they drudge along ;
Nor like the Dandy, turning round,
To look contemptuous on the ground :

Part of the ceiling of the sky,
Happening to fall when Love was nigh,
He made of it an azure car,
And placed on either side a star.

His chariot opened from above,
For Love sees Heaven and Heaven sees Love ;
But when a *tête-à-tête* he chose
Love bade it like a violet close.

He harnessed Hope and young Desire,
And lest the generous steeds should tire,
With kisses he supplied their fare,
And baited them with capillaire.

Love's wheels were of the sandal tree,
Sweet circles of perfumery ;
Each spoke, entwined with jasmine flowers,
Like Love's sweet dial of the hours.

Dreams curtained little Love around,
And Zephyrs played and Pleasures crowned.
The seats are myrtle—only three ;
For Love himself, for you and me.

Love marvelled when the race was done,
To find the prize so quickly won;
Yet turned contemptuous from the sight,
And plumed his wings with self-delight.

"Why, we, ourselves can better do ;"
So said Love, to me and you ;
There's not a steed beneath the sun,
That Love in rapture, can't outrun." pp. 356, 357.

The next thing which the gallant little god does, is to indite a billet-doux:—

"Love wrote a billet—what do you think
Was Love's paper, pen and ink?
Not such things as mortals use ;—
Ink of sable, quill of goose,
Pewter stand, and paper, wove
Out of rags, won't do for love.
He cut the heart of a dove in two,
And mixed the drops with honey dew ;
In an amber vase he plac'd it then,
And went to seek for a lover's pen.
He plucked a ray from the setting sun,
A plume of light, as the day is done,
For Love is warm, tho' night invades,
And Love is bright among the shades.
He waited till the stars arose,
Ere he his billet would compose ;
He wrote on rose leaves newly blown,
Because their fragrance is his own.
A glass of capillaire he quaffed,
Then laughing wrote, and writing laughed :

"*We were for each other born,*
We are from each other torn ;
Where we should, then let us be,
I with you, and you with me."

Love copied then his Billet-Doux,
One for me and one for you ;
He sealed them with his own dear kiss ;
And sent them by the mail of bliss." pp. 357, 358.

He next falls asleep, and we have his likeness thus pourtrayed :—

"Awake him not—he dreams of bliss,
His little lips put forth to kiss
His arms entwined in virgin grace,
Seem link'd in beautiful embrace.

He smiles, and on his opening lip
Might saints refresh, and angels sip ;
He blushes—'tis the rosy light,
That morning wears on leaving night.

He sighs—'tis not the sigh of wo,
He only sighs that he may know
If kindred sighs another move,
For mutual sighs are signs of love.

He speaks—it is his dear one's name—
He whispers—still it is the same—
The imprison'd accents strive in vain,
They murmur through his lips again.

He wakes—the silly little boy,
To break the mirror thus of joy!
He wakes to sorrow, and in pain—
Oh, Love! renew thy dreams again." pp. 359, 360.

Then follows "Love's Benediction," which (to the scandal of our fair readers) is scarcely worth repeating—and an account of his being made a prisoner in a myrtle bower, and bound with garlands of jessamine. The first stanza of this little poem is very pretty; but the two others are not quite as intelligible, or rather as sensible, as might be wished:—

"The snow-drop is in bloom,
And the young earth's perfume,
    Scents anew the floating air;
It is the breath of love—
Beneath, around, above,
    Young love is there.
Come, let us strive to snare him—see,
Love smiling waits for you and me.

Bind him with the jasmine flower,
Hide him in a myrtle bower,
    On thornless roses let him rest;
See his gracious eyelids move,
Hope and joy are eyes of love,
    Kiss them and be blest,
Love gives his own dear heart to be
One half for you, one half for me.

The tongue may lose its power
As Babel's noisy tower
    Confounded it of yore;
But the language of the eye,
Survives, (though others die,)
    Delicious as before.
Love gives his darling eyes, to be
One eye for you, and one for me." p. 361.

He is seen for the last time upon earth at the Capuchin Chapel, and as, in the next poem, we hear of the Rapids of Love, there is some reason to fear (qu. hope) that he is come to an untimely end in his own cataract, and been sent after the head of Orpheus—"down the swift Hebrus to the Lesbian shore."

The lines entitled "A Dying Mother to her Living Daughter," are very pathetic, and bating some blemishes here and there, perhaps the best in the book:—

"I call'd for thee to bless thee—once I thought
    Thou wouldst have sooth'd this bleeding, breaking heart,
A daughter's blessed consolation brought,
    And ere the ebbing drops did all depart,

I hoped to see thee on the shore of life,
　Where I would linger for thy sweet farewell,
And dying, bless in thee a virtuous wife,
　Then yield me to the flesh-dissolving cell.
I wept before thou wast, that thou might'st be,
　And yet I leave thee, and I cannot weep;
I waked with joy to guard thy infancy,
　Now all I hope for is unbroken sleep.
Thou wert my first, my last, my only child,
　How happy was I, blest with only thee.
The treacherous favour, murdered as it smiled,
　I could have wished for more—unconscious me ;
Yet, pardon me—it was the flush of shame,
　That mantling o'er this frozen cheek of mine,
Called forth the accents of reluctant blame ;—
　Thou hast my pardon, daughter—yield me thine.
Come let me bless thee, with my last, last kiss ;
　These cold, cold lips, inhaled thy infant breath.
They hailed thee virtuous, with exstatic bliss,
　Tho' fallen they bless thee, 'mid the pangs of death." p. 377.

Among these "occasional poems," there is one purporting to
be an extract from "Kitty, an unpublished manuscript." The
following paragraph is prefixed to this fragment. "In New-
York, they have Fanny ; in Boston, Sukey ; and why should we
not have Kitty in Charleston ? We can give at present but a
glimpse of her." Now, with great deference, we submit that
the fact mentioned at the beginning of the paragraph, was the
best of all possible reasons why we should *not* have a glimpse
of her. We think that all three of these damsels, (two of them
certainly) might have been kept at home in single, or rather
solitary blessedness, without any loss to mankind. Of Sukey,
it is due to candour to confess, that we judge according to the
rule, *noscitur a sociis*. Fanny we have read, and Kitty. The
latter is a great deal worse even than its prototype. It is a bad
thing badly imitated—the exaggeration of a caricature. Lord
Byron with his Beppos' and Juans' has done infinite mischief in
the rhyming world. There never was a more striking example
of the *decipit exemplar vitiis imitabile*. Nothing is so easy as
to rival the noble poet in his slip-shod, zig-zag, desultory style,
and doggrel versification—but nothing is more difficult than to
pour out, with such perfect *nonchalance*, strains of the most
beautiful poetry, and sallies of incomparable wit. The humor of
a man of genius, however eccentric and even extravagant, is one
thing, and the buffoonery of an awkward mimic, is quite another.
Beppo and Don Juan possess attractions of the most interesting
kind. They exhibit genius in sport. The mighty frame, the
imposing air, the noble proportions are there, and all the strength,
and the grace and the beauty—but there is no artifice or constraint, or pretension, or effort. These works bear the same relation to Childe Harold, for instance, or the Corsair, as the conver-

sations of a great orator (who happens to excel in conversation) to his harangues before public assemblies on solemn occasions. There is the same talent; but one is more charmed, and even struck, with its wonderful readiness, vivacity and point, in familiar impromptu table-talk, than with its more perfect, perhaps, but more stately, and as it were, theatrical exhibition before the world. But it is a grievous mistake to suppose, as Lord Byron's imitators seem to do, that any body may rival Beppo or Juan, by making himself perfectly at home, and writing away at random with visible and invincible determination to transmute doggrel and absurdity into the rarest wit in spite of Minerva. What, for instance, can be said of such lines as these—

> "I love the Fourth of July, that is true,
>   And when it comes, 'twill be in vain to say,
> That I shall stay at home and darn and sew,
>   Nor promenade on that triumphant day.
> So bring my shawl, my parasol and bonnet,
> Since head, and heart, and feet are set upon it." p. 346.

Or these—

> "I like the short coats, and the long coats too,
>   The cocked hats, and the hats that are not cocked,
> I love the green, the red, the grey, the blue,
>   The scattered yagers, and the artillery locked,
> Their hands in brotherly affection meeting,
> Like parted lovers at a happy greeting.
>
> I love a horseman on a likely horse,
>   But precious few of these, alas! there are;
> I have seen better, but I ne'er saw worse,
>   For either purpose, whether peace or war.
> 'Tis rather strange, since ev'ry one is able
>   To hire a good one at a livery stable.
>
> I love the march majestic, long and slow,
>   When the pois'd sword attests the due salute.
> I love the big drum, and the small drum too,
>   And I admire the shrill note of the flute.
> But much do I pity the peaceable mutton
> Whose garments these drums are so cruelly put on." p. 347.

Or these—

> "The night was dark, but Kitty must be seen,
>   So to the Fireworks trippingly she went;
> Such as they kindle, on the Inspection Green,
>   To show the crowd, and then the firmament
> For when the *Fourth of July's* in the socket,
> They send to its relief a blazing rocket,
>
> Needs it to tell, that Kitty then went home,
>   As other modest maids are wont to do;
> For tho' all day they gad about and roam,
>   It does not follow that they at night do so.
> Kitty reclined, fatigued upon her pillow,
>   A pensive, drooping—not a weeping willow." p. 349.

Turn these lines into plain prose, which may be done without making any sensible change in them, and every body would acknowledge them to be the dullest trash that was ever printed—what is there in the *metre* to recommend them? Do nonsense and vulgarity cease to be so, because they are aggravated by doggrel?

The other writings of Mr. Crafts preserved in this collection, are orations on various occasions, and fugitive essays, moral and sentimental, or literary and humorous.

The former, although certainly not free from blemishes of taste, are uncommonly good in their kind. We will remark in reference to these compositions, that the class to which they belong,—that, namely of demonstrative eloquence—which circumstances have made far more common in the United States than any where else, is to be treated with a more indulgent criticism than the oratory either of the bar or of the popular assembly.* As they are calculated only for a sort of holiday ceremony of parade and amusement, they are not confined to that severe and simple style which is essential to effective public speaking upon matters of business. The epithet "lyrical," happily used by the author of the "Memoir" in reference to Mr. Crafts' orations, would be quite absurd if applied in the way of compliment to the style of a debater. A fourth of July orator finds it hard enough, even with the assistance of a little poetry, and the whole artillery of tropes and figures, to say any thing that can be listened to, or deserves to be printed. And so it is of other similar occasions. But although all this is certainly true, yet we must not allow these "fancy" speakers to abuse their privileges so sadly as they have been in the habit of doing on this side of the Atlantic. We do not suppose that it would be possible in any other country under the sun, or at least in Christendom—not even excepting Spain—to make such a collection of vapid bombast and rhodomantade, blended with every vice of style for which grammar or rhetoric furnishes a name, as might easily be got up in any single city in the United States under the title of "American Eloquence." It is wonderful what a rage there is amongst us for exhibitions on the rostrum. Societies are formed, apparently, for no other purpose but to afford young gentlemen an opportunity of "coming out." What an immense accession to the stock of the national literature did the deaths of Messrs. Jefferson and Adams occasion! Nor is this to be wondered at when we consider the vast multitude of funeral orations and eulogies upon very common persons that have been published at different times, and the eagerness with which every oppor-

---

* Genus demonstrativum, (says Cicero somewhere) poëseos licentiam quodam modo viudicat. Isocrates says the same thing in still more pointed language— περι Αντιδοσεως.

tunity is laid hold of to inflict a harangue upon our beloved "friends and fellow-citizens." In short, our society resembles in this particular a Court of Equity, and almost every one you meet with, is, or has been, or may be "your orator."

Mr. Crafts composed his orations with great facility. He had quite a gift in that way, and his elocution was, for such purposes, of the very best kind. But it must be reckoned among his greatest misfortunes that this could be said of him. He was always making orations either for himself or for others, and, by the applause he was sure to excite, was encouraged in all those faults to which, whether as a man or a public speaker, he was most prone. He became as fond of conceits as the Seicentisti. What for instance can be in more wretched taste than the following paragraph from one of the orations preserved in the volume before us. "When they (videlicit, great and good men) disappear, their memory stands in the place of their presence—although cold, they still are luminous—and having gladdened us like the sun in the meridian, they yield from the night of the grave the chaste, pensive and consoling splendor of the stars." Such things are absolutely inconsistent, both with effective speaking and with fine writing, of which the only sure basis is sound, manly good sense.—*Sapere est, et principium et fons.*

We select, as specimens of Mr. Crafts' manner, the following passages, with the remarks of his biographer upon them :—

"In the year 1817, he delivered the annual address before the Phi Beta Kappa Society in Harvard College. It is true an awful weight was imposed upon him, not only by public expectation, but also by his succession to the rostrum, from which Buckminster, Dehon, and others of the same mint, had stretched out a fostering, forming, and guiding hand over the young literature of our country. The subject selected by Mr. Crafts was *the influence of moral causes over national character.* Whether it was too abstract for his image-loving mind to cope with, or he was too impatient to give it that deliberate consideration which such a subject required, it must be confessed that he did not entirely *come round it.* There are, certainly, about the composition, many marks of effort, and of a consciousness, on the part of the author, that he had much to accomplish. The paragraphs are all brilliant, and the sentences all pointed. No common talent could have been employed in its production. It was delivered in the speaker's best style. But, as he proceeded, the audience continued rather to be expecting than receiving the whole of their anticipated gratification. Neither was his subject precisely announced, nor was it clearly developed in the course of discussion. Bead after bead dropped glittering, yet unthreaded, from his hand. With much elegant common-place were mingled many valuable and beautiful reflections ; yet no stranger to William Crafts, then present, would have known of what he was capable, had it not been for his affecting, his unrivalled peroration.

"Tidings had just been received from Charleston, announcing the premature decease of Bishop Dehon, by the fever of the climate. Few names were so dear as his to the Phi Beta Kappa Society, or even to the country at large. And it was an affecting coincidence of events, which brought Mr. Crafts, his townsman, his parishioner, his friend, his associate in some of the higher gifts of genius, to proclaim the account of his death on the spot, where, but a few years before, the deceased himself had impressed every hearer with feelings of profound admiration. How vividly Mr. Crafts felt the whole interest of his position, and how happily he discharged the duty it involved, will be manifest from the following extract, which is inserted with the greater pleasure, as, for reasons above suggested, the entire oration is omitted from our selection.

"Gentlemen of the Phi Beta Kappa Society.—When, in connection with the pleasure of revisiting, after a long interval, the scenes of my boyhood, and the land of my ancestors, I contemplated the danger and difficulty of addressing this fraternity of scholars and critics, I shrunk intuitively from a feast, where the sword of Damocles was suspended over me. Political pursuits had estranged me from the path of letters; and to recal me was only to shew how far I had wandered. But I knew that I could rely on the hospitality of Massachusetts—I thought that I could rely on the hospitality of letters—and rescuing something from indolence, and something from ambition, I came, with the feelings of the prodigal son, to ask forgiveness of the Muses.

"And I wish that I had not been afflicted with a more melancholy errand. It was my misfortune to apprize his relatives of the death of one of our brethren,* who, not many years since, in this place, so much more appropriate for himself than me, addressed and delighted you. I need not name him, who was distinguished in yonder seminary for his early talents and virtues; and who employed the learning he there acquired in the service of religion, in reclaiming the sinful, in confirming the pious, in convincing the sceptical and in soothing the mourner. I need not name that pure and spotless man, whose example illustrated all the precepts he so eloquently uttered. Cut down in the midst of his days, from the object of universal love, he has become, alas! the object of universal lamentation.

"He sleeps, by his own request, under the altar where he ministered—in life, as in death, adhering to the Church. The sun shines not on his grave, nor is it wet with the morning or the evening dew. But innocence kneels upon it—purity bathes it in tears—and the recollections of the sleeping saint mingle with the praises of the living God. Oh! how dangerous it is to be eminent. The oak, whose roots descend to the world below, while its summit towers to the world above, falls with its giant branches, the victim of the storm. The osier shakes—and bends—and totters—and rises, and triumphs in obscurity. And yet, who of you would owe his safety to his insignificance?

"Beneath that living osier not an insect can escape the sun. Beneath that fallen oak the vegetable world was wont to flourish—the ivy clung around its trunk—the birds built their nests among its branches, and from its summit saw and welcomed the morning sun—the beasts fled to it for refuge from the tempest—and man himself was refreshed in its shade, and learned from its fruit the laws of nature. Oh how delightful it is to be eminent! To win the race of usefulness—to live in the beams of well-earned praise—and walk in the zodiack among the stars.

"Fame, with its perils and delights, my brothers, must be ours. Welcome its rocky precipice! Welcome its amaranthine garlands! We must wear them on our brow—we must leave them on our grave. We must, we will, fill our lives with acts of usefulness, and crown them with deeds of honor; and when we die, there will be tears on the cheek of innocence, and sighs from the bosom of virtue, and the young will wish to resemble, and the aged will lament to lose us.

* 'The Right Rev. Theodore Dehon, Bishop of the Diocess of South-Carolina.'

"No person present on that occasion can ever forget the electrical emotions produced by the delivery of these passages—particularly of the last, in which the orator's voice arose to the highest pitch of enthusiasm, while exclaiming—"We must, we will, fill our lives with acts of usefulness, and crown them with deeds of honour"—and then again sank, from one musical, sweet, and melancholy cadence to another, until it reached a murmur, which the deepening silence alone of the multitude rendered audible, as he uttered—"and when we die, there will be tears on the cheek of innocence and sighs from the bosom of virtue, and the young will wish to resemble, and the aged will lament to lose us." pp. xxxi–xxxiv.

"Having now, in so many ways, acquired the admiration of his fellow-citizens, it was in the course of only the succeeding year (1814) that, by performing a melancholy duty of friendship, he secured a still larger portion of their affections and esteem.* His "Eulogy on the Rev. James Dewar Simons" is to this day alluded to much more frequently than any of his other orations, and is regarded indeed as a kind of landmark to his reputation:—a proof of how much deeper are the impressions made upon the heart, than those upon the merely intellectual faculties. On repeatedly perusing this celebrated eulogy, we have missed discerning in it that peculiar stamp of originality and literary excellence, which we have generally held in view, as a standard in the compilation of the present volume. For much of the effect with which it was received and remembered, it must, we think, have been indebted to the nature of the occasion, to the imposing night-solemnities of the surrounding funeral scenery, and to the fond and glowing, but undoubtedly correct delineations, presented by so engaging a speaker, of a most amiable, and extensively beloved and admired young clergyman. The reflections are on the whole very obvious, and the principal interest belonging to the production is not at all of a general description. We have deemed it proper to state these reasons for omitting the performance in question, as as apology to many readers, who, we believe, were expecting its insertion. Yet in justice to them, to the author, to the subject, and to our own feelings, we cannot resist transcribing one or two impressive and characteristic extracts:—

"This is the exordium:—

"Death has been among us, my friends, and has left a melancholy chasm. He has torn his victim from the heart of society, and from the altar of the living God. He has triumphed over the blushing honours of youth, the towering flight of genius, and the sacred ardour of devotion. Virtue, philanthropy, religion are bereaved, and in tears. Death, terrible and insatiate, hath been among us, and we are met to pay him tribute.

"O thou destroyer of human hope and happiness! was there no head, frosted by time, and bowed with cares, to which thy marble pillow could have yielded rest? Was there no heart-broken sufferer to seek refuge from his woes in thy cheerless habitation? Was there no insulated being, whose crimes or miseries would have made thee welcome! who had lived without a friend, and could die without a mourner?

"These, alas, could give no celebrity to thy conquests, for they fall, unheeded as the zephyr. Thy trophies are the gathered glories of learning, the withered hopes of usefulness, the tears of sorrowing innocence, the soul-appalling cries of the widow and the orphan. Thou delightest to break our happiness into fragments, and to tear our hearts asunder. We know that thou art dreadful, and unsparing, and relent-

---

* "In this year also appeared his "Ode to Alexander," some stanzas of which immediately fastened themselves on the memory of every lover of poetry in our country."

less—else our departed friend would have continued with us. His tomb would have been where our hopes had placed it, far distant in the vale of years. Still would his manly and generous affections warm and delight the social circle—still would his pure and spotless manners invite the praise and imitation of our youth—still would he fill that sacred desk, with its appropriate virtues—still would his impressive eloquence illustrate the truths of Christianity, with the countenance of an angel, and the fervour of a saint—still would he be the assiduous servant of religion—the golden cord of connubial affection would gain strength and beauty from time—and still his children would call him father. Vain and deceitful illusion!

> "For him no more the blazing hearth shall burn,
> Nor tender consort watch with anxious care;
> No children run to lisp their sire's return,
> Nor climb his knee the envied kiss to share."

"Towards the conclusion, occurs the following passage, gliding with a certain Attic rapidity, and closely crowded with rhetorical beauties:—
"If some ingenuous youth, marking the gloom which pervades our city, should inquire, what dread calamity has damped the public feeling—why our churches are clad in mourning, 'and woman's eye is wet, man's cheek is pale'—tell him that these are the sorrows which embalm the virtuous. These are the sensibilities, which honour the living and the dead. These are the signs, which speak the bleeding heart. And if he ask, what aged benefactor of the land has fallen into the grave? What time-struck venerable head has bowed beneath the scythe of death? Tell him, the object of our mourning was a youth, like himself, who by the excellence of his disposition, and the purity of his life, had conciliated universal esteem, and had rendered essential services to the cause of religion—that his days, though short, had been full of charitable actions—that his perpetual aim was to enlighten, and reform, and save mankind—that we mourn not for him, but for ourselves. We know that he was innocent; we believe, that he is happy. We weep for the community. Tell him, this is the godlike influence of virtue; and if he would thus live, and thus die—and, if he would be thus canonized in the affections of men—let him follow the bright example of our friend—let him keep himself unspotted from the world—let him devote his talents to the service of God—let him cling around, and support the tottering edifice of religion, and the prayers of the pious shall ascend for him—he shall live in honour, and if, (which Heaven avert!) he should be thus early called from this mortal scene, the gracious drops of pity shall bedew his urn, and he, too, shall be welcomed by the angels to the mansions of eternal joy." pp. xxvii, xxx.

The "essays" which occupy much more than half of the volume, will be read with interest. Many of them are written with uncommon felicity—and all of them bear the stamp of a decided talent for that sort of composition. But they are, generally, mere fugitive pieces, very short, and evidently thrown off in haste, and without revision. When we first read them through, it was our intention to have made copious extracts from them, but, upon a second perusal, we doubt whether it would be quite fair to single out a few passages, and expose them to the severe criticism which the preference implied in such a selection is so apt to provoke. However, it may not be amiss to furnish a few specimens—merely *as specimens* of his general manner.

The following is an effusion on "Spring :"—

"It is pleasing to turn aside from the jarrings of party and political strife, to the welcome and auspicious harmony of nature. Now, when the zephyrs are fanning with their wings the fragrant air—when the birds are carolling their songs of gladness—when the green earth is putting forth its flowery perfume, and its vegetable harvest—when the painted insects of the atmosphere revel in their wonted sweets, and a smiling and a gracious sky looks down as if to bless this beautiful development of the Creator's goodness, what an opportunity of calm contemplation, and of peaceful repose, is afforded to him, who, loving as he may, with the purest philanthropy, the institutions of men, perceives with melancholy, their inevitable imperfections, and resorts for truth, and beauty, and order, to the harmonious design of the universe. Here is, indeed, a constitution that requires no amendment. Here is a theme that admits of no party dissensions. The universe, without exception, is loyal to its Maker. It obeys his mandates without murmuring—it produces and reproduces as he has ordered—it exults in the glorious livery of Heaven. And all these beautiful results, why were they designed except for the happiness of man ? All the productions of earth have been placed gratuitously within his reach, and, invested with rich and radiant forms and colours, to allure his pursuit, and to gladden his enjoyment. In these doth *Spring* abound. Welcome then, thou season of the heart, so full of the sources and the suggestions of gratitude to the Almighty, and of gratulation among mankind." pp. 234. 235.

There is quaintness, and perhaps, bad taste in the following contrast between the land and the ocean, in an essay on the "Mariner's Church," yet, both the thoughts and the language are very striking :—

"The chief attributes of the Deity, are power and goodness; and it has seemed to us that while the former is strikingly exemplified in the grand and tempestuous ocean—the latter remained to be illustrated on the firm and staple earth. Love is never the offspring of fear, and there is too much to dread in the tumults of the sea.

The ocean is bleak and destitute of fire, which is essential to life—it is fickle and tempestuous, and affords no habitation for man—its bosom is barren, and it yields no harvest—its paths are devious and obscure, and it confounds the traveller—when agitated by storms, it exhibits the Almighty in his anger, and man in the depth of humility and insignificance—when calm and serene it images to the mariner the short-lived repose of a sleeping lion, who may at any moment awake and destroy him—it is lonely and desolate, without the joys or the protection of civilized society. If, therefore, we suppose a being endued with reason, to have been conversant with the ocean only, we may well imagine him impressed with humility and awe, at the visible majesty of the divine *power*. And a belief of this is one of the elements of religion.

"The land is the theatre of the *mercies* of God, and forms an amiable counterpart. Its bosom yields us sustenance—its fields afford us fruit—its forests provide us shelter—its fleeces supply us with clothing—its cities civilize—its schools instruct—its institutions guard—and its religious temples enlighten us in the duties of this and of another life. Here is learned the science which designates the paths of the sea, and conducts the mariner in safety to distant parts of the same world ; and here are instilled the doctrines, which fit us alike for this world and the future. And if it be hospitable to throw out to the distressed mariner the signal of welcome as he approaches the borders of repose, is it not amiable and praiseworthy to hold out to his wandering spirit the signal of salvation? And if we teach him the knowledge of the stars, that he may pass the waters in safety, shall we not instruct him in the knowledge and love of Him who created the stars, and before whom they are dim?" pp. 237, 238.

There is great force and justice in the following remarks upon "Lord Byron," whose perverse conduct and licentious muse were, on more than one occasion, the subject of Mr. Crafts' reprobation. The work, to which these strictures had immediate reference, consisted of the 3d, 4th and 5th Cantos of Don Juan :

"If ever Lord Byron, in a serious, not a misanthropic mood, shall reflect on the high mental gifts and graces, with which he was favoured by Heaven, the power to discern, feel, and pourtray, in the glowing and animated colours of song, the outward mould of nature, and the more mysterious and hidden shapes of thought and passion, imprinted on the innermost heart of man—if, with the conscious possession of the moral influence which great genius exercises over mankind, and a sphere of exertion the most alluring and popular, enhanced by the further auxiliaries of birth, and rank and fortune—if aware of all these rare endowments and high responsibilities— aware too of the favour, applause and admiration which followed his efforts, and bore him at once to the throne of modern poetry, amidst the innocent chorus of youths and virgins—if Lord Byron, called now to account to his conscience and God for the use of these peculiar and honoured privileges, should search his life for an answer, what could he reply ? How shall genius, which is the heaven-sent light of truth to guide and to save, excuse itself for the voluntary extinction of its purity and fire, in the chilling and loathsome damps of error, which allows it to re-appear only for mischief and ruin ? How shall Poetry, the refined companion of the Graces and Virtues, with Honour on her brow, Inspiration in her bosom, and Immortality in her right hand—palliate her abandonment of her high destiny, and polluting intercourse with sin and infamy ! That the chaste lyre should echo the song of sensuality—and the harp, that was wont to inspire the patriot and the hero, should become the gratuitous pander of base licentiousness ! That great ability, should be evinced only in mischief—great fruitfulness, in the growth of poison—and the clear and beautiful expanse of corruption become a nauseous, slandering pool of corruption and pestilence ! These are the achievements and triumphs of Lord Byron, patronized by Heaven, only that he might abuse its favours—exalted by genius, only that he might degrade it—admired by the innocent, only that he might insult them—and blest with reputation, only that he might throw it away and trample it under foot." pp. 254, 255.

We close our extracts with the following humourous description of a certain renowned sand-bank in the neighbourhood of this city :

"The little city of Moultrieville, the *Sybaris* of the South, rapidly renews its luxurious population, and is the general resort of the indolent, and refuge of the invalid.

"As a body politic, it enjoys the most perfect leisure for experiments in government.

"It is a state subsisting without a revenue—because taxes are unnecessary ; without labour, for the soil can produce, and the inhabitants will do nothing. It is a city asleep for all the uses and purposes of life, except ease. It has no shops—no public library—no museum—no court-house— no jail—and only recently a church. You can neither buy nor sell there—

so there is no bank. There is no traffic except of cake, which gets hard, and ice, which melts in its voyage from Charleston. There are no town-meetings there, except a medley of carriages, chairs, cavalry and pedestrians, collected in the evening at the cove, to witness the departure of the sun, and of the steam-boat. There is no Custom-House—there being nothing to collect but sand, which the wind gathers and disperses. They have no press, wherein they do suffer much imposition, being compelled to swallow the absurd crudities of the Charleston prints. They have a fort where they all resort on the approach of a storm. Quere: would they do so on the approach of a battle? They have no fee-simple of the soil, their tenure being at the will of the State, and by courtesy of the air and water. It is famous for crabs that are not aquatic, and fiddlers* that make no music. They have no bell "to fright the Isle from its propriety," no watchman to disturb their slumbers, and no militia duty to annoy their leisure. There is a great scarcity of trees, so they enjoy the full benefit of the sun, and they can at any moment be flooded, if they wish to make salt. It is a bad place for horses who cannot digest its sand—equally so for cows, salt marsh having a tendency to produce salt milk. Pigs used to thrive there, it is said, until they were deprived of the freedom of the city.

"An hour's idleness may obtain you a curlew, and, having blistered your fingers, you may catch a sheephead. The Island air rusts metals, destroys shoe leather, and inspires verse-making. It is not the ocean air, nor the land air, but a mixture of both, and not so good as either. It is of doubtful benefit to the lungs, but has a good effect upon the appetite, and is an excellent specific against the yellow fever. The Island itself is known in history, and will long remain so. Moultrieville can give a reason for its name, which is generally not an easy matter. It was derived from the intrepid valor of Moultrie and his associates, who, in the morning of the revolution, on that spot, defeated the British invading squadron, thinking that, barren as it was, it was too good for the enemy." pp. 297–299.

We here close our observations upon the character and writings of Mr. Crafts. We have discharged our duty, we trust, with candor and fairness. Where we thought his example calculated to do harm, we have spoken with the freedom, and even the severity of criticism; but none, we are persuaded, entertain a higher opinion than we do of his natural endowments, and the gentleness and kindness of his disposition, or are less inclined to dwell upon recollections which charity should bury him with in the grave. We will add, that the very laudable object which has mainly induced his friends to publish this little volume, can scarcely fail to secure for it the patronage of the public.

[Hoc decus, [historiæ renovandæ] ut decebat, qui primi amiserant, patriæ suæ restituere aggressi Itali, Leon. Aretinus, Bembus, Sigonius, Folieta, et alii, stimulosque et faces subjecernut aliis gentibus, ne hac laude sua cujusque patria careret, et certatim ex monumentis, pulvere et situ obsitis, tantam materiem congessere, ut ex illa bene disposita et decore ornata opus aliquod perfectum extrueretur: Galli quoque Paullum Æmilium, Ferronum, Thuanum: Hispani Osorium et Suritam, jactare audent: neque nos Belgæ, licet parum acuti et ingeniosi reliquis nationibus videamur, hac laude studionum ita deficimur, ut non magna nomina Junios, Douzas, Grotios, Emmios, Pontanos et plures ostentare possimus,

---

*A small animal of the Crab kind.

qui per vestigia veterum decurrentes ingenti beneficio patriam et pos
teritatem devinxerunt: Britanniæ vero, etsi semper insigni proventu-
virorum ingenio et eruditione, præstantium floruit, nescio tamen qua sor-
tis malignitate acciderit, ut ad Latini sermonis elegantiam, et dictionis
nitorem tam pauci, si cum aliis gentium eruditis componantur, aspiraverint.
Guilielmum quidem Camdenum inter Historicos suos, principe loco collo-
care solent; neque nos intercedimus, quin egregiis ornatum dotibus et
doctrina non vulgari et bonarum artium studiis eruditum ostentent; sed
nemo tamen eum ad elegans illud et accuratum scribendi genus acces-
sisse, aut ulla in parte cum Italis, Gallis aut Belgis comparari posse,
adfirmare audebit. Singulare enim est, et quod a multis observatum
memini, Latinæ linguæ cultum numquam ita fuisse inter Britannos cele-
bratum, ut non modo solutæ et liberæ orationis laude non potuerint super
alios eminere, sed nullos etiam hanc insulam, vel certe paucos, protulisse,
qui Poëtices et culti carminis gloria quæ tot Italos, Gallos et Belgas
decoravit conspicerentur; sive id patriæ linguæ pervicax et nimia medi-
tatio, sive singularis quædam indoles et populi habitus, sive multum ab
aliis discrepans scholarum et Academiarum, antiquæ adhuc et exoletæ
disciplinæ pertinaciter inhærentium, conditio eos in diversa abstulerit;
sive denique occulta quædam ratio et vis gentem, aliis in rebus multo
feliciorem, hac sola gloria ceteris inferiorem esse voluerit. &c.—*Burman's
Preface to Buchanan.*]

TRAVELS OF THE DUKE OF SAXE-WEIMAR.

Travels through North-America, during the years 1825 and 1826. By his Highness, BERNHARD, Duke of Saxe-Weimar Eisenach. 2 vols. 8vo. *Philadelphia.*

IT is impossible to read this book without being charmed with
the *bonhommie* and simplicity of "His Highness, Bernhard,
Duke of Saxe-Weimar Eisenach." At the first glance, indeed,
we were so much struck with these qualities, as to be forcibly
reminded of the inimitable epistles of Mrs. Letitia Ramsbottom
to Mr. Bull. We shall, perhaps, have occasion to exemplify
this resemblance in the course of our subsequent remarks; indeed, we were at first disposed to make a collection of the most
notable things in this kind under the title of "Weimariana,"
which, we are persuaded, would have been quite equal, as a
specimen of gossiping *naiveté,* to any thing the language affords.
Whatever inclination, however, to raillery or ridicule this extreme simplicity may occasionally have excited in us has been
repressed or mitigated by the esteem, we might even say the
affectionate regard, with which the native amiableness and candor, the truly catholic charity, that pervade the whole work,
have inspired us.

The form, which the Duke has adopted, is the simple one of
a journal or diary. He assures us in his preface doubtless, with
more truth than is usual in such cases that "it was by no means
originally designed for publication. I wrote it (he continues)
during my travels, partly to recal past incidents at a future period, partly to give with more ease and certainty information
to my much honoured parents, my relatives and friends, on any
subject on which inquiry might be made. After his return the
book was read by several persons," who, the reader may be
sure, insisted upon its publication so strenuously, that his Highness found it quite impossible to resist their solicitations, especially after he had had the good fortune to meet with a certain
councellor Luden, a person, in every respect well qualified to be
the editor of the precious manuscript. Great exceptions, as we
perceive from some of our daily journals, have been taken to
this simplicity in the form of the work—but we are by no
means sure that they are well founded. This is the age of dissertation; every thing runs out into prosing common-place, and

takes the shape of a scholastic diatribe. A history, written after the manner of Thucydides or Xenophon, does not suit us; we must have, not a mere narrative of facts, with such a development of their causes as may be necessary to a proper understanding of the events recorded, but withal ponderous disquisitions about political economy and national wealth, excursions on the march of intellect, and the state of letters and science, &c. And this confounding of two things, or rather of many things, as distinct as possible in their nature, is what we call "philosophical history." So it is with biography. The life of an individual of any consequence is sure to present a succinct view, in two or three volumes, at least, of every thing connected with the history of the period during which he flourished, and perhaps, of some centuries before his birth. Books of travels, too, have followed the same fashion—nothing will do but "Classical Tours," and we are disappointed if our itinerant philosophers do not take occasion, in the course of their peregrinations, to empty their common-place books of the hoarded results of years of study and research. Certainly, if our ideas are formed upon such models, the modest journal of his Highness, Duke Bernhard of Saxe-Weimar, by no means comes up to them. He indulges very little in speculation. He favours his readers with no fine-spun theories and no high-flown rhetoric. He gives his evidence with all possible simplicity, brevity and caution. He tells just what he saw and heard himself—very rarely what he heard of—and then, generally, puts us upon our guard by apprising us that it is hearsay. If all this wariness and moderation have not saved him from many blunders, we may judge how little confidence is to be reposed in the more specious elaborate works of those who substitute their own random speculations for facts, and build their conclusions upon the loosest *on dits*, as confidently as if they were demonstrative evidence. It is true, a traveller passing rapidly through a country may and must often be deceived by first appearances—but such errors can seldom be so gross and extravagant as those into which fancy or rumour so often betrays less cautious tourists—especially where, as in the present instance, the writer has the candor to advertise us that he pretends to do nothing more than to cast a hasty glance over the surface of things.

We confess it was with no little curiosity that we took up this book. It was enough to excite our interest in it, that the writer was a German, and a man of very high rank. We were anxious to see what impression our young country, our republican institutions and simple manners had made upon a mind accustomed to a state of society, in every point of view so different. To such a man, a visit to this new world, of which so little that can be depended on has been heard in Europe, must reveal almost as

strange things, as Voltaire's inhabitant of Saturn saw, when he
came down to our little planet. The *naiveté* with which, as we
have already remarked, Duke Bernhard lets his wonder escape
him on all occasions, enhances very much the interest excited
by such a situation. The other circumstance, however, of his
being a German, was still more important. The Germans are,
of all nations that ever existed, the fairest in their criticisms
upon others. Their studies are too enlarged for bigotry, and
excessive nationality has never, we believe, been numbered
among their faults. This remark is strikingly exemplified in
their literary opinions. The glowing admiration, the profoundness and originality, with which they have studied and illustrated the beauties of Greek literature, and defended those
immortal master-pieces against the flippant ignorance of the
Parisian wits, will at once occur to every one versed in such
subjects. If any other instance were necessary, it would be found
in their intimate knowledge and just appreciation of the English
and Spanish classics, and, especially in the homage they were
the first among strangers to offer up to the genius of Shakspeare
and of Calderon. To us, peculiarly situated as we are, to be by
a foreigner looked at with any thing like impartiality seemed
rather to be desired than expected. In the very nature of things
no country needs so many allowances to be made for any imperfections in its manners and institutions, as one actually engaged
in felling its forests, laying out towns, and providing itself with
the necessaries of life—yet none has been treated with less indulgence. Our visitors have distanced Smelfungus in absurd
petulance and querulousness. Nothing but absolute impossibilities
could satisfy them. They have exacted of youth the maturity
of age; of poverty, the splendour and magnificence of hereditary wealth. They have been offended with the spirit of equality
under a democratic government, and (*negabitis posteri*) have
lost all patience with the constitution of a great nation, because
the servants of New-York and Boston insist upon, being treated
and addressed as "helps!" The majority, it is true, of these
illuminati, have been vulgar cits and adventurers of no character;
travellers of the Cockney school ! It must be admitted that the
things, published of us by the Fauxs and the Fearons, were
precisely such as might have been expected from writers of that
stamp, and we have been sometimes amused at the wrath which
condescended to break such insects upon the wheel. But we
have had some, and even much reason to complain of the treatment we have received from other and higher quarters. Things
appear to have lately taken a different turn ; still it will be a long
time before we can expect perfect justice—not to speak of favour
and indulgence—from British writers of any class. Naturally
regarding the standard set up in England, as the only right one

for all the forms and institutions of society—where society is, in its general character, English—they can scarcely fail to condemn every deviation from it as *ipso facto* an imperfection, without giving themselves the trouble of inquiring how far it is rendered necessary or fitting by the circumstances of the country, or other the like causes. A striking instance of this proneness so to consider every thing on this side of the Atlantic, which is not in vogue on the other, is furnished by what are called "*Americanisms*" in language. The fact is that most of the peculiarities, noted as such, are to be found in the older English authors, and even in common use at this day among certain classes of society in England, but, as they have been generally disused there by literary men, it is hastily taken for granted that they had no place in the vocabulary which the first settlers brought hither with them, but are arbitrary and uncalled for innovations of a later period.

But to our story. On the 4th of April, 1825, Duke Bernhard of Saxe Weimar set out from Ghent to Antwerp, on his way to Hellevoetsluis, where he was to embark in the corvette Pallas, for the United States. Our readers will be happy to learn that this vessel was furnished him by his government, and provided with every thing necessary to the comfort of his Highness, who was established in the captain's cabin, and had a cot suspended at night for his sleeping place." After a short "sojourn" at Hellevoetsluis this distinguished traveller crossed the channel, and having visited in England, Portsmouth, Plymouth, Falmouth, &c., was again at sea, on the 18th of June, on his way to Boston, where he arrived on the 26th of July. Nothing, it seems, of any great importance occurred, during this voyage, except it were the loss of a midshipman overboard, and the administering of relief to the American ship Schuylkill, in distress for water and provisions. But its consummation was hailed with all the rapture befitting so memorable an event, and perhaps, since the first arrival of Columbus, the shores of the western world have never been approached with equal joy. The following very circumstantial and glowing description can scarcely fail to be interesting to the sentimental reader.

"It was ten o'clock on the morning of the 26th July, when I first placed my foot in America—*upon a broad piece of granite!* It is impossible to describe what I felt at that instant. Heretofore, but two moments of my life had left a delightful remembrance—the first was, when, at seventeen years of age, I received the cross of the Legion of Honour after the battle of Wagram—the second, when my son William was born. My landing in America, that country, which, from my earliest youth, had been the object of my warmest wishes, will, throughout life *remain* a subject of pleasing recollection!"

The thrilling effects of the broad piece of granite were not yet

over, before his Highness established himself at the Exchange
Coffee-house, kept, we are informed, by a man who had been
"a volunteer colonel in the last war, and who, according to the
custom of the country, still retained his old title, without feeling
himself above his present business.   Here he found himself in
excellent quarters, and soon began to experience those polite
and hospitable attentions for which our good friends in Boston
are so justly renowned.   "He had imagined that no one would
take the least notice of him in America."   We are not informed how he came to conceive this extravagant notion, but it gives
us great pleasure to state, in his own words, that "he soon found
himself agreeably disappointed."   In the truly refined, because
enlightened and literary society of Boston, he could not fail to
pass his time very pleasantly, and we are favored with a sufficiently minute account of the principal objects of curiosity in
and about the capital.*   We must not omit some things that
seem to have made a particular impression upon the mind of the
Duke.   Thus, he gave the attendant, who conducted him, two
dollars, and he was so much gratified by this surpassing generosity, that when they were in the chapel, the cunning fellow
"whispered to the organist, who immediately played God save
the King"—at the which, his Highness "was much surprised"—
though we own we are not.   With Mr. Quincy, the Mayor, he
visited the public schools, and thus expressed his approbation of
them; it is a fair specimen of that philanthropic spirit which
breathes through the whole work, and imparts to it a secret
charm in the midst of many blemishes and defects.

"I was pleased both with the kind manners of the teachers and the modest, correct and easy deportment of the scholars.   The boys generally had
handsome faces, and were all of an animated phisiognomy.   With this
they combine, as I was *frequently* convinced, the greatest respect for their
parents and teachers.   It appears to me impossible that young people who
receive so liberal an education, can grow up to be bad or malicious men.
I was indeed affected when I left the schools, and could not but congratu-
late Mr. Quincy, from the bottom of my heart, on such a rising generation.
Capt. Ryk, who accompanied us, participated in my views and feelings."

The Duke and his companion, Mr. Tromp, left the hospitable city of Boston, with grateful hearts, on the ninth of August,

" * The society, especially *when ladies are not* [?] *present*, is uncommonly fine
and lively; both sexes are very well educated and accomplished.   So much care
is bestowed upon the education of the female sex, that it would perhaps be considered in other countries as superfluous.   Young ladies even learn Latin and
Greek, but then they can also speak of other things besides fashions and tea-table
subjects; thus, for instance, I was at a party of Mrs. General Humphreys, which
was entirely in the European style, without cards, dancing, or music, and yet it
was lively and agreeable.   Many of those gentlemen, who are met with in such society, have travelled in Europe, sometimes accompanied by their ladies : Europeans are frequently present, and thus there is no want of materials for conversation.   The generality of the houses, moreover, offer something attractive in the
fine arts," &c. p. 50.

in the mail-coach (of which he does not fail to give an accurate description) for Albany, by way of Worcester and Northampton. This journey was not without its perils. They crossed several *small* rivers and rivulets, on wooden bridges, which are very slight, though they are built with a great waste of timber. The planks [horresco referens] are not even nailed upon the beams, so that his Highness began to be somewhat fearful, especially as the carriage drove rapidly over. This was not all ; for they were overtaken by a *"considerable* thunder storm"—and about a mile from Northampton they had to pass the Connecticut river, five hundred yards wide, in a small ferry-boat, "which as the night had already set in, was not very agreeable." And what was, if possible, worse than all this, they left Northampton to visit the government armory at Springfield, "under the most oppressive heat, with *five* ladies and two gentlemen in the stage-coach, into which they were crowded *somewhat* like those that were shut up in the Trojan horse." He would fain have deviated from his route fourteen miles for the purpose of visiting New Lebanon, but, a person from whom he wished to hire a carriage being "so extortionate as to ask ten dollars," he determined, as he expresses it, "in order to avoid a new Yankee trick, to prosecute his journey in the stage-coach directly for Albany," where, in due season, he arrived and took lodgings at Cruttenden's.

From Albany the Duke went to the Falls of Niagara, and down the St. Lawrence as far as Quebec. A part of the journey to the Falls was performed in a canal packet-boat. The following description shows that his Highness was not perfectly at his ease in that new situation.

"The day was intolerably warm, and our company was very numerous. I confined myself to writing the whole day as much as possible, but in consequence of the heat, I could not avoid sleeping. In the evening, we fortunately had a thunder storm, which cooled the air. During the night, as there was a want of births, the beds were placed upon benches, and as I was the tallest person, mine was put in the centre upon the longest bench, with a chair as a supplement. It had the appearance of a hereditary sepulchre, in the centre of which I lay as father of the family. I spent an uncomfortable night on account of my constrained posture, the insects which annoyed me, and the steersman, who always played an agreeable tune upon his bugle, whenever he approached a lock."

We are next favored with an account of their manner of living on board these boats, the behavior of the guests at table, the furniture, &c. Every one must help himself as he can—there are no napkins—and except the spoons, no silver on the table. The forks, it seems, have two prongs, and their handles, like those of the knives, are of buck's horn. His Highness thinks it, as it no doubt is, an excellent rule that no one, on departing, is bound to give money to the servants. p. 66.

In the further prosecution of this journey, we need scarcely

say that many very remarkable things, besides the most stupendous of cataracts presented themselves to our curious traveller.
At a village called Manlius, for instance, he met with a farmer,
the descendant of a German emigrant, who spoke the language
used in Germany about a hundred years ago, and who thought
the Duke's German too high. (p. 68.) At Waterloo, he saw at
the tavern "a large, beautiful young eagle which had been caught
in his nest and tamed." (p. 69) He also witnessed an amusing
military spectacle. "It consisted of a militia parade consisting
of thirty men, including seven officers and two cornets. They
were formed like a batallion, into six divisions, and performed a
number of manœuvres. The *members* were not all provided
with muskets, but had ramrods instead. Only the officers and
the rifle company, four men strong, were in uniform. The band
consisted of sixteen men, and was commanded by an officer
with a colonel's epaulettes and a drawn sword!" Nor must we
forget to mention a circumstance of so rare a charrcter that we
doubt very much whether it be possible to find a parallel to it,
except in the well-known adventure of the fulling-mill in
Don Quixotte. The Tonnawanta creek runs through a dense
and beautiful forest, which had never been violated by the axe,
until a few trees were cut down on its borders to make place for
a tow-path. The Duke sat in the bow of the boat during the
whole of the passage. Every thing inclines the traveller to pensiveness and meditation. "Nothing interrupted the solemn silence——except—the *chattering of the boatmen's teeth,* who
are often severely afflicted, in this unhealthy part of the country,
with intermittent fevers."

The passage down the St. Lawrence appears to have been one
of the most interesting parts of this tour. The rapids are descended in batteaux or Durham-boats, which are small, flat vessels of about forty tons, have but a half-deck, and draw eighteen
inches of water. The Duke embarked in one of these, which,
by a very singular coincidence, happened to be called "the Flying Dutchman." His fellow passengers are worthy of notice.
"They were, principally, of the lower class of comedians, who
spoke bad French, somewhat like the Walloon." There was
also a personage of a more remarkable description; to wit: "a
lively, young, black bear, three months old, on board." p. 85.

The following description of a scene, on the St. Lawrence, is
executed in a more ambitious style than is usual with the Duke.

"Our captain had businesss at the custom-house: he stopped, therefore,
for an hour, during which I had time to look at the fort; after which, we
continued our course in a strong wind, which was brought on by a thunder
storm. The shores and islands of the river are generally covered with
cedar trees, and amongst them we discovered some neat houses and
churches, with bright tin roofs. At the village of Coteau des Cedres, we
were obliged to encounter the last and most dangerous rapid, called the

Cascades. The waves were uncommonly high, and our vessel passed over the dangerous parts with incredible velocity. Along these rapids, there is also a canal, provided with locks and intended to facilitate the ascent of vessels. If these rapids are viewed from the shore, it appears incredible that a canoe should venture in without being swallowed up. Such a misfortune, however, does not happen, as we had just proved. Below this rapid, the river, where it receives the Ottawa, again spreads out so as to form another lake called Lac St. Louis. North of this lake, and at the place where the Ottawa unites with the St. Lawrence, it forms another lake, Lac des deux Montagnes, which is separated from Lac St. Louis by three islands, called Jesus, Perrot and Montreal. The thunder storm passed close by us; the wind blew *heavy*, but favorably. We met a steamboat, having a corpse on board, and her flag at half-mast! this was a bad omen!!—Another steam-boat got ahead of us as we were passing towards La Chine, and excited our desire to sail faster; but suddenly we saw a terrible storm approaching. In an instant, every hand was endeavoring to take down the sails, and the small one was fortunately drawn in before the *arrival* of the squall, but the large once, in consequence of its bad cordage, was only half way down when it struck us. Near us we observed a sound, with a dangerous cliff which it was necessary to avoid by steering to the left; but we were driven directly towards it. Six men could scarcely manage the helm. Half of the sail floated in the water, and our destruction appeared inevitable. No one knew who commanded; the sailors thought themselves better qualified than the captain, and every thing was hurry and confusion. I deemed it best to remain silent, and commit myself to Providence, who guides the destinies of man. At length, a sailor climbed the mast and cut the cord, so that the sail could be taken down, by which time we had fortunately passed the sound. The storm also, which altogether did not last more than *five* minutes, began to abate, &c. Immediately after the storm, during which it had rained, we observed a remarkable phenomenon, viz. a fall of white-winged insects, of which a great quantity fell upon our boat. It continued during five minutes. These insects had, in all probability, been driven from the neighboring forests," &c. p. 87.

Notwithstanding the dreadful omen of the corpse, and the dangers which followed it so speedily, our traveller arrived safe and sound, and was rewarded for his courage and perseverance, by the many curious things he saw at Montreal and in its vicinity. Among others, as a military man, he was particularly struck at the parade, with a new mode of making ready. "At the command 'ready,' the soldiers levelled their muskets, cocked them in this position; at the command 'fire' they brought them slowly to their cheeks." p. 89. The following remark is quite just, and cannot but be acceptable to Americans:

"Generally speaking, the towns in Canada bear a very poor comparison with those of the United States, and will never arrive at the same point, because the settlers in Canada are mostly poor Scotchmen and Irishmen, who come out at the expense of the government; they receive land, and are oppressed by the feudal system, which opposes all prosperity: emigrants, however, who possess some property and have an ambitious spirit, settle themselves in the United States, where nobody is oppressed; on the contrary, where all laws are in their favor." p. 96.

We extract the following account of "the Shakers," for the

benefit of such of our readers as may not be acquainted with the history and principles of that singular sect:

"The Shakers are a religious sect originally from England: it was founded by Anne Lee, the daughter of a Manchester blacksmith, and wife of the blacksmith Stanley, of the same place. Her chief doctrines are community of goods, a perfect continence with regard to the sexes, and adoration of the Deity by dancing. Anne Lee pretended to higher inspiration, performed miracles, announced the speedy re-appearance of Christ on earth, spoke of the Millennium, and of similar glories. She commenced in England by making proselytes among the lowest classes, who followed her when she preached in public, held noisy prayer, or rather dancing meetings, and thus disturbed the public peace. This worthy prophetess was, therefore, with her friends, at different times imprisoned; the impatient and unbelieving public even began once to stone her. The good soul, whose convulsions were said by the wicked world to be the effect of ardent spirits, wandered, therefore, in 1774, with her family and several of her friends, to New-York, where she settled. But her husband was wearied with the sisterly connection in which he lived with her, and resolved to divorce his sisterly wife and marry another. Whereupon, the repudiated wife wandered towards Albany, settled first at Watervliet, and held meetings. These meetings, however, appeared to the Americans so suspicious, (it was during the time of the revolution) that the good lady was arrested at Albany, with several of her friends, and transported to the neighborhood of New-York, in order to give her in charge to the English, who then held the city. But she soon returned again to Watervliet, and her faithful adherents bought land near Niskayuna, between Albany and Schenectady, and settled there. A large part of this people, those particularly who had joined the sect in America, founded the colony of New-Lebanon. Anne Lee died in Niskayuna in 1784. The colony numbers about six hundred members, who are divided into families, some of which contain about one hundred individuals of both sexes. Each lives in a groupe of houses, with an elder at its head. The elders of all the families form a council, which watches for the public good. They have for divine service, a sort of preachers, two of each sex, who hold forth on Sundays. The greatest cleanliness prevails in the houses, equalled perhaps, only by the hospital of Boston; the brethren live on one side, and the sisters on the other. They have a common eating-room, in which again, each sect has its own side, but different working places. Both the brethren and the sisters live, generally, two in a room, and two also sleep in the same bed. Many of the sisters, however, notwithstanding their good food, were pale and wan.

"When a family wishes to join the Shakers, the relation of brother and sister must immediately take place between husband and wife. The children are then brought up on Shaker principles. Orphans also find a home with them; still, however, unfavourable reports are circulated about the origin of these orphans. Of course, if the principles of these people should prevail, which, however, may Heaven prevent! the world would soon be depopulated. In countries, however, with too great a population, it might, perhaps, be of service to receive missionaries of this sect and promote proselytism." [We hope Mr. Malthus will profit by this hint.]
*   *   *   *   *   *

"They pay also much attention to the breeding of cattle; make good butter, and particularly good cheese, great quantities of which they sell. Their hogs are remarkably handsome, and cleanliness is also extended to them. It is a rare pleasure to walk about in a Shaker pig-stye." pp. 107–108.

Of the servants in the city of New-York, the Duke remarks that—

"They are generally negroes and mulattoes; most of the white servants are Irish: the Americans have a great abhorrence of servitude. Liveries are not to be seen; the male servants wear frock-coats. All the families complain of bad servants and their impudence, because the latter consider themselves on an equality with their employers. Of this insolence of servants, I saw daily examples. Negroes and mulattoes are abundant here, but they generally rank low and are labourers. There are but few slaves in the State of New-York, and even these are to be freed in the year 1827, according to the law passed by the Senate [?] of the State. There are public schools established for the instruction of coloured children, and I was told that these little ape-like creatures do sometimes learn very well. In the city there are several churches belonging to the coloured population; most of them are Methodists, some Episcopalians. A black minister, who was educated in an Episcopalian seminary, is said to be a good preacher. But there is, in this country, a great abhorrence of this class of people, who are obliged to live almost like the Indian Parias." p. 126.

With Philadelphia, and other towns in Pennsylvania, especially Bethlehem, the Duke seems to have been particularly pleased. He was received with the greatest kindness and civility by the literary society of the metropolis, and mentions, with high commendation, the "Wistar Party", a small circle of Savans, which owes its existance to the late Dr. Wistar. His translator, however, is exceedingly dissatisfied with the Duke's taste in painting, and sets him down for but an indifferenr virtuoso, because he does not fall into ecstasies at Mr. West's "Christ healing the Sick." It must be admitted, that if his not admiring our American collections is to be taken as conclusive against the judgment of his Highness, he is any thing but a connoisseur, for his opinion of them is not at all flattering. (pp. 122–140–146–177, v. i. and 179, v. ii.) But without pretending to much skill in such matters ourselves—although we have surveyed, and attentively too, the master-pieces of some of the greatest artists—we may be allowed to "hesitate" assent to the Duke's estimate of our pretentions to virtù. We are as ready as other people, to boast of the talent of some of our native artists, and South-Carolina has produced more than one painter, who wanted only the opportunities and encouragement of a great European capital, to have been as celebrated as her Allston. But certainly, as a nation, we have made scarcely any progress in such things. More ought not to be expected of us by others—we ought not to pretend to it ourselves. We have hitherto had neither the time, nor the money, nor the taste necessary to the cultivation of the Fine Arts with success—at least, to any considerable extent.

On the subject of prison discipline, to which the people of Philadelphia have paid so much attention, the Duke makes some sensible observations. We submit the following to our readers:

"I do not now wish to enter upon the question whether it is advisable to abolish capital punishment altogether or not, but I maintain that this solitary confinement, in which the prisoner is prohibited from all human converse, without work, exercise, and almost without air, is even worse than punishment by death. From want of exercise, they will certainly become sickly; from the want of work, they will become unaccustomed to labour, and, perhaps, lose what skill they may have possessed heretofore in their trade, so that when restored to the world, they will be useless for any kind of business, and merely drag out a miserable existence. No book is allowed them but the bible. It appears therefore to me perfectly possible, that this insulation of the prisoner will be injurious to his mind, and drive him to fanaticism, enthusiasm, and even derangement. When Mr. Vaux asked my opinion of this prison, I could not refrain from answering him that it reminded me of the Spanish Inquisition, as is described by Llorente. Mr. Vaux answered, that it was only an experiment to ascertain whether capital punishment can be abolished, but, notwithstanding this philanthropic view, the experiment appears to me to be an expensive one, because the building has already cost three hundred and fifty thousand dollars, and the State of Pennsylvania will have to expend annually for its support an immense sum. The first great object of a government ought to be to provide for the welfare of its good citizens, and not to oppress them with taxes: on the contrary, to relieve them as much as possible, as it is hard for the good citizens to have to maintain vagabonds for the sake of deterring others by example, or to render convicts harmless. In this view, it ought to be the object of governments, to arrange the prisons, so that convicts can maintain themselves," &c. p. 145.

In Washington, the Duke attended a ball, given by General Brown, on which occasion, he pays the following high tribute to the officers of our little army:

"There is scarcely an army in Europe in which the corps of officers is better composed, than in the small American army; since, in the United States no one can on any account be an officer, if he *is* not well-educated. The officers, are exclusively taken from the Military Academy at West-Point, no subaltern officer is promoted. The greater part of the inferior officers who were advanced during the late war, have been dismissed. Such a measure is in this country unavoidably necessary, where none but people of the lowest class enlist as soldiers in the army; without such an interval between the officers and the rank and file, discipline could not be maintained. Therefore, if a young man is seen in the uniform of an American officer, it may with confidence be inferred, that he is in every respect fit to maintain his place in the best society." p. 180.

In his journey through Virginia, our traveller visited Mr. Jefferson, with whom, however, he does not appear to have been as much struck as he had been with the late Mr. Adams. The Natural Bridge he pronounces "one of the greatest wonders of nature he ever beheld"—albeit he had seen "Vesuvius and the Phlegrean Fields, the Giant's Causeway in Ireland, the Island of Staffa, and the Falls of Niagara." "Finally," (to use a favourite mode of expression of his own) he is amazed at the profusion of militia titles in Virginia, which almost persuaded him that he was at the head-quarters of a grand army, and at the aristocratic notions of some of the gentlemen in the same state, who make no secret of their taste for primogeniture laws and hereditary nobility.

He passed through North-Carolina too rapidly to do anything like justice to the many remarkable things which that respectable state has to boast of. Accordingly, his observations are principally confined to the inns where he stopped, the roads over which he travelled, and the mere exterior of the towns and villages which the stage-coach traverses in its route. He is of opinion, from what he saw in that region, that "it would be a good speculation to establish a glass manufactory in a country, where there is such a want of glass, and a superabundance of pine trees and sand." It had almost escaped us, that he here for the first time made the acquaintance of a "great many large vultures, called buzzards, the shooting of which is prohibited, as they feed upon carrion, and contribute in this manner to the salubrity of the country." This "parlous wild-fowl"* has the honor to attract the attention of his Highness again at Charleston, where he informs us that its life is, in like manner, protected by law, and where it is called from its resemblance to another bird, the turkey-buzzard.

He at length arrives at Columbia, viâ Camden, and takes lodgings at our friend Clarke's, whose style of entertainment he pronounces "merely tolerable." We venture to predict that, if he revisit "mine host" in his new establishment, he will make him the amende honorable, and suppress this offensive passage in all his future editions. In Columbia, he became acquainted with most of the distinguished inhabitants, of whose very kind attentions to him he speaks in high terms. The following good-natured hint too may not be altogether useless: "At Professor Henry's a very agreeable society assembled at dinner. At that party I observed a singular manner which is practised; the ladies sit down by themselves at one of the corners of the table. But I broke the old custom, and glided between them: and no one's appetite was injured thereby." Perhaps, a traveller, so remarkable for the precision and circumstantiality of his narratives, may consider it not unimportant in us to notice several minute errors into which he has fallen, in his account of things in South-Carolina. 1. Columbia—It contains instead of four hundred inhabitants, almost as many thousands. 2. Judge De Saussure's father was not a native of Lausanne, nor uncle of the celebrated naturalist. It was his grandfather, we believe, who emigrated to this country from Geneva. 3. Colonel Blanding is not his

[* Polydore Virgil as to *ravens*; and in England.]

step-son, but his son-in-law. 4. The name of the President of the Senate is not Johns, but I'On. The last two errors, we suspect, ought to be imputed to the translator. 5. Mr. Herbemont never was Professor of Botany in the South-Carolina College, nor is any such professorship known there. 6. The mill of Mr. Lucas, in one of the suburbs of Charleston, was not by any means, the first ever built in Carolina. His Highness also does great injustice to the motives of the Professor of Astronomy, who neglected to introduce him into the Observatory, as well as the College Library, which contains (for this country) a very good and choice collection of books, particularly, a very complete series of Greek and Roman classics of the very best editions.

The Duke visited Charleston in December, and staid here but a short time. His observations upon our city are few and general.

The second volume, which contains the tour from Charleston to New-Orleans, and thence up the Mississippi and the Ohio, back to New-York, is, we think, more interesting than the first. It is characterized by the same amusing simplicity of style, and the same benevolent and amiable temper. We must except, however, out of this remark, his opinions concerning Georgia, which appear to us as extraordinary as they are unjust. We suspect he had imbibed these notions in more northern latitudes, where, for certain reasons, the name of our southern sister was then becoming particularly odious to those who exercised a control over public opinion. Governor Troup, who is alluded to in no very respectful terms by his Highness, has no reason to regret the part which he acted in that memorable controversy. We believe, if ever a *questio vexata,* of some difficulty and most disagreeable character was settled by the concurrence of all candid minds, in favor of the injured party, that controversy was such a one; and just in proportion to the calumny and dishonor which were heaped upon the meritorious individual referred to, during the contest, ought to be the glory of his triumph, and the gratitude of those whom he served so faithfully and firmly.*

Nothing, in truth, can be a stronger exemplification of the difficulties under which a stranger labors, in his efforts to acquire a knowledge of a country new to him, than the perpetual mistakes which our distinguished traveller commits in his brief notices of Georgia. With the best intentions, he appears to labor under constant error, often the result of previous misinformation or misapprehension. Hence, Savannah, one of the most beautifully laid out, and one of the best built cities for its size in the

* The Duke, would, probably, apply to Governor Troup a maxim, which he elsewhere quotes, "Fortuna *audacibus* juvat." Latin, we apprehend, that would scarcely pass muster at Gottingen or Weimar, v. ii. p. 47.

United States, one increasing and destined to increase in commerce, wealth, and all their concomitant advantages, was considered not worthy of his notice. Even the complexion of the people of Georgia displeased him, and, coming from a Court where French was not only the fashionable but the common language of social intercourse, he considers the education of women neglected, because they are not taught that language in situations where they might never have occasion to use it.

We shall not pursue his narrative any further, we have given extracts and remarks sufficient to indicate the general merits of the work.

Upon the whole, with all its twaddle and occasional *niaiserie* this book will convey some knowledge to Europeans, and should give some pleasure to Americans. For the author himself, it is impossible to entertain any other sentiments than those of the highest esteem.

Upon the general merits of the translation, we have no opinion to give. But we suggest to the publisher that it would be just as well in a future edition to use "drunk" instead of "drank," for the participle of "drink"—to distinguish between "sit" and "set" and "lie" and "lay"—to omit "on" before "next day," and not to speak of persons "assembled *to* a ball." p. 209, &c.

THE DISOWNED.

1. The Disowned. By the Author of "Pelham." 2 vols. 12mo. *New-York*. 1829.

2. Tales of the Great St. Bernard. By the Author of "Salathiel." 2 vols. 12mo. *Philadelphia.* 1829.

"PELHAM" might, perhaps, be said to belong in some sort, to a class of novels, which, for want of a better appellation we shall designate as the Beau-Brummel School. Their professed object is to hold the mirror up—not to nature—but to what, according to their representation of it, is the very reverse of nature, viz. English fashionable life. They purport to be a revelation of its esoteric rites and of its most sacred mysteries—to paint it in all the extravagance and exaggeration of its follies and impertinences—in its grotesque mixture of aristocratic hauteur and voluntary self-abasement, of an ambitious meanness and cringing insolence—in its absurd affectations, its slavish etiquette, its studied trifling, its pompous inanity, its disgusting pretension, its heartlessness, recklessness, apathy and *ennui*. We have not the means of judging how far these pictures which have so much the appearance of travesty and caricatures, are to be relied on. We verily believe, however, that—whatever may be the state of the fact as to this—at no other period in the history of polished society, could such stupid extravagances—such vapid and coxcombical imbecility, (mainly, it would seem too, on the strength of the impudence with which they are accompanied) be palmed upon the world, not only as good manners, but as the very perfection of the *suprème bon ton.* Yet what must the worshippers be where the god is a monkey? The success of that celebrated personage, whose name we have just mentioned, is a social phenomenon, quite *sui generis.* It has not failed to attract the attention of those philosophers who have found nothing better to do than to speculate upon the rise and fall of fops and fashions. The author of Vivian Grey, for instance, treats the subject with a gravity and profoundness, befitting its singular importance, and highly edifying to connoisseurs in this department of liberal knowledge—so too, the author of Pelham has found the attraction of Brummell's star irresistible. He delights to dwell upon the fortunes of the illustrious exile— to catch "the farewell sweet" of his philosophical counsels and reflections—to kindle with him over the visions of his departed glory—and to hear him utter such lofty strains of unconquerable pride and revengeful self-complacency, as would scarcely be tolerated in the mouth of Napoleon at St. Helena, or Prometheus Vinctus in a Greek tragedy. Although reduced to very short commons in an obscure corner of Boulogne-sur-Mer, our ill-fated hero *has* tasted the pleasures, and still feels all the conscious superiority of a well-bred *gourmand*. Although a fugitive from his country, and an outcast from society, he *has* seen the day when the former rang with his unrivalled fame, and the latter trembled at his Olympian nod. Although now "none so poor to do him reverence," he did whilom revel in the intoxication of autocratic sway over the "foremost men of all the age" —cracked a joke and a bottle with princes, set his foot upon the necks of dukes and peers, and without rank, or title or family himself, like another Sampson, "made *arms* ridiculous," and became the fountain of honors and distinctions, more envied than the stars and coronets of men descended from Norman barons !

Now, call it rusticity or what you will, we cannot, for the very life of us, contemplate the character and career of such a creature as this with any sort of patience—much less with that strange degree of toleration, or complacency rather, with which some writers alluded to, evidently dwell upon them. We beg his pardon—there is one, and only one of his feelings which we know how to appreciate, and in which we perfectly sympathize. It is the profound contempt which he manifestly entertained for the society, that is, the *clique*—if we are to judge from appearances, at once the most supercilious and the meanest in the world—upon whose dignity and intelligence, his whole conduct was one continued and insufferable outrage. Such extravagant impertinences had never before been tolerated except in those professed fools or zanies, one or more of whom used to be kept, a few centuries ago, in the train of every great man, for the express purpose of beguiling his leisure hours, with licensed absurdity. Indeed, this visible contempt for those about him, we suspect it was, that mainly contributed to our hero's success. It came up to La Rochefoucault's notion of the elevation which does not depend upon fortune—*le prix qus nous nous donnons insensiblement à nous-memes*. Brummel seems to have studied profoundly the character of fashionable society in England. He saw that it was not founded, as it had formerly been in France, on the mere love of elegant conversation and refined pleasures, which a truly polite noblesse did as much as they could to promote, by admitting without reserve into their circles, all whose talents and accomplishments were fitted to delight and adorn them. He perceived that the disease—the all-devouring, epidemic disease—of the *bonne compagnie* in Eng-

land, was *vanity*—that all the forms and habitudes, and arts and
embellishments of life, were contrived not for pleasure, but for
ostentation merely—that the only earthly object of a man of *ton*
was to be considered as a man of ton, and so he could but be
ranked among the *distingués* and the *recherchés*, as they are
called in the fashionable jargon, it was a very minor consideration to him, whether his society were good or bad, agreeable
or disagreeable, intelligent and accomplished, or rude and stupid.
The badges—the insignia of the order were all he wanted.
To be admitted at Almack's—to be in demand at every *select*
party, (the *name* is enough)—to be a sort of *lion*, in short, was
the whole drift and study of his vacant, listless, yawning existence—an αξιωτος ξιος, if there ever was one. Hence every thing
in such a state of society, is capricious and eccentric—*outré* exaggeration and abrupt change. The leaders endeavour to distance all pursuit, or to turn so suddenly as to throw their
followers off the trail. Every thing becomes vulgar that is at
all common—whatever is touched by one of the uninitiated, is
desecrated and defiled for ever. All the ties, duties and charities
of life must be sacrificed without mercy, if they interfere with
your interests in the saloon—you are to shun your best friend
like a pestilence, if he be *cut* by the Brummel of the day—and
the murder of an unfashionable father were almost excusable
homicide in a man of ton!

Something of the same kind, doubtless, takes place in all
countries among people ambitious of this sort of distinction. It
is especially to be remarked in that class which is at once the
most despicable and the most insolent every where—the class
of pretenders—of *nouveaux riches*—the fag end of fashionable
life, if, indeed, they belong to it at all. Their footing there is
too precarious to admit of anything like ease or freedom in their
motions. It is quite as much as they can do to get along
themselves, and they will not, for anything in the world, add to
their difficulties by attempting to help others. They are climbing
up a steep hill, and the operation is tedious enough in all conscience, without loading themselves with unnecessary burthens.
Your *parvenu* is horribly fastidious about his associates—he has
the quickest and the surest instinct in regard to the rank and
consideration of his neighbours—he is the very last to countenance the rising merit of one of his own *farina*, and the very
first to run away at the alarm of bankruptcy and a fall among
his friends.

> Sed quid
> *Turba* Remi? Sequitur fortunam, ut semper, et odit
> Damnatos.

This characteristic of the sort of people alluded to, is very
well hit off by our author in the work before us, and his remarks

upon the subject are quite just, considered as mere *general* remarks, though, for reasons which we shall proceed to state, we doubt their being applicable in their whole extent to the fashionable society of England—at least, *if that society is well described in Pelham, and other novels of the same kind.* "My sister (says the gipsey king) was miserably ashamed of me. She had not even the manners to disguise it. In a higher rank of life than that which she held, she would have suffered far less mortification; for I fancy great people pay but little *real* attention to externals. Even if a man of rank is vulgar, it makes no difference in the orbit in which he moves; but your "genteel gentlewomen" are so terribly dependent upon what Mrs. Tomkyns will say—so uneasy about their relations and the opinion they are held in—and, above all, so made up of appearances and clothes—so undone, if they do not eat, drink and talk *à-la-mode*, that I can fancy no shame like that of my poor sister's, at having found and *being found with* a vulgar brother." pp. 36-38.

Now we think that if there is any truth at all in such works as Almack's, and the rest of that sort, great people *do* in England—far more, at any rate, than great people do in some countries, or should in any—attach some and even the highest importance to externals. According to these works, even a patent of nobility is no passport into "select society"—nay, a Bohun or a Mowbray, if any such there were—a hereditary Lord High Constable or Earl-Marshal of England—might be black-balled by a Brummel. Their professed object is to distinguish between the weight and consideration of a nobleman upon his estates, or in the House of Lords, and his rank in the artificial hierarchy of fashionable life. From the moment that he comes within the magic circle of Bond-street and St. James', the peer of the realm, it seems, is merged in the courtier and the man of fashion, and is measured by a new and most arbitrary standard, set up, it may be, by some presumptuous and vulgar coxcomb who happens to play the "Master of the Revels" for the time being. Even the nobility are thus deprived of their inseparable privilege—an ascertained rank. They, too, must be upon their good behavior—upon the *qui vive* for their places. They must do as they are bidden by their betters. Their whole system of life must be chalked out for them by the constituted authorities. "They must eat, drink and talk *à-la-mode ;*" or quietly submit to the contempt and exclusion—the *"odi et arceo,"* which await the rest of the profane vulgar.

Although it is very possible we may have pushed the matter too far in the preceding remarks, there can be no doubt, we conceive, that they are just to a certain extent. The classes condemned to what is technically called "climbing," are far more extensive in England, than on the continent of Europe. The whole exterior of society exhibits traces of this peculiarity in its character. Nobody seems to have any confidence in himself. "Mrs. Tomkyns" is the terror of the whole vicinage—of the high as well as the low. These, in like manner, are a terror to one another. A rich *parvenu* is afraid that a poor man of fashion may turn up his nose at his awkward stateliness and his bran-new finery. The poor man of fashion is horrified at the sight of this sudden greatness, which "overcomes him like a summer cloud," and but too surely threatens, before the end of a generation, to intercept the rays of public favor and eclipse him altogether. Like true bullies, however, they put the best face upon it. Their interchange of civilities is such as takes place between Abdiel and the rebel angels—it is "hostile scorn" on the one side and retorted scorn on the other. Still, at the bottom of his heart, each knows how to estimate and to respect the peculiar excellencies (for so we must call the advantages) of the other. *Satis clarus est apud timentem, quisquis timetur.* Sir Mordecai Molasses would be very glad to exchange his daughter and her portion for the ready-made respectability of the honorable Mr. Decay—who is still more ready to demean himself, on such terms, by contaminating the blood of his children. They are driven into this compulsory alliance, by the dread of common enemies, who are ever on the watch to take advantage of circumstances, and who wage a war of extermination against all pretenders to "gentility," who have been up and are going down, or who, being down, are struggling to get up. How vicious and perverted is such a state of things! How inconsistent with that "assured and liberal state of mind," as Burke expresses it, which is essential to all true dignity of character and conduct! How inexpressibly despicable in comparison of the unbought nobility of nature—"the old and elegant humanity of Greece"—or even of that exquisite, though more artificial and effeminate refinement in France, under the ancient *régime*, so winning, so gentle, so accessible, so unpretending!

Perhaps, this system of manners, in which no man trusts his neighbour or relies upon himself—in which the heart is quailing and grovelling, even while insult and defiance lower upon the brow—this war of all against all in the petty hostilities of social intercourse, may have contributed somewhat to the success of Brummel. His usurpation in this small way was submitted to, for the same reason that greater usurpations have been borne. There could be no concert among his subjects. Each looked upon his neighbor with distrust, and was afraid to move by himself. This whimsical tyranny thus stood upon the same foundation as Robespierre's. The terrorists built up their system on the simple principle that what is every man's business is no man's business, especially where there is any danger in the way. Make it extremely probable that the first malcontent, who attempts to get up an opposition will be betrayed and cut off, (or *cut,*) and you are secure against the rebellion of the most formidable multitudes.

English fashionable life, thus deformed by all manner of *charlatanerie,* pretension, eccentricity and flippancy, seems to us to be as unfit for exhibition in a novel, (except by way of satire) as the habits and manners of the Athenians were unfavorable to comedies of character. "Pelham," we think, is decidedly the best thing in this kind that we have seen, but the *kind* is miserably bad. "Almack's," for instance, is the stupidest trash that ever took the shape of a work of fiction. "Vivian Grey" has merits of a much higher order, and is, indeed, a very clever book, but its popularity and reputation were out of all proportion beyond its deserts. It owed these, undoubtedly, in a good degree, to the belief that it was not only an accurate representation of "the living manners" of the day, but, what is still more piquant, of living characters of some celebrity. This latter circumstance would have given currency to any work, though its only recommendation had been malignity and mischief, which, when directed against individuals of note and consideration, amply supply the place both of vivacity and wit. "Pelham," dived much deeper below the mere surface of life, and mixed up, with the portraiture of its follies and frivolites, more of profound pathos and more of permanent and universal interest. The character of Reginald Glanville is powerfully drawn. His disclosure of the facts, that led to his unrelenting and mysterious pursuit of the murdered Tyrrel, rises to a strain of far "higher mood" than any thing in "Vivian Grey." As for the morality of the part he acts, that is of course out of the question. We are speaking only of the dramatic interest excited by the personage, and the situations in which he appears, and we need not say, that to excite that sort of interest a character is all the better for having a few human frailties.

In the "Disowned," the author has gone, we think, beyond the pitch of his first performance. Not that, taken as a *whole,* this novel is better executed, or even more interesting than Pelham. Its plot is not so well ordered, and much of the dialogue, especially in those parts where his fashionables take the parol, is less spirited. But there is more pathos and more power—a loftier eloquence in many passages—and every where something bolder and more adventurous, both in conception and in style. He dwells very little upon the vapid impertinences of which we have been speaking—and which are, indeed, the only dull part of the book, except the character of Morris Brown—a vulgar and intolerable bore. But it is when he transcends the boundaries of that narrow and sterile field, and expatiates at large amidst all the variety and magnificence of the moral and material world, that he puts forth his powers to the greatest advantage. He then every where discovers a mind at once enriched with poetic imagery, overflowing with a tender sensibility and the love of beauty and virtue, and disciplined in the profounder and severer speculations of philosophy. There is a vein of deep Platonic musing, running through many of his meditations, which imparts to them a solemn grandeur and elevation. It is true that his style is not always perfect: he is, sometimes, hyperbolical : he sometimes falls into a mawkish sentimentalism—he is often, in comparison of our classic writers, diffuse and feeble—but his diction is, generally, copious and elegant, and eminently well adapted to give full effect to his peculiar turn of thought and feeling.

But the superiority of this work, as the author himself very justly observes in his introduction, mainly consists in "a far deeper and more novel delineation of character—scenes of more exciting interest and vivid coloring—thoughts less superficially expressed—passions more energetically called forth—and, (as he adds, with much more diffidence) if not a greater, yet a more pervading and sensible moral tendency than would have been compatible with the scheme and design of Pelham." He has, indeed, in these respects, if any thing, overcharged the picture. It is a deep tragedy—almost drowning the stage in tears and blood. The *dramatis personæ* are killed off one after another, without mercy. Two of them are assassinated and four hanged, besides many that die in their beds. But there are events in it more touching—more thrilling—more terrible than death.— Every feeling that can agitate and wring the bosom—the grief that leaves the heart desolate, and the burning fever of disappointment which maddens the brain—the wild energies of a misdirected and fanatical zeal—the fond aspirations, the glowing dreams, the life-consuming toil and assiduity of youthful ambition, excited only to delude and to destroy utterly—the diabolical and remorseless malignity of a fiend in the shape of a hardened criminal, attempting to corrupt the virtue which he ought to have relieved, and at length to ruin because he failed to corrupt it—the struggles of that virtue against all the instincts of nature stimulated and goaded to frenzy by unutterable suffering, and those struggles issuing too late, in a worthless victory and more embittered anguish—such feelings as these, exhibited in striking situations, and managed with unquestionable talent, to say no more, could not fail to impart a far graver, deeper and intenser interest to the "Disowned," than has ever before been attempted, or indeed could, by any possibility, be achieved in a mere fashionable novel.

As for the moral tendency of the work, the too obvious disclosure of it, in the novel before us, is, perhaps, even to be reckoned amongst its faults. The "heroic virtues," as a great man expresses it, "go at too high a market for humanity," and it is easy or rather common, in works of fiction, to slide into exaggeration in this particular. For instance, we have always felt dissatisfied with the heroes of Metastasio and Alfieri on this account. Their conduct is rather *too* godlike—their language, although they say only what they are going to do or have done in fact, swells into rhodomontade and extravagance— they are so very Roman, that they cease to have human feelings, or to excite human sympathy. There is nothing, to be sure, so objectionable as this in Mordaunt's character; but we felt, while reading the book, that the thing was somewhat overdone. We will remark, however, that it is no objection to the instructive and salutary moral tendency of the novel, that it does not distribute what is called "poetical justice" among its chief personages. We have always thought that nothing was, at once more fallacious in a philosophical point of view, and more at variance with the analogy of nature and of human life, than such a principle. We have not space to add any further remarks of our own upon this subject—but we cannot refrain from subjoining those of the author before us, which he puts into the mouth of Mordaunt:—

"I looked around the world and saw often virtue in rags and vice in purple; the former conduces to happiness it is true, but the happiness lies *within*, and not in externals. I contemned the deceitful folly with which writers have termed it poetical justice to make the good ultimately prosperous in wealth, honour, fortunate love, or successful desires.—Nothing false, even in poetry, can be just. Virtue is not more exempt than vice from the ills of fate, but contains within itself, always, an energy to resist them and sometimes an anodyne to soothe. To repay your quotation from Tibullus—

Crura sonant ferro—sed canit inter opus.

"When in the depths of my soul, I set up that divinity of this nether earth, which Brutus never really understood, if because unsuccessful in its efforts, he doubted its existence, I said in the proud prayer with which I worshipped it—"poverty may humble my lot, but it shall not debase thee; temptation may shake my nature, but not the rock on which thy temple is *based*; misfortune may wither all the hopes that have blossomed around thy altar, but I will sacrifice dead leaves when the flowers are no more. Though all that I have loved, perish—all that I have coveted, fade away, I may murmur at fate, but I will have no voice but that of homage for thee. Nor while thou smilest upon my way, could I exchange with the loftiest and happiest of my foes. * * * Vol. ii. p. 100.

These sentiments might be expressed with more simplicity and force (for the style is objectionable), but nothing can be more just and philosophical.

We shall now proceed to take a cursory notice of some of the prominent characters of the novel.

We will premise that we were strongly reminded in the course of it, of what our author himself calls the "Magnificent Fable of Melmoth."* The hero of the "Disowned" is very much in the same situation with the young Spaniard of the family of Monçada, whose adventures constitute so prominent a part in Mr. Maturin's novel. The dreadful temptations of poverty to which Mordaunt is exposed, also, have their archetype in the same work, and the part, which Crauford—only a Melmoth of a less unearthly kind—acts, is altogether worthy of an incarnate Dæmon. Although, however, it is probable that the first conception of the characters and situations was suggested to our author by Mr. Maturin's book, there is quite enough in the turn which is given to them here—in the manner in which they are wrought up and appropriated, to support his claim to a good degree of originality in them.

There is nothing very peculiar about the character of the hero. His situation surrounds him with difficulties which he successively overcomes, by marvellously lucky coincidences and unexpected turns of fortune brought about as such things have been used to be from time immemorial—for the heroes of romance. He is cast off by his father, he knows not why, and sent away with a thousand pounds in his pocket to seek his fortunes. His adventures are very various—but the most important of them is his making the acquaintance of a rich bachelor in a very out-of-the-way sort of society at Mr. Copperas', and, after getting into the good graces of the old gentleman, happening very providentially to save his life when in imminent danger, from two desperate burglars. He is immediately taken into favour by his grateful patron; a place is procured for him in a diplomatic mission to the Continent, where he spends some years and gets into good company; he returns at length, falls in love with a beautiful young lady of noble family, and is, for a little while rather a "lion" in "high life." Meanwhile a certain Lord Borodaile pays his addresses to Flora, the mistress of Clarence Linden, (the Disowned ;) seeks an opportunity to insult the latter on the score of his unknown origin—shoots him in a duel, and brings him into such disrepute with the family of the young lady, that he is forbidden to enter their doors, and has the additional mortification soon to hear that his arrogant rival is to be married to his adored in a very short time. That time, of course, never comes. Borodaile gets into a fray with a fanatical politician of the name of Wolf, which terminates in the death of the former, who is precipitated by the enraged democrat from the brow of a steep descent. While Borodaile is on his death-bed, Clarence procures conclusive evidence that he is the brother of that unfortunate nobleman, and the heir-at-law of his title and estates—that his

* Vol. ii. p. 88.

real name is Clinton L'Estrange—and that he was cast off by his father on a suspicion, not conceived it must be confessed without very good colour, that the sire *de facto* of young Master Clinton was not, as he ought to have been, the sire *de jure.* In short, Clarence or Clinton becomes Earl of Ulswater, and makes Flora Ardenne his countess, with the consent and blessings of all parties.

This is a very succinct outline of the plot—but there is (not to speak of episode upon episode) an important *underplot,* far more interesting in every point of view than the story of the hero's fortunes. It is a picture of Madame de Staël's ideal love— *l'amour dans le marriage*—in its holiest purity, its most rapturous enthusiasm, its most heartfelt fidelity and devotedness— a love, which every effort to extinguish it only inflamed the more, and which the very sufferings it led to seemed to consecrate and sanctify—such a passion as the most exalted natures only are capable of—such an adoration as is offered up to loveliness and virtue, by honorable and true hearts kindling with the fervor and chastened by the refinement of a poetical and romantic imagination.

The persons between whom this ill-fated attachment sprung up were Algernon Mordaunt and Isabel St. Leger. Their characters are pourtrayed as follows :—

"Algernon Mordaunt was the last son of an old and honorable race, which had for centuries back numbered princes in its line. His parents had had many children, but all (save Algernon the youngest) died in their infancy. His mother perished in giving him birth. Constitutional infirmity and the care of mercenary nurses contributed to render Algernon a weak and delicate child; hence came a taste for loneliness and a passion for study, and from these sprang on the one hand the fastidiousness and reserve, which render us unamiable, and on the other the loftiness of spirit and the kindness of heart, which are the best and earliest gifts of literature, and more than counterbalance our deficiencies in the 'minor morals' due to society by their tendency to increase our attention to the greater ones belonging to mankind. Mr. Mordaunt was a man of luxurious habits and gambling propensities; wedded to London, he left the house of his ancestors to moulder in desertion and decay: but to this home Algernon was constantly consigned during his vacations from school; and its solitude and cheerlessness, joined to a disposition naturally melancholy and thoughtful, gave those colours to his temper which subsequent events were calculated to deepen, not efface.

"Truth obliges us to state, despite our partiality to Mordaunt, that when he left his school, after a residence of six years, it was with the bitter distinction of having been the most unpopular boy in it. Why, nobody could exactly explain, for his severest enemies could not accuse him of ill-nature, cowardice, or avarice, and these make the three capital offences of a school-boy; but Algernon Mordaunt had already acquired the knowledge of himself, and could explain the cause, though with a bitter and swelling heart. His ill health, his long residence at home, his unfriended and almost orphan situation, his early habits of solitude and reserve, all these so calculated to make the spirit shrink within itself, made him, on his entrance at school, if not unsocial, *appear* so:—this was the primary reason of unpopularity; the second was that he perceived, for he was sensitive (and consequently acute) to the extreme, the misfortune of his manner, and, in his wish to rectify it, it became doubly unprepossessing; to reserve it now added embarrassment; to coldness, gloom; and the pain he felt, in addressing or being addressed by another, was naturally and necessarily reciprocal, for the effects of sympathy are no where so wonderful, yet so invisible, as in the manners.

"By degrees he shunned the intercourse which had for him nothing but distress, and his volatile acquaintance were perhaps the first to set him the example. Often in his solitary walks he stopped afar off to gaze upon the sports, which none ever solicited him to share ; and, as the shout of laughter and of happy hearts came, peal after peal, upon his ear, he turned enviously, yet not malignantly away, with tears, which not all his pride could curb, and muttered to himself,—'And these, these hate me !'

"There are two feelings common to all high or affectionate natures, that of extreme susceptibility to opinion, and that of extreme bitterness at its injustice. These feelings were Mordaunt's; but the keen edge which one blow injures, the repetition blunts ; and, by little and little, Algernon became not only accustomed, but, as he persuaded himself, indifferent to his want of popularity; his step grew more lofty, and his address more collected, and that which was once diffidence, gradually hardened into pride." Vol. i pp. 49-50.

"Figure to yourself a small chamber, in a remote wing of a large and noble mansion—the walls were covered with sketches, whose extreme delicacy of outline and colouring told that it was from a female hand that they derived their existence ; a few shelves, filled with books, supported vases of flowers, whose bright hues and fragrant odours gratefully repaid, while they testified, the attention daily lavished upon them. A harp stood neglected at the farther end of the room, and just above hung the slender prison of one of those golden wanderers from the Canary Isles, which bear to our colder land some of the gentlest music of their skies and zephyrs. The window, reaching to the ground, was open, and looked through the clusters of jessamine and honeysuckle which surrounded the low veranda beyond, upon thick and frequent copses of blossoming shrubs, redolent of spring, and sparkling in the sunny tears of a May shower, which had only just wept itself away. Embosomed in these little groves, lay plots of 'prodigal flowers,' contrasted and girdled with the freshest and greenest turf which ever wooed the nightly dances of the fairies; and, afar off, through one artful opening, the eye caught the glittering wanderings of water, on whose light and smiles the universal happiness of the young year seemed reflected.

"But in that chamber, heedless of all around, and cold to the joy with which every thing else equally youthful, beautiful and innocent, seemed breathing and inspired, sat a very young and lovely female. Her cheek leaned upon her hand, and large tears flowed fast and burningly over the small and delicate fingers. The comb that had confined her tresses lay at her feet, and the high dress which concealed her swelling breast had been loosened, to give vent to the suffocating and indignant throbbings which had rebelled against its cincture—all appeared to announce that bitterness of grief when the mind, as it were, wreaks its scorn upon the body in its contempt for external seemings, and to proclaim that the present more subdued and softened sorrow had only succeeded to a burst far less quiet and controlled. Wo to those who eat the bread of dependence—their tears are wrung from the inmost sources of the heart!

"Isabel St. Leger was the only child of a captain in the army, who died in her infancy; her mother had survived him only a few months: and to the reluctant care and cold affections of a distant and wealthy relation of the same name, the warm hearted and pennyless orphan was consigned. Major-General Cornelius St. Leger, whose riches had been purchased in India at the price of his constitution, was of a temper as hot as his curries, and he wreaked it the more unsparingly on his ward, because the superior ill-temper of his maiden sister had prevented his giving vent to it upon her. That sister, Miss Diana St. Leger, was a meagre gentlewoman of about six feet high; and her voice was as high and as sharp as herself. Long in awe of her brother, she rejoiced at heart to find some one whom she had such right and reason to make in awe of herself; and, from the age of four to that of seventeen, Isabel suffered every insult and every degradation which could be inflicted upon her by the tyranny of her two *protectors.* Her spirit, however, was far from being broken by the rude shocks it received; on the contrary, her mind, gentleness itself to the kind, rose indignantly against the unjust. It was true that the sense of wrong broke not forth audibly; for, though susceptible, Isabel was meek, and her pride was concealed by the outward softness and feminacy of her temper; but she stole away from those who had wounded her heart, or trampled upon its feelings, and nourished with secret but passionate tears the memory of the harshness or injustice she had endured." Vol. i. pp. 72-73.

As soon as these amiable and tenderhearted personages had an inkling of the feelings which Mordaunt entertained for Isabel, they of course lost no time in interposing their *veto.* The result is, after the usual preliminary negotiations, an elopement and a marriage. In a short time, however, Mordaunt is reduced to utter beggary by a law suit, and his next appearance is under the assumed name of *Glendower,* in the capacity of a famishing author, dependant upon the caprice of book-sellers for his daily bread, and for that of his wife and infant daughter. We present here to the reader the following touching picture :—

"The writer was alone, and had just paused from his employment: he was leaning his face upon one hand, in a thoughtful and earnest mood, and the air which came chill, but gentle, from the window, slightly stirred the locks from the broad and marked brow, over which they fell in thin but graceful waves. Partly owing, perhaps, to the waning light of the single lamp, and the lateness of the hour, his cheek seemed very pale, and the complete, though contemplative rest of the features, partook greatly of the quiet of habitual sadness, and a little of the languor of shaken health; yet the expression, despite of the proud cast of the brow and profile, was rather benevolent than stern or dark in its pensiveness, and the lines spoke more of the wear and harrow of deep thought, than the inroads of ill-regulated passion.

"There was a slight tap at the door—the latch was raised, and the original of the picture we have described entered the apartment.

"Time had not been idle with her since that portrait had been taken: the round elastic figure had lost much of its youth and freshness; the step, though light, was languid, and in the centre of the fair, smooth cheek, which was a little sunken, burned one deep bright spot—fatal sign to those who have watched the progress of the most deadly and deceitful of our national maladies; yet still the form and countenance were eminently interesting and lovely; and though the bloom was gone for ever, the beauty which not even death could wholly have despoiled, remained to triumph over debility, misfortune and disease.

"She approached the student, and laid her hand upon his shoulder—
" 'Dearest!' said he, tenderly yet reproachfully, 'yet up, and the hour so late, and yourself so weak? Fie, I must learn to scold you.'
" 'And how,' answered the intruder, 'how could I sleep or rest while you are consuming your very life in those thankless labours?'
" 'By which,' interrupted the writer, with a faint smile, 'we glean our scanty subsistence.'
" 'Yes,' said the wife (for she held that relation to the student), and the tears stood in her eyes, 'I know well that every morsel of bread, every drop of water is wrung from your very heart's blood, and I—I am the cause of all; but surely you exert yourself too much, more than can be requisite. These night damps, this sickly and chilling air, heavy with the rank vapours of the coming morning, are not suited to thoughts and toils which are alone sufficient to sear your mind and exhaust your strength. Come, my own love, to bed: and yet, first, come and look upon our child, how sound she sleeps! I have leant over her for the last hour, and tried to fancy it was you whom I watched, for she has learnt already your smile, and has it even when she sleeps.'
" 'She has cause to smile,' said the husband, bitterly.
" 'She has, *for she is yours!* and, even in poverty and humble hopes, that is an inheritance, which may well teach her pride and joy. Come love, the air is keen, and the damp rises to your forehead—yet stay, till I have kissed it away.'
" 'Mine own love,' said the student, as he rose and wound his arm round the slender waist of his wife; 'wrap your shawl closer over your bosom, and let us look for one instant upon the night. I cannot sleep till I have slaked the fever of my blood; the air hath nothing of coldness in its breath to me.'
"And they walked to the window and looked forth. All was hushed and still in the narrow street; the cold gray clouds were hurrying fast along the sky, and the stars, weak and waning in their light, gleamed forth at rare intervals upon the mute city like the expiring watch-lamps of the dead.
"They leaned out, and spoke not; but when they looked above upon the melancholy heavens, they drew nearer to each other, as if it were their natural instinct to do so, whenever the world without seemed discouraging and sad.
"At length the student broke his silence; but his thoughts, which were wandering and disjointed, were breathed less to her than vaguely and unconsciously to himself. 'Morn breaks—another and another!—day upon day!—while we drag on our load like the blind beast which knows not when the burthen shall be cast off, and the hour of rest be come.'
"The woman pressed his hand to her bosom, but made no rejoinder: she knew his mood—and the student continued." Vol. i. pp. 231–233.

By the interference of a banker of the name of Crauford— the Rowland Stevenson of his day—whom Mordaunt had met with in his travels on the continent, and mortally offended by some aristocratic slight, and who is, besides, bent upon making the unfortunate man the instrument of his own villainy in a grand scheme of embezzlement and fraud—even this scanty and precarious resource is soon cut off. Then opens one of those scenes so common "in Melmoth." Crauford tries every art—exhausts every topic to persuade the unhappy Mordaunt to accept of relief at his hands. He tantalizes him while his body is agonizing with famine and his mind distracted and desperate, with prospects of sudden enjoyment and unbounded opulence. But all his efforts are vain. Mordaunt endeavours to escape from temp· tation by changing his place of residence. He is again discovered—again, tortured by the same sufferings, he is subjected to the same trials—and again triumphs over the arts of his tempter and his own despair. At length the measure of his calamities seems to be filled up. A crisis in his fate is at hand :—

"Struggling with want, which hourly grew more imperious and urgent ; wasting his heart on studies which brought fever to his pulse, and disappointment to his ambition ; gnawed to the very soul by the mortifications which his poverty gave to his pride ; and watching with tearless eyes, but a maddening brain, the slender form of his wife, now waxing weaker and fainter, as the canker of disease fastened upon the core of her young but blighted life, there was yet a high, though, alas ! not constant consolation within him, whenever, from the troubles of this dim spot, his thoughts could escape, like birds released from their cage, and lose themselves in the might, and lustre, and freedom of their native heaven.

" 'If the wind scatter, or the rock receive,' thought he, as he looked upon his secret and treasured work, 'these seeds, they were at least dispersed by a hand which asked no selfish return, and a heart which would have lavished the harvest of its labors upon those who know not the husbandman, and tramples his hopes into the dust.'

"But by degrees, this comfort of a noble and generous nature, these whispers of a vanity, rather to be termed holy than excusable, began to grow unfrequent and low. The cravings of a more engrossing and heavy want than those of the mind came eagerly and rapidly upon him ; the fair cheek of his infant became pinched and hollow ; his wife—(O woman ! in ordinary cases, so mere a mortal, how, in the great and rare events of life, dost thou swell into the angel!) his wife conquered nature itself by love, and starved herself in silence, and set bread before him with a smile, and bade him eat.

" 'But you—you ?' he would ask inquiringly, and then paused.

" 'I *have* dined dearest: I want nothing: eat, love, eat.'

"But he eat not. The food robbed from her seemed to him more deadly than poison ; and he would rise, and dash his hand to his brow, and go forth alone, with nature unsatisfied, to look upon this luxurious world, and learn *content*.

"It was after such a scene that, one day, he wandered forth into the streets, desperate and confused in mind, and fainting with hunger, and half insane with fiery and wrong thoughts, which dashed over his barren and gloomy soul, and desolated, but *conquered not*. It was evening : he stood (for he had strode on so rapidly, at first, that his strength was now exhausted, and he was forced to pause) leaning against the railed area of a house, in a lone and unfrequented street. No passenger shared the dull and obscure thoroughfare. He stood, literally, in scene as in heart, solitary amidst the great city, and wherever he looked—lo ! there were none !

" 'Two days,' said he, slowly and faintly, 'two days, and bread has only once passed my lips: and that was snatched from her—from those lips which I have fed with sweet and holy kisses, and from whence my sole comfort in this weary life has been drawn. And she—ay, she starves— and my child, too. They complain not—they murmur not—but they lift up their eyes to me and ask for——. Merciful God ? thou *didst* make man in benevolence ; thou *dost* survey this world with a pitying and paternal eye—save, comfort, cherish them, and crush *me* if thou wilt.'

"At that moment a man darted suddenly from an obscure alley, and passed Glendower at full speed; presently came a cry and a shout, and the rapid trampling of feet, and, in another moment, the solitude of the street grew instinct and massed with life." Vol. ii. pp. 3–7.

The crowd at length disperses, and silence and solitude are restored.

"He looked quietly on the still night, and its first watcher among the hosts of heaven, and felt something of balm sink into his soul; not, indeed, that vague and delicious calm which, in his boyhood of poesy and romance, he had drunk in, by green solitudes from the mellow twilight, but a quiet, sad and sober [feeling,] circling gradually over his mind, and bringing it back from its confused and disordered visions and darkness, to the recollection and reality of his bitter life.

"By degrees the scene he had so imperfectly witnessed, the flight of the robber, and the eager pursuit of the mob, grew over him; a dark and guilty thought burst upon his mind.

" 'I am a man, like that criminal,' said he, fiercely. 'I have nerves, sinews, muscles, flesh; I feel hunger, thirst, pain, as acutely; why should I endure more than he can? Perhaps, he has a wife—a child—and he saw them starving inch by inch, and he felt that he *ought* to be their protector—and so he sinned. And I—I—can I not sin too for mine? can I not dare what the wild beast, and the vulture, and the fierce hearts of my brethren dare for their mates and young? One gripe of this hand—one cry from this voice—and my board might be heaped with plenty, and my child feed, and *she* smile as she was wont to smile—for one night at least.'

"And as these thoughts broke upon him, Glendower rose, and with a step firm, even in weakness, he strode unconsciously onward.

"A figure appeared; Glendower's heart beat thick. He slouched his hat over his brows, and for one moment wrestled with his pride and his stern virtue; the virtue conquered, but not the pride; and even the office of the supplicant seemed to him less degrading than that of the robber. He sprang forward, extended his hands towards the stranger, and cried in a sharp voice, the agony of which rang through the long dull street with a sudden and echoless sound, 'charity—food!'

"The stranger paused—one of the boldest of men in his own line, he was as timid as a woman in any other; mistaking the meaning of the petitioner, and terrified by the vehemence of his gesture, he said, in a trembling tone, as he hastily pulled out his purse—

" 'There, there! do not hurt me—take it—take all!'

"Glendower knew the voice, as a sound not unfamiliar to him; his pride, that grand principle of human action, which in him, though for a moment suppressed, was unextinguishable, returned in full force. 'None' thought he, 'who know me, shall know my full degradation also.' And he turned away; but the stranger, mistaking this motion, extended his hand to him, saying, 'take this, my friend—you will have no need of force!' and as he advanced nearer to his supposed assailant, he beheld, by the pale lamplight, and instantly recognized his features.

" 'Ah!' cried he, in astonishment, but internal rejoicing—'ah! is it you who are thus reduced!'

" 'You say right, Crauford,' said Glendower suddenly, and drawing himself up to his full height, 'it is *I!* but you are mistaken;—I am a beggar, not a ruffian!'

" 'Good Heavens!' answered Crauford; 'how fortunate that we should meet! Providence watches over us unceasingly! I have long sought you in vain. But'—(and here the wayward malignity, sometimes, though not

always, the characteristic of Crauford's nature, irresistibly broke out)—
'but that you, of all men, should suffer so—you, proud, susceptible, virtuous beyond human virtue—you, whose fibres are as acute as the naked
eye—that *you* should bear this, and wince not !' " Vol. ii. pp. 5-7.

The indefatigable Crauford now returns to the charge more
vigorously than ever, but is at length, after having approached
fearfully near to the accomplishment of his purpose, compelled
to desist in despair. Meanwhile the death of the only son of
that relative, who had deprived Mordaunt of his estate by the
law-suit, opens to the latter the way to the inheritance of his
fathers, and he receives a letter from his kinsman, inviting him
to enter immediately into possession. The bearer of this letter,
Mr. Morris Brown—general go-between and *commissionaire* in
all negotiations, where the author of "The Disowned" cannot
provide a better messenger—has great difficulty in finding the
miserable hovel to which Mordaunt has slunk to hide his wretchedness, and to perish by famine.

"An old crone, leaning out of an opposite window, with matted hair hanging over a begrimed and shrivelled countenance, made answer, 'No one,'
she said in her peculiar dialect, which the *digne citoyen* scarcely comprehended, 'lived there or had done so for years;' but Brown knew better ; and, while he was asserting the fact, a girl put her head out of an-
nother hovel and said that she had sometimes seen, at the dusk of the
evening, a man leave the house, but, whether any one else lived in it, she
could not tell. Again Mr. Brown sounded an alarm, but no answer came
forth, and in great fear and trembling he applied violent hands to the
door ; it required but little force—it gave way—he entered ; and, jealous
of the entrance of the mob without, reclosed and barred, as well as he
was able, the shattered door. The house was *unnaturally* large for the
neighbourhood, and Brown was in doubt whether first to ascend a broken
and perilous staircase, or search the rooms below : he decided on the latter ; he found no one, and with a misgiving heart, which nothing but the
recollection of the great Turkey carpet could have inspired, he ascended
the quaking steps. All was silent. But a door was unclosed. He entered, and saw the object of his search before him.

"Over a pallet bent a form, on which, though youth seemed withered,
and even pride broken, the unconquerable soul left somewhat of grace
and glory, that sustained the beholder's remembrance of better days—a
child, in its first infancy, knelt on the nearer side of the bed, with clasped
hands and vacant eyes that turned towards the intruder, and remained
rivetted on his steps with a listless and lack-lustre gaze. But Glendower,
or rather Mordaunt, as he bent over the pallet, spoke not, moved not ; his
eyes were rivetted on one object ; his heart seemed turned into stone, and
his veins curdled into ice. Awed and chilled by the breathing desolation
of the spot, Brown approached, and spoke, he scarcely knew what ; the
habitual nature of his thoughts, which cast something ludicrous into his
words, doubled as it were, the terror, because it took from the exaggeration of the scene. 'You are' he concluded his address, 'the master of
Mordaunt Court ;' and he placed the letter in the hands of the person he
thus greeted.

"Awake, hear me ! cried Algernon to Isabel, as she lay extended on the
couch ; and the messenger of glad tidings, for the first time seeing her
countenance, shuddered and knew that he was in the chamber of death.

" 'Awake, my own, own love ! Happy days are in store for us yet; our misery is past; you will live, live to bless me in riches, as you have done in want.'

"Isabel raised her eyes to his, and a smile, sweet, comforting, and full of love, passed the lips which were about to close for ever. 'Thank Heaven,' she murmured, 'for your dear sake. It is pleasant to die now and *thus* !' and she placed the hand that was clasped in her relaxing and wan fingers, within the bosom which had been, for anguished and hopeless years, his asylum and refuge, and which now, when fortune changed, as if it had only breathed as a comfort to his afflictions, was, for the first time, and for ever, to be cold, cold even to him.

" 'You will live—you will live,' cried Mordaunt, in wild and incredulous despair—'in mercy live ! You, who have been my angel of hope, do not, O God, O God ! do not desert me now !'

"But that faithful and loving heart was already deaf to his voice, and the film grew darkening and rapidly over the eye, which still, with undying fondness, sought him out through the shade and agony of death. Sense and consciousness were gone, and dim and confused images whirled round the soul, struggling a little moment before they sank into the depth and silence where the past lies buried. But still mindful of *him*, and grasping, as it were, at his remembrance she clasped closer and closer the icy hand which she held to her breast. 'Your hand is cold, dearest—it is cold,' said she, faintly, 'but I will warm it *here* !' And so her spirit passed away, and Mordaunt felt afterwards, in a lone and surviving pilgrimage, that her last thought had been kindness to him, and her last act had spoken a forgetfulness even of death, in the cares and devotion of love." Vol. ii. pp. 59, 60.

Mordaunt now retires once more from the world, into a retreat endeared and consecrated to him by the most touching recollections, to brood over the memory of his blighted love, and to cherish and revive the virtues of his lost Isabel, in an infant daughter, who had inherited all the beauty and the loveliness, as she bore the name of her mother. It was a considerable period after he had been established at his country-seat that Clarence paid him a visit there.

"When Clarence rang at the ivy-covered porch, and made inquiry for Mordaunt, he was informed that the latter was in the park, by the river, where most of his hours, during the day time, were spent.

" 'Shall I send to acquaint him that you are come, Sir ?' said the servant.

" 'No,' answered Clarence, 'I will leave my horse to one of the grooms, and stroll down the river in search of your master.'

"Suiting the action to the word, he dismounted, consigned his steed to the *palefrenier*, and, following the direction indicated to him bent his way to the 'river.'

"As he descended the hill, the brook (for it did not deserve, though it received a higher name,) opened enchantingly upon his view. Amidst the fragrant reed and the wild flower, still sweet, though fading, and tufts of tedded grass, all of which, when crushed beneath the foot, sent a mingled tribute, *copia narium*, to its sparkling waves, the wild stream took its gladsome course, now contracted by gloomy firs, which, bending over the water, cast somewhat of their own sadness upon its surface—now glancing forth from the shade, as it 'broke into dimples and laughed in the sun'—now washing the gnarled and spreading roots of some lonely ash, which, hanging over it still and droopingly, seemed, the hermit of the scene, to moralize on its noisy and various wanderings—now winding round the hill, and losing itself at last amidst thick copses, where day did never more than wink and glimmer—and where, at night, its waters, brawling on their stony channel, seemed like a spirit's wail, and harmonized well with the scream of the gray owl, wheeling from her dim retreat, or the moaning and rare sound of some solitary deer.

"As Clarence's eye roved admiringly over the scene before him, it dwelt at last upon a small building, situated on the widest part of the opposite bank: it was entirely overgrown with ivy, and the outline only remained to show the gothic antiquity of the architecture. It was a single square tower, built none knew when or wherefore, and consequently, the spot of many vagrant guesses and wild legends among the surrounding gossips. On approaching yet nearer, he perceived, alone and seated on a little mound beside the tower, the object of his search.

"Mordaunt was gazing with vacant yet earnest eye upon the waters beneath; and so intent was either his mood or look, that he was unaware of Clarence's approach. Tears fast and large were rolling from those haughty eyes which men, who shrank from their indifferent glance, little deemed were capable of such weak and feminine emotion. Far, far through the aching void of time were the thoughts of the reft and solitary mourner; they were dwelling, in all the vivid and keen intensity of grief which dies not, upon the day when, about that hour and on that spot, he sate, with Isabel's young cheek upon his bosom, and listened to a voice which was now only for his dreams. He recalled the moment when the fatal letter, charged with change and poverty, was given to him, and the pang which had rent his heart as he looked around upon a scene which spring had just then breathed, and which he was about to leave to a fresh summer and a new lord; and then that deep, fond, half-fearful gaze, with which Isabel had met his eye, and the feeling, proud even in its melancholy, with which he had drawn towards his breast all that earth had now for him, and thanked God in his heart of hearts that *she* was spared.

" 'And I am once more master,' thought he, 'not only of all I then held, but all which my wealthier forefathers possessed. But she who was the sharer of my sorrows and want—oh, where is she? rather, ah! rather a hundred fold that her hand was still clasped in mine, and her spirit supporting me through poverty and trial, and her soft voice murmuring the comfort that steals away care, than to be thus heaped with wealth and honour, and *alone*—alone, where never more can come love, or hope, or the yearnings of affection, or the sweet fullness of a heart, that seems fathomless in its tenderness, yet overflows! Had my lot, when she left me, been still the steepings of bitterness, the stings of penury, the moody silence of hope, the damp and chill of sunless and aidless years, which rust the very iron of the soul away; had my lot been thus, as it had been, I could have borne her death, I could have looked upon her grave, and wept not—nay, I could have comforted my own struggles with the memory of her escape; but thus, at the very moment of prosperity, to leave the altered and promising earth, 'to house with darkness and death;' no little gleam of sunshine, no brief recompense for the agonising past, no momentary respite between tears and the tomb. Oh, Heaven! what—what avail is a wealth which comes too late, when she who could alone have made wealth, bliss, is dust; and the light that should have gilded many and happy days flings only a wearing and ghastly glare upon the tomb?' " Vol. ii. pp. 78–80.

He devotes himself in this solitude more than ever to the study of philosophy, not only as the charm of a contemplative life, but as the best discipline for active pursuits—becomes a member of Parliament of great weight and consideration, and is at length murdered by the republican Wolfe, who mistakes him for one of his Majesty's ministers.

From this summary of the part of the fable relating to the fortunes of Mordaunt, we think our readers will agree with us, that it abounds in striking situation and pathetic incident, and from the specimens of the author's style that have been submitted to them, that his execution upon the whole, is not unworthy of so interesting a design. The best portions of it, decidedly, are those in which the ineffable affection of those devoted beings for one another, and especially the deep romantic and adoring love of the philosophic and imaginative Mordaunt, are pourtrayed— in these, we have no hesitation in saying, that the author has been perfectly successful. In parts wherein the subject itself was less inviting—in those especially, in which it was revolting and disgustful, as in some of the interviews with Crauford, he does not appear to us to have done by any means so well. The character of this man himself is at once *outré* and commonplace—it is a disagreeable jumble of contrary qualities. He has the mischevious malignity of Mephistopheles or Melmoth, without their supernatural attributes, and talks of his vast projects and his towering ambition in the *bourgeois* tone of Lombard street and the 'Change. Nothing makes a character, which is out of nature, go down at all, but extraordinary power displayed in the delineation of it. This is the case of the Meg Merrilies of Walter Scott, of Caliban and the Weird sisters; it is even true of that singular, but powerful production, so often mentioned in this article, Melmoth the Wanderer. But we are not satisfied with "The Disowned," in this particular. For the expression of dark and malignant energies merely, there is nothing in this novel to be compared with the portraiture of Glanville in 'Pelham,' and especially to his 'confession,' except it be the character of Wolfe, to which we shall presently advert. Another exception that we take to the part of the work is, that Mordaunt is too metaphysical—too often, "deep contemplative." Our objection is not to the thing itself, which is very pretty, but only to the excess of it, which makes many pages of the work prosy and heavy, in spite of the deep interest we learn to feel in every thing relating to that very interesting personage. The following may be taken as a favorable specimen of these effusions, in which, from our own "love of holy musing," we confess that, whatever may be its faults, we think there is, after all, a certain sweet and soothing melancholy :—

"Fondly and full of thought Mordaunt surveyed the scene before him. 'Beautiful night!' said he. 'What are the day and gaudy sun to thee! Stars, shade, stillness, it is in you that the heart hoards its dearest and holiest treasures of memory and thought! With you they are dormant through the common and garish day—with you they awaken to consecrate the hour when nothing is around us but our dreams! Oh, that in the madness of those dreams there was more a method. We are told that the mind has worked out, from its strong and breathing fancies, shapes which do picture the dead, so that it has been deceived by its own phantasma, and clasped the visions of the overheated brain for the very substance of a fearful truth; and hence have been traced, to a natural origin, the forms and spectral things which the living have deemed shadows from the grave!'

" 'But if it be thus, wherefore come not even those mockeries of our senses unto me? Have not my thoughts, for ever and for ever, sate brooding upon the teeming and fertile past, and dreamt, to delirium, over all that time and the harsh tomb have snatched from my grasp! Have I not called unto the wandering air, and the mystic night! Have I not for days made myself exempt from nature's food, and fasted upon fiery hopes and unearthly desires? Have I not held vigil upon vigil till the eye seemed parched and shrivelling from the unnatural want of the dews of sleep? And then, when the soul was literally wearing itself away from this shroud of flesh, and so growing fit for a kindred commune, have I not invoked, and prayed, and knelt, and sent a voice of agony and wo unto the land of spirits, and heard no echo in return?—none! All—even thy love, my lost, my unforgotten—thy love, which once seemed to me eternal—all was silence, darkness, death! My heart looked from this world unto the world of dreams, and in vain: there, as here, a pilgrim in a peopleless desert, girt with a heavy and burning air, and sinking beneath the palpable weight, and dread, and horror of an eternal loneliness!'

" 'But this is more than idle—beautiful night! with thy balm and softness, and thy maternal love, spreading over this troubled earth with a deep and still sanctity—and you, fresh-breathng winds, and fragrant herbs and grass, and matted trees, which the sun never pierces, and where a vague spirit moving calls, as a tribute tenderness from meditation, and poetry from thought—forgive me for I have wronged you. It is from you that the dead speak, and their whispered and sweet voices have tidings of consolation and joy—it is you, and the murmur of the waters, and the humming stillness of noon, and the melodious stars, which have tones for the heart, not ear, and whatever in the living lyres of the universe have harmony and intelligence—it is you, all of you, that are the organs of a love which has only escaped from clay to blend itself with the great elements, and become with them, creating and universal! O beautiful and soothing mystery of nature, that while the spirit quits the earth, the robes, which on earth it wore, remain to hallow this world to the survivors! remain not only to moulder and decay, but to revive, to remingle with the life around, and to give, even in the imperishability of matter, a type of the immortal essence of the soul!'" Vol. ii. pp. 161–163.

Among the subordinate characters of the novel, there are three particularly entitled to the readers attention. These are Talbot, as described by himself in the "History of the Vain Man," (vol. i. p. 128.)—Warner, or the "Ambitious Artist"—and Wolfe, the stern, fanatical republican, and radical reformer at that time.

Talbot's account of himself is extremely spirited and characteristic—and, bating a little extravagance in what relates to his boyish days, is unquestionably a picture not less just than lively of the contradictions and absurdities of a morbid vanity. Let it not be said that his barbarous treatment of a woman, whose grace he had been at so much pains to win, is unnatural or exaggerated. No man, we are persuaded, who has any knowledge of the world or of the human heart, will think so. The maxim of La Rochefocault is undoubtedly true—*Il n'y a point de passion où l'amour de soi-même regne si puissamment que dans l'amour.* Let any one who doubts this only be at the pains of analyzing the nature and origin of jealousy, and especially its effect, (so well understood by coquettes,) when mingled even in the smallest quantities with the tender passion, to keep it seething and effervescing in an almost preternatural degree. In a word, it is the hardest thing in the world, even for the most experienced *conoscenti*, to discriminate between the effects of self-love and of love in a *liaison* of the sort.

The character of poor Warner is a striking, and to us, a novel conception. He is a young artist, devoured and consumed with the love of fame. Man delights him not, nor woman neither. The honors, the riches of the world, are dross to him. He lives only in the future—he "paints for posterity"—he thirsts and pants after immortality, as the hart panteth after the water-brooks. He would make any worldly sacrifice, and count it nothing, so it enabled him to produce a master-piece. At length, he conceived the plan of an historical picture—the subject was to be the trial of Charles I. in Westminster Hall. The glowing images crowd into his mind, like airy spirits about the wand of an enchanter—they disturb his sleep, they haunt his dreams, they visit him as in a vision by day, and people his solitude with an ideal train. Perpetually engaged in his all-engrossing and too pleasing task, the work grows apace. It becomes that one absorbing passion—that single, predominant idea, so long dwelt upon until the mind confounds it with reality, which causes or constitute madness. At length it is finished, and, in the fondness and confidence of youthful ambition, the poor artist contrives to get the opinion of a connoisseur, (Sir Joshua Reynolds) upon its merits. That opinion was unfavourable—the veteran thought the young aspirant not without talent, but altogether without the discipline and judgment necessary to its success—the picture he condemned to the flames. The unexpected shock is too much for the sensitive and melancholy mind of Warner, wrought up into a fever and delirious emotion, by the hopes which he had so long and so vainly cherished—by the confident persuasion which he had felt but a moment before, that his success was infallible, and "those immortal garlands,"—the reward and the crown of genius—already blooming for his brow. His despair is madness—"madness laughing in its ireful mood" at what were once its dearest illusions. His interest in all things ceases—his enthusiasm is succeeded by languor and dejection—his health rapidly decays—a hectic flush upon the cheek reveals the slow fever which is consuming his vitals. He is enabled by the assistance of friends to make a pilgrimage to Italy—but neither the balmy climate, nor the master-pieces of the art which now engross his attention, and even awaken his fatal talent once more, nor the tranquillity of his feelings, which resignation to his disappointments, and the healing influences of time seemed at length to have restored—availed him anything. He dies at Rome. Such is the outline of the picture—which is filled up in a highly interesting and even forcible manner, though we feel that there is occasionally something frigid and exaggerated in the style.

Perhaps, however, the most vigorously executed, if not the most original in the conception, is the character of Wolfe—a madman of a different, and at the supposed period of these events, a far more common kind. He is a man of powerful but undisciplined understanding and strong passions, who is become an enthusiast of liberty. But we will let him speak for himself;—

"'You consider then, sir, that these are times in which liberty is attacked,' said Clarence.

"'Attacked !' repeated Wolfe—'attacked !' and then suddenly sinking his voice into a sort of sneer—'why, since the event which this painting is designed to commemorate—I know not if we have ever had one solitary gleam of liberty break along the great chaos of jarring prejudice and barbarous law which we term, forsooth, a glorious constitution. Liberty attacked ! no, boy—but it is a time when liberty may be gained.'

"Perfectly unacquainted with the excited politics of the day, or the growing and mighty spirit which then stirred through the minds of men, Clarence remained silent; but his evident attention flattered the fierce republican, and he proceeded.

" 'Ay,' he said slowly, and as if drinking in a deep and stern joy from his conviction in the truth of the words he uttered—'Ay—I have wandered over the face of the earth, and I have warmed my soul at the fires which lay hidden under his quiet surface; I have been in the city and the desert —the herded and banded crimes of the old world, and the scattered, but bold hearts which are found among the mountains and morasses of the new; and in either I have beheld that seed sown, which, from a mustard grain, too scanty for a bird's beak, shall grow up to be a shelter and a home for the whole family of man. I have looked upon the thrones of kings, and lo, the anointed ones were in purple and festive pomp; and I looked *beneath* the thrones, and I saw want and hunger, and despairing wrath gnawing the foundations away. I have stood in the streets of that great city, where mirth seems to hold an eternal jubilee, and beheld the noble riot, while the peasant starved ; and the priest build the altars to Mammon, piled from the earnings of groaning labor, and cemented with blood and tears. But I looked farther, and saw in the rear chains sharpened into swords, misery ripening into justice, and famine darkening into revenge; and I laughed as I beheld, for I knew that the day of the oppressed was at hand.'

"Somewhat awed by the prophetic tone, though revolted by what seemed to him the novelty and the fierceness of the sentiments of the republican, Clarence, after a brief pause, said—

" 'And what of our own country ?'

"Wolfe's brow darkened. 'The oppression here,' said he, 'has not been so weighty, therefore the re-action will be less strong; the parties are more blended, therefore their separation will be more arduous; the extortion is less strained, therefore the endurance will be more meek; but soon or late the struggle must come: bloody will it be, if the strife be even; gentle and lasting, if the people predominate.' " Vol. i. pp. 101, 102.

A scene which afterwards occurs between him and the haughty Lord Borodaile, displays, still more strikingly, the terrible energies of this *tête volcanique.*

"With a motion, a little rude and very contemptuous, the passenger attempted to put Wolfe aside and win his path. Little did he know of the unyielding nature he had to do with; the next instant, the republican with a strong hand, forced him from the pavement into the very kennel, and silently and coldly continued his way.

"The wrath of the discomfitted passenger was vehemently kindled.

" 'Insolent dog!' cried he in a loud and arrogant tone, 'your baseness is your protection.' Wolfe turned rapidly, and made but two strides before he was once more by the side of his defeated opponent.

" 'What were you pleased to observe?' said he, in his low, deep hoarse voice.

"Clarence stopped. There will be mischief done here, thought he, as he called to mind the stern temper of the republican.

" 'Merely,' said the other, struggling with his rage, 'that it is not for men of my rank to avenge the insults offered us by those of yours?'

" 'Your rank,' said Wolfe, bitterly retorting the contempt of the stranger, in a tone of the loftiest disdain; 'your rank, poor changeling! And what are you, that you should lord it over me? Are your limbs stronger? your muscles firmer? your proportions juster? or, if you disclaim physical comparisons, are your mental faculties of a higher order than his who now mocks at your pretensions, and challenges you to prove them? Are the treasures of science expanded to your view? Are you lord of the elysium of poetry, or the thunderbolts of eloquence?—Have you wit to illumine, or judgment to combine, or energy to control? or are you, what in reality you appear, dwindled and stunted in the fair size and sinews of manhood—overbearing, yet impotent—tyrannical, yet ridiculous? Fool! fool!—(and here Wolfe's voice rose, and his dark countenance changed its expression of mockery into fierceness)—go home, and revenge yourself on your slaves for the reproof you have drawn down upon yourself! Go!—goad! gall! trample—the more you grind your minions now, the more terrible will be their retribution hereafter; excite them beyond endurance, with your weak and frivolous despotism, the debauched and hideous abortions of a sickly and unnatural state of civilization! Go! every insult, every oppression, you heap on those whom God has subjected to your hand, but accelerates the day of their emancipation—but files away, link by link, the iron of their bondage—but sharpens the sword of justice, which, in the first wrath of an incensed and awakened people, becomes also for their conquered oppressors the weapon of revenge!'

"The republican ceased, and pushing the stranger aside, turned slowly away. But this last insult enraged the passenger (who, during the whole of the reformer's harangue, had been almost foaming with passion) beyond all prudence. Before Wolfe had proceeded two paces, he muttered a desperate, but brief oath, and struck the reformer with a strength so much beyond what his slight and small figure appeared to possess, that the powerful and gaunt frame of Wolfe recoiled backward several steps, and, had it not been for the iron railing of the neighbouring area, would have fallen to the ground.

"Clarence pressed forward; the face of the rash aggressor was turned towards him; the features were Lord Borodaile's. He had scarcely time to make this discovery, before Wolfe had recovered himself. With a wild and savage cry, rather than exclamation, he threw himself upon his antagonist, twined his sinewy arms around the frame of the struggling but powerless nobleman, raised him in the air, with the easy strength of a man lifting a child, held him aloof for one moment, with a bitter and scornful laugh of wrathful derision, and then dashed him to the ground, and, planting his foot upon Borodaile's breast, said—

" 'So shall it be with all of you: there shall be but one instant between your last offence and your first but final debasement. Lie there: it is your proper place! By the only law which you yourself acknowledge,—the law which gives the right divine to the strongest. If you stir limb or muscle, I will crush the breath from your body.'

"But Clarence was now by the side of Wolfe, a new and more powerful opponent.

" 'Look you,' said he: 'you have received an insult, and you have done yourself justice. I condemn the offence, and quarrel not with you for the punishment; but that punishment is now past, remove your foot, or—'

" 'What?' shouted Wolfe, fiercely, every vein in his countenance swelling, and his lurid and vindictive eye, from its black and shaggy brow flashing with the released fire of long-pent and cherished passions.

" 'Or,' answered Clarence, calmly, 'I will hinder you from committing murder.'

"At that instant, the watchman's voice was heard, and the night's guardian himself was seen hastening from the far end of the street, towards the place of contest. Whether this circumstance, or Clarence's answer, somewhat changed the current of the republican's thoughts, or whether his anger, suddenly raised, was now as suddenly subsiding, we know not: but he slowly and deliberately moved his foot from the breast of his baffled foe, and, bending down, seemed endeavouring to ascertain the mischief he had done. Lord Borodaile was perfectly insensible." Vol. i. pp. 206-8.

After "giving the word" and "testifying" much for "the good old cause," both in public and in private, to very little purpose, among a sinful and perverse generation—for it was only in France that the age of reason was come, and all the blessings of the political millenium were, of course, reserved for that favored land—Wolfe determined to make short work of his reforms, by assassinating, at once, two of the obnoxious ministers. He accordingly lies in wait for them—but mistaking our heroes, Clarence and Mordaunt, for them, unfortunately kills the latter, and is hanged for the misplaced homicide, on the same gallows with Crauford and his clerk Bradly, convicted at last of their fraudulent practices.

The scenes in the encampment of the Gipseys, and the character of King Cole, are very well done—as is also the description of the high life below stairs at "Copperas' Bower."

The fashionable tittle-tattle is rather stupid—at least it is not so good as the same thing in Pelham. We found the St. George's and the Aspedens and the Quintowns, all great bores—as also the Trollolops, the Calythorps and the Findlaters. We had almost forgot to mention that we are introduced into one of those famous circles in which Burke and Beuclere, and Johnson and Goldsmith, and Garrick figured in the last century—but the author has not made much of it; as, indeed, what author could? or what fiction come up to the naked truths as it is revealed in the invaluable Omnium Gatherum of that first of biographers and of boobies, the incomparable Bozzy?

We have hitherto made our quotations exclusively with a view to our reader's edification. We shall be indulged, therefore, in adding but a single one for the gratification of our own peculiar taste. It is a panegyric upon supper, executed with great spirit, and altogether *con amore*. It may be accepted, though a little out of place, as a sort of doxology to our article on M. Ude's book. It came over our own souls with a most refreshing and balmy unction—"like a steam of rich distilled perfumes." We think nothing comparable to suppers—*petits soupers* arrayed in all their appropriate charms of delicate wit, delicate wines, and delicate viands. We are so enthusiastic on the subject, that we have often wondered why, in the never-ending controversy about the comparative merits of the ancients and the moderns, no champion of the former has thought of urging it as an unanswerable proof of their superiority that their principal meal was supper *eo nomine*. It may be thought, perhaps, that our dinners by candle-light, are much the same thing—but we humbly conceive not—no more than a "fashionable" man's residence, in what he is pleased to nickname a "cottage," makes him taste the pleasures of a true "Cotter's Saturday Night."—But we must let our author say the rest, for to do any thing like justice to our own feelings, upon this subject, would require a seperate article.

"That was the age of suppers! Happy age! Meal of ease and mirth; when wine and night lit the lamp of wit! O, what precious thing were said and looked at those banquets of the soul. There, epicurism was in the lip as well as the palate, and one had humour for a *hors d' œuvre* and repartee for an *entremet*. In dinner, there is something too pompous, too formal, too exigent of attention, for the delicacies and levities of *persiflage*. One's intellectual appetite, like the physical, is coarse, but dull. At dinner one is fit only for eating, *after* dinner only for politics. But supper was a glorious relic of the ancients.

"The bustle of the day had thoroughly wound up the spirit, and every stroke upon the dial plate of wit was true to the genius of the hour.— The wallet of diurnal anecdote was full, and 'craved unloading. The great meal—that vulgar first love of the appetite—was over, and one now only flattered it into coquetting with another. The mind, disengaged and free, was no longer absorbed in a salmi, or burthened with a joint. The *gourmand* carried the nicety of his physical perception to his moral, and applauded a *bon mot* instead of a *bonne bouche*.

"Then too one had no necessity to keep a reserve of thought for the after evening; supper was the final consummation, the glorious funeral pyre of day. One could be merry till bed-time without an interregnum.

Nay, if in the ardor of convivialism, one did—we merely hint at the possibility of such an event—if one *did* exceed the narrow limit of strict ebriety, and open the heart with a ruby key, one had nothing to dread from the cold, or what is worse, the warm looks of ladies in the drawing-room; no fear that an imprudent word, in the amatory fondness of the fermented blood, might expose one to matrimony and settlements.— There was no tame trite medium of propriety and suppressed confidence, no bridge from board to bed, over which a false step (and your wine cup is a marvellous corruptor of ambulatory rectitude) might precipitate into an irrecoverable abyss of perilous communication or unwholesome truth. One's pillow became at once the legitimate and natural bourne to 'the overheated brain;' and the generous rashness of the cœnatorial reveller was not damped by untimeous caution or ignoble calculation.

"But 'we have changed all that now:' Sobriety has become the successor of suppers; the great ocean of moral encroachment has not left us one little Island of refuge. Miserable supper lovers that we are, like the native Indians of America, a scattered and daily disappearing race, we wander among strange customs, and behold the innovating and invading dinner, spread gradually over the very space of time, in which the majesty of supper once reigned undisputed and supreme!" Vol. i. pp. 111, 112.

—

For the "Tales of the Great St. Bernard," we find that we have left ourselves quite too little space. They are said to be by the author of 'Salathiel,' and will certainly increase his reputation. In point of *style*, for example, they are very superior to the more elaborate work which we have just been reviewing—there is far more spirit, simplicity and force in Mr. Croly's composition—in short, it is a nearer approach to the perfect propriety and chastened elegance of our classical authors.

The two volumes contain eight tales of various character and extent—though the second entitled "Hebe," is almost as long as all the rest put together.

These tales come up somewhat after the manner of those in Bocacio's Decamerone. A number of travellers casually meet at the Hospice of the Great St. Bernard, where they are detained, although it was the *belle saison*, by one of those sudden changes in the atmosphere, so common in the fitful climate of the Alps. Our traveller had entered it on "a day made in the prodigality of the finest season of the year. The snowy scalps of the hills were interspersed with stripes of verdure that had seen the light for the first time within memory." The bee (the surest harbinger of summer, says the book) was roaming and humming away among the thistle-down and mosses, which even an Alpine frost could not kill—and the soft gales from the mountains seemed to breathe the voluptuous fragrance of Italy. But he had not been two hours under the roof of the Hospice, before the whole face of nature was changed. A violent storm of wind hurled down upon the convent a tremendous avalanche from the sides of Mount Velan. "The sun was blotted out of the heavens; snow in every shape that it could be flung into by the most furious wind, whirlpool, drift and hill, flashed and swept along. Before evening it was fourteen feet high before the Hospice."

The following description of the interior and inmates of that venerable asylum, during the tempest, can scarcely fail to be interesting to our readers:

"As the night fell, the storm lulled at intervals, and I listened with anxiety to the cries and noises that announced the danger of travellers surprised in the storm. The fineness of the season had tempted many to cross the mountain without much precaution against the change, and the sounds of horns, bells, and the barking of the dogs, as the strangers arrived, kept me long awake. By morning the convent was full; the world was turned to universal snow; the monks came down girded for their winter excursions; the domestics were busy equipping the dogs: fires blazed, cauldrons smoked; every stranger was pelissed and furred up to the chin, and the whole scene might have passed for a Lapland carnival. But the Hospice is provided for such casualties; and, after a little unavoidable tumult, all its new inhabitants were attended to with much more than the civility of a continental inn, and with infinitely less than its discomfort. The gentlemen adjourned to the reading-room, where they found books and papers, which probably seldom passed the Italian frontier. The ladies turned over the port-folios of prints, many of which are the donations of strangers who had been indebted to the hospitality of the place; or amused themselves at the piano in the drawing-room, for music is there above the flight of the lark; or pored over the shelves to plunge their souls in some "flattering tale" of hope and love, orange groves, and chevaliers plumed, capped, and guitarred into irresistible captivation. The scientific manipulated the ingenious collection of the mountain minerals made by the brotherhood. Half a dozen herbals from the adjoining regions lay open for the botanist; a finely bound and decorated album, that owed obligations to every art but the art of poetry, lay open for the pleasantries, the memorials, and the wonderings of every body; and for those who loved sleep best there were eighty beds." Vol. i. pp. 8-9.

Every thing went on very well for a few days—but the storm obstinately continued to rage, an antedated winter seemed to have set in, and the sojourners of the Hospice of the Great St. Bernard began to suffer from a plague, against which its hospitable walls afforded as little protection, as if they had been those of a palace. To relieve himself from the *ennui* which all felt, our traveller sought the acquaintance of an English gentleman of his own school, who, in the course of their conversation, told him the "Squire's Tale," to illustrate the "Woes of Wealth."

This is the first, and in our opinion the best of the series. It bears a strong resemblance to the Vicar of Wakefield, and is not altogether unworthy to be mentioned in connection with that charming novel, not only for the general drift and structure of the fable, but for the simplicity of its style, the candor and *bonhommie* with which the hero tells his story, and a certain sly and quiet humor that pervades it throughout.

The gentleman begins by informing our traveller that "he had run away from England, not through taste, but through absolute compulsion. He was too lucky, too important, and too rich to be able to live at home—so that he was come abroad to be nobody, to be good for nothing, and to be happy." He had been bred to the bar, and practised in Westminster Hall, for some years, "with what was considered a remarkable success in the profession." That is to say, when he was of no more than five years standing at the bar, he was, "neither in debt nor in despair," and was actually able, by the sheer profits of his practice, to indulge himself in the luxury of a new wig and gown. Such rare good fortune naturally excited a great deal of sensation of one sort or other, and the future honors of the lucky novice were predicted with confidence by the experienced, and fully anticipated by himself. There is too much reason to suspect, however, that he never had at bottom any very sincere love for that captivating profession ; else he had not been induced to abandon it on such slight grounds, and betake himself to obscurity and five hundred a year in the country. The reasons he gives for foregoing all his high hopes at the very moment when "the tide, which taken at the flood leads on to fortune," was setting so strongly in his favour, are briefly summed up as follows :—

"In the same midsummer circuit when I saw six king's counsel and two judges give way to the respective demands of gout, dropsy and asthma, the natural fruit of success in their trade, I was seized at Lincoln by the fen-fever, which, after chaining me to my bed for six months, left me in such a state of debility that, on taking the advice of my pillow against the advice of all 'my friends,' I abandoned the hope of ever dying lord chancellor.

"The law had, however, taught me one thing, that every man who will take the trouble of judging for himself, is the best judge of his own affairs. It taught me another too, that there is no crime more easily forgiven than the retirement of a rival. Armed thus against the regrets of my cotemporaries, and the advice of my most pertinacious friends, I made up my mind at once ; sold off my law-books, rendered invaluable as they were by many a fragment of random poetry, the product of briefless hours, and occasionally illuminated with pen and ink caricatures of some of the most formidable blockheads of the profession ; and finally shook off the dust of my feet against the gates of Westminster." Vol. i. p. 12.

So he hies him to his few paternal acres about fifty miles from London, and, in three days from his bidding farewell "to all his greatness," we find him "sitting at a casement overlooking a quiet valley, covered with cows and clover, and discussing a cool bottle of wine to the song of gold-finches and linnets, without a tear for operas, silk-gowns, or debates in Lords or Commons." We are not suprised to find this romantic apostate from black-letter and special demurrers, in spite of these pretty rural sights and sounds, soon languishing for want of some engrossing interest. He found one—we should think, (judging from our own feelings) absolutely the only one that can keep any rational being (the choir of poets always excepted,) alive in the country. But he shall tell his own story.

'Arthur Young advises a settler in the country to make his first application to the parson; but a writer on husbandry can think of nothing but tithes. I made my first application to the parson; but it was to marry me. In one of my annual visits, I had found a pretty creature straying among my carnations and roses, as blooming as themselves, and as innocent as the butterfly that shook its yellow wings over them. She fled like a fawn, and though I was not sportsman enough to pursue, I did what was just as absurd; I took her image with me, and saw it for the next six months impasted on the brown pages of my folios. The sylph-like shape started upon me from the statutes-at-large; and many a time I saw the coral lip and blue eye gleaming from parchment as wrinkled as her grandmother.

"The heart of man has been long said to be a craving thing, a void that must be filled. The virtuoso fills it with Roman potsherds, buttons of King Brute, and farthings of Queen Elizabeth. The connoisseur fills it with undoubted portraits of Shakspeare manufactured within the week, noseless statues, and canvass covered with deformity. The old bachelor is proud of being the last possessor of a queue, of adhering to powder with a fidelity strong even to the grave, and of exhibiting the most ridiculous figure that walks the round world. The old lady, destitute of other delights, satiates her vacuity with cats, china, and the affections of canary birds.

"But my tastes did not lie in those directions, and yet I had my vacuity too. Neither the love of law, nor the ambition of the woolsack, had stopped up the gulf, though they prevented its spreading, like the gulf of Curtius, to the absorption of the whole man. The hubbub of the courts, where glorious uncertainty sits of old, and like Milton's fiend, by "decision more embroils the fray," might deafen for the hour my acute perception of those whisperings which told me of the folly of wasting life on the fooleries and fallacies of mankind, of turning my brain into a box of black letter and dusty bitterness, and of struggling through forty or fifty years of obsolete study, obscure quarrel, and exhausted lungs, only to die of the gout at last; but the moment of my quitting the clamour of the noonday Themis, for my lonely chambers in the temple, always brought back my rustic fantasies; and nothing but a fortitude worthy of a dancing bear, or of a monarch standing out the bows and congratulations of a levee day, had often prevented my inlaying my brief with bucolics, and turning poet during term. Now, however, the self-denial was at an end. I had registered a vow against "making the worse appear the better reason" for the rest of my days; and, on a day propitious to the affairs of the heart, I discovered that my sylph had no objection to be married, and that she would as soon be married to me as to any one else. She was the thirteenth daughter of our curate, a sound divine, who served three churches on seventy pounds a year. He was honest enough to feign no hesitation where he felt none; and I was made, as the world phrases it, a happy man.

"I may be forgiven for talking of this period of my life, for it was my pleasantest. My sylph had laid aside her wings without giving up her playfulness. She was pretty and fond; she thought me by much the wisest and most learned personage the sun shone on; and grieved as she was by the superior finery of a sugar-baker's establishment, whose labours sweetened half the coffee of Europe, and whose wealth unluckily overflowed in a new mansion and preposterous demesne within a stone's throw of our cottage, she preserved, at least, the average temper of the matrimonial state. While she was busy with domestic cares, I was plying my pen; and statesmen yet unborn may thank me for the gratuitious wisdom of the hints that I threw out in the shape of pamphlet and paragraph. But the world is an ungrateful one after all; and I was not summoned to the privy council.

"In this primitive way I glided on for twenty years; famous for the earliest roses, the largest cucumbers, and the two prettiest daughters in the county. I played the castanets, spoke French and interpreted a turnpike-act, all better than any man for fifty miles round. I was applied to for cheap law by the ploughmen, wisdom by the puzzled magistrates; and was even occasionally consulted in his Greek by the excellent curate, whose Oxford recollections were considerably rubbed out by the wear and tear of half a century: even the sugar-baker, in his less exalted moments, admitted that I was rather an intelligent kind of person for a man of five hundred a year. Yet if this mighty refiner's praise were flattering to my vanity, his opulence was fatal to my peace. The liveries, equipage and banquets of Mr. Molasses disturbed my wife's pillow; and every new dinner of three courses turned our bread into bitterness.

"But the county election drew on: and the sugar-baker, rich enough to purchase the souls and bodies of a province, began his canvass by a double expansion of his hospitality. Laced liveries twice as deep, dinners twice as sumptuous, balls twice as frequent, and guests flocking in crowd's, stimulated my wife's vexation to the utmost pitch. Many a keen glance was levelled at the humiliating contrast of our woodbine-faced cottage with the mighty mansion of yellow brick that towered like a mountain of flame above our trees; many a murmur I heard at the folly of abandoning a profession in which a man "might be a lord" instead of being extinguished by a trader; and, from time to time, a curtain lecture exploded so directly on my head, that, if I were younger, I might have been frightened into flying the country, burying myself in parchments again, and dying a chancellor after all." Vol. i. pp. 12, 15.

This long extract has, as Falstaff says, "a two-fold virtue in it." It is, in the first place, a fair specimen of the vivacity and sprightliness which distinguish the style of this tale; and in the next, it carries the reader at once into the very midst of things. This Mr. Molasses and his household are quite as important in the Squire's story, as they could possibly be ambitious of becoming in society. Every thing turns upon them in the sequel. The thirteenth daughter of the poor curate is never at ease while Mordecai sitteth at the king's gate. She is become the wife of a retired gentleman, and so, clearly entitled, in her own opinion at least, to look down upon the up-start fortunes of her vulgar neighbours. But in this perverse world, unhappily, *le pouvoir n'est jamais ridicule;* and when she laughed at their awkward display of finery and fashon, it was on, what is expressively called in a homely phrase, the wrong side of her mouth. In short, the poor woman, who was as ambitious and fidgetty as her husband was tranquil and philosophic, was dying of envy. Her day of triumph, however, was at hand. The death of a rich nabob, a distant relative of our hero, whom the latter had never seen but once, brings him a windfal of ten thousand a year— The tidings are communicated to him by a solicitor who came post-haste for the purpose.

"Never was solicitor received as was this man of mire on his introduction to my family. The whole household were in ecstacy. My wife, no longer the sylph culling lilies and roses, but a handsome, solid matron, deep in the secrets of the cuisine—my daughters, two tall and glowing creatures, on the verge of womanhood—the very house maid under my roof saw, with the quickness of her sex, the whole glittering future. I, too, philosopher as I thought myself, was not without my splendid follies : and when at length we sat down to our supper, not even the din of Mr. Molasses' closing festival, the rattling of carriages, and the squabbles of footmen, were heard in the strife of delighted tongues, the scorn of my wife for the mushroom money of trade, and the rapture of my fair daughters at the prospect of a season in London.

"The solicitor, too, happy that his neck was not broken, relaxed from his professional grimness, and told bar stories, valuable for at least their age. My best bottle of claret was broached ; and, before I bade the world good night, there was not a more exhilarated sensorium under the canopy of the stars.

"The hour ought to have been happy, for it was the last [happy one] that I ever experienced." Vol. i. p. 17.

Here begin the "Woes of Wealth," which are all, however, we are happy to inform our readers, very much of the same stamp with the "Miseries" of our renowned friend, and we may say fellow-townsmen, Sensitive and Testy.* The traveller and his sylph begin themselves now to be objects of envy to their neighbours, who imagine they plainly perceive a difference in their deportment since they got up in the world. Censure, ridicule and misrepresentation behind their backs—rudeness, peevishness, captious irritability, and other instances of incivility to their faces, begin to be their portion. Our hero, in spite of his philosophy, finds it impossible to live in peace with the world— his friends take offence, and drop off one after another, and the whole neighbourhood is presently in arms against him.

Meanwhile, his situation at home is scarcely less disagreeable. The whole arrangement of his house and household is altered. His wife is determined to live up to their rank in the world, and to feed her old grudges for the unprovoked outrages of the Molasses', who had presumed to display their wealth so near her when she had none to show in return. Milliners, upholsterers, *et id genus omne* were straightway put in requisition.

"But had I no home ? I had, and one so suddenly sumptuous, that I dreaded to touch any thing for fear of dismantling fifty invaluable things of or-molu, japan, and china ; *chefs d' œuvre* every trinket of them. My chairs were figured satin, too costly to be looked at ; for they were enveloped in eternal bibs and tuckers of canvass, and too delicate to bear any of the rustic usage, the leanings, loungings, and book burdens, that to me constituted the whole excellence of a chair. Wherever I trod, there reposed some specimen of the arts too exquisite for human feet ;—and after having once in my hasty entrance from the garden trodden, black as gunpowder, the Brussels countenance of the great Blucher on a carpet un-

* Mr. Berresford, author of "The Miseries of Human Life," is or was a native of Charleston.

matched on this side of the Channel, I interdicted myself the pleasure of treading on carpets for the time to come.

"I liked quiet. The hand of the workman was in full activity from morning till night. I hated to be driven from my customary room. A new ukase had ordered it to be fitted up in the style of a library comporting the lord of ten thousand a year. It was fitted up accordingly, and I never knew comfort in it again. My rough-backed old books were driven into banishment for strangers in morocco, which I never desired to touch ; and my rambling pencil-sketches, my treasured letters, my rather dusty memoranda, all the clinging recollections, the pleasant records of old days, old dreams, and old friends, were put under sentence of eternal exile.

"Twenty years were extinguished in a week of papering, painting, and general renovation; and to make the change more unpalatable still, the whole was under the superintendence of a Decorator, a 'professor' of puttings up and pullings down, a coxcomb from London, of supreme authority in matters of taste, and who made himself commander-in-chief of every soul in the house from the moment of his alighting from his 'britchska.' This Raphael of paper-stainers I was, by regular contract, obliged to entertain at my table, where he exhibited himself so perfect a connoisseur in claret and champagne, that I had only to swallow my wine in silence ; and talked so familiarly of princes and dukes, whom he had whitewashed into elegance, that he half turned the heads of my wife and daughters. He rode my horses, taught my maid-servants how to rouge, established a billiard table in my house, to which he gave a general invitation to his professional acquaintances ; and by his dinner converse inflamed my four footmen into a demand for an increase of wages, and an allowance for eau de Cologne.

"I bore all this for a while. Strong inclinations to kicking the puppy out sometimes nearly mastered me. But I kept my foot in peace ; until one evening, straying to find a quiet moment in a lonely part of my garden, I heard the fellow ranting a tragedy speech in the most Parisian style. The speech was followed by a scream, and the sight of my younger daughter Emily rushing towards me in the highest possible indignation. The Decorator followed half tipsy. I interrupted his speech by an application to his feelings from the foot that had so long been kept in reluctant peace. He was astonished, but he had mingled with too many potentates to feel much abashed. His natural ease speedily returned, and he actually made his proposals for my daughter on the spot. It was answered by a repetition of the discipline. The puppy grew impudent, and talked of country bumpkins. He had fully earned a third application to his sensibilities, and he got what he earned. My last kick sent him down the steps of my hall-door.

"I had now satiated my wrath, done my duty, and cleared my table of a nuisance. But what is to be had for nothing in this world of debt and credit ? On the other side of the account, I had laid grounds for an action; I had sent a puppy to scatter scandal like wildfire wherever he showed his impudent face ; and I had left my house half furnished within a week of a masquerade, which, in all my scorn of mankind, my wife had insisted on giving, for the acknowledged purpose of returning the fêtes that my luckless legacy had already brought upon us, but, as I verily believe, with the pious intention of breaking the hearts of the whole Molasses dynasty finally and for ever,

" 'The fête was inevitable ; for, in the very hour in which I expelled the Decorator, the cards had been despatched ; and I had the indulgence of receiving at once the compliments of the dynasty that they would be 'proud of the honour,' &c., a horse-load of billets to the same effect from our whole population, and a notice of action for 'an assault on the person of Augustus Frederic Byron Ultramarine, Esq., damages laid at five thousand pounds !'

"Here was a consequence of being just twenty times as rich as I ever expected to be. I could muster up a show of resolution now and then; and, like a falling Cæsar, in this extremity of my dictatorship, I determined to show the original vigour of my character. I became a reformer of the house, ordered my four footmen into my presence, and gave them a lecture on general conduct, which, if they had the sense to understand, would have been worth all the lace on their livery. They bowed, withdrew, and in the next five minutes sent a paper signed by the four 'requesting their *congé*.' I never signed anything in my life with half the pleasure. The female authorities below stairs were beyond my province and my hope; but the dignified resignation of their flirts rendered it a matter of delicacy that the ladies of the scullery should send in their resignation too. It was most graciously accepted. I turned them out root and branch, and, on that night sat down in a house containing not a female but my wife, daughters, and an old housekeeper, too purblind to flirt, and too lame to run away. A neighbouring cow-boy was summoned to tend my horses, and I had the honour of locking my own hall-door." Vol. i. pp. 31–34

Having thus made *maison nette* of his whole establishment, the difficulty was to provide for the reception of their guests at the contemplated fête, or if that were impossible, to dispense with their company upon some decent pretext :—

"In a grand council held over the breakfast-table, we revolved the several expedients to escape the calamity. Flight, sudden illness of the principals, a violent contagious fever broken out among the domestics, all were suggested, and all found wanting. It was shown that, where the ladies of the vicinage were determined on a party, they would not be repelled by a bulletin of the plague, signed by three king's physicians. The only plausible expedients seemed to be my own, and those were, in the first instance to declare that my London banker had failed, and carried off my thousands, as usual on those occasions to America—an intimation, which, in London, I had seen strip a man of every acquaintance on earth in the course of a single revolution of the sun. But this was overruled, as, in the country, if friendships were not more firm, routs were rarer; and we should have the whole dancing population on us as merry as ever, if we were not worth sixpence in the world. My favourite expedient was to set the house on fire; the true mode after all. But the council broke up without coming to a combustion. The fact was that the women had ordered dresses from the supreme *artiste* of Paris, while the sugar-baker's wife had only ransacked London. Triumph was certain, and the female votes carried it that the evil must be endured, and could be at worse only one night's suffering. With a heavy heart I prepared to be the gayest of the gay.

"Time hurries on in spite of all the reluctance of mankind, and the dreaded night came. It was all that I had expected it to be, with the exception that, from one of the serenest days of summer, the weather changed at a moment's warning into a tempest worthy of the north-west passage. Our fête chàmpetre was blown into a thousand fragments. Our lamps, festooned among our elms, were sent flying like chain-shot through our windows; our 'grand emblematic' transparency, the master-piece of a London Apelles, and which cost, I dare not confess how much, was ripped from top to bottom at the first onset, and discharged with the force of a steam-engine down the 'grand staircase' on the heads of an ascending column of quakers, devils, Jews, and Spanish grandees. The uproar was tremendous; and from my study, in which I had lingered till the first concourse should be quiet and I might venture forth with safety to my limbs, I heard the general crash, not undelighted with the anticipations of its clearing my house.

"Mr. Ultramarine's sudden retreat had left all our ornamental exploits half-born. The cascade, painted to a fac-simile of Tivoli, was carried away by the burst of the rivulet that we had been nursing for the occasion. The *superbe fontaine* on the model of the grand tronc of Versailles, after flinging up half a dozen convulsive jets which burst into the drawing-room windows and extravagated over the company, refused to play a drop more. The organ, expressly brought down from London to captivate us by unseen harmony from a grotto, for which the wall of my study was broken down, firmly resisted the touch of human finger during the night, or gave signs of life only in a succession of alternate screams and groans. The crowd was enormous, the heat stifling, the noise deafening, and the crush hazardous to life and limb. To move, much less to dance, and least of all, to get a glass of wine or a fragment of biscuit without a fair combat, became rapidly out of the question. Fixed, like one of my own candelabra, in the corner to which I had first worked my way, I saw, to my infinite alarm, the crowd increase with out measure. The mask had sanctioned every thing and every body; and I could soon discover through all its pasteboard, that a multitude had made good their entrée who had no invitation but their own. As the throng thickened, its materials seemed palpably to degenerate; the malice of my village friends had mustered the rabble for my fête; nameless figures, whose natural garb served them as masquerade habits, and who played the clown with the truth of nature, fought their way through the mass of bantling and bruised shepherdesses, Dianas, and sultanas. To resist was soon hopeless, and in the act of inquiring by what right a tall ruffian with a watchman's coat and rattle, had made his appearance in my house, I at once received a volley of language that made all my belles clap their hands on their ears; a grasp behind, which left my coat skirtless; and a push before, which deprived me of an old and favourite repeater, that I would not have given for the fee-simple of the corporation.

"A new uproar from below announced that a reinforcement was at hand, in the shape of the footmen, coachmen, and grooms, whom the storm had driven within the house. Like the invasions of the Goths and Vandals, this new irruption of barbarians drove forward the old; disorder "sat umpire of the night." The temporary orchestra, left unfinished by our Decorator, found itself unable to sustain the weight of well-fed beauty that fled to its benches for refuge, and came down, fidlers and all, with a crash of expiring harmony. The "grand" supper-table, after having been fought upon for a considerable time, at length gave way to a grand *assaut* of the principal champions, and after a heave or two rolled the whole batallia to the ground, and itself on the top of them. The conflict was doubly reviewed on the rising of the combatants; decanters, ten guineas a pair, flew like meteors against pier-glasses a hundred guineas a piece. My matchless Hockheim tumblers, ancient as Albert Durer, painted and cut with all indescribable griffins, virgins and boars' heads, "invaluable to the antiquary and man of taste," and whose sale broke the heart of the landgrave that had drained them from his cradle to his climacteric; those my muniments and treasures, that I had reserved for an heir-loom to satisfy my remotest generation of the refinement of their ancestor, and that nothing should or could have won from my safe-keeping, but my wife's begging and praying to have something to show on the table which defied Mr. Molasses and all his money to have, and which would consequently bow down to the dust his and his still prouder wife's hearts; those exquisite emblems, that an ancient Roman would have consecrated in the temple of Bacchus, and that I ought to have refused to all human threats and tears, I saw flashing through air, ground between teeth, trampled under heels, and finally levigated into their original sand.

"The supreme catastrophe of the route at length roused me to a sense of my duty. The chandelier, a huge pile, whose galaxy of prisms, drops and stars would have raised the envy of the Great Mogul, had given early signs of tottering. Our Decorator, 'tis true, had pledged his neck to us for its security, and I had reposed on the pledge, presuming it the more valuable to a fellow who had nothing but his neck to lose. He had even given himself an experimental swing from its chain, and, as neither its time nor his was yet come, he had been suspended in safety. But the general concussion, in which the very walls danced, at last reached the ceiling; a flying-claret jug gave the finishing blow, and down thundered the chandelier in a whirlwind of dust, plaster, and or-molu.

"In real alarm, I extricated myself from the chaos to ascertain the fate of my family, and found my unfortunate wife doubly overwhelmed by the general discomfiture, and the fall of an immense screen, which one of the village architects had, in the fullness of his ingenuity, converted into a partition between the *salle de danse*, as it was announced in our *programme*—for we had a *programme* too—and the supper-room; and which of course the first inundation of belles and beaux had swept away as if it had been gossamer.

"Rescuing the partner of my joys and sorrows from the ruin, with the loss of a whole revenue in lace, feathers, and gros de Naples undone for ever; and, leaving the ground covered over with a full crop of beads and bugles, I bore her, fainting and frightened out of all hope of glory for the night, up to her chamber, which I found already invaded by a festive crowd, whose chief amusement was the examination of every little recess of those shrines in which beauty keeps her secrets against the ravages of time." Vol. i. pp. 35-39.

Notwithstanding these little "woes" at their first setting out, they continue to get along very well in the world, until a further accession of fortune, with a title, comes to lift up the aspirations of the ambitious wife of the new baronet, to still higher objects than as yet had excited them. Among other things, she prevails upon her husband, very much against his better judgment, to squander an immense sum of money in a county election for a seat in Parliament. The motive which overcame his reluctance, was an affront put upon his wife and daughters at a ball, by the family of a haughty patrician, who had hitherto been in the habit of disposing, at his own good will and pleasure, of the representation of the shire. To add, if possible, to the effect of this weighty reason, the Duke took it into his head to patronize the Molasses dynasty, and even to procure for the head of it, the title of Sir Mungo. Lady Molasses—"the better part" of her husband in every sense of the word—was determined he should write himself M. P. as well as Baronet. A tremendous contest ensues, in which our hero is successful. The election protested—new difficulties and troubles ensue. The member elect is overwhelmed with applications for his interest, and with the concerns of every body in the shire. His revenue, great as it was, fell alarmingly short of his expenditure, and his whole financial system threatened to be soon irretrievably deranged. Harrassed and perplexed beyond all sufferance by matters with which he had nothing to do, domestic "woes" of a more formidable character than he had ever yet known, await him. His son elopes with his governess—a *soi-disant emigrée* of figure and fashion, but in fact a *soubrette* player of the lowest class and the loosest morals, with a husband already on her hands ; while two foreigners of distinction—with visages buried in whiskers and mustachios, afterwards discovered to be the assumed disguises of two villainous actors—hatch a plot to run away with his daughters, without their consent, which, only intelligence, most providentially communicated to him, enabled him, with the assistance of the police, to frustrate. And, finally, upon his arrival in London to take his seat in the House of Commons, he finds that his Majesty has been graciously pleased, for important reasons of state, to dissolve the Parliament! New writs of course issue. Sir Mungo takes the field again—and our hero, taught by his sore experience, determines to escape from temptations too strong for flesh and blood to resist, by running away to the continent, where we have had the happiness to hear his strange eventful history.

It will be perceived at the first glance, that "The Squire's Tale" is the very antitheton and antidote of a "fashionable novel." In this respect too it resembles the Vicar of Wakefield. Our readers will recollect the precious farce enacted at the Flamboroughs' by those distinguished personages, Lady Blarney and Miss Carolina Wilhelmina Amelia Skeggs—which, burlesque as it is, is not more extravagant than the dull impertinences and flippant balderdash of Almack's & Co. Indeed, we suspect these latter owe all their success to the very reason, which the author just mentioned gives, for favoring us with that delectable specimen of "high life," viz. "that every reader, however beggarly himself, is fond of high-lived conversation, with anecdotes of lords, ladies, and knights of the garter."

We have not space to say anything more of these interesting tales. We will just add, that the second—entitled "Hebe, or the Wallachian's Tale"—is the most elaborate, (as it is by far the longest of any)—with a strong dash of orientialism in it. It presents some very pleasing pictures of Turkish life and manners, with a great variety of striking incidents, in a uniformly elegant and agreeable style. Of the minor tales, that entitled "The Married Actress," is, in our opinion, decidedly the best. It is *perfectly* well told, presents a just view of human character, and conveys an instructive moral lesson.

CICERO DE REPUBLICA.

1. The Republic of Cicero, translated from the Latin ; and accompanied with a Critical and Historical Introduction. By G. W. Featherstonhaugh, Esq. Fellow of the Geological Society of London; of the American Philosophical Society; of the Lyceum of Natural History of New-York, &c. &c. &c. *New-York. G. & C. Carvill.* 1829.

2. M. Tvllii Ciceronis de Repvblica, librorvm reliquiœ e palimpsesto. Ab Angelo Maio, nvper ervtæ ad editionem Romanam diligentissime expressæ. *Boston. Everett.* 1823.

We should be very sorry to consider this pretended *translation* of Cicero's Republic, by a "Fellow of the Geological Society of London," as a fair specimen of the scholarship of New-York. Although it may argue ourselves unknown, we candidly confess we had not the honour of knowing Mr. Featherstonhaugh, even by name, until we took up this little volume. Our expectations were, therefore, any thing but extravagant. We had not the most distant hope of seeing in it a version worthy of the original. We were even willing to forego a comparison which an author would seem fairly to provoke, by treading in the footsteps of Middleton and Melmoth. But we took it for granted that he had measured his own strength with some degree of caution, before he undertook his labors. We gave him credit for a decent share, as it is called—for some little tincture at least —of classical learning. We thought that at any rate, he could construe and parse a plain sentence, and that, if he were not very profoundly versed in Roman antiquities, he had been at the pains of acquiring, for the nonce, such an acquaintance with them, as his subject made absolutely necessary, and as a boy in the fourth form would not be very vain of possessing. To translate any part of Cicero indeed, in a style at all approaching to the excellence of the original, requires gifts such as it would be quite satirical to mention in connection with Mr. Featherstonhaugh's name. But to interpret him faithfully—to *do* him into good, intelligible, appropriate English—is a task which a man might very well perform, albeit he were, as the slave in the play says, "Davus and not Œdipus." We felt, therefore, every disposition to do justice to the merits, and make all reasonable allowance for the defects of the work. We sat down to our examination of it with a conscientious and solemn impartiality, which the event made absolutely ludicrous. We collated the translation with the original, sentence by sentence, for pages together, until we were entirely satisfied that any further prosecution of the disgustful labor was altogether supererogatory. Indeed, we might have augured as much from the "*Critical* and Historical Introduction," as the author facetiously calls the puerile and trivial common-place prefixed to his version. Although the great fault of this part of the work is its total want of all merit, yet we thought we saw in it some very decided, positive blemishes. We are told, for instance, that Clodius brought forward a law that "whoever had taken away the life of a Roman citizen uncondemned should be interdicted *bread* and water." We have heard of such a thing as a man's being interdicted "water and *fire*"—we know that Cicero speaks of himself as having incurred this interdict at the instance of Clodius—and that *interdicere* is used *absolutely*, for *aqua et igni interdicere* —but we had never heard of an interdiction of "bread and water," until we had the good fortune to read this "*Critical* and Historical Introduction."

The body of the work, however, is worse than one would anticipate even from such omens. Our readers have a right to expect that we shall make out this charge. They will bear with us, therefore, for a few moments, while we execute this very unpleasant but necessary part of our office, and inflict a well-merited chastisement upon a hardy and presumptuous offender. We verily believe, as we have said over and over again in the course of our labors, that we shall never do any thing as a literary people, worthy to be had in remembrance by posterity, until we shall have prepared the way by a course of classical education, very different from the wretched system under which the time of the child and the money of the parent have been hitherto, alike, so prodigally and so uselessly squandered. But zealous as we are in this great cause of learning, of truth and of excellence—deeply as we regret and deprecate the vain wisdom and false philosophy of those who have lent whatever of authority or influence their studies have given them, to the disparagement and depression of this most vital branch of discipline—there is one thing which, if possible, we abominate still more. It is the enemy in our camp. It is the absurd pretensions of sciolists and smatterers, whose ignorance has made scholarship among us the by-word of vulgar scoffers. One such example of a practice, scandalously at variance with profession, does more harm, in such a country as this, than the speculative opinions of a hundred men like Dr. Rush and his school—of considerable cleverness and information in other departments of knowledge, but more than suspected of speaking quite conjecturally, however dogmatically, upon this subject. Classical studies are good for no-

218   CICERO DE REPUBLICA.

thing unless they be elaborate and critical. Better a thousand
times that they were altogether exploded—that a boy should
never so much as look into a Greek or Latin grammar—than
waste upon the acquisition of such an imperfect knowledge of
them, as for any practical purpose, just amounts to no knowledge at all, eight or ten of the most precious years of his life.
What might he not acquire in the same period, if his attention
were confined to his own language! How much more profitably
would he be occupied in awaking his imagination and his sensibilities, in forming his taste, and storing his memory with the
beauties of Shakspeare, and Milton, and Spenser; of Barrow,
Jeremy Taylor, Hume, Addison, Atterbury, than in learning to
repeat by rote a few uncouth grammar rules in a dead language,
and making English nonsense of the matchless eloquence and
poetry of antiquity! The system of education, we repeat it,
which obtained universally in this country a few years ago, and
is far from being entirely reformed even now, was the most profligate and insane waste of time and money, that was ever tolerated by an intelligent people, and we regard *him* as the very
worst enemy of classical studies who preaches a different doctrine, or does any thing that has a tendency still further to debase the standard of excellence where it is already so much lower than it ought to be. But to our task.

The following is the first paragraph of this translation :—

"For without the strong feeling of patriotism, neither had G. Duelius,
Aulus Atilius or L. Metellus freed us from the terror of Carthage; or the
two Scipios extinguished with their blood the rising flame of the second
Punic war. Quintus Maximus would not have weakened, nor M. Marcellus have crushed *the one which was springing up* with still greater strength :
or P. Africanus turning it from the gates of this city, have borne it amid
the walls of our enemies. Yet it was not thought *unbecoming in M. Cato*,
an unknown and a new man, by whom all of us who emulate his course
are led as a bright example of industry and virtue, to enjoy the repose of
Tusculum, that healthy and convenient situation. That insane man, however, as some have considered him, preferred when urged by no necessity,
to contend amid those waves and tempests to extreme old age ; rather
than pass his days in the most agreeable manner, amid so much ease and
tranquillity. Men without number I omit, each of whom were benefactors
to the State, and who are not far removed from the remembrance of this
generation. I forbear to commemorate them, lest any one should reproach
me with neglecting to speak of himself or his immediate friends. This one
truth I would mark, that nature has so strongly implanted in man the necessity of virtue, and so powerful an inclination to defend the common
welfare, that this principle overcomes all the blandishments of voluptuousness and ease."

Now, to say nothing of the poverty and inelegance of the
style—an objection which it is a sheer waste of words to make
here—the ignorance of all sorts discovered in these few lines is
really lamentable. Fabius Maximus and Marcellus are represented as crushing a war "which was *springing up*" *after* that

in which Cnæus and Publius Scipio had perished. If Mr. Featherstonhaugh had ever looked into Livy he would have known that the Scipios were cut off in Spain in the course of the very same year that Marcellus took Syracuse—namely, the sixth or seventh of the second Punic war. However, it might be exacting too much of such a writer to require him to think of any thing *dehors* the record, as lawyers express it, and we are will ing to excuse any deficiency of this kind, provided always that he comprehend the text of his author. But unhappily he was, in this instance, misled by that very text, in which the word *excitatus* happens to be used in rather an uncommon sense. The words of Cicero are—"Non duo Scipiones oriens incendium belli Punici secundi, sanguine suo restinxissent nec *id* (i. e. *idem*) *excitatum* majoribus copiis aut Q. Maximus enervavisset aut M. Marcellus contudisset, &c.* This "Fellow of the Geological Society of London" does not know that *excitatus* sometimes means "increased," "aggravated," "inflamed," "raised to a higher pitch or degree," &c. So he takes the meaning of the word which seems to approach nearest to the vernacular, and translates it "springing up" in utter contempt of historical truth, and the obvious exigency of the context. So the other line printed in italics is a gross *contre-sens*. The author, speaking of the influence of that virtue which prompts to heroic achievement and self-sacrifice, exemplifies it in the conduct of the elder Cato, who might, had he been so disposed, have remained at Tusculum, (his birth-place) taking his pleasure in ease and quiet, but who chose rather to be tossed about in the storms of political life, even to an extreme old age, than to enjoy that blissful but inglorious repose.

> M. Catoni, &c., certè *licuit* Tusculi se in otio delectare, &c.

But it will make our remarks more intelligible to print a page or two of the translation, with the original *en regard*, beginning at the second chapter.

"Nec uero habere uirtutem satis est, quasi artem aliquam, nisi utare. Etsi ars quidem, *cum ea non utare, scientia tamen ipsa teneri potest ;* uirtus in usu sui tota posita est ; usus autem eius est maximus ciuitatis gubernatio, et earum ipsarum rerum, quas isti in angulis personant, *reapse, non oratione, perfectio.* Nihil enim dicitur a philosophis, *quod quidem recte honesteque dicatur,* quod *non* ab his partum confirmatumque sit, a quibus ciuitatibus iura descripta sunt. Unde enim pietas ? aut a quibus religio ? unde ius aut gentium, aut hoc ip-

"Yet to possess virtue, like some art, without exercising it, is insufficient. Art, indeed, when *not effective, is still comprehended in science.* The efficacy of all virtue consists in its use. Its greatest *end* is the government of states, and the *perfection*, not in words, but in deeds, of those very things which are taught in the halls. For nothing is propounded by philosophers, *concerning what is esteemed to be just and proper*, that is not confirmed and assured by those who have legislated for States. For, from whence springs piety, or from whom

---

* It must be owned that Cicero himself seems to have confounded the dates of these events; but he does not say what his translator put into his mouth.

sum ciuile quod dicitur? unde iustitia,
fides, aequitas? unde pudor, continentia,
fuga turpitudinis, adpetentia laudis et
honestatis? unde in laboribus et peri-
culis fortitudo? nempe ab his, qui hæc
disciplinis informata, alia moribus con-
firmarunt, sanxerunt autem alia legibus.
Quin etiam Xenocraten ferunt, nobilem
in primis philosophum, cum quæreretur
ex eo quid adsequerentur eius discipuli,
respondisse, ut id sua sponte facerent
quod cogerentur facere legibus. Ergo
ille ciuis qui id cogit omnes imperio le-
gumque poena, quod uix paucis persua-
dere oratione philosophi possunt, etiam
his, qui illa disputant, ipsis est præfer-
endus doctoribus. Quæ etenim istorum
oratio tam exquisita, quæ sit antepo-
nenda bene constitutæ ciuitati, *publico
iuri, et moribus?* Equidem quemadmo-
dum urbes magnas atque inperiosas,
ut appellat Ennius, uiculis et castellis
praeferendas puto, sic eos qui his urbi
bus consilio atque auctoritate praesunt,
his qui omnis *'negotii publici expertes'*
sint, longe duco sapientia ipsa esse an-
teponendos. Et quoniam maxime rapi-
mur ad opes augendas generis humani,
studemusque nostris consiliis et laboribus tutiorem et opulentiorem uitam hominum reddere, et ad hanc uoluptatem
ipsius naturæ stimulis incitamur; ten-
eamus eum cursum, qui semper fuit
optimi cuiusque; neque ea signa audi-
amus, quæ receptui canunt, ut eos etiam
reuocent, qui iam processerint."

religion? Whence the law, either of
nations, or that which is called civil?
Whence justice, faith, equity? Whence
modesty, continence, the dread of tur-
pitude, the love of praise and esteem?
Whence fortitude in trouble and dangers? From those who, having laid a
foundation for these things in early
education, have strengthened some of
them by the influence of manners, and
sanctioned others by the influence of
laws. Of Xenocrates, one of the noblest
of philosophers, it is said, that when he
was asked what his disciples learnt of
him, he replied, 'to do that of their own
choice, which the laws enjoined them
to do;' therefore, the citizen who obliges every one, by the authority and
fear of the law, to do that which philosophers, by reasoning, with difficulty
persuade a few to do, is to be preferred
to those learned men who only dispute
about these things. For which of their
orations, however exquisite, can be compared in value to a well constituted
State, to public *right and to morals.*
Truly as great and powerful cities, *as*
Ennius says, are, *as* I think, to be preferred to villages and castles: so those
who stand pre-eminent in those cities,
in authority and counsel, are to be esteemed far before those in wisdom, who
are altogether *ignorant of the conduct of
public affairs.* And since we are chiefly
urged by a desire to increase the possessions of the human race, and seek
by our counsels and labors, to surround
the life of man with gratification and
security, and are incited by the instincts
of nature to these enjoyments; let us
hold the course which was always that
of the best men: nor attend to those
signals which speculative philosophers
make from their retirement, to allure
back those who are already far advanced." pp. 34, 35.

It is scarcely necessary to remark that the passages printed
in italics are palpable blunders. Indeed, it is difficult to imagine
anything worse in the way of translation. What is the meaning
of—"the greatest end of virtue is the government of States, and
the perfection not in words but in deeds, of those very things
which are taught in the halls." The sense of the original is extremely clear. Cicero affirms that virtue does not consist in contemplation—that it is not a mere speculative accomplishment or
art, which may very well exist in the mind—in theory, though
it never be called forth into practice—that its being is inseparable
from its use, and the most exalted use of it is the administration
or government of a State, and the practical application of those

very things about which philosophers are wont to prattle so much, and to so little purpose in their closets. He then goes on to maintain, not as the translator makes him say, "that nothing is propounded by philosophers *concerning what is esteemed to be just and proper*," but that "nothing is advanced by philosophers, *at least nothing is rightly and properly advanced* by them, "or" nothing that *can be considered as just and fit* is* advanced by them*, (for that is the effect of the subjunctive *dicatur* used with *nihil quod* in this connection) but what may be found more impressively exemplified in the institutions of civil society. His idea is that laws are the recorded morality of nations, and law-givers the most effective teachers of virtue—that they give to the abstractions of philosophy, so to express it, a tangible and living form—clothe maxims, embracing the most important truths and the most refined ethics, with the awful authority of a public sanction, and bring their precepts to bear upon the conduct of life and the interests and business of mankind, with the plastic and controlling influence of a daily, permanent, and authoritative social discipline. We have no time to bestow even a passing remark upon Cicero's philosophy—our present occupation is the humble one of the philologist, and we have our hands full with this *soi-disant* translator. We have to inform Mr. Featherstonhaugh that "perfectio" in this passage does not mean "perfection," or the state of being perfect, but the *act* of perfecting, or accomplishing, or doing perfectly—as in that sentence of the Treatise de Finibus, lib. iii. c. 9. "Ea quæ, &c. *suspectione* primâ, non *perfectione* sunt judicandæ." And many other instances of the same kind might easily be collected. So, nobody talks about the "*orations* of philosophers"—for *oratio* includes *sermo* as well as *concio*—nor do we see very clearly why these orations should be opposed "to public *right* and to *morals*," though they may be a less efficacious discipline than "public law and national manners and customs," which is all that Cicero undertakes to say of them. *Mores*, when used in connection with *jus*, is not to be rendered '*morals.*' It means the *jus moribus constitutum*, public opinion, general usage, the great body of customary or unwritten law, by which positive institutions are supplied or superseded in all nations. So *expers* does not necessarily import *ignorance*, but merely "having or taking no part in, &c." quasi *expars*, ἄμοιρος. Those of our readers, who are sufficiently conversant with Latin to relish the exquisite elegance and felicity of the Ciceronian diction, need not be informed how completely successful "the Fellow of the Geological Society of London" has been in destroying the beauties of the last sentence of the para-

---

* We need not remind scholars that *honestus* means a great deal more than "honest". See Cic. de Fin. ii. 14.

graph quoted—especially the animated and expressive allusion
to the signal of retreat in the last member of it.

"His rationibus tam certis tamque inlustribus *opponuntur* ab his, qui contra disputant, primum labores qui sint republica defendenda sustinendi : leue sane impedimentum uigilanti et industrio; neque solum in tantis rebus, sed etiam in mediocribus uel studiis uel officiis uel uero etiam negotiis contemnendum. Adiunguntur pericula uitae, turpisque ab his formido mortis fortibus uiris opponitur : quibus magis id miserum uideri solet, natura se consumi et senectute, quam sibi dari tempus, ut possint eam uitam, quae tamen esset reddenda naturae, pro patria potissimum reddere. Illo uero se loco copiosos et disertos putant, cum calamitates clarissimorum uirorum, iniuriasque iis ab ingratis impositas ciuibus colligunt. *Hinc* enim illa et apud Graecos exempla, Miltiadem uictorem domitoremque Persarum, *nondum sanatis uolneribus iis,* quae corpore aduerso *in clarissima uictoria* accepisset, uitam ex hostium telis seruatam, in ciuium uinclis profudisse: et Themistoclem patria, quam liberauisset, pulsum atque proterritum, non in Graeciae portus per se seruatos, sed in barbariae sinus confugisse, quam adflixerat. Nec uero leuitatis Atheniensium crudelitatisque *in amplissimos ciues* exempla deficiunt: quae nata et frequentata apud illos, etiam *in grauissimam ciuitatem nostram dicuntur redundasse.* Nam uel exilium Camilli, uel offensio commemoratur Ahalae, uel inuidia Nasicae, uel expulsio Laenatis, uel Opimi damnatio uel fuga Metelli, uel acerbissima C. Mari clades, principum caedes, uel eorum multorum pestes, quae paulo post secutae sunt. 'Nec uero iam meo nomine abstinent.' Et credo quia nostro consilio ac periculo sese in illa uita atque otio conseruatos putant, grauius etiam de nobis queruntur et amantius. Sed haud facile dixerim, cur cum ipsi discendi aut uisendi causa maria tramittant." * *

"Against these reasons so certain and so clear, *it is* urged by those who are opposed to us : *first*, the labour to be undergone in preserving the public welfare; a slight impediment to the zealous and industrious, not alone in matters of such high import, but in inferior things ; whether in studies or in official stations; and to be despised even in affairs of business. To this they add the dangers to which life is exposed, and the dread of death, which brave men scorn ; being wont to view it as more wretched to waste away by infirmity and old age, than to seize an occasion to devote that life to the advantage of their country, which one day must be rendered to nature. It is here, however, they deem themselves most successful and eloquent, when they bring forward the calamities of eminent men, and the injuries heaped upon them by their ungrateful countrymen. *Here come* the instances in Grecian history. Miltiades, the conqueror and subduer of the Persians, with those *wounds yet streaming*, which he received in front, in the *height of victory:* preserved from the weapons of the enemy, to waste away his life in the chains of his countrymen. And Themistocles proscribed and driven from the country he had freed, flying, not to the harbours of that Greece he had preserved, but to the barbarous shores he had harrassed. Nor indeed are instances wanting among the Athenians, of levity and cruelty towards *great numbers of their citizens;* instances which, springing up repeatedly among them, are said also to *have abounded too conspicuously in our city.* For either the exile of Camillus, the misfortune of Ahala, the ill-will towards Nasica, or the expulsion of Lenas, or the condemnation of Opimus, is remembered ; or the flight of Metellus, the sad overthrow of C. Marius, the cutting off of the most eminent citizens, or the destruction of many of them, which soon after followed. Nor indeed is my name forgotten. And I judge that, deeming themselves to owe both life and ease to my peril and counsel, they have a more deep and tender remembrance of me. But it is not so easy to explain how they who cross the seas for the sake of observing or describing" * *

If our readers succeed in torturing the first sentence or two of this extract into the confession of any intelligible meaning, they will be far more fortunate than we profess to have been. To us they appear to exhibit such a union of vulgarity and nonsense, as is rare even in the writings of Mr. F., remarkable as he seems to be for a *curiosa felicitas* in that style. We say nothing of the elegance of "here comes the instances of Grecian history," or of the propriety of rendering "nondum sanatis volneribus"—a chaste and beautiful expression—by such a misplaced hyperbole as "wounds yet streaming." There is no disputing about tastes in such matters, and the translator probably has his own reasons for thinking the style of Cicero tame and languid. But we should like to know why "clarissima victoria" is rendered "in the height of victory"—or how "in nostram civitatem *redundasse,*" is made to signify "have *abounded* too conspicuously in our state"—or where authority can be found for converting "amplissimos cives" into "a great number of citizens." In the same way, we suppose, "vir amplus" would be translated "many men"—so that, in Mr. F's Latin, every man of dignity and consequence is a sort of monster—a Geryon or Briareus—his name is Legion.

We might go on with our criticisms to the end of the volume. We shall trouble our readers, however, with but a few additional specimens of the scholarship of our Geologist. In the fifth chapter, the following sentence occurs in the original. "Quam ob rem neque sapientis esse, &c., neque liberalis, cum impuris atque inmanibus adversariis decertantem, vel contumeliarum verbera subire, vel *expectare sapienti non ferendas injurias.*" The words in italics are thus rendered, "or a wise man hope to withdraw from such a contest without injury." In chaper VII. "Ac tamen siqui sunt, qui philosophorum auctoritate moueantur, dent operam parumper atque audiant eos, quorum summa est auctoritas apud doctissimos homines et gloria: quos ego existimo, etam si qui ipsi rem publicam non gesserint; tamen quoniam de re publica multa quaesierint et scripserint, functos esse aliquo rei publicae munere," is translated, "Nevertheless if there are any who are governed by the opinions of philosophers, let them turn their attention for awhile, and listen to those who enjoy a proud pre-eminence among learned men, even when they have not borne any charge in the republic; still whom I deem from the extent of their studies, and their writings on government, to have been invested with functions appertaining to the public interest." In chapter VIII. for "in qua nihil fere quod *magno opere* ad rationes omnium rerum pertineret," we have "in the which I think scarce any point was omitted that belongs to the consideration of these *great matters.*" In chapter IX., we are informed that "P. Africanus, the son of Paulus, *established Latin holidays* in his gardens. The *feriæ Latinæ* we had always understood to

date from the earliest period of Roman history. But Mr. Featherstonhaugh is no antiquarian, and it is certain that *constituo*
sometimes means to establish. To be sure, when used in that
sense, it never governs the ablative case ; but this is no Hamil-
tonian version for the use of schools, and the author did not
think it necessary to descend to such minutiæ. The words just
quoted, therefore, must be received as a very *liberal* translation
of what means strictly this, "P. Africanus was determined (or
had made up his mind) to spend the Latin holidays in his gardens." So we hear of "Timæus of Locram," (c. xi.) though we
have not been so fortunate as to have ever heard of "Locram" itself. Scipio, who was the son of Paulus Æmilius, but passed
into the family of Africanus (his maternal grandfather) by adoption, is made to speak of both his *parents,* as if he meant his
father and mother. The text is, utriusque *patris.* lib. iii. c. 1.
In the same place mention is made of a writer, hitherto unknown,
we believe, even to Fabricius : it is one "Zethus, the author of
Pacuvius." This is a truly ludicrous blunder. The text of the
original is, "Zethum illum Pacuvi." "Zethus in the tragedy of
Pacuvius." Zethus ille Pacuvianus, as the same author designates the same personage elsewhere.* If Mr. Featherstonhaugh
(we wish his name were shorter) will only open the 18th epistle
of the first book of Horace's Epistles, at the 41st verse, and read
three or four lines together with the notes of the Dauphin editor,
he will learn something more of this "Author of Pacuvius."

But of this *satis superque.* We should make our readers an
apology for troubling them so long with this very minute examination of a worthless book, but for one reason. We have recently heard great complaints made against the form and style
of the periodical criticism of the present day. Reviews, it is
said, are mere set dissertations, in which, the work *nominally*
censured, is only mentioned at the head of the article, in a sort
of *ac etiam* clause to found the jurisdiction upon. We have
been ourselves, more than once, guilty of this heinous offence
against primitive manners and models, and have, therefore, endeavored to atone for our past sins, by this specimen of a legitimate critique, which, we trust, will be graciously received as a
sufficient expiatory sacrifice for them all.

We are happy to find the Boston edition of "The Republic,"
more accurate than the Ernesti edition of Cicero's works reprinted there some twelve years ago. The latter appeared to us
to reflect very little credit upon a city which seems destined to
the double honor of being the cradle of liberty and of letters in
the western world ? But why were not the *prolegomena* of Mai
retained ? Such is the scarcity of books of a certain description

* De Orat. l. ii. c. 37.

in this part of the country, that we have not been able to lay our hands upon the account—an object, in every point of view, of so much interest—which the scholar, to whose enlightened and fortunate researches—we are indebted for this treasure-trove, has given of his own discovery.

Our readers, are, no doubt, generally informed from other sources, that Signor Mai was advanced, on account of some previous researches of a similar kind in the Ambrosian library at Milan, to the place of librarian of the Vatican—that the MS. of this important fragment was preserved in the Monastery of Gobio in Liguria—that the first edition of it was given to the world in 1822—that its faded characters, which had been written over with a commentary of St. Augustin upon the Psalms, were decyphered by means of chemical agents—and that parchment or paper, thus "contrived a double debt to pay," was called even in the time of Cicero himself, a *palimpsest*.* It may be worth while to remark, by the way, that the example of this learned Italian may possibly lead to important discoveries. The spirit of inquiry on the subject of ancient MSS., which had been so long comparatively slumbering, may be awakened, for aught we know, to an animation not unworthy of the age of Petrarch or of Poggio Bracciolini. The hopes of scholars—so far as thay depended upon other resources—were almost extinguished. The monasteries, and such like repositories in Europe, had been so completely ransacked, that little or nothing could be expected from them. On the other hand, the euruption of Vesuvius which overwhelmed Herculaneum and Pompeii, seems to have been so preposterously slow and gradual, as to admit not only of the escape of their inhabitants, but of the removal of almost their whole stock of goods and chattels. And in spite of all the assiduity and (in this matter especially) vaunted sagacity of the German literati, it is not likely that they will ever do much with the Tironian notes. But it is difficult to set bounds to our anticipations from this unexplored, subterraneous region of the palimpsest—these "catacombs of living death," as they may be well enough described in an *outré* metaphor of Curran's. The mighty revolution in opinion, which as early, at least, as the sixth century, involved, in one indiscriminate sentence of ban and anathema, all the genius and taste of classical antiquity, produced it is certain, many and many similar instances of sacreligious spoilation by holy hands. It is true that we are indebted to the same hands, for the preservation of much that remains to adorn our libraries—but who shall balance the

* There is some difference of opinion as to the etymology of this word. We are satisfied with Facciolati's—παλίμψηϛος from πάλιν rursum and ψάω abstergo. Some write *palinxestus* from ξέω rado.

account between what was saved by the liberal, and what was destroyed by the ignorant or bigoted zealot—between the copies made and the MSS. effaced by monks and priests? At all events, a general search-warrant ought to go forth against every inch of parchment occupied by the Gregorys and the Ambroses, the Jeromes and the Chrysostoms. There is proable cause enough for this grand *conceptio furti*. And, notwithstanding all that Gibbon says to reconcile us to the supposed destruction of the Alexandrian library by the Saracens, we must still be permitted to express the strongest desire to see these inquiries prosecuted with success. Conceding that, with some few exceptions, the most celebrated writers of antiquity have been preserved to us, yet what valuable—what boundless stores of information may, nay must be buried in the compositions of those of less note! The works of mere erudition—the thesauri and the bibliothecæ —the voluminous collections of plodding compilers—what would they not do to clear up the doubtful passages in the history of those times, and to expose the futility of many learned conjectures in ours? What should we not gain, for instance, (to go no further) by the discovery of the works of Varro, and the Origines of Cato? And how refreshing would it be to the hearts and the eyes of scholars to witness the resurrection of Menander and Alcæus—to see them restored to the freshness and vigour of a renovated life, after so many centuries passed in oblivion and darkness, like wounded warriors upon some battleground, disengaged by a lucky chance from the heaps, and rescued from the grave of the slain,—or, to make our simile more pointed, like Er, the Armenian, in the sublime rhapsody of Plato, snatched from the funeral pile to reveal the visions of that deep and perilous trance, and gladden the witnesses of his resuscitation with a bright and ravishing dream of elysium and of immortality.

This first discovery of Mai is unfortunately' little better than an earnest of what we may expect in future. It is a mere *torso*— a deformed and mutilated fragment. Including all the scraps preserved by the grammarians and the fathers, we are presented with a paltry duodecimo of a hundred and forty pages. Of these, the first two books, which are in a far better state of preservation than the others, occupy a hundred and eight. But even they are horribly maimed and disfigured. Everv discussion ends in a hiatus, and the reader is scarcely warmed with one subject, before he is compelled to give it up and betake him to some other to just as little purpose. According to the conjectures of the learned editor, not fewer than a hundred and twenty or a hundred and thirty pages are lost of these two books alone. All that remains of the third are a few sentences from Nonius and Priscian, and two paragraphs from St. Augustin de Civitate

Dei. The fourth and fifth are made up of much the same sort of materials, and fill together about sixteen pages. Of the sixth, scarcely any thing is preserved but that noble fragment, the Somnium Scipionis, for which we are indebted to Macrobius, and which has long been the admiration and delight of scholars. It is manifestly impossible to form a satisfactory estimate of the merits of the work, from such a remnant, and those writers who have not scrupled to express their dissatisfaction with the whole treatise, because the discovery of Mai has not been as complete as it might have been, are surely emulous of the wiseacre in Hierocles, showing about his brick as a sample of a house. It is certain at least, that the opinions of those who saw the work in its perfect state do not agree with the dogmatical *divination* of these writers. Cicero himself is known to have set the highest value upon this treatise, to which he frequently refers in his other works, with an evident complacency and predilection.

One cause of complaint particularly dwelt upon is that the author repeats the early legends of Rome without any appearance of incredulity. Mr. Niebuhr, no doubt, flattered himself with the hope of finding all his scepticism justified by this treatise. The contrary has been the fact. There are some passages in this dialogue which shew the general belief of the educated people of those times, as well as the grounds upon which it was founded, to have been far stronger than is altogether consistent with the sweeping scepticism of the present day. Thus, in the thirty-first chapter of the second book, the books of the Pontiffs, and those of the augurs, are referred to as evidence that under the royal government an appeal lay from the king to the people. So in the fifteenth chapter of the same book, Manilius asks Scipio whether he believes the tradition that Numa was a pupil of Pythagoras. The other replies with great confidence, that it was a mere figment, the fact being not only not at all probable, but even demonstrably impossible. He then proceeds to state the reasons of his opinion, and shews that, as to the order of succession, the length of the reigns, &c., no doubt was entertained among people of the better sort at Rome. Atticus had written an abstract or epitome of Roman history, from the foundation of the city, in which, says Cicero, he has omitted no events of importance and has arranged them all in the most accurate chronological order, through a period of seven hundred years.* The orator speaks of this compilation as saving him a great deal of trouble—indeed, as entirely superseding the necessity of his going into the same inquiry again. Atticus, therefore, took the same view of the Roman history that Cicero does. There are many legends of the earlier times, which our author considers as altogether fabulous—such, for example, as the appearance of Castor

* Brutus, 34.

and Pollux at the battle of Regillus. But he seems to entertain no doubt of the great bulk of his country's annals. He even speaks (in the person of Scipio) of the apotheosis of Romulus, as being the most remarkable, inasmuch as it took place only six hundred years before, and in an enlightened and inquisitive age.* There is a single sentence in the fragment before us, wherein he is supposed to admit that no reliance can be placed on the early annals of Rome. Speaking of Ancus Martius, Lælius observes, that the history of their country was obscure, for, he continues, we know who was the mother of that king, but not who was his father. To this, Scipio makes the following reply. "Ita est; sed temporum illorum tantum fere *regum* illustrata sunt nomina." That is to say, as we translate it, generally speaking the names of the *kings only* in those times were illustrious enough to be transmitted to posterity. There are those who lay the emphasis on the word *nomina*, and who construe the sentence as importing that nothing was known in those times but the *names* of the kings, all the recorded transactions, civil and military of their reigns, being entirely apocryphal. We think the context calls for the construction we put upon the words, while any other would be wholly irreconcileable with the passages already referred to. We need not add, that we are by no means disposed to make the early history of Rome an article of faith. We know that some of the evidence upon which we should have to depend is very irregular and exceptionable—not unlike that upon which the Knight of La Mancha rests his belief in the existence of the venerable Doña Quintañona,† that is to say, such as might be adduced, not unplausibly, to establish the æra and exploits of those renowned worthies, Tom Thumb and Jack the Giant Killer. But when we find what is said to be mere popular tradition, adopted by Cicero and Atticus, who, it is probably, only followed the Catos and the Varros, we cannot but hesitate before we pronounce that there was *no truth* at all in it. We take it that Livy states the case as fairly as possible at the beginning of his sixth book— and what he there says of the early history of Rome is just as applicable to that of every other nation under the sun. But having examined this subject at large, on a former occasion,‡ it is sufficient for our present purpose to have made such remarks only as are suggested by the work under review.

As it is our purpose to avail ourselves of some future oppor-

---

* Lib. ii. c. 10, de Rep.

† Mi acuerdo que me decia una mi agüela de partes de mi padre quando veia alguna dueña con tocas reverendas; aquella, nieto, se parece á la Dueña Quintañona; de donde arguyo yo que la debia de conocer ella, o por lo menos debio de alcazar á ver algun retrato suyo; says the knight in the cage to the doubting Canon.

‡ Southern Review, No. II. Art. 2.

tunity to consider, in detail, the philosophical writings of Cicero, we shall confine our observations it this article to his political opinions, and especially to those opinions as they are expressed in "The Republic." Except a little volume on Invention, written while he was yet a young man, and the Treatise de Oratore, published about the year 698, this was the earliest of his literary productions. It was given to the world A. U. C. 700, just before its author set out for his proconsular government in Cilicia. He was then in his fifty-third year. Formed by nature for philosophical pursuits, and always more or less addicted to them, he felt his taste for them growing upon him with his age, and confirmed by the circumstances of the times. They had been the discipline of his youth; the effective auxiliary of his riper powers; the ornament of his prosperity and greatness— they now filled up the measure of their blessed influence, and were his solace and his refuge in despondence and gray hairs. He began to be weary of the world—to be disabused of its illusions—even (though not without many a struggle of rebellious nature) to look with some indifference upon its masks and mummeries, its grandeur and its honours. Above all, he was filled with gloomy forebodings for his country—for that country which no patriot ever loved with a purer love, which no statesman ever watched over with a more filial solicitude. There was but too much in the state of affairs to excite his apprehensions. All the elements of society were thrown into disorder, and those clouds had been long gathering which soon burst forth in wrath and desolation. The laws were violated with impunity by the bad—were trampled upon with scorn by the powerful. Pompey dictated to the Senate—Clodius rioted with the mob. This ruffian, at the head of an infuriated gang of slaves and gladiators, mixed with the dregs and sweepings of the populace, infested daily the streets and public places. The forum—the campus— the via sacra—were a scene of disorders and abominations such as no government, that deserved the name, could have tolerated for a moment, and few civilized nations have ever been condemned to suffer. Cicero saw his brother's house burnt down by these wretches in broad day-light. He was himself pursued by them as a victim, and narrowly escaped being murdered under the eyes of the magistrates. He was afflicted with the deepest sorrow at this state of things, and frequently gives vent to his sensibility in epistles to his friends, written about this time. From one of them, in which he speaks, among other things, of the composition of this very work,* we translate the following passage:—"I endeavour to dismiss evey thought about public affairs from my mind, and to devote myself entirely to letters: yet I will confess, what, however, I have been especially desi-

* Ad. Q. Frat. lib. iii. Epist. 5.

rous of concealing from you. I am grieved, my dearest brother, I am grieved that the commonwealth is no more—that there is no longer any administration of justice—that the very period of my life which ought to be crowned with the highest senatorian consequence and dignity, or occupied with the most active forensic labours, or sustained by literary studies at home, that which has been the object of all my pursuits even from my childhood—'Αἰεν ἀριϛεύειν χ̓ ὑπερειρόχον ἔμμεναι ἄλλων,'—is irretrievably lost for me," &c. In another, written soon afterwards,—"I bore the result of that trial with the greatest equanimity. This advantage I begin at last to reap, that I am now scarcely discomposed by those evils in the state, and that licentiousness of reckless men which used once to overcome me quite. For nothing can be more hopelessly abandoned than these people—than this age. So that as it is now impossible to take any pleasure in public affairs, I really do not know why I should be vexed at them. Literature and study and ease and my villas are now my delight, and more than all these, our two boys."* In a letter to Atticus,† in which also he mentions the work before us, he expresses himself to the same effect, though with an affectation of indifference and levity very awkwardly assumed, and more expressive, than the strongest avowal in direct terms could possibly have been, of that deep mortification of a wounded spirit which it was intended to disguise. Referring to the issue of the same trial, (that of Gabinius) in which the administration of justice had been perverted by Pompey's influence, he says,—"but you will ask, how do *you* bear these things? Very well indeed, and I give myself great credit for doing so. We have lost, my Pomponius, not only all the vigorous and robust health,‡ but the very complexion and semblance of our pristine constitution. There is nothing in public affairs to delight, nothing to content me. And do you bear that patiently, you will say. Yes, even that. I recollect how well the State went on for the short period that I was at the head of affairs, and how I was requited for it. It is no affliction to me that one man is invested with unlimited power: *they* are breaking their hearts about it, who once grieved because I had some little influence. There are many things to console me; and that without any change in my habits and situation. I betake myself to that way of living which is most conformable to nature—to literature and study," &c. Our readers will have remarked that the cause of all this dissatisfaction and despondency was the influence of Pompey, who enjoyed at that time, whether in or out of office, a power nothing short

---

* Ibid. Epist. 9.

† Ad. Attici, lib. iv. 16.

‡ Succum ac sanguinem, appropriate and expressive as it is in Latin, would be rather *strong* in a more literal translation.

of dictatorial. Cæsar was still in Gaul, training his legions to discipline and victory; but nobody yet saw or even imagined in the conqueror of Ariovistus and the Nervii, the fated chief of Pharsalia. Alas for the fears and the foresight of man! who can reflect, without emotion, that a day was at hand, when the fulfilment to the letter of the very worst of Cicero's forebodings might have been reckoned as mercy and deliverance for Rome, and for the world—a day of slaughter and shame, and hopeless, irremediable servitude—when the bands of the faithful were to be scattered in every battle, and the "last of the Romans" should "invoke death with vows as their chief good and final hope," and the gory head of the orator himself should be set up in mockery upon his own Rostra, a hideous trophy of parricide, drunk with its bloody orgies, and ruffianing in its unhallowed domination; and the very name of his adored Republic should be blotted out and gone forever, and ages of despotism and degradation and vice and barbarous ignorance should come like primordial night and cover up, as with a cloud, the whole face of the earth!

> O dark, dark, dark,
> Irrecoverably dark—total eclipse,
> Without all hope of day!

It was under such circumstances and in such a state of mind that Cicero "sought to the sweet, retired solitude" of his Cuman and Pompeian villas to compose his treatise De Republicâ. He seems to have felt it as a very serious undertaking. In the letter to Atticus, from which we quoted a passage just now, he speaks of it as a work requiring much time and labour : and it appears, accordingly, to have cost him more than he ever afterwards bestowed upon the composition of any of his philosophical writings. Most of these we know to have been published in the course of a single year. It may convey some idea of the rapidity with which he wrote them, as well as of the uncommon accuracy of his knowledge, to mention that he dispatched his *Topica* during a short excursion at sea. But he composed "The Republic" with great deliberation and pains. Not to mention that he still felt somewhat of the anxiety of a *débutant*, he no doubt wrote it under deep and serious impressions of duty, and not without the hope of doing something by it to enlighten and to correct pnblic opinion. The object and spirit of his work, as we shall presently have to remark more particularly, were highly patriotic. He wished to bring the constitution back to its first principles, by an impressive exposition of its theory—to inflame his contemporaries with the love of virtue by pourtraying the character of their ancestors in its primeval purity and beauty— and, while he was raising a monument to all future ages of what Rome had been, to inculcate upon his own times what it ought

still to be.   We know it to have been his original purpose to
make it a very voluminous work, for he expressly tells his brother,
in an Epistle already referred, to,* that it was to be extended to
nine books.   Ernesti thinks that they were all given to the world,†
although Cicero, in a letter to Atticus, on which that most
learned and accurate scholar makes this very remark,—speaks
of them as his *six* pledges or sureties for his good behaviour.
Whether the MS. throws any light upon this subject we are unable to say, as we have not had the advantage of seeing the editor's
account of it ; but it seeems to be taken for granted by later
writers that the three last books were never published.

Cicero had some difficulty in determining upon the form of
the work.   It appears, from one of the Epistles just vouched,
that, after having finished the first and second books, he read
them (as was the custom at Rome) to some friends assembled at
his Tusculan villa.   They were then, as they still are, in the
form of a dialogue.   Sallust, who was one of the party, strongly urged the propriety of changing it into that of a continued discourse in the first person.   He thought that the name of Cicero—
not a Heraclides Ponticus—a mere speculative and scholastic
philosopher, but a man of consular rank and of great experience
in affairs, would add authority to his sentiments—that whatever
might be ascribed to such antiquated personages, as the interlocutors selected for his dialogue, would necessarily have the air
of fiction—that, in his book de Oratore, indeed, it was very well
to attribute his rhetorical precepts to persons of another generation
and of established reputation for eloquence, but that even they
were such as he had himself seen and known ; and finally, the
example of Aristotle's Politics was alleged in support of the same
views.   To these considerations, another of still more weight
was added by Cicero himself.   This was that some of the most
important events that had ever occurred in the political history
of Rome had taken place since the supposed epoch of the dialogue.   Perhaps, however, it was this very consideration that
determined him finally to adhere to his original purpose.   He
was afraid of touching upon facts, which, however interesting
in themselves, were too intimately connected with present interests and opinions to be handled without danger of giving offence
to many of his contemporaries.   Add to this the trouble of re-
casting a work composed with so much pains, and the decided
predilection which he seems always to have entertained for the
form of dialogue—a species of composition, at all times attractive, but which had the additional advantage, in antiquity, of
conforming to their mode of communicating instruction in the
schools of philosophy, in an easy, colloquial way, by question
and answer.   As in the treatise De Oratore, Cicero had put his sen-

* Ad. Q.—Frat. iii. 5.   † Ep. ad. Att. vi. 1. in not. 14.

timents into the mouths of Crassus and Antony—the two greatest orators that had ever appeared in the forum before his time—so in this he was not less attentive to a sort of dramatic propriety in the choice of his personages. His chief interlocutors are the younger Africanus, Lælius, Philus and Manilius, the last a lawyer of great eminence for that day. These were accompanied by as many young men, viz: Q. Tubero, P. Rutilius Rufus, Scævola and Fannius—all of them persons of the very highest rank and consideration. Tubero became an eminent jurisconsult. Scævola was the renowned augur under whom Cicero, when he assumed the *toga virilis*, was placed by his father to be initiated into forensic pursuits and the study of the civil law. P. Rutilius Rufus was also celebrated for his knowledge of the laws, for (without having had time to compare dates with any precision) we take him to be the same to whom Gravina assigns the highest rank in his *Jurisprudentia Media*, and whom he pronounces, for many instances of exalted virtue in public life, a *togatus et consularis Socrates*. The æra, too, of the supposed conversation was, for the object which Cicero appears to have had in view, the most favorable that could have been selected. The elder Scipio, says Paterculus, opened to us the door to power—the younger, to luxury. Whatever may have been the ultimate consequences of their victories, their æra—the interval, especially, which elapsed between the triumph at Zama and the fall of Numantia—exhibits the happiest instance, that is to be found in the annals of any nation, of a union of unsurpassed military glory with the stern morals of a primitive, and the graces of a polished age. Even while Cato thought with more than a censor's severity, and lived with more than a Roman's virtue, the pupils of Carneades and Panætius were becoming imbued with the elegance and philosophy of Greece. The literary productions of the age, to which the old censor himself (who is said, be it remembered, to have studied Greek at a very advanced age) contributed not a little, show how rapid was the progress, and how wide the diffusion of improvement. At the same time the voice of civil discord was mute—the tribune almost forgot how to pronounce his *veto*—the very name of Dictator was falling into desuetude. From the beginning of the fifth century, when the Plebeians may be considered as fairly relieved from all constitutional disabilities, until the seditions of the Gracchi—some apprehensions only of which are hinted in the work before us—the history of the Republic is one bright record of virtues and achievements, almost too heroic for the infirmities of human nature. It was at the close of this most extraordinary period, in the annals of mankind, that Polybius went to Rome to study her constitution, and to write her history—that is to say, to illustrate what he considers as the unrivalled excellence of the former by its best fruits made visible in the latter. He became the *protégé* and companion of the Scipio and Lælius who figure in this dialogue, and who exemplified, in their own character and pursuits, the happy union of qualities, of which we have just spoken. They were the most accomplished men of the day, and they stamped their own character upon their age; of which they ever have been regarded as the fittest representatives. As Terence was supposed by some of his contemporaries to have been indebted to their assistance for the grace and elegance of his style, so there can be little doubt (and we have been forcibly struck with the idea in reading this fragment) that the Greek philosopher just mentioned, derived from them many of his very judicious opinions concerning the government of Rome. Such men might well be supposed to contemplate the constitution of their country through the happiest medium, from the "regions high of calm and serene air" in which they seemed "to live insphered." For this reason we have always felt that there was as much propriety as beauty and grandeur in the *Somnium Scipionis.* It costs no great effort of the imagination to conceive of the Scipios as transfigured into "those immortal shapes of bright ærial spirits", who, without mingling in the passions of the world, watch over all its concerns with a tutelary care and interest. The high tone of sentiment—the enlightened love of country—the heroic self-sacrifice—the wisdom and moderation—the philosophic dignity and repose, that pervade that fine vision, are just what we should expect to characterise any thing uttered in the form of advice and exhortation by one Africanus to the other. And never, surely, did a noble theme inspire a loftier strain! The whole soul of Cicero seems to kindle up into enthusiasm at the contemplation of those great men. He sees in them the *beau idèal* of the Roman character—the image of his country, in all her original brightness, "glittering like the morning star, full of life and splendor and joy." It was impossible that he should have selecta better æra or more suitable characters. Still further, to excite the interest of his readers in this dialogue, he very seriously assures them that they are by no means to regard it as a mere fiction of his own; the substance of it having been communicated to him in conversation of several days, at Smyrna, by that very P. Rutilius Rufus, of whom we have already spoken as one of the *dramatis personæ.*

It is commonly supposed that Cicero wrote his book De Republica, and the supplementary dialogues De Legibus, in imitation of Plato. There is very little doubt but that the idea of composing two works, under these titles, was suggested to him by the example of the Greek philosopher. His philosophical compositions are almost, without exception, mere abstracts of the doctrines taught in the schools of Athens—but for Plato, especially, he entertained the most enthusiastic and unbounded admiration. In every part of his writings, this feeling breaks forth unrebuked. He frequently speaks of the Divine Athenian in a style which appears absurdly hyperbolical in our cold Anglo-Saxon idiom, as a *god* among philosophers.* He declares in one place that he never mentions the excellencies of others, without a mental reservation in favor of Plato, and, in another, expressly subjects even Aristotle himself to that exception.† But although he no doubt had Plato's Republic in his eye when he first conceived the idea of his work, and although there are every where in the details manifest imitations, and even translations from the Greek philosopher,‡ yet do these two productions, as Cicero himself frequently remarks in his, differ as widely as possible in their objects and character. Let us first speak of the Greek Utopia.

To say of Plato's Republic that it is the idea of a perfect commonwealth is not to give, by any means, an adequate or even a just description of it. It is, in one sense, to be sure, a dream of social and political perfection, and so far its common title is not altogether inapplicable to it; but it bears hardly any resemblance to the things that generally pass under that name—to the figments, for example, of Harrington and Sir Thomas Moore. Compared with it, Telemachus, though a mere epic in prose, is didactic and practical—the Cyropædia deserves to be regarded as the manual of soldiers and statesmen, and as the best scheme of discipline for forming them. Plato's is a mere vision, and that vision is altogether characteristic of his genius as his contemporaries conceived of it. It is something between prose and poetry in the style§—it is something made up both of poetry and philosophy in the plan and design. But a very small part of it is given to any topics that can pretend to the character of political. Indeed, Socrates expressly says that the institution of a commonwealth is but a subordinate object with him. His principal aim is to unfold the sublime mystery of perfect justice. The title of the work is Πολιτειων η περι Δικαιs. The latter is unquestionably the more appropriate designation. If it were possible to have any doubts after reading the work, the repeated and emphatic declarations of the philosopher himself would remove them. It is in the second that he first alludes to the Commonwealth, and then the purpose for which he professes to treat of it is unequivocally explained. He compares himself to one

* Ad Attic. ubi. sup. Deus ille noster, etc. Nat. Deor. lib. ii. 12.
† Platonem semper excipio. De Fin lib. v, c. 3.
‡ For instance, the noble passage in the sixth book of Plato's Republic, pp. 557 and seq., in which he draws a picture of popular licentiousness carried to excess, is copied almost word for word by Cicero. De Rep. lib. i. c. 43.
§ Aristotle apud Diog. Laert. in Platon.

who, not having very good eyes, is required to read a text, at some distance from him, written in distressingly small letters, and who prepares himself for his task by conning over the very same text which he happens to find set forth somewhere else in larger characters. The justice—the high and perfect justice— whose nature he is endeavoring to penetrate and unfold, exists not only in individuals but, on a grander scale, in the more conspicuous and palpable image of that artificial being, a body politic.* This idea is perpetually recurring. Thus it runs through the whole eighth book, which, it may be remarked by the way, is a dissertation of incomparable excellence, and decidedly the most practical part of the work. In this book he treats of *injustice*. He again resorts to the larger type—to the capital letters. He illustrates the effects of that vice, or rather of that vicious and diseased state of the soul, by corresponding distempers and mutations of the body-politic. We are told that the form of government is an image of the character of the citizen—that whatever may be said of the democracy or the oligarchy applies as strictly to the democrat and the oligarchist†—that there are as many shapes or species of polity, as there are types or varieties of the human soul‡—that, as the most perfect commonwealth is only public virtue embodied in the institutions of a country, so every vice generates some abuse or corruption in the state—some pernicious disorder—some lawless power, incompatible with rational liberty.

In running this parallel between the individual and the corporate existence, he unfolds his idea of the τὸ δίκαιον, not in a prologue as Tiedeman affirms, but throughout the whole body of his work. He begins by shewing that there can be no happiness without it here ; and ends by a revelation of other worlds and a state of beatific perfection, which it fits the soul to enter upon hereafter. We must take care, however, not to confound this sublime justice with the vulgar attribute commonly known by that name. Plato's justice is that so magnificently described by Hooker—in a pas-

* Lib. ii. p. 368. d. Tiedeman a German professor, who, at the instance of Heyne wrote "Argumenta Exposita" of Plato's dialogues, i. e. abstracts or summaries of them with critical observations, published in the Bipont edition of 1786, quarrels, outright, with Socrates about this passage. His remarks are worth inserting here for the benefit of scholars who may not have the edition. "Quæ si, prout verbis sunt exposita, accipiamus; totam de republicâ disputationem justitiæ tantum declarandæ causa instituti, facile nobis persuadeamus ; id quod secus tamen revera sese habet, cum absurdum sit, tam longum ordiri sermonem, adeoque prolixe de republica ordinanda disserere, aperiendæ justitiæ, quæ brevioribus potest exponi, cuusa. Quod igitur quæritur de justitia, prologi tantum locum tenet ; nec recte Plato quid sibi vellet his libris *occuluit* aut legentium saltem oculis subtraxit ; cum scriptoris, præsertim philosophici, longam ingredientis orationem, sit, quem sibi proposuerit finem ante exponere, ut quo tendant singula lector intelligens, etc. This is excellent, truly. It is as if Proclus, or any other dreamer of the Alexandrian school, should insist on making Homer a mystic in spite of himself.

† See about p. 550.   ‡ Lib. iv. Sub. Calc. cf. ib. id. 256–372.

sage which has been hackneyed by legal writers as if it had been the text of a code, but of which no familiarity can diminish or impair the truly Platonic grandeur—"that law whose seat is the bosom of God, and whose voice, the harmony of the world—to which all things in heaven and earth do homage—which angels, and men, and creatures of every condition, though each in different sort and manner, yet all with uniform consent, admire as the mother of their peace and joy." In this noble passage, the author of the Ecclesiastical Polity,. whose mind was rapt and glowing with the visions of his Athenian prototype, touches upon the great leading idea, the true theme and sense of his Republic. The whole dialogue is a Pythagorean mystery. It is the work of one formed in the Socratic school of Milton—

> "There thou shalt hear and learn the secret power
> Of harmony in tones and numbers hit
> By voice or hand, and various measured verse,
> Æolian charms or Dorian lyric odes."

Plato finds the key of the whole universe in the doctrine of number and proportion. He sees them pervading all nature, moral and physical—holding together its most distant parts, and most heterogeneous materials, and harmonizing them into order and beauty and *rythm.* Socrates declares his assent to the Pythagorean tenet, that astronomy is to the eye, what music is to the ear.* The spheres, with the Syrens that preside over them,† and the sweet melodies of that eternal diapason—the four elements combined in the formation of the world—the beautiful vicissitudes of the seasons—light and darkness, height and depth, all existences and their negations, all antecedents and consequences, all cause and effect, reveal the same mystery to the adept. Man is, in like manner, subject throughout his whole nature, to this universal law.‡ Of the four cardinal virtues, take *temperance* for an example. What is it but a perfect discipline of the passions, by which they are all equally controlled—or rather a perfect concord or symphony in which each sounds its proper note and no other—in which no desire is either too high or too low—in which the enjoyment of the present moment is never allowed to hurt that of the future, nor passion to rebel against reason, nor one passion to invade the province, or to usurp the rights of another.§ The το δικαιον goes somewhat further. It is that state of the soul wherein the three parts of which it is composed, the intellectual, the irascible, and

---

* Ib. l. vii. p. 530, d. e.   † Ib. l. x.

‡ For the mystical creation of the human soul according to number and proportion, see the Timæus. The same dialogue applies to the rest of our remarks.

§ ὥςε ορθ'ιτατ' ἄν φαῖμεν ταύτην τὴν ὁμόνοιαν, σωφροσύνην εἶναι, χείρονός τε χ ἀμείνονος κατὰ φύσιν συμφωνίαν, &c. l. iv. 432.

the sensual, exercise each its proper function and influence—in which the four cardinal virtues are blended together in such just proportion, in such symphonious unison—in which all the faculties of the mind, while they are fully developed, are so well disciplined and disposed—that nothing jarring or discordant, nothing uneven or irregular, is ever perceived in them. And so in the larger type—a perfect polity is that in which the same proportion and fitness are observed—in which the different orders of society move in their own sphere, and do only their appointed work—in which intellect governs, and strength and passion submit, that is, counsellors advise, soldiers make war, and the labouring classes employ themselves in their humble, but necessary and productive calling.* On the other hand, the most fearfully depraved condition of society is that which Polybius calls an *ochlocracy*—an anarchy of jacobins and sansculottes—where every passion breaks loose in wild disorder, and no law is obeyed, no right respected, no decorum observed— where young men despise their seniors, and old men affect the manners of youth, and children are disobedient to their parents, wives to their husbands, slaves to their masters—in short, where the very cattle that are within their gates, the ox and the ass, wander about as they list, without any dread of being treated as a public nuisance by the police, or even of being distrained *damage feasant* by the injured.† The justice of which he speaks, is not, therefore, the single cardinal virtue known by that name. It is not commutative justice, nor retributive justice, nor (except, perhaps, in a qualified sense) distributive justice. It does not consist in mere outward conformity or specific acts—in the execution of a contract of *do ut facias* or *facio ut des*. Its seat is in "the inmost mind"—its influence is the music of the soul—it makes the whole nature of the true philosopher, a concert of disciplined affections—a choir of virtues attuned to the most perfect accord among themselves, and falling in with all the mysterious and everlasting harmonies of heaven and earth.‡

This general idea is still further illustrated by the scheme of education in Plato's Republic. It is extremely simple—for young men it consists only of music and gymnastics—for adepts of an advanced age, it is the study of *truth*, pure *truth* the good, the τὸ ὄν, the divine monad, the one eternal, unchangeable. It is in the third book that he orders the former division of the scheme. It is necessary to cultivate with equal care both the

---

* Lib. iv. 443. Be it remembered by political economists, that the *division of labor* is a fundamental principle of Plato's legislation, and is enforced by very severe penalties. He considers it as in the highest degree absurd—as out of all reason and proportion—that one man should pretend to be good at many things.
† Lib. viii. p. 557.

‡ καὶ δὴ τὸν ἄλλον τῆς φιλοσόφου φύσεως χορὸν, &c. l. vi. p. 490. The parts in this *choir* are filled by ανδρια, μεγαλοπρεπεια, εὐμάθεια, μνήμη. Cf. l. iv, 442.

parts of which it is composed—and to allow of no excess or imperfection in either. They who are addicted exclusively to music, become effeminate and slothful; they, on the other hand,
who only discipline their nature by the exercises of the gymna-
sium, become rude and savage.* God gave us these great correctives of the soul and of the body, not for the sake of either
separately, but that all their powers, and functions and impulses
should be fully brought out into action ; and above all, be harmonized into mutual assistance and perfect unison.† Plato's
whole method and discipline is directed to this end. He ban-
ishes from his ideal territory, the Lydian and Ionic measures as
"softly sweet" and wanton—while he retains for certain purposes, the grave Dorian mood and the spirit-stirring Phrygian.
So in like manner, he expels all the poets, (except the didactic)
with Homer at their head. The tragic poets were, in reference
to moral education, especially offensive to him.‡ In conformity
with the same principle, he proscribes all manner of deliciousness and excess—Sicilian feasts, and Corinthian girls and Attic
dessert and dainties—as leading to corruption of manners and
to the necessity of laws and penalties, of the judge and the executioner. No innovation whatever is to be tolerated in this system of discipline—especially in what regards music and gymnastics; the slightest change in which Plato affirms to produce decided, however secret and insidious, effects upon the
character and manners of a whole people.§ When his citizens
divided into four orders, to correspond with the cardinal virtues,
have gone through their preparatory discipline, and discharged
in their day and generation the duties which were respectively
allotted to them, they (at least the better sort of them) must, in the
calm of declining life, turn to the study of the true philosophy.
Not such as is taught by mercenary sophists—mere shallow
fallacies, mountebank tricks to impose upon ignorance, vile arts
to ingratiate one's self with that SAVAGE BEAST, (a favourite
image with the ancient writers,) the wayward and tyrannical
Demus. Nor such a philosophy as bestows its thoughts upon

---

* Lib. iii. p. 410. c. d.   This music, as Tiedeman observes, is mystic and mathematical. Pythagoras and Plato thought every thing musical of divine origin. l. ii.
    † ἀλλ᾽ ἐπ᾽ ᾽ἐκεῖνο ὅπως ἂν ἀλλήλοιν συναρμοσθῆτον, επιτείνομενω και ανειμένω
μεχρι τοῦ προσήκοντος. Ib. 411. e. cf. 413 e. Sub. Calc.
    ‡ In the Minos, Socrates pronounces some story, about the old Cretan of that
name, "an Attic and *Tragic* fable."
    § He traces the progress thus, ἠρέμα ὑποῤῥεῖ πρὸς τὰ ἤθη τε κ᾽ ἐπιτηδεύμ-
ατα, ἐκ δὲ τούτων εἰς τὰ πρὸς ἀλλήλους ξυμβόλαια μεῖζων ἐκβαίνει, εκ δὲ δὴ
τῶν ᾽ζυμβόλαιων ἔρχεται ἐπὶ τοὺς νόμους καὶ πολιτείας σὺν πολλῇ, ὦ Σώκρατες,
ἀσελγεία. l. 4. 424. We ought, perhaps, to apologize for quoting so much
Greek ; but the *ipsissima verba* are important in such discussions, and every
scholar may not have Plato at hand.

the depraved manners of men, or the fluctuating and perishable objects around us; but that deep wisdom, that rapturous and holy contamplation which abstracts itself from the senses and the changeable scenes of life and nature, and is wrapt up in the harmony and grandeur of the universe—in communing with the First Good and the First Fair—the infinite and unutterable beauty,* fountain of all light to the soul—"the bright countenance of truth" revealed to the purified mind "in the quiet and still air of delightful studies." By such contamplation the soul shall attain to the perfection of virtue—ὁμονοητικῆς ϗʹ ἡρμοσμένης τῆς ψυχῆς ἀληθὴς ἀρετή,—and be prepared for the great moral change, the glorious transfiguration that is to crown its aspiring progress to beatitude and immortality; while, in the meantime, spirits of a higher order wait upon her as upon chastity in Comus—

> A thousand liveried angels lackey her,
> Driving far off each thing of sin and guilt;
> And, in clear dream and solemn vision,
> Tell her of things that no gross ear can hear;
> Till oft converse with heavenly habitants
> Begin to cast a beam on the outward shape,
> The unpolluted temple of the mind,
> And turns it by degrees to the soul's essence,
> Till all be made immortal.

Such, we think, is a just idea of Plato's republic, and we flatter ourselves that we have made out the proposition with which we began our analysis of it. The author himself, it ought to be added, or rather Socrates in the fifth book,† disavows all idea of its feasibility, unless the day should ever come when government should be committed to adepts in that true philosophy just described; that is to say, a period very like the Millennium of the Christian system. His treatise "De Legibus," is a far more practical work, and deserves on very account the profound attention of the philosopher and the scholar.

Cicero had reason, therefore, to deviate from Plato's model, even supposing him capable of producing any thing in the same kind, which we more than doubt. His genius, indeed, had "a true consent" with that of the Athenian philosopher, and owed it much of its beauty and elevation. In the course of this very work, too, there are, as we have said before, many imitations of Plato, and several passages upon subjects treated by him, replete with the moral grandeur, the magnificent musings, the ravishing and sublime poetry, in short, of that "Homer of philosophers."‡ But Roman genius was, at best, a very different thing from Greek—and Plato's was a phenomenon even at

---

* ἀμήχανον κάλλος. At this passage Glauco interrupts the rapture of Socrates, and calls it δαιμονία ὑπερϐολή.

† p. 472. 6.

‡ Tusc. Qu. i. c. 32, a saying of Panætius.

Athens—and the Republic is, perhaps, that work of his in which his peculiarities appear most strikingly, because somewhat unexpectedly displayed. If the whole work of Cicero were before us now, we have no doubt, that notwithstanding the points of resemblance, or rather of imitation, just alluded to, it would furnish a most notable exemplification of that difference. Certainly what remains goes far to do so.

The object of the author, in this dialogue, was to show that the Roman constitution, according to its true theory, and as it had existed in the practice of an uncorrupted age, was the most perfect system of government which the wit of man had ever devised—or more properly speaking, to prove that the wit of man had never devised, and could not devise any thing so perfect. Hence he quotes, with great approbation, a saying of the elder Cato, that the true cause of this superiority was, that—whereas other states had owed their institutions to the wisdom of some single legislator, to a Lycurgus, a Solon, a Minos—*theirs* had been the work of time and of circumstances; and, thus growing up out of the exigencies of particular occasions, had been adapted with the utmost precision to the character and condition of the people—in short that, instead of being the hasty and half-formed product of speculative genius, it was the fruit of practical and experimental wisdom, brought forth in full maturity at proper seasons. This idea—which Polybius repeats without acknowledging whence he had borrowed it*—is the basis of the whole treatise *De Republicâ*. The first book is little more than a prologue, embracing such topics as the comparative happiness of an active and contemplative life, the general state of affairs at Rome, &c. But, in the second, Scipio enters fully into his subject, and, beginning with the foundation of the city, delivers an elaborate panegyric upon the wisdom of the Roman people, as displayed in their policy and laws. In the third, as we have always known through St. Augustine, and as we now perceive from the fragment in hand, the question, how far it were profitable to individuals and to states to prefer justice to utility, was discussed, Philus undertaking to repeat the sophisms of Carneades in favor of successful villainy, with the old story of the ring of Gyges and Pacuvius' chariot drawn by winged serpents (c. 9.) In this discussion, which was no doubt a close imitation of that carried on in the first and second books of Plato's Republic, between Lysimachus and Glauco on the one side, and Socrates on the other, Lælius is the champion of orthodoxy. His panegyric upon justice is rapturously praised by Scipio, and we have no donbt but that the loss of it has deprived us of one of the most beautiful effusions that ever delighted a sound taste in morals and literature. The subject of the

*Hist. Rom. l. vi.

fourth book—of which but a single leaf remains—is supposed
to have been education. Nothing else is ascertained of the work,
except the dream of Scipio in the sixth book.

From this outline of the fragment *De Republica*, we have
reason to think that it bore a greater resemblance to the Discourses of Macchiavelli, than to the Dialogue of Plato which we
have just examined : or rather it would seem to have been a sort
of medium between those celebrated productions. If it was
more sober and practical than the Greek philosopher's, it was far
less so than that of the Florentine Secretary. The Somnium
Scipionis, for instance, would have been quite out of place in the
Discourses. Macchiavelli had no *sentiment* and very little imagination. His unrivalled excellence (for unrivalled he is) consists in a cold, calculating, "long-sighted and strong-nerved" reason—seasoned, as is proved by Belfagor and Mandragola, with a
good deal of vivacity and wit. "But there was no more faith
in him than in a stewed prune." He was a heartless Italian di-
plomatist, who had learned to be a *speculative* republican—where
Milton, and Sidney, and Harrington afterwards imbibed their
more sincere love of liberty—in the schools of antiquity, and
whose head was full of the notion, so rife at that time in Italy,
of the superiority of the antique over the gothic model, and of
the Pseudo-descendants of the Romans over the whole race of
Ultramontane barbarians. The merit of his discourses we admit
to be of the very highest order. They are the best work of the
kind extant—less metaphysical than Aristotle's Politics—more
philosophical and comprehensive than our own Federalist—and
not to be degraded by a comparison with the random epigrams
of Montesquieu. It would have been a curious thing to have
collated Cicero's exposition of the Roman government and policy,
with a work upon the same subject, written at the end of fifteen
centuries, without any of those advantages which his æra and
situation gave the Roman consul and philosopher. From the remark of Tubero, however, in the dialogue *De Republica*,* that
Scipio had, so far, rather delivered a panegyric on the Roman
constitution, than a political discourse of general application and
practical tendency, we doubt very much whether the latter had
made, by any means, so full an analysis of the subject as the
commentator upon the first Decade of Livy.

The excellence of the Roman polity, according to Cicero,
consisted first, in its being of a mixed form—and, secondly, of
a very aristocratic spirit and character. These may be regarded
as the two grand postulates of the political science of antiquity.
The Greek and Roman authors are all agreed without, (we believe) a single exception, upon the first point. All the simple
forms they consider as radically vicious and unstable ; and Plato,

* Lib. ii. c. 36.

and, after him, other writers have traced the transmigration of governments from one of these forms into another with much ingenuity, according to laws which they consider as quite ascertained and invariable. For example, an unchecked democracy they regarded as the infallible source of usurpation and tyranny. It deserves to be remarked, too, that they express themselves on the subject of popular government in this unmitigated form, in a tone of aversion and disgust, approaching even to horror. They represent it as the very worst sort of tyranny, and hesitate not to prefer to it a kingly government, which indeed, they universally pronounce the best of the simple forms. Plato, we have seen, speaks of the people, in one of those fierce and lawless democracies, as a great wild beast, untamed, intractable—"the armed rhinoceros, or the Hyrcan tiger." Cicero uses this same image in the work bafore us. Polybius characterises democracy as θηριώδης καὶ χειροκρατικός.* Aristotle represents the people, under such a government, or rather *no* government, as the most despotic and capricious of masters, differing from single tyrants—from the Perianders and Dionysius'—in no respect except by exceeding them in recklessness and cruelty. King Demus, he affirms, keeps as slavish if not as polite a court as other monarchs; has just as good an appetite for flattery, except that there is much more of the glutton in him than the gourmand, and that a "fishy fume" is as savoury to his nostrils as the breath of frankincense and myrrh—and is surrounded, in his demagogues, by the coarsest, basest, most servile and unprincipled sycophants—the dirtiest toad eaters, in short, that ever disgraced the erect form of man, or profaned the awful name of liberty.† Some of these courtiers of the mob aimed at, and attained to, supreme power, as Pisistratus at Athens, who was as much the darling of the rabble there as his antitype, in times more recent, citizen Robespierre, was at Paris— but the great majority of them were satisfied, of course, with much lower wages for their prostituted and infamous subserviency. Demagogues, happily for us, can never, in the nature of things, have such influence under our government, as in the wild and turbulent democracies of antiquity. But we cannot fail to recognize in Aristotle's Parasites, the true *idea* and type of those "firm and undeviating republicans, *par excellence*," those exclusive "friends of the people," who deafen us with their self-proclaimed virtues and obstreperous humility whenever there is a scramble for place in the commonwealth—whose only conception of popular government seems to be as of a great state lottery for the distribution of office to indigent patriots—who, considering every means as justifiable in the pursuit of so exalted an object, make it their business to inflame every tempo-

* Lib. vi. c. 8.   † Pol. lib. iv. c. 4.

rary excitement, to comply with every vulgar prejudice, to suppress all truth, to propagate all falsehood—who adhere to no
party that is not triumphant, cringe to every majority that is
fully ascertained, and sacrifice, without scruple, to promote the
ends of some worthless popular leader, the eternal principles
of justice, law and liberty. It is strange that such men do not
feel themselves to be the vilest of slaves—that they should even
presume to talk of the sycophants of Czars and Sultans, and
thank God that they are not like those publicans. It is still
more strange that they who thus worship in our temples, with
false fire, and, do all that in them lies, to profane and corrupt
the institutions of the land, should not be held in the execration
and contempt they deserve. We agree heartily in the views
of this subject lately presented to the public, in a contemporary journal, by the most eloquent writer of his country—
perhaps of his day.* True liberty, like true eloquence, is founded on the most elevated moral sentiments, and is incompatible
with any other. C'est le culte des ames fières, as Madame Roland nobly expresses it. But it requires something more even
than this sublime spirit, rare as that is. Liberty is law—liberty
is truth—liberty is reason, and "always with right reason dwells,
and from her, hath no dividual being." The greatest men, in
such a country as this, ought to be considered, (what they really
are) as completely insignificant in comparison of the smallest
principle. It is of the very essence of republican government,
that the laws, which all are free to choose, should be implicitly
obeyed by all. And as law has been defined to be "reason
without passion," so those who administer and execute it should
partake of the same unblemished nature. It is in this respect
that Washington stands without a similar or a second. He was
living law—the very personification of the purest, the sternest,
the most dispassionate, the most sublime republicanism. In
this point of view, his character does not seem to have been
sufficiently contemplated—we mean, contemplated with fervid
admiration as an object at once of taste and example—under
the head of the sublime and beautiful, as well as of moral duty.
We hope it has been reserved as a subject for a hand worthy
of treating it—and that we shall see the "awful goodness" of
that incomparable man transmitted to posterity in contrast with
Napoleon's guilty and little ambition, and fitly associated with
the grandeur of Milton's genius.

The democracy, of which the ancient political writers concur
in drawing so frightful a picture, is described by one of them as
a government in which *decrees* stand in the place of *laws*—that
is to say where the popular assembly exercised judicial powers

---

* Dr. Channing. Honor and glory to the man who exerts such talents for such
ends.

in the shape of legislation, and passed statutes, not only for general rules, but for particular cases. This confounding of the executive and judicial powers is the very definition of tyranny under every kind of polity—but we may not so readily perceive why it should have been more intolerable in a popular than a monarchical or aristocratic form. These philosophers, however, had ample opportunities of comparing them in the petty States of Greece. Aristotle, for instance, is said to have examined upwards of a hundred and fifty different constitutions by way of preparation for his great work on politics. They saw that, as Burke expresses it, "a mob has no heart," for the same reason that a corporation is said, by Lord Coke, to have no soul. It retains only the harshest features, the most fearful and repulsive energies of the individuals that compose it. It may be good for attack and defence—for sueing and being sued—for grasping at acquisition, and keeping whatever it acquires locked up in perpetual mortmain—but it has no bowels of mercy and compassion—no amiable weaknesses—no compunctious visitings of nature. The individual feels—perhaps weeps, to think what his duty as a member of an artificial body requires of him. But, in this metaphysical way of abstracting himself from himself, the root of the whole mischief is to be found. He finds all his purposes strengthened and consecrated by it. He considers himself as representing others, and as having no discretion. His very repugnance to an act is a motive for committing it. His conduct, as a public man, is sanctified in his own eyes by the tears which it makes him shed in private. He looks upon himself as a Brutus or a Manlius, and glories in being able to controul the instincts of nature by a comprehensive reason and an unconquerable sense of duty. When he attains to this sublime degree of perfection, and has added to it an *intrepid confidence in his own opinions,* he is what we understand by the word, *jacobin.* Many of those cannibal monsters were men of the gentlest natures and most inoffensive lives. But they had learned the metaphysics of a mob—they became corporators—they got the freedom of the city of Paris, a glorious exemption from all the weaknesses of undisciplined and simple hearts. They thus stopped up, completely, "the access and passage to remorse." The end sanctioned every means—they were ready to sacrifice, to the wildest speculative opinion, all that is held venerable and sacred and dear among men—and their holy covenant of regeneration was to have been sealed and solemnized—not, as Cataline's conspiracy is said to have been, by the blood of a single human victim—but, if need were, by the massacre of half the population of France. Nothing can be imagined more cold-blooded, inexorable and exterminating than this sort of philosophical fanaticism—not even that of the Dominicans in the first fervor of their zeal. The disease is the most incurable because its seat is in the head. It is the madness of Ravaillac and Sands. The following is a genuine specimen of jacobin morals and philosophy. It is the language of Gracchus Barbœuf, who got up the conspiracy of—Floreal, ann. 4, for the purpose of restoring the blessed Reign of Terror. Robespierre he regarded as the wisest and best of men—a prophet sent upon a special mission for the redemption of mankind from the bondage of prejudice and abuse, and raised, himself, above all the common infirmities and errors of our nature. We should translate it if we durst—but no language but his own can do justice to the cold atrocity of such doctrines. "Le salut de vingt cinq millions d'hommes ne doit point être balancé, &c. Un *régénerateur doit voir en grand ;* son devoir est de faucher tout ce qui le gène, tout ce qui obstrue son passage, tout ce qui peut nuire à sa prompte arrivée au terme ; fripons, imbécilles, présomtueux ; c'est égal, tant pis pour eux : pourquoi se trouvaient ils là? Il est vrai que ce principe pouvait nous écraser, toi et moi, mais le bonheur commun devait être la suite de son execution rigoureuse." The mischief of this sort of philosophy is that it bears an imposing resemblance to the highest republican virtue. The difference consists in this—that the jacobin considers himself as infallible, and has the most profound contempt for the understandings of the rest of mankind, and for all established institutions and received opinions, merely *as such.* So that, whenever a fit of *regeneration* takes him, he has no sort of scruple about putting the most important interests of society to the hazard of the wildest experiment in government, which his own conceits may dictate.

When to these considerations we add, what has been justly remarked, that there is no feeling of responsibility—no fear, no shame in multitudes, even for avowed crimes, while the passions which animate them are contagious, and, in the supreme legislative assemblies of a democracy, uncontrollable ; and, when we further reflect how very excitable the Greeks were, and how imperfect was their social civilization in comparison with that of the present times, we shall cease to wonder at the sentiments of their political writers in relation to this species of tyranny. Any mob is bad—a mob of philosophers, on the principles just explained, as bad as any other—but there was a morbid activity, a feverish restlessness in the Athenians, which made their mob particularly mischievous. The following observation of Burke is fully warranted by the history of the ancient democracies, as well as of those which existed in Italy some centuries ago. "Of this I am certain, that, in a democracy, the majority of the citizens is capable of exercising the most cruel oppressions upon the minority, whenever strong divisions prevail in that kind of polity, as they often must; and that oppression of the minority will extend to far greater numbers, and will be carried on with much greater fury, than can almost ever be apprehended from the dominion of a single sceptre. In such a popular persecution, individual sufferers are in a much more deplorable condition than in any other. Under a cruel prince, they have the balmy compassion of mankind to assuage the smart of their wounds; they have the plaudits of the people to animate their generous constancy under their sufferings; but, those, who are subjected to wrong under multitudes, are deprived of all external consolation. They seem deserted by mankind—overpowered by a conspiracy of their whole species." In the petty Italian commonwealths there was a standing party of banished citizens—Fuorusciti.

How far this state of things affected the freedom of thought and opinion, in the republics of antiquity, is a question equally curious and important. Following out the reasoning of the great man just quoted, we should infer that an unmitigated democracy were, to a certain extent, most unfavorable to this highest sort of liberty. Few men have the firmness to be right alone. The sympathies, the concurrence of mankind, are as necessary to us in matters of opinion as any other. If we have these, there is nothing terrible—there is something even attractive in the persecutions of men in power. *Punitis ingeniis gliscit auctoritas,* is a profound sentence of Tacitus. But the tyranny of Demus had the advantage even here. It attacked liberty in its seat and citadel. It shook the confidence of a man in his own opinions. The firm persuasion that he was right would have supported him against a single despot, and he would have been willing to suffer and to die for the truth. But how could it be the truth where the majority was against him? How presumptuous and criminal—what an obstinate heretic—to persevere in opinions condemned by the common sense of mankind! We find, accordingly, that great complaints are made by the Athenian writers upon this subject. It is the burthen of the song with Demosthenes that nothing is tolerated from the Bema but flattery and falsehood, and that all the public speakers of his day were systematic dealers in them. On the other hand, Isocrates, in one of his orations,* declares that liberty of speech is allowed to none but the *demagogues* and the comic writers. We know from Aristophanes that nothing could exceed the license allowed to the latter; and, were it not for this *caveat* of Isocrates, we should infer that the Athenians extended the same privilege to all other classes of writers and speakers. Nay, this very orator, in his Areopagiticus, ventured with impunity to tell the people to their face that their democracy was become a wild and tyrannical anarchy. This passage of his oration, it is true, is remarked on by

* Περί Ειρηνῆς.

Dionysius of Halicarnassus,* as a singular instance of daring, though if we knew all the circumstances, perhaps, we should see less cause to wonder at it. Upon the whole, the most reasonable conclusion seems to be, that in merely *speculative* matters, a sufficient freedom of thought was tolerated by the people—but that, in every thing that related to the administration of affairs, it was necessary to approach them with extreme caution ; except in the license of the stage, where Demus excused any thing for wit. A striking instance of the former is found in the writings of these very political philosophers. Their whole history abounds in examples of the latter. Still, as all might hope to lead in the popular assembly, this sort of despotism did not degrade the understandings, however it may have perverted the morals of the citizens.

But as an unmitigated democracy was considered by the ancient writers as the worst form of government, so they extolled a well-balanced republic as the best. Aristotle calls the latter a *polity* κατ᾽ εξοχην.† Plato, in one of his works, describes the mixed government which he prefers.‡ It corresponds singularly with our own in many important characteristics. It would appear, however, that, provided there were real checks in a constitution—that is to say, opposing and equally balanced interests, they were not very curious about the form or name of the government. They thought with Rousseau—"I call every state a republic which is governed by laws, under whatever form of administration it may be—for there only the public interest governs, *et la chose publique est quelque chose.* Every government of laws is republican."§ Plato says so expressly in the dialogue "De Republica." The same inference is deducible from the constitutions which are pointed out by all these writers as the best in practice. These were the Spartan, the Cretan, the Carthaginian, and (by Polybius and Cicero) the Roman. The only point in which all these governments coincided was that, while the democratic spirit was strong enough to give vigor and animation to the whole system, it was too much repressed and controlled to do any mischief. It must be owned, however, that they were all of a more oligarchical, or, at least, aristocratic character, than we approve.‖ Thus Cicero praises the wisdom of Servius Tellus for having attained that *quod semper in republicâ tenendum est, ne plurimum valeant plurimi.*

This leads us to the second point, in which the political philosophers of antiquity generally concur. They were, as we have

* Jud. de Isocr. x. ἡ.
† Pol. l. iii. c. 5. l. iv. c, 8., &c. 7.   See also Plato de Legib. l. iii., &c.
‡ De Legib. l. vi.
§ Contrat-Social, ii. 6.
‖ Aristotle characterizes representative governments, however, as aristocratic. Pol. l. iv. c. 14.

said, rather more inclined to aristocracy, or more properly speaking, to oligarchy, than to popular goverment. Harrington, who learned his republicanism in a good degree from these doctors, expresses their universal sentiment in a passage, in which he declares, that "there is something, first in the making of a commonwealth, then in the governing of it, and, last of all, in the leading of its armies, which (though there be great divines, great lawyers, great men in all professions) seems to be peculiar only to the genius of a *gentleman :* for it is plain, in the universal series of a story, that if any man founded a commonwealth he was first a gentleman ;" as he takes good care to add that Oliver Cromwell was. And, in another place, he does not scruple to make "that victorious captain and incomparable patriot, Olphaus Megaletor say, in reference to the constitution of Oceana, "I will stand no more to the judgment of lawyers and divines in this work, than to that of so many *other tradesmen*." Thus Plato and Aristotle both consider what is called in Greek, ϐαναυσία, that is, the exercise of any mechanic art, as altogether inconsistent with the character of a freeman and a good citizen.* A curious instance of this same prejudice, which shows how deeply rooted it was in the whole system of ancient manners and opinions, is furnished by Philostratus in his Life of Isocrates. It had been whispered that the veteran rhetorician was originally a flute-maker (αὐλοποιὸς). But that, says his biographer, is clearly false, for he had a statute erected to him at Olympia, which could not be, had he ever been engaged in any illiberal vocation. They did not, however, confine the objection to the more humble trades. Every profession, of which the object is to make money, was regarded as illiberal—*their* word for ungentlemanlike. Thus, merchants were proscribed by Plato. There was an exception (in Greece) in favor of those who excelled in the arts of imagination and taste. Actors, for instance, were very often entrusted with the highest offices of the government. They thought no occupation degrading, of which the end was to imitate *la belle nature,* and to which of course, a profound study of beauty, grace and excellence was necessary. These opinions may be considered as the great vice of antiquity, and one among other causes of the superiority of modern institutions—that is to say, where feudal principles and notions have been exploded. What would Harrington have thought of our first Congress—of that truly Roman Senate, which declared our independence, and which carried us through the war of the Revolution ? To speak disparagingly of professional men and tradesmen, as the founders of a commonwealth, in the country of Henry and Rutledge, of Franklin and Sherman, of Laurens and Morris, would be to advance a paradox not worth the pains of

* Plato de Legib. l. v. Aristot. Polit. l. vii. c. 9. Cic. Off. l. i.

refutation. The best form of government is undoubtedly that in which all the *interests* of society are fairly represented; the best for efficiency, for freedom, for happiness. The various classes of society operate as checks and correctives of one another—profound learning and speculative genius are tempered by the shrewd common sense and "sage experience" of men of business—and the soundest and healthiest part of every community, (where extraordinary causes have not produced a different result) the great middle class of moral, substantial people, below ambition, above a bribe, too virtuous to do wrong wilfully, too wise to be easily imposed upon, is felt in every department of the public administration. A representative government, founded upon such principles, and taking care to provide for the moral education of the people, is the only scheme which holds out any hope of rational and permanent liberty. As for the effects of oligarchical institutions upon the character and destinies of a people, they may be read in every page of Roman history from the æra of this dialogue to the battle of Philippi. Sallust, especially, draws a terrible picture of them in his history of Cataline's conspiracy—which was emphatically a plot of *gentlemen*—of bankrupt patricians and traitorous magistrates. Clodius, too, was as good a gentleman as any at Rome, and frequently sneers at Cicero as an upstart man of Arpinum. This view of the subject was taken by that writer, who, of all the ancients, seems to have had the justest and most comprehensive ideas of the social condition of mankind. Aristotle has a dissertation expressly to shew that the whole people, (under a well balanced polity, of course,) are necessarily better judges of every matter, whether of reasoning or of taste, whether in government, in morals, or in art. than even the best educated and most highly gifted individual can pretend to be. His Demus is a man with a vast multitude of organs, senses and faculties—a sort of male Pandora, in whose composition all kinds of men, all orders of society, have been laid under contribution for perfections.* Macchiavelli probably had this part of Aristotle's work in view, when he wrote the chapter in his Discourses, of which the title is "Che la Moltitudine è più savia e più costante che un principe"—and which presents a noble and powerful defence of popular government.

We will add another remark of some importance in this connection. The idea of liberty among the ancients was very different from that which we attach to the word. This difference, as well as the aristocratic sentiments adverted to just now, sprung undoubtedly out of the institution of domestic slavery, and that principle of their *jus gentium*, which doomed captives in battle to perpetual bondage. From whatever causes, the Ionian and Do-

* Lib. iii. c. 7. Plato, contrà.

rian races—but especially the former—attained to a remarkable superiority over the rest of mankind. In the neighbourhood of despotisms, they established popular and limited governments; in the midst of darkness and ignorance, they cultivated philosophy and the arts which body forth ideal beauty, while the hosts of the Mede sunk beneath their prowess in the field. The other great race, with whose institutions and modes of thought we are made familiar by our early studies, without excelling as much in merely intellectual pursuits, carried the preeminence which civilization gives in war and in policy, to a still higher pitch. "Their empire comprehended the fairest part of the earth, and the most civilized portion of mankind," and kings and tetrachs were glad to become their clients and retainers. That these privileged and illustrious races should be conscious of their unquestionable advantages—that they should look down upon the rest of mankind with an insolent sense of their own superiority, and should even be unwilling to acknowledge themselves of the same origin and species, is not much to be wondered at—at least, may readily be conceived. Accordingly, their whole literature breathes this spirit. It is taken for granted, by their orators, in harangues, of which this opinion inspires the eloquence—by their philosophers who built their systems and theories upon it—that Greeks were created to conquer and to control barbarians. Aristotle, in a grave inquiry, whether slavery be consistent with the law of nature, decides that it is so where one race is by nature inferior to another, and even justifies war, if it be necessary to subject the predestinated bondman to his chains.* In that famous burst of eloquence in which Cicero gives vent to his indignation and horror against Verres for the crucifixion of Gavius, it is evident that he lays the whole emphasis upon the circumstance of his being a Roman citizen, and that this circumstance entitles the offence, in the orator's estimation, to cap the whole climax of crimes and atrocities which he had to unfold, enormous as they were. His language is a precise expression of the sentiments which we impute to the ancients upon this subject. O nomen dulce libertatis! O sweet name of liberty—but what liberty? This question is answered by the next words. *O jus eximium nostræ civitatis.* It was not the violence done to the principles of natural right and justice—it was not that an innocent man had been punished, or that a guilty man had been *cruelly* tortured and disgraced: it was that the Portian and Sempronian laws had been broken—that the sacred privilege of citizenship had been despised—that a ROMAN had suffered as if he had been a Sicilian or a barbarian.† The feel-

* This curious passage which classes the conquest of these *natural slaves* with the hunting of wild beasts, is to be found. Pol. Lib. i. c. 5.

† Justinian darkly hints that slavery is against the law of nature, though agreea-

ing expressèd by the orator is precisely such as one feudal baron would have experienced at witnessing the body of another gibbeted by the king's justice in eyre. Liberty, in short, was rank and nobility among the ancients; and inspired the same sentiments for good and for evil. It was considered as the birthright—the hereditary dignity of certain races—but the idea that, it was part and parcel of the law of nature and nations—that it was due in common justice to all mankind, seems to have occurred to very few, and to have been acted upon by nobody.* This accounts for that fierce and jealous love of liberty which characterized the Athenian democracy, and (whatever may have been its other effects) gives such a noble spirit and such lively interest to their whole literature.

Cicero, as we have said, thought that he saw in the constitution of his country, as it existed during the happy and glorious period before alluded to, the best of all possible schemes of government—a perfect model of the well-tempered and balanced polity, imagined by philosophers in their visions of perfectibility, but never successfully reduced to practice by any other great people. He was willing to take it with all its imperfections on its head—with all its apparent anomalies, irregularities and defects. Its fruits had been good, and that was enough for him. The *imperium in imperio*, the *plebiscitum*, and the veto, which a systematic politician, working by plumb and rule, would have condemned as an absurdity, struck him as the best balance that could be devised. He was not alarmed at the power, or even the necessity, of resorting now and then to the despotism of the dictator, or the decree of *ne quid respublica detrimenti capiat*, which, in more recent times, was substituted for it in practice. He regarded these very irregularities as among the chief excellences of the government in an uncorrupted age. They were a proof that it had not been formed upon visionary and superficial principles, without reference to the wants, the habits, or the character of the people. He had not the presumption to suppose that he could devise *a priori* a scheme of polity better than that which had been so fruitful of good for centuries together. He had no faith in political metaphysics. He knew that nothing was more deceptive and dangerous than the affectation of mathematical exactness in matters which have less to do with quantity than with any other of the ten categories. He had never heard of the three *bases* of the philosophical constitution of France—of the basis of population, the basis of contribution, or the basis of territory; and the rest of that magnificent but senseless jargon. It did not occur to him that (as the specu-

ble to the *jus gentium*. Inst. Lib. i. tit.—and Socrates says something to the same purpose, but with some qualification. Xenoph. Mem. Lib iv. c. 2.

* Hoc teneo, hic hæreo, judices, hoc sum contentus uno, &c.

lative politicians of these times seem to think) there is a sort of mystic or magical power in the mere forms of a polity, and that a government may be altered as often as the most capricious levity shall dictate, without any danger of disturbing the settled order of society, and with a perfect foresight of all the effects of such changes. He knew, that the *mores*, the manners, opinions and character of a people, are by far the most important part in every political problem, and that no constitution can be either stable or efficient which is not in harmony with these. He had adopted, in short, that rule, which a great man—whose speculations have exhausted this subject, and occur to us whenever we have occasion to contemplate it—considers as fundamental with every good patriot and every true politician. Spartam nactus es; hanc exorna. Cicero would have felt the whole force and beauty of the following period. "By adhering in this manner and on these principles to our forefathers, we are guided not by the superstition of antiquarians, but by the spirit of philosophic analogy—in this choice of inheritance, we give to our frame of polity the image of a relation in blood; binding up the constitution of our country with our dearest domestic ties, adopting our fundamental laws into the bosom of our family affections; keeping inseparable, and cherishing, with the warmth of all their combined and mutually reflected charities, our state, our hearths, our sepulchres and our altars." The compliment he pays the government of Rome is, therefore, as full of wisdom as of patriotism, and may be taken as his protest against that pest of our times, SPECULATIVE POLITICS.

HALL'S TRAVELS IN NORTH-AMERICA.

Travels in North-America, in the years 1827 and 1828. By Captain Basil Hall, Royal Navy. 2 vols. 12mo. *Philadelphia. Carey, Lea & Carey.* 1829.

Our only motive for reviewing this book is the general expectation that we shall do so. It is to us, on many accounts, a most unpleasant task. We are by no means sure that the majority of our readers will concur with us in some of our views, and we have too much reason to fear that there are many individuals in every part of the country to whom all of them cannot possibly prove acceptable. But we have learned by experience the truth of Seneca's lines,

> Sæpe vel linguà magis
> ————muta libertas obest—

and since we must needs speak, we shall even speak out.

We will begin by confessing that we have been greatly scandalized at the fuss that has been made about Captain Hall and his book. If there were nothing more in it, this fidgety and prurient anxiety about what he has been saying of us behind our backs, is rather a provoking confirmation of what he reports of our efforts to extort his approbation of us before our faces. But our mortification arises from a more serious view of the matter. For our humble selves, we declare, with great sincerity, that none of the impertinences which have been published about our country and its institutions, in England or elsewhere, have ever given us the smallest uneasiness, nor do we conceive how they should disturb the tranquillity of any rational mind. If the remarks of a stranger convey salutary truths, we feel it a duty to acknowledge, as it is our interest to profit by them. But what possible harm can his errors or his falsehoods do—except indeed, to those who are sensitive enough to be angry with them? Even in the case of an individual, it would infer a great want of self-respect to be so excessively alive to the opinions of others—much more to think of retaliating upon a vulgar calumniator in his own way. But what is undignified in the case of an individual becomes quite absurd in a whole people—especially in a people full of a prophetic confidence in its destinies, and every day, as we are taught to believe, marching with such gigantic strides to the fulfilment of them. Surely it is unworthy of such a people to think of making any other answer to the misrepresentations of a prejudiced, or theoretical, or lying traveller, (as the case may be) than the pregnant one conveyed in the line of Dante—

Taci, e lascia volger gli anni. *

We cannot say that we found any single passage in these volumes more offensive to us than the following:—

"The fact of the greater part of all the works, which are read in one country, being written for a totally different state of society in another, forms a very singular anomaly in the history of nations—and I am disposed to think that the Americans would be a happier people if this incongruous communication were at an end. If they got no more books or newspapers from us, than we do from France or Spain, they would, I really believe, be much happier as far as their intercourse with this country has any influence over them." Vol. i. p. 243.

Yet there is, unfortunately, but too much truth in it. For all our hyperbolical vauntings about our own superiority to the rest of mankind, we do defer too much to English criticism, and suffer ourselves at once to be governed and to be made unhappy by it. We have too much national vanity, and too little of the far nobler feeling of national pride. There can be no true greatness either in individuals or in multitudes without self-reliance. Enthusiasm must be too intense to quail at ridicule, genius must soar above criticism, or there is no hope of excellence. We must learn to think only of truth and nature in what we do and say, and to be contented with the applauses of our own people. Instead of clipping and paring away our energies to suit ourselves to the taste of foreigners, let us give them free scope, and trust to the sympathies of our neighbours, our friends, our brethren. What Frenchman expects to be admired at London, or cares a straw about the opinions of English and Scotch censors? For him the whole world lies between the Alps, the Pyrenees and the ocean. We are, in this respect, too fortunate, did we but know and appreciate our own advantages. Ridiculous as some of our anticipations, bottomed upon the "geometrical ratio" may be, there is one which cannot fail. Beyond a doubt, in the course of half a century more, the audience to which American genius shall address itself (great as it already is) will be far more numerous—the theatre more vast and imposing, if not altogether so brilliant as that of the parent country. At the end of yet another half century it will be said of England, with truth, *pars minima est ipsa sui.* Her language will become a dialect. It will be to the great Anglo-Saxon tongue, spoken on the banks of the Missouri and the Hudson, at best, what the Attic was to the Hellenic or common Greek. The majority, with anything like equality of force and advantages,

* Paradiso, ix.

will govern in this as in other things. The adoption into good
use in England of very many words, but the other day rejected
and ridiculed.as Americanisms, shews already what is the inevitable tendency of things.   And, after all, what does it signify to
us whether that language shall be intelligible and agreeable or
not to a foreign ear.* Happy the men who shall lead the way
in the formation of a national literature—who shall strike the
chord to which so many millions of American hearts shall vi-
brate forever, and leave a name to be re-echoed

> "With a shout
> Loud as from numbers without number, sweet
> As from blest voices, uttering joy."

We begin by avowing frankly that we have been, upon the
whole, agreeably disappointed in Captain Hall's report of us.
From all that we had heard of his conversations and deportment
while among us, we had been led to expect a great deal of misrepresentation and acrimony in his book.   We must do him the
justice to say that there is very little of the former—in the way
of any positive *suggestio falsi* at least—and nothing at all of
the latter.   Most of what he states as matter of fact we believe
to be substantially true.   Our readers will understand us.   We
would carefully distinguish between his statements and his inferences—between the journal of the Traveller and the common-
place book of the Tory philosopher.   That he should be dissatisfied with our political institutions was quite a matter of course.
What Englishman or Scotchman, or any other loyal subject (we
say nothing of a salaried functionary) of his Britannic Majesty,
could ever tolerate popular government in any shape ?   Or why
should we, who utterly abominate their polity, and give ourselves so little trouble to conceal our aversion to it, deny the
same privilege to them?   We were fully prepared, therefore, for
his diatribes upon this subject, and all that we felt ourselves at
liberty to exact from him was what every gentleman owes to
his own reputation, viz. that he should state our case fairly.   It
would be going too far to say that he has done this exactly.
It would be, perhaps, expecting too much of him to require it.
He came hither with preconceived opinions—he is an *homme à
système*, and visited us for the purpose of collecting facts to
support his theory.   He has accordingly seen everything with
a partial and prejudiced eye.   There is no doubt about this, so
far, we mean, as our political constitution and its effects on society are concerned.   On another vital subject, as we shall presently have to remark more particularly, he does not seem to have
adhered so pertinaciously to his opinions.   But, on this great
subject of popular institutions, he looks at all the phenomena
through a false medium, and draws conclusions the very reverse

* See remarks of Captain Hall on this subject, at vol. i. p. 241

of those which would seem fairly deducible from his own premises. When we say, therefore, that he has not, to our knowledge, been guilty of any important misrepresentation, our proposition is, of course, subject to the qualification, that he has suffered his inveterate opinions to throw a false colouring over the objects of his inquiry, and to betray him into the exaggeration and unfairness of a professed advocate. Thus, it is undoubtedly true, that with some few exceptions the speeches of our members of Congress are intolerably long-winded, rhetorical and common-place, although it may be true that the subject, by the time it has passed through a discussion of fifty orators and at least as many days, is as fully elucidated as it could be by as many Pitts and Cannings. So, it is certainly true that the great democratic principle, as it is called, of rotation in office, operates rather too actively to admit of a very mature experience in most of our politicans—and yet it does not necessarily follow but that our raw recruits in legislation are quite a match for the disciplined veterans of other countries. Again, our worthy Captain is lamentably behind the spirit of the age—of the nineteenth century—in his notions about an establishment and the union of the Church and State ; yet he admits that he saw every where the most profound respect for religion, and he is only apprehensive, *a priori*, lest (to verify his theory) things will not long go on in the same train.

Let it be remembered, too, that he visited us at a juncture as inauspicious for the country, as it was well suited to the supposed purpose of the tourist. He was here in the very "torrent, tempest and, as I may say, whirlwind of our passions." He was an eye and ear-witness of many of those disgusting and disgraceful abominations which have made the late presidential election forever memorable—may it be forever unparalleled—in our history. He heard of nothing else wherever he went. The rancorous hostility, the atrocious calumnies, the systematic misrepresentation, the violation of every decency of life, that distinguished the party warfare of the day, pressed upon his observation on all sides. He saw the daily press teeming with ribaldry and falsehood, until the very sight of a newspaper became loathsome to every body that had any sense of shame left. He heard of eaves-droppers reporting conversations—of friends publishing the letters of their correspondents—of guests violating the rights of hospitality, and the sanctity of the fireside and the festive board. He saw this ruthless and unprincipled warfare carried into the very bosom of domestic life, and even female sensibility and honour assailed by remorseless ruffians, apparently with the countenance of men who ought to have blushed at the bare idea of such an alliance. This baleful spirit pervaded everything, disturbed everything, corrupted everything.

It is impossible for any good citizen to contemplate this subject without anxiety and alarm. What is to become of the country if it is to be eternally distracted by the most slavish and degrading of all sorts of political party, that, namely, in which the fundamental maxim of republican government is reversed, and all principles are sacrificed to men? Captain Hall has given anything but an exaggerated account of this mighty evil in a passage which we are about to cite. *Pudet hæc opprobria nobis!* We know that there are men, and those probably, among the busiest and basest actors in such scenes, who would as little scruple to deny their existence, as to get them up again whenever their own ends could be answered by it. But protestations of this sort, however vehemently patriotic they may sound, cannot restore the peace, the dignity, and the morals of a people thus excited and misled. We see no remedy for these things while the daily press is conducted as it is—and while good citizens shrink from the responsibility of denouncing the mean or unprincipled expedients resorted to by their own party, and every through-paced partisan, on the contrary, acts as if he thought success the only test of merit, and failure the only sort of dishonour worth avoiding.

"The most striking peculiarity of this spirit, in contradistinction to what we see in England, is that its efforts are directed more exclusively to the means, than to any useful end. The Americans, as it appears to me, are infinitely more occupied about bringing in a given candidate, than they are about the advancement of those measures of which he is conceived to be the supporter. They do occasionally advert to these prospective measures, in their canvassing arguments in defence of their own friends, or in attacks upon the other party; but always, as far as I could see, more as rhetorical flourishes, or as motives to excite the furious acrimony of party spirit, than as distinct or sound anticipations of the line of policy which their candidate, or his antagonist, was likely to follow. The intrigues, the canvassing for votes, all the machinery of newspaper abuse and praise, the speeches and manœuvres in the legislature, at the bar, by the fireside, and in every hole and corner of the country from end to end, without intermission, form integral parts of the business—apparently far more important than the candidate's wishes—his promises—or even than his character and fitness for the office.

"All these things, generally speaking, it would seem, are subordinate considerations; so completely are men's minds swallowed up in the technical details of the election. They discuss the chances of this or that State, town, or parish, or district, going with or against their friend. They overwhelm one another with that most disagreeable of all forms of argument—authorities. They analyze every sentence uttered by any man dead or alive, who possesses, or ever did possess, influence; not, it must be observed, to come at any better knowledge of the candidate's pretensions as a public man, but merely to discover how far the weight of such testimony is likely to be thrown into their own scale, or that of the opposite party.

"The election of the President, being one affecting the whole country, the respective candidates for that office were made the butts at which all political shafts were aimed, and to which every other election was rendered subservient, not indirectly, but by straight and obvious means. It was of no importance, apparently, whether the choice to be made, at any given election, were that of a governor, a member of Congress, or to the Legislature of the State—or whether it were that of a constable of an obscure ward of an obscure town—it was all the same. The candidates seldom, if ever, that I could see, even professed to take their chief ground as the fittest men for the vacant office—this was often hardly thought of—as they stood forward simply as Adams men or Jackson men—these being the names, it is right to mention, of the two gentlemen aiming at the Presidency. Although the party principles of these candidates for any office, on the subject of the Presidential election, could not—nine cases in ten—afford any index to their capacity for filling the station to which they aspired, their chance of success was frequently made to hinge upon that matter exclusively. Thus, the man who could bring the most votes to that side of this grand, all-absorbing Presidential question, which happened to have the ascendancy for the time being, was sure to gain the day, whether he were or were not the best suited to fill the particular vacancy.

"More or less this interference of Presidential politics in all the concerns of life obtained in every part of America which I visited. There were exceptions, it is true, but these were so rare, that the tone I have been describing was absurdly the predominant one every where. The consequencewas that the candidates for office, instead of being the principals, were generally mere puppets—men of straw—abstract being, serving the purpose of rallying points to the voters from whence they might carry on their main attack in the pursuit of an ulterior object, which, after all, was equally immaterial in itself, but which served, for the time being, to engross the attention of the people as completely as if it were of real consequence to them. In these respects, therefore, the Presidential contests in America resemble those field sports in which the capture of the game is entirely subordinate to the pleasures of its pursuit." Vol. i. pp. 248-250.

As for that peevish disposition, which the worthy Captain manifests on other points, it is partly to be accounted for by his political theory, and partly by the simple fact that he is an Englishman. We say Englishman, because we know that every North-Briton affects to be thought so, if possible. If the edu·cation of the more opulent classes is defective—if domestic discipline is lax and feeble—if the speeches in Congress are prosy and bombastic—if, the roads are rough—if the stage-coaches have hard seats and only one door, or, perhaps, none at all—if every body "gobbles up" his dinner in a trice, and goes about his business—if, in a country-inn or a cheap boarding-house in town, "the dangerous practice" of eating with a broad-sword, nicknamed a knife, instead of a silver fork, and without any napkin, is still kept up here, as it was in England until very recently—it is all owing to that accursed spirit of democracy, the mighty leveller, the universal defiler. So, if the gentlemen do not smooth their hats, are very superficially versed in the neck-clothiana, and seem far less concerned than they ought to be about the cut of their coats. The emphasis, which is laid upon these things by so very intelligent a person, will surprise the uninitiated; but his complaints, on another head, are more frequent and lugubrious. It is, we are grieved to say, but very seldom that he finds a bill of fare satisfactory to his distinguished appetite, or more distinguishing palate.   The good gentleman talks of the boys, at Captain Partridge's Academy, bolting their dinner like cormorants.   We do not pretend either to dispute his statement, or to defend such heathenish manners—but, if some little envy did not enter into this criticism, we have read this book to little purpose.   We never, in all our experience, heard so much about eating, except in a passage across the Atlantic, with a company of French *gourmands*, whose daily practice it was to supply a very scanty and unsavoury dinner, by the "bare imagination of a feast."   We should say that Captain Hall was laboring under as confirmed and violent *gastrimargia** as honest Sancho. Another annoyance of which he complains bitterly, is, that he was constantly put to the torture until he confessed what he thought of every thing that he saw and heard, and, if his answer happened to be less rapturous than was desired, he uniformly had the mortification to perceive that he had given great offence. We are glad to find that he was relieved from this bore as soon as he got as far southward as Baltimore, and was allowed, during the rest of his journey, to bestow or to withhold his admiration as he saw fit.   There is, no doubt, a great deal of truth in the remark that Americans do not bear criticism well.   We know this from our own very limited experience, and we think the account given of it by Captain Hall is substantially correct.†

We readily conceive that the last mentioned grievance is a serious one, and he has all our sympathy when he dwells upon it.   But really, nothing but the proverbial querulousness of Englishmen, especially when travelling in foreign countries, can excuse or rather account for some of our tourist's complaints. Grumbling seems to be John Bull's prescriptive privilege, whether at home or abroad.   Whoever has happened to meet with him on the Continent of Europe, knows that Poco-Curante himself was not harder to please.   Voltaire paints him very pleasantly in the following lines:—

> "Ce fut là qu' á table ils rencontrèrent
> Un brave Anglais, fier, dur, et sans souci * * *
> Parfait Anglais, voyageant sans dessein [?],
> Achetant cher de modernes antiques,
> Regardant tout avec un air hautain,
> Et meprisant les saints et leurs reliques.
> De tout Français c'est l'ennemi mortel—
> Et son nom est Christophe d'Arondel.
> Il parcourait tristement l'Italie;
> Et se sentant fort sujet à l'ennui
> Il amenait sa maitresse avec lui
> Plus dédaigneuse encore, plus impolie," &c.

---

* We do not know that this word has been yet naturalized, but it has quite as much right to the *jura civitatis*, as "gastronomy," &c.

† Vol. i. p. 241.

If there were nothing more in it than this, we should have less cause to complain of the treatment we have received at their hands.   But the fact is that, for obvious reasons, we are subject to the utmost rigor of this peevish and splenetic criticism.   We certainly do not imagine—what Captain Hall says is a prevalent idea in the Northern States, and what is often repeated in fourth of July orations every where—that the English, still sore under their defeats in the revolutionary war, are anxious to revenge themselves upon us as well as they may, by these and other annoyances.   We know, by actual intercourse with them, that this is a most ridiculous notion : the fact is truly stated in the volume before us.   The people of the mother country are profoundly, and, we may add, disgracefully ignorant of every thing that relates to the history and condition of their quondam colonies, and perhaps of their present ones too.   We have reason to believe, what a celebrated compatriot of our traveller is reported to have said to Mr. Madison, that many well informed persons, in all parts of Great-Britain, have never so much as heard of the last war, which was so fruitful to us of signal triumphs and proud recollections.   It is not the resentment of the English (we are sorry to confess it) that we have to apprehend in this matter of criticism, so much as another feeling far less complimentary, which we do not care to mention.   Even when they roam through countries strictly foreign—that is of a different origin and language—they rarely do more, as we have already remarked, than tolerate their peculiar usages and manners.   Still they do make some allowances on this score, while strange idioms, which they seldom comprehend very perfectly, conceal or disguise some of the most remarkable features of national character.   But with us nothing escapes their observation, and everything is tried by false weights and measures.   It is by no means enough that we should be all that can be expected under existing circumstances—nay, that our manners should even come up (if they do come up, which we neither affirm nor deny) to the standard of propriety recognised by polite society all over the world.   We must be in the latest fashion of the West End.   Our clothes must be cut by Stultz, our language must be learned in the slang-dictionary, some Brummel must be our model in the *suprème bon genre.*   Take the important example of the silver fork.   It is not very long ago since this great comfort came into very general use in England, if it can properly be said to be so even now.   But, since it is reckoned by the better sort there a badge of vulgarity to put steel into one's mouth, a British traveller draws the same inference here, as a matter of course, quite overlooking the ocean between us, and, what is yet more important, quite forgetting that his own father must probably come in for his share of the condemnation.   Language is another and a very striking example of the same blind propensity. Certainly there is no line of demarcation between vulgar people, and people of *comme il faut* so palpable, as the use and abuse of the vernacular. Between the inhabitants of the same country the test is quite infallible. But here, too, the English traveller forgets that he is out of his latitude; and is forever wondering why we should not express ourselves in the current slang of the day, instead of speaking a language which no Englishman can comprehend. He never once suspects that he knows nothing about the matter—that it is we who have preserved our mother tongue in its primitive purity, while it has been debased or corrupted among them by recent innovations. Yet so, in many cases, it undoubtedly is. For example, we were quite amused at Captain Hall's dissertation upon the word "Fall," which it seems we use in the place of "Autumn," and which he gravely recommends to the adoption of his countrymen, for poetical purposes at least. Now it so happens that our common ancestors had anticipated his discovery in its whole extent by some centuries, and that the traveller has mistaken, as other people have done before him, his ignorance for originality.

In a word, it is taken for granted by every Englishman, that every thing in America differing in anywise from the same thing in England, is *ipso facto* wrong, and conclusive against the intelligence and taste of the people. This transporting us beyond the seas for trial would be, even under the most favorable circumstances, a very outrageous proceeding, but its injustice becomes still more glaring, when we consider by what law we should be judged. We hazard nothing in saying that, with all the admirable characteristics of her people, which have raised England to such a pitch of glory and power, there is no where to be found in christendom, a state of society in many respects so artificial, exclusive and disagreeable—in short, so widely at variance, if we may be indulged in the expression, with the *jus gentium* of polished life. One very striking feature of it is the stress they lay upon the merest minutiæ of dress and manners; which are regulated by a most arbitrary and fluctuating standard, so that it is utterly impossible for any but the regularly initiated to be sure of conforming to it in all respects. It is not to be wondered, therefore, that Captain Hall, who came expressly to play the censor, should appear so vastly fastidious and faultfinding. We must confess that we sometimes find it difficult to repress a smile when we think of his performance in that character—there is something so *outré* in the notion of a blunt, bluff, opiniated, though we admit very shrewd and clever Scotch sailor, giving himself the airs of an effeminate and priggish dandy. How far, however, his political prejudices contributed to the severity of his criticism, is obvious from the excellent part in which he takes the roughest usage on the northern side of the St. Lawrence and Ontario.

Still it must be confessed that he seems in many respects to have struggled hard against his feelings, which were such as any philosopher might make a boast of curbing; though it is another instance to shew that the γνωϑι σεαυτον was a divine precept, that the author of this book has actually persuaded himself, that he came hither prepossessed in favour of the country! He confesses freely, and with all suitable professions of gratitude, that he was every where treated with kindness, nay, that he was sometimes *overwhelmed* with it, especially in the matter of sight-seeing in the Northern cities. But wherever he went— in crowds or in solitudes, in the maritime capitals, or in the wildest backwoods, he never encountered a human being who did not greet him hospitably, and, if need were, serve him cheerfully. Let it be borne in mind, too, that he made no secret at all of his opinions, but went about sketching, scribbling, sneering, scolding to our very faces, without encountering so much as one ruffled temper, or one uncivil answer.* No greater eulogy, it appears to us, could possibly be passed upon any people. Indeed, highly as in duty bound, we shall ever think of our beloved countrymen, the statement seems to us scarcely credible. What, we should like to know, would be the reception of a foreigner in England under similar circumstances? The remarks of our author upon all the public, but especially the charitable institutions of the country are, also, highly favourable to it. According to this account of us, neither pains nor expense are spared to perfect them—no difficulties, no discouragements damp our philanthropy, or make us weary of well-doing. Captain Hall has done us full justice, too, in another most important particular. He has been at no pains, we think, to disguise the fact, that, bad as its government is, the country is in a very flourishing condition. At least, whatever he may say in occasional passages, this is the necessary inference from his whole statement taken together. He thinks, indeed, that if we had remained under the royal government, we should have had a more prosperous, though not so populous a country. As respects one devoted part of this confederacy, we are sorry to say, we entertain no doubt about the truth of the proposition—but, it is some consolation to reflect that the spoils of that part are blazing forth in the improvements and accumulated opulence of the rest, and nothing can be more wild than Captain Hall's notion, considered in reference to the state of the Union at large. Charleston and

---

* Perhaps the manners of a noble Roman would be vulgar in Grosvenor Square, and the morality of a heathen be despised by those who enjoy the advantages of an established church, but there is *something* after all in the following precept: Peregrini officium est nihil præter suum negotium agere, nihil de alieno anquirere, minime que in aliena essa republica curiosum.—*Cic. Off.* i. 34.

Savannah, and even Norfolk, would no doubt, have been flourishing capitals, instead of mouldering away, in silence, amidst
the unavailing fertility of nature ; but would New-York have
contained two hundred thousand inhabitants, and done the business of the whole continent? Would the carrying trade, and
the East-India trade, during the recent wars in Europe, have
converted, in the course of a single generation, the economical
"store-keepers" of Boston into Venetian magnificoes, and covered the rocks of New-England with exotic luxury and splendor?
As for the great Valley of the Mississippi, its comparative condition must of course, depend in some degree, upon that of the
older States, but it is impossible for any one who understands
the genius of colonial government to imagine that, under such
a system, Cincinnati would have been already counting her tens
of thousands, and the waters of the Ohio and the Mississippi
been covered with upwards of a hundred steamboats? The
very absenteeism which is now helping to desolate the South,
but which would, under a colonial government, have prevailed
over the whole country, (though in a far less degree with *us*
than it does at present) would have been a very serious obstacle
to improvement.

By far the greater part of the second volume of these travels
is devoted to the discussion of two subjects, to which the worthy
Captain seems to have mainly directed his attention. These
are, first, our political institutions and their effects on the national character: secondly, the peculiar domestic institutions of the
Southern States. We shall confine our remarks, in the remainder of this paper, principally to these points.

As to the former, we certainly do not mean to argue it with
Captain Hall, in mood and figure. Whatever may be thought
of it in England, we do not consider it as an open question here.
We have taken it for granted that, under a constitution imposing
proper restraints upon the ebullitions of popular passion, and
so contrived as, in the long run, to throw a preponderating influence into the hands of the virtuous and enlightened, man—at
least the great Anglo-Saxon race within the borders of this republic—is capable of self-government. We restrict, perhaps, the
hopes of humanity to too narrow a compass by the above qualification, yet we must be allowed to say, once more, that we have
not much faith in the "march of intellect," and would not, if
possible, pitch our anticipations in too high a key. But, so far
as our own country is concerned, we have no wish to be disabused of this glorious and ennobling illusion, if that can be
called an illusion which the history of whatever is renowned in
antiquity—which the opinions of the wisest and the best men—
which all the gifts and aspirations of human nature—which our
own experience and discipline in freedom for two centuries, (not

forty years) forbid us to question.   We feel that it would be re-creant to despair in this all important interest of millions upon millions yet unborn, even were appearances a thousand times more against us than they are represented to be.   We dare not express a doubt, in the language we speak, "our English," as Milton calls it, "the language of men ever famous and foremost in the achievements of liberty."   Our ideas of popular govern-ment are, thank God, far different from those which Captain Hall avows.   We would excuse him, who tells us candidly that he judges only from his own crude and unassisted conceptions—which, it is very manifest, have never been lifted up to the height of this great argument by the sublime testimony of the mar-tyrs and confessors in "the good old cause."   But he will allow us to say that our respect for his understanding was put to a se-vere trial by his astonishing paradox, that popular institutions are inconsistent with the highest social and intellectual improve-ment.   Inconsistent !   Those institutions which, even in their very worst form, were reverenced by a people whose genius has never been rivalled, as the nurse of all that is sublime in conception and character—ή δημοκρατία τῶν μεγάλων ἀγάθη τιθήνος. "That free government which we have so dearly purchased, a free commonwealth, held by wisest men in all ages, the noblest, the manliest, the equallest, the justest government, the most agree-able to all due liberty and proportioned equality, both human, civil and christian, most cherishing to virtue and true religion."* We believe that such a government is the *beau idéal* of society, and, like all perfection, equally difficult to attain and to preserve. We are deeply sensible of our unspeakable privileges.   We can-not look back into the history of the past, or look around us at the actual condition of the world, and not feel that it is a rare and glorious distinction—far beyond all nobility—to be free.   We are not propagandists of revolutionary doctrines, and we do not pretend to anticipate what is to be the fate of other nations who have already followed, or may hereafter follow our perilous ex-ample—for perilous, all revolution undoubtedly is.   The general theory of popular government, we leave in the keeping of the great men of antiquity, and their mighty disciples, the Miltons, the Machiavels, the Sidneys, the Harringtons—who, "as a guard cherubic placed," have defended through all time, with a flaming sword of genius and eloquence, this godliest heritage of man. We shall confine ourselves, in the few remarks which we have to make upon this subject, to things as they exist around us—to our own hearths and altars.   "What we have spoken," however, to borrow the awful and prophetic words with which Milton closes his last appeal on behalf of the Commonwealth of Eng-land, then drawing towards its dissolution, while we abominate

* Milton.

the augury from the bottom of our hearts: "What we have spoken is the language of that which is not called amiss "the good old cause;" if it seem strange to any, it will not seem more strange, I hope, than convincing to backsliders. Thus much I should, perhaps, have said, though I were sure I should have spoken only to trees and stones; and had none to cry to, but with the prophet 'O earth, earth, earth!' to tell the very soil itself, what her perverse inhabitants are deaf to. Nay, though what I have spoken should happen (which thou suffer not, who didst create mankind free, nor thou next, who didst redeem us from being servants of men) to be the last words of our expiring liberty. But, I trust, I shall have spoken persuasion to abundance of sensible and ingenuous men; to some, perhaps, whom God may raise up to these stones to become children of reviving liberty, and may reclaim, though they seem now choosing them a captain back for Egypt, to bethink themselves a little and consider whither they are rushing; to exhort this torrent also of the people not to be so impetuous, but to keep their due channel; and at length, recovering and uniting their better resolutions, now that they see already how open and unbounded the insolence and rage is of our common enemies, to stay these ruinous proceedings, justly and timely fearing to what a precipice of destruction the deluge of this epidemic madness would hurry us, through the general defection of a misguided and abused multitude."*

It is a shrewd observation of Machiavel,† that those who find fault with the tumults occasioned by the differences between the nobility and the commons at Rome, quarrel with the main cause of all her freedom and power. These superficial thinkers, he adds, attend only to the din and uproar of the mighty conflict, instead of looking at its influence in forming the balance of the constitution, and, in effecting the conquest of the world by the enthusiasm which it kindled, the energies which it called forth, and exercised, the vivifying impulse which it communicated to the minds of men, and the salutary jealousy which it kept awake between the various orders of society. This remark is an answer to all Captain Hall's complaints. The great maxim of all popular government is *ex fumo dare lucem*. It is a mighty maze, but not without a plan. Like the system of the universe, to whose laws it seems most conformable, its partial evil is universal good, its discord only a more perfect, because more complicated harmony, while all its ceaseless vicissitudes eventuate in order and uniformity.

> If plagues and earthquakes break not heaven's design,
> Why then a Borgia or a Catiline?

* The Ready and Easy Way to establish a Free Commonwealth.
† Discorsi, lib. i. c. 4, et seq.

Our test of excellence in politics, is the same as Paley's in morals—utility in the long run. We believe that, under a well-balanced popular government, a greater sum of happiness and improvement is produced than under any other kind of polity, a greater number of the people made, "in mind, body and estate," what their Creator intended them to be, and that those who take the lead among them must, in general, be indebted for it to mere dint of superior energy and usefulness, to illustrious service, to cultivated genius, or to exemplary virtue. It is true, and not more true, perhaps, than desirable, (for some such spur is always wanted) that unworthy persons do frequently thrust themselves forward into more conspicuous places than they have accomplishments to grace ; and such objects are sure to be the first to attract a stranger's observations. But nothing is more shallow and absurd than to draw inferences from such partial appearances. It is the French way of criticising Shakspeare. They have no conception at all of the comprehensive unity of design which harmonize these apparent irregularities. They acknowledge no genius that is not every where stately, decorous and elegant. It is in vain that you appeal to nature—that you dwell upon all that makes the peerless bard a standing intellectual miracle. They answer your eulogies upon Hamlet, by a jest upon the grave-digger's buffoonery, and think of nothing in Macbeth but the absurdity of a plot concocted in the witches' cauldron, and consummated by the march of a forest to take a castle by storm ! The best of it is, that England—*cette isle*, as Bossuet sublimely expresses it, *plus orageuse que les mers qui l'environnent*—is treated by continental philosophers, precisely as we are by her own. We remember that, in 1819, the wise men of the day at Paris were confidently predicting the speedy wreck of her whole system, because the Manchester rioters had to be put down by the yeomanry, and Lord Russell and others of the whigs were pelted with brickbats at the hustings in Westminster ! They are utterly unable to comprehend that queer compound a *tête Anglaise.** We do not wonder at that ; but it does seem passing strange that one, brought up in that school of license and uproar, should be so sensible of somewhat similar, though by no means so outrageous excesses here. And it is still more strange when we find the same person actually willing to see even the ignorance, stupidity and prejudice of the whole realm, fairly represented in the House of Commons, though the result were that very few places might be left open for the accommodation of suitable leaders for such a rabble ! †

Captain Hall affirms that our government is still a mere experiment, of which it is quite impossible to anticipate the result,

* Madame du Deffand.
† See Captain Hall's speculations at the end of the second volume.

as it is only forty years since its foundation, and it has, even since then, been altered in its most important feature, the appointment of the Executive. So far as regards the Federal Constitution there may be some truth in this. We confess that, within these few years last past, we have occasionally been led to entertain some gloomy forebodings upon that subject. We also admit that the cause of the Union may well be considered as the cause of all our liberties, since there can be no doubt but that its dissolution would make their duration far more uncertain than it is now. But this is the utmost extent of our concessions upon this subject. There are some parts of the country, New-England for instance, which we have no doubt would maintain their popular institutons in spite of that dreadful catastrophe. There are other parts of which, from some peculiarities in their situation, the destiny would be much more uncertain. But we have no reason to despair of any. The first, almost the only question in such matters is are the people prepared for free institutions. It is the national character that is to be looked to when we talk of constitutions—it is the national history that is to regulate our conjectures about the future. Now we must remind Captain Hall that our experience on this subject is exactly as great, that is to say, the very same as that of England. We both date from the Petition of Right, two hundred years ago. The parent country never knew the *placidam sub libertate quietem*, until she got rid of the Stuarts. Her history, until 1688, full as it is of high and heroical examples of patriotism and devotion to the great cause, is very far from encouraging. On this side of the Atlantic, the love of liberty is unsophisticated and virginal. The children of the Puritan and the Huguenot have never ceased to breathe the spirit which animated the first Pilgrims—the spirit of Naseby and Marston-Moor, of Montcontour and of Ivry. The only attempt that was ever made to exercise an unconstitutional power, over us, we resisted with a seven years' war, and resisted successfully. Let it be remembered what was the character of that conquest ; one, not of desperate necessity or excited passion, but of pure, in one sense, almost, of speculative principle—let it be further considered that, after the Revolution, as it is called, no violent innovations, no popular commotions of any kind occurred ; and that when at length it was felt to be necessary to reorganize the system of confederation, it was done with a gravity, a deliberation, a critical examination, a comprehensive discussion of the exigencies of the times and the situation, all indicating precisely that frame of mind which best fits men for the enjoyment and the defence of rational liberty, and we think it will be confessed (though God forbid we should ever have to make the experiment) that the republican institutions of the States would not necessarily perish even with the present general government. We need not add, however, that nothing can possibly endanger the latter, but such a degree of infatuation in our rulers as shall make them altogether lose sight of the just and moderate principles, and the hearty and generous sympathies, the truly brotherly love in which it had its origin.

We have seen that Captain Hall imputes to the form of government every thing which seems to go amiss in the country, while he gives it no credit for any of the blessings we enjoy. He professes to have discovered the cause of all the evils that afflict us. It is that a degenerate people have made a pure democracy of what was designed by its founders to be a well-balanced republic. His reasoning upon this subject is sufficiently ingenious, but it has a fatal defect—no very uncommon one, to be sure, among over-zealous disputants—viz. that it is all a *petitio principii.* He represents the delegate, whether in Congress or the State Legislature, as the mere agent of his constituents, acting under perpetual surveillance and constraint, without any free-will of his own, and consequently, without any sense either of dignity or responsibility. This notion of Captain Hall's, we undertake to say, is quite erroneous. It is most true that, through the frequency of elections, the people exercise a greater controul over their representatives here, than they do in any part of Great-Britain, and so much the better. But they allow much more discretion to their public servants, and are much more under their influence than a stranger would be apt to imagine. It is not true, that the right of instruction is universally admitted here. On the contrary, we believe that there is no honest man in the country—none who is sure of a place in the national or state councils—who would not blush at the idea of compromising with his conscience or his principles upon the plea of compliance with the will of his constituents. During the many discussions which arose in Congress, in relation to the election of Mr. Adams, those of the (then) opposition, who denounced it upon the ground that the will of the people had been despised and set at nought, expressly distinguished the case of the presidential election from the ordinary duties of legislation. We were among those whose wishes in that contest could not blind them to the fallacy of this notion, supported as it was by some of our ablest statesmen. We have ever regarded the argument of Mr. McLane, of Delaware, in reply to a gentleman, whose talents are justly the pride of this State, as entirely conclusive, even upon that part of the subject. But none but the most miserable of party tools would submit in practice to the principle, carried as far as some wild theorists among us have sometimes been disposed to push it. The true distinction is a very simple one. Before an election, the people have a right to know, if they desire it, all the opinions of a candidate in reference to public matters. Any thing like concealment or evasion in a candidate, under such circumstances, would be *dolus malus*—a fraud upon the rights of the electors. But, in all cases whatsoever, where the representative stands uncommitted at the time of his election, (and he will take care to be so in all difficult questions) or, we will add, where he has good reason to believe that subsequent circumstances would have induced a change in popular opinion, he is under the most solemn obligation to follow the dictates of his own judgment. Any other doctrine would undoubtedly produce all the evils which Captain Hall has so ably pointed out. It would make a debate in Congress the most solemn, and the stupidest farce that was ever enacted by mountebanks for the amusement of a gaping and ignorant multitude. It would convert our republic not into a democracy exactly, but into something, perhaps, in one respect, at least, nearly as bad if not worse, inasmuch, as the interests and local prejudices which would govern everything, would be far more incorrigible than if the whole people could be gathered together in one vast *champ de Mars*, and addressed fairly by able men of the opposite sides. We should have greater hopes of repealing the tariff, if the voice of the South—the voice of reason, pleading eloquently, because with the deep earnestness of a wronged and suffering people—could be heard by the misguided yeomanry of New-England and New-York, instead of having to address men who coolly shrug up their shoulders, and reply to unanswerable argument, by pleading the instructions of a prejudiced or half-informed people. Under such circumstances, there is no responsibility either in the delegate or the constituent. Such an instance as this, shews that even the concession we have just made, as to the right of the people to be informed beforehand, what are the opinions of a candidate, must be received with a very important qualification. Whatever this right may be in the abstract, it is plainly inexpedient to exercise it, except on extraordinary occasions; and we believe, accordingly, that the people of the United States do, in fact, exercise it with exceeding moderation. We insist upon this point the more, because it is one of immense practical importance. Some experience and observation in public life have convinced us that this sham plea of the will of the constituent is made use of by time-serving and unprincipled politicians far oftener than facts warrant. We believe that there never was a people from whom a representative, who does what he deems his duty fearlessly, and dares to meet his constituents face to face, with a candid exposition of his motives, had less to fear. In almost all cases, popular excitement is got up by demagogues at home to answer their own purposes. If the representative, whose conduct is impeached, meets the opposition boldly, and encounters and exposes its authors in open discussion, his victory is generally a sure and easy one. If, on the contrary, mistaking the clamours of a few for the voice of the whole, he shrink from the contest—if, what is still worse, and by no means unheard of, he cry out *peccavi*, and strike in with the apparent humor of the day, either to secure his re-election, or give to his future conduct the color of acting under the constraint of imperative instructions, what marvel if the majority go with him, and what was at first only the passion of the moment settle down into a confirmed public opinion? However, it is certain, that Captain Hall prodigiously overrates this evil—which is, we think, far more apparent in Congress than in the State Legislature, that is to say, more apparent *to us*, who have the happiness to live in a part of the country where things are, in general, ordered somewhat differently. But conceding his position in its utmost extent, the government would still be essentially different from that scene of wild impulse, and tyrannical misrule—a pure democracy. There is too much delay, division and variety in our system, to admit of some of the greatest evils of that sort of polity. The very existence of two distinct governments, sharing the attributes of sovereignty, and of a public opinion formed of so many different opinions, and acting, when formed, with such tremendous power, is an element in such a problem of incalculable importance.

Captain Hall supports his notion, that our system has been every day getting more and more democratical from the formation of the constitution to the present time, by various little facts of no great moment, either singly or together. The two features of the times, however, on which he dwells, with the greatest emphasis, are universal suffrage, and the unpopularity of the Judiciary. As to the former, our objection to it is the very reverse of Captain Hall's, and, of course, as we conceive, more just. We regard it as of an aristocratic, or rather oligarchical character. Its direct tendency is, at some future day, to throw an immense weight into the scale of wealth. So far, upon the whole, its operation has probably been the other way, because the population of the country is so thin, that, even at the North, a servant acknowledges himself only a "help." But, in the great capitals, our experience is ample to shew, that this ultra-democratical measure is destined, as all extremes do, to "fall on the other side." It is one of those sophisms or fallacies, of which some, according to Aristotle, are peculiar to each distinct form of government, and produce effects, as he ingeniously shows, the very reverse of what are expected from them.[*]

* Pol. lib. iv. c. 13. The whole passage is well worth consulting and meditating upon.

With respect to universal suffrage, then, the case stands thus. As long as the country continues thinly peopled, it does no great harm, if any, especially in the slave-holding States, and, as soon as our numbers shall have swelled up to anything like a European redundancy, it will operate as a check upon the *real* democracy of the country, whether for good or for evil, we are as yet unprepared to say. We shall not complain of it, however, if its tendency be, as some affirm, to postpone this result to a later period than might otherwise be assigned for it, by elevating the feelings of the poor and habituating them to the exercise of a practical independence.

As to the unpopularity of the Judiciary, we are deliberately of opinion that the evil does exist, and that it is one of the very worst symptoms of our case. The Legislatures of the States are everlastingly reforming this branch of their government, which they spare no pains, as it would appear, to bring into hatred and contempt with the people. There are two prominent causes of these discontents. The first is that the judges, who interpret the constitution and the laws, are, of course, obliged to comply with them, in times of popular excitement, whatever offence it may give to the party leaders of the day. They must adhere to principles, while every body around their judgment-seat is inflamed with passion—they must be weighing little scruples and technical niceties in golden scales, when impatient patriotism, clamorous for a sacrifice at whatever price, rebels against every restraint, and represents the smallest delay as fatal to the commonwealth. It is not very strange, therefore, that petulant, short-sighted politicians, should be uneasy under this salutary control, nor that the vexation and chafing occasioned by the curb, should be frequently visited on those whose office it is to hold the reins. It is the old complaint against every government of laws—and what makes it so very difficult to enjoy that inestimable blessing. Livy puts it into the mouths of the young conspirators who would have restored the Tarquins, that they might have something to hope from their favour and indulgence, instead of being subject to an inflexible rule, along with the mass of the people. Leges rem surdam, inexorabilem esse, salubriorem melioremque inopi quam potenti, nihil laxamenti nec veniæ habere. Every predominant faction has a taste for the same sort of license, and prefers its Tarquins to truth and justice. But the other cause is, perhaps, more active and incessant in its operation. It is that every legislative body in the country is filled with professional lawyers, the inferior sort of whom, as it is well known, are rather a pragmatical and noisy than a very enlightened class of people, and who seldom forget, in their public or corporate capacity, the wrongs they have suffered, or imagine they have suffered in their private business.

The loss of a cause through ignorance, a demurrer overruled, a sally of passion reproved—such are the motives which too frequently lead to attempts at momentous reforms in this most important department of civil government. In the absence of such motives, the mere love of change, or a spirit of discontent, or the self-conceit, characteristic of those who make it a profession to correct abuses in established institutions, leads to the same result. It is lamentable to witness the effects of this fault-finding disposition. Judges, even in States, where their tenure is during good behaviour, live in perpetual anxiety for their safety, or indignation at their wrongs. They have scarcely any of that authority which their station ought to confer. If their own characters are above reproach, there is an infallible means of making them feel the effects of popular hatred, or what is scarcely less terrible, of the hostility of demagogues and innovators. If the constitution forbids the judge to be taken from the office, it does not, it is said, prevent the office being taken from the judge. This wretched sophism has had too many advocates in our councils. At the end of a long period of service, on a pittance dignified with the name of a salary, when he is unfitted by long disuse for the labours of the bar, and has no hope, no refuge left him, he is in perpetual danger of being cast off by some freak in legislation, and consigned to poverty in his old age. This contest between the bar and the bench is fearfully unequal. Everything is in favour of the assailants, who exercise an incalculable control over public opinion. Everything is against their victims, to whom a species of odium attaches, because they seem to be the only irresponsible agents in the commonwealth, and their decrees are represented not unplausibly as superseding the sovereignty of the legislature. Even where the constitution *nominally* secures to a judge his office during good behaviour, this state of things is sufficiently harassing and humiliating. But our reformers are not satisfied with the sinister power they already possess. The trouble and difficulty of altering the constitution, although not by any means so great as they ought to be, are still a serious, practical restraint. The term of service, therefore, must be limited, so that the magistrate whose opinions ought to be formed and delivered without fear, favour or affection, may be placed as much as possible under the influence of such motives. What can we expect from such a state of things in the end, but the utter degradation of the bench, in spite of whatever talents and learning may occasionally adorn it? And how is it possible that the law should not fall into contempt, along with those who administer it—until the tenure of property become altogether precarious, and no rule or principle of justice be left to regulate the conduct and the sentiments of mankind?

We do not mean to insinuate that these consequences have as yet occurred to any material extent. On the contrary, so far as we have been able to inform ourselves, nothing can be more blameless and exemplary, than the conduct, both public and private, of the great majority of our judges. We speak only of the *tendency* of a state of feeling which, we think, is beginning to exist among us. We fear that what has been justly called the most contemptible of all characters, a popular judge, will not long be a very rare one. For instance, a practice, is creeping in among us, having its origin undoubtedly in the very feelings to which we allude, though, at first sight, apparently at variance with them, which strikes us as shockingly indecorous. It is that of calling a meeting of the bar at the end of a circuit, to proclaim to the people the astonishing intelligence, that their humble servant, his Honor, has actually done his duty ! There must be something radically wrong in the situation of the parties, where one of them can presume to offer, and the other stoop to accept, such certificates of good behaviour. In spite of this downward tendency, however, such has been the efficacy of the restraints imposed in our constitutions upon the will of the legislatures, that attempt after attempt has been everywhere made in vain to introduce the principle of an elective judiciary, and very few of the States are yet cursed with such a system. So much for our unchecked democracy ! We may hope, therefore, that this odium, under which the bench labors, is destined to pass away without doing any permanent or extensive evil, and that experience will at length teach the people, or rather their *mis*-leaders, how to appreciate the first of all civil advantages, an upright, enlightened and learned magistracy. For ourselves, if we were asked what single circumstance would go farther than any other to give stability and security to our institutions, we should not hesitate to name such a magistracy. Without considering the effects of their example, and the immediate influence of an order of men set apart to be distributors of justice among their fellow-citizens, upon the morals of the people, the single fact that a learned bench will infallibly create a learned and enlightened bar is of itself conclusive. It has been said of this country that it is not priest—but lawyer-ridden. That the profession has an immense influence here is undeniable. We may apply to them, by the help of a pun, the line—

Agnosco rerum dominos gentemque togatam.

But our case is by no means a singular one. Lawyers—the interpreters of the legislative will, and the arbiters of the all-pervading interests of *meum et tuum,* have had and ever must have the same ascendancy in all free countries. The liberties of England, and, both remotely and immediately, our own, are more due to this than to any other class of men. Whoever has studied the most important period, except one other, of modern history, the progress of the Revolution in the parent country, from the accession of Charles I. to its consummation in 1688, will be fully convinced of this. He will find Lord Coke, at one end of this period, reporting the Petition of Right, and Lord Somers at the other, drawing the Bill of Rights, and adjusting the balance of the Constitution, while all the intermediate space is filled up with the learned and patriotic labors of men like Selden, White-locke, and Prynne. Our own Revolution was brought about in the same way. Indeed, the influence of the profession, for good or for evil, is so great, that everything connected with its char-acter, is matter of the most serious public interest. It has been reckoned a profound stroke of king-craft in Augustus, that he committed the authoritative interpretation of the law to a select number of juris-consults appointed by himself, with that pliant tool, Ateius Capito at their head ; for the purpose of insensibly fashioning and accommodating public opinion to the new order of things. To keep up the old order of things here, we would pursue the same policy. We would select the ablest lawyers and best men, and only such, to be judges of the people. We would clothe them with authority and awe. We would conse-crate them as a priesthood, and exact of them the same purity and holiness of living. As drunkenness in an Archon was pun-ished with death at Athens, so no man should sit on the judg-ment-seat of a free people, who was not exempt even from those blemishes which are sometimes treated as venial in other men. But above all, he should be penetrated, while in the discharge of his duties, with the solemnity of his office and the majesty of the law, whose oracles he is appointed to deliver. This is the grandest feature of popular government ; nor can we imag-ine, on the other hand, a type more strikingly and disgustingly illustrative of that government in its corrupt and degraded form, than a weak or unprincipled judge, prostituting his high office to the interests or opinions of a day ; or an ignorant judge ma-king law a snare and right a mockery. We have dwelt upon this topic the longer, because, we fear, it is not supererogatory to do so ; happy, if our poor remarks should bring but one in-considerate person to serious reflection upon a subject, beyond all comparison, the most important that can engage the attention of a free people. We do not mean to say, that the administra-tion of justice should be exempt from criticism. Far from it— but we protest against systematic efforts to excite popular pre-judices against the bench, by indiscriminate and furious denun-ciation, misrepresentation and calumny.

To return to our text. If we were disposed to point out the characteristic, in which it seems to us, that we differ most from our fathers, whether for better or worse, we should pitch upon our rage for innovation, and our overweening confidence in what are called *principles* in politics. We have already advert-ed to the extreme *sobriety* and moderation of the revolutionary statesmen. This trait was most remarkable. It had, indeed, eminently distinguished the revolution, and even the rebellion in England; but not, we think, in an equal degree. Had the Congress and other legislative bodies of that age been filled with philosophers of as enlarged views as those who composed the Constituent Assembly of France, what a deluge of innova-tion had swept over the land—what a fantastic model of theo-retical perfection would have been proposed for the government of our new-born republics, "with centric and eccentric scrib-bled over, cycle and epicycle, orb in orb."* Our fathers were, after all, but plain, practical statesmen, and it is not to be won-dered at that succeeding generations, and especially the present, have found their work so very imperfect. The light of political metaphysics has been let in upon every part of the social fabric, and nothing will hereafter be allowed to stand, that shall only have experience and authority on its side. There is against all our institutions, a standing "rule to show cause" why they should not be altered or abolished. The rotation or *rotatory* system is thus creeping on from offices to the government which confers them—from men to principles. It is not enough that everything, as it is, be "very good"—we are dissatisfied as long as something better may be imagined. The human mind, we believe, to be marching, *au-pas-de-charge* towards perfection—why should government and law not partake of the universal progress? Brilliant as these ideas are, we confess we have serious doubts whether they ought to be acted on until intellect shall not only have advanced a little farther—but (what is very material) made sure of its conquests, and turned them to some account. We should be sorry to trust our rice-fields to such theoretical geni-uses, and we very much doubt whether as matters stand at pre-sent, we gain anything by our "constancy in nothing but change," engaged, as we are, in a work, like that long ago sung—

————————Of thorough reformation,
Which always must be carried on
And still be doing, never done;
As if *"Republics"* were intended
For nothing else but to be mended.

A very striking instance of Captain Hall's prejudice is to be found in his remarks upon the state of education in this coun-

* We have before us, at this moment, one of these *projets de Constitution*, on mathematical principles, that beats the Ptolomean system hollow. We wish we could give it entire for the use of our speculative politicians. It may be found in Mignet's History of the French Revolution.

try. He admits, that what he calls elementary, that is popular, education is successfully cultivated and universally diffused; but he affirms, that the attainments of young men, who go regularly through the grammar school and the college, are lamentably superficial. This he considers as an undoubted effect of our levelling principles,—an opinion altogether irreconcilable with the facts of the case, and even with the account of this matter which Captain Hall has himself given in a passage hereafter to be submitted to our readers. Now we do not pretend to repel the imputation: we have too often said as much on previous occasions, not to consider ourselves fairly estopped on this subject. There are very few' men of science and still fewer scholars among us—we speak, of course, in reference to the European standard. But how many were they under the Provincial Governments, with all "appliances and means to boot" furnished by the right of primogeniture! A dozen or two young gentlemen from Carolina, not so many from Virginia, and still fewer (if any at all from the North of the Potomac, were sent to English schools and universities.* The *élite* of these became accomplished scholars up to a certain point. The late General Thomas Pinckey, for instance, was, we have no doubt, the very best Hellenist (of a young man) that any part of America has ever had to boast of;† though we do not know that he became extensively read in Greek learning. Just before the breaking out of the Revolution, a cluster of accomplished young men, contemporaries of the distinguished person just mentioned, returned to Carolina from their studies in England, and, true to the spirit imbibed in the writings of the ancients, contributed greatly to the independence of their country. We are far, very far, from disputing their merit—they were an honor and blessing to the State, and they formed a society far superior, in some interesting respects, to anything that has succeeded it in any part of the Union. But the system was essentially aristocratic and exclusive, as the improvements it led to were altogether *exotic*. Those who were born to large fortunes were thus educated in England; but what was done for learning at home? What was done to prepare the soil here for future cultivation and productiveness? What seats, what seminaries of science were endowed in the Provinces—we mean the Southern more particularly. No means at all of acquiring knowledge, or next to none, were provided by the government for people of moderate fortunes. When, therefore, the

---

* A memorial was presented to the King at this period by his Majesty's American subjects then in London. Of the thirty who signed it, *seventeen* were citizens of Charleston—and sent thither for their *education.—See Garden's Anecdotes, Second Series*, p. 4.

† This gentleman was pre-eminent in his classes at Westminster, and was for a long time Captain of the Town-Boys.

separation from the mother country, and the abolition of the right
of primogeniture put an end to the practice of educating young
men at English grammar schools, there was an end to all scholarship, for the simple reason, that there were no grammar
schools on this side of the ocean, at which more than a smattering of Greek and Latin could be acquired. The people of the
South now began to send their children to Northern colleges,
where the standard of classical learning had never been high,
even under the old *régime*, because the fortunes of the people
did not admit of their giving their youth a foreign education,
and where until, very recently, it continued to be exceedingly
low. Here is an explanation of the whole affair. Following
mechanically the old system, we have confined our boys almost
exclusively, during their whole elementary course, to the very
studies which it was impossible they should cultivate successfully. We have insisted on making them classical scholars, and
nothing but classical scholars, when there was no such thing as
a classical teacher to be had in the whole country for love or
money. The first fifteen or sixteen years of life were thus thrown
away almost entirely—childhood, and a good part of youth were
struck out of existence, for all purposes of solid improvement ;
for, a young gentleman was sent to college, as a matter of course,
ignorant of every thing but a few grammar rules, which he did
not know how to apply, and a few scraps of Greek and Latin
(hideously mispronounced) which he did not know how to construe. Of the four years allotted to the college course, a very
considerable portion was thrown away upon the same mockery
of classical studies; but it would be injustice to deny that something more was acquired at the same time. Before the young
man was admitted to his first degree, he had a fair chance of
picking up a little geometry, a little chemistry, a little school-
logic, and quite as much as was desirable of Scotch metaphysics.
These various attainments, surmounted with a suitable stock of
self-sufficiency, and a lofty contempt of prejudice and authority,
fitted him to enter with advantage upon the duties of active life.
The truth is, however, that the root of this execrable system is
not to be sought in the discipline of the college, which, as things
go, is a mere hospital of incurables. We must begin at the beginning. A boy, when he is matriculated at a university, ought
to be already an accomplished scholar, in the highest sense of
the word. He ought to be critically versed in Latin and Greek
as well as in English, that is to say, he ought to be able to *write*
them all with correctness, and have his mind deeply imbued
with the beauties which a knowledge of them reveals to the
adept. But if he have acquired nothing, before he go to a college, what can the most assiduous and learned teacher make of
him there in a few years, but a smatterer and a *charlatan?*

Such is the true historical explanation of the fact; and now we ask, what has *democracy* to do with it? We venture to say, that if by any magic, three such schools as Eton, Westminster and Winchester, or the Charter-House, could be established in the three great divisions of the Atlantic States, in the course of ten years, at the outside, a total change would have taken place in the state of literature all over the country. We speak advisedly, from the wonderful progress which, without such a help, we have made in the same period just elapsed. But we need not tell a Scotchman how difficult it has been found to get up a good grammar school, even under a monarchial government, and in the "modern Athens," itself. Indeed, it is strange enough, but not so strange as ridiculous, to hear the objection to our want of classical learning coming from such a quarter. We should like to be informed how many scholars could be found, on the most accurate survey, between Johnny Groat's House and the Tweed! In education as in other things, the beginning is half the work. If we are still behind hand in this important concern, it is owing to causes growing out of the situation of the country, not of the form of government. The people considered either in their individual or collective capacity, have been anything but indifferent to education and letters. It is almost superfluous to cite examples to shew this. What can be more magnificent, than the liberality which Harvard has experienced from the opulent merchants of Boston? And where can any society be found more entirely devoted to liberal pursuits, than that of the city just mentioned? The same spirit has prevailed in every part of the country—even where circumstances have been far less favorable to its development. This State, for instance, appropriates annually much more than a tithe* of its whole revenue to the instruction of its people. She has founded at great expense a college which has been justly complimented by Captain Hall, and furnished it with a most excellent library. She annually appropriates to the support of it, about $15,000. By this means, the advantage of attending the lectures of some of the most learned men in America, is extended to all who can afford a small annual advance out of their own funds. To the education of the poor, in free schools, we give nearly $40,000 per annum. All this for a population of only 240,000 whites. This is only one out of many other equally shining examples in the Atlantic States, while in the West, whole townships of land in those rising commonwealths, have been consecrated to letters, and the education of youth provided for by a solemn covenant, and placed beyond the reach of chance or change, among "the canon laws of their foundation."

* More accurately a *sixth.*

So who does not see from Captain Hall's own shewing that the reason why a greater number do not become literary men by profession is that they have something, at least, more agreeable to do.

"Every thing in America, as I believe I have before mentioned, appears to be antedated—every thing and every body is on the move—and the field is so wide and so fertile, that no man, whatever be his age, if he possess the slightest spark of energy, can fail to reap from the virgin soil an adequate harvest. By the word adequate, I mean a sufficient return for his own maintainance and that of a family. Thus the great law of our nature, be fruitful and multiply, having no check, supersedes every other, carrying before it classics, science, the fine arts, letters, taste, and refinements of every description, in one great deluge of population.

"This is hardly any figure, being almost literally the fact. As applied to education, its effects are somewhat of the following nature. A boy who hears and sees nothing at all around him but independence, and individual license to do almost any thing, very soon becomes too wild for his father's house; and off he is sent to school. When there, he is restless himself, and the cause of restlessness in others; for he worries his parents till he accomplishes his purpose of going to college. This point gained, his object is to run through the required course as fast as possible, get his examination over, and take his degree, that he may be at liberty to follow the paths of his predecessors, and scamper away to the fertile regions of the west or south, where, whatever betides him, in whatever line of industry his taste or talents may be cast, he is sure of being able to support a wife and children.

"This appears to be going on, with slight shades of difference, over the whole United States, and is in truth the inevitable consequence of their geographical and political situation. The Americans assure us that it cannot possibly be altered. Perhaps not. At all events, it must be submitted to, but whether for good or for evil is not now the question. The real point is, whether or not any modified restraint can be placed upon the operation of such powerful principles of human action in the case of the young men of that country, so as to give them, along with their present advantages, those also which spring out of classical knowledge?—I fear not.

"What answer, for instance, can be made to a lad of sixteen, who sees before him so wide and tempting an area for his immediate exertions to expand themselves in—who is certain that if he marries to-morrow, with scarcely a dollar in his pocket, he may rear up half-a-dozen children in as many years, and maintain them in abundance, till they are in a state to shift for themselves? Or who begs you to tell him in what respect Greek and Latin, or the differential calculus, will advance his project of demolishing the wilderness, and peopling the ground where it stood? Or how a knowledge of the fine arts will improve the discipline of a gang of negroes on a rice or cotton plantation? You can really say nothing in reply. For what instruction you give him in reading and writing he is most grateful; but for all the graces of literature, or the refinements of science, or the elegancies of polished societies, he cares not half a straw. In fact, they are so much in his way, that if he chanced to have picked any of them up, he feels tempted afterwards to fling them from him as troublesome encumbrances, only tending to excite distrust in those unqualified to appreciate such attainments." Vol. i. pp. 304–305.

If, however, this young Rapid had been made *nolens volens* to acquire an adequate fund of classical learning while he had yet nothing else to do, and before he got such high-flying notions into his head, viz. at a grammar-school, we will answer for it, the whole complexion of his destiny had been altered. But, educated as we are in this country, it is too late to think, at eighteen or nineteen, of going back to our accidence. None but those who are very fortunately circumstanced, can attempt such a laborious and disheartening enterprize, and even they may have cause to repent of their aspiring efforts at improvement, when they come to discover how unequal a chance they stand in a country where there are so few to sympathize with them. But what, we ask again, has democracy to do with this? It is human nature that is to blame—it is those feelings which Milton so feelingly alludes to in one of his letters—"Why should not all the fond hopes, that forward youth and vanity are fledged with, call me forward more powerfully, than a poor, regardless and unprofitable sin of curiosity should be able to withhold me, whereby a man cuts himself off from all action, and becomes the most helpless, pusillanimous and unweaponed creature in the world, the most unfit and unable to do that which all mortals aspire to, either to be useful to their friends, or to offend their enemies." How can we wonder then that active life, with all the present and tempting rewards which it holds out to ambition and enterprize, should draw into its vortex almost all the available talent of the country. If, even under the most favourable circumstances, literary pursuits, however elevated, and ennobling, and congenial to his own incomparable spirit, were felt by Milton to require an effort of self-denial, what shall be said of them in such a country as this? But, under all these disadvantages, inseparable and accidental, a life of contemplation would have vastly more attractions, were each of our larger cities filled with gentlemen, well-grounded in classical learning at school, though they went no further, giving countenance and support to literary men.

Upon the whole, the question about the operation of a government is a practical one, and can be decided only by experience. Who would suppose, *à priori*, that the much injured close boroughs should have been so often, we may almost say uniformly, the refuge of distressed parliamentary reform-men, driven off the field of a county election by an ungrateful people, with "sad overthrow and foul defeat?" Who could imagine that a tribunal of justice could owe its independence to the very venality of its places—as was undoubtedly the case with the Parliament of Paris? The causes which produce any given effect in politics are far too complicated and obscure to be discovered by the *coup d'œil militaire* of a philosopher of the quarter-deck, galloping through a country at the rate of twenty-odd miles a-day, Sundays included. There is no *experimentum crucis* to detect them, even for the benefit of more cautious inquirers ; and the highest wisdom amounts here to no more than a sage empiricism—acquiescing as our fathers did in an established order of things until its evils become insufferable, and then making just such changes as the occasion calls for, and no more. Those who judge from superficial appearances or general maxims will be forever blundering. Every republic will pass with them for a licentious democracy, and every republican "have the manners of a Swiss bred in Holland." While, on the contrary, to those accustomed to popular institutions, the very name of royalist will be synonimous with sycophant and slave, and the whole scheme of monarchical government appear incompatible with dignity and virtue. Would the rudest and coarsest citizen of this country gain by exchanging places with the creature, painted by Count Hamilton in the following sentence, as best fitted to make his way to preferment in an English court? "Il jugea qu'au milieu d'une cour florissante en beautés et abondante en argent, il ne devait s'occuper que du soin de plaire à son maitre, de faire valoir les avantages que la nature lui avait donnés pour le jeu et mettre en usage de nouveaux stratagêmes en amour." Yet even Captain Hall would scarcely venture to deny that many hundreds of such men hold up their heads with all the insolence of conceded superiority in Bond-street and the Park, and that a stranger in England is apt to hear more of them than of any other class of people. As a further illustration of the danger of trusting to first appearances, we would add the changes that are made at every election in the composition of Congress and the State Legislatures. Captain Hall has very naturally exaggerated the importance of this fact. He takes the mean ratio, and finds it less than three years ; then infers that there can be no experience at all in our statesmen. Now this may be very good arithmetic, but it is very bad politics. The fact is that these changes are almost exclusively confined to the inferior men—the cyphers of the house. It very rarely happens, that a representative of conspicuous talent or services, fails of a re-election, if he desire it. In the Southern States, at least, there is as much stability in this respect as could be expected or even desired. Neither must it be forgotten that most of our politicians in Congress go through a previous noviciate in the Legislatures of the States, and bring with them into their new business a considerable stock of experience. Although, therefore, there be some inconveniences arising out of this frequency of change in the constitution of those bodies, they do by no means amount to any very serious evil.

On the subject of Southern institutions, we have been most agreeably surprised by the opinions of Captain Hall. We had every reason to expect, from what we heard was his manner of expressing himself while among us, a far more uncompromising hostility to this part of our social polity, even than to the spirit of democracy itself. We were aware, however, that he was doing all he could to inform himself fully upon the subject—that he conversed freely and frequently about it with some of our most experienced and intelligent men, and that he went "poking about," as he terms it, into every hole and corner where anything connected with the condition of the slave or the master was to be seen or heard. It is gratifying to us to be able to state that the result of this investigation, thus undertaken with a prejudice against us, is precisely such as we think all reasonable men must come to, who examine the question in any other spirit than that of a jacobinical and murderous fanaticism.

It is, indeed, one of the most extraordinary revolutions that has ever occurred in the history of the human mind—the change of opinion on this subject within the last forty years. Before that time, the voice of a few philanthropists was heard, here and there, amidst the busy hum of a prosperous commerce, pleading for the victims of that infernal traffic, by which the great trading nations of Europe were endeavoring to swell the mass of colonial produce for their own benefit. Virginia, now so deeply intent upon the means of getting rid of this evil, in vain exerted herself to prevent it. It was decreed by those who had our destinies in their hands that the Southern regions of America should be crammed with this barbarous and abominable population—the commercial navy of the whole world vomited it forth upon us by hundreds of cargoes—every capitalist embarked in the profitable speculation—every insurance office greedily snatched at the premium paid for indemnity against the chances of this traffic in blood and tears—and, in the most rational department of modern jurisprudence, the question was seriously entertained whether "these beings with immortal souls" might not, in case of necessity, be flung overboard like any other merchandize according to the *Lex Rhodia de Jactu!* As long as colonial possessions were held in high estimation, there was no portion of mankind worth mentioning, but partook in the guilt, whatever it was, of this commerce. The whole world was implicated in it. It was a conspiracy of all Europe and the commercial part of this continent, not only against Africa, but, in a more aggravated sense, against these Southern regions. The sternest justice can demand no more than that we should be thought *as bad* as those who brought this evil upon us. But, in a more considerate view of the case, the pander even of a confessedly vicious appetite, is worse than the libertine whose lusts he is base enough to subserve; and it is an absurdity without a parallel in the whole history of human extravagance and folly, to hear the people of Old England or New England, or of any other portion of Christendom, coolly lecturing *us* upon the sin of keeping our fellow-men in bondage ! *They* accuse us of violating the law of nature, who, by the law which they themselves prescribed, drew us into this supposed offence ! *They* talk about the imprescriptible rights of mankind, and question the very *titles* which they became bound to warrant, by selling us the property ! A father, whose vices had entailed disease upon his offspring, and who should cast him off for this hereditary uncleanliness, presents something like a parallel—the only one we have been able to imagine—to this instance of prodigious effrontery.

Whether slavery is, or is not reconcilable with what is called by philosophers the law of nature, we really do not know. We find the greatest theoretical publicists divided upon the subject, and it is, no doubt, a very good thesis for young casuists to discuss in a college moot-club. We shall not undertake it, for we have no taste for abstractions. We will not quote Grotius or Huber. It is enough for us that, when the Southern people consented to receive the African race into their territory, it was upon the express condition of perpetual service, and that this condition was then as lawful as any other arrangement of civil society. *Servitus est constitutio juris gentium.* It was a Christian Emperor, zealous above all men, to promote the manumission of slaves, who laid down this rule, five centuries after Christ had positively enjoined obedience upon *slaves, eo nomine.* * It was emphatically the law of nations. No people, from the most remote antiquity, had ever thought of calling it in question. They all deduced the right of holding an enemy in bondage, from that of murdering him in battle, as in all things else whatever is greater contains the less. They could see nothing very absurd in the conduct of him who went out to destroy, if he saved a life, by which his own country was to gain as much as the enemy lost. His intents, perhaps, were not very charitable, but his reasoning was certainly consequential. The Thracian or Theban captive, instead of being devoured by the vultures became a useful labourer in Attica. The modern world has kept up the greater sin ; but it affects to shudder at the minor—it concedes the premises in this dreadful enthymeme, but thinks it criminal to adopt the conclusion. This may be all very well for some people; but *we* must be allowed to hold on to the old logic a little longer. We have still occasion for it in justifying, not ourselves, but our present revilers, if possible, in their own eyes. They told us that they had conquered these slaves in bat-

* This is the proper translation, and were the Bible read in the original Greek or in a literal version, we should, probably, be less troubled with the ravings of fanatics upon this subject.

tle—that they had acquired them fairly *jure belli*—at least, that they had delivered them out of the hands of victorious and cruel enemies. They will not wonder, therefore, if we are steadfast in our original convictions, and do not yet see how property, recognized and confirmed by all mankind in all ages, can be no property at all—especially after it has passed into the possession of a *bonâ fide* purchaser, has been consecrated by an uninterrupted prescription from time immemorial, and identified with the whole frame and constitution of civil society.

Captain Hall, as will appear from the extracts we shall presently make, considers this great question altogether in a *practical* light. He will not consent to take it up in the abstract, as if it were *res integra*. The following passage, in which he quotes a member of our own fraternity, will serve at once, as an expression of his own opinion and our own.

"A few days afterwards, in the same State, I had an opportunity of conversing with a gentleman of whose candor I had an equally high opinion with that of my friend above, but whose views, I think, are rather more sound.

" 'Force—power—or whatever name you give it', said he, 'by which one nation gains the ascendancy over another, seems to be, in the practice of life, the grand rule which regulates the intercourse of man with man. Civilization beats the savage out of the woods by its superior intellectual resources. Free and well-governed nations acquire a power over those which are mismanaged. The sovereigns, whether they be the many or few, who have got the upperhand, give the law and the inferior party submits. This may not appear just, but so it is; such is the order of our moral and political nature. It has been so from all time, and will continue, so long as there remain any distinctions between human beings. The slave question is merely one of the varieties of this principle. The blacks were brought to America when these matters were not treated philosophically; they have since extended themselves far and wide, and have now become, to all intents and purposes, an integral part of our society.'

"The masters and the slaves, from long habit, and universal usage, have fallen into certain modes of thinking and of acting relatively to one another; and, as this understanding is mutual and complete, the whole machinery goes on with the greatest uniformity, and much more cheerfulness than you will at first believe possible. At least an equal period of time, but perhaps ten or a hundred times as long a period may be required, to unwind the thread again, and to free the country from this moral and political entanglement.

"In the mean time, it is in vain to deny that—circumstanced as they now are—the negroes belong almost to a different race—so different, that no philanthropist or abolitionist, however enthusiastic, pretends to say that an amalgamation can take place between them and the whites. There is no reasoning upon this point—it seems a law of our nature, and is felt, probably, as strongly in other countries as here. What English gentleman, for example, would give his daughter in marriage to a negro? But the prejudice, or whatever it be, is just as strong in the Southern States of America, with respect to a political community of rights and privileges. And if changes in this respect are ever to be brought about, they can only be accomplished by the slowest conceivable degrees. In the State of New-York, the negroes have the privilege of voting; and you will see over the country many mulattoes: but these are mere drops in the ocean of this dark question; and we are still centuries before that period which many very sincere men believe has already arrived.

"No one can tell how these things will modify themselves in time. There may be many bloody insurrections aided by foreign enemies—or the States may separate, and civil wars ensue—or servile wars may follow—or the blacks and whites may, in process of ages, by the combination of some moral and political miracle, learn to assimilate; but in the meantime, I suspect the present generation can do nothing of any consequence to advance such an object. The blacks, who form the labouring population, are so deplorably ignorant, and so vicious, that in almost every instance where freedom has been given to them, they have shown how unfit they are to make a right use of it. The practice of manumission is, in consequence, every where discouraged, and in many places rendered by law impossible, except in cases of high public service."

We can add nothing to this condensed, yet satisfactory view of the subject. Whatever may be his feelings or opinions in relation to slavery in the abstract, no sensible or conscientious man would undertake to *act* upon them in so vital a concern, without looking fully into the consequences. Innovators or Revolutionists, who go only for an imaginary abstract rectitude and symmetry in government, are always dangerous, and sometimes the greatest curse with which heaven in its wrath can visit an offending people. There is some excuse for them, however, when they are liable to suffer the consequences of their own presumption and folly. The destruction of a pestilent madman, who has been the means of converting a whole country into a scene of conflagration and blood, is to be sure, but a poor atonement for such unutterable horrors. But language affords no suitable epithet for the cowardly and atrocious wickedness of wretches, who, under the pretext of a sympathy with one order or portion of a community with which they have nothing to do, presume to recommend or to dictate changes, of which they can neither judge of the propriety, nor feel the consequences. When one contemplates the character of a ruthless and reckless jacobin, like Marat or Danton, the idea that he was destined, at last, to perish by his own measures, redeems him in some small degree from the horror and execration which his crimes excited. *L' Ami du Peuple* might be rewarded for his philosophic patriotism, as he deserved to be, by the knife of the guillotine. But when Brissot came out as *l'Ami des Noirs*, an ocean rolled between this canting hypocrite and the frightful scenes occasioned soon after, by the application of his doctrines. It is of this that the slave-holders of the English West-India Islands have had so much reason to complain. Men were declaring war, without peace, truce or quarter, against them; whose persons, assuredly, were never to be exposed to the dangers of war, and whose appetites, for their dinners would not have been in the smallest degree, affected by the intelli-

gence, that every slave-holder in the world had been exterminated.   We are even disposed to doubt, whether, their exalted
ideas of poetical justice would be quite satisfied with anything
short of this.   There was a time, however, when these very
men held the following language.   "The negroes are truly the
jacobins of the West-India Islands—they are the anarchists,
the terrorists, the domestic enemy. Against them it becomes rival
nations to combine, and hostile governments to coalesce.   If
Prussia and Austria felt their existence to depend on a union
against the revolutionary arms in Europe (and who does not lament, that their coalition was not more firm and enlightened?)
a closer alliance is imperiously recommended to France and Britain, and Spain, and Holland, against the common enemy of civilized society, the destroyer of the European name in the new
world.   We have the greatest sympathy for the unmerited sufferings of the unhappy negroes; we detest the odious traffic
which has poured myriads of them into the Antilles : but we
must be permitted to feel some tenderness for our European
brethren, although they are white and civilized, and to deprecate
that inconsistent spirit of canting philanthropy, which, in Europe,
is only excited by the wrongs or miseries of the poor and the profligate ; and, on the other side of the Atlantic, is never warmed
but towards the savage, the mulatto and the slave. Admitting all
that has been said against the planters, and their African provi-
ders, we are much of the opinion which Lord Bacon has expressed in the following sentence—"it is the sinfullest thing in the
world to forsake a plantation (colony) once in forwardness, for,
besides, the dishonor, it is the guiltiness of the blood of many
commiserable persons."[*]
Either the sad depression of colonial produce, however, or
their own advancement to a much higher degree of philosophical illumination, has subsequently changed the views of these
writers.   And this is another instance, in which we have to
felicitate ourselves upon our separation from the parent country.   Now-and-then, indeed, the Legislatures of some of the
non-slaveholding States have so far forgotten what is due to
our relations under the confederacy, and to the ties of consanguinity, as to insult us by a formal declaration of their opinions
and wishes upon this subject. But, as yet, a very becoming
degree of forbearance has been exhibited by the people of those
States.   It is most unfortunate for us that the District of Columbia should have been subjected to the legislation of Congress.
It is too evident that that spot so governed is destined to be the
hot-bed of infinite mischief—the laboratory of all sorts of political quackery and imposture. So far as this unfortunate Ten-
miles-square is concerned, we may lay our account with some

[*] Edinburgh Review, No. 1. Art. 27.

trouble in this matter, and what shall be the effect of such projects, will depend very much upon the spirit in which the debate shall be carried on. It may be well, therefore, to let it be distinctly known that our people take up this subject just where Captain Hall does. We avow it as our deliberate opinion, in his language, "that we cannot and OUGHT not [consistently with our own duty] to disentangle ourselves from the obligations which have devolved upon us, as the masters of slaves." All virtue is relative, and consists not in visions of ideal perfection, not in a puling and sickly sentimentalism, but in making the most of our situation, whatever it may be, for purposes of improvement and benevolence. The conscientious slaveholder, as our author well remarks, deserves a larger share of the sympathy of those, who have sympathy to spare, than any other class of men, not excepting the slave himself. And we think, paradoxical as it may sound, that one great evil of the system, is its tendency to produce in process of time, laxity of discipline, and consequently, disorders and poverty in a country, by the excessive indulgence of careless or too scrupulous masters. In the course of a generation or two, the family relation, the tie of a sort of *homage ancestral* between master and slave, becomes so intimate, and so affecting, that the sternness and rigor absolutely necessary in the management of men, not under the spur of necessity, sensibly abate, and with them there is a corresponding falling off in the cheerful and ready obedience, and of course, in the happiness as well as the usefulness of the slave. It is impossible to look around us, and not see that some of the worst symptoms of the times are owing to this ill-judged, but we fear, inevitable facility and indulgence.* Nothing, indeed, can be more superficial than the idea, which generally prevails, and seems to possess even Captain Hall's mind, that no affection or confidence can grow up between the master and the slave—that the former is necessarily a tyrant, and the latter always a conspirator. Such a notion is a satire upon human nature, but an unmerited one. The very feeling of *loyalty*, about which this author discourses so philosophically, is sure to spring up on the one side, and a sort of parental or patriarchal kindness on the other. During the Revolutionary war, instances of the most devoted fidelity were every where exhibited by slaves— and, at that time, be it remembered, the treatment of this class of people, was, in every respect, harsher and more severe, though we will not say (in the long run) less humane than it is at present. Nor is this any evidence, as some may think, of their degradation. It by no means follows that, because a man is not a Hampden, ready to resist and resent the slightest instance of arbitrary power, as a personal insult, he has, there-

* Plato—de Legib. lib. vi.—has some excellent remarks on this subject.

fore, no moral principle, no elevated virtues left. Was there no exultation, no heroism in the Vendean, or the Spanish patriots, because they were priest-ridden and degraded, and so blind as to fight for despotic princes? Was the Celtic Clan less devoted to its chieftain, for his exorbitant powers, and his occasional freaks of tyranny? According to the Jewish law,* slaves were adopted into the family of their master, but hired servants never; and it is remarkable that, throughout the scriptures, whenever an example of oppression is wanted, allusion is made to the condition of the latter. The truth is, that *parcere subjectis* was not exclusively a Roman virtue. It is the usual characteristic of all undisputed power.† It is a law of human nature, and in this very law of our hearts, as we verily believe, is to be sought a great mitigation of the evils of slavery—that compensation which exists in all the ordinances of Providence, and by which Infinite Wisdom is ever bringing good out of apparent evil. There are very few men who do not feel the whole force of that beautiful and touching appeal—"Behold, behold, I am thy servant," and no scenes of tenderness, which we have ever witnessed, can exceed what we have seen on plantations, about to be given up by their hereditary owners. We do not agree with Captain Hall that allusions to the poor's rate, and the parish work-house are as unsatisfactory as they are invidious. The Quarterly Review has, in a recent paper, shewn that every labourer in the kingdom is in a greater or less danger of ending his wretched life in those receptacles of wo and want, the last refuge of a worn-out body, and a broken spirit. Compare this hideous prospect with the easy, cheerful, comfortable old age of the negro slave, made free by the very causes which bring the free operative down to the worst of bondage. To say that this does not as yet occur in America, is no answer to our view of the question, which is bottomed upon the inevitable tendency of the system, if it be successful in producing the so much desired results of accumulated capital and dense population. Such a frightful mass of evil as now exists in England— so much bodily suffering and mental anguish—so many crimes prompted by the desperation of utter want, and punished with the unrelenting rigour of a stern and necessary policy, shew that, even under the most propitious circumstances, a large portion of mankind are doomed to servitude and misery. We are sincerely sorry for it, but so we are for all the evil, moral and physical, in the universe, and can only bow with deep humility before the inscrutable wisdom which orders or permits it. We will add, that the contract by which, according to Grotius, the

*Exod. xii. 45—οἰκία δε τέλειος ἐκ δούλων χ᾽ ἐλευθέρων. Arist. Pol. l. i., c. 3.
† And hence it is that, of the vicious forms of government, monarchy has been found most bearable, and prevailed most universally.

master has a right to the services of his slave, in consideration of providing for his perpetual maintenance, is, except in very peculiar circumstances, a most losing one for the former.* So much so that there can be no doubt the gradual extinction of villainage all over Europe is to be accounted for in this way. It is the *euthanasia* of slavery, and those who are for bringing our institutions to a violent and tragical end, would do well to ponder upon this view of the subject. Another piece of inconsistency, in Captain Hall, is his sentimentalism about the use of the lash, whilst, in another part of his work, he undertakes to prove, and, we think, does prove that, in naval and military discipline, it is at once the most efficacious, and the most merciful of punishments.†

We will now submit some extracts on this subject, without pointing out more particularly wherein we differ with him.

"I have no wish, God knows, to defend slavery in the abstract; neither do I say that it is the best state of things which might be supposed to exist in those countries: but I do think it is highly important that we should look this great and established evil fairly in the face, and consider its bearings with as little prejudice as possible. There is no other chance for its gradual improvement, I am well convinced, but this calm course, which has for its object the discovery of what is possible—not what is desirable.

"One of the results which actual observation has left on my mind is that there are few situations in life, where a man of sense or feeling can exert himself to better purpose than in the management of slaves. So far, therefore, from thinking unkindly of slave holders, an acquaintance with their proceedings has taught me to respect many of them in the highest degree ; and nothing, during my recent journey, gave me more satisfaction than the conclusion to which I was gradually brought, that the planters of the Southern States of America, generally speaking, have a sincere desire to manage their estates with the least possible severity. I do not say that undue severity is no where exercised: but the discipline, taken upon the average, as far as I could learn, is not more strict than is necessary for the maintenance of a proper degree of authority, without which, the whole frame-work of society in that quarter, would be blown to atoms. The first and inevitable result of any such explosion, would be the destruction of great part of the blacks, and the great additional misery of those who survived the revolt.

"The evils of slavery are, indeed, manifold. Take a catalogue of the blessings of freedom, and, having inverted them all, you get a list of the curses of bondage. It is twice cursed, alas! for it affects both parties, the master and the slave. The slave, in bad hands, is rendered a liar and a thief, as a matter of course ;—he is often systematically kept in ignorance of all he ought to be acquainted with, from truths of religion, to the commonest maxims of morality ; he is sometimes treated like the beasts of the field, and like them, only better or worse, according to the accidental character of his proprietor. On the other hand, there is in our nature a mysterious kind of reaction, which takes place in all circumstances, from the oppressed to the oppressors, the result of which is, that no man can de-

* A friend reminds us of Don Quixotte's reflection—"Duerme el criado y esta velando el señor pensando como le ha de sustentar mejorar y hacer mercedes."
† Vol. ii. pp. 167-171.

grade another, without, in some degree, degrading himself. In Turkey, for example, where the women are systematically debased—what are the men; I have the less scruple in taking this view of the matter, because it is one which, though not quite new to me, was brought to my notice on many occasions by the planters themselves, who, almost without exception, admitted to me with perfect frankness that there was more or less of a deleterious effect produced on their own character by the unfortunate circumstances inseparable from their situation. They are compelled, at the hazard of their lives and fortunes, to maintain a system, often in the highest degree revolting to their better nature. Like officers on service, they are forced on many occasions to repress their best feelings, and act with a sternness of purpose, which, though every way painful to them, cannot be relaxed for one instant.

"I confess, for my own part, I have seldom felt more sincerely for any set of men, when I heard them lamenting with bitterness of spirit the evil influence of the system alluded to, infusing itself, daily and hourly, into the minds of their children, in the very teeth of their own strenuous efforts to prevent such contamination. It is a curious, and perhaps instructive fact, that the slaves themselves delight in encouraging 'young master,' or even 'young mistress,' to play the tyrant over them! What at first is mere sport becomes in due time serious earnest. The difficulties, accordingly, of right education in those countries, at all its stages, are magnified to a degree, of which people in happier climates can hardly have any idea.

"In condemning slavery, and scorning slave-holders, we are apt to forget the share which we ourselves contribute towards the permanence of the system. It is true we are some three or four thousand miles from the actual scene. But if we are to reproach the planter who lives in affluence in the midst of a slave population, it ought to be asked how he comes by the means to live at that rate. He gives his orders to the overseer, the overseer instructs the driver, who compels the negro to work, and up comes the cotton. But what then? He cannot make the smallest use of his crop, however luxuriant it may be, unless upon an invitation to divide the advantages with him—we agree to become partners in this speculation—the result of slave labor. The transfer of the cotton from Georgia to Liverpool, is certainly one step, but it is no more than a step in the transaction. Its manufacture into the goods which we scruple not to make use of, and without which we should be very ill off, is but another link in the same chain, at the end of which is the slave.

"I shall be grievously misunderstood, if it be supposed that I wish to lessen the general abhorrence which is felt and expressed in the northern parts of America, and in England, for slavery. But I have a very great wish to see the subject properly viewed, and not shuffled aside, as it too frequently is, when all the matters at issue are taken for granted. My reason for desiring to see it so treated, arises from a conviction of there being no other way to do any good in the matter except by considering it with steadiness and temper, and by giving due consideration to the interest and the feelings of the parties most closely connected with it—who, after all, are in strictness not one whit more culpable than ourselves, and are very often, in spite of all our abuse, the most zealous practical friends of the cause we pretend to have so much at heart. It costs us nothing to vituperate slavery and the slaveholders; and, therefore, we play with the subject as we please; indifferent, very often, to the interest or feelings of those persons, who alone have power to do any good. It would be far better policy to obtain their co-operation by trying to show them in what their true interest consists; but it is quite vain to expect them to listen with coolness, while we are putting in jeopardy every thing they hold in the world."
Vol. ii. p. 234-236.

"The political problem, relating to the blacks, which the practical men, who shall be alive a hundred years hence, may be called upon to solve, will, in all probability, be very different from that which it becomes the present generation to attempt. Whatever posterity may do, however, we of the nineteenth century, if we really expect to advance the cause of humanity, in a proper and effective way, must not sit still, and scold or weep over the system of slavery, either in the abstrac:, as it is called, or in the practice.

"The idle things I have heard on the subject of slavery, by people who had not seen a dozen black men in their lives, have sometimes reminded me of a pompous fellow who pretended to be a great sailor, till being once cross-questioned as to what he would do in a gale of wind, if it were necessary to take in the main top-sail—'O, sir', said he, 'I would man the tacks and sheets—let all fly—and so disarm the gale of its fury!' Now, it is just in this fashion that many well-meaning people hope to disarm this hard slavery tempest of its errors, by the mere use of terms, which, in truth, have not the smallest application to the subject.

"The planters, who are men of business, and know better how to treat the question, set about things in a more workman-like style. Their first step is to improve the condition of the negro; to feed and clothe him better—take better care of him in sickness—and encourage him, by various ways, to work cheerfully. The lash, it is true, must still, I fear, be used; but it may be handled with more method, and less passion. These things, properly brought about, beget generous sympathies in both parties; for here, too, the reaction I spoke of formerly, soon shows itself—the slave works not only more, but to better purpose, and as the master feels it his interest, it soon becomes his pleasure, to extend the system further, which again leads to fresh advantages and fresh reactions, all of the same salutary description.

"The effect of better treatment raises the character of the slave, by giving him better habits, and thence invests him not exactly with a positive or acknowledged right to such indulgences, but certainly with a tacit or virtual claim to them. This is a great step in the progress of improvement; because the slave will now try, by good conduct, to confirm the favors he has gained, and to draw them into established usages. The master's profit, in a mere pecuniary point of view, arising out of this introduction of something like a generous motive among his dependants, I have the very best authority for saying, is in most cases indubitable. If experience proves that such consequences follow kind treatment, and that human nature is not dissimilar in the case of the blacks from what it is in every other, these advantages, which at first may be only casual, or contingent upon the personal character of a few masters, must in time become the usage over the plantations generally. Thus one more step being gained, fresh improvements in slave discipline—taking that word in its widest sense—would then gradually creep in under the management of wise and benevolent persons, whose example would, of course, be imitated, if the results were productive. This progress, I have strong reason to believe, is now in actual operation in many parts of America. Better domestic habits are daily gaining ground amongst the negroes, slowly but surely. More intelligence, better morals, and more correct religious feelings and knowledge, are also steadily making their way amongst that unfortunate race of human beings; and in no instance, I am told, have these improvements taken place without additional profit, and additional security to the master." Vol. ii. pp. 237–239.

In the following passage, he takes notice of an absurd notion which seems to be gaining ground in more Northern latitudes, very much, we fear, to our disadvantage in every point of view. We have no uneasiness at all about the event of any servile war, unless it be complicated with some other kind of war. If our Northern friends will have the goodness to abstain, as with few exceptions they have hitherto abstained, from propagating impracticable and dangerous doctrines about universal emancipation and equality of rights, we shall have not the least occasion for their services in the field. Let the *loyalty* of the slave not be disturbed by jacobinical lectures on the wrongs of which he has never been conscious—and he will not conspire at all. Let his conspiracy be unaided by foreign power, and it will be easily suppressed. Let it break out into open rebellion, and he and his whole race will be exterminated. We deprecate this sort of interference, for the sake of the slave rather than of his master. It will lead to nothing but discontent on the one side, and systematic cruelty on the other—to what Burke admirably characterizes as the "merciless policy of fear".*

"The number of negroes is already very considerable, and they are increasing so rapidly, that some people imagine there will, ere long, arrive a moment of political danger, from their mere physical force. Unquestionably there must always be danger from great numbers of persons combined for such a purpose as we may imagine the blacks to have in view. But I do not believe there is one man alive, who has attended to the subject, and certainly not one who has examined it on the spot, who conceives it possible that any thing but slaughter and misery would be the result of such an attempt on the part of the slaves to redress their grievances, real or imaginary, by means of force alone. Insurrections would, no doubt, cause unspeakable distress and ruin to their present masters; but there cannot be the shadow of a doubt, on any reasonable mind, that the slaves would be speedily overwhelmed, and be either cut to pieces, or reduced to servitude still more galling than they at present endure. Now, although all parties in America admit that this would be the result, there are many persons under the impression that in the event of a servile war in the Southern States, the free inhabitants of that section of the Union, could not subdue the insurgents without the co-operation of their non-slaveholding brethren in the North. This, however, I take to be a mere chimera, without any foundation whatever in fact. The armed militia of the slave holding States is abundantly strong for all the purposes of self-defence, even considered in a mere physical point of view. True security, it must be remembered, as far as force is considered, does not consist in numbers, but in that compact unity of purpose which cannot exist among slaves; but is maintained at all times amongst the free inhabitants of the South.

"It is of the highest importance to the peace of those countries that the truth of the above positions should be felt and acknowledged by the slaves themselves; because there seems every reason to believe, that precisely in proportion to their advancement in knowledge, so is this conviction strengthened. But as long as they are kept in a state of ignorance, they are perpetually liable to be worked upon by designing men, who instruct them in nothing, but in the extent of their numbers; and whose logic commences with the fallacy that sixty persons are necessarily stronger

* Cf. What Aristotle says about the Helots of Sparta, lib. i. c. x.

than six. If, however, these six have confidence in one another, and have arms in their hands, it is perfectly clear that they are superior in power, not to sixty, but to six hundred persons who can place no reliance on one another. As the slaves advance in knowledge, therefore, and learn to understand the true nature of their situation, they will only become more and more aware of the utter hopelessness of any remedy arising out of violence on their part. When this conviction is once thoroughly impressed upon their minds, they will not only be far less disposed to revolt, at the instigation of agitators, but will be in a better frame of mind to profit by those ameliorations in their condition, to which I have before alluded, as tending to the mutual advantage both of master and slave." Vol. ii. pp. 241-243.

To conclude—the principles laid down by the Supreme Court in the case of Johnson vs. McIntosh,* in relation to Indian titles, settles the law of the subject under consideration. In his able and luminous exposition of that doctrine, the Chief Justice shews that whatever we might think, were it *res integra*, of the equity and reasonabless of such maxims, it is too late to discuss that question now. The *jus gentium* has anticipated and precluded it. The uniform practice of the country—the universal concurrence of all nations in the same policy—the rights acquired by individuals and by States in reference to the law, and under expectations excited by it—in short, whatever can ratify and consecrate a conventional principle have given this power to the civilized man over the original possessors of the soil. The outcry raised against the people of Georgia and Alabama on this subject is of a piece with the cant about slavery. At the end of two centuries, after these wanderers have been remorselessly driven back from every point on the Atlantic shore, until their very names are almost forgotten in the thickly settled countries of the North, those States, which have still some of them to get rid of, are taunted and denounced by their more fortunate predecessors in this very course, for acting on their own maxims. Civil society could not get on a year, if the ravings of such besotted imbecility were listened to in the conduct of the commonwealth. Every institution, every ordinance of the State might be drawn into question and shaken to its foundations in the same way. Why, for instance, should not the galley-slave come in for his share of this quixotic sensibility? Who gave the majority of a people the right to legislate at their discretion for the minority—and especially to subject their fellow-citizens to ignominious punishments, for indulging themselves in little liberties, which they are pleased to stigmatize and denounce as crimes? What but necessity, "the tyrant's plea," can be alleged in favour of capital punishments in any case, and how loudly ought the blood of whole hetacombs of victims to our tyrannical legislation to cry to heaven against the civilized world for

* 10 Wheaton.

so many solemn judicial massacres, perpetrated under the forms of law, in all ages and countries! We really wonder that no vows have been offered up in the temples of this new "Goddess of Reason"—that no crusade has been preached up by these revolutionary zealots, for the delivery of thieves and footpads—that judges have not been denounced as suborners of assassination—that juries, in all parts of Christendom, have been found so lost to all sense of humanity and religion, as to find verdicts of "guilty" upon such barbarous indictments, and that no writ of attaint has ever been sued out against them! Above all, what shall we say of war and the whole body of the *jus belli*, so fully recognized by all mankind, except one sect remarkable for avoiding, most scrupulously, the shedding of their own blood, and for having very little repugnance to do what they know must lead to the shedding of other people's?

Upon the *right* of our Southern States, in all good conscience, before God and man, to uphold their hereditary institutions, we have not the shadow of doubt in any view of the question. Of their *duty* to do so, against any foreign interference, we have still less. They are called upon to maintain them by every thing which can bind a man to his ancestors and to his posterity—by everything which makes him feel that he has a country, and that he is bound to stand by her to the death, in all times of peril and difficulty. We take it for granted that he considers himself as identified with the commonwealth—that he looks upon its safety and glory as the only foundation of his own hopes. Such a man will feel any attempt of foreigners—by which we mean all who are not bound up with us in the destinies of the same body politic—to interfere with this fundamental institution of our land, as the most unjustifiable of outrages, as the most unequivocal declaration of hostility. If those foreigners happen to sustain a very intimate relation to us, and so to lie under peculiar obligations, not only not to disturb our peace, but to defend us in case of need—if they be those who have always gone out to battle with us against our enemies, and partaken in our trials and our trophies—if they be bound to us by the ties of consanguinity, and have established with us a perpetual covenant of union, "to insure domestic tranquillity and secure the blessings of liberty to *ourselves* and our posterity"—far from acknowledging the right, insanely claimed for them on this very ground, by some inconsiderate persons, to interfere in this peculiar local interest, we should regard any such interference on their part with the most sensitive jealousy, and meet it with the most uncompromising opposition. Instead of shrinking from such a contest, if such a contest should ever be forced upon us, we should go into it with every advantage on our side. We should feel confidence in the righteousness of our own cause.

We should be armed with invincible strength by our just indignation against the mad and atrocious wickedness of our enemies. Appealing to the constitution of our country—to the spirit in which that covenant was formed, and the objects which it was intended to accomplish—to all the recollections which hallowed, and all the hopes that endeared the conception and consummation of that sublime work of peace and brotherly love, we should call heaven and earth to witness that, not upon *our* heads—not upon the heads of those whose course had ever been one of self-sacrifice, until necessity made it one of self-defence—but upon those whom no compact could bind, and no argument or entreaty dissuade from a gratuitous and unprincipled interference with what concerned *them* nothing, but was *our* whole estate, and life, and being—should rest the guilt and the curse of turning that peace into a sword. But we repeat it, there is as yet no reason to impute such mischievous folly and malignity to the people of the non-slave-holding States in general, whatever a few pestilent jacobins among them may be inclined to say or do ; nor is it just to *presume* against them such dark and diabolical fraud.

If any change, then, is to be made in Southern institutions, it must be brought about exclusively by the people of the States immediately interested in this tremendous question. We have no right, certainly, to quarrel with our neighbours about their own domestic arrangements, however dangerous to us the example of some of them may be. If the people of Maryland or Virginia, of Kentucky or Tennessee, deem it their interest, to abolish this fundamental law, we shall, certainly, not declare a war *quia timet* upon them. But we are sufficiently interested in the subject to conjure them to reflect seriously upon what they are doing—to go about such a portentous revolution with the humility which characterizes true wisdom, in matters so far beyond its utmost compass to control—not with the reckless and profligate audacity of self-conceited quacks administering their poisonous nostrums to a charity patient whom they care not if they kill or cure. We would remind them that in politics, more than in any other department of human thought and knowledge, the results of an experiment are wrapt up in darkness and doubt. Man begins a revolution, but its issues are with God alone. The maxim of the true statesman is *festina lente*. The situation in which we find ourselves was not of our own choosing. When we came to the inheritance, it was subject to this mighty incumbrance, and it would be criminal in us to ruin or waste the estate in order to get rid of the burthen at once. That inheritance we are bound to transmit, as far as possible, unimpaired to those who shall owe us their being. We ought never to despair of the republic as it stands, so long as a ray of hope is left us. The counsels of a sage patriotism always take it for granted that the state can be saved without throwing into the sea whatever makes it worth preserving.   The task of a Southern politician is full of difficulty.   The other parts of this country, with a good judicial system to regulate the transactions of individuals, could get along for some time to come almost without any administrative government.   But *we must* be vigilant, and wary, and provident.   We must ask our watchman continually "what of the night."   We must look at the seeds of future events, and the causes which have not yet begun to operate.   Time, which is the wisest of all things, and the greatest of innovators, may possibly convince us, at a future day, that some changes ought to be made.   And we are satisfied that, if we do not spoil his work by our presumptuous and precipitate interference, all will yet go well.   His changes are slow, and gradual, and fit—contraries are insensibly softened down and blended into one another, not without harmony and beauty—and, when it is done, those who only look upon the extent of the mutation wonder how it could have stolen upon their unconscious predecessors, with such an inaudible and noiseless foot.   But the voluntary revolutions of man have almost always been abrupt, violent, and for the worse ; so that the wisdom of antiquity* laid it down, as a maxim, that every fundamental change in a state must needs be bloody and deadly.   We do not mean to say that this truth should make us afraid of doing what freemen sometimes owe to their dignity and rights ; but we do affirm that, even in extreme cases, it ought to inspire us with a deep and awful sense of responsibility.

Before we dismiss this subject entirely, we think it right to correct an egregious mistake of Captain Hall's about the mortality of slaves on rice plantations.   We do not dispute his *data*, but only the inference.   In one or two instances, from local or temporary causes, this result may have taken place, but it certainly is not a general one.   Some of the most remarkable examples that can be cited of increase, by mere propagation, have occurred within our own knowledge upon such estates.   We are not aware that any induction, sufficiently comprehensive to support a general theory upon this subject, has been made by our statists.   There are many other minute errors, but we have neither space nor inclination to correct them.   Some of them have been done away with, we trust, by our general remarks.

Upon the whole, we shut this book with a very high respect for Captain Hall's talents, although, as we began by saying, he is an ultra-tory and full of the prejudices of his party.   Considered as a mere literary performance, the work is liable to many objections.   It is very clumsily put together, and full of *longueurs*. There is an odd mixture of prosing philosophical dissertation and gossipping and garrulous egotism ever and anon breaking

* Εἰσὶ μὲν δήπου πᾶσαί μεταβολαὶ πολιτειων Θανατηφοροι.

out, that becomes in the end quite oppressive.　Add to this an offensive air of arrogance and self-conceit, and a style of reasoning, though sometimes Socratic enough, (for he is a perfect inquisitor at interrogation) certainly anything but *Academical.* We do not believe that his Majesty has a more dutiful, devoted and dogmatical subject.　We were at first inclined to like his style, which is very free and idiomatic.　But, although we prefer decidedly that colloquial ease and simplicity, to what is miscalled elegance by more fastidious critics, we must own he carries it to excess, and deals not only in vulgarisms, but in a disagreeable Tom and Jerry slang.　His jokes are not unfrequently very serious things.　We do not much wonder that our good people did not "take" as readily as our facetious friend could have wished.　We admit (and are very glad of it for reasons that need not be mentioned) that we Americans are a very grave people—but the merriest wag of us would be constrained to say of the Captain what Boileau does of another wit of the same stamp—

> Chapelain est aussi un auteur très plaisant,
> Et je ne sçais pas pourquoi je baille en le lisant.

Note.—In further illustration of our remarks at p. 285, et seq. about the effects of democracy in the long run, we beg to refer our classical readers to the admirable reflections in Cic. de Legib. lib. iii. c. 9, et seq.

[In the reprint of the foregoing article, and the preceding one on "Cicero de Republica," the publishers were without the benefit of Mr. Legaré's revision and marginal notes and corrections, the volume of his set of the Review, containing those articles, being missing.]

EARLY SPANISH BALLADS.

1. History of Charles the Great and Orlando, ascribed to Archbishop Turpin. Translated from the Latin in Spanheim's Lives of Ecclesiastical Writers : together with the most celebrated ancient Spanish Ballads, relating to the Twelve Peers of France mentioned in Don Quixotte ; with English metrical versions. By THOMAS ROOD. In 2 vols. *London.*

2. Floresta de varios Romances sacados de las Historias antiguas de los Doce Pares de Francia. POR DAMIAN LOPEZ DE TORTAJADA.

SINCE the beginning of that struggle, which resulted in the deliverance of German literature from the bondage of French authority and a servile imitation of foreign models, a new order of researches, and almost a new theory of criticism have been proposed to scholars. It has been discovered that there is no genuine, living beauty of composition which springs not spontaneously, if we may so express it, out of the very soil of a country ; which is not connected with the history, animated by the spirit, and in perfect harmony with the character and opinions of its people. It has been found that all imitative or derivative literatures are in comparison of the truly primitive and national, tame, vapid and feeble—that Roman genius, for instance, did but dimly reflect the glories of the Attic muse, and that, even in the *chefs d'œuvre* of the Augustan age of France, replete as they are in other respects with the highest graces of composition, the want of this native sweetness, this "color of primeval beauty," is universally complained of by foreigners. The German critics, therefore, and, after their example, many others have, within the present century, busily employed themselves in tracing the history of modern literature up to its sources, with a view to show its connection with national history and manners. The repositories of antiquarian lore have been ransacked for forgotten MSS. The oldest monuments—the most scattered and mutilated fragments have been brought to light, and collated and compared. The simplest traditions, the wildest fictions, the superstitions of the common people, the tales of the nursery and the fireside, legend and lay, and love-ditty and heroic ballad, have been all laid under contribution, to furnish forth such pictures of national manners, and "to show the very age and body of the times" which produced them, "its form and pres-

sure." These collections, both of metrical and prose "Reliques,"
in English as well as in foreign languages, are multiplying every
day, and becoming more and more generally studied and popular. In short, it is undeniable that the spirit of criticism is, in
this respect, far more liberal now, its views more enlarged and
profound, than they were in the reign of Queen Anne, and during the former half of the last century. The age is gone by
when his display of the beauties of "Chevy Chase" exposed
Addison to "the ridicule of Wagstaffe and the contempt of Den-
nis," and when Dr. Percy found it necessary to use the names of
"many men of learning and character," as "an amulet to guard
him from every unfavourable censure for having bestowed any
attention *upon a parcel of* OLD BALLADS."[*]

There is no country in Christendom whose literature furnishes
such a striking exemplification of these ideas as Spain. Her old
national poetry is second to none—if it is not superior to any in
Europe. Her classical productions of a later date, on the contrary, whatever may be said of them by enthusiasts, and whatever may be, in fact, the merit of some of them, have ever appeared to us, as to the majority of mankind, incomparably inferior to those of her neighbours. We do not mean to repeat the
well known *bon-mot* of Montesquieu, yet we venture to say that,
in spite of Schlegel or Cervantes,[†] it will be long before Calderon, or Herrera, or Garcilaso de la Vega, shall rival Dante, and
Ariosto, and Tasso, in the estimation of the world. But we pity
the man who can read a genuine old Spanish *romance*, and not
feel "his heart," in Sir Philip Sidney's phrase, "more moved than
with a trumpet." For these artless lays are the very language of
nature, at once heroic and simple—the living record of what the
most "renowned, romantic" race of modern men, under circumstances the most peculiar and the most interesting, did and suffered—a picture of "fierce wars and faithful loves," when every
war was a Holy War, waged for hearth and altar, and the stoutest champion that ever drew sword for his country and the cross
would have deemed it a foul blot upon his escutcheon to be
wanting in devotion to his lady-love, and all gentleness and
knightly grace in hall and bower. The intimate connection, especially, which so long subsisted between the Spaniards and
those inveterate enemies of the whole Christian name, their
Oriental conquerors, gives a singular and most attractive colouring to this early literature. From the influence of the church in
the dark ages, and the absence of the diversified interests and
avocations which absorb the attention of mankind, in an advanced state of society, religion mixed itself up with all the pursuits, feelings, opinions, and even the very amusements of those
times. Every thing breathed of it—every thing recalled it to

* Reliques, &c., vol. i., pref. xiv.   † Don Quixotte, c. 6.

the mind and impressed it upon the imagination and the heart. But this zeal for the true faith, or this fidelity to Mother-Church, was perpetually exercised and enflamed by the dangers which were supposed to beset them from the progress and the influence of a rival, though a false creed. In the depth of that starless night, the banners of Mohammedanism had been suddenly displayed in the very heart of Christendom. Sicily and Spain were subdued; Constantinople was repeatedly threatened, and the prowess of Charles Martel seems to have been the only barrier between the hitherto irresistible impetuosity of these martial fanatics and the whole Western world. Never, perhaps, either before or since, were such mighty interests staked upon the issue of a single battle, as depended upon that gained by the hero just mentioned, over the Saracens, between Tours and Poictiers. When at length the tide of conquest was rolled back upon the East, the same fierce and burning spirit of conflict and hostility was kept alive by the Crusades for two centuries together at the very æra of awakening civilization in Europe, and thus pervaded all its institutions and deeply tinctured its character in their first formation. The influence of these wars of enthusiasm upon modern literature has often been adverted to, but cannot be exaggerated. They are to us what Thebes and Troy and the Argonautic expedition were to the Greeks. The particular effect of them, however, to which we are now adverting, was to make an irreconcilable hatred, or at least, perpetual resistance to Islamism, be considered as of the very essence of all true piety. "Mahound and Apolyn," in the old metrical romances, are other names for the incarnate Spirit of Evil. Nor could a good Catholic, in those times, give a better proof of a saving faith in his own religion, or make a surer atonement for his sins, than by visiting the Holy Sepulchre with a warrior's sword and spear, instead of the scrip and staff of a pilgrim. The feelings and opinions of this heroic age are preserved in all its monuments, and were transmitted to succeeding ages, with the exaggeration and enchantment which objects of fancy or feeling are sure to derive from time and distance. To judge from some curious relics of the past, the recovery of Palestine out of the hands of the Infidel was, long after the last of the Crusades, an engrossing interest in Christendom. The idea of the barbarian conquerors, of the execrated *miscreants*, who had formerly struck such terror into Europe—who had overrun so many of the fairest lands, once blessed with the light of the gospel—who had thus been brought into close contact and perpetual and vexatious conflict with the faithful followers of Christ—had "built their seats long after near the seat of God, their altars near his altar—

———— yea, often placed

> Within his sanctuary itself their shrines,
> Abominations"—

this idea took such strong possession of the minds of men as to
be identified with their ordinary pursuits, their daily thoughts,
and their most ruling passions. Thus, in a collection of records
subjoined by Burnet to his History of the Reformation,* we find
the following. It is from "the bidding prayer" in popish times,
and was taken out of the festival printed in 1509, as it is said.
"The Bedes on Sunday. Ye shall kneel down on your knees,
and lift up your hearts, making your prayers to Almighty God
for the good state and peace of all Holy Church, &c. For our
Holy Father the Pope, with all his true College of Cardinals,
&c. Also; ye shall pray for *the Holy Land and the Holy
Cross* that Jesus Christ died on for the redemption of men's souls,
that it may come into the power of Christian men. Again : ye
shall pray for all true pilgrims and palmers," &c. No wonder
that the genius of Tasso—the christian poet *par excellence*—
should have kindled with these feelings, and that the subject of,
by far, the most popular epic of modern times, were the perils
and the triumph of the first Crusade !

But these religious wars, which—important as were their effects, were but an episode in the annals of the rest of Europe—
are the whole history of Spain. For upwards of seven centuries together, this mighty conflict of fanaticism was carried on with
various success, but uniformly the same spirit. From the battle
of Xeres in 712, until towards the end of the tenth century, the
crescent had been in the ascendant, but the faithful few, who had
defended themselves with so much difficulty in their mountain
fastnesses, began, about that period, to act, vigorously and successfully, on the offensive. The exploits of the Cid signalized
the greater part of the eleventh century, and finally decided the
question of superiority, between the Christians and Mahometans,
in favor of the former. The capture of Toledo, in 1085, in
which he was assisted by the flower of European chivalry, has
been justly classed, by Sismondi, with the Crusades soon after
proclaimed, as forming one of the most important eras in modern
history. In the twelfth century, the religious orders of St.
Jago, Calatrava and Alcantara were founded after the example of the Templars and Hospitallers of Jerusalem. One of their
vows was perpetual hostility to the Moslem, and, in every effort
subsequently made to recover their country from its Saracen
conquerors, these martial monks fully acquitted themselves of
that obligation. The knights of Calatrava, second in dignity
and consequence to those of St. Jago, combined in a remarkable degree, the various and apparently incompatible duties of
the camp and the cloister. In their dress and diet, they were

* Vol. ii.

distinguished by the severest simplicity, and even by an ascetic rigor. "They were silent in the oratory and the refectory, one voice only reciting the prayers or reading a legend of battle; but, when the first note of the Moorish atabal was heard by the warder on the tower, the convent became a scene of universal uproar. The caparisoning of steeds and the clashing of armour broke the repose of the cloister, while the humble figure of the monk was raised into a bold and expanded form of dignity and power."* It is easy to conceive how deep an impression such institutions and habits must have made upon the Spanish character, during seven centuries of incessant warfare under the holy banner of the cross. Every encounter with "the Paynim Chivalry," every siege, and battle, and skirmish, during that long period, is invested with somewhat of that romantic character and poetical interest, which are justly ascribed to the adventures of the Croisès; and a crown of martyrdom, in addition to all the other rewards of valor, was reserved for the patriot soldier, who fell by the Moorish scimitar. If christianity and chivalry are, as they have been said to be, the vital principles of modern literature, the old heroic ballads of Spain breathe more of this spirit than any other similar monuments of past times. They are genuine primitive specimens of what the German critics designate as the "romantic" style, and cold indeed, it seems to us, must be the bosom of a reader—of a christian reader, at least—in which this rude minstrelsy finds not an echo for its lofty and thrilling strains!

Besides our immediate interest in Turpin's Chronicle—most of the Spanish ballads having some sort of connection with the leading subjects of the romances of Chivalry, as they are called, it may be necessary to cast a glance at these before we proceed farther in our remarks.

What was the *origin* of the Romances of Chivalry? Is it to be found, as Dr. Percy has ventured to affirm that it "incontestibly" may be, in the mythology of Scandinavia and the lays of the Scalds? Or shall we adopt the (more probable?) opinion of Warton, that, "amid the gloom of superstition, in an age of the grossest ignorance and credulity, a taste for the wonders of Oriental fiction was introduced by the Arabians into Europe, many countries of which were already seasoned to a reception of its extravagancies, by means of the poetry of the Gothic Scalds, who perhaps originally derived their ideas from the same fruitful region of invention. These fictions, coinciding with the reigning manners and perpetually kept up and improved in the tales of Troubadours and Minstrels, seem to have centered about the eleventh century in the ideal histories of Turpin and Geoffrey of Monmouth, which record the supposititious achievements of

* Mills' History of Chivalry.

Charlemagne and king Arthur, where they formed the ground-work of that species of fabulous narrative called romance. And from these beginnings or causes, afterwards enlarged and enriched by kindred fancies fetched from the Crusades, that singular and capricious mode of imagination arose, which at length composed the marvellous machinery of the more sublime Italian poets and of their disciple Spenser."*

But whatever diversity of opinion may exist about the source from which the Romances of Chivalry were derived, there can be none as to their principle subject-matters. These are the two just mentioned in the extract from Warton, viz. the exploits of Arthur's Round Table, and those of Charlemagne and his Twelve Peers. To the fictions, founded upon the fabulous Chronicles of Geoffrey of Monmouth, and the imaginary Turpin, we may add those which sprung up in Spain out of the Romance of *Amadis of Gaul*. These three classes of fictions are altogether distinct from each other.† The last of them is peculiar to the Spanish. To this belong the Florismart of Hyrcania Galaor, Esplandian, &c. They have no pretensions to historical accuracy or verisimilitude. The heroes who figure in them— the Perions, Kings of France, the Languines of Scotland, the the Lisoards of Britanny, exist no where else but in them. The great model of this school as we have already mentioned, is the famous Amadis de Gaul, well known to the readers of Don Quixotte, for the honorable exception made in its favour by the curate and master Nicholas, in the auto-da-fe of the knight's library. This work is ascribed by the Spanish and Portuguese critics to Lobeiras, a Portuguese, who is supposed to have written it about the close of the thirteenth century ; but, as no mention is made in it of the Moors, it seems to be a more probable opinion that it was originally the work of some *Trouvére*, vamped up and enlarged at different times by "various able hands."

We owe to Geoffrey, a Welsh Benedictine, sometime Archdeacon of Monmouth and Bishop of St. Asaph, all that has come down to us in so many various and wonderful tales of King Arthur and his faithless Guenevre or Gwenhwyfar, of Sir Kay, Sir. Launcelot, Sir Gawain, Sir Tristam, and, above all, of that first of seers and sorcerers, the mad eremite of the Caledonian Forest, the enchanter Merlin. Not that Geoffrey composed the substance or even the shadow of all that has been written about these worthies ; but his works, as Mr. Ellis remarks, gave countenance, and as it were authenticity, to the legendary lore

* Hist. Eng. Poet. Diss. I. Sub. cac.

† To these three, we may add with Mr. Ellis, (Specimens, &c. Vol. i. p. 134,) 4. The history of Troy, from Dares Phrygius and Dictys Cretensis, and 5. The Poem of Alexander, from Q. Curtius, but still more from a Greek version of a Persic work, by the Pseudo-Calisthenes, in 1070.

and popular stories of the Bretons and the Welsh, and at once, no doubt, brought out all of these that were already current, and gave occasion to the invention of many similar figments. Thus, in the Chronicle, of which a very copious abstract is to be found in the second series of Mr. Ellis' Specimens,* no mention at all is made of Sir Launcelot, Sir Tristam, Sir Yvain, Joseph of Arimathea, the Sang-réal, the Round Table and its perilous seat, and many other equally important subjects which fill so many invaluable old MSS. The publication of Geoffrey's history was followed by a flood of these Cimric fables which issued from the same great fountain-heads of this sort of literature, Wales and Armorica. Nay, this Chronicle itself was probably nothing more than a *cento* of popular legends and traditions, long separately said or sung by the bards or rhapsodists of the country. It was first brought to England by Gualter, Archdeacon of Oxford, on his return from a tour in France, and put into the hands of Geoffrey to be translated into Latin about the year 1100. The original title of the work was *Brut-y-Brenhined,* or *History of the Kings of Britain,* from the time of the imaginary founder of their dynasty, Brutus the Trojan, down to the demise or disappearance of Arthur, who—as we understand, from Geoffrey's other work, the Life of Merlin—was translated by enchantment to the Fortunate Islands, where, in the never-fading bowers of the Fay Morgana, he still "quaffs immortality and joy," in expectation of once more reigning over his faithful lieges in Britanny and Wales. It seems probable that Geoffrey took some liberties with the Cimric MS., embellishing his paraphrase of it by several additional legends gathered either from popular tradition among his countrymen, the Welsh, or from the communications of his friend, the Archdeacon of Oxford. Of this paraphrase, again, a French metrical version was made about the year 1155, by Wace, to whom the world is under many other weighty obligations of a similar kind. For, without mentioning a metrical history of the Norman Kings in 12,000 verses, and sundry other chronicles of equal accuracy and importance, this Wace was the author of the famous *Roman du Rou* (written in Alexandrines) and the *Roman du Chevalier au Lion,* and is suspected by some writers of having had a hand in the composition of the *Romance of Alexander.* We ought to add that the same service, which this writer had done Geoffrey, was rendered to himself before the close of the twelfth century, by Layamon, who translated his French version into English.

We are now got down to our immediate subject. Arthur and Charlemagne, as Warton expresses it, were the first and original heroes of Romance, and as Geoffrey's history is the grand repository from which every thing relating to the former is either di-

* Edit. 1805, Vol. i. p. 46.

rectly or indirectly derived, so Turpin's Chronicle is the ground-work of all the Ballads and Romances that have been since published about the Emperor and his Paladins. The date of this fabulous book is exceedingly doubtful. It was certainly written before 1122, when it was (dit-on) declared authentic by a bull of Calixtus II. It ought, perhaps, to be referred, as it has been by the French critics, to the latter part of the eleventh century. What we have said of the history of the *Brut d'Angleterre* is, no doubt, equally applicable to the Chronicle before us. It was, probably, little more than a collection of the old ballads and legends that had long been current among the common people, embellished, it may be, as Warton supposes, by an admixture of Oriental fancies communicated to the Armoric bards, through the Saracens of Spain. It is certain that an heroic rhapsody, of which Orlando was the subject, was sung to the Norman troops at the battle of Hastings, to inflame their courage, and Ritson, upon what authority we know not, affirms that it *unquestionably* related to the encounter at Roncesvalles.* As the following remarks of Mr. Ellis, which are quoted by the work under review, throw as much light upon the subject as can be derived from any other single source, we have no scruple in extracting them for the benefit of our readers.

" 'This Chronicle was composed before 1122, with the title of "Joannes Turpini Historia de Vitâ Caroli Magni & Rolandi;' and it may be presumed that the MSS. of such a history were formerly very numerous, though it appears to have principally derived its popularity from its French metrical paraphrases and imitations, some of which were probably of almost equal antiquity with the original, and are alluded to by the subsequent prose translators.

"The earliest of these, according to Fauchet, was written by a certain Jehans, who, at the instance of Regnault, Comte de Boulogne and de Daumartin (then detained as a prisoner by Philippe Auguste), turned into French prose a Latin copy of Turpin, which he found in the archives of St. Denis. A copy of this work is still preserved in MS. in Bibl. Reg., 4. c. xi.

"The next translation was made by Gaguin: it is dedicated to Francis I, and was printed at Paris in 1527, quarto.

"There is a Latin paraphrase of the original in hexameters, many of which rhyme to each other, entitled 'Karolettas,' and preserved in Bibl. Reg., 13. A. xviii.

"The original work was first printed in a collection entitled 'Germanicarum rerum quatuor Chronographi,' Frankfort, 1566, folio.

"Another pretended French translation was afterwards published at Lyons, in 1583, octavo, with the title of 'La Chronique de Turpin, Archevesque et Duc de Rheims, et Premier Pair de France.' This however, which Mr. Ritson supposes to be the work ascribed by Mr. Warton to Michel le Harnes, who lived in the time of Philippe Auguste, contains, as he tells us, the Romance of Renaud de Montauban, and not that of Roland. Per-

* Dissertation on Romance and Chivalry p. xxxv. He quotes the words of W. of Malmesbury, who wrote about the year 1140. Tunc CANTILENA ROL-ANDI inchoata ut Martium viri exemplum accenderet, &c.

haps it may be a conversion into prose of the metrical Romance on the same subject, written, as Fauchet informs us, by Huon de Villeneuve, about the commencement of the fourteenth century.

"Be this as it may, there can be no doubt that numberless fables concerning Charlemange were grafted on the narratives of the supposed Turpin: and, indeed, his translator Gaguin appears to be almost ashamed of the imperfect narrative contained in his original, and is very solicitous to excuse himself for suppressing many particulars concerning his hero, which, though very necessary to be known, the Archbishop had not thought fit to notice. Thus, after mentioning (chapter 26) Olivier, Gondebault Roy de Frigie, Ogier Roy de Dannemarc, Arestaigne Roy de Bretaigne, Guarin Duc de Lorraine, and others, he refers us to 'leurs histoires plus au long descriptés, lesquelles je laisse pour le present à ceux qui lisent les Romans, livres, et autres escriptures.' And, in his concluding chapter, he gives us a sketch of some important events, which, if he had thought fit he could have communicated more at large.

"That such absurdities as these should be accepted in lieu of authentic history in a credulous age, and where better materials could not be had, would excite no astonishment; but, it is very surprising that, for a length of time, they should have usurped the place of the numerous historical documents, which record the glory of a Charlemagne, whose character, when left to the sober voice of truth, is far more amiable and respectable than that of his ideal and romantic substitute. In fact, there is good reason to believe that the name of Charlemagne was first introduced by mistake into a series of fictions, of which the real hero was of a still earlier date; and it is the opinion of Mr. Leyden, an author of much research and information, that the origin of these fictions is to be sought in Britanny. I shall give his sentiments in his own words.

" 'That class of Romances, which relates to Charlemagne and his Twelve Peers, ought probably to be referred to the same source, since they ascribe to that French Monarch the feats which were performed by an Armorican Chief. The grand source, from which the fabulous history of Charlemagne is thought to be derived, is the suppositious history, ascribed to his contemporary Turpin, which, in 1122, was declared to be genuine by papal authority. The history of this work is extremely obscure; but, as it contains an account of the pilgrimage of Charlemagne to Jerusalem, its composition must have been posterior to the Crusades. The Abbé Vellet has shewn that the principal events which figure in the romantic history of that Monarch have no relation to him whatever, though they are historically true of the Armorican Chieftain, Charles Martel. It was this hero, whose father was named Pepin, and who had four sons, who performed various exploits in the forest of Ardenne against the four sons of Aymon; who warred against the Saxons: who conquered the Saracens at Poictiers; it was he who instituted an order of Knighthood; who deposed the Duke of Aquitaine; and who conferred the donation of the sacred territory on the See of Rome. Is it not, therefore, more probable that the history and exploits of this hero should be celebrated by the minstrels of his native country, than that they should be, for the first time, narrated by a dull prosing Monk some centuries after his death? Is it not more probable that, when the fame of Charles Martel had been eclipsed by the renown of Charlemagne, the Monkish abridger of the songs of the minstrels should transfer the deeds of the one to the other, by an error of stupidity, than that he should have deliberately falsified history when he had no purpose to serve? The ingenious author to whom I have referred seems to have pointed out the sense of this error. In the Armoric language meur signifies great, mayne; and marra is a mattock, martel; so that, instead of Charlemagne and Charles Martel, we have Charlemeur and Charlemarra;

names, which, from the similarity of sound, might easily be confounded. A similar blunder has been committed by the Norman trouveur, who transferred the characteristic epithet of Caradoc from the Welsh or Armorican to the Romance language.' " Vol. i. Pref.

We add the following "brief account" of Archbishop Turpin, prefixed to the history.

"Turpin, Archbishop of Rheims, the friend and secretary of Charles the Great, excellently skilled in sacred and profane literature, of a genius equally adapted to prose and verse: the advocate of the poor, beloved of God in his life and conversation, who often hand to hand fought the Saracens by the Emperor's side; he relates the acts of Charles the Great in one book of Epistles, and flourished, under Charles and his son Lewis, to the year of our Lord eight hundred and thirty." Vol. i. p. 1.

This warlike ecclesiastic, in an epistle to Leopander, Dean of Aix-la-Chapelle, which serves at once for preface and introductory chapter to the whole work, explains his motive for writing it, as well as his means of acquiring the very best information on the various matters contained in it. For forty years he had been at the Emperor's side through "the battles, sieges, fortunes that he had passed," and now, on his return from the Spanish campaigns, "his wounds being at length cicatrized !" (says the book) he sits down at Vienne in Dauphiné to indite a particular account of that memorable expedition. The whole chronicle is exceedingly brief, containing in the translation before us little more than fifty duodecimo pages.—But we shall not attempt anything like a full and elaborate abstract of the work. It is as much as we can afford to do to run very hastily over its outlines, and submit to our readers a few of the more remarkable passages, by way of specimens. We may observe, generally, upon it, that it is a true monkish history—half legend, half homily—written with an eye single to the advancement of the Church—telling the most preternatural stories with the most perfect naïveté, and interlarding its incredible narrative with edifying reflections and significant hints, addressed to the impenitent, and especially to those who, in the disposition of their worldly substance, shew how much they prefer the interests of time before those of eternity.

Charlemagne's motive for undertaking this expedition was, of course, a miracle. He had accomplished all his conquests, and was well stricken in years, when, having nothing better to do, he fell to observing "*the* [quære *a*] starry way in the heavens, beginning at the Friezland sea and passing over the German territory and Italy between Gaul and Aquitaine, and from thence in a straight line over Gascony, Béarne and Navarre, and through Spain to Gallicia, wherein, till his time, lay undiscovered the body of St. James." After gazing night after night upon this remarkable phenomenon, a certain beautiful, resplendent vision appeared to him in his sleep, and very affectionately calling him "son," inquired what was "the labor of his thoughts." "And who art thou, Lord," answered Charles. "I am," said the apparition, "St. James the Apostle, Christ's disciple, the son of Zebedee, and brother of John the Evangelist, &c.; my body now lies concealed in Gallicia, long so grievously oppressed by the Saracens, from whose yoke, I am astonished that you, who have conquered so many lands and cities, have not yet delivered it." The object of the vision, therefore, was to excite him to this enterprize, by explaining the sign he had seen in the heavens, and marvelled at so much. That starry way in the sky at once "marshalled him the way that he should go," and prefigured the glory that he was to acquire. Thrice did the apparition of the blessed Apostle of Compostella visit nightly the slumbers of the Emperor, until at length he summoned his Twelve Peers and entered Spain at the head of a grand army.

In this great enterprize, as in so many others, it was only the first step that cost any trouble. For three tedious months, the walls of Pampeluna obstinately resisted the utmost efforts of the beleaguerers; but no sooner had Charlemagne offered up a prayer to God and St. James, than down they came of themselves and left the city to the mercy of its enemies. The report of this miracle convinced the *miscreants*, as well it might, that all further resistance would be fruitless, and so they consented, without more ado, to pay the Emperor tribute; and, before the end of a very short chapter, *he* is bowing at the shrine of St. James, and the good Turpin, traversing the whole country from sea to sea, converting the "Pagans" by thousands, and either putting to death or making slaves of those who refused to embrace the faith. Such is the rapidity with which our holy chronicler, like another Cæsar, despatches whatever his hands find to do, whether in peace or in war, with the sword or with the pen.

Charles, after spending three years in these parts, and collecting a world of money, which he laid out in building churches, appointing abbots and canons to attend them and enriching them with bells, books, robes, and other ornaments, quietly returned to France. But he was hardly gone, before "a certain Pagan King, called Argolander," recovered the whole country. Another expedition, under the command of Milo de Angleris was straightway determined on, but the good Turpin here interrupts his narrative to relate the case of an awful judgment of heaven upon a "false executor," which is as follows :—

"But the judgment, inflicted on a false executor, deserves to be recorded as a warning to those who unjustly pervert the alms of the deceased. When the king's army lay at Bayonne, a certain soldier called Romaricus was taken grievously ill, and, being at the point of death, received the eucharist and absolution from a priest, bequeathing his horse to a certain kinsman in trust, to dispose of for the benefit of the priest and the poor. But when he was dead his kinsman sold it for a hundred pence, and spent

the money in debauchery. But how soon does punishment follow guilt!
Thirty days had scarcely elapsed when the apparition of the deceased appeared to him in his sleep, uttering these words: "How is it you have so
unjustly misapplied the alms entrusted to you for the redemption of my
soul? Do you not know that they would have procured the pardon of my
sins from God ? I have been punished for your neglect thirty days in fire ;
to-morrow you shall be plunged in the same place of torment, but I shall
be received into Paradise." The apparition then vanished, and his kinsman awoke in extreme terror.

"On the morrow, as he was relating the story to his companions, and
the whole army was conversing about it, on a sudden, a strange uncommon
clamour, like the roaring of lions, wolves, and calves, was heard in the air,
and immediately a troop of demons seized him in their talons, and bore
him away alive. What further? Horse and foot sought him four days together in the adjacent mountains and vallies to no purpose; but, the twelfth
day after, as the army was marching through a desert part of Navarre,
his body was found lifeless, and dashed to pieces, on the summit of some
rocks, a league above the sea, about four days' journey from the city.
There the demons left the body, bearing the soul away to hell. Let this
be a warning, then, to all that follow his example to their eternal perdi-
tion." Vol. i., pp. 8–10.

In their first encounter, Charles was utterly overthrown, and
his general, Milo de Angleris, Orlando's father, slain in the battle. The Emperor, however, is rescued by the timely arrival of
four Marquisses from Italy, with four thousand troops, and Argolander now summons all his forces to decide, for good and all,
this mighty contest. The array of the Infidels exhibited a Babylonish confusion of Saracens, Moors, Moabites, Parthians, Afri-
cans and Persians, led by Texephin, King of Arabia; Urabell,
King of Alexandria; Avitus, King of Bugia; Ospin, King of Al-
garve; Facin, King of Barbary; Ailis, King of Malclos; Ma-
nuo, King of Mecca; Ibrahim, King of Seville; and Almanzor,
King of Cordova. The reader of Ariosto will, we ween, be
puzzled to recognize in this host, any of his old acquaintance.

Che fùro al tempo che passaro i Mori
D'Africa il mare, e in Francia nocquer tanto
Seguendo l'ire e i giòvenil furori
D'Agramante lor re.

This great host was defeated by Charlemange in a battle near
Xiantonge, after which Argolander recrossed the Pyrennees and
came to Pampeluna, where he sent the Emperor word "that he
would stay for him." This challenge was accepted, and every
vassal of the Western Empire was summoned to join its standard.

"These are the names of the warriors that attended the king:—Turpin,
Archbishop of Rheims, who, by the precepts of Christ, and for his faith's
sake, brought the people to fight valiantly, fighting likewise himself hand
to hand with the Saracens. Orlando, General of the whole army, Count
of Mans and Lord of Guienne, the King's nephew, son of Milo de Angleris and Bertha, the King's sister. His soldiers were four thousand. Another Orlando likewise, of whom we are silent. Oliver, a General also,
and a valiant soldier, renowned for strength and skill in war, led three thou-

sand troops. Aristagnus, King of Brittany, seven thousand. Another King of Brittany, of whom little mention is made. Angelerus, Duke of Aquitaine, brought four thousand valiant bowmen.

"Gayfere, King of Bordeaux, led three thousand warriors. Galerus, Galinus Solomon, Estolfo's friend and companion; Baldwin, Orlando's brother, Galdebode, King of Friezland, led seven thousand heroes; Ocellus, Count of Nantes, two thousand, who achieved many memorable actions, celebrated in songs to this day. Lambert, Count of Berry, led two thousand men. Rinaldo of the White Horn, Vulterinus Garinus, Duke of Lorraine, four thousand. Hago, Albert of Burgundy, Berard de Miblis, Gumard Esturinite, Theodoric, Juonius, Beringaire, Hato, and Ganelon, who afterwards proved the traitor, attended the King into Spain. The army of the King's own territory was forty thousand horse, and foot innumerable.

"These were all famous heroes and warriors, mighty in battle, illustrious in worldly honor, zealous soldiers of Christ, that spread his name far and near, wherever they came. For, even as our Lord and his twelve Apostles subdued the world by their doctrine, so did Charles, King of the French and Emperor of the Romans, [by his twelve peers,] recover Spain to the glory of God. And now the troops, assembling in Bordeaux, overspread the country for the space of two days' journey, and the noise they made was heard at twelve miles' distance. Arnold of Berlanda first traversed the pass of the Pyrennees, and came to Pampeluna. Then came Astolfo, followed by Aristagnus; Angelerus, Galdebode, Ogier, the king, and Constantine, with their several divisions. Charles and his troops brought up the rear, covering the whole land from the river of Rume to the mountains, that lie three leagues beyond them on the Compostella road." Vol. i. pp. 15–17.*

Charles grants Argolander a truce to draw out his forces and prepare for battle; but, in the meantime, they agree to settle the matter by a combat between a certain number of picked warriors. The Moslem were defeated, but, their King declining to acquiesce in this decision of fortune, nothing remained but the last resort to a general engagement. A truce for a few days, meanwhile, gives room for an interview and most edifying theological controversy, between the two chiefs; Charles piously attempting—and, as he seems to have persuaded himself, not without good hopes—to make a proselyte of his foe. Argolander, however, sends him a Rowland for his Oliver in the discussion, and takes occasion to taunt him with the inconsistency between his professions and practice in his treatment of the poor. The whole chapter is at once so piquant and so characteristic, that we will quote it without abridgment.

"On the third day Argolander attended the King, as he promised, and found him at dinner. Many tables were spread at which the guests were sitting; some in military uniform; some in black; some in priest's habits, which Argolander perceiving, inquired what they were? "Those you see

---

* The names of the twelve Peers, from the metrical romance of Sir Ferumbras in Ellis' Specimens, vol. ii. p. 376, are as follows: Orlando or Roland; Oliver; Guy, Duke of Burgundy; Duke Naymes of Bavaria; Ogier le Danois; Béry l'Ardennois; Fulke; Le Roux; Iron of Brabant; Barnard of Prussia; Bryer of Bretagne, and *Sir* Turpin.

in robes of one color," replied the King, "are priests and bishops of our holy religion, who expound the gospel to us, absolve us from our offences, and bestow heavenly benediction. Those in black are monks and abbots; all of them holy men, who implore incessantly the divine favor in our behalf." But, in the meantime, Argolander espying thirty poor men in mean habiliments, without either table or table-cloth, sitting and eating their scanty meals upon the ground, he inquired what they were? "These," replied the King, "are people of God, the messengers of our Lord Jesus, whom, in his and his apostles' names, we feed daily." Argolander then made this reply: "The guests at your table are happy; they have plenty of the best food set before them; but those you call the messengers of God, whom you feed in his name, are ill fed, and worse clothed, as if they were of no estimation. Certainly, he must serve God but indifferently, who treats his messengers in this manner, and thus do you prove religion false." Argolander then refused to be baptized, and, returning to his army, prepared for battle on the morrow.

"Charles, seeing the mischief his neglect of these poor men had occasioned, ordered them to be decently clothed and better fed. Here then we may note the christian incurs great blame who neglects the poor. If Charles, from inattention to their comfort, thereby lost the opportunity of converting the Saracens, what will be the lot of those who treat them still worse? They will hear this sentence pronounced: 'Depart from me, ye cursed, into everlasting fire; for I was an hungered, and ye gave me no meat; naked, and ye cloathed me not.'

"We must consider likewise that our faith is of little value without good works. As the body, says the Apostle, without the soul is dead, so is faith dead if it produce not good fruit. And, as the Pagan King refused baptism because he found something wrong after it, so our Lord, I fear, will refuse our baptism at the day of judgment if superfluity of faults be found in us." Vol. i. pp. 20–22.

The battle of Pampeluna, in which Charles brought into the field one hundred and thirty thousand men, and Argolander one hundred thousand, results in the total overthrow and death of the latter. Some time after, Charles heard that a certain King of Navarre, called Furra, intended to fight him at Mount Garzim, and immediately prepared for the combat. But, feeling a great curiosity to know who were predestined to fall in the mêlée, he prays to the Lord that they may be designated beforehand. They, accordingly, all appear in the morning marked with a cross on their backs; whereupon, the Emperor, rather impiously, we fear, attempting to jockey the fates, had the designated victims, as he thought, safely locked up in his Oratory. But what was his surprise, upon returning from the field in which he had been completely victorious, to find these hundred and fifty elect, dead to a man! "O holy band of Christian warriors," exclaims the good Turpin in a pious rapture, "though the sword slew you not, yet did ye not lose the palm of victory, or the prize of martyrdom."

We have only one more war to advert to, before we come to the fatal battle, where "Charlemagne and all his peerage fell, by Fontarabbia"—at once the catastrophe and chiefest attraction of this most exact and veracious chronicle. We allude to the war with Ferracute, of which Mr. Ellis has furnished another version, in the metrical Romance of Roland and Ferragus, published from the Auchinleck MS.* Tidings were brought to the French camp that a certain outrageous giant, of the name of Ferracute, and of the race of Goliath, had been sent to Nager by Admiraldus, at the head of twenty thousand "Turks of Babylon," expressly to fight with the victors of Pampeluna. Charlemagne had no hesitation in accepting the defiance, and, with true chivalrous courtesy, went immediately to Nager, to make his respects in person to this Titanian champion. Perhaps he had not been accurately informed, before he made up his mind to do so, what was the dimensions of this "Son of Earth,"—for his stature was twelve cubits, and his face a cubit long; his arms and thighs four cubits; his fingers three palms in length; and he had a nose (though that might have been in the way) that measured a span! Besides this, neither spear nor dart could make any impression upon his body, except in a single spot, and he monopolized the strength of forty men! This dreadful adversary begins by defying the whole chivalry of France to meet him, one after another, in single combat.—Ogier, the Dane, (the Dacian as he is called here) sallies forth first—but the giant, approaching him leisurely, catches him up under the right arm, and as leisurely marches off with him to the city. Rinaldo of the White Thorn—that flower of knighthood and glory of romance—was treated just as unceremoniously. Then Constantine and Ocellus, who went out together, were spirited away—then scores of other warriors by pairs, shared the same fate. Charles was in utter despair, but now Orlando sought and obtained his permission to enter the lists. Like the rest the giant picked *him* up too and seated him quietly upon his steed before him. But, as he was making off with him, Orlando collecting all his strength, and "trusting in the Almighty," seized the terrible miscreant by the beard, and tumbled him off his horse, so that they both came to the ground together. A blow, aimed at the giant, fell upon his steed and cut him through and through; a compliment which the owner of the unfortunate animal presently after returned, by hitting Orlando's horse (which the knight had just remounted) with a blow of his fist, and laying it dead upon the earth. The giant being disarmed of his sword by a well-directed stroke from his adversary's, the combat was kept up until noon, with fists and stones. The mighty infidel then demanded a truce till next day, which Orlando, no doubt, very willingly granted him, and it was agreed that they should return to the encounter on the morrow, without steed or spear.

They did accordingly meet; the giant bringing with him a sword, but Orlando only a long staff (that is, we suppose, a pole

* Specimens, (ed. 1805) vol. ii. p. 307.

or beam) to ward off his adversary's blows, who wearied himself to no purpose. "They now began to batter each other with
stones that lay scattered about the field, till at last the giant
begged a second truce, which being granted he presently fell
fast asleep upon the ground. Orlando, taking a stone for a pillow, quietly laid himself down also. *For such was the law of
honor between Christians and Saracens at that time, that no one,
on any pretence, dared to take advantage of his adversary before the truce was expired, as in that case his own party would
have slain him."** The words printed in italics are worthy of notice, as shewing how early these refined ideas of chivalry began to
be acted on and proclaimed as settled principles of conduct, even
in the intercourse between Christian nations and their deadly and
irreconcilable foes,—to say nothing of the exception which might,
perhaps, have been fairly pleaded, in so anomalous a case as a
contest with a most disproportionate foe.

When Ferracute's nap was over, Orlando (for he also was
awake by this time) rose, and, seating himself by the giant's side,
fell into conversation with him, in the course of which the
son of Anak was indiscreet enough to reveal the secret of his
strength. Their talk was of various indifferent matters, until at
length the Saracen asked the knight what law he followed.
"The law of Christ, so far as his grace permits me." This answer leads to the question who was Christ, and then ensues a
dialogue, continued through five pages, of the most extraordinary character. We will not extract it here, because it is unworthy of the subject, nor shall we attempt a summary of it, because it would be difficult to do so without seeming to fall into
the burlesque. It is enough to say that Orlando undertakes to
explain to his enormous catechumen the most unfathomable
mysteries of the Christian faith—the Trinity, the Incarnation,
the Passion, and the Resurrection—and that the illustrations he
makes use of are exceedingly well adapted to the intellectual
capacity of a giant, which is, we believe, according to a well-
established opinion, in the inverse ratio of his bodily stature.
But, if Ferracute was puzzled, he certainly was not convinced by
his foeman's logic, and he, accordingly, proposed to refer the decision of the controversy to a trial by battle. "Be it so," said
Orlando: whereupon they immediately fell to blows—but the
fatal secret being now revealed, Orlando, dexterously availing
himself of the advantage, gave his adversary a mortal wound,
and scampered away to the camp. The Christians then carried
the city by storm—the wounded giant and his people were put
to death, his castle taken, and all his prisoners set at liberty.

Passing over the diverting "War of the Masks," and the division of the conquests, which forcibly reminds one of the grants

* Chapter 17.

made by Alexander VI., to the discoverers of America, we present our readers with the following portrait of Charlemagne. It may be proper to premise that, in an age of criticism, his true stature has been fixed at six feet one inch and a quarter, English measure.

"The Emperor was of a ruddy complexion, with brown hair; of a well-made, handsome form, but a stern visage. His height was about eight of his own feet, which were very long. He was of a strong, robust make: his legs and thighs very stout, and his sinews firm. His face was thirteen inches long; his beard a palm; his nose half a palm; his forehead a foot over. His lion-like eyes flashed fire like carbuncles; his eye-brows were half a palm over. When he was angry, it was a terror to look upon him. He required eight spans for his girdle, besides what hung loose. He ate sparingly of bread; but a whole quarter of lamb, two fowls, a goose, or a large portion of pork; a peacock, crane, or a whole hare. He drank moderately of wine and water. He was so strong, that he could, at a single blow, cleave asunder an armed soldier on horseback from the head to the waist, and the horse likewise. He easily vaulted over four horses harnessed together; and could raise an armed man from the ground on his head, as he stood erect upon his hand." Vol. i. p. 36.

We now come to the treachery of Ganalon and the battle of Roncevaux.*

"When this famous Emperor had thus recovered Spain to the glory of God and St. James," he returned to Pampeluna, on his way to France. There were at that time, at Saragossa, two Saracen Kings, Marsir and Beligard, "sent by the Soldan of Babylon from Persia to Spain." To these roitelets, Charles despatched Ganalon, requiring them to be baptised and to pay tribute. They complied very readily with the latter part of the requisition, but concerted with the ambassador that diabolical scheme of treachery which was attended with such fatal consequences to the Emperor and his army. The rear guard, in which the whole body of the twelve peers happened to be marching, was cut to pieces. The death, however, of so may gallant spirits did not go unrevenged. Orlando pierced through the thickest array of the Moslem, dealing death on all sides, until he encountered and slew Marsir, one of their kings. The other made his escape by flight, with the shattered remains of his army. Of the Christians, only a few, under Theodoric and Baldwin sur-

---

* The only notice which Gibbon bestows upon an event so important in the History of Fiction, is the following:—"After his Spanish expedition, his rearguard was defeated, in the Pyrenæan mountains; and the soldiers, whose situation was irretrievable, and whose valor was useless, might accuse with their last breath the want of skill or caution of their general."—*Decline and Fall*, c. 49. To this is appended the following note—"In this action, the famous Rutland, Rolendo, Orlando, was slain—cum pluribus aliis. See the truth in Eginhard, (c. ix. pp. 51-56) and the fable in an ingenious supplement of M. Gaillard, (tom. iii. p. 474). The Spaniards are too proud of a victory which history ascribes to the Gascons, and romance to the Saracens." A totally different version of this affair is given by Beuter in the Cronica de Valencia, p. 158, as quoted by the translator of the work before us.

vived.   Orlando himself, covered with wounds, and very much
exhausted with rage and extreme toil, "felt that his hour was
come, and prepared himself to meet his fate in a manner becoming the first of Christian heroes."   There is something very
touching in this picture, in spite of the grotesque coloring of the
Pseudo Archbishop of Rheims.   After scattering the whole host
of the enemy, the Paladin "alighted from his steed and stretched
himself on the ground, beneath a tree, near a block of marble,
that stood erect in the meadows of Ronceval."

"Here drawing his sword, Durenda, which signifies a hard blow, a
sword of exquisite workmanship, fine temper, and resplendent brightness,
which he would sooner have lost his arm than parted with, as he held it
in his hand, regarding it earnestly, he addressed it in these words : 'O
sword of unparalled brightness, excellent dimensions, admirable temper,
and hilt of the whitest ivory, decorated with a splendid cross of gold, top-
ped by a berylline apple, engraved with the sacred name of God, endued
with keenness, and every other virtue, who now shall wield thee in battle ?
who shall call thee master ?   He that possessed thee was never conquered,
never daunted at the foe ; phantoms never appalled him.   Aided by Om-
nipotence, with thee did he destroy the Saracen, exalt the faith of Christ,
and acquire consummate glory.   Oft hast thou vindicated the blood of Jesus
against Pagans, Jews, and Heretics ; oft hewed off the hand and foot of
the robber, fulfilling divine justice.   O happy sword, keenest of the keen ;
never was one like thee !   He that made thee made not thy fellow !   Not
one escaped with life from thy stroke !   If the slothful, timid soldier should
now possess thee, or the base Saracen, my grief would be unspeakable !
Thus, then, do I prevent thy falling into their hands.'—He then struck the
block of marble thrice, which cleft it in the midst, and broke the sword in
twain.

"He now blew a loud blast with his horn, to summon any Christian concealed in the adjacent woods to his assistance, or to recal his friends beyond the pass.   This horn was endued with such power, that all other
horns were split by its sound ; and it is said that Orlando at that time blew it
with such vehemence, that he burst the veins and nerves of his neck.   The
sound reached the king's ears, who lay encamped in the valley still called
by his name, about eight miles from Ronceval, towards Gascony, being
carried so far by supernatural power.   Charles would have flown to his
succour, but was prevented by Ganalon, who, conscious of Orlando's sufferings, insinuated it was usual with him to sound his horn on light occasions.   'He is, perhaps,' said he, 'pursuing some wild beast, and the sound
echoes through the woods ; it will be fruitless, therefore, to seek him.'   O
wicked traitor, deceitful as Judas !   What dost thou merit?

"Orlando now grew very thirsty, and cried for water to Baldwin, who
just then approached him ; but, unable to find any, and seeing him so near
his end, he blessed him, and, again mounting his steed, galloped off for
assistance to the army.   Immediately after, Theodoric came up, and, bitterly grieving to see him in this condition, bade him strengthen his soul by
confessing his faith.   Orlando had that morning received the blessed Eucharist, and confessed his sins before he went to battle, this being the custom with all the warriors at that time, for which purpose many bishops and
monks attended the army to give them absolution.   The martyr of Christ
then cast up his eyes to heaven and cried, 'O Lord Jesus, for whose sake I
came into these barbarous regions, through thy aid only have I conquered
innumerable Pagans, enduring blows and wounds, reproach, derision, and

fatigue, heat and cold, hunger and thirst. To thee do I commit my soul in this trying hour. Thou, who didst suffer on the cross for those who deserved not thy favor, deliver my soul, I beseech thee, from eternal death! I confess myself a most grievous sinner, but thou mercifully dost forgive our sins; thou pitiest every one, and hatest nothing which thou hast made, covering the sins of the penitent in whatsoever day they turn unto thee with true contrition. O thou, who didst spare thy enemies, and the woman taken in adultery; who didst pardon Mary Magdalen, and look with compassion on the weeping Peter; who didst likewise open the gate of Paradise to the thief that confessed thee upon the cross; have mercy upon me, and receive my soul into thy everlasting rest!"—Vol. i. pp. 41–44.

There is a great deal more to the same effect; for Orlando made a most triumphant end. It appears from the following very satisfactory evidence, that on the very day he was slain, his soul was met on its way to heaven.

"What more shall we say? Whilst the soul of the blessed Orlando was leaving his body, I, Turpin, standing near the king in the valley of Charles, at the moment I was celebrating the mass of the dead, namely, on the sixteenth day of June, fell into a trance, and hearing the angelic choir sing aloud, I wondered what it might be. Now when they had ascended on high, behold there came after them a phalanx of terrible ones, like warriors returning from the spoil, bearing their prey. Presently I inquired of one of them what it meant, and was answered, 'we are bearing the soul of Marsir to hell, but yonder is Michael bearing the horn-winder to heaven.' When mass was over, I told the king what I had seen; and, whilst I was yet speaking, behold Baldwin rode up on Orlando's horse, and related what had befallen him, and where he had left the hero in the agonies of death, beside a stone in the meadows at the foot of the mountain; whereupon the whole army immediately marched back to Ronceval."—Vol. i. p. 47.

We omit the lamentations of Charles over the dead body of his nephew, as well as the embalming and subsequent burial of the dead, it different places in France. But it is proper to mention that the Emperor revenged, in the most exemplary manner, the loss which he had sustained, upon those who had been the authors of it. The sun stood still for three days, while he pursued the Saracens to the banks of the Ebro, and slaughtered several thousands of them—with Ganalon, he dealt still more severely. Having ordained a trial by single combat, Pinbel, the traitor's champion, (a caitiff often mentioned in the Orlando Furioso) was vanquished by Theodoric, and the accused himself torn to pieces by four wild horses. The death of Charlemagne, which had been revealed, as usual, to Archbishop Turpin, closes this strange eventful history.

So much for Turpin's Chronicle. We now proceed to the Ballads founded upon it, which occupy the remainder of the first and the whole of the second volume They are supposed, by the translator, to have been published as illustrations of Don Quixotte, in which all of them are mentioned with more or less particularity. We need not add that the point of view in which Cervantes regards them is that of burlesque and caricature. So true is it that in this tragic-farce of human life—this ludibrium rerum humanarum—there is but a single step from the sublime to the ridiculous, and that the most heroic devotedness and the loftiest aspirations of man are excellent game for the wit of the satirist, or the scoffings of the misanthrope. Alas!

> ——————Celsæ graviore casu
> Decidunt turres——

and too often "the paths of glory lead but to"—a jest.

But we are addressing ourselves to those who look at these matters through the medium of a romantic imagination—whose notions of "Rinaldo with his friends and associates,* and of Turpin and the Doseperes," have been formed not in the school of Cervantes, but in that of Boiardo and of Ariosto—who, in short, when they sit down to read a book of fiction consent "to become as little children," and make it a merit to believe, like honest Tertullian, because "the thing is impossible," rather than indulge their "reasoning pride," at the expense of their best interests, in scepticism and profane mockery. To such as have this sturdy faith we can promise a high gratification from the perusal of these Ballads—in the original, we mean, not in this editor's very mean translation of them. He has published the Spanish text on one page and his own work on the other, and it is difficult to imagine a more abominable perversion, than the latter presents. The great charm of ballad-writing consists in telling a metrical tale with spirit, and at the same time, with the perfect simplicity of style, and all the ease of a prose narrative. The smallest appearance of effort or constraint is fatal to its beauty and grace. For this reason the metrical forms of the Spanish Romances are better than those of any other language. The kind of verses almost universally adopted in them are what are called *Redondillas*—composed uniformly of four trochees. These four-footed lines run off so trippingly from the tongue that they are precisely what the Iambics were in Greek dramatic composition, which were chosen because they approached so nearly to prose, that it was difficult not to let them slip even in ordinary conversation. "Thanks to these Redondillas," as Bouterwek expresses it, "any one might sing to his guitar, with scarcely any effort of mind, the sentiments, whether of heroism or of tenderness which possessed his bosom : there was no curious criticism in these effusions, as to the quantity of the syllables, or the exactness of the rhymes. If it were a narrative of facts—a sort of composition, to which at length the name of *romance* became appropriated, verse after verse was uttered

---

* Mas ladrones que Caco, says that slashing and spirited reviewer, the Curate, in the sixth chapter of Don Quixotte, to which the reader is referred for a great deal of curious remark upon these old romances.

just as it occurred to the mind of the *improvisatore*—but when he wanted to express a series of *thoughts* or reflections, they were couched in verses distributed into periods, which produced regular strophes, known by the name of stanzas or couplets." (Estancias y coplas.) In short, "these venerable ancient song editors" took all manner of liberties with the rude prosody of their language, and were quite satisfied, if instead of exact rhyme and quantity, they blundered out a not unpleasing or inharmonious rythm. What aided them greatly in this, was a peculiarity of the Spanish language, which, in this artless versification, admits of imperfect rhymes, formed by a recurrence of the final vowel without the consonant of the preceding line. In this way these Redondillas, equally remarkable for simplicity and variety, took entire possession of the Ballads and almost of the drama of that language. But nothing can be imagined more unequal than the competition between this native simplicity and flowing ease, "which voluntary wake harmonious numbers" and the awkwardness and poverty of a mere uninspired tagger of rhymes like this translator, straining with all his might to make both ends meet in his beggarly versification. Sometimes he is solemn, emphatic and pompous. At other times, in his extremity, he errs on the opposite side, and turns the charming natural graces of the original into downright vulgarity. We take at random the following lines from the ballad of Don Gayferos, to exemplify this criticism.

The knight who was married to one of the daughters of the Emperor, was amusing himself at dice with another of the Paladins. His father-in-law, coming in and seeing him thus occupied, reproaches him in a strain such as Hector addressed to Paris under circumstances somewhat similar. "If you are as good at the use of your weapons, Gayferos, as you seem to be at the dice-board, go rescue your captive wife from the Moors. You know how I, at least, feel for her, for she is my own flesh and blood. Many sought to win her grace; but she smiled on none but you. Since you married her for love, love ought to protect her. Had any other knight been her husband, she would not be where she now is." The conduct of the young hero upon receiving this bitter taunt, is thus described :—

Gayferos que aquesto oyera,	When *renowned* Gayferos heard him,
Movido de gran pesar,	Deeply grieved the speech he bore,
Levantose del tablero	And uprising from the tables,
No quiriendo mas jugar.	*Vowed* that he would play no more.
A manos toma el tablero	And the tables rudely seizing,
Para haverle de arrojar,	*Fain* had dashed 'em to the ground;
Sino por quien con él juega	*But reflection soon returning,*
Que era hombre de linage.	*Kept his rage in decent bound.*
Jugaba con él Guarinos	*With a noble was* he playing,
Almirante de la mar ;	With the Admiral of the fleet ;

Voces dá por el Palacio,	Thro' the palace instant shouting,
Que al cielo quieren llegar.	*Fain* he would his uncle meet.
Preguntando, preguntando	Soon *he heard* that Count Orlando
Por su tio Don Roldan,	Was upon the point to ride;
Hallaronlo en el patio	In the court Gayferos found him,
Que queria cavalgar.	*Just as he had leaped astride.*

A literal prose translation will show how much is strained, emphatic and impertinent in the English lines—the vulgarity and doggrel speak for themselves. "Gayferos hearing this, deeply excited, (by the reproach) arose from the table, for he would play no more. He takes up the table (or board) in his hands, and would have thrown it with violence from him—but for his respect for the person with whom he was playing, who was a man of high rank (or descent). He was playing with Guarin, the Admiral. Then he cried aloud through the palace—so loudly that his voice seemed to mount up to the skies—calling again and again upon his uncle Orlando. He found him in the courtyard, just about to ride."

The dates and the authors of these early Ballads are, it is said, equally unknown. This has been ascribed to the contempt in which they were held by the classical scholars, who, in the course of the fifteenth century, acquired influence enough to give the tone to all literature. They considered these relics of barbarous times, as quite beneath the notice of men who had access to the models of Attic and Augustan elegance. Nobody will wonder at this prejudice who considers what is the invariable progress of the human mind from a state of complete ignorance to that of the highest refinement. The first efforts of genius are, like these before us, the spontaneous effusions of nature, uttered without any idea of rules, or pretensions to excellence, or fear of criticism. Out of the fulness of the heart the mouth speaketh. This is the whole sum and substance of the rhetoric and poetry of rude ages. The warm passion, the glowing conception, break forth in a simple, but fervid and vigorous eloquence.

> "With rude, majestic force they move the heart,
> And strength and nature make amends for art."

But there is more in it than this—there is even a suprising degree of *grace* in the operations of the mind, as in the motions of the body, in this savage state of society. It is the consciousness of perfect equality with those around them—the possession of that unqualified liberty of nature, ubi sentire, quæ velis et quæ sentias dicere liceat—the confidence not of experienced and disciplined talent, but of happy, unrebuked ignorance, that gives to our Indian orators the ease and imposing dignity which have so frequently been remarked in them. They speak well, because they are neither ambitious of speaking well nor afraid of speaking ill. No man is either sheepish, or stately and affected, until he has conceived the idea of a degree of excellence to which he feels that he has not attained, or of the terrors of a criticism to which he is apprehensive of being exposed. In this, as in a graver sense, the δουλιον ἦμαρ—the day which condemns him to feel his inferiority robs him of (more than) half his grace and power. So that, in this view, a little learning is a dangerous thing, for the same reason that what is called the second class of fashionable people are every where the stupidest and most disagreeable of any.

At the revival of letters, pretty nearly the same set of phenomena was exhibited every where. The age of creative genius, of passionate eloquence, of vast and profound and adventurous imaginings came on early. It was immediately after—nay, rather coeval with—that of legends and troubadours—the daybreak, as it were, while twilight, with its spectral imagery and shadowy wonders, still lingered in the vale and the wood. It is such an age that produced Dante and Chaucer. Then came a long period of sterility and blank vacancy—the æra in Italy, of the Filelfos and Poggios and Politians—of plodding, pedantic mediocrity, oppressed by its own acquirements and embarrassed by its own art, with just talent enough to perceive and to avoid the dangers of originality. A still more advanced age generally brings back the simplicity of nature, because it restores the confidence of genius—the Ariostos and the Macchiavellis take the place of the Dantes and Boccaccios, and, making allowance for improvement in minuter matters, extremes in literature—the perfection of discipline and the total absence of it—may be said to meet. In Spain, the age of imitative mediocrity came on about the same time as in other parts of Europe, but it, unfortunately, lasted much longer. Juan de Mena and the Marquisses of Santillana and Villena have been charged, by late critics, with being the first to enroll themselves under the banners of foreigners, and to bring the early national literature into discredit and oblivion. Whoever may have been the authors, or whatever the cause of this revolution, the fact is certain; nor, as we think, was a strain ever again heard within the borders of that land, so true to nature, so sweet, so touching, so heroic, as that of her old minstrelsy.

> "Say, is her voice less mighty than of yore,
> When her war-song was heard on Andalusia's shore?"

But although it may be impossible to assign its proper date to any particular ballad in the Romancero General, or other collections, yet it may be affirmed with confidence, by analogy to what has been observed in other languages,* that the most

* This is remarked of the old English Ballads by Dr. Percy.—Rel. v. iii. p. 5. To which we may add the following remark from the Historia de las Guerras Civiles de Granada, from which it would appear that some of these early ballads

simple, and strictly narrative or historical, are, probably, the most ancient of them. In the earliest stages of society, when there is no history, or indeed any other kind of knowledge, but what is preserved by oral tradition, not only the records, but the very laws of a country are apt to be preserved in verse, in aid of the memory. What is called the poetry of those ages, (that is, its metrical relics) is more subservient to the purposes of truth than of fiction, and, even when the historical outline comes to be filled up with legendary wonders, and coloured with the glow of an improved fancy, there is still, for some time, a closer adherence to fact than is afterwards observed in works of imagination. The bard, the scald, the minstrel, the rhapsodist are the first teachers of mankind and the great repositaries by profession of the experience and memorable doings of their rude tribes. Many examples might easily be adduced to shew how completely the poets of a primitive age fill the place of its philosophers and annalists. Thus, Solon, the law-giver, was so great a master of versification, that, it is affirmed by some one in Plato, he might even have rivalled Homer ; and it is remarked of Homer himself, by a geographer who seems better acquainted with Parnassus than with any other spot on the globe, that his romance was always founded upon, or mixed up with a good share of truth.* This is, at any rate, so far just that the Iliad, for its simplicity, its animation, its minute circumstantiality in description, and the air of earnestness and conviction that pervades its details, approaches, in many places, very nearly to the unaffected narrative style of an old border ballad.† Indeed, we have always felt this to be one of the peculiarities which most advantageously distinguish the Greek bard from his imitators in after times. His is true *epic* poetry—it not only has an *action*, but it is full of action. His narrative does not flag a moment, and, though he recounts very much the same scenes and incidents over and over again, you get through his twenty-four books without a tithe of the fatigue which any other poem of the same kind—not excepting the Gerusalemme—occasions, even to the most indefatigable reader, after the first edge of curiosity has been taken off. No other writer in the world, but this immediate successor of the rhapsodists and minstrels of a primitive age, could have made a readable volume of such length out of such materials ; if, indeed, the volume be (as it no doubt is, however) any thing more than a

were valued merely as history. The book is rather apocryphal, it must be owned—but it is good authority to such a point. Y aunque son Romances es muy buen traerlos á la memoria para los que agora vienen al mundo, porque intiendan la historia porque se cantavan. Y *aunque* los romances *son viejos* son buenos para el afeto que digo. p. 366,

* Ex μηδενὸς δὲ ἀληθοῦς ἀναπτειν καινὴν τετραλογίαν, οὐχ᾽ Ὁμηρικον.—Strabo, lib. i. c. 2. [This remark applicable to all Greek literature.]

[† Aristotle ascribes to Homer what he calls Ψιθομετρια.]

cento of legends and ballads, like Geoffrey's History. In this connection, we cannot refrain from making use of the following apposite observations of Dr. Percy, in his Essay on the Ancient English Minstrels :—"It is to be observed that so long as the minstrels subsisted, they seem never to have designed their rhymes for publication, and, probably, never committed them to writing themselves ; what copies are preserved of them are, doubtless, taken down from their mouths. But, as the old minstrels gradually wore out, a new race of ballad-writers succeeded—an inferior sort of minor poets, who wrote narrative songs merely for the press. Instances of both may be found in the reign of Elizabeth. * * * * The old minstrel ballads are in the northern dialect, abound with antique words and phrases, are extremely incorrect, and run into the utmost license of metre : they have also a romantic wildness, and are in the true spirit of chivalry. The other sort are written in exacter measure, have a low or subordinate correctness, sometimes bordering on the insipid, yet often well adapted to the pathetic ; these are generally in the southern dialect, exhibit a more modern phraseology, and are commonly descriptive of more modern manners." The following lines, from the ballad of Rinaldo of Montalban in this collection, seem to us to exemplify the latter description of poetry. They are so smooth and finished as to smack of an age less rude than that which produced some others of these relics, that of Calainos, for instance.

Quando aquel claro lucero
Sus rayos quiere embiar,
Esparcidos por la tierra
Por cada parte y lugar.

Quando los prados floridos
Suaves olores dán,
A mi preciado vergel
Me fuí para dár lugar
A la triste vida mia
Y muy gran necessidad.

Vida las rosas en flor,
Que querian yá ganar,
Hice una guirnalda de ellas
No hallando á quien la dár.

Por un bosquete despoblado
Comencé de caminar,
Y diera en una floresta
Do nadie suele passar.
En el dulce mes de Mayo
Yo me fuí por descansar,
Por medio de una arboleda
De ciprés, y de rosal.
De una huerta muy florida

"When the glorious sun revolving
Spreads his golden radiance round,
Genial warmth all nature cheering,
Clothes with verdure soft the ground.

Then the meads are all enamell'd,
Then the blooming flow'rs appear ;
Ev'ry eye with rapture glist'ning
Sees sweet Spring approaching near.

I alone to range my garden
Bent my solitary way,
Musing on the life of sorrow,
Still I led each irksome day.

There I saw the roses blowing;
O how lovely was their hue!
And a chaplet twin'd, but no one
Found to give the chaplet to.

Thro' a grove then devious wand'ring,
I perceiv'd a bed of flow'rs ;
'Twas the month of May, and pleasure
Wanton'd in the shady bow'rs.

In a fair alcove I rested
Of the rose and cypress made ;
All around this lovely garden
Was in beauteous tints array'd.

De jazmines, y arrayan,
Los cantos eran tan dulces,
Qué me hicieron parar,
De avecitas que por ellas,
No hacen sino volar,

There the jasmine and the myrtle
Pleas'd in gentle union grew;
Whilst the birds in soft notes thrilling
Form'd a heav'nly concert too.

Long I listen'd with enchantment,
  As they flew from spray to spray,
When the nightingale, sweet singing,
  Thus attun'd his plaintive lay :—

Papagayo, y ruiseñor
Decian en su cantar;

Donde vás el Caballero,
Atrás te quieras tornar,
Hombre que por aqui passa,
No puede vivo escapar.

"Whither art thou wand'ring, whither?
  "Listen to my warning strain ;
"Never Knight yet enter'd hither,
  "And escap'd with life again.

"Pleasure here too fondly reigning,
  "Will the hero's nerves unbrace,
"Circe's wanton cup disdaining,
  "Fly, oh ! fly the fatal place."

Mirando essas avecitas,
Su canto, y armonizar,
A sombra de un verde pino
Me senté por descansar.

I arose, and still I listen'd,
  As along the walks I stray'd ;
Then beneath a shady pine-tree
  Down my listless length I laid."
               Vol. i., pp. 35—39.

We may state in general terms that none of the old Ballads that have been current in Spain date farther back than the thirteenth century, and most of them are probably of much more recent date. In the *Historia de las Guerras Civiles de Granada*, a remarkable book, of which we may say something more by and bye—the distinction of *este Romance antiguo* occurs not unfrequently, and in some instances the *ancient* ballad and a more recent version of it are given together. The three periods of history, to which by far the greater part of these songs of love and war relate, are the invasion of Spain by Charlemagne—the adventures and achievements of the Cid—and the fortunes of the Moorish kingdom of Granada. Charlemagne's æra is the close of the eighth and the beginning of the ninth century. The Spaniards boast a hero contemporaneous with the Paladins, who proved himself, in a contest with Orlando, much more formidable than (as we have just seen) the giant Ferracute had been. This was Bernardo del Carpio, son of Doña Ximena, sister of the king of Leon and of Don Sancho de Saldaña. Beuter, in his Chronicle of Valencia, in a passage which has already been referred to, ascribes to him the honor of having done, or at least consummated, the mischief at Roncesvalles. But, as no allusion at all is made to him in the present collection before us, we shall say no more about him for the present. The Cid, Ruy Dias de Bivar, is the hero of the eleventh century, the very last year of which is made memorable by his death. He is beyond all comparison the most striking object, even in that age of lofty chevisance and wonderful emprize. He was living when the Normans conquered England, and established themselves, by an adventure as romantic as any thing in fable, in Naples and Sicily, and when the rude oratory of Peter the Hermit stirred up all Europe between the Clyde and the Pyrennees to a war, or rather series of wars, to be waged for two centuries together, in a distant region of the earth, for interests not of this world and a crown of more than mortal glory. Every thing dates from this æra—poetry has been inspired by it, romance seeks its heroes there, knighthood was established then, and the proudest nobility of Europe are glad to trace their line to a warrior who fought in Palestine, and to explain their blazonry by the history of a Crusade. The deeds of the Cid were celebrated so long ago as the beginning of the thirteenth century, in a poem which bears his name, and since that time ballads innumerable have diversified or perverted his story. In this Floresta, there is a single *romance* relating to him—the title of it is "The Ballad of the Moorish King who lost Valencia." We will quote some of the first stanzas, with a literal version, opposite:

Helo, helo por do viene El Moro por la calzada, Caballero á la gineta, Encima de una yegua vaya:	Look, look, where comes The Moor riding up the highway, Mounted in gallant style* Upon his fleet bay mare.
Borceguies morroquies Espuela de oro calzada, Una adarga ante sus pechos Y en su mano una azagaya.	His buskins are of morocco, A golden spur is upon his heel, A target before his breast, And in his hand a Moorish javelin.
Mirando estaba Valencia Como estaba bien cercada; O Valencia, O Valencia, De mal fuego seas quemada!	Intently gazed he at Valencia, How well enclosed it was; O Valencia, O Valencia, Mayest thou be given to a devouring fire.
Primero fuistes de Moros Que de Christianos ganada, Si la lanza no me miente A Moros serás tornada.	Thou wert a Moorish city, Ere thou wert conquer'd by Christians, But if my lance deceive me not, To the Moors thou shalt belong once more.
Aquel perro de aquel Cid Prenderlohe por la barba, Su muger Doña Ximena Será de mi cautivada.	For that dog of a Cid, I will pluck him by the beard, His wife Donna Ximena Shall be my slave.
Su hija Urraca Hernandez Será mi enamorada, &c.	His daughter Urraca Shall be my mistress, &c.

"My Cid" overhears this complimentary apostrophe, and bids his daughter show herself at the window, in order to detain the Moor until he shall have saddled his steed Babieca, and girded on his own good sword. Urraca makes her appearance accord-

* That is, with short stirrups, *à la Turque.*

ingly and receives the salutation of the King, which she returns quite lovingly :

Alá te guarde, Señora,
Mi Señora, Doña Urraca.

Allah be with thee, Lady,
My own Lady, Doña Urraca.

Assi, haga á vos Señor,
Buena sea vuestra llegáda ;
Siete años ha Rey, siete,
Que soy vuestra enamorada.

And be he with you too, Sir,
Most welcome in your coming,
'Tis seven long years, O King,
That I have been enamoured of you.

He is paying her back in her own coin with interest, when the footsteps of Babieca are heard. Away he flies like the wind and the Cid after him, until they come to a river, which the Moor crosses hastily in a boat. The Cid coming up to the bank, hurls his javelin at his foeman—addressing him at the same time in these words :

———— recoged yerno,
Recoged aquessa lanza,
Que quizá tiempo vendrá
Que os será bien demandada.

Pick up, my son-in law, pick up this lance—for perhaps the time will come, when it shall be demanded at your hands.

The rest of these Ballads all relate to Charlemagne and his Peers. The first of them is the famous *romance* of Calainos, which Ritson thinks (and with good reason) one of the most ancient among them. It is mentioned in Don Quixotte, and is so well known in Spain, that it is said to be a proverbial expression of contempt there, no *vale las coplas de Calainos*. With the most profound deference, however, for the Señor Sarmiento, upon whose authority this is affirmed, we presume to suggest that this saying may mean nothing more than that that venerable old ballad is in every body's mouth, like the Children of the Wood and Johnny Armstrong, and so it may be with it, as the wife of Bath sagely teaches of conjugal endearments, that "a glutted market makes provision cheap." But it must be owned that this *romance* of Calainos falls very far short of the merits of some of the other pieces in this collection. One of the best of them is the ballad of Gayferos, to which we have already had occasion to allude. Another remarkable one is that of Count Claros of Montalban, the son of the famous Paladin Rinaldo. The story relates an anecdote of one of Charlemagne's daughters, who are all of them known to have been very far above the *vulgar* prejudices of mankind in relation to their sex. Perhaps it is founded, as the translator conjectures, upon the well-known story of his secretary and historian, Eginhart. Those who read Spanish may be edified with the unceremonious gallantry of the following colloquy sublime.

Count Claros has past a sleepless night for love of Doña Clara. So at the first peep of dawn, he leaps out of bed, and calling up his chamberlain, puts on a dress, all glittering with scarlet and gold, and precious stones. His steed is caparisoned in the same gorgeous style, and is, in particular, tricked off with *three hundred* morris-bells jingling about his poitrail with a most delectable din. Thus equipped, he hurries to the imperial palace, and is presently upon his knees before his mistress. She returns his salutation, and goes on to address him—

Las palabras que prosigue Eran parar enamorar; Conde Claros, Conde Claros, El Señor de Montalvan.	Y otro dia de mañana Con cien Moros pelear, Si á todos no los venciesse, Mandassedesme matar.
Como haveis hermoso cuerpo Para con Moros lidiar! Respondiera el Conde Claros, Tal respuesta la fue á dár.	Calledes, Conde, calledes Y no os querais alabar, Que el que quiere servir damas, Assi lo [qu. no] debe hablar.
Mejor lo tengo, Señora, Para con damas holgar. Si yo os tuviesse Señora Esta noche á mi mandar,	Y al entrar en las battallas Bien se suele escusar; Sino lo creis Señora, Por las obras se verá.

He then swears, as Doña Urraca did to the Moorish king who lost Valencia, that he has been for seven years desperately in love with her, with other the like approved *fleurettes*. She tells him he is a gay deceiver, and so forth; but the result is that the Emperor, who is not quite as much pleased with Count Claros and his way of making love, as the princess had been, has him arrested and put in irons, and seated upon a mule ; and, not satisfied with thus disgracing him, though the Paladins all intercede for him, orders him to be sentenced to death by a jury of his peers—which is accordingly done. In this extremity, the Archbishop obtains leave to visit the unfortunate youth in prison, for the purpose of administering to him the usual ghostly consolations. The first words which he addresses to the Count are very chcracteristic of the times and manners. These words were most pathetic, says the book—they are as follows:—

Pesame de vos el Conde, Quanto me puede pesar, Que yerros por amores Dignos son de perdonar.*	I feel as deeply for you, Count, As it is possible I should feel, *For* the sins of lovers Deserve to be pardoned.

He repeats this wise saw again soon after, and tells him he ought to meet death very cheerfully, considering in how good a cause he is to suffer. His Page is so much of the same way of thinking, that he tells the Count he would rather change places with him than with the crabbed old Emperor, who has

---

* Count Claros had probably heard the same thing from his own father, if we may believe what Messer Lodovico says on the authority of the "good Turpin":

Pensò Rinaldo alquanto e poi rispose : Una donzella dunque de' morire, Perchè lasciò sfogar nell' amorose Sue braccia al suo amator tanto desire? Sià maladetto che tal legge pose,	E maladetto che la puo patire. Debitamente muore una crudele, Non chì da vita al su 'amator fedele. [*Orlando Fur.*, Cant. iv., 63.

condemned him to this honorable martyrdom. The Count, however, calls upon his young friend for a much lighter service than to act as his substitute on the scaffold—he only sends by him a request to his mistress to place herself so that his last looks may be turned upon her, assuring her that her presence would disarm death of its terrors and its sting. The Infanta, as she is called in the ballad, is in despair, and her sorrow is extremely well-painted. She rushes forth with the eloquent *abandon* of a woman made desperate by a conflict of high passions, and at length prevails upon her stern father to spare the Count's life on condition of his marrying her, and atoning for the lover's indiscretion by the virtues and fidelity of the husband.

Charlemagne is represented in a still more trying situation in by far the longest, and, perhaps, the most celebrated of these ballads, we mean that of the Marquis of Mantua. He is there made to act the part of the elder Brutus, and to pass sentence upon his own son, Carloto. This is the story which takes possession of the knight's imagination, after he had undergone that unmerciful drubbing from the mule-driver, mentioned in the fourth chapter of Don Quixotte. At the beginning of the next chapter, we see him sprawling upon the ground, from which he was utterly incapable of rising, so dreadfully belabored had he been by that rascally churl. In this uncomfortable situation, he bethinks him, as usual, of his books, and "his anger recalled to his memory the story of Valdovinos and the Marquis of Mantua, when Carloto left him wounded in the mountain—a story known by children, not forgotten by youth, celebrated and even believed by the old, and for all that, as apocryphal as the miracles of Mahomet."

The outline of this interesting tale is as follows :—The Marquis of Mantua—Danes Urgèl el Léal—is engaged in a stag chase, when a violent thunder storm arising, his company is scattered, and he finds himself alone in the midst of the forest. At a loss whither to direct his course, he gives the rein to his gallant steed, who presses forward with such incredible expedition, that Danes Urgèl is presently at the distance of more than ten leagues. Here he enters a wood of pines, and thence descending into a valley—his attention is suddenly arrested by a fearful cry of distress. Dismounting from his steed, he advances on foot a few steps, and sees the carcase of a war-horse, caparisoned as for battle, and horribly maimed in almost every part of his body. A little further onward, he hears a voice uttering a devout and doleful prayer to the Virgin. His curiosity is now worked up to a painful pitch of excitement—he makes an opening by cutting down the thick bushes and foliage, and sees the ground all stained with gore—immediately after, he espies a knight seated under an oak, cased in armour from head to foot, but without any offensive weapon. The Marquis pauses and listens in breathless silence. The first words uttered by the wounded cavalier are those quoted in the chapter of Don Quixotte just referred to. It is, therefore, impossible to repeat them with any gravity, much less in that deeply pathetic tone with which they were, no doubt, uttered by a dying lover.

Donde estás, Señora mia,	"Alas! where are you, lady dear,
Que no te pena mi mal?	That for my pains you do not moan?
O no lo sabes, Señora,	Thou little know'st what ails me here,
O eres falsa ó desleal.	Or art to me disloyal grown."
	[*Ozell.*

This address to his lady fair becomes gradually more affectionate and confiding as it proceeds, and is followed by an apostrophe to all and singular the Twelve Peers, whom he reproaches for not knowing that he stands in need of their assistance—to the Emperor on whose justice he relies, even when it is invoked against his own son—to God, whose mercy he supplicates—to his assassin Don Carloto—to his own mother, and last of all, to the Marquis of Mantua himself. The Marquis now approaches him, and, without disclosing who he is, inquires into the story of his calamity. Baldwin (for it was he) states that he is the son of the King of Dacia, one of the *Doseperes*—that the Marquis of Mantua is his uncle—and that he was married to the beautiful "Infanta Sevilla or Sybilla," whose fatal charms had been the source of all his wo. For the Prince Don Carloto, being desperately enamoured of her, and having hitherto failed in his attempts upon her virtue, had determined to make away with her unfortunate husband, for the purpose of succeeding him in that relation to Sevilla. That, with this design, he had upon some fair pretext, decoyed his victim into the forest, where the unhappy young man was set upon by three assassins, and left in his present deplorable situation. He beseeches the stranger Knight to bear these tidings to his friends. Here the feelings of the Marquis of Mantua become uncontrollable—and he gives vent to them in a truly pathetic manner; for, after loosing all his own children, he had adopted this young man as his heir, and centered his affections in him. But he was now a desolate old man, and would not be comforted. This scene is interrupted by the arrival of Baldwin's squire, bringing with him a Hermit, who dwelt hard by in the forest. The holy recluse was a priest, and he was come to shrive the dying cavalier. After this melancholy office is performed, and Baldwin has breathed his last, the Marquis asks what wood that was and who was its lord.

Tal respuesta le fue á dár:	"Thus the ancient Hermit answer'd,
Haveis de saber señor,	You shall soon hear what he said—
Que esta tierra es sin poblar;	'Know, my lord, from this wild country
Otro tiempo fue poblada,	All the people long have fled.
Despoblóse por gran mal,	

Por batallas muy crueles,
Que huvo en la Christiandad.
A esta llaman la floresta,
Sin ventura, y de pesar;
Porque nunca Caballero
En ellá aconteció entrar,
Que saliesse sin gran daño,
O desastre desigual.

Esta tierra es del Marqués
De Mantua, la gran Ciudad;
Hasta Mantua son cien millas,
Sin poblacion, ni lugar:

Sino solo una Hermita,
Que á seis leguas de aqui está;
Donde yo estoy retraído,
Por el mundo me apartar.

'Once a region fair and fertile,
Till a sad mischance befel;
Fatal wars throughout prevailing,
Their disastrous horrors tell.

'Of distress and lamentation
Is this gloomy forest call'd;
Never Knight its bounds hath enter'd
But some dire mishap enthrall'd.

'To fair Mantua's noble Marquis
Does this country appertain;
'Tis a hundred miles to Mantua,
Yet between no souls remain.

'Six leagues hence, amidst the forest,
Stands a lonely Hermit's cell;
In it, from the world secluded,
There in gentle peace I dwell.'"
Vol. ii., pp. 100—103.

The Marquis now questions the squire, who gives him a detailed account of the treachery of Carloto. He then binds himself by the vow so pleasantly ridiculed by Cervantes in that passage (c. xii. b. 2) where the knight, after his combat with the Biscayan, finding his helmet quite demolished, laying his hand upon his sword, and, lifting up his eyes to heaven, pronounces the following oath, "I swear by the creator of all things, and by all that is written in the four Evangelists, to lead the life which the Marquis of Mantua led when he made a vow to revenge the death of Baldwin; not to eat food upon a table cloth, nor—with many other things which though I do not remember I here consider as expressed,* until I have taken vengeance upon him who has done me this injury."

The second part of the Ballad is an account of the embassy

* This vow being quite a curiosity, we publish it here for the readers of Spanish.

Puso la mano en el ara,
Que estaba sobre el altar,
A los pies de un crucifixo
Jurando comenzó á hablar.

Juro por Dios poderoso,
Y á Santa Maria su Madre,
Y al Santo Sacramento,
Que aqui suelen celebrar.

De nunca peynar mis canas,
Ni de mis barbas cortar,
De no vestir otras ropas,
Ni renovar el calzar.

De nunca entrar en poblado,
Ni las armas me quitar,
Sino fuera solo una hora
Para mi cuerpo limpiar.

De no comer en manteles,
Ni á la mesa me assentar.

Hasta que muera Carloto,
Por justicia, ó pelear,
O morir en la demanda,
Manteniendo la verdad.

Y si justicia me niegan,
Sobre esta gran maldad,
De con mi estado, y persona
Contra Francia guerrear,

Y manteniendo la guerra,
Vencer, ó en ella acabar.
Y por este juramento
Prometo de no enterrar,

El cuerpo de Baldovinos,
Hasta su merte vengar.

sent by the Marquis to the Emperor to demand that the murderer of his nephew should be brought to justice. His delegates were the count of Irlos and the duke of Sanson, men of the highest rank, and "of the twelve who ate together at the Round Table." They have an audience—open their business, and enforce the demand of their principal, by the most persuasive topics. The Emperor, as may naturally be supposed, was in very great tribulation, but he comes to the determination to see justice done, "as it was ever wont to be in France, without distinction of persons."

> Assi al pobre, como al rico,
> Assi al chico, como al grande
> Y tambien al extrangero,
> Como al proprio natural.

He only begs to be excused from personally assisting at the trial, but appoints commissioners, with plenary powers, to conduct it, whether it be by witnesses or by wager of battle. A safe conduct is granted to the Marquis, who comes attended by a brilliant and formidable retinue, and encamps (according to his vow) *without* the walls of the city.

The third part contains the judgment of the court, which is drawn up with all the pedantic formality of the bar. The sentence passed upon the young Prince was less proportionate to his rank than to his base treachery. He is ordered to be dragged on the ground by a wild colt, and beheaded and quartered like a common felon. In great consternation at this harsh and ignominious doom, Carloto writes to his cousin Orlando, who determines to come to his rescue, but, his intention being discovered, is prevented by an anticipated execution of the sentence. The fourth part describes the Exéquies of Baldwin. It is much shorter than the other three parts, but is excellent in its way. The last stanza reminded us of the famous line in the dirge of Sir John Moore—"We left him alone with his glory."

> Lo meten en el sepulchro;   And then they lay him in the tomb
> Como usarse soleá;   As all the dead must lie—
> *Quedando el cuerpo con fama*   Fame dwells there with his cold re-
> Con gloriá el alma subia.   mains,
>   His spirit has soar'd on high.

We are so much beyond the limits which we had assigned to this article, that we must defer to a future opportunity many of the remarks we purposed making in relation to the fortunes and the influence of the Moorish kingdom of Granada. This is the last of the three periods to which, as we remarked just now, these old ballads principally relate. There are few subjects that kindle up our enthusiasm for the romantic and the chivalrous, (and we are not ashamed to confess this fondness) so much as the factions of the Zegris and the Abencerrages, and the duels, jousts and tournaments which continually occurred in that famous *plain*, by the Fuente del Pino, between Moorish or Christian and Moorish knights.* Some of the ballads, relating to those encounters, are most admirable specimens of this simple poetry. Indeed the work just referred to in a note is a mere romance of chivalry, written in what has been called the Varronian style, that is, partly in prose and partly in verse, the former being little more than a loose paraphrase of the latter, or a running commentary upon it. It is just such a chronicle as we may suppose that of Cide Hamete Benengeli—the imaginary authority of Cervantes—would have been. A cursory mention is made of the foundation of the city of Granada in very remote times, and the origin of the kingdom in the thirteenth century—of the eighteen kings who successively held its sceptre—and of the thirty-two noble families which at once adorned and defended it. But the narrative does not properly begin before the reign of the last (the nineteenth) king, Muley Hazen and his son Boaudilin, called the Rey Chico, or Little King. It then unfolds the petty rivalships and jealousies, which at length produced a fatal feud in the court of the latter, and contributed to the conquest of the country by Ferdinand and Isabella. Never did so important an event spring out of causes apparently so insignificant. The honest chronicler writes a mere court calendar—a tale of lord and lady gay—

> ———— races and games
> And tilting furniture, emblazoned shields,
> Impresses quaint, caparisons and steeds;
> Basings and tinsel trappings, gorgeous knights
> At joust and tournament—then marshalled feast
> Served up with sewer and seneschal.

The situation of Granada, in relation to the Christian power in Spain, from the middle of the thirteenth to the close of the fifteenth century, was a highly interesting one. As Toledo, and Valencia, and Cordova and Seville successively fell; as the boundaries of Islam were narrowed down by the progress of the Christian arms, this last strong hold of the Moors received new accessions every day, and ultimately became the asylum of the greater part of the race. It was for the two last centuries a scene of perpetual war—the orchestra of Mars, as Epaminondas called his own Bæotia—and often even in times of truce (for *peace* there was none) would a master of Alcantara or Calatrava—a Saavedra or a Ponce de Leon—gallop in defiance about the vega, or rein up his war-horse before the Alhambra, while

---

* The title of the old fabulous chronicle of this kingdom, which now lies before us, is Historia de los Vandos de los Zegoris y Abencerrages, Cavalleros Moros de Granada, de las civiles guerras que uvo en ella y battallas particulares que se dieron en la vega entre Christianos y Moros, hasta que el rey Don Fernando Quinto gano este Reyno.

each Paynim *gentleman* burned to enter the lists with him, and to exhibit his prowess to the Galianas and the Daraxas, in a joust to the utterance.

Independently of the influence, real or imaginary, which they are supposed to have exercised over modern literature, there is something exceedingly brilliant and captivating in these pictures of Moorish life. The splendor of oriental imagination is there— the soft and bewitching voluptuousness of those bright climes, where the earth is ever gay with flowers and the whole air loaded with perfumes, and the sky lighted up with a cloudless and tranquil glory. The dreams of that "delightful londe of faerie" where the fancy of Spenser lingered so fondly, seem to be realized in these sunny regions. In the garden of Generalife, with its fresh fountains and its myrtle bowers, the very atmosphere breathed of poetry and love. But the sensibility of the Moors of Spain was refined by the imagination which it awakened and warmed. The Ommiades of Cordova, as is well known, rivalled the Abassides in their patronage of letters, and the arts of cultivated taste at once heightened and chastened every enjoyment of a life of pleasaunce.

> Such the gay splendor, the luxurious state,
> Of Caliphs old, who, on the Tigris' shore,
> In mighty Bagdad, populous and great,
> Held their bright court, where was of ladies store,
> And verse, love, music, still the garland wore.
> When sleep was coy, the bard, in waiting there,
> Cheered the lone midnight with the muse's lore;
> Composing music bade his dreams be fair,
> And music lent new sweetness to the morning air.

SIR PHILIP SIDNEY'S MISCELLANIES.

The Miscellaneous Works of Sir Philip Sidney, Knight. With a Life of the Author, and Illustrative Notes. By WILLIAM GRAY, Esq., of Magdalen College and the Inner Temple. 1829.

THE reputation of Sir Philip Sidney, as a knight and a gentleman, is familiar to every body, and may be summed up in the following apostrophe to a Preux Chevalier, which is a perfect picture of that old-fashioned character. "And now I dare say," exclaims Sir Bohort in the Morte Arthur, "that Sir Launcelot there thou liest; thou were never matched of none earthly hands. And thou were the curtiest knight that ever bare shield. And thou were the truest freende to thy lover that ever bestrode horse. And thou were the truest lover of a sinful man that ever loved woman. And thou were the goodliest person that ever came among prece (press) of knyghtes. And thou were the meekest man and the gentillest that ever ate in hal among ladies. And thou were the sternest knight to thy mortal foe, that ever put spere in rest." But his renown as a scholar and a poet, though equally high among his contemporaries, has not proved so enduring; and many of our readers, we have no doubt, will be surprised to learn what immense literary honours have been showered down upon this rival of Bayard, and right worthy successor of Chandos and Du Guesclin. We are informed by his biographers that no fewer than two hundred authors have borne testimony to his merits. He had not attained his twentieth year when he was honoured with the friendship and the correspondence of Hubert Languet—then an old man, universally esteemed in Europe for his learning, integrity and political wisdom. The muse of Spenser, which he patronized, and the graver pen of Camden united in eulogizing him. The two universities poured out three volumes of scholastic lamentation over his untimely grave. The "Royal Solomon," King James I., wrote his epitaph both in Latin and English. An elegant scholar would have no other inscription upon his own tomb-stone, save that he had been "tutor of Sir Philip Sidney;" and Lord Brooke—the well-known Fulke Greville—took the same means of perpetuating the memory of his intimacy with that accomplished person. Some, perhaps a considerable portion, of this popularity and renown, was, doubtless, owing to the favour of

Elizabeth and the influence of Leicester. But, long after these transient causes had ceased to operate, men of learning and taste spoke of his literary talents with high, and even with *exalted* praise. Dr. Young characterizes the "Arcadia," as the "charm of ages." Johnson, in the preface to his Dictionary, associates Sidney with Spenser, as an authority in our language—as a writer, in whose works all the richness, variety and compass of English poetic diction have been displayed. And, what is still more extraordinary, the sober and elegant Sir William Temple speaks of our author as "the greatest poet and the noblest genius of any that have left writings [*subaudi*, of a certain sort] behind them, or published in ours or any other language—a person, born capable not only of forming the greatest idea, but leaving the noblest example, if the length of his life had been equal to the excellence of his wit and his virtues."

It is, on the other hand, quite amusing to contrast with these high-flown panegyrics the dogmatical and contemptuous criticism of Horace Walpole, who treats the reputation of Sidney as a *hum* of the first magnitude. The remarks of this Iconoclast by profession—this wayward and opiniated sceptic whose perverse delight it was to doubt where others believed, and decry what all the world admired—may be found in his Catalogue of Royal and Noble Authors in the notice of Fulke Greville. It is due to him, however, to state that some of our contemporaries have shewn themselves inclined to the same way of thinking. This wide diversity of opinion as to the merits of a person, in every point of view so interesting, is calculated to awaken the liveliest curiosity, and will, no doubt, supersede the necessity of an apology for troubling our readers with a few remarks suggested by the volume under review.

As we shall confine ourselves principally to the literary character of Sir Philip Sidney, and to that character, as it is exhibited in the work before us, we shall only remind our readers that he acted a most conspicuous part in the affairs of his time—that, after receiving a liberal education, he was appointed, at the early age of twenty-one, ambassador to the Court of the Emperor Rodolph—that his influence with Elizabeth's government was deemed considerable enough to be put into requisition by Du Plessis Mornay, on behalf of the Huguenots—that, happening to be at Paris on the dreadful night of the St. Bartholomew, he conceived against the Catholics a hostility unusually intense, even in that age of bigotry and persecution, and, by a remonstrance published in this miscellany, did confessedly more, than any single person, to prevent the marriage of the Queen with the Duke d'Alençon—that his mother was a sister, and himself the favorite relative and presumptive heir of the insolent Leicester—and, finally, that, in the campaign of 1586, against the Spaniards in the Low Countries, he received a mortal wound at the battle of Zutphen, and died, a few days afterwards, the death of a knight and a christian, at the age of only thirty-two years.

It is obvious to observe that the hasty productions of one who died at so early an age, and was so deeply engaged in the affairs of active life, ought not to be brought into comparison with the master-pieces of professed authors. It is not very common to see men of business or men of fashion—and Sidney united in himself both these characters—even in this age of universal authorship—leaving behind them, in the maturity of their faculties, any thing that may challenge the attention of posterity. We are, therefore, bound in fairness to look upon these remains with an indulgent eye—non enim, as Cicero has it, *res* laudanda, sed *spes*. Considering the pieces in the miscellany before us, rather as promises of future excellence, than as the finished works of a ripe mind, we think that they entitle their author, if not to all the praise that has been bestowed upon them, at least to a good share of it.

The pieces collected in the volume before us are all the works of Sir Philip Sidney, except the Arcadia and the Psalms. They are as follows : 1. The Defence of Poesy. 2. Astrophel and Stella. 3. Miscellaneous Poems. 4. The Lady of May, a Masque. 5. A Letter to Queen Elizabeth, in the year 1580, dissuading her from marrying *Monsieur*, (the then Duke of Anjou). 6. A Discourse in defence of the Earl of Leicester. 7. Letters. Of these, the first is the most elaborate of his prose compositions, and, in our opinion, by far the most able and finished of his works. Walpole gives the preference to the Defence of Leicester; but the truth is that he does not seem to have even read the fine essay which we have just mentioned. So far was the vindication alluded to from being regarded by the author and his friends as a master-piece, that it was never published until the Sidney papers appeared in the course of the last century. As an argument, it is admitted to be a failure ; nor, indeed, could it be otherwise, for the conduct of the base and tyrannical favorite was altogether indefensible. Accordingly, Sir Philip takes much more pains to clear up the doubts thrown upon the blood of the Dudleys, than to refute the graver charges set forth in "Father Parson's Green Coat," and other publications of the exiled Catholics. Upon these charges, he takes issue in the old feudal way. He pleads "not guilty" in round terms— tells his adversary he "lies in his throat," and gives him to be informed, that "he (Sir Philip) will be ready to justify upon him in any place of Europe, where he shall assign him a free place of coming, within three months after the publishing of these presents." Certainly we are not to look to a controversy settled by wager of battle, for the very best specimen of dialectics. The letter to Queen Elizabeth is a production, in every point of view, of a much higher order. It is written, as Hume observes, with "unusual elegance of expression, as well as force of reasoning;" and Zouch has not scrupled to claim for it the honor of having rescued England from the tyranny of a foreign race. It is hard to say what determined Elizabeth ultimately to reject her youthful lover, or whether that vain old coquette ever seriously entertained the idea of a marriage so outrageously disproportionate and unsuitable. It is certain, however, that the flirtation was become alarmingly warm and vehement, and that even Burleigh and Walsingham considered the "maiden reign" as at an end, when this young champion came to the rescue. That Elizabeth was far from being indifferent to her suitor, and that it was quite a perilous undertaking to canvass his pretensions too freely, may be inferred from the cruel punishment inflicted on the author and publisher of a pamphlet, written about the same time, entitled, "The Discoverie of the Gaping Gulph, whereinto England is like to be swallowed by a French marriage, if the Lorde forbid not the bands by letting her Majestie see the sin and punishment thereof." These two pragmatical patriots—Stubbs, a member of Lincoln's Inn, and Page, a painter—were condemned to lose their right hands as libellers, and underwent that sentence without mercy. This shocking piece of barbarity was witnessed by the learned Camden. It is, by the bye, a fair specimen of the humanity of those times— distinguished above all others by the cultivation of what scholars call the *literæ humaniores*, and by an astonishing, perhaps, unparalleled development of talent in every intellectual pursuit, whether in active or speculative life.

"The Defence of Poesy" is supposed to have been written about 1581—a year after Spenser is conjectured to have commenced the Fairy Queen, and sixteen years before the first plays of Shakspeare that made their appearance in print—Romeo and Juliet and Richard the Second and Third—were given to the world. We are not disposed to dissemble that we have conceived from this admirable essay—written when its author was only twenty-seven years of age—a very high idea of Sir Philip's talents. It is a masterly exposition of the subject, and, as the book is but rarely to be met with in this country, we shall furnish our readers with pretty copious extracts from it. For, although the *very* cause which is said to have produced it has long ago ceased to operate and even to exist, there is still, and ever will be, a considerable party entertaining the opinions so ably combated here. If we are to take what our author says, *au pied de lettre*, "he had most just cause to make a pitiful defence of poor poetry, which, from almost the highest estimation of learning, was fallen to be the laughing-stock of children." It is certain that, through a long tract of time, her voice had been almost mute in England. With the exception of Surrey, Wyat and Sackville—meritorious, but still inferior poets—two centuries had passed away without producing a single name worthy to be had in remembrance by posterity. Chaucer and Gower, as we observed on a former occasion, had hitherto found as few successors as Dante and Petrarch ; while, in both countries, the national literature, after this period of darkness, "burst forth into sudden blaze" about the same time, or at no great interval. It is not improbable that this coincidence in so striking a state of facts was produced by some general cause—at least, by some cause common both to Italy and England. But however that may be, the revival of poetry had to encounter in the latter, an obstacle altogether unknown in the former country. This was the rigorous, self-mortifying fanaticism of the Puritans. We do not mean to derogate from the merit of the sect, whose stern discipline, like that of their archetypes in heathen antiquity, the Stoics, was so admirably fitted for a period of trial and fiery persecution, and taught so many patriots and heroes, to think, to act, and to die, as becomes men devoted to duty and to liberty. We are too well aware what the world—what we in particular, owe to the Long Parliament, and who *they* were that most zealously promoted the reforms which it made in the Constitutional Law of England. It is no serious objection with us, as it seems to have been with Hume, to Hampden, Vane, Pym, &c., that their leisure moments were devoted to the worship of God, after their own fashion, however uncouth that fashion, instead of being employed, as such moments were wont to be by Brutus and his compeers, in literary studies or elegant social converse. But, highly as we appreciate the political services of these great men, we must be allowed to dissent from some of their views of human nature. Their imaginations were so strongly possessed with what they considered as the abominations of idolatry in those "gay religions full of pomp and gold," from which they were desirous of purging England, that they could tolerate in the church nothing but the most absolute simplicity of forms, and the severest spirituality in worship. The same modes of thought, were naturally extended to other subjects. In this vale of tears, how absurd, how criminal was it to be gay ! How could a being, accountable for every idle thought, indulge his fancy, with impunity, in vain and chimerical figments, in foolish dreams of what he never could expect, or should never wish to see realized ! When every imagination of the thoughts of his heart was evil only, and his whole being was so infected with the taint of original sin, that a life of ascetic abstinence, uninterrupted devotion, and penitential tears, could not, without the influences of His grace, restore his fallen nature—amidst the temptations of the world, the flesh and the devil—was it *safe* to inflame the mind with visions of pleasure and beauty, and to stimulate the senses by the soft delights, the syren melody, the false enchantments of poetry and song? The curse of idolatry was denounced against him, if his hands should make a graven image of divinity; was there no guilt in gloating with secret fondness and almost with adoration upon the indwelling images of false gods and their obscenities, which the books of old bards and a quaint mythology would raise up in his mind? We, of course, speak only of those who pushed these opinions to the greatest extreme. We know that, a generation or two after Sidney's work was published, Milton—puritan as he was in many respects, to his heart's core—maintained the same opinions, and uttered them with incomparably greater power, in his own gorgeous and magnificent prose. We are, also, aware that the biography of Col. Hutchinson and his accomplished wife exhibits the same character, when it had been much softened down by time and social intercourse, in the most amiable and winning form. But, in Sidney's time, there was all the exaggeration of a new-born zeal in that sect. They carried on their hostilities against idols of all sorts, or what they deemed so, *recentibus odiis*, as Tacitus expresses it—with the keenness of personal resentment, with the unsparing fury of a tumultuary insurrection.

But, independently of religious opinions, there is a standing party in all countries—especially in this—which wages war against poetry, as *proving* nothing—as leading to no *practical* results—as doing nothing to advance the "greatest good of the greatest number." This objection comes from the *utilitarian* and the economist, and it is not the first time that we have had occasion to advert to it.

> O foolishness of men! that lend their ears
> To those budge doctors of the Stoic fur,
> And fetch their precepts from the Cynic tub,
> Praising the lean and hollow abstinence.

Our answer to the dogmas of this school is the same that was made to the Stoics two thousand years ago. They aim at a degree of perfection—if apathy *is* perfection—quite inconsistent with the nature of man and his relation to the world about him. They treat him as if he were no-*body*, but all understanding—a mere mathematical machine, whose only object is to *know*, whose only business is to *reason*, and whose whole conduct in life is to be a sort of practical *demonstration*. All instinctive impulse, however generous; all uncalculating affection, however sweet and consoling; all feeling, in short—unguarded, natural feeling—is unworthy of a rational being, much more of a supremely wise man. According to this theory, taste, and the sense of beauty and of melody, were given us in vain. Imagination is no part of our original nature, but a consequence, rather, and proof of its corruption. Nature is lovely in vain. Nay, it is worse than in vain that she has poured her bounties forth with such a lavish hand, and covered the earth with odours, fruits and flowers*—with so many sources of enjoyment—with so many scenes of magnificence and attraction—all, but to delude, to ensnare and to destroy us! Every thing about us, and within us, and above us, is full of poetry—for every thing is full of sublimity and beauty—every thing is calculated to inspire admiration or awaken love in rational creatures and in them alone—yet to enjoy the very pleasures—to cultivate the very perceptions and faculties that most distinguish them from the brutes that perish, is folly or worse, in the opinions of those who talk, in the loftiest strain, of the privileges and pre eminence of human reason! But there is another objection to this prosaic morality, and a more serious one, than that of its being either morose and ungainly in itself, or inconsistent with the constitution and analogies of nature. It tends to harden, and, consequently, to corrupt the heart, by perverting the understanding. There is a saying of Theophrastus, (we believe it is) which, as we interpret it, expresses our idea very pointedly— ἁπάντων μεν ζητοῦντες λόγον, ἀναιροῦσι λόγον. Those who exact a reason for every thing, destroys reason itself.† This is certainly true of morality. No one is in a surer way to become completely *roué*—to use a coarse but expressive word—quibble away all sound principles, and kindly, sincere and generous sensibility, than he who attempts to reduce this utilitarian system rigidly to practice. It is *ex vi termini* calculating. Every thing is summed up in that word. Even supposing a man to do all the duties of life with scrupulous punctuality on calculation, he would be the most unamiable (however respectable) being alive. But the tendency of that system is still worse : it is demoralizing, because, for many of our strongest natural feelings it is difficult to assign any reason, which a subtle dialectician may not render very questionable—and the dialecticians, trained in this cold and heartless school, are sure to be not only subtle, but captious.‡ They are taught to consider every thing as matter of proof, and they soon learn to treat every thing as subject to controversy. Nothing is safe or sacred—there is no sanctuary in the heart into which the profane voice of doubt is not allowed

[* "For immediately there was great and innumerable fruit, and many and divers pleasures for the taste, and flowers of unchangeable hue, and odours of wonderful smell." ii. Esdras, 6, 44.]

† Le raisonnement en bannit la raison.—*Molière.*

[‡ Cf. Arist. Sop. 1. c. 2 ; also Magna Moralia, 13. 1 c. 1., "making virtue ἐπιστήμη excludes ἦθος and πάθος, and so wrong."]

to penetrate—there are no titles to veneration and love, which have been consecrated by universal acquiescence. Whatever the shallow and self-sufficient reason of the sceptic does not fully approve is regarded as a prejudice, and, in his theory, no prejudice can be salutary. The result is universal doubt, and in many cases—chastity for instance—even to *doubt* is to be defiled. *Qui deliberant descivere.* Why should a man love his child with such a blind, doating, self-devoted love? Why should it be considered as so exalted a virtue to love one's country—the most miserable spot on earth, perhaps—an Ithaca for example—so much, as not only to prefer it, as Ulysses did, to one's own immortality; but to regard its prosperity as of more consequence than the happiness of the whole world besides, and to act accordingly? Such feelings, if not, in fact, mere prejudices, are so much like them that it were extremely dangerous to suffer them to be seriously drawn into question. We do not speak theoretically upon this subject. We have seen them drawn into question within the last forty years, and the discussion of them has been attended with precisely such consequences, as we should have anticipated, *à priori.*

True poetry—like true eloquence—is the voice of nature appealing to the heart with its utmost sublimity and power. Its precepts differ from those of philosophy only in their effect. Instead of teaching merely, it persuades, elevates, inspires. It excites a feeling where the other leaves only an opinion or a maxim. It proposes examples of ideal excellence, and raises virtue into heroism. "The Scripture also affords us a divine pastoral drama in the Song of Solomon, consisting of two persons and a double chorus, as Origen rightly judges. And the Apocalypse of St. John is the majestic image of a high and stately tragedy, shutting up and intermingling her solemn scenes and acts with a seven-fold chorus of hallelujahs and harping symphonies; and this, my opinion, the grave authority of Pareus commenting that book is sufficient to confirm. Or if occasion shall lead to imitate those magnific odes and hymns, wherein Pandarus and Callimachus are in most things worthy, some others in their frame judicious, in their matter most an end faulty. But those frequent songs throughout the law and prophets beyond all these, not in their divine argument alone, but in the very critical art of composition, may be easily made appear, over all the kinds of lyric poesy, to be incomparable. These abilities, wheresoever they be found, are the inspired gift of God rarely bestowed, but yet to some (though most abuse) in every nation; and are of power, beside the office of a pulpit, to inbreed and cherish in a great people the seeds of virtue and public civility, to allay the perturbations of the mind and set the affections in right tune; to celebrate, in glorious and lofty hymns, the throne and equipage of God's almightiness, and what he works and what he suffers to be wrought with high providence in his church ; to sing victorious agonies of martyrs and saints, the deeds and triumphs of just and pious nations, doing valiantly through faith against the enemies of Christ. And, lastly, whatsoever in religion is holy and sublime, in virtue amiable or grave ; whatsoever hath passion or admiration in all the changes of that which is called fortune from without, or the wily subtleties or refluxes of man's thoughts from within ; all these things with a solid and treatable smoothness to point out and describe.* Teaching over the whole book of sanctity and virtue, through all the instances of example, with such delight to those especially of soft and delicious temper, who will not so much as look upon truth herself unless they see her elegantly dressed, that, whereas the paths of honesty and good life appear now rugged and difficult, though they indeed be easy and pleasant, they will then appear to all men both easy and pleasant, though they were rugged and difficult indeed."†

But, without pursuing this important speculation any further for the present, we proceed to our quotations.

"And may I not presume a little farther, to show the reasonableness of this word 'vates,' and say, that the holy David's Psalms are a divine Poem ? If I do, I shall not do it without the testimony of great learned men, both ancient and modern. But even the name of Psalms will speak for me, which, being interpreted, is nothing but Songs : then, that it is fully written in metre, as all learned Hebricians agree, although the rules be not yet fully found. Lastly, and principally, his handling his prophecy, which is merely poetical. For what else is the awaking his musical instruments ; the often and free changing of persons ; his notable prosopopœias, when he maketh you, as it were, see God coming in his majesty ; his telling of the beasts' joyfulness, and hills leaping, but a heavenly poesy ; wherein, almost, he showeth himself a passionate lover of that unspeakable and everlasting beauty, to be seen by the eyes of the mind, only cleared by faith ? But, truly, now, having named him, *I fear I seem to profane that holy name, applying it to poetry, which is, among us, thrown down to so ridiculous an estimation.* But they that, with quiet judgments, will look a little deeper into it, shall find the end and working of it such, as, being rightly applied, deserveth not to be scourged out of the church of God.

"But now let us see how the Greeks have named it, and how they deemed of it. The Greeks named him ποιητήν, which name hath, as the most excellent, gone through other languages ; it cometh of this word ποιεῖν, which is *to make* ; wherein, I know not whether by luck or wisdom, we Englishmen have met with the Greeks in calling him 'a maker,' which name, how high and incomparable a title it is, I had rather were known by marking the scope of other sciences, than by any partial allegation. There is no art delivered unto mankind, that hath not the works of nature for its principal object, without which they could not consist, and on which they so depend, as they become actors and players, as it were, of what nature will have set forth. So doth the astronomer look upon the stars, and

[* Cf. Lycurg. in Leocrat. κέ.]
† Milton.

by that he seeth set down what order nature had taken therein. So doth the geometrician and the arithmetician, in their diverse sorts of quantities. So doth the musician, in times, tell you, which by nature agree, which not. The natural philosopher thereon hath his name; and the moral philosopher standeth upon the natural virtues, vices, or passions of man: and follow nature, saith he, therein, and thou shalt not err. The lawyer saith what men have determined. The historian, what men have done. The grammarian speaketh only of the rules of speech; and the rhetorician and logician, considering what in nature will soonest prove and persuade, thereon give artificial rules, which still are compassed within the circle of a question, according to the proposed matter. The physician weigheth the nature of a man's body, and the nature of things helpful and hurtful unto it. And the metaphysic, though it be in the second and abstract notions, and therefore be counted supernatural, yet doth he, indeed, build upon the depth of nature. Only the poet, disdaining to be tied to any such subjection, lifted up with the vigor of his own invention, doth grow, in effect, into another nature: in making things either better than nature bringeth forth, or quite anew; forms such as never were in nature, as the heroes, demigods, Cyclops, chimeras, furies, and such like; so as he goeth hand in hand with nature, not enclosed within the narrow warrant of her gifts, but freely ranging within the zodiac of his own wit. Nature never set forth the earth in so rich tapestry as divers poets have done; neither with so pleasant rivers, fruitful trees, sweet-smelling flowers, nor whatsoever else may make the too-muched loved earth more lovely; her world is brazen, the poets only deliver a golden." pp. 8–10.

After pursuing the same idea somewhat farther, he divides poetry into three great classes: the religious, as the Psalms, and the philosophical or didactic, and the purely *ideal*.

"These he subdivided into sundry more special denominations: the most notable be the heroic, lyric, tragic, comic, satyric, iambic, elegiac, pastoral, and certain others; some of these be termed according to the matter they deal with: some by the sort of verse they liked best to write in; for indeed the greatest part of poets have apparalled their poetical inventions in that numerous kind of writing which is called verse. Indeed but apparelled verse, being but an ornament, and no cause to poetry, since there have been many most excellent poets that never versified, and now swarm many versifiers that need never answer to the name of poets. For Xenophon, who did imitate so excellently as to give us *effigiem justi imperii*, the portraiture of a just empire, under the name of Cyrus, as Cicero saith of him, made therein an absolute heroical poem. So did Heliodorus, in his sugared invention of that picture of love in Theagenes and Chariclea; and yet both these wrote in prose; which I speak to show, that it is not rhyming and versing that maketh a poet; (no more than a long gown maketh an advocate, who, though he pleaded in armour, should be an advocate and no soldier); but it is that feigning notable images of virtues, vices, or what else, with that delightful teaching, which must be the right describing note to know a poet by. Although, indeed, the senate of poets have chosen verse as their fittest raiment; meaning, as in matter they passed all in all, so in manner to go beyond them; not speaking, table-talk fashion, or like men in a dream, words as they chanceably fall from the mouth, but piecing each syllable of each word by just proportion, according to the dignity of the subject." p. 14.

He next proceeds to show that poets are the most effective teachers of morality.

"Now, therefore, it shall not be amiss, first, to weigh this latter sort of poetry by his *works*, and then, by his *parts;* and if in neither of these anatomies he be commendable, I hope we shall receive a more favorable sentence. This purifying of wit, this enriching of memory, enabling of judgment, and enlarging of conceit, which commonly we call learning, under what name soever it come forth, or to what immediate end soever it be directed: the final end is to lead and draw us to as high a perfection as our degenerate souls, made worse by their clay lodgings, can be capable of: this, according to the inclination of man, bred many formed impressions: for some that thought this felicity principally to be gotten by knowledge, and no knowledge to be so high or heavenly as to be acquainted with the stars, gave themselves to astronomy; others, persuading themselves to be demi-gods, if they knew the causes of things, became natural and supernatural philosophers. Some an admirable delight drew to music; and some the certainty of demonstrations to the mathematics; but all, one and other, having this scope, to know, and by knowledge to lift up the mind from the dungeon of the body to the enjoying his own divine essence. But when, by the balance of experience, it was found that the astronomer, looking to the stars, might fall in a ditch; that the inquiring philosopher might be blind in himself; and the mathematician might draw forth a straight line with a crooked heart; then lo! did proof, the overruler of opinions, make manifest that all these are but serving sciences, which, as they have a private end in themselves, so yet are they all directed to the highest end of the mistress knowledge, by the Greeks called ἀρχιτεκτονικὴ, which stands, as I think, in the knowledge of a man's self; in the ethic and politic consideration, with the end of well doing, and not of well knowing only: even as the saddler's next end is to make a good saddle, but his farther end, to serve a nobler faculty, which is horsemanship: so the horseman's to soldiery; and the soldier not only to have the skill, but to perform the practice of a soldier. So that the ending end of all earthly learning being virtuous action, those skills that most serve to bring forth that, have a most just title to be princes over all the rest; wherein, if we can show it rightly, the poet is worthy to have it before any other competitors." pp. 15, 16.

He then compares the poet with the moral philosopher and the historian, and, after pointing out some defects in the methods of these latter, proceeds as follows:

"Now doth the peerless poet perform both; for whatsoever the philosopher saith should be done, he giveth a perfect picture of it, by some one by whom he presupposeth it was done, so as he coupleth the general notion with the particular example. A perfect picture, I say; for he yieldeth to the powers of the mind an image of that whereof the philosopher bestoweth but a wordish description, which doth neither strike, pierce, nor possess the sight of the soul so much as that other doth. For as, in outward things, to a man that had never seen an elephant, or a rhinoceros, who should tell him most exquisitely all their shape, colour, bigness, and particular marks? or of a gorgeous palace, an architect, who declaring the full beauties, might well make the hearer able to repeat as it were, by rote, all he had heard, yet should never satisfy his inward conceit, with being witness to itself of a true living knowledge; but the same man, as soon as he might see those beasts well painted, or that house well in model, should straightway grow, without need of any description, to a judicial comprehending of them: so, no doubt, the philosopher, with his learned definitions, be it of virtues or vices, matters of public policy or private government, replenisheth the memory with many infallible grounds of wisdom, which, notwithstanding, lie dark before the imaginative and judging power, if they be not illuminated or figured forth by the speaking picture of poesy.

"Tully taketh much pains, and many times not without poetical helps, to make us know the force love of our country hath in us. Let us but hear old Anchises, speaking in the midst of Troy's flames, or see Ulysses, in the fullness of all Calypso's delights, bewail his absence from barren and beggarly Ithaca. Anger, the stoics said, was a short madness; let but Sophocles bring you Ajax on a stage, killing or whipping sheep and oxen, thinking them the army of Greeks, with their chieftains Agamemnon and Menelaus; and tell me, if you have not a more familiar insight into anger than finding in the schoolmen his genius and difference? See whether wisdom and temperance in Ulysses and Diomedes, valour in Achilles, friendship in Nisus and Euryalus, even to an ignorant man, carry not an apparent shining; and, contrarily, the remorse of conscience in Œdipus; the soon-repenting pride in Agamemnon; the self-devouring cruelty in his father Atreus; the violence of ambition in the two Theban brothers: the sour sweetness of revenge in Medea; and, to fall lower, the Terentian Gnatho, and our Chaucer's Pandar, so expressed, that we now use their names to signify their trades: and finally, all virtues, vices, and passions so in their own natural states laid to the view, that we seem not to hear of them, but clearly to see through them." pp. 19, 20.

He observes that, in moral teaching, the difficulty lies not in shewing what ought to be done, but in moving men to act up to their admitted principles, by a proper discipline of the heart and the influence of well-tempered affection.

"Now, therein, of all sciences, (I speak still of human, and according to the human conceit) is our poet the monarch. For he doth not only show the way, but giveth so sweet a prospect into the way, as will entice any man to enter into it: nay he doth, as if your journey should lie through a fair vineyard, at the very first give you a cluster of grapes, that full of that taste you may long to pass farther. He beginneth not with obscure definitions, which must blur the margin with interpretations and load the memory with doubtfulness, but cometh to you with words set in delightful proportion, either accompanied with, or prepared for, the well-enchanting skill of music; and with a tale, forsooth, he cometh unto you with a tale which holdeth children from play, and old men from the chimney-corner;* and, pretending no more, doth intend the winning of the mind from wickedness to virtue; even as the child is often brought to take most wholesome things, by hiding them in such other as have a pleasant taste: which, if one should begin to tell them the nature of the aloes or rhubarbarum they should receive, would sooner take their physic at their ears than at their mouth: so is it in men; (most of whom are childish in the best things, till they be cradled in their graves:) glad they will be to hear the tales of Hercules, Achilles, Cyrus, Æneas; and, hearing them, must needs hear the right description of wisdom, valour and justice; which, if they had been barely (that is to say philosophically) set out, they would swear they be brought to school again. That imitation, whereof poetry is, hath the most conveniency to nature of all other: insomuch that, as Aristotle saith, those things which in themselves are horrible, as cruel battles, unnatural

---

* This is conceived to have suggested Shakspeare's exquisite description.

That elder years played truant at his tale,
And younger hearings were quite ravished,—
So sweet and voluble was his discourse, &c.

monsters, are made, in poetical imitation, delightful.   Truly, I have known men, that, even with reading Amadis de Gaule, which, God knoweth, wanteth much of a perfect poesy, have found their hearts moved to the exercise of courtesy, liberality, and especially courage.   Who readeth Æneas carrying old Anchises on his back, that wisheth not it were his fortune to perform so excellent an act?   Whom doth not those words of Turnus move (the tale of Turnus having planted his image in the imagination)

—— fugientem hæc terra videbit?
Usque adeone mori miserum est?—Virgil.

Where the philosophers (as they think) scorn to delight, so much they be content little to move, saving wrangling whether 'virtus' be the chief or the only good; whether the contemplative or the active. life do excel: which Plato and Bœtius well knew; and, therefore, made mistress Philosophy very often borrow the masking raiment of poesy.   For even those hard-hearted evil men, who think virtue a school-name, and know no other good but 'indulgere genio,' and therefore despise the austere admonitions of the philosoper, and feel not the inward reason they stand upon; yet will be content to be delighted, which is all the good-fellow poet seems to promise; and so steal to see the form of goodness, which seen, they cannot but love, ere themselves be aware, as if they took a medicine of cherries."   pp. 27–29.

The following is a passage of frequent reference:

"Is it the lyric that most displeaseth, who, with his tuned lyre and well accorded voice, giveth praise, the reward of vitue, to virtuous acts? who giveth moral precepts and natural problems? who sometimes raiseth up his voice to the height of the heavens, in singing the lauds of the immortal God?   Certainly, I must confess mine own barbarousness; I never heard the old song of Percy and Douglas,* that I found not my heart moved more than with a trumpet; and yet it is sung but by some blind crowder, with no rougher voice than rude style; which, being so evil apparelled in the dust and cobweb of that uncivil age, what would it work, trimmed in the gorgeous eloquence of Pindar?   In Hungary I have seen it the manner at all feasts, and all other such-like meetings, to have songs of their ancestors' valour, which that right soldier-like nation think one of the chiefest kindlers of brave courage.   The imcomparable Lacedæmonians did not only carry that kind of music ever with them to the field, but even at home, as such songs were made, so were they all content to be singers of them; when the lusty men were to tell what they did, the old men what they had done, and the young what they would do.   And where a man may say that Pindar many times praiseth highly victories of small moment, rather matters of sport than virtue; as it may be answered, it was the fault of the poet, and not of the poetry, so, indeed the chief fault was in the time and custom of the Greeks, who set those toys at so high a price, that Philip of Macedon reckoned a horserace won at Olympus among his three fearful felicities.   But as the inimitable Pindar often did, so is that kind most capable, and most fit, to awake the thoughts from the sleep of idleness, to embrace honourable enterprizes.

"There rests the heroical, whose very name, I think, should daunt all backbiters.   For by what conceit can a tongue be directed to speak evil of that which draweth with him no less champions than Achilles, Cyrus, Æneas, Turnus, Tydeus, Rinaldo? who doth not only teach and move

* Ben Johnson, charmed with the beauty of this old song of Chevy Chace, in which the battle of Otterburn, in 1388, is supposed to have been celebrated, was wont to say that he would rather have been the author of that little poem, than of all his own works.

to truth, but teacheth and moveth to the most high and excellent truth: who maketh magnanimity and justice shine through all misty fearfulness and foggy desires? who, if the saying of Plato and Tully be true, that who could see virtue would be wonderfully ravished with the love of her beauty; this man setteth her out to make her more lovely, in her holiday apparel, to the eye of any that will deign not to disdain until they understand. But if any thing be already said in the defence of sweet poetry, all concurreth to the maintaining the heroical, which is not only a kind, but the best and most accomplished kind, of poetry. For, as the image of each action stirreth and instructeth the mind, so the lofty image of such worthies most inflameth the mind with desire to be worthy, and informs with counsel how to be worthy. Only let Æneas be worn in the tablet of your memory, how he governeth himself in the ruin of his country; in the preserving his old father, and carrying away his religious ceremonies; in obeying God's commandments to leave Dido, though not only all passionate kindness, but even the human consideration of virtuous gratefulness, would have craved other of him; how in storms, how in sports, how in war, how in peace, how a fugitive, how victorious, how besieged, how besieging, how to strangers, how to allies, how to enemies; how to his own, lastly, how in his inward self, and how in his outward government; and I think, in a mind most prejudiced with a prejudicating humour, he will be found in excellency fruitful. Yea, as Horace saith, 'melius Chrysippo, et Crantore:' but, truly, I imagine it falleth out with these poet-whippers as with some good women who often are sick, but in faith they cannot tell where. So the name of poetry is odious to them, but neither his cause nor effects, neither the sum that contains him, nor the particularities descendnig from him, give any fast handle to their carping dispraise." pp. 33–36.

The rest of the tractate is a review of the history and condition of English poetry, which was, it seems, so wofully fallen from its high estate, that, as the Troubadours sank at last into jugglers, so poets, in his time, "were in almost as good reputation as the mountebanks at Venice." This part of the essay gives abundant evidence of the good taste and sound sense of the author, as well as of a degree of critical acumen which would do honour to a veteran Aristarch. We would refer, *inter alia*, to his observations at pp. 60, 61, concerning style, which he concludes with some very just remarks in relation to popular eloquence.

"But I would this fault were only peculiar to versifiers, and had not as large possession among prose-printers: and, which is to be marvelled, among many scholars, and, which is to be pitied, among some preachers. Truly, I could wish, (if at least I might be so bold to wish, in a thing beyond the reach of my capacity) the diligent imitators of Tully and Demosthenes, most worthy to be imitated, did not so much keep Nizolian paper-books of their figures and phrases, as, by attentive translation, as it were, devour them whole, and make them wholly theirs. For now they cast sugar and spice upon every dish that is served at the table: like those Indians, not content to wear ear-rings at the fit and natural place of the ears, but they will thrust jewels through their nose and lips, because they will be sure to be fine. Tully, when he was to drive out Cataline, as it were with a thunderbolt of eloquence often useth the figure of repetition, as 'vivit et vincit, imo in senatum venit imo in senatum venit,' &c. Indeed, inflamed with a well-grounded rage, he would have his words, as it were, double out of his mouth; and so do that artificially, which we see men in choler do naturally. And we, having noted the grace of those words, hale them in sometimes to a familiar epistle, when it were too much choler to be choleric.

"How well, store of 'similiter cadences' doth sound with the gravity of the pulpit, I would but invoke Demosthenes' soul to tell, who with a rare daintiness useth them. Truly they have made me think of the sophister, that with too much subtlety would prove two eggs three, and, though he might be counted a sophister, had none for his labour. So these men, bringing in such a kind of eloquence, well may they obtain an opinion of a seeming fineness, but persuade few, which should be the end of their fineness.

"Now for similitudes in certain printed discourses, I think all herbalists, all stories of beasts, fowls, and fishes are rifled up, that they may come in multitudes to wait upon any of our conceits, which certainly is as absurd a surfeit to the ears as is possible. For the force of a similitude not being to prove any thing to a contrary disputer, but only to explain to a willing hearer, when that is done, the rest is a most tedious prattling, rather over-swaying the memory from the purpose whereto they were applied, than any whit informing the judgment, already either satisfied, or by similitudes not to be satisfied.

"For my part, I do not doubt, when Antonius and Crassus, the great forefathers of Cicero in eloquence, the one (as Cicero testifieth of them) pretended not to know art, the other not to set by it, because with a plain sensibleness they might win credit of popular ears, which credit is the nearest step to persuasion, (which persuasion is the chief mark of oratory); I do not doubt, I say, but that they used these knacks very sparingly; which who doth generally use, any man may see, doth dance to his own music: and so to be noted by the audience, more careful to speak curiously than truly. Undoubtedly (at least to my opinion undoubtedly) I have found in divers small-learned courtiers a more sound style, than in some professors of learning; of which I can guess no other cause, but that the courtier, following thatwhich by practice he findeth fittest to nature, therein (though he know it not) doth according to art, though not by art: where the other, using art to show art, and not hide art, (as in these cases he should do) flieth from nature, and indeed abuseth art." pp. 60–62.

Turn we now to "Astrophel and Stella"—from the *ars poetica* to the poetry of Sir Philip Sidney—from his theory to his practice, which, we are fain to confess, differ not less in our author, than they have so often been found to do in other distinguished preachers. It is said that Pope, meditating a discourse upon the history of English poetry, had gone so far as to class the most distinguished writers of his first æra under the following heads:—1. Provençal School. 2. School of Chaucer. 3. School of Petrarch. 4. School of Dante. Under the third of these denominations, he ranked Sir Philip Sidney, along with Surrey, Wyat, and Gascoign. Sir Walter Raleigh also, it seems, calls our author "the English Petrarch." Any one who opens "Astrophel and Stella" will see how naturally such an idea presents itself to a reader of the great father of Italian elegance. The metrical collection, to which our author or his editors have given that appellation, contains no less than a hundred and eight sonnets and eleven songs—an unmerciful infliction in its way, and which, indeed, out-Herods Herod, since even Petrarch himself has to answer for only seventy-six effusions of the former kind, and twenty-odd of the latter.* But the canzoni and the sonnets of Petrarch are very different things from Sir Philip's imitation of them. We are aware that to the description of people, against whom our author defends poetry in general, a whole volume of love-ditties is an object of especial abhorrence and disgust, and there are even to be found, among scholars of unquestionable taste and learning, those who acknowledge that they do not feel in Petrarch the extraordinary excellencies which his own countrymen ascribe to him. Gibbon and Sismondi hold this language. But the former has well remarked that a foreigner—be he never so good a critic—must be very cautious how he sets up his own opinions against those of a whole people, and that people too, in every thing relating to the arts of beauty, a most cultivated and susceptible race. At any rate it is too late, after the lapse of five centuries, to entertain any hope of reversing the decrees of such a tribunal. A discreet man, who has the misfortune not to be satisfied with those decisions, will only take the more pains to become so. He will assume it, as a thing of course, that he is in the wrong; at least, that the presumption is very strong against him, and will proceed accordingly in his search after the truth. Now, we cannot conceive how any one, who shall read Petrarch in this spirit, can fail to award to him all the praise which the best critics among his own countrymen have bestowed upon his sweet and elegant muse. Certainly he is not a poet of the very highest order—he is not equal to Tasso and Ariosto—and there is a gulph "thrice from the centre to the utmost pole," between him and his mighty master and precursor, Dante. Even in the very matter of sonnet writing and erotic sentiment, this unrivalled genius has left some specimens behind him, which show what deep and awakening sounds he could strike from the soft Lesbian lyre. A sonnet of Dante, beginning—"Tanto onesta e tanto gentile pare, La donna mia," &c.—is quite a masterpiece of its kind. There is more heartfelt passion, more of the entire devotedness and the idolatrous adoration of love in it, than in all the finished harmony with which Petrarch, for so many years, fatigued the echoes of Vaucluse. But it is not disparaging any poet to say that he is not equal to Dante—one of the most extraordinary of men, whose "soul was as a star and dwelt apart" from the whole species—far above the highest, brighter than the most shining. But, with all his faults—with all the forced and frigid conceits and the puling sentimentalism that have been imputed to him—there is enough

[* Mistake.]

of tenderness and beauty in the verses of the great laureate, and especially of elegance both in thought and expression, to have given immortality to any poet in any age—especially to one who, in the fourteenth century, could anticipate in his style all the refinement and politeness of the sixteenth. It would be easy, if this were the proper place, to establish our opinion by a minute examination of his works. No impartial man, it seems to us, can read over even the ten or twelve last sonnets of Petrarch, including the fine canzone *Che debb' io far, che mi consigli, amore*, without concurring in our estimate of him. Not to speak of those other strains of his—the fourth *canzone*, for instance—which are animated by a high-souled partiotism worthy of old Rome, and of which Tyrtæus himself might have been proud, addressed to those who had enslaved, or to those who, like Rienzi, were struggling, or thought to be struggling, to awaken and to regenerate Italy.

But whatever may be the merits or the faults of Petrarch, we fear that Sir Philip Sidney has been far more successful in imitating the former than the latter. There are the conceits in abundance, and the affectation and the straining after something fine and striking, but we miss almost all that compensates for them in the Italian poet. We do not think that in this whole collection there is a single sonnet which can stand the test of criticism. It is all cold imitation and abortive effort—without any life or soul. Our author describes himself in the following lines :—

> "You that do search for every purling spring,
> Which from the ribs of old Parnassus flows,
> And every flower, not sweet, perhaps, which grows,
>   Near thereabouts, into your posey wing.
> You that do dictionary's method bring
> Into your rhymes, running in rattling rows :
> You that poor Petrarch's long deceased woes,
> With new-born sighs, and denizen'd wit do sing :
>
> You take wrong ways ; those far-fetch'd helps be such,
> As do bewray a want of inward touch.
>   And sure, at length, stol'n goods do come to light ;
> But if (both for your love and skill) your name
> You seek to nurse at fullest breasts of fame,
>   Stella behold, and then begin t' indite."

In one other important particular, these effusions differ very materially from those of the "famous renowners of Beatrice and Laura." They are not characterized by the same refinement, elevation and saintly purity of sentiment. Without sinking into all the grossness of Catullus, the gallantry of the English poet is strongly dashed with sensuality. This is particularly true of the tenth song, which has been censured on this very ground by Godwin. The Editor thinks such an exception comes with but an ill grace from that quarter—but, whether the husband (was it?) of Mary Wolstoncroft had a right to play the censor's part or not, his criticism is undoubtedly just in this particular. We think he very much overrates the merits of the poetry in other respects. It is, however, one of the best things in the collection, and as it does not sin very glaringly against propriety, even in its most objectionable parts, we venture to extract it without abridgment.

"O dear life, when shall it be,
  That mine eyes thine eyes may see;
  And in them thy mind discover,
Whether absence have had force,
Thy remembrance to divorce,
  From the image of thy lover?

Or if I myself find not,
After parting, aught forgot:
  Nor debarr'd from beauty's treasure,
Let not tongue aspire to tell
In what high joys I shall dwell;
  Only thought aims at the pleasure.

Thought, therefore, I will send thee
To take up the place for me:
  Long I will not after tarry:
There, unseen, thou may'st be bold,
Those fair wonders to behold,
  Which in them my hopes do carry.

Thought, see thou no place forbear,
Enter bravely every where:
  Seize on all to her belonging:
But, if thou would'st guarded be,
Fearing her beams, take with thee
  Strength of liking, rage of longing.

Think of that most grateful time,
When thy leaping heart will climb,
  In my lips to have his biding;
There those roses for to kiss,
Which do breathe a sugar'd bliss,
  Opening rubies, pearls dividing.

Think of my most princely power,
Which I, blessed, shall devour
  With my greedy, lick'rous senses,
Beauty, music, sweetness, love,
While she doth against me prove
  Her strong darts but weak defences.

Think, think of those dallyings,
When with dove-like murmurings,
  With glad moaning passed anguish,
We change eyes; and heart for heart,
Each to other do depart,
  Joying till joy makes us languish.*

[* Beautiful.]

Oh my thought! my thoughts surcease,
Thy delights my woes increase;
 My life melts with too much thinking:
Think no more, but die in me,
Till thou shalt revived be,
At her lips my nectar drinking." pp. 144–146.

In two respects, there was a strong coincidence between Sir
Philip and his Italian master. They both loved, *à la Werther*,
women, whom fate had put out of their reach, by appropriating
them to more fortunate rivals. The case of the English sonnetteer was especially desperate, since, besides the difficulties
which a bachelor would have found in it, he had a wife of his
own upon his hands. The object of this romantic affection was
Lady Penelope Devereux, whom a cruel destiny united to a
course and brutal husband—Lord Rich. His name, of course,
was quite a treasure to a sonnetteer, and Sir Philip makes as
much use of it, as Petrarch does of Laura's. He rings the changes
upon it as follows :—

"My mouth doth water, and my breath doth swell,
My tongue doth itch, my thoughts in labor be;
Listen then, lordings, with good ear to me,
 For of my life I must a riddle tell:
 Toward Aurora's court a nymph doth dwell,
Rich in all beauties which man's eye can see;
Beauties so far from reach of words, that we,
 Abase her praise, saying, she doth excel:

Rich in the treasures of deserv'd renown;
 Rich in the riches of a royal heart;
Rich in those gifts which give th' eternal crown;
 Who, tho' most rich in these and ev'ry part
Which make the patents of true worldly bliss,
Hath no misfortune, but that Rich she is." p. 91.

Another example of this forced and frigid style is to be found
in the forty-ninth sonnet.

"I on my horse, and Love on me, doth try,
Our horsemanships, while, by strange work, I prove
A horseman to my horse, a horse to Love;
 And now man's wrongs in me, poor beast, descry.
 The rein wherewith my rider doth me tie,
Are humbled thoughts, which bit of rev'rence move,
Curb'd in with fear, but with gilt boss above
 Of hope, which makes it seem fair to the eye.

The wand is will; thou, fancy, saddle art,
 Girt fast by memory; and while I spur
My horse, he spurs, with sharp desire, my heart:
 He sits me fast, however I do stir,
And now hath made me to his hand so right,
That in the menage myself takes delight." p. 98.

The four following sonnets strike us as among the best in the volume. There is a certain delicacy of thought and expression which makes them very agreeable trifles of the kind, and although they can hardly be called poetry, they are not without some tincture of a poetical spirit, and the grace of a poetical *tournure*.

> "When far-spent night persuades each mortal eye,
>   To whom nor art nor nature granteth light,
>   To lay his then mark-wanting shafts of sight,
> Clos'd with their quivers, in sleep's armory ;
> With windows ope, then most my mind doth lie,
>   Viewing the shape of darkness and delight ;
>   Takes in that sad hue, which, with th' inward night
> Of his maz'd powers, keeps perfect harmony :
>
> But when birds charm, and that sweet air, which is
> Morn's messenger, with rose enamell'd skies,
>   Calls each wight to salute the flower of bliss ;
> In tomb of lids then buried are mine eyes,
>   Forc'd by their lord, who is asham'd to find
>   Such light in sense, with such a darken'd mind."—pp. 149–150.

> "Leave me, O love ! which reachest but to dust ;
>   And thou, my mind, aspire to higher things :
>   Grow rich in that which never taketh rust ;
>   Whatever fades but fading pleasure brings.
>
> Draw in thy beams and humble all thy might
>   To that sweet yoke where lasting freedoms be,
> Which breaks the clouds, and opens for the light,
>   That doth both shine, and give us sight to see.
>
> O take fast hold ! let that light be thy guide,
>   In this small course which birth draws out to death,
> And think how evil becometh him to slide,
>   Who seeketh heav'n, and comes of heav'nly breath.
>
> Then farewell, world, thy uttermost I see,
> Eternal Love, maintain thy life in me.
>
> *Splendidis longum valedico nugis.*" pp. 199, 200.

The following pair of kisses would not be out of place in Joannes Secundus. They are not quite so burning as those which the amorous bard of Verona snatched from Lesbia's lips to give to immortality in song.

> "Love, still a boy, and oft a wanton is,
> School'd only by his mother's tender eye :
>   What wonder then if he his lesson miss,
> When, for so soft a rod, dear play he try ?
>   And yet my Star, because a sugar'd kiss
> In sport I suck'd while she asleep did lie,
>   Doth low'r, nay chide, nay threat for only this :
> Sweet, it was saucy Love, not humble I.

But no 'scuse serves, she makes her wrath appear
In beauty's throne ; see now, who dares come near
Those scarlet judges, threat'ning bloody pain ?
O heav'nly fool ! thy most kiss-worthy face,
Anger invests with such a lovely grace,
That anger's self I needs must kiss again." p. 115.

"O kiss ! which dost those ruddy gems impart,
Or gems, or fruits, of new-found Paradise :
  Breathing all bliss and sweet'ning to the heart;
Teaching dumb lips a noble exercise.
O kiss ! which souls, ev'n souls, together ties
By links of love, and only nature's art :
  How fain would I paint thee to all men's eyes,
Or of thy gifts at least shade out some part !

But she forbids, with blushing words, she says,
She builds her fame on higher-seated praise :
But my heart burns, I cannot silent be.
Then since, dear life, you fain would have me peace,
And I, mad with delight, want wit to cease.
Stop you my mouth with still, still kissing me." p. 120.

The letters of Sir Philip Sidney are very justly characterized by Walpole as "small matters" There is nothing remarkable in them either one way or another—except the following, in which he is as "curst and brief," as Sir Toby Belch could wish. The extreme insolence of this violent little epistle, is a fair sample of the manners of that time. From the swearing virago on the throne, down through every gradation and class of society, the same haughty and ungovernable temper was perpetually breaking out in the various shapes of formidable outrage or petty annoyance. The treatment, which Sidney himself received from the Earl of Oxford, and which is detailed at length in his Life, is another striking illustration of it. One does not very well conceive how a knight (and such a knight) could have borne that mortal offence, though the De Vere had been of royal estate as well as lineage.

"Mr. Molineux—Few words are best. My letters to my father have come to the eyes of some. Neither can I condemn any but you for it. If it be so, you have played the very knave with me; and so I will make you know, if I have good proof of it. But that for so much as is past. For that is to come, I assure you before God that if ever I know you do so much as read any letter I write to my father, without his commandment, or my consent, I will thrust my dagger into you. And trust to it, for I speak it in earnest. In the meantime farewell. From court, this last of May, 1578.* By me,

PHILIP SIDNEY.
"Indorsed, Mr. Philip Sidney to me, brought 1578, by my lord chancellor ; received the 21st of June."

* "This letter was not written to the steward, as Walpole falsely states, but to the secretary of Sir. H. Sidney, Edward Molineux, Esq., of Nutfield, in the county of Surrey. Sir Philip imagined, erroneously, as he afterwards confessed, that this

Sir Philip's prose was more poetical than his verse; and shews abilities which time might have ripened into the grave authorship of Raleigh, or the political wisdom of Buckhurst.

gentleman had basely betrayed the confidence of his employer and furnished the enemies of the aged lord deputy with matter of accusation against him   Though the above epistle, therefore, is sadly deficient in point of discretion and temper, it shows the intensity of our author's filial regard ; and, whatever may be deducted from our estimation of the coolness of his head on account of it, an equivalent must, we apprehend, be substituted in our increased love and respect for the amiable qualities of his heart."

LORD BYRON'S CHARACTER AND WRITINGS.[*]

Letters and Journals of Lord Byron, with Notices of his Life. By Thomas Moore. In 2 vols. Vol. I. *New-York. J. & J. Harper.* 1830.

The same inordinate curiosity about this work, which, as we are assured, made it absolutely necessary to publish it by piecemeal, will be a sufficient justification for a critical notice of it in its present incomplete state. It is, however, not without some degree of reluctance, that we hazard an opinion as to its merits, before we have fairly heard the author out with his story. The end not only "crowns the work," as the proverb expresses it, but it does something more. It explains, illustrates, reconciles all the parts, and, by discovering fully their relation to each other and to the whole, often shews the fitness and propriety of what at first appeared questionable or unsatisfactory. We are the more disposed to give Mr. Moore the full benefit of this concession, because we humbly conceive that he stands in need of it. We are free to confess that we have risen from the perusal of this volume with a very decided feeling of disappointment, to use no stronger expression. That our expectations—the Life of Sheridan to the contrary notwithstanding—had been raised to no ordinary pitch, we readily admit: and some allowances ought, doubtless, to be made on that score. But how should it have been otherwise? The few notices we had seen of the book, from the English press, were of the most flattering kind, and, independently of these, there was every thing about the author's character and situation—the unhapy failure just alluded to always excepted—to excite the liveliest hopes for the success of the present very popular undertaking. We knew that the "noble poet" had been as intimate with Mr. Moore, as his extreme jealousy and shyness would allow him to be with any body. We knew, further, that our author had been made, by Lord Byron himself, the depositary of certain MSS. of such deep and mysterious import that it was deemed, for the benefit of all concerned—except the gentleman who made this sacrifice—to consign them to the flames. This act of considerate and lofty disinterestedness, as it has always been represented to have been, was, on many accounts, calculated to awaken

[* This view of Lord Byron's character and writings has been *completely* confirmed by Lady Blessington's volumes recently published (1833); which some say are not the *vero*, but all admit are the *ben trovato*.]

great interest in the present work.   To have had it in his power to make such a sacrifice, was, one would think, no small advantage to a biographer.   However false may have been Lord Byron's representations of the conduct of others in this Black Book—however atrocious and unscrupulous his hostility to those who had offended or thwarted or defied him—he both loved himself and knew himself thoroughly; nor is it possible that he should not have impressed the image of his whole character, that he should not have breathed out his inmost soul, upon every page of that dark record of hate and wrath.   We drew a not less favourable inference from the spirit, by which Mr. Moore was supposed to have been actuated in that affair.   He had sacrificed, when in distress, two or three thousand pounds, (so the story went) rather than be accessory to the publication of such "perilous stuff" as the posthumous libel was made up of.   He was a man, therefore, neither to be bribed by any pecuniary interest of his own, nor to be induced, by any overweening partiality for his friend, to be the instrument of his malignity, or to spare his vices.   We certainly expected, from such a man, something different from the awkward, glozing, parasitical apology, which he has given to the public under the equivocal title of "Notices of the Life of Lord Byron"—to say nothing of a determined propensity for bookmaking which appears in it. We repeat it : we may see cause to change or at least to qualify our opinion of the whole work, when the rest of it shall have been published.   But, for the psesent, the impression left upon our minds is that it is just such a full, frank, and manly statement of the whole truth and nothing but the truth, as a jury at the sessions is likely to hear from a hackneyed advocate in a desperate cause.

We have heard it remarked, as something favorable to this work, that it is a rare example of the biography of a great poet, written by one of the most distinguished of his compeers.   In general that would be any thing but a recommendation ; since the life of one literary man is, according to a trite remark, always a dull subject for another, and the only advantage, which a poet, as such, could have in treating his theme, would be not the most auspicious, in the world, to historical accuracy.   Yet, whether the subject was fortunate in his biographer or not, in the the present instance, the biographer was incontestably most fortunate in his subject.   Lord Byron's life was not a literary, or cloistered and scholastic life.   He had lived generally in the world, and always and entirely *for* the world.   The *amat nemus et fugit urbes*, which has been predicated of the whole tuneful tribe, was only in a qualified sense, a characteristic of his.   If he sought seclusion, it was not for the retired leisure or the sweet and innocent tranquillity of a country life.   His retreats were rather like that of Tiberius at Capreæ—the gloomy solitude of misanthropy and remorse, hiding its despair in darkness, or seeking to stupify and drown it in vice and debauchery. But, even when he fled from the sight of men, it was only that he might be sought after the more, and, in the depth of his hiding places, as was long ago remarked of Timon of Athens, he could not live without vomiting forth the gall of his bitterness, and sending abroad most elaborate curses in good verse to be admired of the very wretches whom he affected to despise. He lived in the world, and for the world—nor is it often that a career so brief affords to biography so much impressive incident, or that the folly of an undisciplined and reckless spirit has assumed such a motley wear, and played off, before God and man, so many extravagant and fantastical antics.

On the other hand, there was, amidst all its irregularities, something strangely interesting, something, occasionally, even grand and imposing in Lord Byron's character and mode of life. His whole being was, indeed, to a remarkable degree, extraordinary, fanciful and fascinating. All that drew upon him the eyes of men, whether for good or evil—his passions and his genius, his enthusiasm and his woe, his triumphs and his downfall—sprang from the same source, a feverish temperament, a burning, distempered, insatiable imagination ; and these, in their turn, acted most powerfully upon the imagination and the sensibility of others. We well remember a time—it is not more than two lustres ago—when we could never think of him ourselves but as an ideal being—a creature, to use his own words, "of loneliness and mystery"—moving about the earth like a troubled spirit, and even when in the midst of men, not *of* them. The enchanter's robe which he wore seemed to disguise his person, and, like another famous sorcerer and sensualist—

> ———— he hurled
> His dazzling spells into the spungy air,
> Of pow'r to cheat the eye with blear illusion
> And give it false presentments.

It has often occurred to us, as we have seen Sir Walter Scott diligently hobbling up to his daily task in the Parliament House at Edinburgh, and still more when we have gazed upon him for hours seated down at his clerk's desk, with a countenance of most demure and business-like formality, to contrast him, in that situation, with the only man, who had not been, at the time, totally overshadowed and eclipsed by his genius. It was, indeed, a wonderful contrast ! Never did two such men—competitors in the highest walks of creative imagination and deep pathos—present such a strange antithesis of moral character, and domestic habits and pursuits, as Walter Scott at home, and Lord Byron abroad. It was the difference between prose and poetry—between the dullest realities of existence and an incoherent, though powerful and agitating romance—between a falcon trained to the uses of a domestic bird, and, instead of "towering in her pride of place," brought to stoop at the smallest quarry, and to wait upon a rude sportsman's bidding like a menial servant— and some savage, untamed eagle, who, after struggling with the bars of his cage, until his breast was bare and bleeding with the agony, had flung himself forth, once more, upon the gale, and was again chasing before him the "whole herd of timorous and flocking birds, and making his native Alps, through all their solitudes, ring to his boding and wild scream. Lord Byron's pilgrimages to distant and famous lands—especially his first—heightened this effect of his genius and of his very peculiar mode of existence. Madame de Staël ascribes it to his good fortune or the deep policy of Napoleon, that he had succeeded in associating his name with some of those objects which have, through all time, most strongly impressed the imaginations of men, with the Pyramids, the Alps, the Holy Land, &c. Byron had the same advantage. His muse, like Horace's image of *Care*, mounted with him the steed and the gondola, the post-chaise and the packet-ship. His poems are, in a manner, the journals and common-place books of the wandering Childe. Thus, it is stated or hinted that a horrible incident, like that upon which the Giaour turns, had nearly taken place within Byron's own observation while in the East. His sketches of the sublime and beautiful in nature, seem to be mere images, or, so to express it, shadows thrown down upon his pages from the objects, which he visited, only colored and illumined with such feelings, reflections and associations as they naturally awaken in contemplative and susceptible minds. His early visit to Greece, and the heartfelt enthusiasm with which he dwelt upon her loveliness even "in her age of woe"—upon the glory which once adorned, and that which might still await her— have identified him with her name, in a manner which subsequent events have made quite remarkable. His poetry, when we read it over again, seems to breathe of "the sanctified phrenzy of prophecy and inspiration." He now appears to have been the herald of her resuscitation. The voice of lamentation, which he sent forth over Christendom, was as if it had issued from all her caves, fraught with the wo and the wrongs of ages, and the deep vengeance which at length awoke—and not in vain! In expressing ourselves as we have done upon this subject, it is to us a melancholy reflection that our language is far more suitable to what we *have* felt, than to what we now feel, in reference to the life and character of Lord Byron. The last years of that life—the wanton, gross, and often dull and feeble ribaldry of some of his latest productions, broke the spell which he had laid upon our souls ; and we are by no means sure that we have not since yielded too much to the disgust and aversion which follow disenchantment like its shadow.

The task of Mr. Moore was, in one respect, beset by a very extraordinary difficulty. This we have already alluded to, and it may be still more pointedly summed up in the remark, which has been so frequently made, that all Lord Byron's poems were, in some sort, *auto-biographical*.* He was himself, as our author remarks, uniformly the *dark* sublime he drew. Whatever the subject or the scene, the gloom of his desolate spirit fell in the same broad shadow over the picture. His heroes are all cast in one mould, and the standard of character and conduct which he sets up in his poetry, as we shall presently show, was precisely what he aimed at in his life. At first it seems he treated this opinion as wholly unfounded, and lamented the fate of genius, if it were called to account, in its own person, for whatever, in its surveys of man and nature, it might conceive of guilt and crime. His defence was the trivial one which has been set up for Macchiavelli, and with very much the same degree of reason and propriety. It soon, however, became apparent to his readers, as it does to those of the great political Mephistophiles, that he painted *con amore*. One work after another bore evidence of this, until, in the two last Cantos of Childe Harold, the noble poet scarcely took the trouble to hold up the mask to that sardonic and withering countenance, "thrice changed with pale, ire, envy and despair," which was become so familiar to mankind.† It was this circumstance, indeed—besides their own merit—that for some time excited so powerful an interest in his works. It was as if they who read were listening to accents of living anguish—the breathings, deep and intense as if they had been vented in the solitude of the bed-chamber, of a wounded and wronged spirit in its agony. The charm which has been felt to attach to auto-biography, in every shape, for the supposed truth of its revelations, was heightened here, as in the confessions of Rousseau, by the extraordinary peculiarities of the man, and the wizard tones of genius. It was not only the laying bare, as in tragedy, of that *Hell*, to use Lord Byron's own expression, the human bosom, with all the furies that possess it—its fiercest and fellest passions, in most vehement agitation and conflict—a spectacle so attractive, that all ages have assigned to it, with one consent, nothing less than the very highest place

* Or "auto-graphical," rather, "self-painting."
† "I would gladly—or, rather, sorrowfully—comply with your request of a dirge for the poor girl you mention. But how can I write on one I have never seen or known ? Besides, you will do it much better yourself. *I could not write upon any thing, without some personal experience and foundation ;* far less on a theme so peculiar. Now, you have both in this case, and, if you had neither, you have more imagination, and would never fail."—*Letter* ccxxxii. *to Moore,* p. 460.

among the achievements of creative mind.   It was a living man, equally favored, according to the vulgar estimate, by nature and by fortune—too young, one would have thought, to have experienced the ills of life, or too high to be reached by them—that uttered these ravings, so strangely wild and melancholy, "were ne'er prophetic sounds so full of woe."   At the same time, his whole life and demeanour, as we have remarked before, were calculated to increase the curiosity excited by his writings.   The singularities, which really distinguished them, were exaggerated by report.   Every thing about this solitary heir of an old Norman line, and lord of an antique, ruined pile—still of the same venerable aspect as when its cloisters were the last refuge of the broken-heart, and the quiet nursery of holy thoughts, but now desecrated, it was rumoured, by midnight revelry and the nameless abominations of sin and folly—administered to the vulgar appetite for the marvellous—"and then," to use the words of the poet himself, in his picture of "Lara"—

> ———— his rarely called attendants said,
> Thro' nights long hours would sound his hurried tread,
> O'er the dark gallery, where his father's frowned,
> In rude but antique portraiture around ;
> They heard, but whispered—"*that* must not be known—
> The sound of words less earthly than his own.
> Yes, they who chose might smile, but some had seen
> They scarce knew what, but more than should have been.
> Why gazed he so upon the *ghastly head*,
> Which hands profane had gathered from the dead, &c.*

It is not wonderful that public curiosity should have been always alive about such a man, and that all his movements should have been (as they were) studiously watched and reported.   Accordingly, there is no end, whether in print or in conversation, to "anecdotes of Lord Byron."   In short, we had heard so much of him from himself and from others, and what we had heard was so full of interest and mystery, so extraordinary, so exciting, that we fell upon Mr. Moore's publication with an eagerness scarcely conceivable.   We expected it to prove the most interesting of biographical works—at least, "to rival all but 'Boswells book' below."   But the very circumstances which had excited these expectations, were most unfavorable to the fulfilment of them ; and it may be that no writer could have compiled a Life of Lord Byron, which should have come up to our hopes, or fallen in with our preconceived opinions.

The title of the work is strictly accurate.   It is "the letters and journals of Lord Byron *with* notices of his life."   The staple of the book is all Byron's as our readers will readily conceive, when we inform them that it contains no less than 240 epistles (good and bad) of the poet's, with a great deal of miscellaneous

* For a striking and beautiful picture of his romantic life, see "The Dream."

matter from his other MSS., and his every day tittle-tattle picked up in conversation by his friends. His biographer has done little more than string his materials together in the order to which he has chosen to reduce them. This he has, for the most part, done, as such things are always done, by a few sentences of narrative or explanation; but he takes care, whenever occasion serves, to paint all *couleur de rose*, with many a gloss at intervals, and now and then a set dissertation or *excursus*, in a style of most laboured philosophical rhetoric. Indeed, we must remark upon the style throughout that nothing seems more unaccountable to us than the great encomiums which (as we are informed) have been passed upon it by the English journals. It appears to us the stiffest and most pompous we have ever met with in a work of the kind—a tissue of heavy brocade. Mr. Moore seems to have been frightened out of all confidence in himself by the criticisms on his Life of Sheridan. He was, clearly not at his ease in composing; and, as a matter of course, the composition has neither grace nor nature in it. In avoiding one evil he has run into another. Instead of *poetical license*, the redundancy of figurative language and such like blemishes, which deform the diction of the Life of Sheridan, he has given us here a specimen of dull and pedantic formality. We were often struck with the contrast between Byron's letters, written with the greatest possible vivacity and *abandon*, and the elaborate prosing that comes after them. We can compare it to nothing except it be going out of the elastic open air, in a bright October day, into the atmosphere of a close and crowded room. In taking these steps from the author to the commentator we occasionally experienced a sensation which strongly reminded us of suffocation. Yet there are some passages—some score or two of pages, it may be—in which Mr. Moore has been more felicitous, and which are indeed quite worthy of his poetical reputation.—We shall have occasion to refer to at least one of these in the sequel.

Lord Byron's prose style has always appeared to us excellent. We have read few things with greater satisfaction, in every point of view, but especially in *this*, than his famous letter to Murray on the Pope and Bowles controversy. The besetting sin of his poetry, as we shall have to remark when we come to it, was exaggeration and effort; but nothing can be more off-hand, dashing and lively than his prose. He expresses himself with all the freedom of literary table talk, and one is surprised to find a man of so much and such extraordinary genius, as remarkable as the best of his contemporaries, for that strong common sense, and shrewd cleverness which have not always been attributes of the most gifted spirits. His opinions in literature too meet in general our heartiest concurrence—except that we do not see why he has so *unbounded* an admiration for the "Pleasures of Memory," and think also that he overrates the "Pleasures of Hope." His defence of Pope, against the modern Grub-street, as he expresses it himself, had been worthy of all praise, had he gone a little farther and only gibbetted a few of that great man's detractors in another Dunciad, as an offering to his offended manes. Having tried his own hand at satire, with some degree of success, Byron was the better able to appreciate the matchless excellence of Pope, in his peculiar walk. We must observe, however, as to some of the opinions advanced by the noble poet in the volume before us, that they were those of a very young man, and were no doubt subsequently corrected by "sage experience." One instance of this is expressly noticed by Mr. Moore, and as the change respected the merits of Petrarch, who is rather a pet with us, we saw it with a lively satisfaction. Many, very many of these letters are far from being remarkable in any respect, and we are satisfied that there is much more interesting and characteristic matter to be found in the unpublished correspondence of Lord Byron, as may possibly appear from the subsequent volume of Mr. Moore. We confess, however, we have sad misgivings upon this subject, and doubt very much whether biography, in the hands of so tender a friend as our author, will at all answer the purpose, strongly expressed by Dryden in his own way, of exhibiting the poor erring being "as naked as ever nature made him" The following extracts are submitted as specimens of that we think Lord Byron's happiest manner.

In a letter to Mr. Dallas, he refers to the death of a young man of whom he repeatedly speaks in the same exalted terms. It was written shortly before the publication of the first two Cantos of Childe Harold.

"Newstead Abbey, September 7th, 1811.

"As Gifford has been ever my 'Magnus Apollo,' any approbation, such as you mention, would, of course, be more welcome than 'all Bokara's vaunted gold, than all the gems of Samarkand.' But I am sorry the MS. was shown to him in such a manner, and I had written to Murray to say as much, before I was aware that it was too late.

"Your objection to the expression 'central line,' I can only meet by saying that, before Childe Harold left England, it was his full intention to traverse Persia, and return by India, which he could not have done without passing the equinoctial.

"The other errors you mention, I must correct in the progress through the press. I feel honoured by the wish of such men that the poem should be continued, but to do that, I must return to Greece and Asia; I must have a warm sun and a blue sky; I cannot describe scenes so dear to me by a sea-coal fire. I had projected an additional Canto when I was in the Troad and Constantinople, and, if I saw them again, it would go on; but, under existing circumstances and *sensations*, I have neither harp, 'heart, nor voice' to proceed. I feel that *you are all right* as to the metaphysical part; but I also feel that I am sincere, and that, if I am only to write '*ad captandum vulgus*,' I might as well edit a magazine at once, or spin canzonettas for Vauxhall.

*   *   *   *   *

"My work must make its way as well as it can; I know I have every thing against me, angry poets and prejudices; but, if the poem is a *poem*, it will surmount these obstacles, and, if *not*, it deserves its fate. Your friend's Ode I have read—it is no great compliment to pronounce it far superior to S * *'s on the same subject, or to the merits of the new Chancellor. It is evidently the production of a man of taste, and a poet, though I should not be willing to say it was fully equal to what might be expected from the author of '*Horæ Ionicæ*.' I thank you for it, and that is more than I would do for any other Ode of the present day.

"I am very sensible of your good wishes, and, indeed, I have need of them. My whole life has been at variance with propriety, not to say decency; my circumstances are become involved; my friends are dead or estranged, and my existence a dreary void. In Matthews I have lost my 'guide, philosopher, and friend;' in Wingfield a friend only, but one whom I could have wished to have preceded in his long journey.

"Matthews was indeed an extraordinary man; it has not entered into the heart of a stranger to conceive such a man; there was the stamp of immortality in all he said or did; and now what is he? When we see such men pass away and be no more—men, who seem created to display what the Creator *could make* his creatures, gathered into corruption, before the maturity of minds that might have been the pride of posterity, what are we to conclude? For my own part I am bewildered. To me he was much, to Hobhouse every thing. My poor Hobhouse doted on Matthews. For me, I did not love quite so much as I honoured him; I was indeed so sensible of his infinite superiority, that, though I did not envy, I stood in awe of it. He, Hobhouse, Davies, and myself, formed a coterie of our own at Cambridge and elsewhere. Davies is a wit and man of the world, and feels as much as such a character can do; but not as Hobhouse has been affected. Davies, who is not a scribbler, has always beaten us all in the war of words, and by his colloquial powers at once delighted and kept us in order. H. and myself always had the worst of it with the other two; and even M. yielded to the dashing vivacity of S. D. But I am talking to you of men, or boys, as if you cared about such beings."—p. 219.

We subjoin the following, dated at Patras, 1810, to his friend Hodgson. It is extremely sprightly and one of the most characteristic in the whole collection. The line printed in italics reveals that horror of being ranked with mere authors which he always felt or affected. Mr. Moore admits it has been justly said of him that "he was prouder of being a descendant of the Byrons of Normandy, who accompanied William the Conqueror into England, than of having been the author of Childe Harold and Manfred." But of that more anon.

"Since I left Constantinople, I have made a tour of the Morea, and visited Vely Pacha, who paid me great honours and gave me a pretty stallion. H. is doubtless in England before even the date of this letter—bears a despatch from me to your bardship. He writes to me from Malta, and requests my journal, if I keep one. I have none, or he should have it; but I have replied, in a consolatory and exhortatory epistle, praying him to abate three and sixpence in the price of his next Boke, seeing that half a guinea is a price not to be given for any thing save an opera ticket.

"As for England, it is so long since I have heard from it. Every one at all connected with my concerns is asleep, and you are my only correspondent, agents excepted. I have really no friends in the world; though all my old school-companions are gone forth into that world, and walk about there in monstrous disguises, in the garb of guardsmen, lawyers, parsons, fine gentlemen: and such other masquerade dresses. So, I here shake hands and cut with all these busy people, none of whom write to me. Indeed, I ask it not; and here I am, a poor traveller and heathenish philosopher, who hath perambulated the greatest part of the Levant, and seen a great quantity of very improvable land and sea, and, after all am no better than when I set out—Lord help me!

"I have been out fifteen months this very day, and I believe my concerns will draw me to England soon; but of this I will apprize you regularly from Malta. On all points, Hobhouse will inform you, if you are curious as to our adventures. I have seen some old English papers up to the 15th of May. I see the 'Lady of the Lake' advertised. Of course it is in his old ballad style, and pretty. After all, Scott is the best of them. The end of all scribblement is to amuse, and he certainly succeeds there. I long to read his new romance.

"And how does 'Sir Edgar?' and your friend, Bland? I suppose you are involved in some literary squabble. *The only way is to despise all brothers of the quill.* I suppose you won't allow me to be an author, but I contemn you all, you dogs!—I do.

"You don't know D———s, do you? He had a farce ready for the stage before I left England, and asked me for a prologue, which I promised, but sailed in such a hurry, I never penned a couplet. I am afraid to ask after his drama, for fear it should be damned—Lord forgive me for using such a word!—but the pit, Sir, you know, the pit—they will do those things, in spite of merit. I remember this farce from a curious circumstance. When Drury-lane was burnt to the ground, by which accident Sheridan and his son lost the few remaining shillings they were worth, what doth my friend D——— do? Why, before the fire was out, he writes a note to Tom Sheridan, the manager of this combustible concern, to inquire whether this farce was not converted into fuel, with about two thousand other unactable manuscripts, which of course were in great peril, if not actually consumed. Now was not this characteristic?—the ruling passions of Pope are nothing to it. While the poor distracted manager was bewailing the loss of a building only worth £300,000, together with some twenty thousand pounds of rags and tinsel in the tiring rooms, Bluebeard's elephants, and all that—in comes a note from a scorching author, requiring at his hands two acts and odd scenes of a farce!!

"Dear H., remind Drury that I am his well-wisher, and let Scrope Davies be well affected towards me. I look forward to meeting you at Newstead and renewing our old Champagne evenings with all the glee of anticipation. I have written by every opportunity, and expect responses as regular as those of the liturgy, and somewhat longer. As it is impossible for a man in his senses to hope for happy days, let us at least look forward to merry ones, which comes nearest to the other in appearance, if not in reality; and in such expectations I remain, &c."—pp. 182, 183.

We would remark further in reference to Lord Byron's talents, as what he calls "a proser," (his rather ungracious name for a writer of any sort of prose) that we think his first speech

in the House of Lords, a very promising début for so young a
man. Still it is questionable, whether he could have succeeded as a public speaker—we mean in that particular assembly.
That the same genius, which gave him so great a mastery of the
human heart in his poetry, might easily have been trained to the
most sublime eloquence of the popular assembly, we have no
doubt.   We do not believe in the trivial maxim—*poeta nascitur,*
orator fit, as *it is commonly understood.* No man can make
himself an orator in the proper sense of that word. The eloquence which fires and melts the hearts of men, is at least as
much an affair of temperament as of discipline.   But, in addition
to the sensibility and genius which are requisite for success in
poetical composition, a great public speaker must have dramatic
talents of the highest order ; and the advantages of a fine voice
and expressive countenance if not indispensable, are at least
very important.   How far this latter class of requisites were to be
found in Lord Byron, we have no means of judging. Mr. Moore
attributes the comparative failure of his subsequent efforts, (for
he spoke three times) to what he calls his *sing-song* delivery.
The truth is, no doubt, that Byron wrote his speeches before
they were pronounced, and having committed them to memory,
repeated them by rote like a Harrow-boy reciting his lesson.
This defect in his delivery, so disagreeable and destructive of all
effect in public speaking, might have been corrected in any other
assembly than the House of Lords.   The touch of nature and
passion would have operated upon Byron (had he become a man
of business) in his oratory, as it did in his poetry, like Ithuriel's
spear.   Had he been forced out, in *our* public assemblies, after a
little training at the bar, or without that training, had great and
agitating questions arisen in the land, his soul would have flashed forth with all its smothered fires, and the puny reciter of
memorized common-place, suddenly transformed into an orator,
"collecting all his might, dilated stood."   But no such metamorphosis could possibly have taken place in the House of Lords ;
the very last place, in any country enjoying the advantages of
representative government, in which any thing like eloquence
can originate.   The languid, monotonous and somniferous dignity of that assembly would have chilled even Byron into mediocrity.

We proceed now to make some remarks upon his moral character and his poetical genius and works.   But, first, a word about
his biographer.

Mr. Moore's account of the affair which made him for life
Lord Byron's most grateful and devoted *friend,* (for so let him
be called, *per euphemismum*) and, consequently, the author of
this book, is one of the most amusing things in the volume.
Every body who has read the English Bards and Scotch Re-

viewers remembers the following lines with the note appended
to them.

> "Health to great Jeffrey! Heaven preserve his life,
> To flourish on the fertile shores of Fife,
> And guard it sacred in his future wars,
> Since authors sometimes seek the field of Mars.
> Can none remember that eventful day,
> That ever glorious, almost fatal fray,
> When Little's leadless pistol met his eye,
> And Bow-street myrmidons stood laughing by ?"

Then comes the note.

"In 1706, Messrs. Jeffrey and Moore met at Chalk Farm. The duel was
prevented by the interference of the magistracy; and, on examination,
the balls of the pistols, like the courage of the combatants were found to
have evaporated. This incident gave occasion to much waggery in the
daily prints."

The quizzing and pleasantry which this awkward specimen
of chivalry, (as it was represented) thus gave rise to, led Mr.
Moore to trouble the public with a corrected version of the whole
affair, in the fond hope of spoiling their fun, and, for some time,
he informs us, his letter did seem to have produced the desired
effect. But, "unluckily," as he goes on to relate with admirable
naïveté, "the original story was too tempting a theme for humour and sarcasm to be so easily superseded by mere matter of
fact. Accordingly, after a little time—more especially by those
who were at all willing to wound—the old falsehood was, for
the sake of its ready sting, revived." Although as good-humour-
ed as his own Anacreon, he became at length rather impatient of
what he had to endure in this hornet's nest, and anxiously looked
for some responsible person whom he might make an example
of, and hold up *in terrorem* to the rest. He had suffered under
these torments of the spirit three whole years—with the exception of the momentary repose which his explanation had procured him—when new pungency and venom were given to the
old joke, by the aforesaid passages of Lord Byron's satire.
Still the injured Little, though smarting under his wounds, had
too much discretion to take the steps usually pursued by an
Irishman in such situations, because the satire was not formally
published in the author's name. Very soon after, however,
Lord Byron, tickled with the *éclat* which his success had given
him, sent forth a second edition to the world, and acknowledged
the relation in which he stood to his work. The time for acting
was now come, and Mr. Moore shall tell what he did.

"I was, at the time, in Ireland, and but little in the way of literary society ; and it so happened that some months passed away before the appearance of this new edition was known to me. Immediately on being
apprized of it,—the offence now assuming a different form,—I addressed

the following letter to Lord Byron, and, transmitting it to a friend in London, requested that he would have it delivered into his lordship's hands.

"DUBLIN, January 1st, 1810.

"MY LORD,

"Having just seen the name of 'Lord Byron' prefixed to a work, entitled 'English Bards and Scotch Reviewers,' in which, as it appears to me, *the lie is given* to a public statement of mine, respecting an affair with Mr. Jeffrey some years since, I beg you will have the goodness to inform me whether I may consider your lordship as the author of this publication.

"I shall not, I fear, be able to return to London for a week or two; but in the mean time, I trust your lordship will not deny me the satisfaction of knowing whether you avow the insult contained in the passages alluded to.

"It is needless to suggest to your lordship the propriety of keeping our correspondence secret.

"I have the honour to be

"Your lordship's very humble servant,

"THOMAS MOORE."

"22, Molesworth-street."

"In the course of a week, the friend to whom I intrusted this letter wrote to inform me that Lord Byron had, as he learned on inquiring of his publisher, gone abroad immediately on the publication of his second edition; but that my letter had been placed in the hands of a gentleman named Hodgson, who had undertaken to forward it carefully to his lordship. Though the latter step was not exactly what I could have wished, I thought it as well, on the whole, to let my letter take its chance, and again postponed all consideration of the matter.—p. 229.

It appears, from the foregoing extract, that Mr. Moore took offence not at Lord Byron's ridiculing him as a coward, but at the fact that his Lordship had not been satisfied with Mr. Moore's explanation of the Chalk Farm business. As it was quite probable, however, that the noble satirist had never seen the explanation alluded to, there was, obviously, great room for accommodation without coming to blows. Still it was as well that Lord Byron went abroad, for during his absence a very remarkable change took place in his adversary's feelings, which is related with much ludicrous solemnity, in the following passage. The contrast between Mr. Moore's tenacity about having his explanation believed, and his caution in approaching Byron, appears to us irresistibly comic.

"During the interval of a year and a half which elapsed before Lord Byron's return, I had taken upon myself obligations, both as husband and father, which make most men,—and especially those who have nothing to bequeath,—less willing to expose themselves unnecessarily to danger. On hearing, therefore, of the arrival of the noble traveller from Greece, though still thinking it due to myself to follow up my first request of an explanation, I resolved, in prosecuting that object, to adopt such a tone of conciliation as should not only prove my sincere desire of a pacific result, but show the entire freedom from any angry or resentful feeling with which I took the step. The death of Mrs. Byron, for some time, delayed my purpose. But, as soon after that event as was consistent with decorum, I addressed a letter to Lord Byron, in which, referring to my former communication, and expressing some doubts as to its having ever reached him, I restated, in pretty nearly the same words, the nature of the insult, which, as it appeared to me, the passage in his note was calculated to convey. "It is now useless," I continued "to speak of the steps with which it was my intention to follow up that letter. The time which has elapsed since then, though it has done away neither the injury nor the feeling of it, has, in many respects, materially altered my situation; and the only object which I have now in writing to your lordship is to preserve some consistency with that former letter, and to prove to you that the injured feeling still exists, however circumstances may compel me to be deaf to its dictates at present. When I say 'injured feeling,' let me assure your lordship that there is not a single vindictive sentiment in my mind towards you. I mean but to express that uneasiness under (what I consider to be) a charge of falsehood, which must haunt a man of any feeling to his grave, unless the insult be retracted or atoned for: and which, if I did *not* feel, I should, indeed, deserve far worse than your lordship's satire could inflict upon me." In conclusion, I added, that, so far from being influenced by any angry or resentful feeling towards him it would give me sincere pleasure, if, by any satisfactory explanation, he would enable me to seek the honor of being henceforward ranked among his acquaintance."*

"To this letter Lord Byron returned the following answer.

"CAMBRIDGE, October 27th, 1811.

"SIR,—Your letter followed me from Nott's, to this place, which will account for the delay of my reply. Your former letter I never had the honor to receive;—be assured, in whatever part of the world it had found me, I should have deemed it my duty to return and answer it in person.

"The advertisement you mention, I know nothing of. At the time of your meeting with Mr. Jeffrey, I had recently entered College, and remember to have heard and read a number of squibs on the occasion, and from the recollection of these I derived all my knowledge on the subject, without the slightest idea of 'giving the lie' to an address which I never beheld. When I put my name to the production, which has occasioned this correspondence, I became responsible to all whom it might concern,—to explain where it requires explanation, and, where insufficiently or too sufficiently explicit, at all events to satisfy. My situation leaves me no choice; it rests with the injured and the angry to obtain reparation in their own way.

"With regard to the passage in question, *you* were certainly *not* the person towards whom I felt personally hostile. On the contrary, my whole thoughts were engrossed by one whom I had reason to consider as my worst literary enemy, nor could I foresee that his former antagonist was about to become his champion. You do not specify what you would wish to have done: *I can neither retract nor apologize for a charge of falsehood which I never advanced.*

"In the beginning of the week, I shall be at No. 8, St. James's-street. Neither the letter nor the friend to whom you stated your intention has ever made their appearance.

"Your friend Mr. Rogers, or any other gentleman delegated by you, will find me most ready to adopt any conciliatory proposition which shall not compromise my own honor,—or, failing in that, to make the atonement you deem it necessary to require.

"I have the honor to be, sir, your most obedient, humble, servant,
"BYRON."

* "Finding two different draughts of this letter among my papers, I cannot be quite certain as to some of the terms employed; but have little doubt that they are here given correctly."

"In my reply to this, I commenced by saying that his lordship's letter was, upon the whole, as satisfactory as I could expect. It contained all that, in the strict *diplomatique* of explanation, could be required, namely,—that he had never seen the statement which I supposed him wilfully to have contradicted,—that he had no intention of bringing against me any charge of falsehood, and that the objectionable passage of his work was not levelled personally at *me*. This, I added, was all the explanation that I had a right to expect, and I was, of course, satisfied with it.

"I then entered into some detail relative to the transmission of my first letter from Dublin,—giving, as my reason for descending to these minute particulars, that I did not, I must confess, feel quite easy under the manner in which his lordship had noticed the miscarriage of that first application to him.

"My reply concluded thus :—'As your lordship does not show any wish to proceed beyond the rigid formulary of explanation, it is not for me to make any further advances. We, Irishmen, in business of this kind, seldom know any medium between decided hostility and decided friendship : but, as my approaches towards the latter alternative must now depend entirely on your lordship, I have only to repeat that I am satisfied with your letter, and that I have the honor to be," &c. &c.

Lord Byron, however, showed not the smallest disposition to *fraternize* with the open-hearted Irishman. On the contrary, he received the proposal with the most haughty and repulsive coldness ; when Moore, "somewhat piqued," as he assures us, "at the manner in which his efforts towards a more friendly understanding"—ill-timed as he confesses them to have been—were received, hastening to close the correspondence by a short note, frankly avowing that Byron's carriage towards him had made him feel very awkwardly, and so, having received ample satisfaction touching the principal object of their correspondence, he hoped it would now cease forever. Lord Byron's generosity was affected by this *naïve* appeal to it. He, accordingly wrote Moore a note declaring that he had behaved to him with coldness only because he thought etiquette required it, and concluded with an assurance, that he "should be happy to meet when, where, and how he pleased." The result was a meeting at the house of the poet Rogers, in a *partie carrée* at dinner—consisting of the host, the combatants, and the author of the "Pleasures of Hope ;" at which, Lord Byron astonished his new acquaintance by his rigid abstinence from wine, as well as from every thing in the shape of fish, flesh or fowl.

Such is a brief outline of this singular affair. We will only add that the ascendant, which Byron possessed at the beginning, he obviously retained to the last, in his intercourse with Mr. Moore: and that his biography seems to us to have been written very much in the same spirit as the notes just adverted to—to wit, the spirit of—a dependant, at least—we were going to use a harsher word.

Lord Byron's genealogy was a proud one. He traced his descent on the father's side, from Ralph de Burun, whose name it seems, ranks high in Domesday Book, among the tenants of land in Nottinghamshire : and on the mother's from that Sir William Gordon, who was third son of the Earl of Huntley, by the daughter of James the I.   In more ancient times, his ancestors had distinguished themselves in the field and at court, but, for a considerable period before he came forward to give it immortality, the name of Byron had been under a cloud.   Those who believe in the force of *blood* will attach some importance to the reputations of the two personages to whom he was indebted for his life and estate—his father and his grand-uncle. The latter was tried for one murder, and accused of another ; for the "state of austere and almost savage seclusion," in which he passed the latter years of his strange life, gave occasion and countenance to many horrible stories in the neighbourhood of his residence.   One of these deserves notice : his cruelty to Lady Byron was notorious, and "it is even believed that, in one of his fits of fury, he flung her into the pond at Newstead." "All the kind of the Launces have this fault."   Lord Byron's father, Captain Byron, was twice married.   His first wife was Lady Carmarthen, whom he carried off with him to the continent, and (the Marquis having obtained a divorce from her) subsequently married.   Lord Byron's sister, Mrs. Leigh, was the fruit of this union.   The gallant captain's second choice—avowedly determined by mercenary motives—was Catharine Gordon, only child and heiress of George Gordon, Esq., of Gight.   He squandered her fortune with so much expedition, that, in the course of two years, she was reduced to a pittance of £150 per annum, and soon after retired to Aberdeen, where she took up her residence.   Her husband lived with her there for a short time, but they did not agree—except to a separation, which accordingly took place, *à l'amiable.*   Captain Byron died in '91 when his son was only three years of age, so that the whole task of educating the poet devolved upon his mother.   The character of that mother was an unfortunate one, and peculiarly unsuitable to such an office.   She was full of the most violent extremes, and seems to have been utterly unable to control her feelings.   She was thrown into hysterics by Mrs. Siddons in Isabella—and, on being informed of her husband's death, ill as he had treated her, and firmly as she had resented his misconduct, "her grief bordered on distraction, and her shrieks were so loud as to be heard in the street."   With a temperament thus inflammable, Mrs. Byron was equally destitute of every high intellectual endowment and all the winning graces of society.   Mr. Moore gives us the following, upon the authority of one of Lord Byron's earliest instructors, Dr. Glennie.   "Mrs. Byron was a total stranger to English society and English manners ; with an exterior far from prepossessing, an understanding where nature had not been more bountiful, a mind almost wholly without cultivation, and the peculiarities of northern opinions, northern habits, and northern accent, I trust, I do no great prejudice to the memory of my countrywoman, if I say Mrs. Byron was not a Madame de Lambert, endowed with powers to retrieve the fortune and form the character and manners of a young nobleman, her son." The worst feature, however, of the discipline, or rather *no*-discipline, in which Mrs. Byron trained up her son, was her excessive fondness and indulgence—interrupted, of course, at no very distant intervals, by volcanic explosions of rage. It is due to Lord Byron to quote the following passage :—

"Even under the most favourable circumstances, such an early elevation to rank would be but too likely to have a dangerous influence on the character; and the guidance, under which young Byron entered upon his new station, was, of all others the least likely to lead him safely through its perils and temptations. His mother, without judgment or self-command, alternately spoiled him by indulgence, and irritated, or—what was still worse—amused him by her violence. That strong sense of the ridiculous, for which he was afterward so remarkable, and which showed itself thus early, got the better even of his fear of her; and, when Mrs. Byron, who was a short and corpulent person, and rolled considerably in her gait, would in a rage, endeavour to catch him, for the purpose of inflicting punishment, the young urchin, proud of being able to outstrip her, notwithstanding his lameness, would run round the room, laughing like a little Puck, and mocking all her menaces. In the few anecdotes of his early life which he related in his 'Memoranda,' though the name of his mother was never mentioned but with respect, it was not difficult to perceive that the recollections she had left behind—at least, those that had made the deepest impression—were of a painful nature. One of the most striking passages, indeed, in the few pages of that Memoir which related to his early days, was where, in speaking of his own sensitiveness, on the subject of his deformed foot, he described the feeling of horror and humiliation that came over him, when his mother, in one of her fits of passion, called him 'a lame brat.' As all that he had felt strongly through life was, in some shape or other, reproduced in his poetry, it was not likely that an expression such as this should fail of being recorded. Accordingly, we find, in the opening of his drama, "The Deformed Transformed,"

> "*Bertha.* Out, hunchback !
> *Arnold.* I was born so mother !"

It may be questioned, indeed, whether that whole drama was not indebted for its origin to this single recollection."—pp. 33, 34.

If it is not without reason that so much importance has been attached to the influence of the mother in the formation of a son's character—and we believe that it can scarcely be over-rated—great allowance ought to be made for Lord Byron's infirmities and errors on this ground.

We do not know whether others have felt as we did, in reading this account of Lord Byron's childhood—but we found the situation of the young poet extremely touching. It presents, in some respects, a striking contrast to his future destiny. He was alone in the world—unknown, and friendless, and in poverty. With none to care for him but his unhappy mother, the future heir of Newstead and a title, (for he succeeded to them collaterally, and, as it were, casually) experienced all that makes the lot of the fatherless so commiserable, as it is represented in the scriptures. He, whose voice of woe—wrung from him by the agonies of a self-tormenting spirit still doomed, in every change of circumstance, to suffering—was to reach to the uttermost corners of the earth, and draw tears from the eyes of the stranger and the foreigner, appears to have been an amiable and affectionate boy, of most vivacious and engaging manners (among his familiar acquaintance),* of a spirit remarkably enterprising and intrepid, and, although wild and wayward, and very much inclined to little acts of mischief, still, in general, liked by his teachers, and a decided favourite with his young associates. Yet were the seeds of his future wretchedness already sown. He was shy and sensitive to excess, and his mortification about his lameness—a mortification unspeakable in the young, and in Byron's case, approaching to madness—early superinduced upon him that impatience and even horror of ridicule, and those habits of gloomy seclusion and bitter, misanthropic derision and defiance, which grew with his growth, and became, at length, so fatally inveterate, as to form a part of his very being. The following simple anecdote speaks volumes to those who have studied the human heart.

"I have been told by a gentleman of Glasgow that the person who nursed his wife, and who still lives in his family, used often to join the nurse of Byron, when they were out with their respective charges, and one day said to her, as they walked together, 'What a pretty boy Byron is! what a pity he has such a leg!' On hearing this allusion to his infirmity, the child's eyes flashed with anger, and, striking at her with a little whip which he held in his hand, he exclaimed, impatiently, 'Dinna speak of it.' "—p. 23.

We have heard that, when he first grew up, he used to speak of himself, in reference to the same misfortune, as "accursed of God from his birth," His feelings upon this subject are expressed more fully, though not more powerfully, in the "Deformed Transformed." We have not the least doubt that a good portion of Lord Byron's morbid irritability is to be accounted for in this way. Sir Walter Scott, who labours under precisely the same misfortune, but seems to have borne it much more patiently, because discipline has made him a wiser and better man, has clearly felt a like mortification, though less intense in degree; or he could not possibly have drawn the

* "Few people understood Byron, but *I* know that he had naturally a kind and feeling heart, and that there was not a single spark of malice in his composition." *Dr. Pigot.* p. 70.

"Black Dwarf." That novel appears a piece of fantastic extravagance to superficial readers—it is, on the contrary, a profound and masterly conception, which nothing but such a genius, instructed by personal experience, could have formed. Shakspeare has, no doubt, admirably depicted one of the effects of this cause in Gloster's soliloquy, and, indeed, in the whole character of Richard III. He traces up the wickedness of this tyrant to his deformity. His cruelty to man is despite to God. He rebels against the "dissembling nature" which has *wronged* him—by which he has been

> "Curtailed of this fair proportion,
> *Cheated* of feature"—

and wreaks his capricious vengeance upon her more favoured children. This, as we shall presently have to remark, is the very spirit of Lord Byron's poetry—the spirit of rebellion and despite—the spirit of Cain, the homicide, with the "primal eldest curse upon him!" But Sir Walter Scott has dived much deeper than Shakspeare into this dreadful mystery of the heart. With all that makes him so striking a dramatic hero, there is something vulgar in Richard's wickedness. It is downright *devilry*, to use a homely phrase. There is nothing of the "archangel ruined" there—no glimpse of immortal aspirations dashed down— no ray of "an excess of glory obscured." He is never surprised into "tears such as angels weep." He is of the democracy—the populace of Hell—a head without name in the hierarchy of evil—the thrones, dominations, princedoms, virtues, powers, led on by HIM, "unmatched, save with the Almighty," have not heard of him. There is, of consequence, nothing to awaken sympathy in Richard—our pity is all given to his victims. But, in Scott's terrible picture—in Byron's imaginary, (if we persist in making that unmeaning distinction) but still acute and intense suffering—there is every thing to move us to compassion—much to plead even for forgiveness. It is vain to say that it argues a weak mind and an ill-regulated temper to be so much affected by what is, in the eye of reason, so trifling. Instinct, especially in youth, when character is forming, is too strong for mere unaided reason. Even at an advanced age, and in the midst of his triumphs, it is an undoubted, historical fact that Julius Cæsar was deeply mortified by his baldness.* The feeling, as expressed by Lord Byron to a friend, is that "nature has set a mark" upon the sufferer—held him up to be a show and a laughing stock—a

---

* Suetonius is precise and emphatic. Circa corporis curam morosior, ut non solun tonderetur diligenter ad raderetur, sed, velleretur etiam, ut quidam exprobaverunt; calvitii vero deformitatem *inquissime ferre*, sæpe obtrectatorum jocis obnoxium expertus.—*D. Julius*, 45. He adds, that for this reason, no act of public flattery ever pleased him so much as the being allowed to wear his laurels always—jus laureæ perpetuo gestandæ.

thing for the vulgar to wonder at, point at, scoff at. Byron, we venture to affirm, spoke only the language of all irritable and proud spirits, under a similar misfortune, before time has reconciled them to their fate, when he said, with so pointed an emphasis, what is ascribed to him in the following passage, "But the embittering circumstances of his life—that which haunted him like a curse, amid the buoyancy of youth and the anticipations of fame and pleasure—was, strange to say, the trifling deformity of his foot. By that one slight blemish, (as in his moments of melancholy he persuaded himself) all the blessings that nature had showered upon him were counterbalanced. His reverend friend, Mr. Beecher, finding him one day unusually dejected, endeavored to cheer and rouse him by representing, in their brightest colors, all the various advantages with which Providence had endowed him, and, among the greatest, that of 'a mind which placed him above the rest of mankind.' 'Ah! my dear friend,' said Byron mournfully—'if *this* (laying his hand upon his forehead) places me above the rest of mankind, *that* (pointing to his foot) places me far, far below them.'" There was no affectation in this: there is not more exaggeration than is generally found in expressions of poignant feeling. But the victim here, let it be remembered, was born a poet, with that exquisite sensitiveness and that gloomy and fitful disposition, which have always marked the poetical temperament. The same sensibilities which made him so tremblingly alive to beauty, which kindled up into enthusiasm or were dissolved in tenderness and pathos, where others scarcely felt at all—in short, the peculiar organization, which made Byron what he was, exposed him "to bleed and agonize at every pore"—turned his sadness into moody melancholy, and exalted his griefs into madness and despair. We do not mean to extenuate his vices—we shall not follow the example of Mr. Moore. His conduct, especially after he had attained to mature years, was, in our opinion, wholly indefensible. But if we would be just, we must be merciful to men of genius. It is the interest of human nature to show, where those who have, in some respects, adorned and exalted it most, have gone astray, that their errors may be accounted for, if not excused, by sufficient reasons, and that the highest gifts and accomplishments of man have not been, as if in mockery, thrown away upon *monsters*. There is deep sense as well as pathos in the lines on Sheridan—

> "——— ah! little do ye know
> That what to you seems vice might be but wo!"

We shall not shrink from the solemn duty of exposing, so far as in us lies, the enormous sins of Lord Byron's genius and life—his blasphemy against Providence—his infernal scoffings at human nature—and all that he did to darken our views of the one, and to degrade and pervert and defile the other. Yet far be it from us to join in that unfeeling host who, in his own language,

> "———— track the steps of glory to the grave,
> Watch every fault that daring genius owes
> Half to the ardor which its birth bestows."

We shall, in all we have to say about him, allow him the full benefit of the plea, which, in the same poem, he sets up for the celebrated martyr of undiciplined genius—

> "Breasts to whom all the strength of feeling given
> Bear hearts electric—charged with fire from heaven,
> Black with the rude collision, wildly torn,
> By clouds surrounded and on whirlwinds borne,
> Driven o'er the lowering atmosphere that nurst,
> Thoughts which have turned to thunder—scorch and burst."*

But we fear that it is not in this plea—even urged with all the force of this exaggerated language—to save Lord Byron from condemnation as an unprincipled and bad man.

When we say that he was an unprincipled man, we mean to be understood in the proper sense of that epithet. He alone can aspire to the reputation of virtue, who, besides having good impulses, and what is called an amiable character, lays down settled rules for the government of his conduct, from which it is possible to calculate, with some approach to certainty, what that conduct will be, from day to day, under given circumstances. A man, for instance, who is only charitable by fits and starts—who, at one moment, lavishes his bounty upon the undeserving, and, at another, withholds it from the most meritorious object in the most calamitous situation—may be, naturally, of a very benevolent disposition, but conduct, thus determined by casual impulse cannot be regarded as strictly virtuous. It is for this reason that prudent men often do charity, where they are doubtful about the claims of the object, merely that their own good habits may not be broken in upon, and their principles be supplanted by caprice. But as bad men may lay down inflexible rules for the government of their conduct, something more than this constancy is necessary to the definition of virtue. A man's principles then must be *good* ; that is they must be such as arise out of and confirm the better impulses of our nature, the social and benevolent affections ; and we may add they ought to be, in strictness, merely indications and consequences of those impulses, in every particular instance. In other words, the feeling and the principle ought every where to co-exist. Thus, it is quite conceivable that a man should discharge all the duties of a father,

* Monody on Sheridan,

a husband, a son, with perfect propriety and exactness, and yet, not possess, in any remarkable degree, the sentiments which are natural in those several relations, and which one would be led by his conduct to attribute to him.   Such a man, however, would be strictly virtuous; he would do all that society has a right to exact—and yet, to persons standing towards him in any of those correlative situations, however estimable, he would not be a very amiable object.   They would *lament* the absence of those sweet affections which usually make virtue its own reward, yet they could not justly *complain :* they might not love, but they could not *disapprove.*   Nay, it is very possible that an exemplary man, instead of being blessed with such impulses, should be visited by feelings of the very opposite character ; yet, if he resisted them so successfully as to act up to the standard of nature and right reason, he would still deserve the reward of virtue, for virtue consists in *action* and

> "———— evil into the mind of God or man
> May come and go, so unapproved, and leave
> No spot or blame ————."

Now, making all the allowances, which we admit ought to be made, for a being so peculiarly constituted as Lord Byron, we do not think his fondest admirers would agree to try him by this standard of conduct—at least, we shall put him to the test, presently, in a case or two.   He seems to have been altogether the creature of *impulse.*   Originally, it should seem, his impulses—bating some rather ominous "silent rages"—were amiable and kindly—there was a certain effeminate softness in his disposition, blended with great spirit and energy—above all, love, as he says of Rousseau, love was of his soul's essence, his very being's being.   Had his fortunes continued until his thirtieth year as humble as they were in his ninth, we have no doubt but that his temper had been mellowed down to gentleness and equability.   His was precisely the character over which the discipline of necessity would have exercised its most salutary influence.   The idea that he was likely, in spite of his scepticism, to become enthusiastically religious—that he would kindle with the fervor of the Methodists, or be smitten with the imposing and gorgeous solemnities of the Catholic Church— was founded upon this view of his character.   It is precisely such a mind as Byron's—when it has not been perverted by false principles—that is most apt to give itself up entirely to the impressions of grandeur and beauty, which the magnificent manifestations of Deity throughout all his works are adapted to make upon reflecting beings ; and these impressions are the soul and poetry of all religion.   Even when his vast conceptions came to be always, more or less, deeply tinged with a peevish and petulant misanthropy, they were at home in the immensity of nature. He had a sympathy with her mighty and mysterious powers. Like his own Manfred, he seemed to hold communion from the mountain-tops with the viewless spirits of the air.

> "I live not in myself, but I become
> Portion of that around me; and to me
> High mountains are a feeling, but the hum
> Of human cities torture; I can see
> Nothing to loathe in nature, save to be
> A link reluctant in a fleshly chain,
> Classed among creatures, when the soul can flee,
> And with the sky, the peak, the heaving plain,
> Of ocean or the stars, mingle————."

But his natural tastes were at length perverted, as in other respects, so even in this. There came a time when he saw undelighted all delight, not only among men, but in the material universe. Like the same dark creature of his imagination just mentioned, when he stood upon the summit of the Jungfrau, as the morning awaked around in her gladness and bloom, he could say—

> "My Mother Earth!
> And thou fresh breaking day, and you, ye mountains,
> Why are ye beautiful? I cannot love you.

It was so in every thing else. His whole nature was in process of time perverted and poisoned. The irregularities of his temper and disposition, instead of being corrected by experience, were confirmed by excessive indulgence. From the time he became Lord Byron, he seems to have been entirely emancipated from all control. The authority of his mother, which had never been great, ceased entirely—his guardian, Lord Carlisle, discouraged by his waywardness, or on some other pretext, coldly abandoned him to his fate. He never learned the first, last, great lesson of man's existence—submission. He became more and more impatient of contradiction, rebellious against authority, wilful and obstinate in his course of conduct, peculiar and fantastical in his manner of living. To approve himself worthy of the ancestor from whom he immediately inherited his estate, he armed himself, while quite a boy, with pistols, and began to *play* the out-law which he afterwards *became* in another sense. He gradually learned to refer every thing to himself, like other spoiled children; and to expect that the laws of nature should yield to his wanton caprices. The smallest offence to his pride, or self-love, was to be visited with unmeasured, insatiable vengeance. Nor was it very material against whom he vented his spleen. It was enough that *his* bosom had been made to feel a pang, to justify his offering up, like Achilles, whole hecatombs to his own terrible wrath. For the attack made upon him by the Edinburg Reviewers, he wreaked his vengeance indiscriminately upon all his contemporaries: without, for a moment, reflecting upon the injustice which he was doing to many, and of which he afterwards professed to repent so much. The great exemplar of Byron was Coriolanus in the Volscian camp, before Rome—but Coriolanus, deaf to his mother's prayers. Lord Bacon speaks of a certain excess of self-love which would make a man burn down another's house to roast his own eggs. Byron's was not so mean, but it was equally extravagant: to atone for the smallest affront, he would have reckoned his country but a cheap victim. The hero after his own heart is the parricidal apostate Alp—the traitor Doge Faliero—a man, this latter, of whom it is worthy of remark that the Italian writers speak as of a moral portent, *haruspice dignum.* In a word, the poetry of Lord Byron, which pictures forth his own character, is—to borrow a quaint phrase of Madame de Staël—the very "apotheosis" of self-love. They were considered as grovelling and degraded, these selfish passions, better suited for comedy than ode or epic, before they were raised to a "bad eminence" by his verse. But he has lifted them up to the height of his great genius. He has converted revenge—which was never allowed to be, at best, more than a "sort of wild justice," and which, when disproportionate, is the very spirit of Pandæmonium itself—into a heroic virtue. What dreadful lines are these! and yet hundreds of such are to be found in every part of his works:—

> "Ah! fondly youthful hearts can press
> To seize and share the dear caress;
> But love itself could never pant
> For all that beauty sighs to grant
> With half the fervor hate bestows
> Upon the last embrace of foes, &c.*

It will not do, as we have already observed, to say that Lord Byron is not responsible for the sentiments of his corsairs and renegadoes. The truth is that his whole poetry is steeped—dyed, through and through, with these feelings. They obtrude themselves upon him in the deepest solitudes of nature—they discolor to his eye the most glorious objects of contemplation—they turn the sun into blood and the moon into darkness, and earth into a charnel house, and a den of wild beasts, and a hell before him.

Nothing can be imagined more utterly subversive of all sound principle than such a system. The end of moral discipline is the very reverse of these notions. It is to mortify, to control, to do all but extinguish self-love, and especially that variety of it which the French call *amour propre*—a conceited, irritable, *exacting* self-love. Instead of making a man a god in

* Giaour, 645, et seq.

his own eyes, shaking the spheres, of which he deems himself the centre, with his nod—that discipline teaches him to view himself as much as possible, with the eyes of others, and to accommodate his sentiments and conduct, as Adam Smith expresses it, to the sense of the impartial spectator. Instead of consecrating the absurd conceits of vanity, the bitter moodiness of despite, the wild sallies of vengeance, the spirit of rebellion against restraint; the pride, envy, hatred, and all uncharitableness, which are the accursed brood of this concentrated *égoisme*—it inculcates upon the aspirant that there can be neither happiness nor virtue where there is not resignation, and that it is not more the lot, than it is the duty and the interest of man, to acquiesce in the order of nature and of society. It exhorts him, therefore, to possess himself in patience—to say, with the philosophic Antoninus, "every thing suits me, which is fitted to promote thy harmony, O World. Nothing is either premature or tardy which is in good time for thee. All that thy seasons bring forth, O Nature, is fruit for me. Out of thee are all things, in thee are all things, to and for thee are all things. There are who say, O beloved city of Cecrops: shall none exclaim, O beloved city of God."* This is the language of a heathen philosopher, seated upon the throne of the Cæsars, and absolute master of the Roman world. Yet is it a language which suits all times and nations and degrees in society—the language of christianity, of virtue, and of common sense. But Lord Byron was a revolted spirit, and his school of poetry has been not improperly designated as the Satanic, or, as we should prefer calling it, the *Titanic* School.

That there is a problem in nature of which reason is utterly incapable of furnishing any exact philosophical solution is acknowledged, even by those who do not believe that the mystery has been cleared up by the light of revelation. This problem is the origin of evil, moral and natural.† It has perplexed speculative men in all ages; and, although they have generally come to the same practical result, which we have just seen embodied in the sublime language of the Portico, yet they have come to it by very various, and all of them, blind and thorny paths. These doubts are more painful just in proportion as men are enlightened, and entertain a more exalted idea of the creator and governor of the universe. Among barbarous nations who indulge very little in reflection of any kind, the common feeling upon this subject shows itself only in their popular superstitions. What they suffer is set down to the account of evil spirits or gods of some sort or other. But they are not struck with the apparent incongruity between the boundless aspirations of the soul and the condition to which the body is reduced on earth—between what man imagines and what he experiences,

* Liv. iv.   [† Esdras II. ch. 7. 46.]

his dreams and his doom—in short they have not learned to set
in opposition,

> "An heir of glory ! a frail child of dust!
> Helpless immortal ! insect infinite !
> A worm ! a god !"

Poetry, which is the language of nature, uttered with the least
reserve or disguise, is full of such melancholy reflections. Even
the classical poetry of Greece, though represented, by the advocates of the romantic school, as so cheerful, joyous, and brilliant,
abounds in them; and those "teachers best of moral prudence,"
the tragedians, often say "in Chorus or Iambick," that it were
better for man that he had never been born.*

> Μὴ φῦναι τον ἄπαντα νι–
> κᾶ λόγον· τὸ δ' ἐπεὶ φανῇ
> Βῆναι κειθεν ὅθεν περ ἥκει
> Πολὺ δεύτερον ὡς ταχιςα.
>
> [Soph. Œdip. Colon. 1290.

Yet, it must be owned, that these passages, however frequent,
are still only of occasional occurrence—this melancholy spirit
certainly does not form the basis, if we may so express ourselves, or key-note, of the classical poetry of antiquity. Nor
is there ever any thing beyond *lamentation* in these effusions.
It is Job pouring out his sorrows in magnificent lyrical self-
bewailings, but refusing to "curse God and die." In both these
respects they differ materially from Byron's song. His muse—
unknown among the old nine of Greece—is inspired by, and
inspires, nothing but despair. Robed in her funereal pall, with
her distracted looks and snaky hair, she would be as unwelcome a guest in the Delphic vestibule, as the Furies of Orestes in Æschylus. But not only does his poetry, like an
ill-omened bird, sit brooding over the evil alone which seems
to deform the universe, and proclaiming it to unhappy mortals
with a demoniac despite. It raves and blasphemes. It represents the rebellious spirit of the Titans warring with fate and
heaven. It takes the place of the impious Capaneus.† It curses
the Creator and his creation, and the birth and the life and the
death of man. Nothing in Dante's Inferno, or Milton's, is more
frightful, than the views which Byron presents of human destiny, throughout his works, and the general impression which they
make upon a reader. We never think of them, in reference to
their moral character, without being reminded of the terrible

[* Iliad P. 445. Jupiter and the horses of Achilles. Cf. the words of Arta-
banus to Xerxes weeping on the Hellespont. Herod. 7. 46. Pind. Pyth. 8. 131–
9. Σκιας οναρ ανθρωπος. Cf. the remarkable dialogue of Æschines, περὶ
Θανατου,—all Mimnermus. Herder s Ideen, etc., 12. B. v., p. 162.]
    [† Dante's Inferno.]

lines in which the great Italian bard describes the first confused, hideous sounds of hell, which resounded through "the starless air."

"Quivi sospiri, pianti ed alti guai,
Risonavan, per l'aer senza stelle—
Diverse lingue, orribili favelle,
Parole di dolore, accenti d'ira
Voci alte e fioche, e suon di man con elle," &c.

Young's Night Thoughts are the counterpart of Byron's poetry. But we need not say that they differ as widely in their spirit and their results, as Christianity and Atheism. The former paints, to be sure, a terrible picture of this life—but it is to draw away our eyes to a better and brighter prospect. All is vanity in our pursuits and possessions here—because there is so much more in reserve for us hereafter. Young dwells upon the mournful incidents and evidences of mortality—

"The knell, the shroud, the mattock, and the grave;
The deep damp vault, the darkness, and the worm."

But the grave gains no victory and death has no sting, where all is faith and hope and heaven beyond it. But Byron's only refuge from despair is in desperation. His fate is that of Prometheus Vinctus—without his innocence and philanthropy. He is chained upon a rock, hurling defiance and execrations against Jove, and a vulture is gnawing his vitals, which die not, and yet live only for suffering—but he cannot reflect upon the services he has rendered mankind—he has neither the crown nor the consolations of martyrdom.

Whoever has considered the scheme and drift of Goëthe's famous drama of Faustus, understands the history of Lord Byron. The progress in evil which the aspiring adept makes under the guidance of his familiar spirit—the gradual extinction of his original sensibility, in a bitter, ironical, undistinguishing hard-heartedness—his falling off from grand conceptions and ambitious views, into vulgar wickedness and debauchery—every effect, indeed, which that diabolical discipline was fitted to produce is seen in the successive phases or aspects of Byron's character. His works touch the two extremes of this Titantic style. If in one of them, he is on a level with that grand conception of Æschylus, to which we have just referred—the Prometheus Vinctus—he descends in the other to the fiend-like buffoonery of Candide. Childe Harold is the repository of whatever is most sublime in his sorrow and scorn. The two last cantos especially are full of touching sensibility. Some stanzas it is impossible to read, without forgetting the errors or offences of the writer, in his dreadful sufferings, and the powerful appeals which he addresses to the sympathies of mankind. The following lines— bating the exaggeration and inequality which are the great

blemishes of all Byron's poetry, but especially of this poem—
would not be out of character in the fine tragedy just mentioned.

"It is not that I may not have *incurr'd*,
For my ancestral faults or mine, *the wound*
I bleed withal, and, had it been *conferr'd*
With a just weapon, it had flow'd unbound;
But now my blood shall not sink in the ground ;
To thee [Nemesis] I do devote it—*thou* shalt take
The vengeance, which shall yet be sought and found,
Which if *I* have not taken for the sake—
But let that pass—I sleep, but thou shalt yet awake.

And if my voice break forth, 'tis not that now
I shrink from what is suffered : let him speak
Who hath beheld decline upon my brow,
Or seen my mind's convulsion leave it weak :
But in this page a record will I seek.
Not in the air shall these my words disperse,
Tho' I be ashes ; a far hour shall wreak
The deep prophetic fulness of this verse,
And pile on human heads the mountain of my curse !

That curse shall be forgiveness—Have I not—
Hear me, my mother earth ! behold it, Heaven !
Have I not had to wrestle with my lot ?
Have I not suffer'd things to be forgiven ?
Have I not had my brain seared, my heart riven,
Hopes sapp'd, name blighted, life's life lied away ?
And only not to desperation driven,
Because altogether of such clay
As *rots into the souls of those whom I survey.*

From mighty wrongs to petty perfidy,
Have I not seen what human things could do ?
From the *loud roar of foaming calumny*
To the small whisper of the as paltry few,
And subtler venom of the reptile crew,
The Janus glance of whose significant eye,
Learning to lie with silence, would *seem* true,
And without utterance, save the shrug or sigh,
Deal round to happy fools its speechless obloquy.

But I have lived, and have not lived in vain :
My mind may lose its force, my blood its fire,
And my frame perish even in conquering pain,
But there is that within me which shall tire
Torture and time, and breathe when I expire ;
Something unearthly, which they deem not of,
Like the remembered tone of a mute lyre,
Shall on their softened spirits sink, and move
In *hearts all rocky now the late remorse of love.*

[Childe Harold, cxxxiii. Canto iv.

There is, doubtless, too much of this—nor is it in Byron's very
best vein—yet one cannot help thinking that, had he never writ-

ten in any other, the fond anticipation expressed in the last line might have been fulfilled. But his heart became callous in its vices. The pathos, which gave dignity and attraction to the earlier expressions of his misanthropy, disappeared—and the magnificent lamentations and the tragical despair of the Childe, sank into the gross ribaldry of Rochester. Lord Byron in writing Don Juan, renounced—renounced with foul scorn and beyond all hope of recovery—the sympathies of mankind. He had just the same excuse, as he played the same part, with the murderer in Macbeth, and all other worthies of a similar stamp.

> "————— I am one, my liege,
> Whom the vile blows and buffets of the world
> Have so incensed, that I am reckless what
> I do, to spite the world."

It was, however, neither his gloomy views of nature and destiny, nor native, unmixed wickedness of heart, that made him the savage scoffer which he at last became. It was defeated, mortified, agonizing *pride*. Pride (with a strong infusion of vanity) was his ruling passion—at least, it seems to have swallowed up the rest, from the moment that he stood forth as a man of great consequence in the public eye. The obstinacy and impatience of the spoiled child, had been confirmed and inflamed by the unexpected accession of a fortune and a title. Still, before the attack of the Edinburgh Review, he does not seem to have discovered much acerbity of temper (the 'silent rages' excepted) ; his faults, as yet, had been those rather of levity and mere want of principle, as in his conduct to his mother. But, from the time of publishing his satire, he appears in a totally new light. Then, for the first time, he tasted the intoxicating, Circean cup of public applause. He became confident in his powers, and his poetical temperament (which had not been developed before) and his gloomy and ferocious misanthropy displayed themselves at once, in the first and second cantos of Childe Harold. Here, again, "a change came o'er the spirit" of his life. The unbounded success of that poem seems to have astonished its author. Mr. Moore mentions it as a surprising thing, that Byron did not set a very high value upon the MS., thinking that his *fort* was satire. We confess we see nothing very surprising in this. He had actually succeeded in the one—in which, indeed, a certain ephemeral success is easily commanded, even by malignant mediocrity—and the other was written after a fashion not only as yet untried by its author, but altogether new and adventurous in itself.

When we consider what had been the condition of English poetry for half a century before Scott appeared, we shall know how to appreciate Byron's misgivings about his poetical *outlaw*, for so Harold was in more senses than one. The fruit of its success, however, was unbounded admiration and flattery. Such poetry, written by a young lord who was, at the same time, a rake and a dandy—was, at least, as extraordinary a phenomenon, as a volcano bursting forth from the bottom of the North Sea. In order to estimate the effect which this dazzling and sudden *éclat* produced upon Byron's mind, we must recollect a fact mentioned by Mr. Moore. This was that when his lordship went to the House of Lords, to claim his seat as a hereditary legislator of the land, and a representative of one of its most ancient families, he found himself utterly alone. There was no one even to introduce him in form. His guardian, Lord Carlisle, stood aloof, and he knew nobody else. Few situations can be imagined—none in more humble life—so well calculated to mortify a proud and aspiring man—especially one laying so great a stress upon the advantages which exposed him to that trial.* But his poetry—which he threw off with uncommon *nonchalance*, as if he only rhymed because he could not help it—gave him just such control over the public mind, as was most flattering to his self-love. Byron had not much of a merely literary ambition—no propensity for book-making as such. On the contrary, he was emphatically a lord among wits. We have already cited Mr. Moore's authority to shew that he valued himself much more upon his blood, than upon his *books*, for which he disdained to receive any compensation. We say his *books*, not for the sake of the alliteration, but because it suggests a very important distinction. We fully believe in Lord Byron's contempt for authors and authorship. It was in anology with the rest of his character—and worthy of so genuine a descendant of those feudal barons, who, according to Castiglione— tutti i literati tengono per vilissimi uomini e pare lor dir grande villania a chi si sia, quando lo chiamano *clero*.† But, then, he was exceedingly proud of *being able* to write a better book than any professed author could—by an inspiration which put to shame their "slow endeavouring art." His *genius* was a privilege the more: a distinction, which set him apart from the

---

* "But at the time when we first met, his position in the world was most solitary. Even those coffee-house companions who, before his departure from England, had served him as a sort of substitute for more worthy society, were either relinquished or had dispersed ; and, with the exception of three or four associates of his college days, (to whom he appeared strongly attached) Mr. Dallas and his solicitor seemed to be the only persons whom, even in their very questionable degree, he could boast of as friends. Though too proud to complain of this loneliness, it was evident that he felt it ; and that the state of cheerless isolation, "unguided and unfriended," to which, on entering into manhood, he had found himself abandoned, was one of the chief sources of that resentful disdain of mankind, which even their subsequent worship of him came too late to remove. The effect, indeed, which his short commerce with society afterwards had, for the period it lasted, in softening and exhilirating his temper, showed how fit a soil his heart would have been for the growth of all the kindlier feelings, had but a portion of this sunshine of the world's smiles shone on him earlier." p. 240.

† Il Corteggiano, lib. i.

herd of mankind. It put him above his less-gifted peers—the *noble* vulgar—and it enabled him to write up or write down, just as the mood prompted, their claims to the consideration of the world. There can be no doubt that the antiquity of a distinguished race has a great effect upon the imagination. There is a *prestige* in rank derived from a prescription, whereof the memory of man runneth not to the contrary, which no *created* peerage, of whatever class, possesses. But this advantage is quite ideal, and the prosaic world *will* perversely prefer a Duke or Earl, with a patent but of yesterday—especially if he be rich—even to a descendant of the Bastard or the Plantagenets, who is only a poor baron. This happened to be Lord Byron's situation, and his genius was necessary to turn the scale in his favour as against *them*. His competition with literary men was a secondary object with him, but not an indifferent one. Failure was intolerable to him in any undertaking ; and that no adversary, however humble, was contemptible in his eyes, is manifest from his too celebrated "Sketch." He could have made up his mind, perhaps, without great effort, not to write at all, at least after his reputation was once established ; but he could not bear to write what none could read or approve. Accordingly, Mr. Moore informs us that, upon some mortification or disgust real or imaginary, of the kind, he talked of recalling all his works, and renouncing "the trade" forever. Nothing could be more characteristic than this anecdote. It shews all the sickly sensitiveness, and the impracticable and repulsive pride of his character.

His pride, we have said, was strongly dashed with vanity. Lord Byron did not know that sublime, rational, imperturbable self-esteem—that prophetic confidence in his unaided genius— which Milton felt, and expresses with such a noble candor, in the "Apology for Smectymnus" and others of his prose writings. It is impossible to read the passages to which we allude, without doing homage to the matchless sublimity of this great man's moral character, more especially when we consider under what circumstances it was that he fulfilled his glorious anticipations in the composition of "Paradise Lost." All poets—the classical poets of antiquity, especially—have indulged, without the least reserve, in boastful self-praise. And they have done this in the rapture and revelry of their inspiration—"soaring," to use Milton's own words, "in the high region of their fancies, with their garlands and singing robes about them." But we know not where any of them, "sitting here below in the cool element of prose, a mortal thing among many readers of no empyreal conceit," has ventured to divulge his secret opinion of his own powers, and his bright visions of future glory, with such antique simplicity, such an air of solemn conviction, such an awful sense of the account which, he to whom much is given, will be required to render of its use. To impute vanity to such a being, were nothing short of blasphemy. His character was as grand as his epic. How much is expressed in the single sentence which follows! "And long it was not after, when I was confirmed in this opinion that he who would not be frustrate of his hope to write well hereafter in laudable things ought himself to be a true poem; that is, a composition and pattern of the best and honorablest things; not presuming to sing high praises of heroic men and famous cities, unless he have in himself the experience and the practice of all that which is praiseworthy." Well might such a man expect "to leave something so written to after times, as that they should not willingly let it die." Well might he scorn the "rabble rout" of a prostituted and infamous court of mimes and harlots, and ask only for the few who were "fit audience" for *him*. Well might he console himself "in danger, and with darkness compassed round and solitude," with the reflection that he had incurred the sorest of human calamities, loss of sight, in the service of mankind—"in liberty's defence, his noble task,

"Whereof all Europe rang from side to side."

Contrast with the "honest haughtiness"—the stern, majestic, and, we might almost add, *holy* pride of such a being, the irritable, petulant, worldly-minded, little self-love of Byron, writing a travestie of Southey's Vision and bitter libels upon my lady's nurse!

Burke, if we mistake not, calls Jean Jacques, "the apostle of vanity." The designation is equally just and felicitous. There is no doubt that a good share of Rousseau's madness, (as it is called) is to be ascribed to the extraordinary elevation to which he so suddenly attained, at a rather advanced age. He was entirely beside himself—intoxicated with success. Born in humble circumstances (he had even been a menial servant), his admirable genius did not inspire him with sentiments above the condition of a *parvenu*. He never felt at home in the great world—his immense reputation and popularity did not sit as easily upon him as a suit of livery. He was, accordingly, the victim of a morbid vanity—always doubting the sincerity of the worshipper, even when he was suffocated with the fumes of his incense, mistaking his best friends for assassins, and every social circle for a conspiracy against his reputation, which, of course, entirely engrossed the thoughts of all mankind. Byron has been frequently compared with this "inspired madman;" and not without reason. But we do not know any trait in which he resembles him so much, as his morbid and jealous vanity. The difference between them is, that Rousseau had none of that gloomy and insolent pride which made the vanity of the poet so peculiarly bitter and odious. Byron's "chief humor," like Bottom's, "was for a tyrant," and, whilst he was full of the suspicions of a vain man, he was haunted by all those which are the inseparable companion and "bosom plague" of tyranny, in all its shapes. He challenged the admiration of mankind by every effort and device—from the highest flights of genius to the smallest artifices and affectations of fashionable life—but he challenged it, as an Eastern despot gathers his tributes, with fire and sword. His mighty genius was governed by the paltriest motives, and made subservient to the most despicable ends—yet he could not bear that such a guilty and grovelling abuse of the most sublime powers should bring down upon him the scorn of the wise and the good, and he did every thing he could to disgust and defy them still more. He wrote his finest poetry, as he bought the finest clothes, to make an impression at Almack's and in Bond-street; and, whether he rivalled Milton or Brummel, he affected the same lordly, well-bred indifference about his success, and felt the same burning desire to command it. Pope's powerful picture of the effect of vanity in the Duke of Wharton is applicable to Byron, with the qualifications which we made just now, in speaking of Rousseau. Nothing is so whimsical and contradictory as self-love in this form—it is the most extravagant of coquettes—rejecting what it would make any sacrifice to obtain, were it not offered unsought, deriding the object of its secret affection, but always the most unhappy victim of its own caprices. The curse, however, of its destiny is suspicion. It anticipates the hostility which it has done so much to provoke. It is haunted with hideous imaginings—its way is beset with innumerable enemies—it is hated by the world, wronged, persecuted—and all because mankind, wearied out with its impertinences, leave it to itself and attend to their own business or pleasures, with as much interest and keenness, as if there had never been any such being, in nature, as Byron and Rousseau. Then come the mutterings of wrath and vengeance—"worm-like 'twas trampled, adder-like revenged," &c., and the ravings and scoffing of despair and madness. A brilliant writer has well said—"rien n'est si barbare que la vanité * * * Quand la vanité se montre, elle est bienveillante; quand elle se cache, la crainte de'être découverte la rend amère et elle affecte l'indifférence, la satiété," &c. Byron had much to mortify him. His destiny was a cruel tantalism. He possessed signal advantages—but every blessing was dashed with bitterness, and the suffering from what was withheld was more than the enjoyment from what he possessed. He was a man of the proudest descent—yet he was born in obscurity, and he went into the House of Lords, like an intruder, unknown, unwelcome. He was of high degree but low estate—a nobleman and man of fashion, so straitened in his circumstances, that his house was always beset with duns and bailiffs. He was the most beautiful of men, with a deformity which humbled him to the dust. He had a sublime genius, but undisciplined and irregular—exquisite sensibility, but so perverted as to be alive only to suffering—and, in the full blaze of his glory, "the depreciation of the lowest of mankind was more painful to him, than the applause of the highest was pleasing."*

We quote the following as illustrative of what we have said—

"A resolution was, about this time, adopted by him, which, however strange and precipitate it appeared, a knowledge of the previous state of his mind may enable us to account for satisfactorily. He had now, for two years, been drawing upon the admiration of the public with a rapidity and success which seemed to defy exhaustion,—having crowded, indeed, into that brief interval, the materials of a long life of fame. But admiration is a sort of impost from which most minds are but too willing to relieve themselves. The eye grows weary of looking up to the same object of wonder, and begins to exchange, at last, the delight of observing its elevation for the less generous pleasure of watching and speculating on its fall. The reputation of Lord Byron had already begun to experience some of these consequences of its own prolonged and constantly renewed splendor. Even among that host of admirers who would have been the last to find fault, there were some not unwilling to repose from praise; while they, who had been from the first reluctant eulogists, took advantage of these apparent symptoms of satiety to indulge in blame.

"The loud outcry raised, at the beginning of the present year, by his verses to the Princess Charlotte, had afforded a vent for much of this reserved venom; and the tone of disparagement in which some of his assailants now affected to speak of his poetry was, however absurd and contemptible in itself, precisely that sort of attack which was the most calculated to wound his, at once, proud and diffident spirit. As long as they confined themselves to blackening his moral and social character, so far from offending, their libels rather fell in with his own shadowy style of self-portraiture, and gratified the strange inverted ambition that possessed him. But the slighting opinion which they ventured to express of his genius,—seconded as it was by that inward dissatisfaction with his own powers, which they whose standard of excellence is highest are always the surest to feel—mortified and disturbed him; and, being the first sounds of ill augury that had come across his triumphal career, startled him, as we have seen, into serious doubts of its continuance.

"Had he been occupying himself, at the time, with any new task, that confidence in his own energies, which he never truly felt but while in the actual exercise of them, would have enabled him to forget these humiliations of the moment in the glow and excitement of anticipated success. But he had just pledged himself to the world to take a long farewell of poesy,—had sealed up that only fountain from which his heart ever drew refreshment or strength,—and thus was left, idly and helplessly, to brood over the daily taunts of his enemies, without the power of avenging himself when they insulted his person, and but too much disposed to agree with them when they made light of his genius. 'I am afraid (says he, in noticing these attacks in one of his letters) what you call *trash* is plaguily to the purpose, and very good sense into the bargain; and to tell the truth, for some little time past, I have been myself much of the same opinion.'"

* A MS. note of Lord Byron on Mr. D'Israeli's Work.

"In this sensitive state of mind,—which he but ill disguised or relieved by an exterior of gay defiance or philosophic contempt,—we can hardly feel surprised that he should have, all at once, come to the resolution, not only of persevering in his determination to write no more in future, but of purchasing back the whole of his past copyrights, and suppressing every page and line he had ever written. On his first mention of this design, Mr. Murray naturally doubted as to his seriousness; but the arrival of the following letter, enclosing a draft for the amount of the copyrights, put his intentions beyond question."—pp. 396-7.

Lord Byron's political principles—if his vague, unsettled notions upon such subjects deserve the name of principles, as, according to his own account, they certainly do not—are in perfect keeping with the rest of his character. His maxim was, *aut Cæsar, aut nihil*—he spurned at all control or subordination—the very name of *subject* was hateful to him. That he should be a republican in Europe followed as a matter of course. The love of liberty is the instinct of a haughty spirit, and, as we are firmly persuaded that none but a proud people can be free, so we do not readily conceive, how such a people should long consent to be otherwise. A speculative preference for the republican form, too, seems to be a natural consequence of classical studies; so much so, that Hobbes scruples not to declare that the Greek and Roman authors have done more harm by stirring up men to rebellion against government, than they have ever done good by improving their taste and style. But to be a practical republican of any sort of account one must be a good citizen—and to this unpretending, but most worthy character, at least two constituents are essential, neither of which seems to have been very prominent in Lord Byron's composition, viz. the love of country and "a constant and perpetual disposition" in all things and towards all men—*jus suum cuique tribuere*. That Byron's patriotism was of the most questionable sort, nobody, we presume, will deny. Except the admirable lines in Childe Harold, in which he describes England as the "inviolate island of the sage and free," we do not, at present, remember one syllable in all his works, from the *spirit* of which, it could be fairly inferred that he was even a citizen, much less a hereditary counsellor, lawgiver and judge—one of the privileged and honoured few—of that famous commonwealth. On the contrary, there are many passages both of his prose and poetical writings, from which a stranger would, in charity to his lordship, wish to conclude the reverse.* Yet England had done

* His indifference, not to say aversion to England, discovered itself at a very early age; and in the following letter, written when he was in Greece the first time, he talks of abandoning his country as he would of going from Ravenna to Florence.

"ATHENS, February 28, 1811.

"DEAR MADAM,

"As I have received a firman for Egypt, &c., I shall proceed to that quarter in

nothing to injure him. All his fortune had come down to him from his ancestors, under the protection, nay, favour of her laws: the very name which he bore, and of which he was so proud, linked him in most intimately with her history. And even if he had suffered injustice at her hand—could he have suffered more than Dante, or, suffering less, might he not have blushed to contrast, in this respect, the writings of that immortal victim of persecution with his own? The fact is that the sympathies of Byron were all with *power*—power in its reckless daring and its terrible energies, in its tragical downfal or its voluntary self-sacrifice; but at all events with power. His great favourite, in modern times, was Bonaparte—not, it is to be presumed, because *he* was at all remarkable for what is called, by our party journals, "his undeviating republicanism"—but what was much more acceptable in Byron's sight—he had crushed and trodden upon the mighty ones of the earth—making them drink up the cup of degradation to its most nauseous dregs, passing them under the yoke like captives, chaining them like slaves to his imperial car! But a hero, whom he preferred even to Napoleon, was Sylla—a patrician rebel and usurper—who exercised his power very much as Byron did his own genius, with a very gentlemanlike *nonchalance*—who postponed the most exquisite of mortal pleasures, in Byron's opinion, to duty or to glory—not pausing, in his victorious career in the East, even "to feel the wrath of his own wrongs, or to reap the *due of hoarded vengeance*"—yet after having reaped this *due*—after having gorged himself with the gore of his own countrymen, whom he butchered by thousands in cold blood—in broad daylight—in the very midst of Rome—was so terrible a personage that he could venture to lay down—not with an *atoning* smile," for what *could* atone for such crimes?—"the dictatorial wreath." Byron's enthusiasm for this bloody voluptuary—this most abandoned, because most deliberate and calculating ruffian—this sys-

the spring, and I beg you will state to Mr. H. that it is necessary to further remittances. On the subject of Newstead, I answer, as before, *no.* If it is necessary to sell, sell Rochdale. Fletcher will have arrived by this time with my letters to that purport. I will tell you fairly I have, in the first place, no opinion of funded property; if by any particular circumstances, I shall be led to adopt such a determination, I will, at all events, pass my life abroad, as my only tie to England is Newstead, and, that once gone, neither interest nor inclination lead me northward. Competence in your country is ample wealth in the east, such is the difference in the value of money and the abundance of the necessaries of life; and I feel myself so much a citizen of the world, that the spot, where I can enjoy a delicious climate, and every luxury, at a less expense than a common college life in England, will always be a country to me; and such are in fact the shores of the Archipelago. This then is the alternative—if I preserve Newstead, I return; if I sell it I stay away. I have had no letters since yours of June, but I have written several times, and shall continue, as usual, on the same plan.
        "Believe me yours ever,   "BYRON.
"'P. S.—I shall most likely see you in the course of the summer, but, of course, at such a distance, I cannot specify any particular month." pp.—*Letter l.* 186–7,

tematic corrupter of the people he enslaved—the precursor and pattern, at once, of Catiline and Cæsar—a man, whom we should suppose it impossible for an attentive reader of Sallust, Cicero and Plutarch, to contemplate without horror—throws a deep shade of suspicion upon his praises of Washington. He, no doubt, labors under the vulgar mistake, that the Father of his Country might have made himself her master; and is pleased with the image of such mighty power, resigned with so much *sang-froid*—as if Washington were no better than a Sylla—as yet unstained with blood! In a word, to come out with the whole truth, we believe that envy had a good deal to do with Byron's politics, nor have we any idea that he would have found life tolerable in a republic constituted as ours is. He was a democrat after the fashion of *Count* Alfieri, (a man, by the bye, whom he resembles in more points than one) who expressed the greatest indignation because M. *de* Voltaire*, "a French *plebeian*," presumed to write a tragedy about the second Brutus—it being the exclusive right of the privileged orders, in his imaginary commonwealth, to speak of a descendant of the Junii and the Cornelii.

We think Byron confirms what we have said in the following passages :—

" 'W., and, after him, * *, has stolen one of my buffooneries about Mde. de Staël's Metaphysics and the Fog, and passed it, by speech and letter, as their own. As Gibbet says, 'they are the most of a gentleman of any on the road.' W. is in sad enmity with the Whigs about this Review of Fox (if he *did* review him);—all the epigrammatists and essayists are at him. I hate *odds*, and wish he may beat them. As for me by the blessing of indifference, I have simplified my politics into an utter detestation of all existing governments; and, as it is the shortest and most agreeable and summary feeling imaginable, the first moment of a universal republic would convert me into an advocate for single and uncontradicted despotism. The fact is riches are power, and poverty is slavery, all over the earth, and one sort of establishment is no better, nor worse, for a *people* than another. I shall adhere to my party, because it would not be honorable to act otherwise; but as to *opinions*, I don't think politics *worth* an *opinion*. Conduct is another thing:—if you begin with a party, go on with them. I have no consistency, except in politics ; and *that* probably arises from my indifference on the subject altogether.' "—p. 343.

"Napoleon Bonaparte has abdicated the throne of the world, 'Excellent well.' Methinks Sylla did better; for he revenged, and resigned in the height of his sway, red with the slaughter of his foes—the finest instance of glorious contempt of the rascals upon record. Diocletian did well too— Amurath not amiss, had he become aught except a dervise—Charles the Fifth but so, so—but Napoleon, worst of all. What! wait till they were in his capital, and then talk of his readiness to give up what is already gone!! 'What whining monk art thou—what holy cheat?' 'Sdeath! Dionysius at Corinth was yet a king to this. The 'Isle of Elba' to retire to! Well—if it had been Caprea, I should have marvelled less. 'I see

* Voltaire affected this *de* very much.

men's minds are but a parcel of their fortunes.' I am utterly bewildered and confounded.

"I don't know—but I think *I*, even *I* (an insect compared with this creature,) have set my life on casts not a millionth part of this man's. But. after all a crown may be not worth dying for. Yet to outlive *Lodi* for this !!! Oh that Juvenal or Johnson could rise from the dead ! 'Expende—quot libras in duce summo invenies ?' I knew they were light in the balance of mortality; but I thought their living dust weighed more *carats*. Alas ! this imperial diamond hath a flaw in it, and is now hardly fit to stick in a glazier's pencil; the pen of the historian won't rate it worth a ducat.

"Psha ! 'something too much of this.' But I won't give him up even now ; though all his admirers have, 'like the Thanes, fall'n from him.' "—p. 370.

We subjoin the following, which presents the other side of the same question.

"If I had any views in this country, they would probably be parliamentary. But I have no ambition; at least, if any, it would be 'aut Cæsar aut nihil,' My hopes are limited to the arrangement of my affairs, and settling either in Italy or the East (rather the last), and drinking deep of the languages and literature of both. Past events have unnerved me ; and all I can now do is to make life an amusement, and look on while others play. After all—even the highest game of crowns and sceptres, what is it ? *Vide* Napoleon's last twelvemonth. It has completely upset my system of fatalism. I thought, if crushed, he would have fallen, when 'fractus illabatur orbis,' and not have been pared away to gradual insignificance ;—that all this was not a mere *jeu* of the gods, but a prelude to greater changes and mightier events. But men never advance beyond a certain point;—and here we are retrograding to the dull, stupid old system,—balance of Europe—poising straws upon kings' noses, instead of wringing them off! Give me a republic, or a despotism of one, rather than the mixed government of one, two, three. A republic !—look in the history of the earth—Rome, Greece, Venice, France, Holland, America, our short (eheu !) Commonwealth, and compare it with what they did under masters. The Asiatics are not qualified to be republicans, but they have the liberty of demolishing despots,—which is the next thing to it. To be the first man—not the Dictator—not the Sylla, but the Washington or the Aristides—the leader in talent and truth—is next to the Divinity !—Franklin, Penn, and, next to these, either Brutus or Cassius—even Mirabeau—or St. Just. I shall never be any thing, or rather always be nothing. The most I can hope is that some will say, 'He might, perhaps, if he would. ' "—p. 325.

We add a short, but very significant paragraph about Bonaparte and Brutus. What a jumble! His preference for Napoleon as here expressed, reminded us of Timon's interest in Alcibiades for a like reason.

"Napoleon! this week will decide his fate. All seems against him : but I believe and hope he will win—at least, beat back the invaders. What right have we to prescribe sovereigns to France ? Oh! for a republic ! 'Brutus thou sleepest.' Hobhouse abounds in continental anecdotes of this extraordinary man ; all in favour of his intellect and courage, but against his *bonhommie*. No wonder ;—how should he, who knows mankind well, do other than despise and abhor them.

"The greater the equality, the more impartially evil is distributed, and becomes lighter by the division among so many—therefore, a republic.

*   *   *   *   *   *

"Ah my poor little pagod, Napoleon, has walked off his pedestal. He has abdicated, they say. This would draw molten brass from the eyes of Zatanai. What! 'kiss the ground before young Malcolm's feet, and then be baited by the rabble's curse !' I cannot bear such a crouching catastrophe. I must stick to Sylla, for my modern favourites do n't do,—their resignations are of a different kind."—pp. 361, 391.

The moral character of Lord Byron is exhibited to us, we humbly conceive, in a most unamiable not to say, detestable light, in his intercourse with his mother. The poor woman was certainly not a model for matrons—she was no rival of Cornelia—and her son had a right to complain of her on many scores, but especially for that extreme indulgence which made him so miserable through life. But we do not think it was a good reason for treating her with cold and cruel contempt that she doated with all a woman's fondness upon her only child. That such were her feelings towards Lord Byron—even if we doubted the instincts of nature—would clearly appear from Mr. Moore's own account of her. It is true that, having an ungovernable temper and very bad manners, she occasionally both said and did, in a paroxysm of rage, what a good son would have witnessed, on *her* account, with extreme regret. Things of the sort, however, (not in the same *degree*, to be sure) occur sometimes in the best of families, and it is precisely because they do occur, that such inviolable sanctity is ascribed to all the secrets of domestic life, and that such sacred charities, like good angels, watch over its peace. But who ever thought of treasuring up the hasty expressions of a parent—a mother—of making a hoard of them, and brooding over it with a miser's perverse and sleepless vigilance—of blabbing them to the world with an unfeeling levity—of recalling and repeating them for the purpose of justifying a parricidal alienation of mind, itself wantonly avowed to a stranger in a distant land. We read the following paragraph with a sensation of horror, and thought, involuntarily, of Nero and Agrippina.

"He spoke often of his mother to Lord Sligo, and with a feeling that seemed little short of aversion. 'Some time or other,' he said, 'I will tell you *why* I feel thus towards her.'—A few days after, when they were bathing together in the Gulf of Lepanto, he referred to this promise, and, pointing to his naked leg and foot, exclaimed—'Look there! it is to her false delicacy at my birth I owe that deformity ; and yet, as long as I can remember, she has never ceased to taunt and reproach me with it. Even a few days before we parted, for the last time, on my leaving England, she, in one of her fits of passion, uttered an imprecation upon me, praying that I might prove as ill-formed in mind as I am in body !' *His look and manner, in relating this frightful circumstance, can be conceived only by those who have ever seen him in a similar state of excitement.*"—p. 184.

Now, what Mr. Moore calls *aversion* was, we should say, settled hatred—both from its cause and its effect. It was precisely the point on which Lord Byron's feelings were most sensitive and exacerbated, and, as he had neither forgotten nor forgiven the offence, we may be sure that his hostility—so provoked—was of the most unmerciful character. Indeed, nothing short of the sternest malignity, or a total want of principle, it seems to us, could account for his speaking of such a thing at all. If his mother had really deserved his hatred, and excited it by unnatural conduct towards him, one would have expected him to bury the dreadful secret in the inmost recesses of his bosom—to drive it away from his own thoughts whenever it occurred—to struggle desperately, even against the strongest convictions of his mind and the involuntary feelings of his heart—in short, to treat it, like the inborn hatred of the sons of Œdipus, as a curse from heaven for some unatoned crime of his race, to be expiated, if possible, by sacrifice and repentance. But the truth is that there was nothing extraordinary or tragical in the matter. Mrs. Byron, however violent in her temper, far from having any aversion to her son, always believed him destined to become a great man, and was wrapped up in him, the last, the only object of her desolate affections. At the very time that he, in a foreign country, at an immense distance from her, after an absence that might have softened his heart towards any one—but especially one standing in that sacred relation towards him, and whom, as it happened, he was to see no more—was indulging in these malignant recollections—the object of his hostility, as Mr. Moore informs us, was carefully and fondly gathering up every word of kindness or praise which men spoke, of her child, at home!

"That, notwithstanding her injudicious and coarse treatment of him, Mrs. Byron loved her son, with that sort of fitful fondness of which alone such a nature is capable, there can be little doubt,—and still less, that she was ambitiously proud of him. Her anxiety for the success of his first literary essays may be collected from the pains which he so considerately took to tranquillize her on the appearance of the hostile article in the review. As his fame began to brighten, that notion of his future greatness and glory, which, by a singular forecast of superstition, she had entertained from his very childhood, became proportionately confirmed. Every mention of him in print was watched by her with eagerness, and she had got bound together in a volume, which a friend of mine once saw, a collection of all the literary notices, that had then appeared, of his early poems and satire—written over, on the margin, with observations of her own, which to my informant appeared indicative of much more sense and ability than, from her general character, we should be inclined to attribute to her."—p. 207.

Now there is no imaginable excuse or palliation for such conduct. The practice of civilized nations furnishes no plea, in parricide or misprision of parricide, but the *general issue* ; to *justify* would be to plead guilty. There is no part of Mr. Moore's

396   LORD BYRON'S CHARACTER AND WRITINGS.

book which is more disagreeable to us than the manner in which he glosses over this passage of his hero's conduct—it is the most mawkish toad-eating, and there is a degree of simplicity approaching to *niaiserie* in his way of telling his story. Admitting all that he says on the subject—which from internal evidence we do not—Byron's conduct is not justified, however his mother may, (on his account and through his means!) be censured and degraded in the eyes of the world. It is at best the shepherd's song in Virgil.

Crudelis mater magis, an puer improbus ille?
Improbus ille puer, crudelis tu quoque, mater.

When Lord Byron was about eighteen years of age, Mr. Moore gives the following account of the intercourse between himself and his mother. If our readers recollect any parallel to the fact mentioned in the first paragraph, they are more fortunate or *un*fortunate than we have been.

"Between a temper, at all resembling this, and the loud hurricane bursts of Mrs. Byron, the collision, it may be supposed, was not a little formidable; and the age at which the young poet was now arrived, when,—as most parents feel,—the impatience of youth begins to champ the bit, would but render the occasions for such shocks more frequent. It is told, as a curious proof of their opinion of each other's violence, that, after parting one evening in a tempest of this kind, they were known each to go privately that night to the apothecary's, inquiring anxiously whether the other had been to purchase poison, and cautioning the vender of drugs not to attend to such an application, if made.

"It was but rarely, however, that the young lord allowed himself to be provoked into more than a passive share in these scenes. To the boisterousness of his mother he would oppose a civil and no doubt provoking silence,—bowing to her but the more profoundly the higher her voice rose in the scale. In general, however, when he perceived that a storm was at hand, in flight lay his only safe resource. To this summary expedient he was driven, at the period of which we are speaking; but not till after a scene had taken place between him and Mrs. Byron, in which the violence of her temper had proceeded to lengths, that, however outrageous they might be deemed, were not, it appears, unusual with her. The poet, Young, in describing a temper of this sort, says—

"*The cups and saucers, in a whirlwind sent,*
Just intimate the lady's discontent."

But poker and tongs were, it seems, the missiles which Mrs. Byron preferred, and which she, more than once, sent resounding after her fugitive son. In the present instance, he was but just in time to avoid a blow, aimed at him with the former of these weapons, and to make a hasty escape to the house of a friend in the neighbourhood ; where, concerting the best means of baffling pursuit, he decided upon an instant flight to London. The letters, which I am about to give, were written, immediately on his arrival in town, to some friends at Southwell, from whose kind interference in his behalf it may fairly be concluded that the blame of the quarrel, whatever it may have been, did not rest with him. The first is to Mr. Pigot, a young gentleman about the same age as himself who had just returned, for the vacation, from Edinburgh, where he was, at that time, pursuing his medical studies."--pp. 63, 64.

Mr. Moore takes it for granted (for there is no testimony adduced) that Byron conducted himself, throughout these shocking scenes, with perfect propriety—that is to say, with the most unresisting gentleness and meekness. Now—not to mention that, according to our author's own account, Lord Byron was accustomed, when younger, to do all he could to provoke his mother to anger—we infer that he was, at least, as much in fault as she, from the very letters given in evidence by his friend. No son, capable of writing those letters, could have had a spark of filial love, respect or dutifulness, in his whole composition. They remind one of the autobiographical sketches of Scipio, Raphael, and other worthies of that stamp, in Gil Blas, which contribute so much to make that book the most amusing, as the most faithful picture extant of the dark side of human life, especially among the inferior sort. Lord Byron treats the whole affair as capital fun, and exhibits the angry heroine to all possible advantage, in the broadest burlesque and caricature. We can safely recommend some of these letters as very entertaining pieces of pleasantry. The writer is any thing but sparing in his sarcasm. He returns to the charge over and over again, and always in the same tone. He calls his mother "that amiable Alecto," p. 64; "a *hydra*," p. 66; "that Upas tree, that antidote to the arts, Mrs. B." p. 68; "my *nice* mamma would raise the accustomed *maternal war-whoop*," p. 99, &c. It is worthy of remark, in this connection, that Mrs. Byron used to say that her son resembled Rousseau—and that before he was twenty. So much for his character at that period of his life.

Mr. Moore's general remarks on this subject, are as follows:

"It can hardly have escaped the observation of the reader that the general tone of the noble poet's correspondence with his mother is that of a son, performing, strictly and conscientiously, what he deems to be his duty, without the intermixture of any sentiment of cordiality to sweeten the task. The very title of 'Madam,' by which he addresses her—and which he but seldom exchanges for the endearing name of 'mother'—is, of itself, a sufficient proof of the sentiments he entertained for her. That such should have been his dispositions towards such a parent can be matter neither of surprise nor blame—but that, notwithstanding this alienation, which her own unfortunate temper produced, he should have continued to consult her wishes, and minister to her comforts, with such unfailing thoughtfulness as is evinced not only in the frequency of his letters, but in the almost exclusive appropriation of Newstead to her use, redounds, assuredly, in no ordinary degree, to his honor; and was even the more strikingly meritorious from the absence of that affection, which renders kindnesses to a beloved object little more than an indulgence of self.

"But however estranged from her his feelings must be allowed to have been while she lived, her death seems to have restored them into their natural channel. Whether from a return of early fondness and the all-atoning power of the grave, or from the prospect of that void in his future life, which this loss of his only link with the past would leave, it is certain that he felt the death of his mother acutely, if not deeply. On the night after his arrival at Newstead, the waiting woman of Mrs. Byron, in passing the door of the room where the deceased lady lay, heard a sound as some one sighing heavily from within ; and, on entering the chamber, found to her surprise, Lord Byron sitting, in the dark, beside the bed. On her representing to him the weakness of thus giving way to grief, he burst into tears and exclaimed, 'Oh, Mrs. By, I had but one friend in the world, and she is gone !' "

While his real thoughts were thus confided to silence and darkness, there was, in other parts of his conduct more open to observation, a degree of eccentricity and indecorum which with superficial observers might well bring the sensibility of his nature into question.   On the morning of the funeral, having declined following the remains himself, he stood looking, from the Abbey door, at the procession, till the whole had moved off ;—then, turning to young Rushton, who was the only person left besides himself, he desired him to fetch the sparring-gloves, and proceeded to his usual exercise with the boy.   He was silent and abstracted all the time, and, as if from an effort to get the better of his feelings, threw more violence, Rushton thought, into his blows than was his habit ; but, at last,— the struggle seeming too much for him,—he flung away the gloves, and retired to his room.   *   *   *   *   *

"Among those less traits of his conduct through which an observer can trace a filial wish to uphold, and throw respect round the station of his mother, may be mentioned his insisting, while a boy, on being called 'George Byron Gordon'—giving thereby precedence to the maternal name,—and his continuing to the last to address her as the 'Honourable Mrs. Byron,'—a mark of rank, to which, he must have been aware she had no claim whatever.   Neither does it appear that, in his habitual manner towards her, there was any thing denoting a want of either affection or deference—with the exception, perhaps, occasionally, of a somewhat greater degree of familiarity than comports with the ordinary notions of filial respect.   Thus, the usual name he called her by, when they were on good-humored terms together, was 'Kitty Gordon ;' and I have heard an eye-witness of the scene describe the look of arch, dramatic humor, with which, one day, at Southwell, when they were in the height of their theatrical rage, he threw open the door of the drawing-room, to admit his mother, saying, at the same time, 'Enter the Honourable Kitty.' " pp. 205–207.

Mr. Moore has done very little towards explaining the great mystery of Byron's life—his unhappy separation from his wife. As *he* represents the matter, Lady Byron left her husband upon a temporary visit to her parents, and left him in an unusually affectionate manner.   The letter announcing, some weeks after, her determination to return no more, had been preceded by one full of cordiality and kindness.   That determination was as unexpected, therefore, as it was afflicting, and the necessary inference seemed to be, that Lady Byron had been prevailed upon to take the irrevocable step, by the influence of others.   Lord Byron evidently laid the blame of this fatal interference to the mother of his wife, and that female attendant or domestic, on whom he condescended to wreak his vengeance, in such unmeasured terms, in the "Sketch."   We have lately seen Lady Byron's reply to Mr. Moore ; denying that her parents had any thing to do with the matter, ascribing the kindness of her manner at taking leave to a belief that her husband was insane, and declaring that, as soon as she was convinced of her mistake on this point, she made up her mind, without hesitation, to an eternal separation from him. She is supported in her statement by the evidence, and justified in her conduct by the authority, of a celebrated civilian, and the public are left, by this imperfect disclosure, to imagine the worst of that behaviour which nothing but madness could excuse. That Lord Byron committed the first fault in this unhappy feud, we never entertained any doubt; first, because in all similar cases, the chances are at least ten to one in favour of the lady; secondly, because in the celebrated lines "Fare thee well," as well as in Childe Harold, the poet plainly acknowledges himself in the wrong, and only represents his wife as too stern and inflexible in her indignation: thirdly, because, according to his lordship's own account corroborated by Mr. Moore's, Miss Milbank enjoyed the highest reputation for exemplary conduct, and every virtue that can adorn the character of an accomplished lady: fourthly, because some such result was to have been anticipated from Lord Byron's eccentricities and violence of temper: an instance of this violence, about the period of the rupture, given by Mr. Moore himself, being almost beyond credibility.* To all these, our author adds a fifth reason, which he regards as *instar omnium;* and which he has taken extraordinary pains to elucidate and fortify by every topic of argument, example and illustration. This is, that there is something in extraordinary genius itself, which unfits its devoted possessor for performing the duties and enjoying the happiness of domestic life—and that Lord Byron's case only adds melancholy confirmation to what is, otherwise, the result of universal experience upon the subject.

Boccaccio, in his Life of Dante, undertakes the same thesis, but he does not present it in precisely the same point of view. His objection to matrimony is the trivial one, that it is an impediment to great enterprizes, to literary studies and to the enjoyments of society. The friends of that poet had procured him a wife for the purpose of diverting his thoughts, if possible, from the fate of his lost Beatrice—*his* first love, and if we be-

---

* "For this story, however, there was so far a foundation, that the practice, to which he had accustomed himself from boyhood, of having loaded pistols always near him at night, was considered so strange a propensity as to be in that list of symptoms (sixteen, I believe, in number), which were submitted to medical opinion, in proof of his insanity. Another symptom was the emotion, almost to hysterics, which he had exhibited on seeing Kean act Sir Giles Overreach. But the most plausible of all the grounds, as he himself used to allow, on which these articles of impeachment against his sanity were drawn up, was an act of violence committed by him on a favorite old watch, that had been his companion from boyhood, and had gone with him to Greece. In a fit of vexation and rage, brought on by some of those humiliating embarrassments to which he was now almost daily a prey, he furiously dashed this watch upon the hearth, and ground it to pieces among the ashes with the poker." *Note*, p. 460.

lieve him, the fountain of all his inspiration. But the remedy
proved worse than the disease, and his biographer, the gay
lover of Fiammetta, makes himself, as usual, very merry at the
expenses of holy wedlock. He laments that a man, whose intercourse with the world might be so various and delightful, should
be thus confined to the society of one or of very few—that, instead of enjoying the conversation of kings and philosophers, he
should have to listen to a pert woman's incessant chattering, and,
what was still worse, to seem (if he had any regard to his interest) to assent to and delight in it—that his sweet liberty
should be exchanged for curtain lectures, and the suspicious tyranny of a jealous wife, and his sublime contemplations be disturbed certainly by the cares and the *cries* of a family, and possibly by worse enemies to a husband's peace of mind—which
shall be nameless. Boccaccio concludes this characteristic tirade
by an apology to the ladies, whom he gravely assures that he is
no enemy to wedlock in general, especially to that of rich bache-
lors, lords and country gentlemen—but only to the marriages of
men already betrothed to philosophy. Mr. Moore goes much
more deeply into the philosophy of the matter. He dives into
the abstrusest metaphysics, and traces what he calls, in a rather
euphuistic phrase, "the transfer of the seat of sensibility from
the heart to the fancy"—that is to say, in plain English, the
heartlessness and selfishness—of men of genius to the very
frame and constitution of their minds. Now, that poets, especially—who represent the most sublime and subtilized genius—
are an "irritable race," is a proverb—and we are firm believers
in the effects of physical organization upon the highest sensibilities of our nature. We even conceit that, if a man be born for
great excellence, in oratory, or any other of the arts of imagination, you may feel it in his pulse. But that it can be laid down
as a general rule that genius is inconsistent with the most sacred duties, and the sweetest affections of life, we cannot admit—
notwithstanding the formidable catalogue of precedents, which
Mr. Moore cites in justification of Lord Byron. Many of those
examples prove nothing more than that men of genius may draw
blanks in the great lottery of matrimony, as well as the common
herd of mankind. Some of them prove nothing at all. But
what shall we say to the hundreds of instances the other way,
which are not the *exceptions*, but the rule?—What shall we say
to such exemplary men as Sir Walter Scott, Schiller, Wordsworth,
and Mr. Moore himself—who has generously disclaimed his own
titles to renown as a poet, to secure to his friend the reputation
of virtue? Perhaps there never was a more affecting and beautiful picture of "wedded love," in all its holiness and rapture,
than is presented in the biography of the most sensitive of this
imaginative race of beings, poor Mozart—and Pope, who is call-

ed in by our author as a witness for his doctrine, was at least, the most devoted and affectionate of sons.   In short, men of genius have, in general, strong passions, but there is no reason in the world, why they should not have sound principles, and where this is the case, the evil, in the course of a few years, infallibly works its own cure.   The progress of a warm and vigorous mind, under the discipline of experience, reminds us of that of the sun in this climate, at a certain season of the year— when, if he generally rises in mist, he always melts it away by noonday, and goes down in cloudless and serene brightness.

Mr. Moore speaks of Byron's love as Byron speaks of Rousseau's in Childe Harold.   As the whole passage is not only very applicable here, but strikingly illustrative of the supposed resemblance between these two celebrated men, we quote it the more readily.

> "His love was passion's essence—as a tree
>   On fire by lightning; with etherial flame
> Kindled he was, and blasted; for to be
> Thus, and enamour'd, were in him the same.
> But·his was not the love of living dame,
> Nor of the dead who rise upon our dreams,
> But of ideal beauty, which became
> In him existence, and o'erflowing teems
> Along his burning page, distemper'd tho' it seems.
>
> *This* breathed itself to life in Julie, *this*
> Invested her with all that's wild and sweet;
> This hallow'd, too, the memorable kiss
> Which every morn his fever'd lip would greet
> From hers, who but with friendship his would meet;
> But to that gentle touch, thro' brain and breast,
> Flash'd the thrill'd spirit's love-devouring heat;
> In that absorbing sigh perchance more blest,
> Than vulgar minds may be with all they seek possest.
>
> His life was one long war with self-sought foes,
> Or friends by him self-banished, for his mind
> Had grown suspicion's sanctuary," &c.*

This rapturous description has, at least, one great fault, besides its extravagance.   It is not true.   Rousseau, if we are to believe his Confessions, had often felt (or thought he felt) more

---

* "I think I also remarked in Byron's temper starts of suspicion, when he seemed to pause and consider whether there had not been a secret, and, perhaps offensive, meaning in something casually said to him.   In this case, I also judged it best to let his mind, like a troubled spring, work itself clear, which it did in a minute or two.   I was considerably older, you will recollect, than my noble friend, and had no reason to fear his misconstruing my sentiments towards him, nor had I ever the slightest reason to doubt that they were kindly returned on his part.   If I had occasion to be mortified by the display of genius which threw into the shade such pretensions as I was then supposed to possess, I might console myself that, in my own case, the materials of mental happiness had been mingled in a greater proportion."—*Letter of Sir W. Scott*, p. 445.

extatical and frenzied delight in love, than even *he* had any power to express. In one respect, to be sure, his passion was ideal, and ideal enough. "He saw Helen's beauty on a brow of Egypt." He invested the most ordinary woman with the charms of an imaginary loveliness, and not long after raving about Julie in his Nouvelle Heloïse, with such intoxicating and delirious eloquence, he became the slave (if ever there was one) of a vulgar, ungainly creature, whom he permitted to bear his (then) celebrated name. As for Lord Byron's *idealism* in love, we suspect, it was a match for Rousseau's in deed and in practice. If we are to judge of it, at least, by its fruits, it was as far as possible, from being extravagant. It is not worth while to dream, if our visions fall short even of common place realities. Byron's heroines—with the exception of Angiolina, the paragon of wives, and Gulnare, a girl of so great a spirit, as to disgust a pirate by her boldness—are all mere Circassians. Hundreds of such women, we fancy—in all but their deep, unalterable devotedness—are to be seen in the harems of the East. They are kept—in Byron's poetry—in a sort of Oriental seclusion, like the females in the comedies of Terence. All that they are required to know, think of, do, desire, dream, is love. To be sure, to love such men so fondly and faithfully. may be no ordinary task. For, as it has been well remarked, the women in Byron's tales know no form of· faith, no rule of conduct, but that laid down in the fine lines of his biographer.

> "Oh! what was love made for, if 'tis not the same,
> Thro' joy and thro' torment, thro' glory and shame—
> I know not, I ask not, if guilt's in that heart,
> I know that I love thee whatever thou art."

Maturin has quoted these lines at the head of one of the chapters of "Melmoth," and we have been forcibly struck with what we conceive to be an *exaggeration* (caricature would be too harsh a word) of Byron's *ideal* love, in the passion of Imalee foṛ the preternatural Wanderer. There is more genius, however, in the conception of that beautiful creature, growing up amidst flowers "herself a fairer flower," in such simplicity and spotless innocence, and loving, like Miranda, the first human form that invaded her quiet, sequestered paradise, though that form happened to be possessed by a demon—than in the doating, but still somewhat vulgar, fondness of the Leilas and Medoras. It is dreadful to think of passion so utterly thrown away as Imalee's—of the dismal doom of Melmoth's spirit which would have sympathized in that passion, but could not. Woman, however, in Byron's poetry, although not filling her loftiest sphere—although the object of a fierce, jealous and distempered Eastern love, rather than of that respectful and idolatrous sentiment, with which chivalry has exalted and refined the intercourse between the sexes—is still all-important to man. She is the mistress, not the wife—but through every danger and toil, through fire and flood, the desperadoes, whom Byron selects for heroes, are true to the vow plighted at no altar but love's—and that love is an absorbing, engrossing, devouring passion, which takes absolute possession of their whole being. It is not the gay and frivolous gallantry of France—it is not the soft and blissful voluptuousness—the elysium of the heart—in which the sorceresses of romance, the Morganas and Armidas, in their fairy bowers, "lap the prisoned souls" of captive and captivated knights. The love of Conrad, for example, is his only virtue—the single good passion to which all his other passions—fierce and terrible as they are—yield as to a charm. It is a warm, green spot in that "vacant bosom's wilderness." His dark and guilty spirit takes refuge from its sufferings in this one sweet affection—riots and revels in it—bathes itself in its unfathomable and boundless bliss. All the energies of his nature abused—its principles perverted—its tastes depraved—are redeemed by it. He is at war with God and man, but "his very hate to them is love to her," the adored and adoring—the only being in creation upon whom he bestows a thought, but of hostility and wrath—the only being in creation to whom the secrets of that throbbing bosom are imparted—who knows and feels and soothes the pangs which flash across that burning brow.

> "None are all evil—quickening round his heart,
> One softer feeling would not yet depart;
> Oft could he sneer at others as beguiled
> By passions worthy of a fool or child ;
> Yet 'gainst that passion vainly still he strove,
> And, even in him, it asks the name of love!
> Yes, it was love—unchangeable—unchanged,
> Felt but for one from *whom he never ranged*, &c.
>
> Yes—it was love—if thoughts of tenderness,
> Tried in temptation, strengthened by distress,
> Unmoved by absence, firm in every clime,
> And yet—oh more than all!—untired by time ;
> Which nor defeated hope, nor baffled wile
> Could render sullen were she near to smile."
> Nor rage could fire, nor sickness fret to vent
> On her one murmur of his discontent ;
> Which still would meet with joy, with calmness part,
> Lest that his look of grief should reach her heart,
>
> Which nought removed, nor menaced to remove—
> If there be love in mortals, this is love !
> He was a villain—ay—reproaches shower
> On him—but not the passion, nor its power,
> Which only proved all other virtues gone,
> Not guilt itself could quench this loveliest one !"
>
> [Cors. Canto I. 283.

Now there is nothing ideal in this love but its own purity and perfection, and the character of the person who feels—not *inspires*—it. It is strange enough that a pirate should be so vastly sentimental—a critic might object that this incongruity violates a canon of the schools—

Aut famam sequere aut sibi convenientia finge.

But the prodigy here is the lover, not the beloved ; and, though it would be rather a hopeless pursuit to go among the corsairs of the Mediterranean, in quest of a Conrad, any girl, desperately in love, is fully a match for Medora. We cannot say, therefore, that we see in Byron those lofty imaginations of female excellence or fascination, which nothing existing in *rerum naturâ* could satisfy. It is very remarkable, however, that, in his conceptions of love, as in all his other thoughts and feelings, the dark, exclusive, diseased self-love of the man makes itself visible in every line.

Yet we have no doubt that Lord Byron had an immense capacity for love, and that had his principles been less perverted, he would have been very tractable to a woman of sense. As he was, we are inclined to agree with Mr. Moore that a lady of a certain stamp might have exercised great influence over him, and, perhaps, restored "his fallen nature" to all its original goodness. But we do not think that his biographer has, in his picture of this imaginary lady, hit the mark exactly. Lord Byron did not care about high intellectual or moral attributes in a woman ; his standard of female excellence, as we have endeavored to show, was not a very high one. Beauty, grace, amiableness—but above all, devoted love, and a patience capable even of martyrdom—at least, if inflicted by her lord—such were the chief attributes of his ideal help-meet. In short, he would have tried his wife as the Marquis of Saluzzo in the Decamerone did poor Griselda—for none but a Griselda would have suited, or could have overcome Lord Byron. Now, the lady he married happened to have no taste for martyrdom. "Patient Grizzle" was a part she never expected, and was of consequence quite unprepared to act. She had more unmixed pride, and loftier as well as purer feelings, than her husband—and her cool, decided conduct towards him crushed his tyrannical and selfish spirit to the earth. Lord Byron shows, how perfectly conscious he was of his own uncontrollable and unhappy disposition, by a slight remark of his, recorded in this volume. He says that he had always loved his sister—adding, that it was, probably, because they had been very little together ! Was that because he had an "ideal standard" of sisters, to which Mrs. Leigh did not come up ? The sophistical trash of Mr. Moore upon this subject will not do at all. In this connection, we extract the following remarks of our author.

"In the extracts from his journal, just given, there is a passage that cannot fail to have been remarked, where, in speaking of his admiration of some lady, whose name he has himself left blank, the noble writer says: 'a wife would be the salvation of me.' It was under this conviction, which not only himself but some of his friends entertained, of the prudence of his taking timely refuge in matrimony from those perplexities which form the sequel of all less regular ties, that he had been induced, about a year before, to turn his thoughts seriously to marriage,—at least as seriously as his thoughts were ever capable of being so turned,—and chiefly, I believe by the advice and intervention of his friend Lady Melbourne, to become a suitor for the hand of a relative of that lady, Miss Milbanke.   Though his proposal was not then accepted, every assurance of friendship and regard accompanied the refusal; a wish was even expressed that they should continue to write to each other, and a correspondence,—somewhat singular between two young persons of different sexes, inasmuch as love was not the subject of it,—ensued between them.   We have seen how highly Lord Byron estimated as well the virtues as the accomplishments of the young lady, but it is evident that on neither side, at this period, was love either felt or professed.

"In the mean time, new entanglements, in which his heart was the willing dupe of his fancy and vanity, came to engross the young poet; and still, as the usual penalties of such pursuits followed, he again found himself sighing for the sober yoke of wedlock, as some security against their recurrence.   There were, indeed, in the interval between Miss Milbanke's refusal and acceptance of him, two or three other young women of rank who, at different times, formed the subject of his matrimonial dreams.   In the society of one of these, whose family had long honored me with their friendship, he and I passed much of our time, during this and the preceding spring; and it will be found that, in a subsequent part of his correspondence, he represents me as having entertained an anxious wish that he should so far cultivate my friend's favor as to give a chance, at least, of matrimony being the result.

"That I, more than once, expressed some such feeling is undoubtedly true. Fully concurring with the opinion, not only of himself, but of others of his friends, that in marrriage lay his only chance of salvation from the sort of perplexing attachments into which he was now constantly tempted, I saw in none of those whom he admired with more legitimate views so many requisites for the difficult task of winning him into fidelity and happiness, as in the lady in question.   Combining beauty of the highest order, with a mind intelligent and ingenious—having just learning enough to give refinement to her taste, and far too much taste to make pretensions to learning,—with a patrician spirit proud as his own, but showing it only in a delicate generosity of spirit, a feminine high-mindedness, which would have led her to tolerate his defects in consideration of his noble qualities and his glory, and even to sacrifice silently some of her own happines rather than violate the responsibility in which she stood pledged to the world for his:—such was, from long experience, my impression of the character of this lady; and, perceiving Lord Byron to be attracted by her more obvious claims to admiration, I felt a pleasure no less in rendering justice to the still rarer qualities which she possessed, than in endeavouring to raise my noble friend's mind to the contemplation of a higher model of female character than he had, unluckily for himself, been much in the habit of studying." pp. 358, 359.

One of the best written and most felicitous passages, in this volume, is that in which Mr. Moore explains an effect of Lord Byron's youthful love for Miss Chaworth upon his lordship's imagination. It was perfectly natural that this disappointment should make a deep impression upon his mind, and equally natural, under all circumstances, that the object of his early affection should be cherished, and almost sanctified, in his remembrance. He had loved passionately, and nothing had happened to disenchant him. He had been *disappointed*—without being disgusted. This lady became to him an ideal being—a vision of fancy and feeling—and, amidst his many mortifications and sufferings, he could not fail to look back upon her, as his lost hope—to look up to her image, with feelings somewhat resembling the adoration which Dante pays to the spirit of his own Beatrice—dwelling amid the spheres and inspiring him with holy hopes and aspirations. But, that this disappointment had any other effect—that it *embittered* Byron's existence, when he arrived at years of maturity—we do not believe.

"It was about the time, when he was thus bitterly feeling, and expressing the blight which his heart had suffered from a *real* object of affection, that his poems on the death of an *imaginary* one, 'Thyrza,' were written;—nor is it any wonder, when we consider the peculiar circumstances under which these beautiful effusions flowed from his fancy, that of all his strains of pathos, they should be the most touching and most pure. They were, indeed, the essence, the abstract spirit, as it were of many griefs:— a confluence of sad thoughts from many sources of sorrow, refined and warmed in their passage through his fancy, and forming thus one deep reservoir of mournful feeling. In retracing the happy hours he had known with the friends now lost, all the ardent tenderness of his youth came back upon him. His school sports with the favourites of his boyhood, Wingfield and Tatersall—his summer days with Long, and those evenings of music and romance, which he had dreamed away in the society of his adopted brother, Eddlestone—all these recollections of the young and dead now came to mingle themselves in his mind with the image of her, who, though living, was, for him, as much lost as they, and diffused that general feeling of sadness and fondness through his soul, which found a vent in these poems. No friendship, however warm, could have inspired sorrow so passionate; as no love, however pure, could have kept passion so chastened. It was the blending of the two affections, in his memory and imagination, that thus gave birth to an ideal object, combining the best features of both, and drew from him these saddest and tenderest of love-poems, in which we find all the depth and intensity of real feeling touched over with such a light as no reality ever wore." p. 226.

Before we dismiss the subject of Lord Byron's moral character, we must remark that he seems to have been uniformly kind to his dependents and inferiors—when *they did nothing to offend his pride*. His master passion made no war upon the humble and the weak. His feelings were, as we have said, naturally kind and humane. It was only upon those, who thwarted or wounded his *amour propre*, that he poured out his direful wrath. *Debellare superbos* was his maxim. Merciful to the unresisting, he declared a war of extermination against all who denied his supremacy or opposed his sovereign will.

The literary reputation of Lord Byron has been established beyond all possibility of change or decay. We do not believe—notwithstahding some apparent exceptions—that the opinions of contemporaries, in regard to the works of men of genius, have ever materially differed from those of posterity. But this is especially true of those writers who have addressed themselves more to the feelings of mankind, than to the imagination. Milton, although his works were far more justly appreciated by his own age, than is commonly thought, certainly did not hold exactly as high a rank in general estimation then, as has been conceded to him since. But—besides the character of that wretched age—Milton's poetry is addressed to the learned. It bears, upon every line of it, the impress of vast erudition and consummate art. It is true he is the greatest master of the sublime that any language has to boast of—greater than Shakspeare—greater than Dante—greater than Homer. But it requires study and reflection, objects of comparison and a competent familiarity with literature, to perceive the amazing magnitude of this glorious orb. A vulgar eye might glance over him a thousand times, and still mistake this "ocean of flame"* for a star of an inferior class. This is a great obstacle to his popularity—and it is one not less formidable, that he is deficient in pathos, and in topics of general interest. Byron wrote because he felt, and as he felt. It may be said most justly of his genius—*furor arma ministrat*. Instead of "lisping in numbers", as Pope did, he sighed and groaned and cursed in them. He spoke to the hearts of men, and, however the spirit of most of his productions is to be censured, his voice, whether for good or for evil, has seldom failed to find an echo *there*.

It may, in general, be remarked of his poetry, as of most of that of the present age, that it is not sufficiently elaborated. Many feeble, prosaic, and even unmeaning lines abound every where in his finest compositions. English criticism is less fastidious, in this respect, than that of any other language, and things are pardoned or passed over by it, which would endanger the success of a work in France or Italy, and would have destroyed it at Athens. But it is impossible to read any of Byron's masterpieces along with the best passages of our classical poetry, without being struck with the *general* inferiority and carelessness of his diction, as well as with the great inequality of his style. Compare, for instance, any thing that he has done, (except, of course, some highly wrought passages) in the Spenserian Stanza, with Spenser himself, or with the first part of Thomson's "Castle of Indolence." Whatever may be thought of their relative merits in other respects, we fancy every body, who has either ear or taste, must agree that, as far as mere language goes,

* Addison.

there is a richness, harmony and uniform finish in the works of those masters, which are sadly wanting in Byron. So in satire, he has produced nothing to be talked of in comparison to Dryden's vigorous and bold pen, or the condensed and sententious elegance of Pope. Nothing can be more powerful and pathetic than his poetry in his loftier vein—but the same objection lies here to the want of that *limæ labor*, which entitles a work of genius to be classed among perfect specimens of art. Lord Byron threw off some, probably most of his compositions, with almost as much rapidity as a hackneyed writer for the daily press. Not the less instructive part of Mr. Moore's book is the insight it gives us into his manner of composing—from which the fact just mentioned appears, along with another more important, if not quite so remarkable. This is that many of the greatest beauties of those poems were put in as corrections and improvements, on second thought and with great care—the true secret of the *curiosa felicitas* in all times and tongues. A late writer* mentions that he saw an autograph MS. of Ariosto, at Ferrara, from which it appeared, that that great and fertile genius had actually written over *sixteen* different times the famous octave of the tempest.

"Stendon le nube un tenebroso velo," &c.

We *did* purpose exemplifying our criticism upon this point by a comparison between select passages of Byron, and similar ones from Milton and other classics—between some parts of Manfred, for instance, and Comus, especially the songs, or whatever they are, of the Spirits in each. But we have left ourselves no space for doing that, which cannot be well done without a considerable degree of minuteness and prolixity.

One fault—or rather class of faults—which has been justly imputed to Byron's style, is, as often happens, nearly akin to its greatest virtue. Horace shall say what we mean in three words—*Professus grandia, turget*. His genius is, no doubt, incomparably superior to Lucan's, whose *gazette ampoulée* as Voltaire calls the Pharsalia, we never yet have been able to read through ; but there is the same tone of emphasis and exaggeration in Childe Harold, for example, as in that poem. The famous sentence *victrix causa Diis placuit, sed victa Catoni*, which we have always *felt* to be frigid and extravagant, and now *believe* to be so, since we find the Pére Bouhours of the same opinion, is altogether *Byronian*. There are too much bluster and pretension about this sort of sublimity for our taste. True grandeur is always simple, and even subdued in its tone, as we see Raphael's pictures and in the Philippics of Demosthenes. We were forcibly struck, in reading the "Prophecy of Dante," with a cer-

* Bombet's Life of Haydn and Mozart.

tain swelling and swaggering air about the whole affair, which resembles any thing rather than the oracular and terrible brevity of that great poet.   We shall give an example or two of the extravagance which we take to be Byron's besetting sin, from what is, by some critics, regarded as his master-piece, the third and fourth cantos of Childe Harold—though, for our parts, we have no hesitation in assigning the honour of that distinction to Manfred.   Here is a specimen of downright bombast.

> "—————— Above me are the Alps
> The palaces of nature, whose vast walls
> Have pinnacled in clouds their snowy scalps,
> And *throned eternity in icy halls*
> *Of cold sublimity*, where forms and falls
> The avalanche—the thunderbolt of snow !"
>
> Canto III. 63.

Another instance of the same kind of extravagance.   He is speaking of a tower—

> "Standing with half its battlements alone,
> And with two thousand years of ivy grown,
> *The garland of eternity*, &c.   Canto IV. 99.

Again—

> "Admire, exult—despise—laugh, weep,—for here
> There is such matter for all feeling :—man!
> *Thou pendulum betwixt a smile and tear.*" &c.   Ibid. 100.

Many other examples might be adduced did our limits permit ; but we must observe that what we object to in Byron is not so much a frigid conceit or bombastic expression, here and there, which may be pointed out with precision, but the general tone of exaggeration—a too obvious effort, running through his whole poetry, (in its sublimer strains) to be very strong and very striking.   For instance, the description of the cataract, or rather cascade of Velino, in the fourth Canto, which has been much extolled, has, we confess, always appeared to us extravagant.   It would be so if applied to Niagara :

> "The *hell* of waters! where they howl and hiss,
> And boil in endless torture ; while the sweat
> Of their great agony, wrung out from this," &c.
>
> Ibid. 66.

> To the broad column which rolls on, and shows
> More like the fountain of an infant sea,
> Torn *from the womb of mountains by the throes*
> *Of a new world*," &c. * * * Look back !
> Lo! *where it comes like an eternity*," &c.
>
> Ibid. 71.

In the 72d stanza, there is great beauty as well as power of expression, and the comparisons of the Iris of the falls to "hope upon a death-bed," and "to love watching madness," are such as could have occurred only to a man of genius, yet we think them far-fetched and not remarkably illustrative. With regard to figures of speech, in general, Byron is the most anti-classical of the romantic poets. Instead of drawing his similes, &c., from the natural world to the moral, as the ancients uniformly did, he does just the reverse. Thus, a lake "is calm as *cherished hate*."* Zuleika was "soft as the memory of buried love." The cypress is stamped with an eternal grief, "like early unrequited love."† Beauty or defect, this is a remarkable peculiarity of his.

Of Lord Byron's heroes we have already given an account. They are almost all of them very eccentric personages, uniting the most contradictory qualities and habits. His tales are the "Sorrows of Werther" translated into Lingua Franca. His pirates are as tender as Petrarch, and his Turks, sighing for sentimental love, abjure polygamy and concubinage. But these are the privileges of poetry—they are like the recitativo of the opera. This license once conceded, every thing goes on well. Whether natural or not, Byron's heroes are the most interesting villains that can be conceived. They are just what the heroes of the drama ought to be, according to Aristotle—with "one virtue" to redeem "a thousand crimes."

Byron does not strike us as a poet of very fertile invention. He composed, it is true, with considerable facility, but there is no variety either in his subjects or his style. We doubt, for this reason, whether he could have become distinguished as a dramatic poet, in the modern sense of the term. Besides this, his compositions are rather short sketches of notable objects, or occasional meditations upon them, than complete and well combined works. Still it is hard to say what the author of Manfred might not have done. One thing seems probable—that had he been born at Athens, at the right time, he might have rivalled Æschylus and Sophocles, in tragedy à la Grecque. Two or three heroic *dramatis personæ*, a simple plot, beautiful or powerful narrative and dialogue, interrupted by passionate ejaculation and choral ode—such a task would have been Byron's element.

Upon the whole, excepting the two first places in our literature—and Pope and Dryden who are writers of quite another stamp—we do not know who is to be placed, all things considered, above Byron. We doubt between him and Spenser—but no other name is prominent enough to present itself to us in such a competition. His greatest rival, however, was himself. We throw down his book dissatisfied. Every page reveals powers which might have done so much more for art—for glory— and for virtue!

---

* Childe Harold, Canto IV. 173.   † Bride Abyd. Canto I. 28.

BYRON'S LETTERS AND JOURNALS.

Letters and Journals of Lord Byron, with Notices of his Life. By THOMAS MOORE. In 2 vols. Vol. ii. *New-York. J. & J. Harper.* 1831.

THE second volume of Mr Moore's work is one of the most interesting books in the language. The success of the author is exactly in the inverse ratio of the space which he occupies in his own pages—of which he has, for this time, yielded the almost exclusive possession to the hero of his story. He has, indeed, presented us with the "Confessions" of Lord Byron, made up of the most authentic and least suspicious of all possible materials,—his letters, journals, and the like relics, thrown off with the impression of ever varying mood upon them, and apparently without any intention, or even the remotest idea of giving them to the public. They exhibit, accordingly, without disguise or palliation, a view of his whole course of life during his last residence on the continent. We need not say that the life, of which the secret *post-scenia* and deepest recesses are thus unexpectedly laid bare to the gaze of the world, is that of a man of pleasure—dashed, it is true, with the gloom of a complexional melancholy, or more brilliantly diversified by the mingled glories of genius and literature, and abruptly and prematurely terminating in a high tragic catastrophe—an atoning self-sacrifice, and a hero's grave, A book of this character, it may very well be conceived, will in spite of its attractions, or rather in consequence of them, find a place in the *Index Expurgatorius* of the sterner sort of censors—along with the "Mémoires de Grammont," and the "Amours des Gaules" of the Count de Bussy-Rabutin. Yet it is fit and desirable that such truths should be told. They are passages in the book of life which all would and some *should* read, and, although the example of such a man as Lord Byron is, no doubt, calculated to do much harm to minds of a certain stamp, we must only take care to deny it to such people, as edged tools and dangerous drugs are kept out of the way of children, and adults who are no better than children. In this *naïve* confession, besides, of all the infirmities and irregularities of the grandest genius, burning and bewildered with the most ungovernable passions, there is, we conceive, no artificial stimulant for the morbid appetite of sensuality. It is not addressed to the imagination, to deprave by exciting it. It is a picture of life and manners, with far more of history and philosophy in it, than of voluptuous poetry: Every thing depends, as to the effects of certain exposures, upon the associations which they have a tendency to call up. The nudities of the surgeon's cabinet, or the painter's study, are not those of the bagnio. They are "the simplicity and spotless innocence" of Milton's Paradise, to men who survey such objects with the eye of the artist or the philosopher.

We repeat that we have read this book with intense interest. We do not know where the letters are to be found in any language, which better repay a perusal. Perhaps, as mere models of the epistolary style, they are not so exquisite as some that might be cited. Even of this, however, we are far from being sure. If they do not equal, for instance, in grace and elegance, those of Gray, or Lady Mary—if they are not specimens of that inimitable, ineffable *bavardage*, which makes those of Madame de Sévigné so entirely unique—they fully rival the best of them in spirit, piquancy, and, we venture to add, *wit*, while, like the epistles of Cicero, they not unfrequently rise from the most familiar colloquial ease and freedom into far loftier regions of thought and eloquence. We were particularly struck with this last peculiarity. We scarcely read one of them without being surprised into a smile—occasionly into a broad laugh—by some felicitous waggery, some sudden descent from the sublime to the ridiculous, while there is many a passage in which the least critical reader will not fail to recognize the hand that drew Childe Harold.

Two other general observations have been suggested to us by the perusal of this volume: the first is that, although, as we have already remarked, it exhibits a view of Lord Byron's life when he had abjured the realm and put himself out of the pale of English society, denying its authority, defying its power, setting at nought, with foul scorn, all its conventional decencies and established opinions, he appears to us in a much more amiable and estimable light as a man, than he did in the first part of the work. We are not troubled here with any sham pleas—any labored and abortive apologies of Mr. Moore, for what he must have known to be indefensible, if he had any moral sense at all. There is none of that whining and mawkish hypocrisy which we found so peculiarly disgusting in the history of the earlier part of Byron's life. He does not tell a tale of horror, and affect to palm it off upon his reader as a candid avowal of a peccadillo—he does not charge his hero with what amounts to parricide, and then lament the unfortunate peculiarities of a parent, which, he more than insinuates, were a justification of such a monstrous perversion of nature—in short, he does not confess Byron to have been utterly heartless, by his very attempt (and a most awkward attempt) to find an excuse for him, in the tendency of genius to "mount me up into the brain," as honest Falstaff would say, but, as Mr. Moore most daintily expresses it, "to transfer the seat of sensibility from the heart to the fancy." He tells, or rather he suffers Byron to tell his story here without any grimace or dissimulation. The whole truth comes out in a round unvarnished tale, and yet it is scarcely possible to read these letters and not feel disposed rather to deplore the fate, than reprobate the conduct of the writer—the gifted and miserable possessor of so much that might be envied, admired and loved—"a fallen cherub," not only majestic, but touchingly beautiful and attractive, "though in ruins," with enough of his original goodness as well as brightness about him, to make us feel what transcendent and glorious excellence he has forfeited, by those accidental circumstances or complexional peculiarities, or whatever else it were, by which, like one of his own heroes, "he was betrayed too early and beguiled too long."

The gloomy and fierce passions which inspire the muse of Byron seldom break forth in these letters; and, as it has been said of Garrick that it was only when he was off the stage that he was acting, so, if the epistolary correspondence of the poet is (as we take it to be) a fair specimen of his ordinary conversation, we should be inclined to look rather to the effusions of his imagination, than to those which are supposed to flow more immediately from the heart, for the true image of his character. It is not so with common men—it is not so even with those who, possessing extraordinary talents, are in the habit, from policy or propriety or other motives, of exercising a strong self-control when they appear before the public. But Byron knew no such restraints—and then, all his poetry, as we remarked on a former occasion, was the language of feelings which he had brooded over until they were exalted into madness, and his brain burned as in a feverish delirium. We are glad to have what we then advanced confirmed by the poet himself. From an unpublished pamphlet, of which Mr. Moore has furnished some passages, we extract the following. (p. 255.) His lordship is accounting for his having deviated in his own compositions from the standard of excellence which he maintains in theory. "Those who know me best," says he, "know this, and that I have been considerably astonished at the temporary success of my works, &c. Could I have anticipated the degree of attention which has been awarded, assuredly I would have studied more to deserve it. But I have lived in far countries abroad, or in the agitating world at home, which was not favorable to study or reflection: so that almost all I have written has been mere passion—passion, it is true, of different kinds, but always passion; for, in me (if it be not an Irishism to say so) my *indifference* was a kind of pas-

sion, the result of experience and not the philosophy of nature."*
Nor is what he says in another place, (p. 50,) at all inconsistent
with this avowal—but rather a confirmation of it:—"As for
poesy, mine is the *dream of the sleeping passions ;* when they
are awake, I cannot speak their language, only in their somnam-
bulism; and just now they are not dormant." That is to say,
the first paroxysms of his wild emotions were overpowering,
and he was silent under them—Curæ—ingentes stupent. The
eloquence of the passions does not begin until their sharpest
fury is spent—until the conflict within, the agony of the tor-
mented spirit, has been assuaged and subdued by time and reflection—but never was that eloquence uttered by one who had
not felt what it expresses, and felt it to the very bottom of a
thrilling and agitated heart. This is true of every art which
professes to hold the mirror up to human nature, in the scenes
of its intensest excitement.—The unbounded control which a
first-rate orator or actor exercises over a popular assembly—the
magic of the flashing eye, the expressive countenance, the melt-
ing or piercing tones of a well modulated voice—are these mere
feats of rhetorical artifice—the tricks of a crafty juggler, coldly
practising upon the credulity of the vulgar? By no means.
The self-control which generally accompanies them, and which
makes them so surely and uniformly effective, is, indeed, the fruit
of discipline—but the potent charm, the breathed spell is from
the soul—it is nature and nature alone, which asserts this dominion over the hearts of men—and cool and concentrated as
the successful performer may appear to be, he owes his triumphs
over the feelings of others, to still keener sensibilities of his own
—to the "pulse which riots and the blood which burns" within
him. But if this is true of all men of genius, as it certainly is,
it is more applicable to poets than to other artists, and more applicable to Lord Byron than to any other poet. It is impossible
to cast the most superficial glance over his works, without perceiving that they are the effusions of a morbid and maddened
sensibility—a faithful record of the poet's own experience in
every variety of wild, tumultuous excitement. Dreams, they
may be, of sleeping passion—but they are passions which *have*
been awake, and they are dreams which do but fashion into
more poetical shapes, and array in more gloomy or glowing colors, the images of wo or of bliss, of love or of wrath, of beauty
or of horror and deformity, which have peopled the waking fancies of the poet.

He, therefore, that sees Lord Byron only through the medium
of these letters, will form at once, a very inadequate and a very
erroneous conception of that extraordinary character. He is
looking upon Vesuvius, when his "grim fires" are covered over

* See note, *infra.* p. 16.

with vernal luxuriance and beauty—he is looking upon the ocean, when the zephyr is scarcely breathing upon its glassy surface : how should he be able to picture to himself the sublime terrors of the volcano, vomiting forth its smouldering flames and molten lava, or of the foaming surge, when the lowest depths of the sea have been torn up by the tempest ? Pope excelled all men in point, terseness and condensation, and he was a very great master of prose, as all true poets are—yet, whenever he wished to be particularly terse, condensed and pointed, he preferred writing in verse. Byron's poetry was, in like manner, the natural vehicle of his deepest feelings. Masterly as was his prose style, it was no fit channel for such a burning flood of passion and impassioned thought as he poured out when the *estro* (to use his favorite phrase) was upon him—when he had drunk of love and beauty until he was frenzied with their deliciousness, or some dark fancy, or unfortunate event had occurred to wrap his thoughts in gloom, and "from the bottom stir the hell within him." His dæmon, like him of the Delphic shrine, delivered his inspiration only in numbers. Compare Manfred with some of these playful epistles and such lines as these :

> "My boat is on the shore
> And my bark is on the sea;
> But before I go, Tom Moore,
> Here's a double health to thee.

> "Here's a sigh to those who love me,
> And a smile to those who hate;
> And whatever sky's above me,
> Here's a heart for every fate," &c.

Or these,

> "My dear Mr. Murray,
> You're in a damned hurry
> To set up this ultimate canto;
> But if they don't rob us,
> You'll see Mr. Hobhouse
> Will bring it safe in his portmanteau," &c.

The gulph between them is immeasurable : it separates worlds; yet they are but the two extremes of Lord Byron's moral idiosyncracy : the fitful and strange varieties of an hysterical nervousness. That gay creature, with such redundant animal spirits, so full of glee and wantonness, apparently so docile and placable, and prepared to encounter all the vicissitudes of life with irrepressible buoyancy of spirit—what is become of him? In the twinkling of an eye, he has undergone an entire metamorphosis—

> "For even in his maddest mirthful mood,
> Strange pangs would flash across Childe Harold's brow,
> As if the memory of some deadly feud,
> Or disappointed passion, lurked below"—

a cloud is upon his forehead, and wo is in his heart, and his spirit is agitated and convulsed, as with the agony of a dæmoniacal possession. So we have a right to infer from, what it is impossible to separate from the man, the *poetry of his passions*— which is, at the same time, in perfect analogy with his conduct in certain important particulars, and with his habits of life in his more unsocial and gloomy moods. We, of course, speak rather of the *capacities* of Lord Byron's sensibility, than of any permanent, actual state of it. It is very plain from these letters, as well as from other sources of information, and indeed, from the common experience of men, that "time and the hour ran" with him as they do with the rest of the world "thro' the roughest day." But it also appears that he had his moments of severe anguish, of mortal disgust, of withering *ennui*, dejection and despair—that he felt, when he was scarcely turned of thirty, the blight of a long antedated old age, the weariness, the want of interest, the palled appetite and exhausted sensibility—and that the figments of romance do not often exhibit a combination of personal attributes, or a mode of existence, more strange and peculiar, than those of the poetical exile at Venice or Ravenna.

Smooth and smiling, however, as the surface of these letters generally are, there occur occasionally in the course of them some passages, fraught with all the wrath and acerbity of Byron's 'inner man.' Witness, for instance, the fiendlike joy with which he laughs at the affecting suicide of one of the best and ablest men of whom England has ever had to boast, Sir Samuel Romilly. Be it remembered that the inexpiable offence which drew down upon him this fierce and implacable hostility was, that he had been *professionally* engaged by Lady Byron's friends. To be sure, his Lordship charges him with having previously received his retainer—but then Sir Samuel offered him, we should think, a satisfactory excuse, when he declared (what Lord Byron alleges no reason to disbelieve) that, in the multiplicity of his business, his clerk had not informed him of the fact. It appears to us altogether unreasonable to *presume* a man of honor guilty of such unhandsome conduct, in the first place, and of a base falsehood, afterwards, to excuse it. Lord Byron may have had better grounds than he has chosen to state for his opinion on the subject—at all events, it is difficult to imagine a sterner or fiercer vindictiveness than is expressed in the following passages :

"I have never heard any thing of Ada, the little Electra of my Mycenæ. ********. But there will come a day of reckoning, even if I should not live to see it. I have at least seen *** shivered, who was one of my assassins. When that man was doing his worst to uproot my whole family, tree, branch and blossoms—when, after taking my retainer, he went over to them—when he was bringing desolation upon my hearth, and destruction on my household gods—did he think that, in less than three years, a natural event—a severe domestic, but an expected and common calamity—would lay his carcass in a cross-road or stamp his name in a verdict of lunacy! Did he (who in his sexagenary ***,) reflect or consider what my feelings must have been, when wife and child and sister and name and fame and country were to be my sacrifice on his legal altar—and this at a moment when my health was declining, my fortune embarrassed, and my mind had been shaken by many kinds of disappointment—while I was yet young and might have reformed what might be wrong in my conduct, and retrieved what was perplexing in my affairs! But he is in his grave and ******." p. 153.

The asterisk in the above passage, no doubt, supply the place of some very dreadful words, since Mr. Moore has thought fit to suppress them. Murray, to whom the letter, from which the passage is extracted, was addressed, seems to have expostulated with Byron on the injustice of his censure, or the excessive ferocity of his resentment. The poet replies—

"You ask me to spare ****. Ask the worms. His dust can suffer nothing from the truth being spoken: and if it *could*, how did he behave *to me?* You may talk to the wind, which will carry the sound—and to the caves which will echo you—but *not* to me, on the subject of a **** who wrongs me, whether dead or alive." p. 156.

We feel in duty bound to quote his remarks, in quite a different strain, upon another instance of suicide. The subject of them, it seems, had been an enemy of Byron, and had assailed him, as we are informed by Mr. Moore, "with peculiar bitterness and insolence, at a crisis when both his heart and fame were most vulnerable." Considering this circumstance, they are certainly very amiable and generous.

"Poor Scott is now no more. In the exercise of his vocation, he contrived at last to make himself the subject of a coroner's inquest. But he died like a brave man, and he lived an able one. I knew him personally, though slightly. Although several years my senior, we had been schoolfellows together at the 'grammar schule' (or, as the Aberdonians pronounce it, *'squeel'*) of New Aberdeen. He did not behave to me quite handsomely in his capacity of editor a few years ago, but he was under no obligation to behave otherwise. The moment was too tempting for many friends and for all enemies. At a time when all my relations (save one) fell from me like leaves from the tree in autumn winds, and my few friends became still fewer—when the whole periodical press (I mean the daily and weekly, *not* the *literary* press) was let loose against me in every shape of reproach, with the two strange exceptions (from their usual opposition) of the 'Courier' and the 'Examiner,'—the paper of which Scott had the direction was neither the last, nor the least vituperative. Two years ago I met him at Venice, when he was bowed in griefs by the loss of his son, and had known, by experience, the bitterness of domestic privation. He was then earnest with me to return to England; and, on my telling him, with a smile, that he was once of a different opinion, he replied to me, 'that he and others had been greatly misled; and that some pains, and rather extraordinary means, had been taken to excite them.' Scott is no more, but there are more than one living who were present at this dialogue. He was a man of very considerable talents, and of great acquirements. He had made his way, as a literary character, with high success, and in a few years. Poor fellow! I recollect his joy at some appointment which he had obtained, or was to obtain through Sir James Mackintosh, and which prevented the farther extension (unless by a rapid run to Rome) of his travels in Italy. I little thought to what it would conduct him. Peace be with him!—and may all such other faults as are inevitable to humanity be as readily forgiven him, as the little injury which he had done to one who respected his talents and regrets his loss."—p. 253.

The other general remark suggested to us by the perusal of these letters is, that they show Lord Byron to have been quite as much distinguished by his knowledge of the world, and his acute, practical cleverness, as by the highest attributes of genius. That he should write good, or even admirable prose, is not, in itself, wonderful. Many other poets have excelled in the same way. But Byron's style is distinguished by an ease, simplicity and *abandon*, rarely equalled even by those most practised in composition, and every thing he utters is marked with the most accurate and judicious thinking. It is as good a specimen as we have ever seen of strong healthy English sense— that common sense which is of all things most uncommon—in pure, idiomatic, expressive and vigorous English. It is, in short, *very prose*—and although, as we have said, he occasionally rises into a strain of far loftier mood than is common even in the epistles of the greatest men, his *style* never ceases to be perfectly free from affectation of every kind, and with no more of poetical colouring about than is inseparable from the expression of a glowing thought or a deep feeling. Take the following animated and striking passage as a specimen. It is just one of those occasions, be it remarked, where, as Pope has it,

> "if a poet,
> Shone in description, he might show it,"

and where he would be most sorely tempted to show it. Yet nothing could be thrown off more carelessly. To be sure it is the dash of a master's pencil, and we are not to wonder that the sketch is so spirited and fine.

"In reading, I have just chanced upon an axpression of Tom Campbell's;—speaking of Collins, he says that 'no reader cares any more about the *characteristic manners* of his Eclogues than about the authenticity of the tale of Troy.' 'Tis false—we *do* care about 'the authenticity of the tale of Troy.' I have stood upon that plain *daily* for more than a month, in 1810: and if any thing diminished my pleasuae, it was that the blackguard Bryant had impugned its veracity. It is true I read 'Homer Travestied,' (the first twelve books,) because Hobhouse and others bored me with their learned localities, and I love quizzing. But I still venerated the grand original as the truth of *history* (in the material *facts*,) and of *place*. Otherwise, it would have given me no delight. Who will persuade me, when I reclined upon a mighty tomb, that it did not contain a hero ?* Its very magnitude proved this. Men do not labour over the ig-

[* Cf. the fine lines, Iliad H., 89 et seq., Hector's challenge to the Greek army. Ἀνδρὸς μεν τόδε σῆμα πάλαι κατατεθνηῶτος, etc.]

noble and petty dead: and why should not the *dead*, be *Homer's* dead? The secret of Tom Campbell's defence of inaccuracy in costume and description is that his Gertrude, &c., has no more locality in common with Pennsylvania than with Penmanmaur. It is notoriously full of grossly false scenery, as all Americans declare, though they praise parts of the poem. It is thus that self-love forever creeps out, like a snake, to sting any thing which happens, even accidentally, to stumble upon it." p. 279.

We were greatly struck, the first time we read this passage, with the very few lines in it which relate to Homer and Troy. The style, both of thought and expression, seems to us remarkable for a noble, and even grand simplicity, while the "reclining upon a mighty tomb" presents, in itself, to the fancy of the reader, a complete picture, and brings thronging about it all the great associations of that holy ground of poetry and arms. It reminded us strongly of some imagery in the letter to Murray upon the Pope and Bowles controversy. There is no merit of composition more rare and exquisite, than that of thus exhibiting a perfect image of the object described, suggesting, at the same time, and calling up, as if by enchantment, the whole scene to which it belongs, without any labored pomp of description. Every scholar knows what high encomiums have been deservedly passed by the critics upon a noted instance of the kind in an oration of Cicero, in which he paints Verres, in an effeminate foreign costume, reclining upon the shoulder of a courtezan, and looking out upon a fleet at sea from the shore at Syracuse.* These letters and journals abound with such beauties.

But descriptive talent is not to our present purpose—nor is Byron's merit as a prose-writer by any means confined to his style. He is a sound and most ingenious thinker. It is scarcely possible to open this volume—unequal as familiar epistles generally are—without being struck with this truth, and wondering how so sensible a man could have yielded himself up, in the conduct of life, so unresistingly, to the besetting sins of his temper and temperament. We might easily adduce instances without number—but we shall confine ourselves to one. We mean his defence of Pope—a favorite subject, to which he recurs again and again, with unabated enthusiasm. We venture to back him in this—his chosen vocation of critic and champion of injured genius—against any Aristarchus of the schools from the first downward. We would willingly reprint all that he has said upon this subject,—bating the extravagance to which the zeal of the advocate has, in a single instance, carried him—to aid in the circulation of so much excellent sense and good writing—especially as this volume may be considered, in some sort, as an interdicted book. But we will content ourselves

* In Verrem, act ii. l. 5. c. 33.

with two extracts—one of them containing some curious remarks upon Pope's amour with Miss Blount.

"And here I wish to say a few words on the present state of English poetry. That this is the age of the decline of English poetry will be doubted by few who have calmly considered the subject. That there are men of genius among the present poets makes little against the fact, because it has been well said that, 'next to him who forms the taste of his country, the greatest genius is he who corrupts it.' No one has ever denied genius to Marino, who corrupted not merely the taste of Italy, but that of all Europe for nearly a century. The great cause of the present deplorable state of English poetry is to be attributed to that absurd and systematic depreciation of Pope, in which, for the last few years, there has been a kind of epidemical concurrence. Men of the most opposite opinions have united upon this topic. Warton and Churchill began it, having borrowed the hint probably from the heroes of the Dunciad, and their own internal conviction that their proper reputation can be as nothing till the most perfect and harmonious of poets—he who, having no fault, has had REASON made his reproach—was reduced to what they conceived to be his level; but even *they* dared not degrade him below Dryden. Goldsmith, and Rogers, and Campbell, his most successful disciples: and Hayley, who, however feeble, has left one poem 'that will not be willingly let die' (the Triumphs of Temper), kept up the reputation of that pure and perfect style: and Crabbe, the first of living poets, has almost equalled the master. Then came Darwin, who was put down by a single poem in the Antijacobin: and the Cruscans, from Merry to Jerningham, who were annihilated (if *Nothing* can be said to be annihilated) by Gifford, the last of the wholesome English satirists.

*   *   *   *   *   *   *   *

"These three personages, S**, W**, and C**, had all of them a very natural antipathy to Pope, and I respect them for it as the only original feeling or principle which they have contrived to preserve.—But they have been joined in it by those who have joined them in nothing else: by the Edinburgh Reviewers, by the whole heterogeneous mass of living English poets, excepting Crabbe, Rogers, Gifford and Campbell, who, both by precept and practice, have proved their adherence; and by me, who have shamefully deviated in practice, but have ever loved and honored Pope's poetry with my whole soul, and hope to do so till my dying day. I would rather see all I have ever written lining the same trunk in which I actually read the eleventh book of a modern Epic poem at Malta, in 1811, (I opened it to take out a change after the paroxysm of a tertian, in the absence of my servant, and found it lined with the name of the maker, Eyre, Cockspur-street, and with the Epic poetry alluded to, than sacrifice what I firmly believe in as the Christianity of English poetry, the poetry of Pope.

*   *   *   *   *   *   *   *   *

"Nevertheless, I will not go so far as ** in his postscript, who pretends that *no* great poet ever had immediate fame; which, being interpreted, means that ** is not quite so much read by his contemporaries as might be desirable. This assertion is as false as it is foolish. Homer's glory depended upon his present popularity: he recited,—and without the strongest impression of the moment, who would have gotten the Iliad by heart and given it to tradition? Ennius, Terence, Plautus, Lucretius, Horace, Virgil, Æschylus, Sophocles, Euripides, Sappho, Anacreon, Theocritus, all the great poets of antiquity, were the delight of their contemporaries.

The very existence of a poet, previous to the invention of printing, depended upon his present popularity; and how often has it impaired his future fame? Hardly ever. History informs us, that the best have come down to us. The reason is evident; the most popular found the greatest number of transcribers for their MSS., and that the taste of their contemporaries was corrupt can hardly be avouched by the moderns, the mightiest of whom have but rarely approached them. Dante, Petrarch, Ariosto, and Tasso, were all the darlings of the contemporary reader. Dante's poem was celebrated long before his death; and, not long after it, States negotiated for his ashes, and disputed for the sites of the composition of the Divina Commedia. Petrarch was crowned in the Capitol. Ariosto was permitted to pass free by the public robber who had read the Orlando Furioso. I would not recommend Mr. * * to try the same experiment with his smugglers. Tasso, notwithstanding the criticisms of the Cruscanti, would have been crowned in the Capitol, but for his death.

. "It is easy to prove the immediate popularity of the chief poets of the only modern nation in Europe that has a poetical language, the Italian. In our own, Shakspeare, Spenser, Jonson, Waller, Dryden, Congreve, Pope, Young, Shenstone, Thomson, Johnson, Goldsmith, Gray, were all as popular in their lives as since. Gray's Elegy pleased instantly, and eternally. His odes did not, nor yet do they please like his Elegy. Milton's politics kept him down; but the Epigram of Dryden, and the very sale of his work, in proportion to the less reading time of its publication, prove him to have been honored by his contemporaries. I will venture to assert that the sale of the Paradise Lost was greater in the first four years after its publication than that of the 'Excursion' in the same number, with the difference of nearly a century and a half between them of time, and of thousands in point of general readers." pp 253, 254.

* * * * * * * *

"Pope himself 'sleeps well—nothing can touch him farther:' but those who love the honour of their country, the perfection of her literature, the glory of her language, are not to be expected to permit an atom of his dust to be stirred in his tomb, or a leaf to be stripped from the laurel which grows over it.

* * * * * * * *

' To me it appears of no very great consequence whether Martha Blount was or was not Pope's mistress, though I could have wished him a better. She appears to have been a cold-hearted, interested, ignorant, disagreeable woman, upon whom the tenderness of Pope's heart in the desolation of his latter days was cast away, not knowing whither to turn, as he drew towards his premature old age, childless and lonely,—like the needle which, approaching within a certain distance of the pole, becomes helpless and useless, and, ceasing to tremble, rusts. She seems to have been so totally unworthy of tenderness, that it is an additional proof of the kindness of Pope's heart, to have been able to love such a being. But we must love something. I agree with Mr. B. that *she* 'could at no time have regarded *Pope personally* with attachment,' because she was incapable of attachment; but I deny that Pope could not be regarded with a personal attachment by a worthier woman. It is not probable, indeed, that a woman would have fallen in love with him as he walked along the Mall, or in a box at the opera, nor from a balcony, nor in a ball-room; but in society he seems to have been as amiable, as unassuming, and, with the greatest disadvantages of figure, his head and face were remarkably handsome, especially his eyes. He was adored by his friends— friends of the most opposite dispositions, ages and talents—by the old and wayward Wycherley, by the cynical Swift, the rough Atterbury, the gentle Spence, the stern attorney-bishop Warburton, the virtuous Berkeley, and the 'cankered Bolingbroke.' Bolingbroke wept over him like a child ; and Spence's description of his last moments is at least as edifying as the more ostentatious account of the death-bed of Addison. The soldier Peterborough and the poet Gay, the witty Congreve and the laughing Rowe, the eccentric Cromwell and the steady Bathurst, were all his intimates. The man who could conciliate so many men of the most opposite description, not one of whom but was a remarkable or a celebrated character, might well have pretended to all the attachment which a reasonable man would desire of an amiable woman.

"Pope, in fact, wherever he got it, appears to have understood the sex well. Bolingbroke, 'a judge of the subject,' says Warton, thought his 'Epistle on the Characters of Women' his 'masterpiece.' And even with respect to the grosser passion, which takes occasionally the name of 'romantic,' accordingly as the degree of sentiment elevates it above the definition of love by Buffon, it may be remarked that it does not always depend upon personal appearance, even in a woman. Madame Cottin was a plain woman, and might have been virtuous, it may be presumed, without much interruption. Virtuous she was, and the consequence of this inveterate virtue was that two different admirers (one an elderly gentleman) killed themselves in despair (see Lady Morgan's 'France'). I would not, however, recommend this rigor to plain women in general, in the hope of securing the glory of two suicides apiece. I believe that there are few men who, in the course of their observations on life, may not have perceived that it is not the greatest female beauty who forms the longest and the strongest passions.

"But apropos of Pope,—Voltaire tells us that the Mareschal Luxembourg (who had precisely Pope's figure) was not only somewhat too amatory for a great man, but fortunate in his attachments. La Valière, the passion of Louis XIV., had an unsightly defect. The Princess of Eboli, the mistress of Philip the second of Spain, and Maugiron, the minion of Henry the Third of France, had each of them lost an eye; and the famous Latin epigram was written upon them, which has, I believe, been either translated or imitated by Goldsmith :

'Lumine Acon dextro, capta est Leonilla sinistro,
    Et potis est forma vincere uterque Deos ;
Blande puer, lumen quod habes concede sorori,
    Sic tu cæcus Amor, sic erit illa Venùs.'

"Wilkes, with his ugliness, used to say that 'he was but a quarter of an hour behind the handsomest man in England'; and this vaunt of his is said not to have been disapproved by circumstances. Swift, when neither young, nor handsome, nor rich, nor even amiable, inspired the two most extraordinary passions upon record, Vanessa's and Stella's.

'Vanessa, aged scarce a score,
    Sighs for a gown of forty-four.'

"He requited them bitterly; for he seems to have broken the heart of the one, and worn out that of the other; and he had his reward, for he died a solitary idiot in the hands of servants.

"For my own part, I am of the opinion of Pausanias that success in love depends upon fortune. 'They particularly renounce Celestial Venus, into whose temple, &c. &c. &c. I remember, too, to have seen a building in Ægina, in which there is a statue of Fortune, holding a horn of Amalthea and near her there is a winged Love. The meaning of this is that the success of men in love-affairs depends more on the assistance of Fortune than the charms of beauty. I am persuaded, too, with Pindar, (to whose opinion I submit in other particulars,) that Fortune is one of the Fates, and that in a certain respect she is more powerful than her sisters.'—See Pausanias, Achaics, book vii. chap. 26, p. 246, 'Taylor's Translation.'

"Grimm has a remark of the same kind on the different destinies of the younger Crebillon and Rousseau.   The former writes a licentious novel, and a young English girl of some fortune and family (a Miss Strafford) runs away and crosses the sea to marry him; while Rousseau, the most tender and passionate of lovers, is obliged to espouse his chamber-maid. If I recollect rightly, this remark was also repeated in the Edinburgh Review of Grimm's Correspondence, seven or eight years ago.

"In regard 'to the strange mixture of indecent, and sometimes *profane* levity, which his conduct and language *often* exhibited,' and which so much shocks Mr. Bowles, I object to the indefinite word '*often;*' and in extenuation of the occasional occurrence of such language it is to be recollected that it was less the tone of *Pope*, than the tone of the *time*.   With the exception of the correspondence of Pope and his friends, not many private letters of the period have come down to us; but those, such as they are— a few scattered scraps from Farquhar and others—are more indecent and coarse than any thing in Pope's letters.   The Comedies of Congreve, Vanbrugh, Farquhar, Cibber, &c., which naturally attempted to represent the manners and conversation of private life, are decisive upon this point: as are also some of Steele's papers, and even Addison's.   We all know what the conversation of Sir R. Walpole, for seventeen years the prime minister of the country, was at his own table, and his excuse for his licentious language, viz. 'that every body understood *that*, but few could talk rationally upon less common topics.'   The refinement of latter days,— which is perhaps the consequence of vice, which wishes to mask and soften itself, as much as of virtuous civilization—had not yet made sufficient progress.   Even Johnson, in his 'London,' has two or three passages which cannot be read aloud, and Addison's 'Drummer' some indelicate allusions." pp. 321–323.

There are two short paragraphs in this volume, that let us fully into Lord Byron's theory of the sublime and beautiful in composition.

"I thought Anastasius *excellent:* did I not say so?   Matthew's Diary most excellent; it, and Forsyth, and parts of Hobhouse, are all we have of truth or sense upon Italy.   The letter to Julia very good indeed.   I do not despise * * * * * *; but if she knit blue-stockings, instead of wearing them, it would be better.   *You* are taken in by that false, stilted, trashy style, which is a mixture of all the styles of the day, which are *all bombastic* (I don't except my *own*—no one has done more through negligence to corrupt the language;) but it is neither English nor poetry.   *Time will show.*" p. 240.

"I perceive that in Germany, as well as in Italy, there is a great struggle about what they call 'classical' and 'romantic'—terms which were not subjects of classification in England, at least when I left it four or five years ago.   Some of the English scribblers, it is true, abused Pope and Swift, but the reason was that they themselves did not know how to write either prose or verse: but nobody thought them worth making a sect of. Perhaps there may be something of the kind sprung up lately, but I have not heard much about it, and it would be such bad taste that I shall be very sorry to believe it." p. 248.

It is plain from these passages that he had formed his taste, or nature had formed it for him, upon the models of *Attic*, not of *Asiatic* eloquence—of classical, not of romantic poetry.   His observations upon the styles of the day (his own included) are perfectly just. They *are* all *bombastic*—even Wordsworth's, who loves such infantine simplicity—for even his simplicity is often affected, and always visibly elaborate—as different, as it is possible to imagine any thing, from the naked, unsophisticated nature of the best Greek writers.* As to Lord Byron himself, he has pleaded guilty, in anticipation, to a charge which may undoubtedly be alleged against him with perfect justice. He has done more than any body else to make a vicious style popular. The two last Cantos of Childe Harold have, we believe, generally been considered as his master-pieces. They have been abundantly extolled, and Mr. Moore mentions that one distinguished writer, especially, and he an enemy of Byron, at least, an active adversary of his principles, has pronounced the fourth Canto the most sublime production of human genius. Without subscribing to this extravagant encomium, we flatter ourselves that we feel all the grandeur and pathos of that powerful production. Yet we undertake to say it would be difficult to point out any work of genius of the present age, which is more obnoxious to the sweeping censure pronounced by the author upon himself and all his contemporaries. In a former article, we adduced several instances to exemplify this criticism, but we then remarked, that it was not a frigid conceit, or an extravagant hyperbole, here and there, which we have to find fault with, so much as the general tone of emphasis and exaggeration—a too visible effort apparent throughout the whole work, to be very original and striking, or very powerful, grand and impressive. This straining after effect—which produces what is well described in French as the *style gigantesque*—seems to us more or less visible in every part of the poems alluded to, and, no doubt, greatly impairs their general effect, not to mention the positive faults which it engenders.† Let us cite an example. The description of the Belvidere Apollo, contains some of the finest lines in the poem. The whole picture is a magnificent one and worthy of the subject. It is the idea of the statuary bodi-

---

* Voltaire's prose style is more Attic than that of any writer, we remember, within the last century—except, perhaps, Goldsmith.

† Lord Byron speaks, in one of his letters, of the Childe Harold as his favorite work. We cite the passage more willingly, because it throws still farther light upon the manner in which he identifies himself with his work—the *egoisme*, in short, which is their pervading principle and spirit. "I rejoice to hear of your forthcoming in February, though I tremble for the magnificence which you attribute to the new Childe Harold. I am glad you like it : it is a fine indistinct piece of poetical desolation, and my favorite. *I was half mad* during the time of its composition, between metaphysics, mountains, lakes, love unextinguishable, thoughts unutterable, and the night-mare of my own delinquencies. I should, many a good day, have blown my brains out, but for the recollection that it would have given pleasure to my mother-in-law ; and even *then* if I could have been certain to haunt her, and fling the shattered scalp of my sinciput and occiput in her frightful face."—p. 51.

ed forth in poetical language, or rather a competition between the single visible form and the whole power of words, which shall convey the most perfect image of beauty to the mind—such a contest as Roscius and Cicero are said to have instituted, to try the relative compass of gesture, (or more strictly, mute acting) and oratorical diction. Yet successful as the poet must be admitted to have been in this lofty enterprize, his verse has faults in it from which the statue is free. This comparison is the more important, because as Schlegel says, after Winkelmann, they who wish to conceive a just idea of the standard of excellence which Greek genius proposed to itself, must study the antique in sculpture. The remark is perfectly sound, and we can only say, that Sophocles always occurs to us when we think of the Apollo and *vice versa*. And so we conceive that no modern artist (including the poets) has ever approached so nearly to the severe graces, and the simple grandeur of the antique, as Raphael.* But to proceed with the matter in hand. The description is contained in two stanzas—it appears to us that both begin most beautifully and end faultily; a perfect Apollo sinking (if we may be pardoned a pun, intelligible only to a foreigner) into a *phébus*.

> "Or view the Lord of the unerring bow,
> The god of life and poesy and light—
> The sun in human limbs arrayed, and brow
> All radiant from his triumph in the fight.
> The shaft hath just been shot—the arrow bright
> With an immortal vengeance; in his eye
> And nostril beautiful disdain,† and *might*
> *And majesty flash their full lightnings by,*
> Developing, in that one glance, the deity."

The words in italics do not appear to us either in keeping with the image of the Apollo, or appropriate in themselves. "Majesty flashing its lightnings" might be of questionable propriety, i. e. sobriety, any where—most especially, however, is it so, when applied to this statue. So the epithet *"full"* seems to be quite out of place—and the *"by"* at the end of the line is clearly there only for the rhyme. We may be wrong, but the pleasure we have uniformly derived from this beautiful stanza has always been in some degree marred by these imperfections, as they seem to us. But the second is more objectionable.

> "But in his delicate form—a dream of love,
> Shaped by some solitary nymph, whose breast
> Longed for a deathless lover from above
> And maddened in that vision—are exprest

---

* With deference to Winkelmann, be it said.

† This fine line is a *reminiscence*—in part:
> "Oh what a deal of scorn looks beautiful
> In the contempt and anger of that lip."—*Shakspeare.*

All that ideal beauty ever bless'd
The mind within its most unearthly mood,
When each conception was a heavenly guest—
A ray of immortality—and stood,
Star-like around, until they gathered to a god "

These last three lines may be fine: there may be some secret
meaning in them which we do not seize: we own, however, that
they have always appeared to us vague, mystical and extravagant. Of one thing we are very sure, they contribute nothing
either to the distinctness or vividness of that image of beauty,
which it was the object of the poet to bring out as strongly as
possible, and are not like any thing that is to be found in Greek
poetry—not excepting the odes of Pindar, or the choruses of the
tragedians.   Is it good as "romantic" writing ?

This last allusion leads us to remark upon that distinction between the "classical" and "romantic" styles, which Byron, in one
of the passages quoted above, alludes to as a novel, and condemns as an absurd one.   We are glad to hear an opinion, which
we ventured to advance in our first number,* confirmed by so
high an authority—for if any writer has a claim to a high place
in the new school, it is undoubtedly Byron.   The distinction,
now alluded to, originated in Germany.   It was seized by Madame
de Staël with avidity, as well adapted to her purposes of metaphysical, mystical and ambitious declamation, and it has since
been entertained, with more respect than we conceive it deserves,
in the literary circles of Europe.   A. W. Schlegel, in his valuable Lectures upon Dramatic Poetry, makes it the basis of all his
comparisons between the ancients and the moderns in that art.
His main object is to account for the simplicity of the Greek
drama, and its close adherence to the three unities, as well as
the rigid exclusion from it of every thing comic and incongruous, on principles which shall explain the difference between
that style and the complicated and irregular plots and tragi-
comic mixtures of Calderon and Shakspeare, without supposing
any inferiority in the latter.   It was not enough for him to say,
that ancient taste was too fastidious ; or that ancient criticism
was more severe, as the modern is more indulgent—that the
former exacted of genius more than it can perform, at least without a sacrifice of much of its power and enthusiasm—while the
latter unshackles "the muse of fire" and gives it full scope and
boundless regions to soar in—and that this is the reason, in short,
why Macbeth and Othello are so much better (as *we* say they
are) than the Orestiad or the Œdipus.   This did not suit with
Schlegel's way of thinking, first, because he was a good scholar,
and knew better ; and, next and principally, because he was a
German philosopher, and therefore bound to explain the phenom-

* Article I.—Classical Learning.

enon by some subtile process of reasoning of his own invention. This he has attempted to do, and the result (as we understand it) is that, in all the arts of taste, the genius of modern times is *essentially* different from that of the Greeks, and *requires*, for its gratification, works of a structure totally distinct from those which he admits to have been the best imaginable models of the classic style.

The principle, by which it is attempted to account for this mighty revolution in art and criticism, is *religion*. That of the Greeks, we are told, was "the deification of the powers of nature and of earthly life." Under a southern sky, amidst the sweets of a genial and radiant climate, genius naturally dreams of joy and beauty, and the forms, with which a poetical fancy peopled heaven, were fashioned upon those with which it was familiar on earth. A gay, sensual and elegant mythology grew up under its plastic hands—its visions of ideal perfection were embodied in the idols of superstitious worship,—and Venus, Apollo, Minerva, Hercules, &c., have been individualized as images of certain attributes, and identified with the conception of all mankind, by the master-pieces which they may be said to have patronized, since they were created to adorn their temples or to grace their festivals. But this system of religious adoration was confined to the present life, addressed itself exclusively to the *senses*, exacted of the worshipper only forms and oblations, and confirmed him in the tranquil self-complacency or the joyous spirit which the face of nature and the circumstances of his own condition inspired. Christianity was, in all these particulars, the very opposite of Paganism. It added to the material world, a mysterious world of spirits—it substituted the infinite for the finite, and endless future for the transitory present— at the end of every vista in life, it presents the grave, and it has shrouded the grave itself in a deeper gloom, and made death emphatically the King of Terrors. But Schlegel has expressed himself so well upon this subject, that we are tempted to quote a long passage from him:

"Among the Greeks, human nature was in itself all sufficient; they were conscious of no wants, and aspired at no higher perfection than that which they could actually attain by the exercise of their own faculties. We, however, are taught by superior wisdom that man, through a high offence, forfeited the place for which he was originally destined: and that the whole object of his earthly existence is to strive to regain that situation which, if left to his own strength, he could never accomplish. The religion of the senses had only in view the possession of outward and perishable blessings; and immortality, in so far as it was believed, appeared in an obscure distance like a shadow, a faint dream of this bright and vivid futurity.   The very reverse of all this is the case with the Christian: every thing finite and mortal is lost in the contemplation of infinity; life has become shadow and darkness, and the first dawning of our real existence is beyond the grave.   Such a religion must awaken the foreboding, which slumbers in every feeling heart, to the most thorough consciousness that the happiness after which we strive we can never here obtain: that no external object can ever entirely fill our souls, and that every mortal enjoyment is but a fleeting and momentary deception.   When the soul resting, as it were, under the willows of exile, breathes out its longing for its distant home, the prevailing character of its song must be melancholy.   Hence the poetry of the ancients was the poetry of enjoyment, and ours is that of desire; the former has its foundation in the scene which is present, while the latter hovers between recollection and hope.   Let us not be understood to affirm that every thing flows in one strain of wailing and complaint, and that the voice of melancholy must always be loudly heard.   As the austerity of tragedy was not incompatible with the joyous views of the Greeks, so the romantic poetry can assume every tone, even that of the most lively gladness; but still it will always, in some shape or other, bear traces of the source from which it originated.   The *feeling of the moderns is, upon the whole, more intense, their fancy more incorporeal, and their thoughts more contemplative.*"*

Now, we are disposed to assent, in general, to the justness of these observations.   We think that modern literature does differ from that of the Greeks in its *complexion and spirit*—that it is more pensive, sombre and melancholy, perhaps, we may add, more abstract, and metaphysical—and it has, no doubt, been "sickled o'er" with this sad hue, by the influence of a religious faith which connects morality with worship, and teaches men to consider every thought, word and action of their lives as involving, in some degree, the tremendous issues of eternity.   Macchiavelli has a similar theory of his own.   He refers the existence of democratic government among the ancients, and the almost total absence of it in his time, to the same cause.   The spirit of polytheism he conceives to have been bold, hardy and masculine; that of Christianity to be so meek, lowly and self-abasing, as to fit its professors for any sort of imposition or contumely.†   This notion has been signally refuted by the history of the last three centuries—especially by the exploits of our Puritan and Huguenot ancestors—but the theory of the Florentine secretary is, in practical matters, very much what Schlegel's is, in literature.   Certainly we are more given to *spiritualizing* than the Greeks

* Dram. Lit.—Lect. v. i. p. 15.   † Discorsi.

were—sensible objects suggest moral reflections more readily—the external world is treated as if it were the symbol of
the invisible, and the superiority of mind to matter, of the soul
to the body, is almost as much admitted by the figures of rhetoric and poetry, as in the dogmas of philosophy.   There were
no Herveys and Dr. Youngs at Athens.   The *spirit*, we repeat it,
is changed—the associations, which natural objects suggest, are
different, of course—but does this alter, in any essential degree,
the *forms* of beauty?   Does it affect the *proportions* which the
parts of a work of art ought to bear to each other and to the
whole?   Does it so far modify the relations of things that what
would be fit and proper in a poem, an oration, a colonnade, a
picture, if it were ancient, is misplaced and incongruous now?
In short, has the philosophy of literature and the arts, the reason, the logic—which controls their execution and results as
much as it does the conclusions of science, though in a less palpable manner—undergone any serious revolution?   Schlegel
and the rest of the same school affirm that such a revolution
has taken place.   Their favorite illustration of it is, as we have
already remarked, the drama and the unities; Shakspeare and
Sophocles are the great representatives of the "romantic" and
the "classical"—and they compare the former to painting which
is various, the latter to sculpture, which is of course characterized by singleness and simplicity.   "Why," say they "are the
Greek and romantic poets so different in their practice, with respect to place and time."   The question is an interesting one.
Many solutions may be offered; and the very last we should
adopt would be the following: which, indeed, so far as it is
intelligible, is only a different way of asserting the same thing;
in other words, a very palpable *petitio principii.*   "The principal cause of the difference is the *plastic* spirit of the antique and
the *picturesque* spirit of the romantic poetry.   *Sculpture* directs
our attention exclusively to the groupe exhibited to us, it disen-
tangles it as far as possible from all external accompaniments,
and where they can be altogether dispensed with, they are indicated as lightly as possible.   *Painting*, on the other hand, delights in exhibiting in a minute manner, along with the principal figures, the surrounding locality and all the secondary objects, and to open to us in the back ground, a prospect into
a boundless distance; light and perspective are its peculiar
charms.   Hence the dramatic, and especially the tragic art of
the ancients annihilates in some measure, the external circumstances of space and time; while the romantic drama adorns by
their changes its more diversified pictures.   Or to express myself in other terms, the principle of antique poetry is ideal, that
of the romantic mystical: the former subjects, space and time,
to the internal free activity of the mind; the latter adores these

inconceivable essences as supernatural powers, in whom something of the divinity has its abode."*

We are willing to impute the transcendent, or, if the epithet be preferred, the truly *romantic* nonsense of the last sentence to the translator; but we may conjecture from the context, and from the other parts of his work, what was the drift of the author. M. Schlegel means to say (as he does affirm elsewhere) that this difference between ancient and modern genius, which is thus illustrated by sculpture and painting, or the *plastic* and the *picturesque*, pervades all the departments of literature and art, without exception. In music, for instance, the ancients are said to have preferred melody, the moderns harmony—in architecture, compare the Parthenon or the Pantheon with Westminster Abbey, or the Church of St. Stephen at Vienna—even the sculpture of the moderns, according to the opinion of Hemsterhusius, is too much like painting, as the painting of the ancients was probably too much like sculpture. Now, in the first place, we deny the fact that the taste of the moderns *is* different from that of the Greeks in these particulars. As for the drama, *we* have no tragedies but Shakspeare's, and, if we had, his incomparable genius has settled that part of the controversy irreversibly, so far as popular opinion is concerned. But do not all scholars, without exception, admire and delight in the Greek tragedy? As for music, we suspect that melody is as much preferred now to harmony, as it ever was at Athens; but if it were not, it would be for time to decide, whether the taste of the day were not a transitory and false one. We know too little of the state of that art among the Greeks to enable us to draw any sure inferences from it. Besides the proper comparison would be not between melody and harmony, but between romantic melody or harmony, and classical melody or harmony, since both existed at each of the two great periods, and there can be no fair comparison but between things of the same kind. So with architecture. A Gothic cathedral has its beauties—it has its own peculiar proportions—it has fitness to the solemn purpose for which it was designed—it has gorgeous ornament, imposing massiveness, striking altitude, immense extent—its long-drawn aisle and fretted vault—its storied windows—the choir, the altar, the crucifixes, the confessional of the penitent, the stones of the pavement worn by the knees of pilgrims and crusaders, the air of venerable antiquity and religious gloom pervading the whole interior—a thousand interesting associations of the past and of the future, of history and the church, conspire to make it one of the most impressive objects that can be presented to the imagination of man. The origin of the style was in a dark age; but it has taken root, nor is it at all probable

* Dramatic Lit.—Lect. ix. p. 348.

that, so long as Christianity shall endure, the modern world will ever be brought to think as meanly of these huge piles, as a Greek architect (if one were suddenly revived) possibly might. Still, there are very few builders of the present age who do not prefer the orders of Greece—and, even if they did not, how would that prove that future ages would not? "Time will show," as Byron says, which taste is the more natural and reasonable: and time only, and the voice of the majority, can shew it conclusively.

Meanwhile, let us descend to details: suppose a particular object proposed to be painted or described in the strict sense of those words? Are there two ways of doing that perfectly, and yet as different from each other as the styles in question are supposed to be? A portrait, for instance,—is a classical likeness, a different thing from a romantic one, and yet both are good likenesses of the same thing? Suppose the object described to be twilight. If the pictures were confined to the *sensible phenomena*, it is obvious there *could not be* any variety in them, as any one who doubts what is obvious to reason, may convince himself by comparing parallel passages in the ancient and modern classics— e. g., Milton's lines, "Now came still evening on, and twilight gray", Virgil's beautiful verses on midnight, in the fourth Æneid, Homer's on moonlight in the eighth Iliad. The exquisite sketches of these objects, executed by the great masters just mentioned, are all in precisely the same style, and, if they were in the same language, might easily be ascribed to the same age of poetry. To be sure, if without, or besides describing the object, some striking association of ideas be suggested, that may make a very material difference, because such things are essentially accidental and mutable. For instance, Dante's famous lines on the evening describe it, not as the period of the day when nature exhibits such or such phenomena, which must always be the same while her everlasting order shall be maintained, but by certain casual circumstances which may or may not accompany that hour— the vesper bell, tolling the knell of the dying day, the lonely traveller looking back, with a heart oppressed with fond regrets, to the home which he has just left—very touching circumstances no doubt to those who have a home or have lived in Catholic countries, but still extraneous, and it may be, transitory circumstances.

The same thing may be affirmed of any other particular object, either in the moral or the material world. A picture of conjugal love, for instance, as in Hector and Andromache—of maternal despair, as in Shakspeare's Blanche—of filial devotedness, as in the Antigone. We do not comprehend how it is possible to exhibit such objects in more than one style that shall be perfect— and that the *natural*, the universal, the unchangeable—quod semper, quod ubique, quod ab omnibus. And what is clearly true of the details we take to be equally true of the combinations. The *spirit* may vary, the *associations*, the colouring or complexion; but, substantially, there can be but one form of ideal beauty, with which human nature, that never changes, will rest forever satisfied.

We will borrow an illustration, on this subject, from the learned Michaelis. If any two systems of religion and poetry differ in their spirit, in the associations with which they surround the objects of their adoration and praise, and the effect they produce upon the mind of the votary, it is the Jewish and the Pagan—the one dwelling forever, in its prophetic raptures, upon the sublime unity of the Godhead filling immensity, whose invisible glory it was the guiltiest audacity to degrade by attempting to represent it in any sensible image; the other crowding all space with a mob of thirty thousand deities of every rank and shape. The sacred poetry of the Hebrews, besides, is the great fountain of modern inspiration, strictly so called. Yet, differing as widely as it is possible in the very element of thought and character from which Schlegel deduces such important results, there is no essential difference in the *forms* of Hebrew and Classical poetry. The illustration we shall borrow from the learned author referred to is the following. He remarks that, as the Heathen assigned to Jupiter a chariot and horses of thunder, so the Hebrews have a similar fable, and the Cherubim are expressly the horses of Jehovah's chariot. He is frequently described as sitting upon the Cherubim. He thunders so that the earth shakes—or as Horace might have expressed it,

> "Jehovah per cœlum tonantes
> Egit equos, volucremque currum;
> Quo bruta tellus, et vaga flumina
> Quo Styx et invisi horrida Tœnari
> Sedes, Atlanteusque finis
> Concutitur."*

The same observation holds, in the strictest manner true, of Milton and Dante, the two most sublime poets of modern times, the most Christian in spirit, and the most classical and severe in style.

After all, this classification of styles may be only a more artificial and scholastic way of confessing that those irregular works of modern genius, which are designated as romantic, *par excellence*, in fact, deviate very materially from the Greek standard. Of this no one who has studied criticism in the works of the ancients, can have any doubt at all. Three things were considered as essential to all excellence, in a composition of genius, perfect unity of purpose, simplicity of style, and ease of execu-

* On Lowth's Hebrew Poetry—Lect. ix.

tion—and it is in these things that the literature and art of Greece exhibit their matchless perfection. Other nations have produced works indicating as rare and fertile invention, as much depth of thought, as much vigor of conception, as much intensity of feeling—but no body of literature or of art can be compared to the *antique* for the severe *reason*, the close, unsparing *logic* of its criticism. Unity of design, especially, which is more immediately connected with the subject in hand, ·they rigorously exacted. They considered a work of art always as a *whole*—a sort of organized body—to the very structure of which certain parts and proportions, and none others, were essential, and in which the least violation of this fitness and harmony was a deformity, more or less uncouth and monstrous.* The details were sacrificed without mercy to the general effect. In an oration, for instance, they looked to the end which the speaker had in view, and whatever was not calculated to further that, however brilliant and impressive in itself, was rejected without reserve. The notion of Pythagoras that the sublime order of the universe was maintained by the secret power of *proportion*, by the magic of mathematical relations, probably sprang out of this truly Greek idea of the perfection of art, applied by analogy to the works of creation.† This unity of thought, this harmony in composition, this ἀνάγκη λόγογραφικη as Plato calls it, a sort of necessary connection, like that of cause and effect, between the parts, every thing being in its right place, following logically from what goes before it, leading inevitably to what comes after it, pervades all the monuments of genius which that wonderful race has left behind it. The superiority in their exquisite *logic* of literature and the arts—a logic not a jot less exact and elegant than the demonstrations of their own unrivalled geometry—is, we fear, a lamentable truth, nor will it help us much to call our deformities, peculiarities, and to dignify what is only *not* art with the specious title of the 'romantic.'

This severe study of unity naturally led, it seems to us, to the two other prominent excellencies of Greek style, simplicity and

---

* Plato, Phæd. p. 244. c. Socrates says, οἶμαι, &c. πάντα λόγου ὥσπερ ζῶου συνεςάναι, ςῶμά τι ἔχοντα αὐτον αὐτοῦῶςε μήτε ἀκέφαλον, &c. "I think you ought to say that every composition is, as it were, an animal having a body of its own: so that it should be neither without a head or feet, but should have its various parts, suitable to one another, and composing one perfect whole." μέσά τε ἔχειν ᗒ ἄκρα, πρέποντα ἀλλήλοις ᗒ ςῶ ὅλω γεγραμμένα.

† There is a remarkable passage in Cicero, (de Finib. l. 3. c. 22) in which this idea is brought out very vividly and precisely—Quin enim, aut in rerum natura, quâ nihil est aptius, nihil descriptius, aut in operibus manu factis, tam compositum tamque compactum et coagmentatum inveniri potest. Quid posterius priori non convenit? Quid sequitur quod non respondeat superiori? Quid non *sic aliud exalis nectitur, ut non, si unam literam moveris, labent omnia*? *&c.* We should have translated this, if we could have ventured to take that liberty with what is so perfect in itself, and so strikingly illustrates our text. (3) Ubi. sup.

ease or grace. Their genius was most enthusiastic—their sensibilities were even acute and lively to excess. Let any one
read those passages of their best authors wherein they treat of
poetry, and he will not fail to be struck with the force of their
expressions. They speak of it as a heavenly inspiration, a divine
fury, the revelry and intoxication of the soul—they compare it
to the madness of the Pythoness, the rage of the bacchanal, the
convulsive *improvisations* of the Corybantes awakened by the
peculiar μελος of their God.* But their taste was as refined as
their temperament was ardent, and hence the severity of the restraints which they laid upon their own genius. They seem to
have been conscious of their tendency to exceed, rather than be
wanting, in energy and warmth, and to overstep the modesty of
nature by indulging her impulses too freely. They studied perpetually how to speak the language of soberness and truth. The
smallest appearance of effort or exaggeration was particularly
disagreeable to them, as leading to the vice they most avoided.
The intense love of beauty which possessed them, the influence
of a happy climate and still happier organization, the native inspiration of genius, were common advantages, and those were
enough, they thought, to insure all the *power* necessary, (with
sufficient discipline) to attain to a high degree of excellence.
The artist was supposed to possess *this* qualification as of course.
His aim, therefore, was not to show that he possessed it, by an affected or ostentatious and unseasonable display of it, but to manage it with a wise economy, to turn it to the greatest account in
creating, in whatever might be his province, some perfect form
of beauty. His study of the ideal led him to think, as we have
shown, of the compositions of a *whole ;* for details, however
brilliant, were still mere fragments, and as such were unworthy
of his ambition. Any body could accomplish them, and abundance always creates fastidiousness. But to do all that can be
done by the greatest effort of genius, yet to be free from all the
faults into which genius, when it exerts itself most, is so apt to
be betrayed—to put forth his whole power, yet never to transcend
the limits of reason, and to embody the visions of an excited
imagination in a form so perfect as to defy the most fastidious
criticism of his country, and to challenge a place among the im-
perishable monuments of his art—this was indeed to be a *'maker'*,
ποιητης—this was to be truly Attic and classical. Accordingly,
what is most admirable in that matchless literature is this simplicity and ease, produced by the study of unity and the severe
reasoning on which we have been dwelling. It is, we conceive,
impossible not to be struck with the difference, in this respect,
between its master-pieces, and those of any other language—for
Shakspeare himself frequently falls into bombast and conceit,

* See the truly Dithyrambic effusion of Socrates in Plato's Io.

In short, the strength of Greek genius is never discovered in monstrous contortions or laborious struggles—it wields the mightiest subjects, apparently, without an effort, and with all the grace of conscious superiority. Its beauty is not confined to a single feature, "to a lip or eye," but is emphatically "the joint force and full result of all"—it is not the hectic glow of disease, or the meretricious lustre of a painted cheek, but the lumen juventæ purpureum, the bloom of youth, the proper hue, as the natural effect of a vigorous and robust constitution.

Lord Byron's speculative opinions in literature, were, as we have seen, all in favour of the classical models. His preference of Pope is owing to this; though it must be admitted that, in spite of his extraordinary merits, Pope is, in some degree, a mannerist, and, so far, falls short of absolute perfection. But theory and practice are unfortunately not more inseparable in literature than in other matters, and of this truth there is no more striking example than the author of Childe Harold. We stated in our notice of Mr. Moore's first volume, that Manfred struck us as decidedly the master-piece of Lord Byron. The long analysis, which we have just gone through of the principles of the *ideal*, will, as we flatter ourselves, have done much towards accounting for this preference. The merit of Manfred has been acknowledged by Goëthe, who thinks he recognizes in it a copy, or an imitation rather, of his Faustus.[*] His remarks are furnished by Mr. Moore, and are as follows :

"The following is the article from Goëthe's 'Kunst und Alterthum,' enclosed in this letter. The grave confidence, with which the venerable critic traces the fancies of his brother poet to real persons and events, making no difficulty even of a double murder at Florence to furnish grounds for his theory, affords an amusing instance of the disposition so prevalent throughout Europe, to picture Byron as a man of marvels and mysteries, as well in his life as his poetry. To these exaggerated, or wholly false, notions of him, the numerous fictions palmed upon the world of his romantic tours and wonderful adventures in places he never saw, and with persons that never existed, have, no doubt, considerably contributed ; and the consequence is, so utterly out of truth and nature are the representations of his life and character long current upon the continent, that it may be questioned whether the real "flesh and blood" hero of these pages,—the social practical-minded, and, with all his faults and eccentricities, *English* Lord Byron,—may not, to the over-exalted imaginations of most of his foreign admirers, appear but an ordinary, unromantic, and prosaic personage.

"Byron's tragedy, Manfred, was to me a wonderful phenomenon, and one that closely touched me. This singular intellectual poet has taken my Faustus to himself, and extracted from it the strongest nourishment for his hypochondriac humour. He has made use of the impelling principles in his own way, for his own purposes, so that no one of them remains the same ; and it is particularly on this account that I cannot enough admire his genius. The whole is in this way so completely formed anew, that it

[* See Werther (Goëthe's Works, vol. 16, p. 154). Werther standing on a precipice.]

would be an interesting task for the critic to point out not only the alterations he has made, but their degree of resemblance with, or dissimilarity to the original: in the course of which I cannot deny that the gloomy heat of an unbounded and exuberant despair becomes at last oppressive to us. Yet is the dissatisfaction we feel always connected with esteem and admiration.

"We find thus in this tragedy the quintessence of the most astonishing talent born to be its own tormenter. The character of Lord Byron's life and poetry hardly permits a just and equitable appreciation. He has often enough confessed what it is that torments him He has repeatedly portrayed it; and scarcely any one feels compassion for this intolerable suffering, over which he is ever laboriously ruminating. There are, properly speaking, two females whose phantoms forever haunt him, and which, in this piece, also perform principal parts—one under the name of Astarte, the other without form or actual presence, and merely a voice. Of the horrid occurrence which took place with the former the following is related. When a bold and enterprizing young man, he won the affections of a Florentine lady. Her husband discovered the amour, and murdered his wife; but the murderer was the same night found dead in the street, and there was no one on whom any suspicion could be attached. Lord Byron removed from Florence, and these spirits haunted him all his life after.

"This romantic incident is rendered highly probable by innumerable allusions to it in his poems. As, for instance, when, turning his sad contemplations inwards, he applies to himself the fatal history of the king of Sparta. It is as follows;—Pausanias, a Lacedæmonian general, acquires glory by the important victory at Platæa, but afterwards forfeits the confidence of his countrymen through his arrogance, obstinacy, and secret intrigues with the enemies of his country. This man draws upon himself the heavy guilt of innocent blood, which attends him to his end; for, while commanding the fleet of the allied Greeks, in the Black Sea, he is inflamed with a violent passion for a Byzantine maiden. After long resistance, he at length obtains her from her parents, and she is to be delivered up to him at night. She modestly desires the servant to put out the lamp, and, while groping her way in the dark, she overturns it. Pausanias is awakened from his sleep, apprehensive of an attack from murderers—he seizes his sword and destroys his mistress. The horrid sight never leaves him. Her shade pursues him unceasingly, and he implores for aid in vain from the gods and the exorcising priests.

"That poet must have a lacerated heart who selects such a scene from antiquity, appropriates it to himself, and burthens his tragic image with it. The following soliliquy, which is overladen with gloom and a weariness of life, is, by this remark, rendered intelligible. We recommend it as an exercise to all friends of declamation. Hamlet's soliloquy appears improved upon here." pp. 229, 230.

As to the imputed imitation, Byron (rather implicitly than expressly) disavows it in a letter to Murray:

"Enclosed is something which will interest you, to wit, the opinion of *the* greatest man of Germany—perhaps of Europe—upon one of the great men of your advertisements (all 'famous hands,' as Jacob Tonson used to say of his ragamuffins)—in short, a critique of *Goëthe's* upon *Manfred.* There is the original, an English translation, and an Italian one; keep them all in your archives, for the opinion of such a man as Goëthe, whether favorable or not, is always interesting—and this is more so, as favorable.

His *Faust* I never read, for I don't know German; but Matthew Monk
Lewis, in 1816, at Coligny, translated most of it to me *vivâ voce*, and I was
naturally much struck with it; but it was the *Steinbach* and the *Jungfrau*,
and something else, much more than Faustus, that made me write Manfred.   The first scene, however, and that of Faustus, are very similar."
p. 228.

When we speak of Manfred as the master-piece of Lord Byron, we speak of it as a *whole*.   There are to be found in most
of his other compositions, especially in Childe Harold, many
passages of unsurpassed beauty and power.   But, in the first place,
these passages, in the poem just mentioned, are short, isolated,
uncombined.   The wandering bard describes the remarkable objects, which present themselves to him in his progress, in a sort
of poetical itineracy.   He lavishes upon them, it is true, the
wealth of an exuberant imagination—and, whether it be Waterloo, or the romantic Rhine, or Lake Leman and its magic shores,
or the Alps, or an Italian sun-set, or the tombs of the famous
dead, or the monuments of Roman magnificence, or the master-
pieces of antique art, he is still equal to his subjects, and crowns
them anew with glory and immortality.   But such effusions are
not, *cæteris paribus*, comparable to works, in which the beauty
of design and composition is added to all other beauties.   A lyrical rhapsody is an easier, and much easier thing than a sage
and solemn drama, exhibiting a rare portraiture of character,
combining many incidents, introducing the difficult and even
perilous machinery of magic, incantations, and the spirits of the
air or the deep, and withal unfolding an impressive moral truth.
There is a great deal more both of *invention* and of art, more
creative genius, in short, required in the latter than in the former.
The very necessity of preserving a uniform tone of coloring, the
harmony, the *keeping*, of such a work, is a most important addition to the task of the artist.   We have seen what immense
emphasis the Greeks laid upon this circumstance.   In the next
place, the style of Manfred is more sober and subdued than that
of Childe Harold—and so is, comparatively, exempt from the
faults which we impute to that poem.   It is, indeed, remarkable
for a degree of austere and rugged force, which reminds us as
strongly of Dante, as the spirit and character of the poem itself
does of the Inferno.   When the Italian poet says of the souls in
his limbo, who shut out from the beatitude of heaven, still endure no other punishment, than the total want of all interest or
enjoyment, a consuming *ennui*, a dismal desolation of the heart—
non hanno speranza di morte—"they may not hope for death"—
he pronounces the terrible doom of Manfred, in almost his very
words:

> "Accursed! what have I to do with length of days,
> They are too long already."

As in the Inferno, too, so also in Manfred, the darkness and the desolation that seem to cast a gloom over the whole work, are relieved by gleams of beauty and freshness, ever and anon, breaking forth, the more striking as they are unexpected, the more touching because softened by melancholy associations, and escaping, as if in spite of it, from a mind in which neither sorrow nor pain, nor even despair itself, has been able to quench the deep love of nature. There is an unspeakable charm of the kind in the soliloquy with which the second scene of the first act opens. Manfred is standing alone upon the cliffs of the Jungfrau, as the day dawns and reveals to him the magnificent scenery of that Alpine region, upon which his desolate soul must no more gaze with rapture. He is doomed, henceforth, to see "undelighted all delight"—to know that what he looks upon is beauty, to feel it even, but just enough to make him conscious of the curse that is upon his soul, the blight that has seared his heart, and deadened and destroyed all its capacities of enjoyment.

> "*********My mother earth!
> And thou fresh breaking day, and you, ye mountains,
> Why are ye beautiful ? I cannot love ye.
> And thou, the bright eye of the universe,
> That openest over all, and unto all
> Art a delight—thou shin'st not on my heart*****:
> *   *   *   Beautiful!
> How beautiful is all this visible world!
> How glorious in its action and itself;
> But we, who name ourselves its sovereigns, we,
> Half dust, half deity, alike unfit
> To sink or soar, with our mix'd essence, make
> A conflict of its elements, &c.
> *   *   *   Hark! the note,
> The natural music of the mountain reed—
> For here the patriarchal days are not
> A pastoral fable—pipes in the liberal air,
> Mixed with the sweet bells of the sauntering herd ;
> My soul would drink those echoes.—Oh! that I were
> The viewless spirit of a lovely sound,
> A living voice, a breathing harmony,
> A bodiless enjoyment—born and dying
> With the blest tone which made me !"

So in the second scene of the second act.

> "It is noon—the sun-bow's rays still arch
> The torrent with the many hues of heaven,
> And rolls the sheeted silver's waving column
> O'er the crag's headlong perpendicular,
> And flings its lines of foaming light along,
> And to and fro, like the pale courser's tail
> The giant steed, to be bestrode by death,
> As told in the Apocalypse. No eyes but mine
> Now drink this sight of loveliness ;
> I should be sole in this sweet solitude,

And with the spirit of the place divide
The homage of these waters,—I will call her.
*   *   *   *
Beautiful spirit! with thy hair of light
And dazzling eyes of glory, in whose form
The charms of earth's least mortal daughters grow
To an unearthly stature, in an essence
Of purer elements; while the hues of youth,
Carnationed like a sleeping infant's cheek,
Rocked by the beating of her mother's heart,
Or the rose tints, which summer's twilight leaves
Upon the loftier glacier's virgin snow,
The *blush of earth embracing with her heaven*,—[a conceit.]
Tinge thy celestial aspects, and make tame
The beauties of the sun-bow which bends o'er thee.
Beautiful spirit! in thy calm, clear brow,
Wherein is glass'd serenity of soul," &c. &c.

But what struck Goëthe in this fine poem, and what entitled
it more, perhaps, than its other merits, to the rank which we
assign to it among the productions of its author, is the conception of Manfred's character and situation. To judge from our
own experience, nothing can be more profoundly interesting.
Often as we have read it, it has lost none of its effect. We
never take it up but with some such feeling as we conceive to
have possessed of old the pilgrims of Delphi and Dodona, or
those anxious mortals, who, like Count Manfred himself, have
sought to learn the secrets of their own destiny, by dealing
with evil spirits. The book contains a spell for us, and we lay
our hands upon it with awe. It brings us into actual contact
with the beings that wait upon the hero's bidding. We are
transported, by an ideal presence, to that Alpine solitude in
which this second Cain—this child of an accursed destiny—is
alternately agitated by the furies of remorse, or "wrapt as with
a shroud" in the darkness and desolation of a sullen despair.

"Daughter of air! I tell thee since that hour—
But words are breath—look on me in my sleep,
Or watch my watchings—come, and sit by me!
My solitude is solitude no more,
But peopled with the furies;—I have gnash'd
My teeth in darkness till returning morn,
Then cursed myself till sunset;—I have prayed
For madness as a blessing—'tis denied me.
I have affronted death—but in the war
Of elements the waters shrunk from me,
And fatal things pass'd harmless—the cold hand
Of an all-pitiless demon held me back,
Back by a single hair, which would not break.
In phantasy, imagination, all
The affluence of my soul—which one day was
A Crœsus in creation—I plunged deep,
But, like an ebbing wave, it dash'd me back
Into the gulf of my unfathomed thought,

I plunged amidst mankind—Forgetfulness
I sought in all, save where 'tis to be found."

It would be worth while to compare Manfred in detail with the Orestes of the Greek tragedy.* We regret that it is not in our power to do so at present; but we should be glad if some one, who has more leisure to trace the contrasts and coincidencies of literature, would take our hint.

We will venture a few remarks of our own, having a bearing upon a topic already discussed. Manfred, like the Eumenides of Æschylus, is a picture of remorse, but there can be no better illustration of the difference, which we admit to exist between ancient and modern dramatic literature, than is afforded by the manner in which this affection is exhibited, respectively, in the Greek tragedy and the English Drama.† In the former it is made a sensible object—it is personified—its office is performed by the Furies. They have pursued the wretched parricide with wild rage, until he takes refuge in the Temple of Apollo at Delphi. Here the tragedy opens. The fugitive stained with the blood of his guilty mother, is seen supplicating the protection of the god. The vindictive goddesses, attired in their robes of black, and with serpents entwined in their horrid tresses, are sleeping around him—having apparently sunk under the effort of their long and unremitted pursuit. When the young man has, by the contrivance of Apollo, stolen out of the Temple, to make his way to Athens, where Minerva is to decide finally upon his innocence or guilt, the shade of Clytemnestra, gashed with the fatal wounds, appears, and, calling aloud to the Furies in reproachful language, vanishes again. The Furies, aroused by her voice, discover that Orestes has made his escape. Their rage is greatly excited—they dance about the stage in frantic disorder—they renew the pursuit with fresh keenness, and are next seen at Athens, near the overtaken fugitive, who has embraced the statue of Minerva. They claim his head as justly forfeited to the laws—the goddess listens to both parties, and

[* I wish I had developed the idea more at length. It is difficult to believe that Byron had not a view to the Eumenides.]

† This is worthy of further observation. The *spirit* of Manfred is strictly modern or romantic. The air of abstract reflection, the moral musing, the pensive wo, which pervade it, are a contrast to the sensible imagery and the lively personifications of the Greek play. Yet its *frame and structure* are strictly 'classical.' Byron, in all his dramatic compositions, professed to copy after the Greek models,—as much so as Milton in the Samson Agonistes. But, besides discarding the chorus, he has not in other respects approached those models so closely as Milton. From what he has done, however, and from the character of his genius, we think, as we remarked in a former number, that had he been born an Athenian, he would have excelled peculiarly in that walk. Manfred proves, it—and here we will add that his aerial chorus of sprites and fiends, is quite equal in that kind to any thing in the grandest conceptions of Æschylus, and nothing can be more felicitous, in the way of choral ode, than some of their hymns—witness, especially, the grand anthem in honor of Arimanes.

agrees to become their umpire—the cause is regularly discussed, and the unfortunate young man is at last acquitted by an equality of suffrages.

It is evident that the moral lesson conveyed by such an exhibition as this, is rather the secondary, than the principal object; nor will those, who are versed in the dramatic history of the Greeks, be at all at a loss to account for the apparent dimness of the allegory in which the truth is veiled. Yet, to one who looks attentively into the hidden sense, the picture of remorse thus presented, as it were, by types and sensible images, is equally remarkable for scenic effect and profound philosophical analysis. But Byron in Manfred derives no help from such external symbols—nor does he darkly shadow his purpose in allegory. It is spread out over the whole surface. His hero is alone. He flies from the commerce of his own species, and communes only with those aerial shapes, whose office it is to "tend on mortal thoughts"—to do the behests, to consult the wishes, to echo the voice of their master—in short, to be his slave and his shadow, so long as they are under his spells. This, indeed, is the purpose, and a very important one, which the spirits of the *drama* answer. Manfred really tells his own story—his attendants are no better than the chorus of a Greek tragedy—good listeners. He might have done substantially what he has done in a long *monologue;* or he might have addressed himself, in a voice of lamentation, to the mountains and the desert caves. But a perpetual soliloquy of three acts would have been equally tiresome and irregular, and yet, to have introduced such a being into a common drama—to have represented him as moving in the dull round of life, and interchanging sentiments with vulgar interlocutors, would not have been in keeping with the unearthly grandeur of his character, and would have defeated what we take to have been the great purpose of the poet. Like Faustus, therefore, Manfred, by his aspiring genius, must compass such a knowledge of the visible world, as shall enable him to control the invisible—that he may summon a disembodied auditory from the depths of the sea, or the remotest star in the firmament, and proclaim his remediless woes and his irreversible doom, by this same preternatural agency, to the most distant parts of the universe, and all orders of created being. The machinery of the poem then answers two great purposes—it relieves its monotony, without violating its plan, and it exalts the dignity of the hero without disturbing the characteristic solitude—the essential loneliness of his being. This needs a few more words of explanation.

We have said that this drama is a picture of *remorse;* and so it is, but of a peculiar kind of remorse. It is not self-condemnation for a mere crime or sin committed. Manfred's conscience was made of sterner stuff than that. Above all, it was not, as a late writer supposes,* because his sister, Astarte, had fallen a sacrifice to some diabolical piece of magic, in which she was at once an accomplice and a victim. Byron was not a man to make a book of sentimental raving à la Kotzebue, upon such a fantastical and ludicrous subject. He aimed at exhibiting what may be called his *ruling idea*, in the strongest of all possible forms. That idea is that, without a deep and engrossing *passion*, without *love*, in short, intense, devoted love, no power, nor influence in the world, nor genius, nor knowledge, nor Epicurean bliss, can "bestead or fill the fixed mind with all their toys;" and that a man may be completely miserable for want of such a passion, though blessed, to all appearance, with whatever can make life desirable. This idea is, in reference to very excitable natures, certainly just—and is thus expressed in the soliloquy with which that drama opens.

> "I have no dread,
> And feel the curse to have no natural fear,
> Nor fluttering throb, that beats with hopes or wishes
> Or lurking love of something on the earth."—

Here is evidently "the leafless desert of the soul," "the vacant bosom's wilderness," the dreary vacuity, the mortal apathy upon which so many changes are rung in all his other poems.

But this is not all; for, if it were, Manfred would be no better than the Giaour. The merit that raises him to his bad eminence, among these heroes of "disappointed passion," is two-fold—in the first place, it is darkly hinted that his love was unnatural, or, at least, unlawful, and so dishonorable to her whom he adored; and, secondly, that he was either the wilful or involuntary instrument of her destruction—her blood was upon his hands, and her curse upon his soul.

> †"And a magic voice and verse
> Hath baptized thee with a curse;
> And a spirit of the air
> Hath begirt thee with a snare;
> In the wind there is a voice

* Galt.—We happened to look for the first time into his work a few hours ago and have been quite shocked at a coincidence or two in the previous pages, which were in type before we saw his book.

[† Cf. the ''Υμνος δέσμιος of the Furies in Æschy. Ευμενιδ. v. 300, et seq.

> ἐπὶ δὲ τῷ τεθυμένῳ
> τόδε μέλος παρακοπὰ,
> παραφορά, φρεναδαλὶς
> ''Υμνος ἐξ 'Ερινύων,
> Δέσμιος φρενῶν, ἀφόρ-
> μιχτος, αὔονα βροτοῖς.]

*Shall forbid thee to rejoice;
And to thee shall night deny
All the quiet of her sky;
And the day shall have a sun,
Which shall make thee wish it done.

From thy false tears I did distil
An essence which hath strength to kill;
From thy own heart I then did wring
The black blood in its blackest spring;
From thy own smile I snatch'd the snake,
For there it coiled as in a brake;
From thy own lip I drew the charm,
Which gave all this their chiefest harm;
In proving every poison known,
I found the strongest was thine own.

By thy cold breast and serpent smile,
By thy unfathomed gulfs of guile,
By that most seeming virtuous eye,
By thy shut soul's hypocrisy;
By the perfection of thine art
Which passed for human, thine own heart;
By thy delight in other's pain,
And by thy brotherhood of Cain,
I call upon thee! and compel
Thyself to be thy proper hell!"

Whatever had been the conduct alluded to in these terrible
lines, he clearly regards himself as the murderer of Astarte He
had murdered—by what means, is not material—

"——— her, whom, of all earthly things
That lived, the only thing he seemed to love."

The only tie of existence had been severed—the single feeling that made the world bearable, and, without which, it was no
better than a vast Bastile, had been extinguished—the being
that loved *him* with the devotedness of woman's love, while all
mankind besides were cold or hostile to him, and who was to
him, amidst the weariness of life or its severest wo, real or
imaginary, an interest and a passion and an unfailing resource and
a sweet consolation, had been destroyed—and by *him*. This
catastrophe was, it is evident, a moral suicide, and he became
afterwards, as he expresses it "his soul's sepulchre."   His
hope, his love, his dream of bliss, made more ravishing by the
contrasted gloom of his ordinary life, was gone—he is condemned to that dreariest of all solitudes, the utter loneliness of the
blighted heart—he now, at last, perceives all the guilt of the
coldness, or perverseness, or cruelty, or whatever else it was, that
led to the event which he has such bitter cause to lament—the

[* τὸ χαίρειν μὴ μαϑόντ' ὅπου φρενῶν,
ἀναιματον βόσκημα, δαιμόνων σκιά. v. 301-2.]

worth, the loveliness of his victim is felt in the sufferings which
the loss of her has inflicted—and he repents what he has done
and curses the destiny which ordered or permitted it, and addicts
himself, more exclusively than ever, to the society of evil spirits,
and devotes himself to the tortures of hell as a relief from the
more intolerable agony of. a wounded spirit! *This* is his *re-*
morse! La Rochefoucault says that men repent of their offences
only when they feel, or are likely to feel some inconvenience
from their consequences. Certainly, penitence is made more
lively by a little suffering, and the whole force of this selfish
theory is exhibited in the remorse of Manfred. But in what
heart-rending language is this late awakening of lost love expressed !

> "Hear me, hear me !
> Astarte ! my beloved ! speak to me ;
> I have so much endured—so much endure—
> Look on me ! the grave hath not changed thee more,
> Than I am changed for thee. Thou lovest me
> Too much, as I loved thee : we were not made
> To torture thus each other, tho' it were
> The deadliest sin to love as we have loved.
> Say that thou loath'st me not—that I do bear
> This punishment for both—that thou wilt be
> One of the blessed—and that I shall die ;
> For hitherto all hateful things conspire
> To bind me in existence—in a life,
> Which makes me shrink from immortality—
> A future like the past. I cannot rest ;
> I know not what I asked, nor what I seek :
> I feel but what thou art—and what I am ;
> And I would hear yet once before I perish
> The voice which was my music—speak to me !
> For I have called on thee in the still night,
> Startled the slumbering birds from the hush'd boughs,
> And woke the mountain wolves, and made the caves
> Acquainted with thy vainly echoed name,
> Which answered me—many things answered me—
> Spirits and men—but thou wert silent all.
> Yet speak to me ! I have out watch'd the stars,
> And gazed o'er heav'n in vain in search of thee.
> Speak to me ! I have wandered o'er the earth
> And never found thy likeness—speak to me !
> Look on the fiends around—they feel for me ;
> I fear them not, and feel for thee alone—
> Speak to me !—tho' it be in wrath ;—but say—
> I reck not what—but let me hear thee once—
> This once—once more !"

We must now bring these remarks, which have unexpectedly
run out to an unconscionable length under our pen, to an abrupt
close. But we cannot consent to end this article without doing
Lord Byron the justice to quote the whole of a most animated
and eloquent defence of his conduct, which Mr. Moore has fur-

nished from an unpublished MS. Let him be heard, and let the reader judge for himself.

"My learned brother proceeds to observe, that 'it is in vain for Lord B. to attempt in any way to justify his own behaviour in that affair; and, now that he has so *openly* and *audaciously* invited inquiry and reproach, we do not see any good reason why he should not be plainly told so by the voice of his countrymen.' How far the 'openness' of an anonymous poem, and the 'audacity' of an imaginary character, which the writer supposes to be meant for Lady B., may be deemed to merit this formidable denunciation from their 'most sweet voices,' I neither know nor care : but when he tells me that I cannot 'in any way *justify* my own behaviour in that affair,' I acquiesce, because no man can '*justify*' himself until he knows of what he is accused ; and I have never had—and, God knows, my whole desire has ever been to obtain it—any specific charge, in a tangible shape, submitted to me by the adversary, nor by others, unless the atrocities of public rumour and the mysterious silence of the lady's legal advisers may be deemed such. But is not the writer content with what has been already said and done ? Has not 'the general voice of his countrymen, long ago pronounced upon the subject—sentence without trial, and condemnation without a charge ? Have I not been exiled by ostracism, except that the shells which proscribed me were anonymous ? Is the writer ignorant of the public opinion and the public conduct upon that occasion ! If he is, I am not : the public will forget both long before I shall cease to remember either.

"The man who is exiled by a faction has the consolation of thinking that he is a martyr ; he is upheld by hope and the dignity of his cause, real or imaginary : he who withdraws from the pressure of debt may indulge in the thought that time and prudence will retrieve his circumstances: he who is condemned by the law has a term to his banishment, or a dream of its abbreviation ; or, it may be, the knowledge or the belief of some injustice of the law, or of its administration in his own particular : but he who is outlawed by general opinion, without the intervention of hostile politics, illegal judgment, or embarrassed circumstances, whether he be innocent or guilty, must undergo all the bitterness of exile, without hope, without pride, without alleviation. This case was mine. Upon what grounds the public founded their opinion, I am not aware : but it was general, and it was decisive. Of me or mine they knew little, except that I had written what is called poetry, was a nobleman, had married, became a father, and was involved in differences with my wife and her relatives, no one knew why, because the persons complaining refused to state their grievances. The fashionable world was divided into parties, mine consisting of a very small minority: the reasonable world was naturally on the stronger side, which happened to be the lady's, as was most proper and polite. The press was active and scurrilous; and such was the rage of the day, that the unfortunate publication of two copies of verses, rather complimentary than otherwise to the subjects of both, was tortured into a species of crime, or constructive petty treason. I was accused of every monstrous vice, by public rumour and private rancour : my name, which had been a knightly or a noble one since my fathers helped to conquer the kingdom for William the Norman, was tainted. I felt that, if what was whispered, and muttered, and murmured, was true, I was unfit for England ; if false, England was unfit for me. I withdrew ; but this was not enough. In other countries, in Switzerland, in the shadow of the Alps, and by the blue depth of the lakes, I was pursued and breathed upon by the same blight. I crossed the mountains, but was the same; so I went a little farther, and settled myself by the waves of the Adriatic, like the stag at bay, who betakes him to the waters.

"If I may judge by the statements of the few friends who gathered around me, the outcry of the period to which I allude was beyond all precedent, all parallel, even in those cases where political motives have sharpened slander and doubled enmity. I was advised not to go to the theatres, lest I should be hissed, nor to my duty in Parliament, lest I should be insulted by the way; even on the day of my departure, my most intimate friend told me afterwards that he was under apprehensions of violence from the people who might be assembled at the door of the carriage. However, I was not deterred by these counsels from seeing Kean in his best characters, nor from voting according to my principles; and, with regard to the third and last apprehensions of my friends, I could not share in them, not being made acquainted with their extent till some time after I had crossed the channel. Even if I had been so, I am not of a nature to be much affected by men's anger, though I may feel hurt by their aversion. Against all individual outrage, I could protect or redress myself; and against that of a crowd, I should probably have been enabled to defend myself, with the assistance of others, as has been done on similar occasions.

"I retired from the country, perceiving that I was the object of general obloquy; I did not indeed imagine, like Jean Jacques Rousseau, that all mankind was in a conspiracy against me, though I had perhaps as good grounds for such a chimera as ever he had: but I perceived that I had to a great extent become personally obnoxious in England, perhaps through my own fault, but the fact was indisputable; the public in general would hardly have been so much excited against a more popular character, without at least an accusation or a charge of some kind actually expressed or substantiated, for I can hardly conceive that the common and every-day occurrence of a separation between man and wife could in itself produce so great a ferment. I shall say nothing of the usual complaints of 'being prejudged,' 'condemned unheard,' 'unfairness,' 'partiality,' and so forth, the usual changes rung by parties who have had, or are to have, a trial; but I was a little surprised to find myself condemned without being favored with the act of accusation, and to perceive in the absence of this portentous charge or charges, whatever it or they were to be, that every possible or impossible crime was rumoured to supply its place, and taken for granted. This could only occur in the case of a person very much disliked, and I knew no remedy, having already used to their extent whatever little powers I might possess of pleasing in society. I had no party in fashion, though I was afterwards told that there was one—but it was not of my formation, nor did I then know of its existence—none in literature; and in politics I had voted with the Whigs, with precisely that importance which a Whig vote possesses in these Tory days, and with such personal acquaintance with the leaders in both houses as the society in which I lived sanctioned, but without claim or expectation of any thing like friendship from any one, except a few young men of my own age and standing, and a few others more advanced in life, which last it had been my fortune to serve in circumstances of difficulty. This was, in fact, to stand alone: and I recollect, some time after, Madame de Staël said to me in Switzerland, 'You should not have warred with the world—it will not do—it is too strong always for any individual: I myself once tried it in early life, but it will not do.' I perfectly acquiesce n the truth of this remark; but the world had done me the honour to begin the war; and, assuredly, if peace is only to be obtained by courting

and paying tribute to it, I am not qualified to obtain its countenance.
I thought in the words of Campbell,

> 'Then wed thee to an exile lot,
> And if the world hath loved thee not,
> Its absence may be borne.'

"I recollect, however, that, having been much hurt by Romilly's conduct
(he, having a general retainer for me, had acted as adviser to the adversary, alleging, on being reminded of his retainer, that he had forgotten it,
as his clerk had so many), I observed that some of those who were now
eagerly laying the axe to my roof-tree, might see their own shaken, and
feel a portion of what they had inflicted. His fell, and crushed him.

"I have heard of, and believe that there are human beings so constituted as to be insensible to injuries; but I believe that the best mode to
avoid taking vengeance is to get out of the way of temptation. I hope
that I may never have the opportunity, for I am not quite sure that I could
resist it, having derived from my mother something of the 'perfervidum
ingenium Scotorum'. I have not sought, and shall not seek it, and perhaps it may never come in my path. I do not in this allude to the party,
who might be right or wrong; but to many who made her cause the pretext of their own bitterness. She, indeed, must have long avenged me
in her own feelings, for, whatever her reasons may have been (and she
never adduced them to me, at least), she probably neither contemplated
nor conceived to what she became the means of conducting the father of
her child, and the husband of her choice.

"So much for 'the general voice of his countrymen:' I will now speak
of some in particular.

"In the beginning of the year 1817, an article appeared in the Quarterly Review, written, I believe, by Walter Scott, doing great honour to him, and no disgrace to me, though both poetically and personally more than sufficiently favourable to the work and the author
of whom it treated. It was written at a time when a selfish man
would not, and a timid one dare not, have said a word in favor of either: it
was written by one to whom temporary public opinion had elevated me to
the rank of a rival—a proud distinction, and unmerited; but which has not
prevented me from feeling as a friend, nor him from more than corresponding to that sentiment. The article in question was written upon the third
Canto of Childe Harold, and, after many observations, which it would as
ill become me to repeat as to forget, concluded with 'a hope that I might
yet return to England.' How this expression was received in England itself I am not acquainted, but it gave great offence at Rome to the respectable ten or twenty thousand English travellers then and there assembled.
I did not visit Rome till some time after, so that I had no opportunity of
knowing the fact; but I was informed, long afterward, that the greatest
indignation had been manifested in the enlightened Anglo-circle of that
year, which happened to comprise within it—amid a considerable leaven
of Welbeck-street and Devonshire place, broken loose upon their travels—
several really well-born and well-bred families, who did not the less participate in the feelings of the hour. 'Why should he return to England?'
was the general exclamation—I answer why? It is a question I have occasionally asked myself, and I never yet could give it a satisfactory reply.
I had then no thoughts of returning, and if I have any now, they are of
business, and not of pleasure. Amid the ties that have been dashed to
pieces, they are links yet entire, though the chain itself be broken. There
are duties and connections which may one day require my presence—
and I am a father. I have still some friends whom I wish to meet again,
and, it may be, an enemy. These friends, and those minuter details of

business, which time accumulates during absence, in every man's affairs
and property, may, and probably will, recall me to England; but I shall
return with the same feelings with which I left it, in respect to itself, though
altered with regard to individuals, as I have been more or less informed of
their conduct since my departure; for it was only a considerable time after
it that I was made acquainted with the real facts and full extent of some
of their proceedings and language. My friends, like other friends, from
conciliatory motives, withheld from me much that they could, and some
things which they *should* have unfolded; however, that which is deferred
is not lost—but it has been no fault of mine that it has been deferred at all.

"I have alluded to what is said to have passed at Rome merely to show
that the sentiment which I have described was not confined to the English in England, and as forming part of my answer to the reproach cast
upon what has been called my 'selfish exile,' and my 'voluntary exile.'
'Voluntary' it has been; for who would dwell among a people entertaining
strong hostility against him? How far it has been 'selfish' has been already explained." pp. 249–253.

For our own part, we must say that our opinions have undergone no material change in relation to the essential points of
Lord Byron's character and conduct. No one ever denied that
he was formed for better things—or that he had, with all his peculiarities, what the world calls amiable manners—nay, that his
natural impulses were good, and that he had a heart full of
kindness to those who *did* not, and especially who *could* not
provoke his resentment or mortify his sensitive, selfish and
gloomy pride. But, winning as he is in his moments of good
nature—interesting and amiable, for instance, as he appears
throughout almost the whole of this voluminous compilation of
letters and confessions, we see nothing to make us think differently of his *principles* or his *ruling passion*—the things, by
which a man's conduct in life will, in the long run, be determined. We apply to him, without changing a syllable, his own
lines in relation to Manfred:

"This should have been a noble creature; he
Hath all the energy which would have made
A goodly frame of glorious elements,
Had they been wisely mingled; as it is,
It is an awful chaos—light and darkness—
And mind and dust—and passions and pure thoughts,
Mixed, and contending without end or order."

JEREMY BENTHAM AND THE UTILITARIANS.

Principles of Legislation; from the MS. of Jeremy Bentham, Bencher of Lincoln's Inn. By M. DUMONT. Member of the Representative and Sovereign Council of Geneva. Translated from the second corrected and enlarged edition; with Notes and a Biographical Notice of Jeremy Bentham and of M. Dumont. *By John Neal. Boston.* 1831.

WE do not know whether the publication of this book is to be considered as any proof of the growing popularity of Bentham and Utilitarianism in the United States. But sure we are—if we know any thing of the state of public opinion in this country—that it will do nothing to increase that popularity. The author professes himself, every where, a devoted admirer of his "guide, philosopher and friend," yet it is difficult to conceive a more ridiculous figure than he makes him cut in his pages. It is just such a portrait as a very wicked or very simple *valet de chambre* might be expected to paint of a very absurd hero. If Sancho Panza, for instance, had written the Life of Don Quixotte, with that odd indescribable mixture of reverence and suspicion which runs through his conversations with the knight, it would have been much of a-piece with the biographical sketch before us. Mr. John Neal, indeed, prostrates himself devoutly before his idol—exalts and magnifies him above all Greek and Roman fame—pronounces him, as Lucretius does Epicurus, the great light of the world, and its redeemer from spiritual bondage— yet, when we survey the whole picture together, it is hard to believe that there is not a good deal of waggery in these lofty expressions of homage. We do not think there is a Life in Diogenes Laertius—and that is saying much—which makes philosophy, in the person of one of her most renowned votaries, so despicable and repulsive.

The style in which the author tells his story is full of a quaint pedantic affectation of simplicity. He is as confiding and communicative as "downright Shippen or as old Montaigne." He talks to his reader as if he were writing an epistle to one of Jeremy's private secretaries, and as if the world had nothing to think of but the "High Priest of Legislation and the Lord Bacon of the age." The excessive importance which he attaches to every thing connected with the Reformer and his dogmas redounds, of course, upon his humble self. But he

does not trust to distant inference for his share in the honours of the school. His self-conceit is fully commensurate with his admiration of his betters, and he takes care to garnish his pan-egyric upon his master with an abundance of garrulous egotism. Nobody understands Bentham but Mr. John Neal—"the readers (and the *writers*) of the Edinburgh, Quarterly, Westminster and North-American Reviews, will *now* have, what they never had before—an opportunity of knowing the truth and the whole truth, about the character and opinions, the philosophy and the faith of a man," &c. His object, as he announces it in his pre-face, is twofold. By the first part of his work, "which is nothing more than a familiar biographical sketch," his readers are to be "brought acquainted with the *man* Jeremy Bentham, and by the *last*, which may be regarded as an abridgment of his whole sys-tem of philosophy, with the philanthropist, the lawgiver and the statesman." We hope he knows more about "the *man* Jeremy," than he seems to understand of his translator's language. At page 271, we observe the following *naïve* confession of igno-rance, accompanied by, what appears to us, a very sufficient ex-emplification of it:—"Thus every act of cruelty produced by a passion, the principle of which is in every heart and from which every body may suffer, may cause an alarm which will continue until the punishment of the offender *has removed the danger from the side of injustice.* * * * * * * * *"
Upon which we have the following note:—"The meaning of this I have not been able to make out, with any sort of satisfaction to myself. It reads thus in the original, 'fera éprou-ver une alarme qui continuera jusqu' à ce que la punition du coupable ait transporté le *danger du côté de l'injustice, de l'inimitié cruelle.*'" Whatever we may think of the style, the meaning of this passage is clear enough from the context. Jeremy, or rather Dumont, is speaking of the terror which the unrestrained indulgence of certain passions would inspire. This alarm, he says, will continue until the punishment of one who has sinned through the influence of such passions, has in-spired him, and those like him, with fear, in their turn—until "injustice and malignant hatred" are made, by the law, to feel some of the terror they occasion; literally, "until the punish-ment of the guilty has transferred the danger *to* the side of in-justice," &c. It is strange that any one should set up for an interpreter of French who does not know the effect of the *du* in the phrase, *du côté de*, and it is lamentable to reflect that we, the *uninitiated*, have no other means of understanding the inesti-mable Benthamee, but the translation of a translation by such a druggerman as Mr. John Neal.

The drift of this attempt upon the Life of Jeremy Bentham, is thus explained by the biographer himself.

"Such a portrait is now to be attempted for the lovers of such biography. It will be for them to say whether a magnificent picture, which, by resembling every body, would be a *portrait* of nobody, is worthier of admiration. It may be wanting in dignity—*I hope it may*—but of this the reader may be sure: whatever it wants in dignity shall be made up in truth; and in such truth too as will soon be sought after with deep solicitude, not only here, and in the country of our philosopher, but throughout the whole earth.

"After a few preliminary observations, I shall take up a body of memoranda, now lying before me, which were made every night, and before I slept, after we had passed the evening together, and transferred them, with as little change as possible, directly to these pages. They, therefore, who wish to be acquainted with the lawgiver and the philosopher, and with him only, need not throw away one single hour upon this part of the book, which is intended for such, and for such only as care to be acquainted with the man, but proceed forthwith to the second part, where Bentham and Dumont are occupied with the great business of morals and legislation." pp. 14, 15.

We shall follow the author in the course he has marked out—first, saying a few words about the character of Jeremy Bentham, and then discussing, with all possible brevity, his pretensions to the admiration which is challenged for him by his biographer.

This great luminary of the age was born, it seems, in the year 1747–8. He was the son of an attorney who was, according to Jeremy himself, "a weak man," and to whose mechanical predilection for his own profession, we owe the light which his son has been able to shed upon the philosophy of jurisprudence. To be sure, misfortune—which has ever been the best nurse of genius—had its share in this result; for the man, who was destined to reform the whole body of the law, does not seem to have been fitted to excel in the most important part of it, viz. the application of its principles to practice. "On a particular occasion, (said he to Mr. Neal,) I gave a legal opinion which turned out not to be law, because the law had been altered without my knowledge or consent. I refused to give an opinion after this." p. 61. Whereupon, his biographer remarks, with great simplicity, that "he could not help imagining, as he went through the history of this early error, how *much* of his subsequent *views* of the law, the lawyers, and the judges of England, might be owing to this very incident. * * * * * * * * * *
Most of Mr. Bentham's peculiar views, peculiar habits and peculiar figures; I believe I might say all, may be traced in the same way to incidents connected with his youth—his hatred of English law and of English lawyers, of Blackstone, of Mansfield and of Eldon—to his *fortunate* [qu.] failure in his profession. Other facts of the same nature will appear in the further development of his character." p. 61.

His first work was an expression of his very natural, if not very reasonable grudge against these odious objects. He made, it seems, while yet a very young man (he was in his 28th year) "a masterly attack" on Blackstone's Commentaries.   Lord Mansfield, if we are to believe Mr. Neal, or rather Bentham himself, used to speak of this diatribe in the highest terms, though, on Blackstone's being asked if he intended to reply to it, *his* answer was "no, not if it were better written." His dislike for the author of the Commentaries discovered itself at a very early period. He related to his biographer the following story, "to be repeated in Yankee-land."

"*April* 4. Mr. B. relates a story of Blackstone, to be repeated in Yankee-land. 'As early as sixteen,' said he, 'I began to *query* Blackstone, my Gamaliel, while I was sitting at his feet. He was a stiff, pompous, proud quiz—Mansfield couldn't bear him. I told you, I believe, that he, M., had the whole of the Fragment read to him, and liked it mightily. When Blackstone was Vinerian professor at Queen's College, Oxford, he sent to Dr. Brown, provost of the College, to know what distinction should be awarded to him, or how he should be ranked. Tell him, said Brown, who was a shrewd fellow, tell him he may walk before my beadle,—the beadle that preceded him with a mace, when he walked out. Mr. Eden (the writer on penal law,) afterwards Lord Ackland, and Blackstone did something together once, which Bentham approved. Out of this grew something of Mr. Bentham's, about which Blackstone wrote him, complimenting him rather highly." pp. 133, 114.

In 1788, he published his "Views of the Hard-Labor Bill, with observations relative to Penal Jurisprudence in general," and nine years after his celebrated "Defence of Usury." In 1789 appeared the original quarto edition of MORALS and LEGISLATION, "the ground work of the author's whole fame with Dr. Parr and others of like amplitude and strength of mind." Mr. Neal pronounces it, oracularly, "the *novum organum* of Morals and Legislation'" and he makes the celebrated scholar just mentioned say of it that, since Lord Bacon's great work, there had been nothing in the history of the human mind to compare with it. It is this same treatise, be it remembered, in its most approved form, or rather its quintessence, that constitutes the second part of the volume before us.

After this publication, he favored the world with an immense catalogue of lucubrations of greater or less importance—the *Panopticon* or Inspection-house—or new plan for the construction of penitentiary-houses, prisons, work-houses, lazarettos, hospitals and schools. "These are," it seems, "the celebrated letters on the subject of *Prisons and Prison-Discipline*, to which Europe and America are chiefly indebted for the improvement, made during the last half century in the structure of prisons and treatment of prisoners, and all this without any acknowledgement in favor of the author"—a charge we regret to add, which lies against "our Prison-Discipline Society of Boston, among the rest." This excellent scheme, however, like many of equal promise in the island of Laputa, was, for some reason or other, never put into practice. Then came A Draft of a Code for the Organization of the Judicial Establishment of France, 1790—An Essay on Political Tactics, afterwards embodied in a long work, in two volumes, by M. Dumont—Chrestomathia—Plan of Parliamentary Reform—Papers relative to Codification and Public Instruction—Church of Englandism—The Book of Fallacies—Analysis of the Influence of Natural Religion, published by *Richard Carlisle*, in 1822—an able book, saith Mr. Neal, of which the object was to prove that all religions are equally unworthy of regard. In this connection, our biographer holds the following emphatic language :

"From what I know of Mr. Bentham, I have no doubt of his being an atheist. I have been told so, by those who knew him; a good many of his more youthful followers are so—if they themselves may be credited; and, though we had never had any conversation together that satisfied me, still, as I have said before, I have no doubt of his being an atheist. And I mention this here, that I may not be charged with blindness to what I look upon as not only the greatest, but as the only great error of that man's faith. Not that he *believes* there is no God—I do not say so : but he is not thoroughly satisfied, I believe, that there *is* a God. If he would inquire, and it is not even yet too late, he would perceive what he must delight in hoping, even if it were not proved, the existence of One who is emphatically the Father of such men as he is. Peradventure, it is not so much atheism after all, as it is a mistake with him. He mistakes the uncertainty of one fact, or rather a want of mathematical certainty in one fact, for the certainty of another fact : the *want* of such kind of mathematical proof, as he is habituated to, that there *is* a God, for conclusive demonstration that there is *not*. I know well the nature of his mind ; and I do not scruple to say that I believe this. Not being satisfied as other men are, and not being at leisure, in his old age and just on the shadowy and shifting threshold of another world, to investigate the subject in his own way ; and being imbued with the pestiferous, and most unreasonable doubts of a Frenchman, who was a believer in Voltaire, and the first teacher of Mr. Bentham ; and withal having translated Le Taureau Blanc of Voltaire, without acknowledging it,—nor does he know to this day, probably, that he was ever suspected of it ; and having produced the work on Natural Religion, above-mentioned, which was edited by one atheist, and published by another, (the infamous Richard Carlisle,) it cannot be expected of him that he should now inquire very diligently or wisely, nor that his disciples, whatever *he* might do or say now, would be satisfied. We may be sorry for such things, but, if they are otherwise good men, our sorrow will lead us rather to pity than to rage or hatred for them. As well might we rebuke those who are troubled with fever, as them that require to be convinced by touch, or taste, or ciphering, of the existence of a Deity. Why may not men be suffered to believe what they please, or what they *can* rather, about God and a future state, and all the mysteries of theology, as about any other subject of dispute or inquiry. We do not quarrel with men now about their belief touching wizards, or the motion of the planets, or the origin of the blacks. Why should we, about their belief respecting their Father above ? What I say, I believe. I am no atheist—If I were, I should avow it in the face of heaven and earth, and abide the consequences." pp. 33, 35.

Besides many other works, of which we have not space

enough to repeat the names, some MSS. of Bentham passed through the hands of a clever Frenchman, Dumont, who, (as Mr. Neal affirms upon the authority of Mr. Gallatin,) used to write the very speeches that Mirabeau delivered ! We strongly suspect there is some mistake about this part of the story. But, be that as it may, it is admitted that the best, if not the only means of understanding many of the great Reformer's speculations is to read them in a foreign language. It is difficult to conceive by what species of divination M. Dumont is able to decypher the strange gibberish of his author. According to Mr. Neal's account of the *Benthamee,* no mystagogue ever earned his wages more fairly. The progress, which the philosopher has been gradually making in this corruption of style, is rather a singular phenomenon in itself, but it is not more strange than his biographer's notion that it is to be explained by the tenderness of Mr. Bentham's conscience.

"But to conclude this part of our subject. As Mr. Bentham grew older, he grew more and more dissatisfied with the *inadequacy* of language, with the want of exactness in it ; and he therefore began to prepare a new system of logic for himself—a few chapters of which have lately been booked into a readable shape, by his nephew, Mr. George Bentham, one of the most promising men of the age, both for acuteness and for strength. From this, he went on, growing less and less elegant, and to the careless reader, the novel-reader, or the newspaper-reader, less and less perspicuous every year ; for he went on abridging volumes into chapters, and chapters into tabular views, till it was impossible for any body to understand him, who had not gone step by step through his preliminary demonstrations ; till at last he came to a style, which cannot be defended—such as that of the article he wrote for the Westminster Review. And yet, though all this may be said of that particular paper, it is due to him and to the public to add, that as he has grown older he has grown wiser ; *that the style referred to grows out of his exceeding honesty,*—for he does not allow himself to separate his assertions from their qualifications—so that his periods are encumbered on every subject of interest ; that in ordinary matters where a newspaper style would do, no man alive writes a more off-hand, free or natural style than Jeremy Bentham; and that—after all—the very difficulties we complain of are attributable more to the *subject* handled by him, than to the style in which they are handled; more to the nature of the science treated of, than to any thing else ; and that for people, who are not acquainted with his early works, to complain of *all* his late works for not being clear, is about as absurd as it would be for a man, who had never studied his multiplication table, to find fault with a treatise on fluxions for not being as intelligible, straight-forward and agreeable as a newspaper-essay upon the private character of a political adversary."—pp. 38, 39.

It would be exacting too much of a biographer to require him to write the life of another, without occasionally alluding to his own, and Mr. Neal has, therefore, taken the liberty of detailing, (p. 41,) with the greatest precision, all the circumstances which led to his acquaintance with Jeremy. It was about twelve years ago that he first heard that illustrious name. He was, at that time, "a student at law in Baltimore, Maryland," when it so happened that Mr. Hoffman published his "Course of Legal Study." In this "Course," the works of Bentham were to be studied by the novice, who, in common, he says, with most of the literati of the United States, did not know who or of what country this same Bentham was. But as some of the works alluded to were written in French, our author naturally concluded that the author was a Frenchman ; which, as "he was not very easy with French at the time," must have been rather a discouraging inference. After "many years had gone by," however, and he had attained to his present *proficiency* in that language, "on hearing Mr. Hoffman express a desire that somebody would undertake to render the two volumes referred to, into English," he very readily offered to do so, "if he could find"— that only Mecenas of aspiring genius in these mechanical days— "a publisher." He accordingly wrote to a Mr. Riley, at New-York, "one of the largest law-publishers in the country," undertaking to translate two volumes, Svo. with notes, and so forth, for *three hundred dollars,* one half payable in law-books. But Mr. Riley knew his business, and nobody, knew Bentham. And so, moderate as these terms were, the overture was unceremoniously rejected, and there the matter rested until 1825, when Mr. Neal and Mr. Bentham "were accidentally thrown together in the native country" of the latter. The biographer's account of his first approaches to the awful presence-chamber of the reformer, is too curious and characteristic to be omitted. He began with one of the outposts of the school, the debating-club of the young Utilitarians at the philosopher's house. His picture of this notable scene and assembly is what might be expected from the *dramatis personæ* who figure in it. We beg our readers to remark, in this living instance, the practical tendency of that cynical narrow-minded and degrading philosphy, which professes to do more, than any other, to advance the real happiness of life, by indiscriminately proscribing its highest graces and accomplishments.

"But, although I would have crossed the Atlantic, as I have said before, to enjoy his company for a single evening, had I been able to afford it; still, after I *had* crossed the Atlantic—nay, after I had arrived in the very neighborhood of his house, I could not find a person that knew him, or had ever seen him; and I was there above a twelvemonth, before I knew where he lived, though his habitation was hardly a pistol-shot from my own lodgings, in Warwick-street, Pall-Mall. At last, however, when I had given up all idea of ever seeing the man, for I knew several native Englishmen of high character, who had been trying for years to find the way to his door, as they acknowledged without scruple.—we were brought together by the merest accident in the world ; and I remained with him so long, and knew him so intimately, that, perhaps, it would not be too much to say—probably no person alive knows more of the true character of Jeremy Bentham than I do. Mr. Bowring, and Mr. Mill, the author of British-India, may have known him longer ; but never more intimately. They have seen him at intervals of a week or a month, year after year: but I have been with him every day for about eighteen months, and spent almost every evening with him, from six o'clock, the dinner-hour, till about eleven or twelve at night, for the whole of that time. I have seen him through his changes therefore; and I believe that I know him thoroughly and completely.

On Friday evening, Oct. 22d 1825—I have the very day before me—I was invited to meet with the Utilitarians at his house, for debate,—a body of youthful conspirators against government, order and morality; the fine arts, and all the charities and sympathies and elegancies of life, you would suppose, were you to judge of all by two or three; or even by what is said of all, by those who occupy the high-places in the commonwealth of literature. This formidable band, however, consisted of but seven persons, most of them young men, mere boys in age and experience, and the others below the middle age. They were all, without one exception, I believe, atheists—fixed and irretrievable atheists *in their own opinion*, though of the whole, no one had ever read much, or thought much, or written much, even for a youth. Nor were they otherwise remarkable. As debaters, they were unspeakably wretched; as writers they were nearly as bad, with one or two exceptions; but they were good reasoners; and one of their number was certainly the closest and clearest I ever knew under the age of thirty-five. Yet he was hardly eighteen I believe; certainly not over nineteen. They had a young gentleman to preside, of whom all that I can remember is, that he had very black hair, very bright eyes, and very large teeth; that he was clever, but saucy, and a great lover of paradox. After the business of the society was over, young Mr. Mill, the editor of Mr. Bentham's Rationale of Evidence, then going through the press, read a portion of the manuscript, with two or three of his own notes, which were certainly very surprising for such a youth. Having already learnt to prefer crude Benthamism to prepared Benthamism, I detected the original of much that Mr. Mill, the father, had furnished for the supplement to the Encyclopedia Britannica here. We had almost the whole of his renowned essay on Jurisprudence, in a colloquial form. After this, they had what they called a debate—and such a debate! No wonder the Utilitarians are at daggers drawn with oratory. Of the leaders, not one was ever able to express himself, with power and beauty, even about his own faith; not one converses well, not one is there that speaks with energy, clearness and fluency, at the same time, nor one that may ever hope, under any circumstances, to be distinguished as a speaker. I know them all, and I know what I say to be true. Mr. Bentham is very unhappy in conversation, the moment he leaves preaching and begins to argue; and Mr. Mill, the father, never attempted a speech but once, they say, and then he failed so utterly and so hopelessly that he has been at war with oratory ever since. However, as I have said before, they are almost to a man powerful and acute reasoners, though addicted to questioning the most obvious truth when it stands in their way. This evening the subject was the poor-laws, and the policy of their introduction into Ireland. It was opened by a Mr. P., a good-natured, large, agreeable man, who, like two others in this society of seven, was afflicted with an impediment of speech, and used to stop and breathe between every two or three words. No wonder they sneer at oratory! He was replied to by young Mill, in a very modest, firm, unprepared speech. The reasoning and the language of Mr. M. were both good, though he appeared somewhat anxious; and a part of his pronunciation was that of the North country, waound, raound, &c., for wound, round, &c. He was followed by another, who got up with a sort of fling, and began with a loud, free voice, which died away after a moment or two; when he lost himself entirely, having said this, and this only: Sir, I rise to make a few observations,—and *but* a few. My opinion is decided, and *very* decided. Here he began to talk lower and lower, and soon ran himself out, courage, waggery and all." pp. 43–47.

The school was so very prepossessing, that our young countryman was more curious than ever to be introduced to its visible head on earth. The memorable day at length arrived—the doors of "Q. S. P." (p.55.), which seldom turned upon their hinges to admit the mighty ones of the earth, were thrown open to a friendless foreigner—and it would be difficult to match the quaint and pompous *niaiserie* of the following description:

"After this brief sketch of the Utilitarians I saw gathered together at the hermitage of Mr. Bentham, in Queen-Square Place,—and whom, by the way, it was my lot to oppose, whenever they touched upon theology,—the reader will be prepared to feel as I did, when at the end of another week, as I was sitting by my-self in my landlady's little parlour, a young man whom I knew for the private secretary of Mr. Bentham, and whom I supposed to be one of the two keepers mentioned by the trust-worthy Parry, entered the room, and, after interchanging a word or two about the weather, dropped his voice, and communicated a verbal invitation to me from Jeremy Bentham, as if it were the pass-word for something, which it were a matter of life and death for any body to over-hear. So—I was to dine with the philosopher; and the day fixed upon was the 2d of November (1825); the hour six. But query, said I to my-self, as the day drew near—must I go punctually or not? If I go punctually, who knows but I may be charged with affectation or ignorance; a disregard or want of acquaintance with the usages of the country, not to be pardoned. I knew very well that 'fashion's six is half-past six or seven,' just as 'not at home' is,—I have no time to throw a-way on you. But then the philosopher, they say, is not a man to be trifled with: he is, moreover, somewhat whimsical, and he cares nothing about fashion. Perhaps, therefore, if I do not arrive punctually, I may be reproached for my want of republican virtue, and put off without my dinner. This determined me, and I started in good season; but, owing to the difficulty of finding the way without a guide through Queen-Square Place, the secretary had been obliging enough to say that he would leave the iron gate open for me, which enters on the park. The gate I missed; and I did not arrive therefore till a quarter after the time. But, after I had arrived, there seemed to be little or no prospect of my seeing the interior. I could find nothing that resembled what in our country is denominated a front-door—nothing in the shape or size of a principal entrance. A door I saw, and I marched up to it; but there was no knocker, and, after feeling about in the dark for awhile, I discovered the steps, and circumnavigated the whole premises, including the coach-house, and a part occupied by Mr. Coulson, editor of the Globe. At last I found myself just where I started from. So, for the want of any thing better, I began to pound away at the door with my knuckles. After a minute or two spent in this way, the door opened, and the secretary appeared in a room on the left of the passage-way, seated at a piano—as vile a thing, by the by, as I ever saw, though he had a decided taste for music, and played the organ with a masterly touch for an amateur. We entered into conversation immediately, and were beginning to understand each other, when I stopped to listen to a cheerful trembling voice that appeared to be approaching. The next moment I heard my name pronounced and somebody talking very fast and not very intelligibly at the door, which opened with a nervous, hurried shake, and a middling-sized, fresh-looking old man, with very white hair, a good-humored, though strongly marked face, a true quaker-coat, and a stoop in his gait, entered and began talking to me as if we had known each other for years. A—a welcome to the hermitage—I can't see here (turning away from the light)—a—a—there's my hand—a—a—we must form—a—a—I've heard of you a—a—anti-holy alliance together. I made the best reply in my power, delighted with his cordial strange way, though sorely puzzled to make out what he said. "Just time enough to look at my garden—a—a—" clapping on a large straw hat as he spoke, with a green ribbon to it (the reader will not forget the season of the year,) and grasping a cane. I thought of Parry here, the veracious Parry; but on the whole, as it was very dark, I did not feel much afraid of being mistaken for the keeper of a gray-haired lunatic. Yet I was half afraid to offer my arm at first; and when I did, he threw it aside with a laugh, and I began to prepare for a trot, as described by that facetious gentleman, up one street and down another. Away we went as fast as we could go, he keeping a little ahead, and talking away as fast as ever, though with a slight hesitation of speech hardly perceptible at first. N. B. He is the founder of the Utilitarian school of oratory. This way, this way, said he, as we drew near another part of his large garden, this way now, taking my arm as he spoke; I'll show you—this is classical ground—a—a—much to *classicalize* it. I had no time to bow, nor would he have seen me if I had. Rush was here, a—a—down on your marrow-bones,—a—a—I gave him a piece of the balustrade of Milton's house—a—a there it is (pointing to the back side of a two-story brick house) that belongs to me—a—a—large garden—the largest here that looks upon the park, except the royal-gardens—a—a—now it is dinner-time." pp. 47–49.

Then comes the dinner.

"This over, he led me up to what he called his work-shop: a small crowded room, with a false floor occupying two-thirds of it; a sort of raised platform, with a table on it, just large enough for himself, his two secretaries, and one guest—he never had more. I had what he called the seat of honor opposite the sage, with Mr. Secretary Doane at my right, and the other at my left. I had been told, I know not how many queer stories about the household economy of the philosopher; but they were all very far from the truth. He began with removing a cover—judge of my amazement to see one potato in the dish, and but one. It was large and mealy, to be sure; but hardly a mouthful for a hungry man, who had long passed his regular dinner-hour. But, while I was wondering at the simplicity and straight-forwardness of the philosopher, who fell upon the potato, broke it up, and began peeling it with his fingers, a tureen of capital soup was served; and I was directed to a bottle of Burgundy that stood on my right, and a bottle of Maderia on my left, which, as the philosopher himself never tasted wine, were probably intended for his two secretaries and myself. To the soup succeeded oyster-paties, a very savoury dish, under the management of his cook. Then we had plum-pudding, apple-pie, and beef; and, while he ate of the two former as a first course,* such being the fashion of his youth, we were served with the beef; and, while we partook of the plum-pudding and apple-pie, he *took* beef, as we say here. I mention the courses, and the very dishes, and the order in which they appeared, thus particularly, because of the strange stories that are

* As the old-fashioned of our country still do. You know the law, reader—he that eats most pudding shall have most meat.

abroad on the subject, all of which are not only untrue, but ridiculously untrue. He talked a good deal after the heavy work of the dinner was through ; and his conversation was delightful, not so much on account of the subject or the language, though the former was full of interest, and the latter good enough to satisfy me, as on account of the general, unaffected pleasantry of his manner, with here a dash of good-natured sarcasm, and there a sprinkle of downright roguishness. I should not say of Mr. Bentham that he had much of the manner of the old school, or any thing of a high-bred air; but he had what I cannot help revering and loving much more, a playful and easy manner, like that of one who is tired of being upon his good behaviour, and is glad to let a stranger see the inside of that which all but a very few are only permitted to judge of by the outside—his real character." pp. 50, 51.

As it would be unreasonable to expect that many of our readers should buy this whole book, while it must be owned that some of the anecdotes which it contains are amusing enough, we shall make pretty copious extracts from the biographical sketch.

Every body, we suppose, has laughed as heartily as Lord Byron over Capt. Parry's account of what his lordship facetiously called "Jerry Bentham's cruise." On that subject Mr. Neal mentions what follows :—

"I watched my opportunity this evening, and alluded to Parry— Captain Parry, the authority of the North-American Review, for January, 1828. Captain Parry—*Major Parry* he calls *himself*, said Mr. Bentham, with decided emphasis, and a little anger. He lied—he dined with me, and went away drunk ; we dined at six, my usual hour, instead of eight or nine. The secretary on his right and the secretary on his left, appeared rather blank too, at the mention of Parry." p. 58.

It may be true that Parry threw a *little* exaggeration into his amusing sketch—but, if Mr. Neal is not himself a caricaturist, it *could* have been *very* little. Compare with that picture, the anecdotes and sketches in this book. An old man—an octogenarian—five feet high, bent down under the weight of years, with a plentiful head of white hair streaming like the tail of the pale-horse in the Apocalypse*—hallooing in the heart of a great city as loudly as a man-of-war's boatswain in a storm—"hurrying away in a *respectable* trot," (what *can* that mean ?)—the straw hat, the woollen stockings rolled over the drab cloth trowsers, &c. How is it possible to add any thing to the effect of an image so ridiculous and *outré* ?

"21st. Calls me every day to walk in the garden with him before dinner. Halloos like a man-of-war's boastwain in a storm ; good practice for the lungs—thinks they are strengthened by it, as they undoubtedly are. When he began to halloo, he could not make himself heard in the library; now the whole neighborhood may hear him. I observe to-day that his real stature, before he began to stoop, must have been about five feet six. I do not know that I ever saw a finer picture than this old man, *hurrying away on a respectable trot,* with a cane that he calls *dapple,* after the

* Manfred.

favourite mule of Sancho Panza ; a plain, single-breasted coat of a dark greenish olive; white hair, as white and plentiful, and curved about as much as the mane of a horse; a straw hat, edged and banded with a bright green ribbon ; thick wollen stockings, rolled up over his knees outside of a pair of drab cloth trowsers, (he hates breeches—never could look at himself in breeches without laughing he says;) a waistcoat of thin striped calico, all open at the bosom—a dress, take it altogether, which he wears, not only in the depth of winter, but in the heat of summer." p. 64.

  *   *   *   *   *   *   *   *   *

"This very day, (Aug. 24,) after going out to receive a small annuity, he trotted all the way from Fleet-street to Queen-Square Place, Westminster, a part of the way very fast—not at all tired, though warm. Perhaps he did so to re-assure himself—on the way back from a life-annuity office, of which he was the only surviving annuitant of a particular age." p. 95.

His habits are cynical throughout. His bed, especially, is a fit receptacle for such a body. One would suppose that, like Diogenes of Sinope, he had taken the first hint of his manner of living from a rat.*

"25. Sunday. Mr. B. sleeps standing after dinner; fell once he says, and hurt himself on the elbows; the approaches of sleep are extremely delightful, he adds, being half asleep at the time. He sits up in bed in the morning to enjoy the approaches of sleep—not to sleep. And here it may not be amiss to describe the bed. *The philosopher sleeps in a bag, and sometimes with his coat on ; the bed not being made up for a month together.* p. 66."

  *   *   *   *   *   *   *   *   *

"He shuts the flap of the book-case to hide the hole in the floor, which is occupied by the player at the organ ; the darkness being rather unpleasant to the philosopher, he affects to believe it full of ghosts—not seriously to be sure, but more than half-seriously. He sleeps in his coat now—having ordered the flaps to be cut off, which are too warm for the night, and bring on the heat and itching of the skin, with which he is afflicted after dinner—the *devil* he calls it. Having drawn a line down each side of the middle-seam, with a bit of chalk, he has ordered a strip of the cloth to be cut out, and a cord to be let in, like the lacing of stays, to keep his backbone cool : D.—the mischievous dog he employed for this purpose—having cut off the flaps of the coat and ripped it up in the back, now added the initials of the philosopher's name, as if to provide against his going astray,—putting them in large white letters in the very middle of the back. When I mentioned it, saying—If you escape now, sir, you will be brought home; instead of being offended, he laughed, said it was a foolish joke, and made the secretary rub it off. Such a figure no mortal ever saw before out of a mad-house. I cannot think of it to this day without laughing. I can see him now, it is the fourteenth of June, thermometer 76° ;—There he goes with a pair of thick leather gloves on, woollen stockings rolled up over his knees outside, his coat-tail shaved away like a sailor's round-about, and stooping, with his reverend rump, pushed out like that of a young chicken. I made a sketch of his figure, but am half afraid to publish it. He sleeps now with his feet in a bag. On some occasion, wanting an improvement in the shape of his bed, he told the carpenter to jump in, so that he could judge for himself what was wanted. In the fellow jumped, shoes and all covered with mud,—No idea I could sleep in such a place, added our

* Diog. Laert. in Diog. Sinop.

philosopher, with the most diverting simplicity. On hearing the fact mentioned, I could not help thinking of his regular ablutions every night, and of the cleanliness insisted upon in the Panopticon." pp. 81, 82.

* * * * * * * * *

"I am told to-day that he has his bed made only when he changes the sheets, that is, about once a month—sometimes not for six weeks; that coffee has been spilt on those he now sleeps in—that it is all spotted and discoloured with his fleecy hosiery, which he wears to bed with him, though wet and muddy'; and that sometimes other droll accidents occur, which, added to his peculiar night-dress, the truncated cloth-coat, and the bag for his feet, are indeed examples of idiosyncracy not often to be met with." pp. 83, 84.*

The language of "Q. S. P." is in keeping with the rest of the establishment.

"I must now give two or three specimens of the peculiar phraseology at Q. S. P. Instead of saying to the secretary, on my left, please to touch the bell, or please to ring it, he says *make-ringtion*; and this not merely for the joke, but in sober earnest, though intended for a caricature of his own theory. But he, and the secretary on my left, who has lately betaken himself to the church, are in the habit of substituting words, which, though synonymous at law, are not so in practice. Instead of saying a *rich* paste, they say an *opulent* paste; for *shortness*, they say *brevity*; for veal-pie, the *basis* of that pie is veal; for *good* mutton, *virtuous* mutton; for pretty-good, or apparently good, *plausible*; and so with I know not how many more words; all which from the mouth of Mr. B. the philosopher and the humourist, the great and good, though whimsical old man, is rather diverting than otherwise. But, when repeated by a youth, and with imperturbable gravity, as if a new mode of speech were to be learned by those who had the honour of eating at the table of his preceptor, it was infinitely diverting." pp. 67, 68.

The uncouth jargon is particularly well adapted to the vulgar blasphemy of which it is every moment the vehicle. We have already seen a flat avowal by Mr. Neal, that "this great and good, though whimsical man," is an atheist. But it is not every atheist who is fortunate enough to be able to clothe his doctrines in such an appropriate guise as Mr. Bentham. We could not read the passage which we are about to cite, and which presents so lively an instance of the indecent wantonness and license of this old man's conversation, without being strongly reminded of the lines—

"Nullos esse Deos, inane cœlum
Affirmat Cœlius; probatque
Quòd se videt, dum negat hæc, beatum."

* It is impossible to read these passages, without thinking of Socrates, as he appears even in what may be considered as the flattering representations of Plato and Xenophon. See the beginning of the *Convivium*, where Aristodemus, meeting Socrates in a clean dress and with shoes on, asks him on what extraordinary errand he is bound. So, in the *Memorabilia*,(c. 6,) Antiphon says to him—"You live as no slave could bear to live. Your meat and drink are the worst possible, and your raiment is not only mean and shabby, but the same winter and summer, ἀνυπόδητός τε χᾀχιστων διατελεῖς."

"*June* 12, 1826. Ever hear of a bargain I propose—a—a—a bargain for the future, said he. Some comfort for my death-bed; first year of my death will be the first year of my reign; if you have not, you are the only one of my intimates that has not. I know very well how long I have a right to live at my age; I look at the tables—four years now; the longer I live the harder the bargain God Almighty will drive with me. Now I say—here God Almighty; here are four years: Now I'll give up two of the four, if you'll let me take the other two at such intervals as I like; one hundred, two hundred years hence; I should like to see the effect. Had no answer to the purpose yet—perhaps there may be. Wilberforce or ——— ——— or———, naming several more, they might have one, or others in a more advanced stage of human discovery.

"His health instead of growing worse, would appear to be growing decidedly better. He used to have the tooth-ache, the ear-ache, the head-ache, and always winter-coughs, till within the last two years—now he is entirely free from all these troublesome and wearing ailments. I see no reason why he should not live to a century." p. 85.

*   *   *   *   *   *   *   *

"*July* 7th. A favourite expression of the lawgiver, when he hears any thing new, is, Lord God, only think o' that! accompanied with a shake of his white hair, and a look of eager surprise, with the forehead thrown back, and the whole head thrust forward." p. 87.

It is worth while to extract another passage, which shews that this philosophical Mezentius stands in sufficient awe of the Infernal gods, at least.

"Mr. Bentham is so afraid of death, that he will not allow the subject to be discussed before him—he is afraid of being alone after dark; he is either read to sleep every night, or left to fall asleep with a lamp burning; and he is a believer in what *he* calls ghosts; that is, in a something which makes him uneasy in solitude after dark." p. 114.

In this respect, the reformer of "Q. S. P." resembles Hobbes, and Mr. Neal takes occasion to run a formal parallel between them, much after the manner of Fluellin. His comparison does not strike us very forcibly. The point in which Hobbes and Bentham approach each other nearest, in our opinion, is the perfect contempt for other men's understandings, and the proportionate confidence in their own, which contributes so much to the air of originality and vigor that pervades their respective works. But in reference to this very originality (of which it is our purpose to say much) they differ as widely as any two writers can. Of all men, the philosopher of Malmesbury most detested verbal disputes, technical phraseology, and the mystical and unmeaning jargon of the schools. He thought that the universities, for which he has no great respect at best, were particularly obnoxious to censure on this score. They had substituted words for things, and persuaded mankind that they had learned philosophy, when they had only acquired a strange, perhaps a barbarous nomenclature.* Nothing can be more

*Leviathan, p. i. c. 1. He is speaking of "sensible species," &c., which he denounced as unmeaning and deceptive phrases—"I say not this as disapproving

just than this charge. It is really astonishing to reflect, how much of what was considered knowledge and philosophy once, is utterly passed away, never to be revived or even remembered more. How little, for instance, how very little of the whole stock of learning, (the erudite ignorance, as Voltaire calls it,) that made Thomas Aquinas and Albertus Magnus so famous in their times, is any thing more than the jargon of the schools, very ingeniously (no doubt) and skilfully put together, and requiring as much thought and time to acquire it, as the science of Newton and La Place, but absolutely good for nothing either in practice or in speculation. To go up to the fountain head of all that learning; who that has ever read through Aristotle's logical works can have failed to make the same remark? The amount of intellect expended upon those compositions, is stupendous. Take the Categories for example. It shows wonderful comprehensiveness and acumen, as well as originality of mind, merely to have been able to reduce all affirmation to these ten predicaments. It was considered as a clever thing of Hume to point out the few principles which govern the association of ideas—cause and effect, proximity of time and place, &c.—and Coleridge has thought it worth his while to claim the honor of so great a discovery for the "angelical doctor" just mentioned. But the Categories are a much more complicated and difficult matter, in themselves, and Aristotle could not, at that early period, have had any aid from his predecessors. He was himself the inventor, the creator of this body of philosophy. Nor is it only the original conception that strikes his reader. He is still more astonished at the completeness and harmony in all its parts, and the perfection even in its minutest details, of the system that is built upon it. The boundless copiousness of the Greek language seems exhausted, its utmost capability of refined distinction is tasked, by the philosopher in developing his doctrines through all their shades and ramifications. Yet after all, for any one *substantial* purpose in literature or in life, of what use is all the logic of Aristotle? It is a question we have asked ourselves over and over again, after toiling for three or four hours together over his Analytics, and taking immense pains to possess ourselves of his whole train of thought. Every thing is admirable to look at—but *materiam superabat opus*. The wonderful skill of the artificer strikes us as much as if the work he has erected were destined to answer some of the great ends of society, but science has gone on improving and a day is come, when all his ingenuity, except as matter of philosophical curio-

the use of universities; but, because I am to speak hereafter of their office in a commonwealth, I must let you see, on all occasions by the way, what things should be amended in them, amongst which the frequency of unmeaning speech is one."

sity, is absolutely thrown away.   For is there a man on the face
of the globe, or has there ever been one, who was wiser or abler
either in speculation, or in affairs, for having made himself master of the Analytics, the Topics, or the Metaphysics of Aristotle?
Or of the thousands and tens of thousands of wise and able
men, who have directed the studies, or managed the affairs of
mankind, without giving themselves the trouble once to think
of topic or category, would any one have been the better of a
thorough acquaintance with these speculations?   "How much
of many young men's time (says Locke,) is thrown away in
purely *logical* inquiries, I need not mention.   This is no better
than if a man who was to be a painter, should spend all his time
in examining the threads of the several cloths he is to paint,
&c."* There never was a more just and pregnant observation.

So of the rhetoric of the Stagirite—considered merely *as rhetoric* and not with a view to literary history—and so of all rhetorical and grammatical studies.   All that one learns from them is
language—the names of his tools—that what one speaks every
day is *prose*—that this or that deviation from the *sermo pedes-
tris*, is a trope or figure, with this or that sounding name.   We
do not deny that every scholar would do well to learn these
names; but he will sadly deceive himself, if, after having done
so, he mistake them for things, and set that down as an acquisition of science which is only the accomplishment of a linguist.
In these studies, however, as in logic and metaphysics, great ingenuity and even originality and comprehensiveness of thought,
may be, and have been displayed by celebrated writers—but it is
all comparatively thrown away because the results of such inquiries never can be any substantial addition to the stock of human
knowledge.   They resemble the pleadings (as they are technically called) of the common lawyers.   Nothing can be more
subtle, systematic and logical—nothing looks more like exact
science.   But their merit is simply dialectical.   They are only
an organum or instrument to be used for some purpose, for their
adaption to which and for that alone, they are valuable—and the
remark just cited from Locke strictly applies to them.

That Jeremy Bentham is a most vigorous and original
thinker cannot be denied.   We do not pretend to be familiar
with all, or even the greater part of his works, but we have
seen enough of what he has done, to be satisfied, that, like
Hobbes, he may justly boast of being very little indebted to his
predecessors, either for the conclusions he comes to, or for his
manner of deducing and illustrating them.   Whether these conclusions be discoveries or not for other people, they are so for
himself.   Whether it be difficult or not to establish them, in the
usual way of treating such subjects, it always costs him great

* On the Conduct of the Understanding, 87.

pains to arrive at them.　He has no idea of any intellectual labor-saving contrivance—he carefully eschews the shortest distance between any two points—he hates simplicity, as if it were not the great end of all philosophers to simplify.　We have seen what a jargon is used at his fireside—he adopts a similar one in his ethical and juridical speculations.　His nomenclature or terminology is a study of itself—as complicated, if not quite so systematic, as that of the chemists.　This wrapping up of plain matters in the mysteries of artificial language, which Hobbes detested so much, is Jeremy's great title to the admiration of the world.　He is the Heracleitus of the age.　We cited, in a former number,* a very long passage from the book on Judicial Evidence as a specimen of this truly *original* language.　A great deal of ingenuity may doubtless be displayed in such things, inelegant, unphilosophical and worthless as they are in themselves.　But it is all a wasteful expenditure of intellect—it is dialectical trifling—it is darkening counsel with words without understanding—and puffing up the unhappy *adepts* in the pretended science, with a self-conceit as unbounded, as it is absurd and pernicious.

It may be worth while to add that this same charge was made by the ancient philosophers against Zeno and the Stoics.　The originality of which these latter boasted so much was said to consist only in their arbitrary neology.　"Of all philosophers, (says Cicero in the Dialogue de Finibus) the Stoics innovated most in this respect: and Zeno, their head, was an inventor not of things, so much as of words."†　And, in another part of the dialogue, he makes a Peripatetic say of the same school—"They have stolen from us, not one or two dogmas merely, but the whole body of our philosophy—and, as thieves alter the marks of the things they take, so these men have attempted to pass off our doctrines as their own, under the disguise of new words."‡

In moral philosophy, more than in any other department of knowledge, the field of discovery (properly so called) is, at once, excessively confined and completely preoccupied.　What can you tell a man of himself, which he has not over and over again experienced?　Mechanical philosophy, with the double advantage of experiment and demonstration, may go on improving to the end of time—astronomy may reveal unknown worlds, or make us better acquainted with those already known—and there is manifestly no assignable limit to the analytical researches of the chemist.　But what discovery is to be made in human nature, at this time of day?　What nook has been left unexplored in the heart?—what *terra incognita* in the mind of man?　Accordingly, it is here, if any where, that Hume's pointed observation applies, that "nothing is more usual than for philosophers to en-

* So. Review, No. 10, Art. V. p. 382.　† De Finib. l. iii. c. 1.　‡ Ib. l. v. c. 25.

croach upon the province of grammarians, and to engage in disputes of words, while they imagine they are handling controversies of the deepest importance and concern." The truth of this
observation is, we venture to say, more and more felt every day
that a man lives, whose time is at all given to such studies, and
the great and almost peculiar merit of the incomparable writer,
from whom we quote, consists in his clear perception of it, exemplified by his own practice. His essays contained, in a condensed, simple and intelligible form, the substance of as many
volumes, loaded as such volumes usually are, with wire-drawn
verbiage, dull truism or startling paradox.

We do not mean to say that all ethical compositions are superfluous and uninstructive. Far from it. We beg leave to distinguish. Ethical *literature* is as delightful and as useful as ever.
Paintings of the passions and affections and manners of men—
precepts of morality—whether in prose or in verse, can never
be multiplied to excess. There is always room for eloquence
and poetry—for the drama, the novel, or the essay—for vivid
descriptions of life, and impressive exhortations to duty. Addison and La Rochefoucault, Johnson and Fenelon cannot be superseded—they please as much, and instruct as well now as they
ever did. Our observations apply to ethical *science*, strictly so
called—to inquiries into the *principles* of morals—to such dissertations, in short, as that which constitutes the second part of
the volume before us. We maintain that to talk of Jeremy Bentham as a great *discoverer*, "a Columbus," as he is pronounced
by Mr. Neal, because he teaches that *utility* is the only true
ground of moral approbation, is just as absurd as it would be to
vaunt that sublime doctrine revealed by Shaftesbury to a world
lying in darkness, that ridicule is the test of truth—with this
difference, by the by, that there really is some smartness and novelty, in the latter proposition, and that there is not a particle of
either in the former. The following is a specimen of the language in which the admirers of Jeremy Bentham express their
belief in his extraordinary powers :—

"This magnificent rule of conduct, which may be regarded as the greatest discovery in morals that ever was made, did not originate with Bentham. Ages ago, people talked about the *fitness of things;* and Helvetius,
that extraordinary Frenchman, had got his foot upon the shadow of the
pyramid, and was preparing to measure its altitude for the benefit of all
who were at sea, in the vast ocean of morality, when Mr. Archdeacon
Paley appeared, and brought forth a new instrument, under the name of
Utility, and gave us what we required—a name for that, which will hereafter be a guide for the nations, a pillar of light, for the journeying ages
that are to follow in the footsteps of this.

"And after Paley came Bentham, who looking abroad with the eye of
one that is able to read the universe of thought like a map and fixing upon
two or three first principles, in Morals and Legislation, as clear and as
satisfactory, as the law of gravitation in physics, laid the foundation of a

new science, which, for the want of a better, we may call by the name of UTILITY." pp. 120, 121.

As to the wonderful merit of this discovery, it is curious to compare what Paley himself says of his own originality, with what Mr. Neal says for him. The most sensible writer excuses himself for frequently omitting the names of the authors whose sentiments he makes use of, on the ground that "in an argumentative treatise and upon a subject which allows no place for discovery or invention, properly so called, and in which all that can belong to a writer is his mode of reasoning or his judgment of probabilities," he thought it superfluous.* Yet Paley's doctrine of obligation really had some novelty (and we think just so much error) in it—whereas Bentham's, so far as we are able to perceive, has none at all—except, perhaps, in its spirit and tendency, of which we shall speak by and by. A great philosopher—and that neither Helvetius nor Paley—who has, we venture to affirm, exhausted the subject of utility, and put it in the justest and the clearest point of view—appears to regard "the greatest happiness principle" as any thing but a mystery. "It seems (he says) so natural a thought to ascribe to their utility the praise which we bestow on the social virtues, that one would expect to meet with this principle every where in moral writers, as the chief foundation of their reasoning and inquiry. In common life, we may observe that the circumstance of utility is always appealed to," &c.† This position we are persuaded, could be fully made out by any one learned enough to gather up, like Grotius, the expressions of the common sense and feeling of mankind, which are to be found scattered through the literary monuments of all ages. Thus, when Horace tells the Stoics that their great paradox—the equality of crimes—is repugnant alike to the common sense of mankind and to *utility*, which is (almost) the mother of justice and equity, &c.

> Sensus moresque repugnant
> Atque ipse utilitas, justi *propè* mater et æqui. *Sat. li.* 3. 97.

he enunciates, in a single line, the proposition which Hume establishes. "Whatever is expedient is right," says Paley, and so Socrates, in Plato's Meno, affirms that "whatever is right is expedient." παντα τ'αγαϑα οφελιμα· ουχι ;‡ Nor is this an accidental inconsiderate *dictum*, thrown out without any view to consequences; for the question discussed throughout the whole dialogue is whether virtue be an affair of the head or of the heart—whether a good man is or ought to be guided in the discharge of his duties by enlightened reason, rather than by the in-

---

* Pref. to his Philosophy, p. 13.

† Hume's Essays, v. ii. c. ix. p. 20; and cf. his Essay on "Justice," "Civil Society."   ‡ 87, &c.

stincts of a generous nature, or the inspiration of heaven itself—
by a comprehensive view of consequences, rather than a spontaneous, but infallible impulse of the soul.   So there is a discussion of great length in that admirable dialogue, "Protagoras or
the Sophists," of which the very end is to prove that all moral
virtue is *prudence*, and consists in balancing, with judgment,
good against evil or a greater against a lesser good, and bestowing the preference where it is deserved.   In like manner Polybius traces the origin and growth of the sense of justice and the
το` χαλον from the selfish feelings of the heart,* and there never
has existed a code of laws in which the greatest happiness principle" (under proper limitations however,) was not implied, nor
a language of civilized man, in which it has not been mentioned
with assent and approbation.

It is really curious to see how all the artificial arrangement
and elaborate dialectics of Bentham lead to results, of which no
man, in his senses, ever entertained any doubt.   Let the reader
turn to the book before us at p. 247, and he will find the author
of the Principles of Legislation treating at great length of the
"secondary circumstances which influence our sensibility"—sex,
age, rank, education, habitual occupations, climate, race, government.   He then proceeds to the practical application of his
theory.   It consists in making due allowance for the effect of
such things upon our sensibilities—is a mere *rifacimento* of
Aristotle's distributive justice and may be all summed up in
two lines of Tasso.

> "Vario è l'intesso error ne'gradi vari
> E sol l'igualità giusta è co'pari."

The same observation, it seems to us, applies to the whole
treatise.   We have searched in vain for any substantial addition
which it has made to the previous stock of knowledge upon the
subject—whether for theoretical or practical purposes.   The
form is novel and peculiar—the substance is quite *banal*.   If
specificatio or the giving a new shape to an old thing, be a
legitimate source of property in literature as the civilians allow
it to be in law, this theory is all Mr. Bentham's.   It is the very
thing Horace meant in the disputed passage, communia proprié
dicere.   But otherwise, we see nothing *new but the quackery*—
the absurd affectation of mathematical exactness, in a matter
which does not admit of it.   "To multiply pleasures and diminish pains," he tells us, is the whole business of the legislator—
and this he is taught by the Utilitarians to do according to
Cocker !

"It is proper to observe that the *principle of sympathy and antipathy*
may often coincide with that of *utility*.   To feel affection for those who

* Lib. vi. c. 4.

benefit us, and aversion for those who injure us, is the universal disposition of the human heart. Thus, from one end of the earth to the other, the common sentiment of approbation for benevolent acts, and of disapprobation for hateful acts. Morals and jurisprudence, guided by this instinct, have therefore most frequently reached the great object of utility, without having any clear idea of the principle. But these sympathies are not sure and invariable guides. Let a man refer his blessings and his evils to an imaginary cause; and he is subject to groundless affection and to groundless hatred. Superstition, quackery, the sectarian spirit of party, depend almost entirely upon blind sympathy or antipathy." p. 205.

   *   *   *   *   *   *   *   •

"According to this principle, legislation is a matter of study and of calculation: according to the ascetics, it is a matter of fanaticism: according to the principle of sympathy and antipathy, it is an affair of caprice, of imagination or of taste. The first ought to please the philosophers, the second the monks, the third the people, the wit, vulgar moralist, and men of the world." pp. 206, 207.

   *   *   *   *   *   *   *

"Would one estimate the value of action? He must follow in detail the operations that have just been described. They are the elements of the moral calculation, and legislation becomes a matter of arithmetic. The *evil* caused is the expense: the *good* that one produces is the profit. The rules for this calculation are the same as in every other." p. 238.

   •   *   *   *   *   *   *   *

"This theory of moral calculation has never been fully explained; but it has always been followed in practice; at least, wherever men have had a clear idea of their own interest. What constitutes the value of a lot of ground? Is it not the amount of pleasure to be drawn from it? And does not that value vary according to the greater or less duration that we are able to promise ourselves in the enjoyment of it? according to the proximity or distance of the period, when we are to enter into the enjoyment? According to the certainty or uncertainty of the possession?" p. 238.

Merely speculative, philosophical principles have seldom had any sensible effect upon the conduct of educated men. Yet they *may* do much harm in practice. When, for instance, they are promulgated in times of trouble and excitement, and are preached to the mob in a popular and plausible style, as in the first French revolution—they shake all the institutions of society to their foundation. So in the case of an individual—if his taste be perverted, if his temper be bad, if his natural propensities be base and grovelling—a theory of morals, which is at all Jesuitical, may lead to the worst crimes. Much depends, too, upon the *spirit* in which a doctrine is preached and the purposes and the character of those who inculcate it. Take this very principle of utility for an example. In the hands of Paley, it is quite harmless—it is even, in one point of view, a beneficent and consoling principle. It presupposes the perfect goodness and wisdom of God; for the rule of moral conduct, according to that Divine, is His will, collected from expediency. This—whatever we may think of its philosophical correctness—is a truly christian doctrine, christian in its spirit and its influences, no less than in its origin and theory. There is nothing in it to harden the heart, to pervert the understanding, to inspire a wilful domineering self-conceit or a jacobinical fanaticism. It merely affirms a proposition—which we believe to be, by the great fundamental laws of nature, both in the moral and material world, strictly true—that virtue and happiness are synonimous terms, that our interest and our duty are identical, and that whatever promotes the prosperity of all, in the long-run, is right, because it were a solecism and a contradiction, on the supposition of God's benevolence, to believe that any thing wrong or vicious could promote the prosperity of all.

We need not say that "the greatest happiness principle," in the teachings of Jeremy Bentham and his school, differs, in its origin and spirit, from the utility of Paley, as widely as atheism and christianity. But, in their tendency and pretensions, they differ, at least, as much. The object of Paley is merely to explain the sense of obligation in a manner more satisfactory to himself, than by referring it to an original principle of human nature. Perhaps, it was to furnish an additional topic in favor of christianity. It was not enough, in his opinion, to say that men *feel* the beauty or deformity of character and behaviour, just as they feel the beauty or deformity of natural objects, and that this susceptibility of moral impressions—this inborn love of virtue—is one of the essential attributes and the most glorious privileges of a rational being. He thought the "moral sense" too variable a criterion to depend upon in matters of so much importance, and that a spontaneous compliance with the impulses of the heart was inconsistent with the very idea of *obligation.* "A man," according to him, "is said to be obliged when he is urged by a violent motive, resulting from the *command of another.*" That violent motive was the expectation of being rewarded or punished after this life, and that command was the voice of God himself. We think this doctrine, as we have already observed, and shall presently show, radically erroneous; but it is, at best, in Paley's system a speculative, rather than a practical one. When he proposes utility as the test of duty, he is explaining a phenomenon of nature, not laying down a rule of conduct. He plainly regards it as a mere abstraction, and accordingly touches upon it, as Mr. Neal observes, very slightly and briefly. The *practical* rule which this philosopher proposed was the decalogue and the gospels. His followers were not left to their own shallow and fallible understandings, to deduce, by refined argument and nice calculation, by a comparison of distant contingencies and possible effects, inferences utterly unsafe to depend on, which were to guide them in their most important duties, and to supply the place of the unerring and eternal instincts of the heart. They had a written text and a settled law to go by. But that law, text, gloss and commentary, is exploded by the Benthamites—together with that other law engraved upon the heart of man—quam non didicimus, accepimus, legimus, verum ex naturâ ipsâ arripuimus, hausimus, expressimus—ad quam non docti, sed facti; non instituti sed imbuti, sumus.* In this new system of "mental pathology and intellectual dynamics," every thing, as we have seen, is reduced to mathematical precision. A sin, a vice, a crime, is only an error in arithmetic—not, perhaps, a very venial one, because it were a foul reproach not to know, what it is so easy to learn, the multiplication-table of this infallible school!

The presumptuous and reckless confidence, which such views must needs inspire, is not the least pernicious of their effects. A thorough bred Utilitarian, or rather Benthamite, is never wrong; for he goes by "arithmetic," and figures cannot lie. He is absolutely sure, in every imaginable situation, what the greatest happiness of the greatest number requires at his hands. Propose to him the most puzzling problem in casuistry ; he solves it in a moment—the most difficult and momentous question of public policy, he feels not the smallest hesitation. Let the life of his father or the existence of his country be at stake—he has no scruple about sacrificing them to what he *knows* to be the interest of the majority. It is vain to speak to him of the fallibility of the human understanding—he has never been conscious of it himself. Talk to him of the voice of nature or the instincts of the heart, he laughs outright at such childish and ridiculous superstition. To say that his sensibilities have been extirpated by the stern discipline of his school, is only to say that he is an Utilitarian—but a worse effect, if possible, of this discipline, is the inevitable extinction of that chastity of moral feeling, which has never sinned even in thought—that "pious awe and fear to have offended," though but in a dream—that PUDOR, as Hume expresses it, which is the proper guardian of every kind of virtue and a sure preservative against vice and corruption. The whole system of the Utilitarian, when reduced to practice, is a system of Jesuitical sophistry and compromise ; and it appears to us next to impossible that a mind, accustomed to consider every thing that should be sacred as subject to controversy, and to entertain, with complacency, ideas that are, and ought to be revolting to every unsophisticated heart, can long retain a very lively sense of moral distinctions.

When we speak thus of the system of the Utilitarians, we would be understood to address ourselves especially to that system, which Mr. John Neal applauds so highly in the volume before us—the system of Jeremy Bentham, and the "horrid crew" of Q. S. P. It is not because they attach great importance to the principle of utility, that we hold them and their doctrines in

* Cic. pro Milon.

utter detestation—for in that respect, as we have seen, they are not peculiar. It is because they attach importance to nothing else—because they make war upon the highest graces of the human character, and the most generous and ennobling sympathies of the heart—because, in short, their whole philosophy is "of the earth, earthy," leading directly to a sordid and calculating (and what is worse, miscalculating,) selfishness and drawing off its votaries from the contemplation of the τὸ Καλον— of the sublime and beautiful in morals—of all that is best fitted to elevate the soul of man, and fill it with the enthusiasm of virtue. Nil generosum sapit atque magnificum, as was long ago said of the Epicurean philosophy.*

Indeed, the doctrine of the Utilitarians is precisely the same as that of Epicurus—with this difference, however, that Bentham has deformed and debased it with an infusion of his own cynical coarseness and vulgarity. The agreeable, if not elegant, philosophy of the Gardens becomes, in his hands, so sordid and ungainly, that a reader of Lucretius might wonder how it could inspire poetry at all—much less *such* poetry. The soothing images of retired leisure and philosophical repose of mind, which enter into our idea of a blissful Epicurean life, and which have been wrought up into an enchanting fiction in Thompson's Castle of Indolence, are certainly not awakened by the mention of Q. S. P. Bentham is a compound of Antisthenes or Crates and Epicurus. But with this qualification, there is a perfect coincidence between his philosophy and that of the sect just alluded to. In both, pleasure and pain are the *end*—the τελος— of all human action ; and the test of virtue is its tendency to increase or secure the former, to diminish or exclude the latter. In both, the pleasures of the imagination and the arts, which minister to them, are proscribed, and all the poetry, the grace and the elegance of life.† Atheism is an ingredient in both— more essential, indeed, to the system of Epicurus, of which the very foundation is a knowledge of physical causes and perfect freedom from all superstition—but flowing naturally enough from the sheer worldliness, and the grovelling *ègoisme* of the Benthamites. *Utility* plays the same part in the Epicurean philosophy as "the greatest happiness principle" in the "Morals and Legislation" of the new school. *Prudence*, of which the very end and office is to take care of the interests of life—is the first of the cardinal virtues—the prime good of Epicurus.‡ *Temperance* and *fortitude* are subordinate to it, and formed by its discipline and controlled by its dictates. *Justice* is, for our pur-

---

* Cicero. † Cic. de Finib. l. i. cc. 5. 7. 20.

‡ Τούτων δὲ πάντων ἀρχὴ ϰ͵ τὸ μέγιϛον ἀγαϑόν φρόνησις. See the tenth book of Diogenes Laertius and the Commentary of Gassendi. Philosoph. Epicur. l. iii.

poses, a better illustration still. Gassendi, in his laborious work
on the "Philosophy of Epicurus"—to which we refer those of
our readers, who have any curiosity on these subjects, for a full
exposition of its doctrines—has a very interesting dissertation to
shew that utility is what Epicurus affirms it to be, the origin and
test of all justice and law.*   We wish Mr. Neal would read this
dissertation, and then tell us what he thinks of the wonderful
discoveries of "the philosopher" in this unexplored region of
morals!

It is certain that the philosophy of Epicurus was the most
widely diffused of all the ancient systems and that the succession of its school was kept up, long after the others were fallen
into decay.† The eloquent Lactantius, adverting to this fact,
attempts to account for it by shewing that that philosophy addressed itself, by turns, to every vice of man's nature.   "The
slothful it forbids to cultivate letters—the avaricious it exempts
from the expenses of the popular largess—it tells the unambi-
tious that they must abstain from public affairs—the lazy, from
athletic exercises—the timid, from war.   The irreligious man
is taught to despise the gods—the unfeeling and the selfish, to
do nothing for the benefit of others, since a truly wise man acts
with a view exclusively to his own interests.   To one who
shuns the crowd, the charms of retirement are painted in fascinating colours—a stingy fellow learns that he may get through
life perfectly well upon bread and water.   If you hate your wife,
you hear of the advantages of celibacy—if you have bad children, you are told what a blessing it is to be, without them—if
your parents be not affectionate as they ought to be, you are ab-
solved from the obligations of nature," &c.   Lactantius speaks
in this passage the universal sentiment of antiquity in respect to
the tendency of the Epicurean doctrine.   Torquatus, in the Dialogue de Finibus,‡ affirms that Cicero is singular in not detes-
ting the head of their school, however much he disapproved of
its dogmas.   This general odium could not exist without a sufficient cause—nor do we think that such a cause has been assigned by Gassendi, and after him by Bayle,§ in the active hostility and great influence of the Stoics—"the Pharisees of paganism".   The truth is, that the doctrine of *utility* is found to be
essentially selfish and licentious, the moment it is attempted
to reduce it to practice.   No matter what may be its form

---

* The expression of Epicurus is somewhat different and more just. "Natural
justice is the symbol or test of the useful," If just, then useful. Τό τῆς
φύσεως δίχαιόν εςι σύμβολον του συμφέροντος. See infra.
† Diog. Laert. ub. sup—Cic. de Fin. l. i. c. 5. l. ii. c. 15.—Lactant. (apud Gassendi) l. iii. c. 17,
‡ De Fin. l. i. c. 5. quod Epicurum nostrum, non tu quidem oderis, ut fere faciunt
qui ab eo dissentiunt, sed certe non probes.
§ Bayle Dict. Art. Epicure.

and complexion—whether it allure us by the charms of Epicurean ease and voluptuousness—or take the coarse, cynical and, if we may so express it, ruffian shape of the "greatest happiness principle" of Q. S. P.—no man, it appears to us, can act systematically upon calculation and compromise—can regard the principles of morality as a subject for perpetual cavil and controversy—can treat the holiest feelings of nature, as so many rank superstitions, and violate them without scruple upon any presumptuous notion of expediency—in a word, no man can be a *practical Utilitarian* without imminent risk of falling into a loose casuistry, and forfeiting, in a greater or less degree, as by eating of the fruit of some forbidden tree, the primeval loveliness and innocence of his character.* And, although in persons very happily born and carefully educated in other respects, the effects of such a doctrine may not always be very visible, yet the propagation of it among the great mass of mankind can scarcely fail of being extremely pernicious. Even were it philosophically just in the abstract (which it is not) it is so liable to be at once misunderstood in theory and abused in practice! "Your encomiums upon pleasure, (says Seneca to the Epicureans,) are dangerous, because what is good in your precepts, is hidden—what corrupts, obtrudes itself upon the view."† The observation is strictly applicable to the Utilitarianism of our own day—the worst, because the most exaggerated and extravagant form of it.

But *every* theory which affects to resolve all obligation into the single principle of utility—that is to say, utility existing and *perceived* in each particular instance—is radically wrong, as being either insufficient to account for the phenomena, or something worse. "Why am I obliged to keep my word," asks Dr. Paley. His answer is "because it is the will of God." But why am I *obliged* to conform to the will of God? Because you will be eternally punished if you do not, replies the same philosopher. We see very clearly, that it is our *interest* to avoid this consequence, and there can be no doubt that a rule of conduct, enforced by such a sanction, is more apt to prevail among the bulk of mankind than any other. But how is the *feeling* of *moral* obligation explained in this way? How am I made to love the "beauty of holiness" by such a motive? It were just as accurate to affirm that a hungry man is *morally* bound to eat his dinner, when we only mean that he cannot chose but yield to the natural appetite. In vulgar parlance, indeed, one is said to be *obliged*, whenever he is *compelled* to act: but surely this confusion of terms—which, so long as it is confined to common discourse, is very excusable—is quite shocking when it creeps

*See a disgusting instance of this in the volume before us, p. 146.
† Hoc est, cur ista voluptatis laudatio perniciosa sit, quia honesta præcepa intra latent; quod corrumpit, apparet,—De Vita. Beat. c. 13.

into a philosophical system. According to Paley's doctrine, there is no morality at all without religion, and a Manichean, we suppose, is *bound in conscience* to worship one of his gods as much as the other, and, of course, to conform his actions to this divided empire of good and evil in those whose will may determine the reward, and so must give the rule of his conduct.

Now, to suppose that man—whose chief end and highest attribute are *moral* responsibility—is not prepared for that responsibility by the very frame and constitution of his nature—by some original, inherent principle—which, however reason may enlighten and education control or modify it, is still quite independent of either and inseparable from the idea of such a being—is, as it seems to us, to doubt that very wisdom and goodness of God assumed by Paley for the foundation of his whole doctrine. Such a creature would be an anomaly in the universe. If, for instance, instead of the instinctive love which springs up in a mother's bosom, as soon as she has an infant to press it for nourishment—a love pervading all animated nature and necessary to its preservation—she had to settle a previous question—to work an algebraical equation of utility—miserable, indeed, would be the boasted privilege of reason! But it is not so, and a woman that should have to argue herself into the performance of that holiest of duties, would justly be regarded as a monster deserving the execration and horror of all mankind. It is true, that some philosophers affect to explain these, apparently, instinctive determinations of nature by the force of habit and the association of ideas. They resolve the principles of all actions ultimately into utility and self-love; but they admit that a virtuous man becomes, at length, quite unconscious of any such connection. The later Epicureans introduced this improvement, as they considered it, into their system.* This sort of "philosophical chemistry" is, in its very nature, entirely speculative and therefore harmless and immaterial. We have no great objection to Utilitarianism, until it is reduced to *practice*—until it becomes the professed object of its teachers to *awaken* the mind to the consciousness of its self-love and to make a calculation of interests, with arithmetical precision, the rule of conduct in all cases. This is the odious boast and peculiarity of the Benthamites. We shall not quarrel with any body because he imagines that what he admits to be, in practice. *social* affections, are in their origin or *genesis*, selfish. This may be so, just as the Rev. Mr. Allison has endeavored to resolve the emotions of sublimity and beauty into the associations of ideas. In either case, the origin of the *sentiment* is within, and its ope-

---

* *Cic. de Fin.* l. ii. c. 26. Attulisti aliud humanius *horum recentiorum, nunquam dictum ab ipso illo,* quod sciam; primo utilitatis cansâ amicum expeti, cum autem usus accessit, tum ipsum amari propter se, etiam omissâ spe voluptatis, etc.

ration is what is commonly called instinctive or mechanical—and therefore not liable to the objection of explaining that by *reason,* (or by "a violent motive resulting from the command of another" as Paley has it)—which must be resolved into an original law of nature. We beg leave, in this connection, to quote a passage from Hume. "Though reason, when fully assisted and improved, be sufficient to instruct us in the pernicious or useful tendency of qualities and actions; it is not alone sufficient to produce any moral blame or approbation. Utility is only a tendency to a certain end; and were the end totally indifferent to us, we should feel the same indifference towards the means. It is requisite a *sentiment* should here display itself, in order to give a preference to the useful above the pernicious tendencies. This sentiment can be no other than a feeling for the happiness of mankind and a resentment of their misery; since these are the different ends which virtue and vice have a tendency to promote. Here, therefore, *reason* instructs us in the several tendencies of actions, and *humanity* makes a distinction in favor of those which are useful and beneficial." To deliver precepts of morality to men, if they had no original perception of moral distinctions, whould be neither more nor less absurd, than to lecture to the blind about the colours of the rainbow. A moral sense—an innate sensibility to the beauty and deformity of conduct—is quite as much presupposed in the one case, as the use of the bodily organ in the other.

It is to this division of the offices, which *reason* and *sentiment* perform in morals, that we owe the discussion of a question, which (as we have seen) frequently arose, at Athens, between Socrates and the Sophists; whether virtue were an art or science, capable of being reduced to exact rules and principles, or an impulse of the soul, an inspiration from above. The sublime, though visionary, genius of Plato leans obviously to the latter opinion, His sages have that wisdom which is from above, and are all θειοι—divinely inspired. It is certainly not the object of that great writer to underrate the importance of an enlightened understanding, in all matters of moral conduct or opinion. He argues that side of the question too strongly to be supposed not to have very fully considered it. But Plato, as we should conclude from the general scope and spirit of his speculations, thought that the great desideratum of moral discipline was, not to shew what are the duties of life, but to dispose men to perform them, and rather to make them enthusiasts in the love of virtue, than casuists and cavillers about the subtleties of doctrine. He seems to have thought it easy enough, in these matters, to convince the mind by argument, but hard to persuade the heart, to win over the affections, to fortify the soul against the temptations of the world, and to raise it above the grovelling influences of sense and selfishness. His philosophy, therefore, has a poetical colouring. It is delivered in a lofty and glowing strain, and addresses itself to the imagination, which it inflames and elevates with visions of perfection and hopes of bliss. He is persuaded that such are the attractions of virtue— so ravishing is moral beauty—that, if mankind could but be persuaded to lift up their eyes from the meaner objects which too constantly engross them, and fix them upon the only one that is really worthy of their aspirations, they could not fail to be smitten with the deepest love. When we read the writings of St. Paul, we are struck with the resemblance they bear, in this respect, to the dialogues of Plato. The faith, hope and love (commonly translated *charity*), which good christians are exhorted to cultivate and cherish, are dwelt upon in a strain as rapturous as any in which Socrates pours out his eloquent admiration of the First Good and the First Fair. Indeed, to inspire a certain degree of enthusiasm, a divine fervour of feeling, a holy intenseness of purpose, is the very end of all christian discipline, and it is because that discipline abounds in the means of accomplishing this end, far more than any scheme of philosophical teaching, that its moral effects are so conspiciously beneficial. What, indeed, is the love of God, the great pervading principle of christianity, but a new motive—a sublime and solemn enthusiasm—counteracting the downward tendencies of self-love—the evidence of a regenerated nature purified from the contaminations of the world and the body, acting under the influence of grander views, and reasserting its original glory and perfection?

The aims of Utilitarianism are the very reverse of all this. It seems to be taken for granted, in that discipline, that *sentiment* has no share in moral approbation, and ought to have no influence upon moral conduct. Its inevitable tendency, if not its avowed object, is to chill enthusiasm, to extinguish sensibility, to substitute wary, and even crafty calculation, for the native goodness of an uncorrupted heart. They are not satisfied with laying down general principles of conduct or forming habits of virtue. An account-current of consequences is always open before them and their love and their hatred, their approbation and censure, vary with every appearent change in the balance-sheet. Their sage never forgets his arithmetic for a moment— the most sublime instances of heroic self-devotion, the most touching pictures of benevolence and charity, are examined with the same *sang-froid* with which a beautiful body is cut up in the dissecting-room. A cockney tradesman associating the recollections of Cheapside with the scenery of Switzerland—a rude hind, noting the vicissitudes of the seasons, the rising and setting of the heavenly bodies, and all the glorious phenomena of nature only as they are connected with his vulgar occupations,—such is the image of an Utilitarian contemplating the sublime and beautiful in morals.   Like Mammon, he is

> "—— The least erected spirit,
> That fell from heaven: for, even in heaven,
> His looks were always downward bent, admiring more
> The riches of heaven's pavement, trodden gold,
> Than aught divine or holy else enjoyed
> In vision beatific."

The whole complexion and character of Utilitarianism, as a practical system of discipline, is determined by its fundamental maxim, that whatever is expedient is right.   We certainly do not deny the truth of this proposition—but we do object to the form in which it is enunciated, and the emphasis that is laid upon it.   Whether we arrive at the conclusion, with Paley, by reasoning *à priori* from the assumed or established attributes of Deity, or by experience and observation, we have no doubt but that utility (properly understood) and virtue are one and the same thing, or—to express it in a more familiar way—that honesty is, and must forever be, in the long run, the best policy.   It is, in this respect, that the utility of Paley differs from that inculcated by Lysimachus, in Plato's Republic, and by Carneades, in his famous discourses or prælections at Rome, so often alluded to in the dialogues of Cicero.   The *utile* thus considered is always opposed to the *honestum* or to fitness and propriety. But that is a short-sighted Machiavelian policy—the utility of the footpad and the usurper, of Jonathan Wild, and Borgia or Bonaparte.   We admit that Jeremy Bentham has not gone so far as openly to profess *this* science, but we contend that, however he may affect to distinguish his doctrines from those of the true Newgate school, they have, in practice, an awful squinting the same way.   If he had only affirmed that whatever is right is expedient, we should have found no fault at all with the dogma.   But this proposition would not have suited his purposes.   It is entirely too consonant to truth and nature.   It would be only repeating what every body has said for, at least, three thousand years, and would leave mankind as much under the influence of those superstitions, miscalled natural feelings, as if no "Bacon of the age" had ever been vouchsafed to them. Those ingenious gentlemen, who are disposed to moot questions, which, according to Aristotle, ought to be answered by a jack-ketch instead of a dialectician,* would have had no room

---

* This passage of the Stagirite is remarkable enough to be quoted.   It is to be found in the Topics, l. i. c. 11.   "It is not every problem or thesis that deserves consideration: but such only as are matters of doubt to men, who want to be enlightened by argument, not to those who are worthy of punishment, or without some of the senses.   For they who doubt, for instance, whether they ought to honor the gods, or love their parents, deserve to be punished—they who doubt

at all for their innocent paradoxes, or been confined in their discussion of them to a plea at the Old Bailey.   It is the boast of
Jeremy that, by his version of the maxim just cited, he has
exploded altogether what he calls the system of sympathy and
antipathy—that his disciples can very coolly argue propositions,
of which the bare idea is revolting to people whose consciences
are more nice than wise—and that, if his sect spread, civilized
nations may not long have to envy savages the right of destroying their sickly children and superannuated parents, or Mr.
Mill, jr. or Mr. Francis Place, or any other good Malthusian,
boggle about teaching and practising infanticide as "the sovereign'st remedy on earth" for a glut in population.

True philosophy, we repeat it, is studious to inculcate not
that whatever is expedient is right—but that whatever is right
is expedient.*   The rules of morality are few and simple.   Follow nature, as the oracle said to Cicero.   Love your neighbour,
and indulge, without fear of consequences, the promptings of an
honest heart.   The duties of life are, generally speaking, plain
and obvious to any man of common capacity, and woe to those
who consider them as problems, as matters of recondite and perplexing science, which all the powers of algebra are required to
settle!   The true seat of intelligence and wisdon, in morality,
is (where the ancients placed it in all things) the heart.   It does
not occur in one case out of a thousand, perhaps ten thousand,
that the advice of a casuist is wanted even in the weightiest
concerns of life.   To talk of a system of ethics, built upon the
everlasting feelings of nature, as "arbitrary," or "mutable," appears to us to be abusing language.   The differences in the morality of civilized nations, in spite of all the causes that seem to
conspire to aggravate them, are very slight, and those (be it
remembered) occasioned not by the *feelings* of men, but by
what is called their *reason*—by *policy*—by positive legislation
and instituted rule.   These, indeed, continually fluctuate and
vary infinitely—as every thing founded upon the conclusions of
Utilitarian logic will ever be found to do.   But the great bulk
and body, if we may so express it, of the morality of nations—
the *jus gentium* of civilized people—springing, as it does, out of
feelings which are inherent in the heart wherever it beats—is
perpetual and uniform.   The same taste in literature, which pronounced Homer the first of poets in his own times, has survived
all the vicissitudes of empire and manners.   Nature does homage
to his genius still, because his genius is always true to nature.

whether snow be white or not, are destitute of a sense." This reminds us of
Cyril, who said, that a man must be a Jew to insist upon reasons, and ask *how*
upon mysterious subjects, and that this same *how* would bring him to the gallows.
Bibliot. Univers. vii. 54.

[* Jambl. Ch. Vita Pythag. No. 204-5. Porphyry Id. No. 39.]

His pictures of virtue and vice are as just and as pleasing now
as they ever were, and time has made far greater changes in the
spot where his heroes fought—the face of the great globe itself—
than in the sentiments which their achievements and their sufferings are fitted to awaken.   School-boys are still taught to repeat
the heroic exhortation of Sarpedon, and to study, in Hector, the
model of every public and private excellence.

The intellectual discipline of the Utilitarians is of a-piece
with the moral.   Its professed object is the same, and so are its
effects.   It aims at cultivating the understanding alone, at the
expense of the imagination and sensibility.   It proscribes poetry
and eloquence, and we have Mr. Neal's authority for saying that
this part of the system, at least, has been completely successful.
Here, too, they are at war with nature, and their "vast Ty-
phœan rage" vents itself indiscriminately upon whatever most
embellishes society and refines and exalts the spirit of man.
Why is there so much about us to inspire genius, and to make
the heart "o'erflow with fragrance and with joy?"   Why is
nature vocal with sweet music, and clothed all over in beauty,
as with a bridal garment, so that the most useful objects in creation are still the most distinguished for grandeur and loveliness,
and there is one glory of the sun, and another glory of the moon,
and yet another glory of the stars, and "great and innumerable
fruit, and many and divers pleasures for the taste, and flowers of
unchangeable colour, and odours of wonderful smell?"*   Why,
we ask, is this ; and what is still more, why was a being placed
in the midst of all this magnificence and deliciousness, with a
moral and intellectual constitution in perfect harmony with the
external world thus adorned and pleasant, and with every capacity for enjoying it, if his whole duty was to be self-denial, and
his highest perfection, insensibility?   The truth is, that poetry
is a part, and an essential part, of human nature ; and he who
can look out upon the material world, as it lies before him in
its grandeur and beauty, or read of the heroic doings of the
mighty dead, without feeling his bosom warmed with that
enthusiasm which is the soul of poetry, falls, so far, short of
what man ought to be.   The ordinary relations and duties of
life are surrounded with associations which have a like effect
upon the imagination and the heart.   "Honor thy father and
thy mother" is a precept of universal morality, and even an
Utilitarian, we suppose, would *generally* assent to its reasonableness—but what a difference is there between a cold compliance with the letter of the law,—between such conformity as
"the greatest happiness principle" exacts of a politic "arithmetician"—and the religious veneration, the fervid and holy love,
the entire devotedness of soul which Sophocles has consecrated

* Esdr. ii. 6, 44.

in the person of Antigone! It is this *poetry* of the affections—
thus protecting and cherishing the virtue which it adorns—that
is seared and blighted by this churlish and cynical doctrine.
"All the decent drapery of life," to borrow the felicitous language of Burke, "is rudely torn off," and the beauty which
gives to moral excellence its highest attraction, and the love
which makes duty happiness, and the endearing sensibilities,
without which the most scrupulous propriety of conduct is cold
and ungainly, wither away beneath its influence. If, by some
sudden change in our own constitution, or in that of the material world, whatever, in sensible objects, now charms the eye
and the ear, and, through them, the imagination and the heart,
were to become indifferent to us—so that all music and beauty
should cease to be, and sight and hearing should inform us
merely of the existence of nature, without filling us with such
transports of pleasure and admiration as her works are fitted to
inspire—how deformed and desolate would this magnificent universe become! Such is precisely the effect of the discipline in
question—such is the havoc which it makes in the soul of man.

But enough of Utilitarianism—a philosophy, the very reverse
of that so justly, as well as beautifully described in Milton's
Comus :

> "How charming is divine philosophy—
> Not harsh and crabbed as dull fools suppose,
> But musical as is Apollo's lute
> And a perpetual round of nectared sweets."

CODIFICATION.*

A History of English Law, or an attempt to trace the rise, progress and successive changes of the Common Law; from the earliest period to the present
time. By George Crabb, Esq., (of the Inner Temple) Barrister at Law, author of the English Synonymes Explained, &c. First American edition :
with Definitions and Translations of Law Terms and Phrases, additional
references, dates of successive changes, &c. Burlington Chauncey Good-
rich. 1831.

We avail ourselves of the appearance of this History of the
Common Law—a mere abridgment of no great mark or likeli-
hood—to say a few words upon a subject which has recently attracted a good deal of attention in this country—Codification.

Reform, it is said, is the order of the day. It has shaken
down thrones and convulsed empires. It has smitten and shivered to pieces the idols of the nations on the other side of the
Atlantic—broken up their "shrines, abominations"—let in day-
light upon their most awful and, therefore, most profitable mysteries—and turned their mummery into a mountebank's farce
for popular amusement. The same aspiring and overruling spirit of improvement, we are told, pervades every art of life and
every department of knowledge—why should not the great *scientia civilis*—the science of sciences—that which is not a mere
episode, but the history—not an embellishment, but the very
foundation of society itself—viz: legislation and judicature—
why should that alone be stationary amidst this universal progress, and affront, with its uncouth darkness and its antiquated
and barbarous deformities, the light of the nineteenth century?

They, who recommend the turning of the whole body of our
jurisprudence into written law, ask this question as triumphantly as if it were quite unanswerable. And so it would doubtless
be, if the *fact* assumed in it were conceded. But who that is
at all versed in the common law—who that has read the volume before us, or any other history of the origin and progress
of that venerable body of jurisprudence—does not know that the
picture which Jeremy Bentham and his followers have drawn
of it, even as it stands at this day in England, is a broader caricature, by far, than the "Clouds of Aristophanes?" And yet the

[* For a striking and complete confirmation of the whole article, see Lettres sur
la Chancellerie d'Angleterre, published by M. Royer-Collard.]

advocates of Codification scruple not to repeat the same language in reference to its condition in this country, in spite of all the changes that have been made in it. They talk of it as a mere heap of feudal abuses, long after tenures, with all their fruits, have been abolished, and when, of our *corpus juris,* what relates to the doctrine of real estate, is so far from being the whole, that it constitutes but a small and even a subordinate part of the multifarious mass. They tell us that it is a tissue of *lies* and gravely quote the innocent forms of the action of ejectment, and the pledges of Doe and Roe, to prove it. The theory of its pleadings they denounce as a system of paltry quibbling and chicanery, and its practice as a vast scheme of extortion and fraud. It is in vain to urge the necessity of this form of statement to the making up of a single issue, and the necessity of such an issue to the perfection of our justly preferred mode of trial by jury. It is enough that no man can be well versed in this branch of the law, without profound study, and that the inequalities created among men, by talent and perseverance, savor of privilege and monopoly. By way, therefore, of relieving us from abuses, which do *not* exist here, and exist only to a certain extent even in the less commendable practice of Westminster Hall, and, we suppose, of restoring things to the simplicity which is the perfection of art, they would substitute for the precision, directness and brevity of the declaration and the plea, the loose vague and cumbersome generalities of the bill or the libel !*

It is obvious to observe that, even if all this were admitted, it would not help the cause of Codification in this country. That the law of England is susceptible of great improvements, and, indeed, in certain branches of it, calls loudly for unsparing reform, nobody of our acquaintance has ever pretended to deny, and is admitted by the very changes which have been universally made in it throughout these States. The expense of litigation is so great there as to amount to a denial of justice to all but the rich or the adventurous. The forms of conveyancing are too verbose and complicated. The mere subtleties of pleading— such as go not to the merits, but to immaterial allegations, and are (generally) confined by the statute of Elizabeth to special demurrers—are too much encouraged. The record being paid for, and most extravagantly paid for, according to its extent,† is the excuse for this, but it were better that no necessity for such an excuse existed, as none exists here, where, to borrow a phrase of our own courts, "the law mechanic" is paid a lumping price by the job. Some technical rules, too, there are in different branches of the law, which might be profitably replaced by others

[* Pref. to Lettres sur la Chancellerie, p. liv.]
† Bristow *vs.* Wright, Douglas (or Cowper)—a case which is not law here *ces-sante ratione,* &c.

more rational, at least more consonant to the common understanding of mankind. In short, it would be well for England, if she would copy after most of our judicial reforms, so far as they may not be inconsistent with the frame and policy of her constitution ; and it is, no doubt, a very great compliment to the wisdom of our predecessors that there is a marvellous coincidence between the reforms projected in that country by her ablest men, and those which have been so generally adopted among us. But how very uncandid or absurd it is in those who recommend to us the transferring, or rather the transformation, of our whole law into one great statute, to argue from the abuses, redundancies and imperfections of the English system. Yet this is a topic of declamation, for argument it cannot be called, perpetually insisted on by the advocates of Codification. They express themselves upon the subject of our law, precisely as if they were holding forth to a radical meeting in London. Feudal barbarism, especially, is forever in their mouths, just as if every word of Littleton were as much the law now, as when he wrote—just as if the learning of the year-books were not almost entirely obsolete among us—just as if the whole law of contracts—beyond all comparison the most important part of our jurisprudence as of every other—covering such an immense field, and branching out into such infinite ramifications, were not either derived, through Bracton and the old writers, and since, through Lord Mansfield, and other great judges, from the Justinian collection, or from the enlightened commercial policy and opinions of an advanced state of society, and were not strictly speaking, a part of the *jus gentium* of cultivated nations !

The truth is that the only department of the law, in which the least trace of feudal doctrine is visible, is the learning of remainders, escheats and a few other the like subjects. Even with these, its connection is slight and indirect. It is not at all necessary that one should be a profound feodist to understand them perfectly well for most practical purposes ; as is proved by the admitted fact, that Lord Coke was very little versed in the book of Fiefs. To be sure, to know the grounds and reasons of the law—to feel strong in a new case, and to be able to go, with a firm tread, beyond the footsteps of our technical predecessors, it is an advantage to have meditated upon this old learning—to have drunk at its fountain-head, and have traced its course through the different doctrines with which it has mingled. And, furthermore, we venture to affirm that the branch of our law, which is, of all others, the best settled and most systematic—in which there is least excuse for being wrong, and a counsellor ought to be able to advise his client with the greatest confidence—in a word, in which jurisprudence must display its boasted approach to the exactness and certainty of demonstrative science, is precisely this. Fearne's book is the most satisfactory volume, and one of the clearest, in a lawyer's library. We may not always think the policy of a given rule good or reasonable—but about the rules themselves nobody, who will be at the pains of following him through his masterly criticisms upon cases, can entertain any doubts. We speak now more particularly in reference to *deeds*, as to which we see principles applied in all their rigor—because, in the case of wills, the English judges, by endeavouring to reconcile the inflexible rules of a feodal conveyance, with the principle that the intention of the testator should be the law of the testament, did, involve themselves in much confusion and perplexity. The statute of 1824 restored our law to its primitive simplicity in this respect. Even in regard to devises, however, we are yet to learn wherein the rules as to the vesting and contingency of legacies have any advantage with respect to precision and certainty, over those which control the testamentary disposal of real estates.

But suppose that too much of feodal principle is mixed up with our law of land property, how does it follow that the whole of our jurisprudence ought, on that account, to be turned into a statute or series of statutes? The obvious remedy would be to abolish all distinction between realty and personalty, and reduce things to the condition in which they stand in the civil law, where the heir, whether by law or by testament, is the representative of his testator or intestate as to every right and responsibility, without discrimination : in universum jus quod fuit defuncti succedit. Some changes, in addition to the mighty ones that have already been made in our law, are still necessary. Let them be made. All our statutes ought to be revised, condensed, amended, explained, digested. They are in a sad state, it must be confessed. Let them receive such improvements, and be reprinted at large, or reduced into the form of a code, with the interpretations which they have received from the courts, embodied in it. So there is much dissatisfaction expressed in regard to our penal law—not altogether without reason—let us, if we please, adopt Mr. Livingston's code, or the code Napoleon, or, if we prefer it, venture upon a new one for ourselves. But is there any necessity or occasion for undertaking to codify the whole body of our common law ?

This, we humbly conceive, is quite a distinct question, and altogether a *practical* one, to be decided according to circumstances. We shall examine the policy of making such a change in the law, just as we should do, were it submitted to a legislative body in South-Carolina ; for a great advantage is given to the advocates of codification by discussing it in the abstract. They always argue it as if those who are sceptical about its utility, in the actual state of things, deny altogether its practicability; or its expediency, under any imaginable circumstances. As to its practicability, nothing could be more absurd than to call it in question, (at least in the common acceptation of that word, though we shall shew that it is to be used in this connection with some very important qualifications,) when so many examples of it are before our eyes. There is certainly no reason in the world, why the common law of South-Carolina, should not be condensed and republished by legislative sanction, in a single volume, in the same manner, and just as well, as the five codes of France—provided, always, nevertheless, that we find as able jurists for our *rédacteurs.* But *cui bono* undertake such a gigantic and difficult work? Is there any thing in the actual condition of our law which makes such an enterprize necessary? Is there any thing in the promised advantages of a code which makes it desirable? This we take to be the true question. That we shall hazard much in the attempt, nobody, we presume, will deny—that landmarks may be obliterated, and distinctions confounded and order be turned into chaos by an incompetent lawgiver, is obvious. Indeed, one of the ablest and most strenuous advocates, for a code in the abstract, candidly confessed to us that he entertained great doubts about the expediency of attempting it in this State. We beg to be pardoned for indulging in rather a more general scepticism. And then, we ask, is there any sufficient reason why we should encounter so great a hazard?

There was in Louisiana. Mr. Livingston, in his admirable Introductory Report, to his System of Penal Law, has made that very plain. There was in France. No nation was ever so much distracted by the conflict of discordant laws. General and local customs together, there were as many, we believe, as two hundred and fifty different systems of jurisprudence in that country before the revolution.* This was a great and intolerable evil—nor is it at all to be wondered at that, after that mighty convulsion had thrown down all established institutions, and obliterated the monuments of the past, the first thought of her new rulers should have been to unite "the people, one and indivisible", under a single uniform rule of right and duty. It would, indeed, have been strange if this reform had not been attempted, and, fortunately for France, she had in her courts a body of accomplished lawyers, who have, with great judgment, incorporated in their compilation, whatever was most instructive in the discussions, or most profitable in the experience of their predecessors. Far be it from us to derogate from the exalted merit of such men. It is our deliberate opinion, from an exa-

[* Il y avait en France deux cent quarante coutûmes *generales,* non compris les coutûmes locales. Pref. aux lettres sur la profess. d'avocat—Ed. M. Dupin.]

mination of various parts of the *code civil*, that its provisions are almost preferable to those of the Justinian collection when they happen to differ in particular instances, while it is immeasurably superior to the latter in method and arrangement. Besides these cardinal merits of the work itself, the development of the morality and reason of the law, in the *Exposition des Motifs* which accompanies the codes, is worthy of all praise. The schools of philosophy have never taught a system of severer and purer ethics, in language more impressive and beautiful.

As to the Justinian collection, it is familiarly referred to by every apostle of reform, as a most triumphant example of codification—though we must be permitted to think, without a sufficient examination of its pretensions as a code. ✱ We do not mean to question, for a moment (what, indeed, it would be absurd to question), that the study of the civil law has done much—more, perhaps, than any other single branch of study—to enlighten and civilize the modern world. Neither do we mean to affirm that its great luminaries in antiquity, Papinian, Paullus, Ulpian, Modestinus, Julianus, Caius, and others, were not worthy of all the admiration which their immediate successors awarded to them and which still lives in a general tradition and consent of mankind. But it does not follow, because the principles which may be gathered from the immense compilations of Justinian are perfect as rules of right, or have been pregnant with lessons of improvement and usefulness, that the *collection* as such is a good one—and that is all that we have any thing to do with here. On the contrary, there are many learned men,* who have thought, as Jortin bluntly expresses it, that Justinian did more harm than good to the civil law, by his slovenly and unphilosophical method of compilation, and by substituting, in so many instances, the language of his own degenerate and barbarous age, for the elegance of a more fortunate era.

It is our intention to dwell more at large, in some future number, upon the history and the most striking characteristics of that famous body of jurisprudence. But it is not beside our present purpose to remark that the Augustan age of the Roman law, if we may use the expression, was about the beginning of the third century of our era—the reigns of Septimius Severus, and his immediate successors—just three hundred years before Tribonian was employed to gather up the fragments which fell from the tables of such men as Papinian and Ulpian. In this long interval, the seat of empire had been removed to another climate, and the language, in which a nation of conquerors had dictated its laws, ceased to be spoken at the Court of the Cæsars. The Goth, the Vandal, the Frank, the Hun had spread them-

[* *Now* the general opinion. See Lettres sur la Chancellerie d'Angleterre, c. c. 29. 20.

selves over the whole western world, and made one blot of it. Genius had long since been an obsolete word, but now taste was barbarous. All literature that deserves the name—all original, living, creative literature, springing from, and addressing itself to the refined and lofty sensibilities of human nature—was utterly perished. The spirit of man was broken, and, of course, his understanding narrowed and enfeebled—and, by a singular and expressive coincidence, the same emperor, who has stamped his inglorious name upon the immortal labors of the men of other times, might boast the sinister distinction of abolishing the very title of Roman consul, and shutting up, forever, the schools of Athenian philosophy.* Another coincidence, not less striking, deserves to be pointed out. A few years before Justinian set about his labors as a compiler of the laws, that is, in the seventh year of the sixth century, Alaric, King of the Visigoths, whose dominions extended from the southern bank of the Loire, beyond the Pyrennees, undertook, for the benefit of his Roman subjects (for they were still indulged in an option between their hereditary institutions and those of their rude masters), to compile a code of his own. This *Corpus Alaricianum*, as it is called, of which all the fragments have been laboriously gathered up by Schultingius, in his *Jurisprudentia Anti-Justinianea*, comprised abridgments of the Hermogenian and Gregorian codes as well as of that of the younger Theodosius—some novels, an epitome of the Institutes of Caius, excerpts from the sententiæ of Paullus and the writings of Papinian—together with voluminous commentaries upon the whole; these last, it is needless to add, deeply stained with the barbarism of the age, and containing any thing but a just interpretation of the text. The author of this collection is supposed to have been one Anianus, a high officer of the Gothic court.† We are indebted to the modesty with which he undertook to improve what he had not the understanding to appreciate, for a corrupt and mangled edition of the Institutes of Caius‡—a work which had been long used as a text book in the law-schools, and was confessedly the pattern of the Institutes of Justinian.

The opinion which we have expressed concerning the merits of the Greek emperor's compilation, is, we think, that of the most judicious of modern (the *more* modern) civilians—Heineccius, for example. Hottoman, the author of the Anti-Tribo-

---

* If the portrait, which Agathias has drawn of one of the professors of philosophy in his time, is a fair representation of them all, Justinian, tyrannical and barbarous as was his act, did no great harm to the world. It reminds one forcibly of the description which Gil Blas gives of the school of that unrivalled pedant, Doctor Godinez of Oviedo.—*See Agath.* l. ii. c. 28.

† This is denied by Godefroy. Prolegom. Cod. Theodos. c. v. De Breviario Codicis Theodosiani, quod vulgò Aniani *perperam* dicitur.

[‡ Confirmed by the recent discovery of these Institutes. Lettres, &c. 29. 30.]

nianus, and the great Cujas are at the two opposite extremes—
the former denouncing the arch codifier in unmeasured terms
of reprobation and scorn, the latter exalting him to a level with
the very best of his predecessors. But his work speaks for itself. It consists, as every body knows, of three distinct parts,
the code, the pandects and the institutes. The *code,* which was
first published, was so unsatisfactory that it had to be done over
again; even in its present shape, admitting it to be perfectly well
executed, it is a mere digest of the *statute* law.* The commissioners were instructed to compile all the imperial *constitutions,*
extant in the Gregorian, Hermogenian and Theodosian codes, as
well as those subsequently issued from the throne—to omit pre-
amble and superfluities, to condense what was prolix, to explain
what was doubtful, to omit what was obsolete, to avoid repetition, to reconcile contradictions, and to comprehend under a single sanction, and reduce to one enactment, the various precepts
that might be found concurring in their objects and character—
the whole to be arranged in strict chronological order with the
day of each date, and the names of the consuls carefully set
down. Such a compilation may, or may not be a work of greater
utility than the "statutes at large," according to the manner of its
execution, and, in this respect, Justinian's commissioners have
not escaped criticism. The learned Godefroy, in his *prolegomena* to the Theodosian code, expresses himself very freely upon
the subject. He speaks of the liberties which they took with
the works of their predecessors as, in very many instances, neither sensible nor profitable—as sometimes betraying ignorance
in the reformer, at other times, not effecting his intentions, and
often, entirely misrepresenting or falsifying the original statute.†
The *pandects,* or *digest,* is a collection of the dicta, sententiæ,
or sayings and commentaries of the most distinguished jurisconsults, huddled together in fifty books, with little or no regard to
any principle of philosophical classification. Nor is this to be
wondered at. Justinian allowed his commissioners *ten* years for
the completion of their work ; and the allowance, as Schultingius remarks, was any thing but extravagant. They chose to
hurry it over in *three.* The *institutes* is a mere elementary
work *in usum juventutis.* It is much better arranged than the
other two, and really exhibits "no contemptible order" as Gibbon
expresses it; though every body must admit that it falls very
far short of a high scientific standard and that, to borrow a remark of D'Aguesseau, 'M. Domat would have done it much more
perfectly than Monsieur Tribonian.'

Most English and American lawyers derive whatever know-

* De Novo Cod. faciend. s. ii. Ad Senatum urbis Constantinopolit. In this
epistle, or *message,* Justinian sets forth the design of this work
† Ubi supra c. iv. De Justiniani Instituto et Triboniani facinoribus circà Cod.
Theodosian. in Oriente.

ledge they have of the civil law, not from the original text, but from modern commentaries and versions, especially from the writings of Domat and Pothier. It is no wonder they have formed a very exalted idea of the Justinian collection, viewing it, as they do, through the most favorable medium. The two writers just mentioned are, beyond all comparison, the most useful guides to a systematic and comprehensive knowledge of jurisprudence, that the generality of readers can have recourse to. It has been well remarked of the former, by a very high authority, that whoever has made himself master of what he has written, would be if not the most learned of jurists, at least the soundest of judges.* Of Pothier we have no language to express our admiration. The highest compliment that can be paid him is to state that the *rédacteurs* of the French code have generally followed his opinion in cases, where there is any difference of sentiment among jurisconsults, as the Roman emperor enjoined it upon his judges to abide by that of Papinian. It is the good fortune of the civil law that, after having been collected, however imperfectly, into one body, it has passed through the hands of such men. It has been made, in every part of Europe, a branch of academic education, and enthroned, with philosophy and learning, in the most venerable seats of science. Paris and Padua, and Bourges† succeeded to the honors of Rome, Constantinople and Berytus—the most erudite professors, men who devoted their whole lives to the science, with an intensity and enthusiasm, of which this degenerate age can scarcely form an adequate idea, have collated, criticised, expounded and *arranged* its principles—and, since the revival of the study in the twelfth century, so many editions, glosses, commentaries, paratitla, systems, abridgments, abstracts, have been published, that as many camel-loads of lumber, of all sorts, have been created by the work of Justinian, as it is said to have superseded and sunk. A memorable lesson to those who declaim against the multitude—inevitable under any system—of our common law reports and treatises!

Before the invention of the art of printing, compilations and abridgments were much more necessary than they are now. A library—even in these times, a costly instrument—was then the privilege of a very select few, and it is quite conceivable that even a bad or imperfect code was preferable to a common law, of which the memorials were comparatively rare, and all in MS. and a statute book filled with the capricious and atrocious absurdities of such wretches as Commodus and Caracalla.‡ It

* D'Aguesseau.
† Bituricensium Academia veteris Berythi æmula, &c. Gravina.
‡ Yet the wisdom of Papinian dictated some of the constitutions of the latter and the attempt made, in a subsequent age, to abolish them all, did not succeed.

deserves to be mentioned, too, that the Roman courts had no respect for decided *cases*. They were governed by the opinions of distinguished jurisconsults to which we shall presently have further occasion to allude—by the *rescripts*, edicts, *pragmatic sanctions*, &c., of the emperor for the time being, whose *will* enlightened the judge when he was at a loss for the rule—and, in earlier times, by the arbitrary (as it often happened) and superficial notions of the Prætors, in their annual vicissitudes of jurisdiction. It is really surprising that their prætorian law, or equity, as it may be called, was not reduced to a permanent system until the reign of Adrian, who compiled the Perpetual Edicts.

We confess, therefore, that we are not very much impressed with this example of codification—the more especially as we have no evidence whatever to shew us how it worked in practice. The Justinian collection never took root in the Western empire at all—except a few spots in Italy, which had not been overrun by the Lombards, such as the Exarchate of Ravenna and Magna Græcia, where, it is said, the codes and the novels were received. In the East, clouds, darker and deeper, every day gathered over the prospects of the empire, while its limits, more and more contracted by the encroachments of Sclavonian or Mohammedan invasion, were, at length, reduced to little more than the suburbs and city of Constantinople. It is not probable that, in such calamitous times, any principle of reason, or any rule of right was much respected. And, at all events, we know that, in the ninth century, Basil, the Macedonian, and his son, Leo, judged it expedient to supersede the boasted labours of Tribonian, and to publish an entirely new *corpus juris* under the title of *Basilica*.

So much for authority and precedent, and we do not think they are all conclusive upon the point, considered as a practical one. But what, after all, are the promises held out by the advocates of a code? Or rather, to begin at the beginning, what are the grounds of their discontent with the present state of the law?

They are, in brief, that nobody knows what the common law is, or where it is to be found—that it is scattered over a thousand or it may be ten thousand volumes which it is almost impossible to collect—that by far the greater part of it is, what is called in one of their phrases, "judge-made" law, and that it still indulges the bench in an arbitrary and tyrannical latitude of discretion—that the citizen who ought to know the rules of his civil conduct, as well as those of morality and religion, is forever in danger of doing what he ought not to do, or leaving undone what he ought to do, from sheer ignorance, and *that* incurable ignorance—and, lastly, that lawyers profit exceedingly, at the expense of the "lay gents", by the mystery in which they have contrived to involve their practices, which accounts, it is said, for their being, to a man, irreconcilably opposed to every plan of reform, and bitter persecutors of the best friends of mankind, the codifiers. In short, codification is to make every man his own counsellor and every judge infallible—or rather, it is to supersede, in a good degree, the necessity of both. They begin, as Dick the butcher says to Jack Cade, by killing all the lawyers, and we are not sure but the projected reform is more acceptable on this account than for any other benefit which it promises.

Now is this last desirable result, especially, to be expected even from the most perfect code? We concede, for the present, that such a work shall be executed in the best possible manner, and so that there will be no danger in attempting it—will it abridge the study necessary to make one an accomplished lawyer—or lessen the discretion of the judges—or diminish the expenses of litigation, or expedite the business of the courts—in fine, will it answer any good purpose which a body of unwritten jurisprudence (supposing that, too, to be perfect of its kind) could not? We do not think it will—with the exception of what is properly called the public law of a country, and especially the law of crimes and punishments, which ought to be made as simple as possible, and put into every body's hands. Mr. Livingston, we perceive, admits that there is a very material difference between a civil and a penal code, and that strong objections lie against the former, which do not apply to the latter.* Let us examine the subject a little more narrowly.

As to the study of the law, we do not know by our own experience, that it is easier to master any given number of statutes, than an equal portion of the unwritten law, and we are disposed to think it is just the reverse. Every professional man must have recognized, in the course of his practice, the wisdom and justness of Lord Coke's saying, that, if asked what were the common law as to a case put, he should be ashamed not to answer without book—but, if the question were concerning the meaning of a *statute*, he should be ashamed to answer without examining its provisions for the nonce. Perhaps this may be explained as follows.

The difference between written and unwritten law—or, to use less ambiguous terms, between statute and common law—consists not in the shape in which they ultimately appear, so much as in the manner in which they originate.† That is called

* Introductory Report to the System of Penal Law, &c. Part i. p. 65, et seq. [Cf. D'Aguesseau, Dissertation sur l'erreurs de droit. Œuvr. Tom. 9.]

† The Spartan laws were never written, for Plutarch, in the Life of Lycurgus, says it was one of the fundamental constitutions of Lacedemon not to commit their laws to writing. Yet Schultingius (ad Caii Inst. l. i. n. 7. de jur. natur.) well observes that, being positive commands of the lawgiver, they are to be considered as *statutes*—leges—not common law, *mores*.

written or statute law, which is arbitrarily prescribed and
promulgated, in a certain definite form, by a lawgiver, whose
mere authority binds the people. *Sic volo, sic jubeo, stet pro
ratione voluntas.* You shall not dispose of your property by
will, unless you reduce it to writing, and publish it before
three or more witnesses who shall sign it in your presence,
neither shall you revoke it when made, except, &c., in the
presence of as many witnesses, who shall see you sign. The
question arising upon such a law is not what is reasonable,
but what is commanded—and, in the case of a *contract*, not
what the community at large understand by a given form of
words, but what the author of the statute meant. The business
of the interpreter is that of a grammarian and philologist—he is
an *auceps syllabarum*, required to extract from a given number
of letters and syllables, the intention, more or less clear, of a self-
willed dictator. In the case of a single statute, it is often impossible to come to any satisfactory conclusion—because it may
be absolutely impossible to derive any assistance from general
reasoning on the analogies and policy of the law. The memory,
therefore, is not assisted by the usual helps of philosophical connection and arrangement. To remember, with any advantage,
you must remember *verbatim.* When a principle of the common law is ascertained, it may be fearlessly pushed out to all its
consequences—but, in a statute, a subsequent provision may
come in conflict with the prior, because the legislator did not
see, or did not choose to adopt, the true theory in its whole extent. Thus it is that the common law is said to be reason and
the perfection of reason : that is to say, it is the application of
common sense, disciplined and directed by certain established
principles, to the affairs of men. Take the case of remainders,
for example. All that is wanted is a definition of a fee—a particular estate—and one or two maxims in relation to the freehold
never being in abeyance, and the necessity of its vesting in somebody to do the feudal dues, and answer to a *præcipe.* It is astonishing how many conclusions, in this complicated branch of
law, are deduced with the greatest clearness and certainty from
such apparently slender premises. There is, in truth, as we
remarked on a former occasion,* a surprising analogy in this
respect between jurisprudence and the exact sciences. It is true
that an entire code gives far more scope for such reasonings than
a single statute, because one part of it may derive light from
others. But it appears to us that, in this respect, a body of unwritten reason, of which the great outlines are precisely designated, and the first principles well settled, must necessarily have
an advantage over a system or collection of positive enactments,
for the reason just stated. Hence it is safe to say that, with the

* Southern Review, No. 3, art. iii.

exception of a very few instances of arbitrary, or rather obsolete rules, which are every day becoming still fewer, nothing that is not reasonable is good law. And hence we venture the additional assertion that no written law ever approaches to perfection, either in respect of theoretical beauty, or practical fitness, until it has been reduced to the form of unwritten or common law—until the refractory and inflexible matter of the original statute, if we may so express it, has been melted down and moulded into a more convenient shape, by the plastic hands of the commentator or the judge.

A striking illustration of this remark is found in the history of the Roman law. The *matrix* of the whole *corpus juris civilis* was the laws of the XII tables. Then came the *senatus consulta*, the *leges*, passed by the *comitia centuriata* or the whole people, partricians included, and the *plebiscita*, adopted by the commons alone, but binding upon all. To these we may add the edicts of the Prætor and the Edile. All these together constituted a body of written or arbitrary law. But out of these beginnings sprang up what is properly called the *jus civile*, or common law. These various statutes or enactments were considered and commented on and applied, with a sage discretion, to particular cases, by the learned jurisconsults whose authority was binding upon the judges. The pandects, as we have seen, are a collection of these. And thus it was, that the *responsa prudentum*—the interpretations of the learned—came to be the most copius fountain of that jurisprudence which has refreshed the whole earth with its healthful and invigorating waters—and thus, too, it was that, whereas our statutes are engrafted upon the common law which they derogate from, or change or control, *their* common law grew up out of their statutes, and was as an atmosphere of light superinduced upon, and circumfused about them, or like that beautiful luxuriance of foliage and fruit which Virgil describes as shooting forth under the hand of the engrafter from a bald and barren stock, and towering up the skies.

> "Nec longum tempus et ingens
> Exiit ad cœlum, ramis felicibus arbos
> Miraturque novas frondes et non sua poma."—*Georg.* ii.

Then, as to the uncertainty of the law and the discretion of the judge. It is altogether chimerical to suppose, that a written text can exempt us from these evils, if it be ever so well executed, and if it be otherwise, it will multiply them beyond expression. We have seen that the great bulk of the civil law was really "judge-made" law, although it had its origin in statutes. Let us adduce some other examples. Barrington, in his amusing book upon the statutes, records it, as a saying in Westminster Hall, that the exposition of the statute of frauds had cost one hundred thousand pounds; and we have very little doubt that it did, for a respectable volume has been compiled of cases that have arisen under it. One of the questions it has given rise to is among the most memorable in the history of our law. The statute requires, as is well known, that wills disposing of lands shall be attested by three or four credible witnesses. Under this apparently simple clause, a doubt was started, in the case of Anstey *vs.* Dowsing,* whether a benefit to a witness, at the time of his attestation, should annul his testimony, though at, or after the testator's death, he should have become disinterested by a release of his legacy or the receipt of its value. It was held that the condition of the witness, at the time of the attestation, should be regarded. This led to the statute 25 Geo. ii. c. 16, which avoids the legacy in such a case, and makes the witness competent. About the same time (the decisions were somewhat later) the celebrated difference of opinion arose upon these very words of the statute, between Lord Mansfield, and Lord Camden—the former, in Wyndham *vs.* Chetwynd,† deciding that the clause only exacted competency in the witness, and that at the time he should be called to testify in court—the latter in Hindon *vs.* Kersey,‡ holding with the doctrine in Strange. It is difficult to imagine any thing better reasoned than the judgments of these great men, and, to this moment, we are not satisfied what was the will of the lawgiver. Such a question might possibly arise at common law ; but could a more perplexing one be imagined ? And yet the language of the statute out of which it sprang seems as plain and intelligible as its author could have employed. The saying of Lord Hardwicke with regard to the statute of uses is well known ; the only effect of it has been to add three words to a conveyance. Reformers and philanthropists will, no doubt, see in this, another reason for declaiming against the tyranny of judges—but surely it affords us very little ground to hope that the reducing of the law to a written text will be sufficient to control those usurpers.

Compare with the difficulties, which the Courts encountered in the construction of these statutes, those which presented themselves to Lord Mansfield in building up, by a series of luminous decisions, the Commercial law of England. That judge is celebrated as the founder, and, as some think, the author of this part of our law ; and this, we suppose, is one of the most flagrant and most unpardonable instances upon record of judicial legislation. But the truth is that it was no legislation at all. What could the court do ? Two merchants have entered into a contract of insurance or affreightment—the one demands, the other refuses, performance of the contract, because they differ as to its meaning and effect. The decision of the controversy is, of

---

* Strange, 1254. † 1 Burr. 414 ‡ 4 Burn. Eccl. Law, 97.

course, referred to the judge. It is clear that he has no alternative but to decide it—that is to say, to do justice between the parties according to their own agreement, by interpreting the agreement as it *ought* to have been understood between them. And how was this to be done, seeing that the form of the contract had not been prescribed by the legislature, and no precedent was to be found among the judgments of the courts? The common law furnished every means necessary to the effecting this purpose in the most satisfactory manner. A special jury of merchants is empannelled at Guildhall—the usages of trade and the general opinion of the mercantile community are ascertained by other merchants called up as witnesses—these are found to be confirmed by the lights of foreign judicature, and the experience of practised lawyers, who are resorted to for assistance by the judge—the verdict of the jury is conformable to the evidence, and both are sanctioned by the wisdom of the bench. The meaning of the contract is ascertained—or, in other words, it is ascertained what the parties ought to have understood each other as meaning—the law which they have chosen to lay down for themselves is manifest. What remains to be done? Simply to lend the aid of the court to enforce that voluntary law of the parties—which it does, as a matter of course, in all cases of agreement either by an action of covenant, (if it be under seal,) or by an action on the case, if it be not under seal, and there be a sufficient consideration.

Now let it be remarked that these decisions took nobody by surprise. On the contrary, we doubt whether any judgment of the King's Bench, in the interpretation of the plainest statute, ever gave such universal satisfaction, by conforming perfectly to the common sense of mankind and the expectations of the public. It is an error to call Lord Mansfield an inventor. With all his great talents as a jurist, and his bold and adventurous spirit of inquiry, he did no more than apply principles, which had been fully ascertained and settled, with judgment and discretion, to cases as they arose. And there is hardly a rule laid down by that judge, which Valin, Emerigon, and other continental writers have not discussed—except where the usages of trade in England forbad his drawing upon such resources, or modified their results.

But, even under the best code that ever has been formed, judges must often find themselves in the same situation with Lord Mansfield, without the same means of executing the true purposes of the parties whose differences are submitted to them. We shall cite the highest possible authority to this effect, M. Portalis. In his '*exposition des motifs*' of the law relative to the publication of statutes, &c., he uses these identical words. He is discussing the subject under the particular head of *règles pour les juges.* "There is then," says he, "necessarily a multitude of cases in which a judge finds himself without a law. It is necessary, therefore, to leave to the judge a power of supplying the law by the natural lights of integrity, (droiture,) and good sense. Nothing were more puerile than to take such precautions as would prevent a judge from having any thing more to do, than to apply a precise text. To prevent arbitrary judgments, we should expose society to a thousand iniquitous judgments, and, what is still worse, we should run a risk of having no justice administered at all; and, with the wild notion of deciding all cases, we should make of legislation an immense labyrinth in which reason and memory would be equally lost."

Again. "We speak as if legislators were gods, and judges not even men."

"The judges then must never stop: a question of property cannot remain undecided."

"The judge who shall refuse to decide, upon a plea of the silence, or obscurity, or insufficiency of the law, shall be liable to impeachment for a denial of justice." *Code Civil*, No. 4.

M. Faure, another distinguished counsellor, in his address to the *Corps Legislatif*, upon the same subject, holds the following language:

"In a word, as to every matter, whether civil or criminal, either the law speaks, or it is silent. If the law speaks, the judge decides in conformity to it. If it is silent, he must still decide, but with this difference, that, when the matter at issue is a mere civil right, the judge must be governed by the rules of equity, which consist in the maxims of natural law, of universal justice and of reason, and that, when it is a criminal case, the accused ought to be acquitted in consequence of the silence of the law."

This last distinction is undoubtedly a sound one, and is, as we have seen, recognized and developed by Mr. Livingston, in his introductory Report to the Penal Code of Louisiana. But we ask whether any advocate of the common law ever dreamed of claiming for its judges a larger charter of interpretation, than this. And yet the *people*, who are so deeply concerned, it seems, in the issue of this question, are led to believe that all they have to do is to swell the bulk of the Statute Book in order to bring the law within the compass of the uninitiated!

This suggests to us an alternative important to be adverted to. When a code is finished, like all other statute laws, it has to be interpreted and applied to the cases as they arise. It is, of course, subject to misinterpretation.

"No written law can be so clear, so pure,
But wit may gloss, and malice may obscure;
Not those indited by his first command,
A prophet graved the text, an angel held his hand;"

says Dryden, with as much truth as force, and suggesting a very apt and pregnant illustration of his position. Interpretation is the great business of Courts, and it may suggest useful matter for reflection to consider how just Blackstone's remark is, that, in giving effect to the intentions of testators, fifty cases (we should say five times fifty) of difficulty arise about the construction of the words, to one involving a pure question of law, applicable to the disposition, when the intention has been once fully ascertained.

A new statute is passed—what does it mean? Any man may guess at the purpose of the lawgiver—a learned counsellor may be pretty confident that he has hit upon it, after deliberate consideration—but, after all, so arbitrary are such enactments, so much depends upon nice verbal criticism, and so little upon broad views and a scientific comparison of analogies, that it is hard to say what effect any given argument can have upon a judge's mind. There is no sea-room—not scope enough for bringing to bear upon him the whole artillery of cognate and subsidiary learning. His conclusion is apt to be fortuitous and fanciful. Still his conclusion settles the *case*. Now is it, or is it not to settle the *law*? If it is not, the wildest confusion, the most inextricable difficulties, the most interminable litigation is the consequence. The *jus vagum et incognitum*—the miserable slavery of anxious and agitated minds ensues; all confidence is banished from among men, and the repose and order of society are at an end. Black-acre goes to A.—White-acre to B. under the very same title, and the same circumstances; for no reason in the world, but that it is better to have a virgin code, untainted by judicial contamination, than to sacrifice such beautiful abstractions to the vulgar interests of mankind in the old fashioned way of our forefathers.

But, if the interpretation of the judge is to be, so to express it, embodied in the code—if *stare decisis* is to be the rule, as it must be, or anarchy and ruin ensue, then what becomes of the boasted benefits of reform? How does it exclude judicial legislation? Ask M. Portalis and his compeers—ask the very men upon whose authority this enormous delusion is attempted to be practised upon the creduility of mankind.

But then the common law—the common law—with its antiquated trumpery—and its technical jargon—and its quaint subtleties, and its black letter, and its Norman French, and its scraps of bad Latin, and its Egyptian mystery, and its fictions, and its formulary! Verily she hides her truths at the bottom of a deep well, and her ways are past finding out! And so does all truth lie at the bottom of a well. Do the advocates of codification mean to dispute either of these two propositions: 1st. That no code that ever has existed, or that can be conceived to exist, can bring the law down to the level of the great bulk of mankind, so as to dispense with professional lawyers, or to relieve these from the devoted and laborious study of a whole life, in order to entitle themselves to public confidence ;—and 2d. That as great lawyers, that is to say, men as profoundly and thoroughly versed in their science, and as perfectly prepared for a skilful application of it to particular cases, have existed in Westminster Hall, as ever expounded the codes of Justinian or Napoleon.* Is it pretended, for instance, that any jurist, now distinguished in the *Palais de Justice*, knows more about the law in France, or can more confidently predict the result of a cause, than Coke or Plowden, even in that most technical and pedantic age, knew of the common law and its application? Or, are lawyers less necessary now, and is the bar less a road to distinction in life than in the days of Loyseau and Du Moulin? One advantage, we admit, the code has. In every thing relating to the public law of France—to the rights, duties, and liabilities of the *citizen* as such—the people have, in ordinary cases, the means of informing themselves without consulting a legal adviser. Almost all this part of our law is in our statute book, and as it is in general more simple, and, at all events, more necessary to be known than any other, we have always desired a digest of it, either with legislative sanction or otherwise. Nothing is risked, and every thing is to be gained by such reform. It is inconceivable, to those who have not had much experience, how difficult it is to find out what is the law on any of these subjects, among the loose and scattered, and often contradictory enactments of different legislatures. But does any one imagine, especially after the passages which we have cited from the French authorities, that every man in Paris is his own lawyer, or that the head of a professional man is less stored with recondite and extensive reading and his pocket with liberal fees, than formerly? Nobody, we presume, can be under such a persuasion with regard to the Justinian collection. The very sight of the *corpus juris civilis* is appalling. We have already alluded to the studies of its professors—to the immense erudition of the Cujas' and the Godefroys. And we will only add that Justinian himself exacted a novicate of *five* years in his law schools. We suspect that few of our young advocates had gone through as many months of solid study, before they passed muster as junior counsel.

As to the common law being scattered over so many volumes, it is just as reasonable as to say that the decalogue and the gospels are spread over whole libraries, and can only be learned through them because whole libraries have been written upon them. The cases, which exhibit the rule in one important application of it, and which must be profoundly meditated by

[* French Bar fallen off since the code. See Lettres, &c., Pref. lxv.]

every one who aims at something more than being able to repeat a dry formulary like a parrot, are, indeed, to the honor of the law, numerous enough—almost as numerous as the infinite variety of human concerns require them to be. But the rules themselves are comparatively few. The proportion is precisely that between a report running through some scores of pages, and the marginal enunciation of the doctrine in as many lines, or words, it may be. Fearne's book may be cited as an example of this. The first two hundred pages are taken up with the discussion of little else than the rule in Shelley's case. Let any one who wishes to see how many volumes the *principles* of the common law, (and they are all that can be codified,) fill up, only make the experiment for himself. He will find that the whole doctrine of contingent remainders lies within a very narrow compass, however refined the questions may be that arise out of it.

Then why not codify it? We answer simply because it will cost a great deal to do so, and because, in the present state of our law, it can do very little good, and may do much harm. The digests, which have already been executed by private hands, and which are improving every day, wholly supersede the necessity of such a work for professional purposes. If one of these were brought so near to perfection as to want only a legislative sanction to make it a code equal to that of the French, we should not desire to see it take that shape. Our objection depends upon the difference between written and unwritten law, and the danger arising out of the essential character of the former. The difference, as we have endeavoured to shew, is between what depends upon general reasoning and what depends upon verbal criticism. A rule is laid down in a digest: if it be inaccurately enunciated you go to the *case* which has settled it. Your remedy is in the report—you detect the error, and rectify it; and the precision and uniformity of the law is maintained. But, from the moment you *enact* all those rules, they are adopted and promulgated as positive law and must be interpreted as such. You are to make a great bonfire of your libraries, and take a new start. If there is the least change or obscurity in the language, verbal criticism begins, every thing that has been settled is afloat once more, and the glorious uncertainty continues until as many more camel loads of reports take the place of the old ones. Even supposing a code perfectly well done, we do not think the game worth the candle in the actual state of things—but, if it be inartificially executed, the labours of six centuries are utterly thrown away.

But we are told none of these consequences can take place, because we shall retain the common law nomenclature and still resort to it, for collateral light and illustration. Indeed! But how very imperfect and ineffectual such a reform would be. We have seen that all the conclusions of law are deduced, by a train of reasoning analogous to that of the mathematicians, from *definitions.* To retain the nomenclature, therefore, if we understand the meaning of that term, would be in fact to retain the whole body of the common law; and to have recourse to its text writers and reporters would be only to aggravate the evils of which we complain.

Upon the whole, we would recommend to our younger friends a profound study of our jurisprudence as it stands, rather than the ambition of reforming it. A thorough knowledge of that jurisprudence is a highly profitable and glorious distinction among men—especially in an intellectual and free country. In our own land, it is the way to every thing desirable, and must ever be so—and, though practical cleverness and dexterous empiricism may, with the help of good fortune, achieve much, there is no hope so solid as that bottomed upon an honest, thorough-paced knowledge of the science. It is better than talent—but it helps talent—it is fuel for its fires, a lamp to its feet, and a staff of strength in its right hand.

PUBLIC ECONOMY OF ATHENS.*

The Public Economy of Athens, in four books; to which is added a dissertation on the Silver-Mines of Laurion. Translated from the German of Augustus Boeckh. *London.* 1828.

In his preface to this work, (which was first published at Berlin in 1817,) Professor Boeckh, as we are informed by the translator, pronounced the knowledge of the ancient history of Greece to be still in its infancy. The observation, we have no doubt at all, is perfectly just. It is but of late years, and first and principally in the universities of Germany, that the researches of scholars have been directed by the spirit of a distinguishing and comprehensive philosophy. They have made dicoveries in fields of inquiry which one would have thought exhausted long ago. They have poured out a flood of light upon every controverted point, and, on the other hand, have shaken many an established dogma, and exposed many a consecrated error. They were not content to learn their lessons by rote, with implicit acquiescence as was the fashion even with very erudite men, a century ago. They took it for granted, or to speak more properly, they reasonably concluded, from what the genius and judgments of the ancients had done in every variety of intellectual achievement, that what appears incongruous and absurd in their institutions or their conduct and opinions, is not so in reality, that the presumption against our knowledge is stronger than against their sense, and that we ought to have a care how we indulge our supercilious fancies with regard to such men, lest we incur the old censure of the *damnat quod non intelligit*. It is quite inconceivable to those, who have not looked narrowly into such matters, what a revolution this school of philosophical erudition has brought about in them. Examples might easily be cited in every department of literature—but we will confine ourselves to one about which we are now principally concerned—that of historical criticism. Their inquiries in this branch of learning have united two things that were very rarely found together before, immense erudition, with acute scepticism and discriminating judgment. It is very clear that, in the hands of such men,

[* When I wrote this article I had not read Niebuhr's *prologomena* to his history, with which my introductory remarks sometimes so strangely coincide.—Brussels, November 10th, 1834.]

classical studies afford scope even now for the highest order of minds. Far from being worn out, the soil has not been well enough cultivated to bear its best fruits, and mines of unexplored wealth lie hidden beneath the surface, which has been for centuries together (so to express it) the great highway and thoroughfare of scholars.

Much that has been said in disparagement of this branch of study has been provoked, and in some measure warranted, by this singular fact. But the objection, however plausible, was obviously not well founded. The complaint was that too much time had been bestowed upon the remains of antiquity—that scholars knew too much of the remote past, and too little of present interests and existing institutions. The truth is, however, that they never have known enough of that past—their fault has been not an excess, but a deficiency of solid learning. So far, indeed, as taste and style were objects of their discipline, they were eminently successful, for nothing can surpass the elegance of such writers as Lambinus and Muretus, or Addison and Atterbury. So, too, in the mere accumulation of facts or figments and data—the gross amount of acquirement, if we may so express it—the erudite men of the sixteenth and seventeenth centuries, the Scaligers, the Casaubons, the Salmasius', the Gronovius', have not been surpassed, if they have been equalled, by their successors. But they were not philosophers, and that is saying every thing—they were not even critics, in the highest sense of the word—they were, in most essential matters, as ignorant and prejudiced as their vulgar contemporaries, who spoke no language but their mother tongue, and had little knowledge of any thing beyond the legends of the nursery. Men of shining abilities many of them were, but the whole discipline of their schools, as the temper of the times was unfavourable to those inquiries, which enable us to distinguish what is true or probable, from what is merely mythical and fictitious in the traditions of the past—to look through the sign to the thing signified, through accidental forms to the enduring substance of things, through bizarre and arbitrary customs to the true genius and spirit of laws and institutions. They looked upon the vast mass—owing to the loss of so many libraries and other monuments, a mutilated, undigested and shapeless mass—of antiquities that lay before them, with the eyes of verbal grammarians, or slavish compilers, or at best, of mere laborious archæologists. The view they presented of the history and society, and even literature of the Greeks, was altogether unsatisfactory in theory, because not agreeable to the experience of mankind in other times and countries. Still less was it safe to reply upon it in practice, because practice calls for precise information, and it is in practical matters especially that a "little knowledge" and still more erroneous and perverted, or even superficial views are a "dangerous thing."* Thus, they could repeat Livy's history, it may be, by heart, and let out a deluge of learning, pertinent or otherwise, upon each disputed reading; but did they think of asking how far the whole story was credible, and what reliance was to be had upon it as a record of man's experience? So, they wrote diatribes upon the democratical and oligarchical parties, upon the influence and contests of Athens or of Lacedæmon, and yet we venture to say, in our author's language, that their knowledge of the polity and social state of those nations was still in its infancy. Even in mere literary researches there is the same want of a philosophical spirit. Their learned dissertations, for instance, upon the Athenian theatre, were satisfactory enough as to mere externals, the mask and the mummery, the costume and the chorus, but what have they written of the drama of Sophocles or Aristophanes that is at all worthy of the subject, or even to be compared with the more recent speculations of Schlegel?

The truth is that, considering the state in which the remains of antiquity are come down to us, to acquire the kind of knowledge, which every enlightened man ought to aim at in such things, requires much more than industry. A wary judgment—a penetrating sagacity—an enlarged understanding—a fertile and even inventive genius must be exercised, and all the results of modern science be brought to bear upon the materials of an erudition at once exact and immense. The scholar must be able to turn every hint to account—to gather the most scattered fragments that relate to each other and put them together, like a dissected map. The science and skill of the comparative anatomist, who can sketch the form of the whole animal from a single bone, must be his. † His business is to re-construct the fabric of Greek society—to give the body of those times its very form and pressure—to enable us clearly to perceive how far their institutions and opinions agreed with our own, or differed from them— to reveal to us the secrets of their thoughts, to translate the very language of their affections into our modern tongues, to make them objects of sympathy, and examples for conduct to us—in short, to bring their little world before us, not as an empty pageant, or a wild phantasmagoria, having neither relation nor resemblance to the things about us, but with all the force and impressiveness of a sober and ascertained, yet vivid and living reality. Unfortunately the men who had the minds best fitted for such investigations, have, in general, been destitute of the

---

* Macchiavelli's incomparable *Discourses* would seem to refute what is here said. But they do not. The Cyropœdia or any other figment would have answered his purpose as well. He wanted only a *canvass.*

[† This very illustration is used by Niebuhr. Römische Geschichte. v. 3. p. 135.]

necessary erudition. Bayle is the only exception that occurs to us; but even he was too much absorbed in metaphysics and theology to do much as a historical critic. Hume's essay on the "Populousness of Ancient Nations" is a very promising performance, but it only shews what that great writer might have done had the fashion of the times—hostile to all learning—or his own indolent disposition, permitted him to inform himself sufficiently on any subject requiring much research. As for the rest of the philosophers of the eighteenth century, with all their unquestionable talents, and their enlarged, and, in the main, just views of society and human nature, they were universally as ill qualified for such inquiries as Hume. Nothing can be more ridiculously superficial and absurd than Voltaire's notions about Greek literature, and nothing but his inimitable wit could have saved them from the contempt they deserve.

But a knowledge of the whole body of Greek history can only be attained by fully investigating some subordinate departments of it; and the work now under review is offered by Mr. Boeckh as a compilation of that sort. The subject treated of is a very important one, and hitherto but little understood, and we are glad that it has fallen into the hands of a master. On many difficult and disputable points the reader may see cause to differ with the author—even on such points, however, we are mistaken if he will not dissent with hesitation and deference— while there is not a subdivision of the inquiry which does not call forth a profusion of the most accurate learning, controlled and directed by the soundest criticism. The translator laments indeed that his author is not sufficiently versed in political economy and that, with some unimportant exceptions, there is scarcely any thing in the book which a well educated Grecian of the time of Aristotle might not have written. There is something in the objection undoubtedly, but it is too strongly put and too much insisted on. We cannot perceive how "the value of the first book, either considered by itself, or as a ground-work for his subsequent researches, has been thus diminished," though we admit that it would have given an additional interest and finish to his discussions on prices, profits, wages, &c., if his great diligence and accuracy in collecting the materials had been helped by a more scientific arrangement and vocabulary. After all, however, this defect is one rather of form than substance; and although Mr. Boeckh may not be as much of a political economist, as it were desirable he should be, it is going too far to speak of him as wanting the lights of modern science. It would have been impossible for any one, who had not profoundly reflected upon the whole frame and constitution of society as it is treated of by modern publicists, to have conceived the plan of such a work. He has brought together (generally speaking) all the *data* necessary to form a complete idea of the Public Economy of Athens and he has discussed them with judgment and ability. A writer of a more speculative turn might, out of such materials, have made a different book, or, it may be, several different books (for such things present themselves in various aspects to various minds), but surely that does not diminish the value of the volumes before us.

The work is divided into four books. The first relates to prices and property in Athens. It is, of course, very miscellaneous, treating of the precious metals—their quantity and value—of the population and extent of Attica—of agriculture and commerce—of the lands, mines, houses, slaves, cattle, corn and bread, wine, oil, salt, wood—of food, dress, furniture and implements of all kinds—of the sum necessary for the maintenance of life and the proportion of the same to the national wealth—of the wages of labour, the interest of money, money-changers and mortgages of land—of bottomry, rent, &c. The subject of the second is the public expenditure. The last two books are a most learned and elaborate exposition of the ways and means to meet that expenditure—the revenues, regular and extraordinary, of the Athenian State, and of the peculiar financial measures of the Greeks. At the beginning of the third book, the author remarks that in the inquiries involved in the latter half of his work he had been nearly unassisted by the labours of any predecessor, with the exception of what had been written on the subject of the Liturgies, and what Manso, (Sparta, vol. ii. pp. 493–5) had adduced in reference to the period of the Peloponnesian war. Yet, by this voyage of discovery into regions so entirely unexplored, he has accomplished the most important results, while he pursues his course in the midst of all the difficulties and perplexities incident to such an enterprise, with the steadiness and assurance of practised skill.

The science of political economy cannot properly be said to have existed at all among the ancients. In the Economics, attributed, falsely it is thought, to Aristotle, the *word* occurs, but nothing more, for the few brief and imperfect remarks about revenue and taxation it contains, under that head, surely deserve no serious consideration. Yet rules for practice, as Mr. Boeckh observes, were not wanting, and these varied in complexity and importance, according to the situation of different States, or of the same State at different times. Sparta, for instance, with her simple form of government, and a fundamental policy calculated rather for security and defence, than for foreign conquest and colonial dominion, had but little occasion for a regular system of finance. It was not so with Athens; and, in that city, from the end of the Persian war, when she became the head of a great confederacy, until she lost her national independence under the successors of Alexander, the Public Economy of Greece is seen upon its largest scale. It is, therefore, to the interval between those two epochs that Mr. Boeckh has confined his inquiries— touching only occasionally upon the events of earlier or later times, and the affairs of other States. Even within the period referred to, however, the financial system of the first of Greek commonwealths was (as every reader of these volumes must perceive) extremely irregular and imperfect.

We do not think we can better consult the interests of the general reader than by extracting from the first book several passages throwing much light upon some subjects of perpetual occurrence in this department of study, with which it is, therefore, important that he should be as familiar as possible.

The value of the Athenian coins is thus settled :

"Coined metal, or money, is, as well as uncoined metal, a commodity; and it is obvious that in the ancient days of Greece, as well as in modern times, it would be an object of trade with the money-changers. If we exclude the arbitrary value which individual states are able to give to a particular kind of coin for the use of their own citizens, the current value of money is determined by the fineness of the standard: and upon this point, in reference to the Greeks, and to Athens in particular, I will only say so much as appears necessary to make what follows intelligible to the reader. In Attica, and in almost all the Grecian states, and even out of Greece, the talent contained 60 minas, the mina 100 drachmas, the drachma 6 oboli. At Athens the obolus was divided into 8 chalcûs, and the chalcûs into 7 lepta. As far as the half obolus downwards, the Athenian money was generally coined in silver : the dichalcon, or ¼ obolus, either in silver or copper; the chalcûs, and the smaller coins, only in copper. Upon a single occasion, in the early times of the Republic, copper was coined instead of silver, probably oboli, but they did not long remain in circulation. When in later writers, in Lucian for instance, we read of copper oboli, they should not on any account be considered as ancient Athenian money. Among the larger silver coins, the tetradrachms are the most common, called also staters. The value of the Attic silver talent has been differently determined by different writers, as they set out upon the weight and fineness of different tetradrachms ; for all agree that the early coins are better than the more recent. According to the enquiries of Barthélemy, which seem preferable to those of Eckhel, the ancient tetradrachms, coined in the flourishing times of Athens, weigh 328 Paris grains, (nearly 269 Troy grains, i. e. about 67¼ to a drachma,) if we reckon in four grains, which they might have lost by wear in the course of so many centuries. The silver is nearly pure, for Athens did not, like other states, alloy it with lead or copper, on which account this money was particularly valued, and every where exchanged with profit. It appears, however, probable that the average was not so high as represented by Barthélemy, even without allowing four grains for wear ; and that it is safer to take the Attic drachma at 65 Troy grains; which, as the shilling contains about 80¾ grains pure silver, is nearly equal to 9⅔d. of English coinage; whence the mina amounts to £4 0s. 6⅔d. and the talent to £241 13s. 4d. It may be moreover observed that, as the Romans reckoned in sesterces, so the Greeks generally reckoned in drachmas; and where a sum is mentioned in the Attic writers, without any specification of the unit, drachmas are always meant." pp. 23-26.

Again—

"The ancient writers frequently reckon in Euobic talents, which appear to have come into use in the Italian colonies of Magna Græcia, chiefly on account of the spreading of the Chalcideans, and which for that reason frequently occur in the treaties of the Romans with other nations, as well as in Herodotus, who evidently composed or altered many parts of his history after his migration to Thurii." pp. 27, 28.

"As to the Euboic talent, Herodotus, if the present reading is correct, reckons that the Babylonian talent contained 70 Euboic minas, Pollux 7000 Attic drachmas. Here then the Attic and Euboic talents are considered as equal. According to Ælian, on the contrary, the Babylonian talent contained 72 Attic minas, a statement which is evidently of more weight than the uncertain account of Pollux; and it thence follows that the Euboic talent was somewhat greater than the Attic. At the same time this statement may not be mathematically accurate; for, according to it the Attic talent is to the Euboic as $72\frac{1}{2}$ to 75 (70 to 72,) agreeably to Herodotus' computation of the Babylonian talent in Euboic minas. It is probable, however, that Solon, when he wished so to change the Attic money, that 100 drachmas should be coined from the same quantity of silver as had formerly been made into 75, intended to make the Attic silver talent equal to the Euboic, which had been for a long time in general circulation. According to this supposition, the Euboic talent would, before the time of Solon, have been to the Attic talent in the ratio of 75 to 100. Since, however, the money of Solon proved actually to be the ancient Attic money in the ratio of $72\frac{32}{99}$ to 100, strictly speaking, the new Attic silver talent must have been to the Euboic as $72\frac{32}{99}$ to 75, that is, as 70 to $72\frac{9}{20}$: but as, upon an average, the new Attic was to the old Attic talent as 73 to 100, in the same manner it might be assumed that the proportion of the new Attic to the Euboic was, in round numbers, as 73 to 75, which nearly coincides with the ratio obtained from Herodotus and Ælian, of $72\frac{1}{2}$ to 75, or 70 to 72." pp. 30, 31.

The proportion of gold to silver in ancient times appears to have been most generally as ten to one. This ratio, Mr. Boeckh remarks, seems rather low, considering the scarcity of gold in early times. The price of it, however, gradually rose, partly on account of the proportionally greater increase of silver, until it came to be (subject to occasional variations) $13\frac{1}{2}$ and even 15 to 1—as in modern Europe.

The following passage is worthy of consideration:

"The meaning of the terms talent and mina, when applied to gold, has been frequently a subject of enquiry. According to Pollux, the gold stater was equal in value to a mina; a statement which seems wholly inexplicable, unless, with Rambach, we understand gold coins of eight or ten drachmas in weight, which would certainly agree with the value of a silver mina. But Pollux is speaking with particular reference to the common gold stater of two drachmas in weight; unless then he confuses the entire question, according to some method or other of computing, a weight of two drachmas of gold must have been called a mina. That, however, in speaking of gold, an entirely different language must have existed, is probable from the circumstance that the same grammarian in two other places calls three Attic gold staters, or a chrysûs, a talent of gold. The reason which prevents me from receiving the emendation proposed by Salmasius is that Pollux repeats the same statement twice. I am therefore inclined to follow the opinion of J. F. Gronov, that a weight of six drachmas of gold was called a talent, according to an idiom customary upon certain occasions, perhaps, as it has been conjectured, because this was the value of a talent of copper, the ratio of gold to copper being as 1000 to 1. This small gold talent could only have contained three minas, each two drachmas in weight. This supposition is completely established by the fact of the talent of Thyateira being equal to three gold staters: and Eustathius even calls two chrysûs, and Hero of Alexandria one chrysûs, a talent. Probably the goldsmith reckoned by these small talents; and when we read of golden crowns of many talents in weight, this smaller kind is doubtless intended. Who can believe that the Carthaginians presented to Damarete a crown of a hundred talents of gold, if a talent of gold were the usual weight of the silver talent, or even only a portion of gold equal in weight to the value of the silver talent? Are we to suppose that the inhabitants of the Chersonese would have given a crown of 60 talents to the senate and people of the Athenians, if the silver and gold talents were of the same weight? and how vast must the size of such crowns have been? And even if we suppose that 100 talents of gold were equal to 600 gold drachmas, and 60 talents of gold to 360 drachmas, these crowns still remain of considerable weight. Excepting the crown of Jupiter at Tarracona, 15lbs. in weight, and that which the Carthaginians sent to the Capitoline Jupiter in the year of the city 412, of 25lbs. of gold (1875 Attic drachmas,) and the immense one in the time of Ptolemy Philadelphus, of 10,000 gold staters (which, at a festival in the time of that king, was laid upon the throne of Ptolemy Soter,) together with another, 80 cubits in length, of gold and precious stones, I find no example of such large crowns as those two were, even if they only weighed 600 and 360 drachmas. In the Acropolis of Athens there were golden crowns of 17½, 18½, of 20, and 25 drachmas or rather more; also another of 26½; four of which the joint weight was 135½ drachmas; one of 29, others of 33, 59, and 85 drachmas. A crown, which the celebrated Lysander sent as a sacred offering to the Parthenon of Athens, weighed 66 drachmas 5 oboli. Two crowns, honorary gifts to Minerva of the Acropolis, weighed, the one 245 drachmas 1½ oboli, the other 272 drachmas 3½ oboli. Another for the same goddess weighed 232 drachmas 5 oboli. A crown, dedicated to the Delphian Apollo at the great festival which was celebrated every fourth year, cost only 1500 drachmas of silver; and, consequently, if the workmanship is estimated at the lowest possible rate, can hardly have weighed a hundred drachmas of gold. According to these facts, then, the talents, in which the weight of the Carthaginian and Chersonetan crowns is stated, must have been small talents of six drachmas of gold. Yet there can be no question but that as much gold, as was equal to the value of a silver talent, is often called a talent of gold: as also that a quantity of gold weighing 6000 drachmas was known by the same name; which therefore in this case is manifestly independent of any relation to the value of silver." pp. 37–40.

The area of Attica, calculated according to the map of Barbié du Bocage, published in 1811, is (including Salamis and Helena, the former containing twenty-six, the latter five square miles,) six hundred and fifty-six English square miles. Taking the English geographical mile to the statute mile as four to three, the whole area of Attica, including those islands, would be only eight hundred and seventy-four square miles—something more than the one-thirtieth part of the small State of South-Carolina, and much less than the single district of Charleston. This small space is admitted on all hands to have been well peopled, but there has been some diversity of opinion as to the precise amount of its population. That the number of citizens, who were entitled to receive compensation for assisting at the public assemblies, was thirty thousand, was generally assumed from the time of the Persian to the end of the Peloponnesian war. This appears from a passage which we had occasion to cite, on a former occasion, from the Ecclesiazusæ of Aristophanes,* and some other authorities, to the same effect, have been added by our author. He thinks, however, that this was an exaggeration, and, after collating and examining a number of texts which have a bearing upon the subject, adopts the usual mean average of twenty thousand. The following passage embodies the result of this very able and interesting discussion:

"Soon after this an enumeration of the people occurs, which is the very one to which the number, mentioned in Plutarch, of the citizens who remained and were disfranchised in the reign of Antipater, was adapted. It was carried on by Demetrius Phalereus when Archon in Olymp. 117.4. and yielded, according to Ctesicles, 21,000 citizens, 10,000 resident aliens, and 400,000 slaves. From this very important statement the whole number of the population of Attica has been variously determined. According to the usual rule of Statistics, the adults have been generally taken as a fourth part of the population. This gave for the citizens 84,000, and for the aliens 40,000. But when they came to the slaves, these calculators fell into an embarrassment: for, according to the same or somewhat lower proportion, their number came out far above what could be deemed probable. Hume, wishing to shew that the population of ancient times has been greatly overrated, contends with many reasons against this number of slaves, and ends by substituting 40,000 in the place of 400,000 whom he considers as the adults, to which it would be then necessary to add the women and children. But his arguments are partly inconclusive, and partly founded upon false suppositions. Thus all that he says concerning the national wealth of Attica, that it was only equal to 6000 talents, is completely false; and, in the next place, slaves were not computed by adults or fathers of families, which is a term wholly inapplicable to slaves, but they were counted, like sheep or cattle, by the head, and were regarded in the same light with property, as Gillies has already observed, for they were in the strictest sense a personal possession, 400,000 is therefore the sum total of the slaves; and the population of Attica would amount, on this supposition, to 524,000 souls. Wallace's computation is higher, for he makes the whole population amount to more than 580,000, and Sainte Croix goes as far as 639,500. The latter writer erroneously adds 100,000 children to the number of slaves, and likewise 4½ and not 4 for every male adult or father of a family, so that the free as well as the slave population is made more numerous. As however this proportion appears to be more correct for southern countries, the citizens with their families may be fairly taken at 94,500 and the resident aliens at 45,000. In order however not to proceed solely upon the period of Demetrius, but upon the mean average of 20,000 citizens, I reckon only 90,000 free inhabitants and 45,000

* Ve. 1124. Southern Review, No. 4,—Art. Rom. Orators.

resident aliens. With regard to the total amount of slaves, it is stated too much in round numbers for perfect accuracy; the historian doubtless added whatever was wanting to complete the last hundred thousand, although the correct number might not have been so great by several thousands. It will be sufficient to reckon 365,000 slaves together with women and children, which latter however were proportionally few. Adding to these 135,000 free inhabitants, we may take as a mean average of the population 500,000 in round numbers; of whom the larger proportion were men, since fewer female than male slaves were kept, and not many slaves were married." pp. 50-52.

The distribution of this population, which is the next object of inquiry, is involved in as much difficulty as its amount. The circumference of Athens, including the Piræus and Phalerum, was equal to two hundred stadii, and the city itself contained ten thousand houses. In general, only one family lived in a house, and Mr. Boeckh, on the authority of Xenophon (Soc. Mem. ii. 7. 2.) takes a family of fourteen free persons to have been a large one. There were συνοιχίαι, however, which—whether we interpret the word as meaning *lodging-houses*, or a collection of houses—contained a greater number of inhabitants, and the factories of various sorts, for which Athens was renowned, were, no doubt, filled with many hundred of slaves. The mines, too, were in a space sixty stadii wide, and are known to have been worked by a vast multitude of hands. For these our author allows twenty thousand people, and to the city and the two seaports, one hundred and eighty thousand—two hundred thousand for the thirty-two square miles included within both. There then remain three hundred thousand for the other six hundred and eight square miles—which gives something less than four hundred and ninety-three and a half to a square mile. This is an immense population—but Mr. Boeckh thinks that, considering the number of small towns or market places, villages and farms in Attica, it is not to be wondered at. Since the publication of his work, (as we are informed by the translator) this whole subject has been examined by several writers, one of whom concurs very nearly with our author, another[*] differs so widely as to set down the whole population of Attica at only two hundred and twenty thousand; but the reasonings of the latter are glaringly inconclusive, and his positions wholly untenable.

If the estimate of Mr. Boeckh is to be relied on, the supplying such a population with food must have been one of the most serious and pressing concerns of State, and accordingly we find that the corn-laws of Attica were remarkable for a most jealous spirit and a stern and even tyrannical severity of enactment. Admitting, as our author alleges, that the soil of Attica was not quite so sterile as has been generally supposed, still it is certain

[*] M. Lebronne—Mémoires de l'Académie des Belles Lettres. Tom. vi.

that eight hundred thousand medimni (about twelve hundred thousand bushels) of foreign corn were imported into Athens.* We are not to wonder, therefore, that, in an age when the great truths of Political Economy were wholly unknown even to philosophers, legislators adopted what our author is pleased to call "judicious arrangements" to prevent the scarcity with which the country was always threatened.   Not to speak of the expenses incurred for fortifications and convoy-fleets, with a view to the protection of the corn-trade, the exportation of all grain was absolutely prohibited.   Two-thirds of the corn imported into the Piræus were required to be brought to Athens—that is to say, only one-third could be sent away to other countries.   Engrossing was laid under severe restrictions.   The buying more than a certain quantity of corn at a time was prohibited on pain of death, and purchasers were compelled to resell at an advance of only an obolus on the medimnus.   This sort of people were very odious at Athens, and Mr. Boeckh expresses himself in regard to them with an earnestness of censure that is quite diverting.   This particular branch of trade—instead of being, like all other commodities, under the inspection of the Agoranomis,—was committed to an especial magistracy, the Sitophylaces, and, to insure or increase the importation of corn, there was a general law that no money should be lent upon any vessel which would not bring back to Athens a return cargo of corn, and that no Athenian should ship corn to any other market.†

With regard to this last law there is a difference of opinion between Salmasius and Mr. Boeckh, which we advert to here because it has an important bearing upon a question we are about to discuss.   Salmasius thinks that it refers exclusively to the corn-trade, and we confess that we were strongly inclined to agree with him, until we read over again the oration of Demosthenes against Lacritus, upon which he relies.   The words of the statute are cited by Mr. Boeckh.   He thinks it apparent, on the very face of it, independently of some cogent reasons which he adduces to establish the inference, that this oppressive regulation extended to all contracts of the kind (bottomry or respondentia) whatever might be the subject of them.   The words of the law itself might bear another construction, but we are constrained to admit that no other interpretation than Mr.

---

* Demosth. in Leptin.   Mr. Boeckh states it at a million of medimni—equal to a third part of the whole consumption.

† ἴσε γὰρ δήπου, ὦἄνδρες δίκαςοὶ, τον νόμον ὡς χαλεπός ἐςιν, ἐάν τις 'Αθηναιων ἄλλοσέ πη σιτηγήση η Αθήναζε, ἤ χρήματα δανείση εις ἄλλο τι ἐμπόριον ἤ τὸ 'Αθηναίων, οἱαι ζημίαι περι του'των εισιν, ὡς μεγάλαι και δειναι.   Demosth. in Lacrit. 941.

The client of Demosthenes might well characterize such a statute as χαλεπός.

Boeckh's is consistent with the context of the speech and the case of Lacritus itself. It is greatly to be regretted that the other heads of the statute, which are alluded to in this pleading, are not extant. As it is, we are left to conjecture what could have been the object of so odious an enactment. Why should the State prohibit contracts of *fœnus nauticum,* where the return-cargo was to be delivered at any other port than that of Athens? We confess that, notwithstanding the words of the law and the speech referred to are comprehensive enough, as we have said, to include all contracts of the kind, we strongly suspect the motive of the lawgiver to have been some indirect encouragement of the corn-trade, and that he thus acted on a high ground of public policy. This leads us to the point which we intimated, just now, our purpose to discuss.

Was freedom of trade the standing policy of Athens? And if it was, was it so upon principle, or only because the simple and elegant reason of the Greeks had not gone deep enough into the theory of social life to discover the benefits of a system of monopoly and exclusion? There are those who talk of a Romantic or Gothic school in literature as contradistinguished from the classical. It would be curious to trace a similar contrast in matters of philosophy and government, and to shew that we are indebted, for the barbarous, narrow-minded, narrow-hearted, unchristian restrictions to which the intercourse of mankind, and the exchange of the common blessings of nature have been subjected in modern times, to an age of darkness, anarchy and violence, when the poverty of necessitous kings compelled them to traffick away to the burgers of petty corporations the right to truck and huckster in their turn, at the expense of every body else, upon their own terms,* and to transmit the same fraudulent privileges and selfish spirit to their successors, even down to this period of universal illumination. In this connection, we quote the following passage :

"Among the many proposals for the advancement of commerce, which Xenophon makes in his Treatise upon the Revenues,† there is no where an exhortation to restore the freedom of trade: either this was not one of the points which lay within the knowledge of antiquity ; or it must have existed without any limit. The latter supposition is nearly maintained by Heeren: "they were ignorant," says he, "of a balance of trade, and thus all the violent measures that flow from it naturally remained unknown. They had custom-duties as well as ourselves ; but their only object was to increase the revenues of the state, and not, as with modern nations, by prohibiting this or that article, to give a particular direction to the course of industry. You will find no prohibition to export raw produce. no encour-

*See the instance adduced by Hallam. Mid. Ages. v. i. p. 165 and seq.
[†Read and meditate the 3d Chap. of this Treat. of Xenophon, which seems to me quite conclusive upon the subject of the balance of trade and the exportation of the precious metals, which, it is, obvious the Athenians considered as an evil. Πορoι.γ.]

agement of manufactures at the cost of the agricultural classes. In this sense then there was a complete freedom of industry, of commerce, and of intercourse. And this was not the result of accident, but was founded upon principle. At the same time, where every thing was determined according to circumstances, not according to theory, persons may find individual exceptions, perhaps discover particular cases in which the state may for a time have assumed to itself a monopoly. But yet what a wide difference is there between this and our mercantile and compulsory system." I am ready to acknowledge that there is a great deal of truth in these remarks; but the other side of the question must also be considered. According to the principles of the ancients, which were not merely scientific, but were recognised by the whole of the people, and deeply rooted in the nature of the Greeks, the state embraced and governed all dealings between man and man. Not in Crete and Lacedæmon alone, two states completely closed up and from their position unsusceptible of free trade, but generally throughout the whole of Greece, and even under the free and republican government of Athens, the poorest as well as the richest citizen was convinced that the state had the right of claiming the whole property of every individual : any restriction in the transfer of this property, regulated according to circumstances, was looked upon as just ; *nor could it properly be considered an infringement of justice, before the security of persons and property was held to be the sole object of government ; a light under which it never was viewed by any of the ancients.* On the contrary, all intercourse and commerce were considered as being under the direction of the community, inasmuch as they originally owed their existence to the establishment of a regular political union : and upon the same basis was founded the right of the state to regulate trade, or even to participate in the profits of it.* Any person who dissented from these principles was not a member of the state, and would by the bare avowal be considered as detaching himself from it. It was upon the same principle that the national monopolies were founded which do not appear to have been unfrequent in Greece, although of short duration ; their productiveness had been tried in the cases of private individuals who had obtained them by engrossing particular articles." pp. 71–73.

There is much good sense in these observations of Mr. Boeckh, and the lines printed in italics, especially, are as profound as they are just. He proceeds to adduce a variety of instances which go to shew how far the government felt itself authorized, upon any notion of State-necessity or of mere expediency, to interfere with the rights and interests of individuals. Among others, he cites the law just now referred to, disannulling or avoiding contracts of *fænus nauticum* (bottomry and respondentia) if the return-cargo were not shipped for Athens. We have already spoken to that case, and we will add, with regard to most of the others, that they are political, not commercial or economical measures. Some of them, for example, proceed upon the principles of contraband of war. Such as the prohibiting the exportation, to the Peloponnesus, of timber, tar, wax, rigging, and leather,†

[*Property *pub. juris*—trade disgraceful.]

[† ασκωματα, leather used for oars, etc. Athenæ xi., cvii., cites Herod. lv. The Argives and Æginetæ bound themselves to use nothing Attic. μη δε κεραμον, αλλ' εκ χυτριδων επιχωριων το λοιπον αυτοθι ειναι πειναι.]

articles which were particularly important, as our author remarks for the building and equipment of fleets. We think this quite plain from the very text which he cites,* and, even if the prohibition were not confined to a case of actual or proclaimed hostilities, what was the whole existence of Athens but war in fact, or "in procinct"—especially in her relations with Lacedæmon and its dependencies? Others of the restrictions mentioned were intended to operate in the way of *non-intercourse*, as coercive measures, such as the famous decree of Pericles against the people of Megara, upon which Dicæopolis comments, with such effect, in the Acharnenses† of the comic poet just referred to. The policy of the corn-laws has already been the subject of remark, and there were cases in which certain branches of commerce were prohibited or restrained upon grounds of morality or religion.‡ So, it is true that inland traffic and the daily business of the markets were laid under many restrictions with a view to police, which, according to the same high-prerogative notions of the ancients, in matters of government, meddled with things of the kind, if with nothing else. The ideal commonwealths of the philosophers, in which scarcely any thing is left *unregulated* sufficiently attest their opinions, at least as to the *right* of a body politic to control the pursuits of its members. There is a remarkable passage in Plato de Legibus,§ which seems to have escaped Mr. Boeckh, but which furnishes an illustration exceedingly apposite in every view of this subject. In this second commonwealth (as it is called) the philosopher distinctly declares that there shall be no duties either on imports or exports—yet, he immediately adds that the importation of frankincense and other costly perfumes, fetched from distant countries for the sacrifices, and purple and foreign dyes, and the materials of arts, that minister to luxury, shall be altogether prohibited, as also the exportation of things that are necessary at home (corn, we suppose, for instance). So the trade in arms, and the implements and munitions of war, was to be committed to the special care and discretion of certain military officers of high rank. He then goes on to lay down rules for the government of the retailers in the markets, which would be not a little irksome and offensive in a *real* commonwealth.

Upon the whole, it seems to be a fair inference from all the *data* which we possess that free-trade, as such, was the policy—the systematic *economical* policy—of the Athenians, but that the power of government to interfere with all the concerns of the citizen, in the most absolute and arbitrary manner, was impli-

---

* Aristoph. Ran. 360–363. We have Brunck's edition which is without the Scholia. The line immediately following those cited by Boeckh, is as follows:
ἢ χρήματα ταῖς τῶν ἀντιπάλων ναυσὶν παρέχειν τινὰ πείθει. v. 364.

† Acharnens. 510–538.   ‡ Herod, L. v. 83.   § De Legib. l. viii. sub fin.

citly admitted, and that this power was, in fact, often exercised to the great detriment of commerce. It might seem strange that a power, so despotic and dangerous, was not only conceded to the body politic, or, which is the same thing, to the majority, real or constructive, of the body politic, or, which is still the same thing, more accurately expressed, according to the experience of mankind, to the reigning Demagogue of the day, if we did not know that Demus had as high a notion of his prerogatives as any other monarch, and that it is but in our own times that the true theory of government—that which calls upon it for nothing but protection from force and fraud—has begun to be received even among educated people. Mr. Boeckh is right in saying that freedom of trade depends upon precisely the same principles as the security of private property and exemption from unnecessary, and therefore, oppressive and vexatious legislation. The tyrannical prerogative of the Eminent Domain, the right of appropriating to the use of the public or otherwise disposing of the substance of any individual member of the society, without his consent and without making full compensation for it—is at the bottom of all these abuses. The right has been universally admitted by publicists, and, in cases of extreme necessity, no doubt, does exist, because the *salus populi* must be preferred to all personal considerations. But necessity is always an exception, and our constitutions, in requiring government to make compensation, in every case, for any trespass which it may have been constrained to commit upon the property or the rights of individuals, have disavowed the most odious privilege of this despotism, and consecrated, in a solemn manner, a high canon of political justice. Yet there is much to be done to perfect the scheme of a free commonwealth, even in this favored land. We must disavow that other privilege, which the philosophers of antiquity conceded to the body-politic—we must declare all legislation which is not necessary, to be *ipso facto* oppressive and therefore unconstitutional. With regard especially to restrictions on commerce, imposed with a view to foster domestic industry, they are, if there be any virtue in political economy, the exercise of a power which no free government can be supposed to possess without a contradiction in terms—a power to levy a tax without an adequate object—to take away a greater amount of property from some classes in order to secure, without any benefit to the public, a smaller amount of property to others. It does appear to us to be the veriest solecism in politics to talk of such measures as consistent with any constitution written or unwritten, of which the object is the happiness of the governed, and not the gratification of a wanton and tyrannical lust of power in the ruler. We express these sentiments with the greater emphasis at this interesting juncture, because, if we do not sadly mistake the indications of the times, they are destined soon to become the sentiments of the whole American people. We exult in a persuasion so honorable to the national character, so full of hope and promise for the future: nor do we rejoice the less, now that the whole country is beginning to ring, from side to side, with the pæans of this anticipated triumph of reason and justice, because we have uniformly lent our humble aid to promote that first, great interest of civilized society, moderation in government.*

A considerable part of the first book is taken up, as we hinted at the beginning, in retailing the prices of particular commodities in Attica, (pp. 83–147) from a comparison of which with prices in our times, the author seems to have persuaded himself that he could draw some safe conclusion, as to the relative wealth of Attica. For obvious reasons, as the translator has well observed, this collection of details is more curious and interesting than useful, at least for this purpose. It appears, however, to be a fair inference from the *data* furnished here that all commodities which come under the description of the necessaries and comforts of life were very cheap—but there were luxuries upon which taste or fashion had set an extravagant value, such, for instance, as Chian wine, and especially ointment—the dearest article, by far, in use at Athens, a cotyla of it costing from two to five minas. The price of slaves varied very widely, according to the talents, education, beauty and other personal qualities of those unfortunate people, and—since by a barbarous and detestable law of nations, all prisoners of war fell, of course, into that condition—in an age of perpetual war, the slave-market was always well supplied, and the range of choice presented to a purchaser in it, was as great as the distance between ignorance and brute nature, and the highest cultivation of taste and talent. Ordinary house-servants and slaves, who did the meanest sort of labour, sold as low as two minas. The author quotes from Lucian a ludicrous valuation of the philosophers, in which Socrates is estimated at two talents, a Peripatetic at twenty, Chrysippus at twelve, a Pythagorean at ten, Dion of Syracuse at two minas, and Philo the sceptic, at one mina—he being destined for the mill. It may be remarked here that the wages of labour were exceedingly low, and that the gangs of slaves, maintained by the wealthy, and employed in every branch of trade and manufac-

* The following passage from Cicero's Republic, which has just occured to us, deserves to be brought to the view of the reader, in this connection. It will be seen that Rome exercised the right of protection as a right of conquest, and that the first of her statesmen and philosophers regarded it as a plain violation of justice:—"Nos vero justissimi homines, *qui transalpinas gentes oleam et vitam serere non sinimus, quo pluris sint nostra olivela notræque vineæ*; quod cum faciamus, prudenter facere dicimur, *justè non* dicimur, ut intelligatis discrepare ab æquitate sapientiam." *Cic. de Repub.* lib. 3. § 9.

ture, kept the poorer citizens* out of work, and thus, reducing them to a state of absolute dependance, made them the ready instruments and accomplices of unprincipled demagogues. The same effect upon the labouring classes is noticed by Tacitus, at Rome, and it was mainly to remedy this very evil—which seems inseparable from the institution of domestic servitude, under certain circumstances—that the Gracchi undertook their "reforms." The following extract shews forth some of the consequences which we should anticipate a *priori* from such a state of things:

"The national wealth of the Athenians, exclusive of the public property and the mines, I have estimated, in a succeeding part of this work, according to a probable calculation, at from 30 to 40 thousand talents; if of this only 20,000 talents are reckoned as property paying interest, each of the 20,000 citizens would have had the interest of a talent, or, according to the ordinary rate of interest, an annual income of 720 drachmas, if property had been equally divided, which the ancient philosophers and statesmen always considered as the greatest good fortune of a State; and, with the addition of the produce of their labour, they might have been all able to live comfortably. But a considerable number of the citizens were poor; while others were possessed of great riches, who from the lowness of prices and the high rate of interest were able not only to live luxuriously, but at the same time to accumulate additional wealth, as capital increased with extreme rapidity. This inequality destroyed the State and the morals of the inhabitants. The most natural consequence of it was the servility of the poor towards the rich, although they thought that they had the same pretensions as their superiors in wealth; and the wealthy citizens practised the same canvassing for popular favour,† as was the custom at Rome, with different degrees of utility, or rather of hurtfulness. A citizen might perhaps adopt beneficial means for obtaining his end, as Cimon for example, the first man of his age, who besides his great mental qualities imitated Pisistratus‡ in leaving his lands and gardens without any keepers, and thus the produce of his farms and his house became almost the property of the public; he used also to provide cheap entertainments for the poor, to bury the indigent, to distribute small pieces of money when he went out, and to cause his attendants to change clothes with decayed citizens.§ Yet these were the very means by which the sovereign citizens were reduced to a miserable state of beggary and dependance. Even this however might have been tolerable; but, as every statesman had not the means of making such large outlays from his private fortune, and liberality to the people being necessary to purchase their favor, the distribution money at the festivals, the payment of the soldiers, the Eclesiasts, Dicasts, and senators, the costly sacrifice, and the Cleruchiæ,‖ were introduced by the demagogues: the allies were compelled to try their causes at Athens, among other reasons for producing more fees to the Dicasts, and employment for the other citizens: of every oppressive act committed against the allies public crimes were the consequence, which the demagogues pretended that they were driven to by the poverty of the people. And when the necessary consequence and punishment of their tyranny arrived in the defection of the allies, the helpless condition of the State had increased; for the multitude had forgotten their former activity, and been gradually

[* Poor citizens kept out of work by slaves—therefore an equal division of property.]

[† Servility ?   Slavery of the rich.]

[‡ Nicias.]

[§ Magnificent liberality of Cimon.]

[‖ Demagogue stock.]

accustomed to ease and refinement* ; no course therefore remained but to struggle to regain their former ascendency. Add to this the envy which the poor entertained against the rich, and the joy and readiness with which they divided their possessions†, upon which, after bribery had been tried in vain, the whole rage of the multitude vented itself. Xenophon, in his treatise upon the Revenues, understood perfectly that it was necessary to promote the welfare of individuals ; but, leaving out of the question the insufficiency of his proposals, Athens, even if her power in foreign parts could have been restored, was lost beyond all hope of recovery, as the minds of her citizens could not be so easily recalled to a state consistent with her desired prosperity." pp. 154–156.

The interest of money at Athens was not regulated by law— the lowest rate of it was, according to our author, ten—the highest thirty-six—the ordinary, from twelve to eighteen per cent. This will doubtless strike the reader as exorbitant ; and Mr. Boeckh attempts to account for it by the high profits of stock in every branch of industry. He adds, however,—what is, in our opinion, a more important consideration—that credit was at a low ebb, because, under such a government as the Athenian, no confidence could be reposed in the administration of the laws, and because, as will appear in the sequel, the immorality, the faithlessness, the libertinism of the people, both public and private, was such as it is difficult for the imagination of a modern even to conceive. Even the legislation of Solon, (which seems to have been unscrupulous enough, as Mr. Boeckh remarks,) had a tendency to produce this state of things. He abolished imprisonment for debt—we give no opinion as to that—but the famous measure of the Seisachtheia proves that the State, under his administration, had no great respect for the obligation of contracts and the security of property, whether, in our author's language, by this ordinance, merely the value of the currency was depreciated, or the rate of interest also was diminished, or whether, in certain cases, at least, a complete annihilation of all claims of debt was effected by it. Add to these difficulties of the law and of the manners, those which grew out of the situation of Attica, involved in perpetual war, and exposed to desolating inroads and ravages from enemies at her very door—sweeping away all moveable property from the face of the earth, and, of course, greatly impairing the value of land security. The consequence of such a state of things was, as the translator suggests, that there was perhaps, no such thing as *interest* properly, so called at Athens ; for interest is what the lender exacts as a remuneration for the mere *use* of his money, without taking into the account any risk or uncertainty, as to the punctual payment, according to the contract, either of interest or of principal. Another consequence was, that almost all money transactions fell

[* People corrupted by the spoils of Greece.]
[† Confiscation.]

into the hands of bankers and exchange-brokers by profession—who, besides their dealings in foreign coins at an agio, carried on an immense business in trading upon borrowed money. They were generally low fellows—freedmen, aliens, and so forth—but, by great exactness in meeting their engagements, they acquired a wonderful degree of credit, and, even in such an age and such a state of society, were common referees in matters of dispute and depositaries of the contracts and effects of others. On the other hand, they exacted the "due and forfeit" of their own bonds with the sternest rigor, and became objects of as much popular odium as usurers have been in more recent times.

We close our remarks upon this introductory book, with some extracts from our author, which show what was the ordinary rate of living at Athens.

"From the preceding particulars it is possible very nearly to determine the sum which was requisite for the maintenance of a respectable person in the best times of Athens. The most moderate person required every day for opsom one obolus, for a chœnix of corn, according to the price of barley in the age of Socrates, a quarter obolus, making altogether in a year of 360 days, 75 drachmas; and for clothes and shoes at least 15 drachmas; a family of four adults must therefore at the lowest have required 360 drachmas for the specified necessaries; which sum for the age of Demosthenes, when the price of corn was five drachmas, must be increased by about 22½ drachmas, for each person, and for four persons by about 90: to this the expense of house-room is to be added, which, if we reckon the value of a house at the lowest at three minas, taking the ordinary rate of interest of 12 per ct., gives an outlay of 36 drachmas: so that the poorest family of four free adults spent upon average from 390 to 400 drachmas a year, if they did not live upon bread and water. Socrates had two wives, not indeed at the same time, as has been fabulously reported, but one after the other; the first was Myrto, whom he married poor, and probably without a dowry; the second Xanthippe; he had three children, of whom Lamprocles at the death of his father had reached the age of manhood, while Sophronicus and Menexenus were minors; for himself, after having sacrificed his youth to unceasing endeavours after knowledge, he followed no profession, and his teaching did not produce any pecuniary return. According to Xenophon he lived upon his own property, which if it had found a good purchaser (ὠνητής) would together with the house have readily produced five minas; and he only required a small contribution from his friends: whence it has been inferred that prices were most extraordinarily low at Athens. It is, however, evident that Socrates and his family could not have lived upon the proceeds of so small a property; for, however miserable his house may have been, it cannot be estimated at less than three minas, so that, even if the furniture is not taken into consideration, the rest of his effects only amounted to two minas, and the income from them according to the ordinary rate of interest to only 24 drachmas, from which he could not have provided barley for himself and his wife, not to mention the other necessaries of life and the maintenance of his children." pp. 147, 148.

"If in the time of Socrates four persons could live upon 440 drachmas, they must have passed a very wretched existence, and to live respectably it was necessary even then, and still more in the time of Demosthenes, to be possessed of a larger income. According to the speech against Phænippus, the plaintiff and his brother inherited from their father 45 minas, upon which the orator says it was not easy to live, that is upon the interest, which according to the common rate amounts to 540 drachmas." p. 151.

"The expenses of Demosthenes himself when a youth, of his young sister and of his mother, amounted to seven minas a year, exclusively of the cost of house-rent, as they lived in their own house: but the cost of Demosthenes' education was not paid out of this sum, as it remained owing by the guardians. After Lysias has finished speaking of the fraudulent account rendered by the guardian of Diodotus' children (who for example had charged more than a talent for clothes, shoes, and hair-cutting within eight years, and more than 4000 drachmas for sacrifices and festivals, and at the termination of his office would only surrender three minas of silver and 30 Cyzicenic staters), he remarks that, "if he charges more than any person in the city ever did for two boys and a girl, a nurse•and female servant, he could not reckon more than 1000 drachmas a year;" which would give not much less than three drachmas per day. This is equal to about two shillings and three pence in our money, a sum which certainly must appear too large for three children and two female slaves in the time of Lysias. In the age of Solon an obolus must have gone very far, for that legislator prohibited any woman from carrying with her upon any procession or journey more than would buy thus much of food, together with a basket which was more than an ell long: and the Trœzenians appear to have made a liberal donation, when, according to Plutarch, they decreed to allow two oboli to every one of the old-men, women, and children, who had fled from Athens at the time of the invasion of Xerxes. But, in the flourishing times of the State, one person could live but moderately upon two or even three oboli a day; upon the whole, however, the cheapness and facility of living were considerable. From the piety of the Greeks towards the dead, the death of a man, with his funeral and monument, often cost more than many years of his life, for we find that private individuals frequently spent, for that purpose, as much as three, ten, fifteen, or even 120 minas." pp. 152–153.

Having, in the first book furnished a valuable mass of collateral preparatory information, Mr. Boeckh proceeds in the second to enter upon his subject, which he pursues to the end of his work. He first addresses himself to the *Expenditure* of the State, with regard to which he regrets that we have not the same means of attaining to precise knowledge, as with respect to its income; but which, we think, he has done much to ascertain.

A preliminary question suggests itself to the author, which is curious enough to engage the attention of our reader. "Whether, in ancient times, the operation of the financial system was of the same general and predominant importance, and exercised that influence upon the welfare and decline of nations, which it is found to possess in modern days." It may readily be admitted that the ancients had nothing which deserves the name of an elaborate and scientific system of finance. They stood not in need of such a system. Their wars—those of the Greeks, at least, at the period to which this work is confined—were sudden irruptions, mere predatory excursions, in comparison of

those of the last century and a half. If they were ever so
much prolonged,—the Peloponnesian for instance,—still each
campaign seemed, in a manner, separate from the others, as
every reader of Thucydides must have remarked.* The bud-
get of their Chancellor of the Exchequer, therefore, was a very
unceremonious affair. Hear Demosthenes tell the Athenians
how they are to fit out an expedition to Thrace or Macedo-
nia—read the still more striking, because more general and comprehensive view, which Pericles presents, of the ways and means
at the breaking out of the long war just mentioned. It is the
simplest thing in the world. The condition of Europe, under
the feudal system, is somewhat in point. The revenues of
kings at that time—all that did not spring out of their own domains—were merely the fruits and incidents of tenure. Such
an income (stinted as it was), together with the obligation of
every vassal to serve forty days in the year, might enable them
to carry on war, according to the fashion of the times, when
war looked more like a border foray and lifting of black-mail,
or a sanguinary tournament and a gorgeous pageant, than (as
we see it) a vast scheme of national ruin, concerted with the
profoundest calculation, and combining and commanding all
the resources, with which wealth and science have armed the
destructive passions of the species. Any one who will compare
the ordinary revenues of the king of England—that is to say,
the feudal dues and "flowers of prerogative" here alluded to—
with his *extraordinary* revenues, as the annual taxes paid by
his people are called in our law books, will perceive what an
immense difference there is between the exigencies they are calculated to meet. Thucydides accounts for the length of the
seige of Troy by the poverty of the beleaguerers. So mighty a
host, he thinks, would have reduced the city much more speedily, had not the greater part of it been all the while employed in
procuring supplies for the camp, by cultivating the Chersonesus,
or by plundering the islands, and the coasts of the continent.†
This was primitive enough, it must be owned, but old Cato's
saying—so much applauded in its day—that his war should
support itself, shews that, even under a government formed for
the conquest of the world, the policy of the heroic age, was not
quite obsolete.   Plunder, indeed, was at all times, a most important head in the financial system of antiquity. It is mentioned
by Xenophon, in his life of Agesilaus, that of the spoils, gathered
by that Captain in Asia, the tithe sent to the temple at Delphi
amounted to one hundred talents. And we shall see in the sequel that the rapacity and violence, which thus supplied the
Greeks with the instruments of mischief abroad, were quite as

* This is applicable, at least, to the first ten years of the war.
† Hist. l. 1 10.

much practised in the department of the interior, as in foreign war.

It is very conceivable, therefore, that the *legitimate* wants of the State were comparatively few, and supplied by coarser machinery, than in this age of vast empires and a systematic balance of power.* But we cannot admit the position, which seems to be countenanced by Mr. Boeckh, that in the commonwealths of antiquity revolutions and civil disturbances were less frequently caused by taxation (of one sort or other) than among modern nations. This is a great and fundamental error. Extortion surely does not suppose much skill in finance, and one of the most memorable struggles in the annals of the world—that which produced Magna Charta—was mainly occasioned by the exactions of the monarch and other great lords, in an age whose whole political economy may be summed up in the good old rule" and "simple plan" of Rob Roy.† Our author does not see how a revolution could have arisen in the republics of antiquity, from a refusal to pay taxes—because the imposers and the payers were the same persons. This sounds speciously enough. But what was the fact, according to his own shewing (as will presently appear) and according to the universal testimony of the ancient philosophers and historians?‡ Why, that there was a perpetual war§ between the rich and the poor—that a destitute, and, withal, a dissipated and dissolute populace, with an appetite for plunder, "wolfish, starved and ravenous," were forever breaking through the barriers of the law, to prey upon the substance of their neighbours—and that their sycophants, the demagogues, lost no opportunity of glutting their rapacity, by offerings of forfeiture and confiscation at home, and a division, with or without a pretext for hostilities, of the territory of their oppressed and subjugated allies.‖ To refer, again, to the ideal commonwealths of the philosophers. Equality of fortune seems to be considered, in all of them, as a condition indispensable to their repose. Aristotle, in his admirable strictures upon Plato's Republic, objects to a part of the plan, that it did not guard sufficiently against inequalities of property—which he declares to be a never-failing source of discord and sedition¶—while, in a passage referred to

* *Systematic*, we say, because the *idea* of a Balance of Power is too obvious not to have occurred to mankind in all ages, and in Greece it was frequently and understandingly reduced to practice. See Isocrat. ad Philip.

† Wordsworth.　　‡ Aristot. Pol. v. 5—Isocrat. de Pace—Plato, passim.

[§ War of poor on rich—Καὶ μαλιστα τῷ πλουτεῖν ἑαυτὸν υφορωμένος μη διὰ τοῦ παθη τιθειναι. Dion. Halicarn. Λεινορχ. B.—And read what Charmides says in his praise of poverty in Xenophon. Conviv. c. i. v. 29, 32. Cf. the Economics of the same. C. I—The rich were perfect *slaves*. Cf. the horrible case of the Milesian Γεριυιδαι mentioned by Athenaæ. l. 12. c. 25.]

‖ See v. ii. pp. 144, 127, 129, 172, and v. i. 289 to 292.

¶ Pol. l. ii., c. 4.

by M. Boeckh, he highly commends the scheme first introduced
by Phaleas of Chalcedon, as better calculated to correct that besetting sin of society.* We shall illustrate this subject more
fully when we come to treat of the Property Taxes, the Liturges
and the Cleruchiæ.

This book begins with a very learned inquiry concerning the
officers engaged in conducting the fiscal concerns of the government. The general administration of those concerns, subject to
the supreme legislative power of the people, was committed to
the Senate of 500. The farming of the revenues was under
its superintendence. Those who were indebted for public, or
sacred property, were bound to make payment to it. The treasurers delivered in an account of moneys received and due to
the same assembly, and it was charged even with such matters
as the salary of poets, and the support of the impotent poor. It
would not be very edifying to the general reader to mention the
numerous officers concerned in the financial department, the
more especially as it is not always easy to define their various
functions. We will only specify the Manager of the Public Revenue (ἐπιμελητὴς τῆς κοινῆς προσόδυ) a sort of Comptroller-General,
and the Hellenotamiæ, who had charge of the tributes of the
allies, or common treasury of the Athenian confederacy, to which
we shall have occasion to advert in the sequel. It is worth while
to add that every officer almost without an exception, nay, that
every person whatsoever, that had exercised any function, or been
clothed with any authority, or dignity by the State, was bound
to render in a strict account of his stewardship. If he neglected
to do so, he was not allowed to go abroad, nor to make a will,
nor to be adopted into another family, nor to dedicate offerings to
the gods, and his whole property was under a tacit hypothec to
the commonwealth, until he had undergone this examination.†
He was, besides, subject to other disabilities, as the reader may
inform himself by consulting the oration of Æschines against
Ctesiphon. Yet with all these jealous and vexatious precautions
it is lamentable to reflect upon the scene of official profligacy
exhibited in the annals of Athens.

"From what has been said it is evident that there was no want at Athens
of well-conceived and strict regulations ; but what is the use of provident
measures where the spirit of the administration is bad ? Men have at all
times been unjust and covetous and unprincipled, and above all the Greeks
distinguished themselves for the uncontrolled gratification of their own desires, and contempt for the happiness of others. If any competent judge
of moral actions will contemplate their character without prejudice, and
unbiassed by their high intellectual endowments, he will find that their
private life was unsocial, and devoid of virtue ; that their public conduct
was guided by the lowest passions and preferences ; and, what was worst
of all, that there existed a hardness and cruelty in the popular mind, and

* Ib. c. 5.   [† Xenophon.]

a want of moral principle to a far greater degree than in the Christian world.* The display of noble actions, it is true, has ceased, and will never re-appear with the same brilliancy; but the principles of the majority of mankind have been elevated, even if we allow that some distinguished individuals in ancient times were as pure as the most exalted characters of modern days; and in this general elevation consists the progress of mankind. When we consider then the principles of the Greeks, which are sufficiently seen from their historians and philosophers, it cannot be a matter of surprise that fraud was used by public officers at Athens in so great a matter as the regulation of the days: in the early times of the republic Aristides accused his contemporary Themistocles of this deceit; it was even the common opinion that there existed a certain prescriptive right to the commission of this fraud, and a person who had scruples on the subject was censured for his too great strictness. Every where we meet with instances of robberies and embezzlement of money by public officers; even the sacred property was not secure from sacrilegious hands. The Romans had at least a period in which fidelity and honesty were practised and esteemed; but among the Greeks these qualities will be sought for in vain. All officers of finance were bound by a solemn oath to administer without peculation the money entrusted to their care : "but if, in Greece," says the faithful Polybius, "the State entrusted to any one only a talent, and if it had ten checking-clerks, and as many seals and twice as many witnesses, it could not ensure his honesty." The officers of finance were therefore not unfrequently condemned to death or to loss of property and imprisonment; sometimes indeed unjustly, when money had accidentally been lost; but the Logistæ allowed themselves to be disgracefully bribed in order to enable the offender to evade the legal penalty. Even the great Pericles does not appear to have been free from the charge of peculation, if at the least the story is true which represents Alcibiades to have said, on hearing that Pericles was occupied in preparing his accounts for the people, that he would be better occupied in endeavoring to render none at all. The comic poets, who undermined the fame of every distinguished person, have also brought against him charges which are doubtless exaggerated; for example, Aristophanes in the comedy of the Clouds, misunderstands and ridicules an item in the account of Pericles which he had rendered in his capacity of general, although in this instance he was free from all blame. The truth is that he had charged ten talents without specifying the particular object to which they had been applied; but the charge was allowed by the people, as it was well known that they had been used for purposes of bribery, and that the names of those who had received them could not be mentioned without offending Pleistonax the king of Sparta, and the Harmost Cleandrides.† There is however a very general tradition that Pericles was in great difficulties with his accounts. Before the breaking out of the Peloponnesian war, Phidias the sculptor was subjected, by means, as it appears, of a conspiracy, to an examination respecting some gold which he was accused of having embezzled; on that occasion Pericles extricated himself and Phidias from the difficulty. But other attacks were made upon him for the purpose of annoyance; and at last, when the Athenians were dissatisfied with his expenditure, they required an account of his financial administration. The importance of this transaction is evident from the proceedings which were proposed for it: the account was to have been referred to Prytanes; and, according to the decree of Dracontides, the judges were to vote from the altar upon the Acropolis, which was the most solemn

[* Official profligacy—defaulters—bad morals of Greeks.]
[†Rogues all.]

method of deciding. This last ceremony was dispensed with by the interference of Hagnon, and it was directed that five hundred judges should
sit in judgment upon this case, in which was uncertain whether there
had been peculation or some other offence. In order to put an end to
this contest, in which he was in danger of falling a sacrifice to both party
rage and individual perfidy, Pericles is said to have engaged his country
in a war; a severe accusation, which however will be in some degree
diminished, if it is considered that several causes contributed, and that this
selfish motive might only have added strength to other inducements. I
am the less inclined wholly to acquit Pericles of this charge, because Aspasia is also said to have contributed to the undertaking of the Samian
war." pp. 260–263.

　The pursuits of a people, like those of an individual, are seen
in the objects of their expenditure, and the disbursements of the
public money at Athens will challenge the profound attention of
a philosophic reader. They are extremely characteristic. Pleasure, the arts, magnificence in public edifices, rewards for genius
and valour, and above all, distributions of money among the
people, under the various forms of pay, pension and bounty.
There was, to be sure, no community of goods *eo nomine* established by law—but one might suppose it the covert object of
the whole administration of affairs to bring about the same result in practice. Demus, like other kings, had his privy-purse,
as Mr. Boeckh expresses it, as well as his exchequer—and we
are not to wonder if we sometimes find every branch of the
public service stinted, every serious national interest neglected
and suffering, while a heedless and remorseless prodigality lavished the resources of the country upon the *menus plaisirs* of
that wanton and voluptuous, however elegant and refined despot.
　The regular expenditure is arranged under the following
heads:—Expenses of public buildings—police—celebration of
festivals—donations to the people—pay for certain public services in time of peace—maintenance of the poor—public rewards—and the providing of arms, ships and cavalry in time
of peace. Extraordinary expenses, which were occasioned by
war, are treated of at the end of the book. The first item has
been made especially interesting to us by the half defaced monuments that even now attest its magnitude. There is a famous
passage in the oration of Demosthenes against Aristocrates,*
which deserves to be quoted as a *locus communis* on this subject. He reminds his hearers that in the time of their fathers
every thing in the city that belonged to the public was costly
and magnificent, while there was no distinction among private
individuals—that the houses of Themistocles and Miltiades differed in no wise from those of their neighbours, while the
national edifices and other property of the commonwealth were
such that succeeding generations had been able to add nothing

* Page 689.

to their splendor, these Propylæa, says he, the Docks, the Porticoes, the Piræeus, and other things with which you see the city adorned. But, now, they who administer the affairs of the commonwealth accumulate such fortunes, that some of them have built them houses more magnificent than many of the national edifices, others have bought up more land than all of you in this court, put together, possess—while the public buildings which you are erecting are so paltry and contemptible, that one is absolutely ashamed of them. This passage, making every allowance for the peevishness of a declamatory censor, states, probably, the historical truth of the matter, and we subjoin another, from the work before us, which will shew how important an interest, at Athens, the Public Buildings were, and why it was that her matchless orator was so fond of dwelling upon "the Parthenon and the Propylæa."*

"The public buildings, the magnificence and splendid execution of which still excite astonishment even in their ruins, were constructed at so great an expense, that they could not have been attempted without the treasure derived from the tributes: their maintenance alone required a considerable standing expense. I will only mention the building of the Piræeus by Themistocles, the fortification of it together with the other harbours, the market-place of the Hippodamus, the theatre and the many temples and sacred edifices, in the Piræeus ; the docks, in which the ships lay as it were under cover cost 1000 talents, and after having been destroyed in the Anarchy by the contractors for three talents, were again restored and finally completed by Lycurgus. A splendid edifice in the Piræeus was the Arsenal built by Philon and destroyed by Sulla (ςχευοθήχη, ὁπλοθήχη). The fortifications of Athens were enormous ; besides the Acropolis, the city and the Piræeus with Munychia were respectively fortified ; the two latter embraced a circumference of eight English miles, with walls sixty Grecian feet high, which Pericles wished to make as much as double this height ; and at the same time so wide that two carriages could easily pass one another upon them ; they were built of square stones without cement, joined together with iron cramps ; the city and the harbour were also connected by the long walls, the longer of which was equal to forty stadia (five English miles), the shorter to thirty-five ; built upon marshy ground raised with stones. And these immense works were restored after their destruction in the time of the thirty tyrants : for which purpose the Athenians were, it is true, assisted by a donation of money from Persia. To these were added, in time of war, ramparts of earth, trenches and parapets, for the strengthening of the works ; together with the fortification of smaller places in Attica. Thus Eleusis was fortified as being an ancient, and formerly an independent city ; also Anaphlystus, as we learn from Xenophon and Scylax ; so again Sunium was fortified in the Peloponnesian war, as well as in Thoricus and Œnoë a stronghold upon the Bœotian frontier : together with the secure defences of Phyle ; lastly Aphidna and Rhammus, which, in the time of Philip, together with Phyle, Sunium, and Eleusis, were used as places of refuge. But how great was the number of splendid buildings which the city and its environs contained ; if we consider the spaces used for the assembly, the courts of justice, and markets, the highly ornamented porticoes,

---

* Æschines in Ctesiph.

the Pompeum, Prytaneum, Tholus, Senate-house, and other buildings for the public offices ; the innumerable temples, the Theatre, the Odeum, wrestling-schools, Gymnasia, Stadia, Hippodromes, aqueducts, fountains, baths, together with the buildings belonging to them, &c. And again how great must have been the expense of the works upon the Acropolis. The entrance alone, the Propylæa, which occupied five years in its construction, cost 2012 talents. Here too the numerous temples, the Temple of Victory, the Erectheum, with Temple of Minerva Polias and the Pandrosium,· and splendid Parthenon, all these were adorned with the most costly statues and works of art, and enriched with gold and silver vessels. And, besides these great works, how many were the perpetual small expenses, of which *we* have scarcely any notion, that occurred in an ancient State ; for example, the building of altars, which were always erected for certain festivals. Here we may also mention the construction of roads, not only as regards the paving of streets in Athens, but the formation of the roads to the harbors, of the sacred road to Eleusis and perhaps to Delphi as far as the boundary, since it is asserted that the Athenians first opened the road to this place." pp. 268–271.

Police, considered as a part of penal jurisprudence, is not congenial to free institutions, and that of Athens was no exception to the rule. Not that offences, real or imaginary, against the law, escaped with impunity, for the want either of prosecutors or tribunals. Far from it—on the contrary, every citizen, in that jealous democracy,* was allowed by law, and seemed disposed by inclination, to accuse, and there existed undoubtedly, in political matters and every thing connected with them, a spirit of intolerance and treachery upon a large scale, scarcely less fatal to the confidence of social life, and to all liberty of speech, than the systematized espionage† of despotic governments.‡ Witness the case of Socrates. He was put to death, as Æschines openly affirmed in the public assembly, because he had educated Critias,§ that is to say, we have no doubt, because of those very discourses upon government, which the divine eloquence of his disciple, the founder of the academy, has commended to the admiration of all time.‖ But it is the business of police to prevent rather than punish crimes, and in this respect there does not seem to have been any institution of the kind at Athens. We may except, indeed, a city-guard of from three hundred to twelve hundred public slaves (for the number varied at different periods), who lived in tents in the market-place, and afterwards on the Areopagus, and kept watch and ward over the peace of society.

The public festivals were the occasion of a prodigal expenditure. It is not to be denied, however, that it was attended with great benefits, by cultivating the sentiments of natural religion, the elegant humanity of social intercourse, and the genius and taste for literature and the arts, which made the Athenians, em-

[* Aristophanes—equites-aves.]
[† *Espionage*—De Tocqueville—democracy an Argus.]
‡That is to say, on *political* subjects. See Apology for Socrates.   § In Timarch.
[‖ Cf. Miller's Dorians, v. 2. p. 196.]

phatically, a peculiar people. The splendid pageantry of the procession and the chorus, the decorations of the temple, the music and the gymnastic games, the intellectual pleasures and the scenic pomp of the theatre, the sacrificial banquets for which hecatombs of victims bled, the costly perfumes that smoked upon the altars, the golden crowns and tripods bestowed upon the victors in the games—such were the principal items of the lavish and luxurious, but refined profusion, that beguiled the leisure hours of that wonderful antithesis* "the Demus of Erectheus."†

The theatre, especially, was a source of enormous expense. They laid out upon it sums sufficient to equip and maintain armies. "If it were calculated, says a Lacedæmonian in Plutarch, what sum each play cost the Athenians, it would be found that they had spent more treasure upon Bacchæs, and Phœnissæs, and Œdipuses and Antigones, and the woes of Electra and Medea, than upon wars undertaken for empire and for freedom against the Barbarians." The cost of wars for freedom is not to be counted, but how many millions, wrung from the sweat and tears of the industrious, have been squandered, in the course of the last century, upon projects of conquest and of commercial aggrandisement, of which all the benefits put together are not worth the Œdipus or the Phœnissæ !

The chief of the popular donations were the Theorica—a fatal innovation of Pericles—of which the unavoidable, however unforseen, result was utterly to deprave and intoxicate the people by the mingled indulgencies of pleasure, of power and rapacity. Distributions of corn, and the division, by lot, of the lands in conquered countries (cleruchiæ), together with the public revenues from the mines, were inveterate evils, but the illustrious Demagogue, just mentioned, was the first to reveal the *arcanum imperii* of that fierce democracy—to commend to their lips the worse than Circean cup which wrought so great a change in their nature—by which "they lost their upright shape and downward fell" into an equally grovelling and ferocious herd, "trapped with liquorish baits fit to ensnare a brute," and hurried on, in a wild, feverish delirium, from one excess to another, while some designing sycophant, their minion for the time being, played the master of the revels, and the Agora might almost be likened to those dark haunts of Comus—

> "——Whence, night by night,
> He and his monstrous crew were heard to howl
> Like stabled wolves, or tigers at their prey,
> Doing abhorred rites to Hecate."

[* Iliad B. 547—a verse (with many following it) condemned by Knight. See note *in loc.*]

† Plato, Alcib., I.

If any of our readers think that we have painted the effects of this system of corruption in exaggerated colours, let him examine—not what is *called* the caricature, though we think it the authentic testimony, of Aristophanes*—but what sober history records of these Athenian demagogues. Let him consider the character and career of Demades, for example—the most gifted of them—a man, of whom no less a person than Theophrastus pronounced that he was *above* a city of which Demosthenes was only "worthy"—let him trace this man's progress through his uniform course of prostituted and unprincipled sycophancy—first under the tyranny of the mob, and afterwards under that of its destroyer, Antipater—for, with a disgraceful, though natural consistency, he was equally the toad-eater of both. Or, to omit others, let him hear what Theopompus, a witness above exception—in a single passage, fortunately preserved out of a whole book of his history, in which he discoursed at large of the popular leaders at Athens—says of Eubulus of Anaphlystus, renowned above all his compeers for the part he took in bribing the people with the gratifications bought by this same misapplied fund—the Theorica. "He was," says the historian, "a celebrated demagogue, active and indefatigable in his vocation, but during his administration, and by his distributions of money, Athens sank to the lowest state of inactivity and indolence, exceeding even Tarentum in extravagance and debauchery." It is needless to add that, in such a state of public morals, political libertines did not suffer the vast sums of money, expended upon these worthy objects, to pass through their hands, without retaining a suitable compensation, for their own merit in procuring the expenditure. They contrived, like most of their antitypes, the jacobins of France, to enrich themselves by their disinterested service of the commonwealth. Yet it is melancholy to reflect upon the fate of such exemplary patriots. They, almost without an exception, ended like Wolsey and Sejanus;† for the tyrants they served were of precisely the same stamp—jealous, capricious, sudden and quick in quarrel, violent in the excesses of passion, and too fond of pelf and pleasure, not to covet and to employ every means of obtaining them. As soon, therefore, as their ministers became rich enough to be suspected of *incivisme*, they fell victims to the cupidity they had so studiously awakened, and were compelled, by an ungrateful multitude, to pay back in fines and forfeitures whatever they had accumulated by years of diligent peculation. Mr. Boechk has cited, in another part of

[* Robbing demagogues squeezed by Demus—Aristophanes—authority—Athenæ—Athenæi, lib. ix. sub fin. Dinarch. Κατα Δημοσθ. *m.*]

[† I find myself anticipated in this rapprochement by Camille Desmoulins in the Vieux Cordelier—No. 3, C. 58, he quotes Aristophanes as to some bird, and says he rejoices to have such authority (εχεγγυωτατοϒ μαρτυρ).]

his work, many instances of this poetical justice, executed, upon their panders and betrayers, by a depraved and injured people.*

The following account of so important an institution as the *Theorica* cannot but be acceptable to our readers:

"The distribution of the Theorica, which, as we have seen, produced such fatal consequences to the Athenians, took its origin from the entrance-money to the theatre. The entrance was at first free, and crowds and tumults having arisen from the concourse of many persons, of whom some had not any right to enter, it was evidently to be expected that, in a theatre constructed of wood, which was the only one that Athens then possessed, the scaffolding would break; and this accident in fact took place; to avoid which evil it was determined to sell the seats for two oboli; but, in order that the poor might not be excluded, the entrance-money was given them, on the delivery of which each person received his seat. Persons of high rank no doubt at first disdained this as well as other donations; although in the age of Demosthenes they received the Theoricon. It is possible that the entrance-money for the theatre was introduced before the Theoricon was first paid by the State: it may be fairly supposed that the citizens, having for a time defrayed it at their own expense, the State undertook to pay for the poor; and the introduction of the entrance-money may be fixed without improbability as early as the 70th Olympiad, at which time the scaffolding fell in suddenly, when Pratinas and probably also Æschylus were representing in the theatre. But the payment of the Theoricon out of the public money was first introduced by Pericles; and, when Harpocration calls Agyrrhius the author of the Theoricon in the extended sense of a distribution of money, he refers to an increase of it, made at a later period, of which I shall presently speak. This distribution of the Theoricon filled the theatre. We may observe that the entrance-money was paid to the lessee of the theatre (θεατρώνης, θεατροπώλης, ἀρχιτέκτων), who was bound to keep the theatre in repair, and who paid something to the State for rent, as we see in the case of the theatre at Piræeus. Ulpian, a writer on whom very little dependence can be placed, affirms that one obolus was given to the lessee of the theatre, or, as he calls him, to the Architecton, and that the citizens received the other for their support; this statement however is without foundation, for, according to Demosthenes, the regular entrance-money was two oboli; although it is so far true that a separate payment of Theoric was made for the banquet of the citizens. It might also be supposed that, as Demosthenes reckons the entrance-money among the smaller revenues of the State, the payment was received on the public account, and not for the lessee; but, even though the tenant received it, it might have been enumerated among the national profits, inasmuch as he paid a rent to the State; so that this example from Demosthenes, who only speaks in general terms, and without any great precision, proves nothing in contradiction to my opinion. The privilege of receiving the Theorica was obtained through registration in the book of the citizens (ληξιαρχικὸν γραμμ-ματεῖον); the distribution was made both individually and by tribes, absentees receiving nothing; and it took place in the assembly, which was sometimes held in the theatre, particularly when the business related to the celebration of the Dionysia. The application of the Theorica was soon extended, and money was distributed on other occasions than at the theatre, though always at the celebration of some festival; and, as either a play or procession was invariably connected with it, the name still continued applicable. Under the head of Theorica were also comprised the

* Volume ii., p. 115. [See also Aristoph. Eq. 1112, 1150.]

sums expended upon sacrifices and other solemnities.   Not only at the Panathenæa, but at all the great festivals (ἱερομηνίαι), Theorica were distributed. In the Choiseul Inscription we find that in Olymp. 92. 3., from the public treasure alone (probably however on condition of repayment), in the first seven Prytaneias, 16 talents 4787 drachmas were paid to the Hellenotamiæ under the name of Diobelia, which formed a part of the Theorica.   The citizens were thus enabled to celebrate the festival with greater luxury ; and from this various application of the money there has arisen an uncertainty whence the Theoricon took its name ; and Ammonius, in direct contradiction to Cæcilius, denies that it had reference to *spectacles* (θέαι)." 292-296.

Mr. Boeckh thinks that at least eight thousand out of the twenty thousand citizens received this public largess—so that it amounted to a talent a day.   This again multiplied by twenty-five or thirty—the number of days on which the distribution was probably made—gives twenty-five or thirty talents for the whole amount of the expenditure.   In process of time, however, it was greatly increased.   All the money destined for the exigencies of war was *by law*—by a deliberate act of the people, in their sovereign capacity, prescribing rules for future legislation—solemnly appropriated to this purpose, and it was made death, for any orator even to *propose* to the assembly the diverting of the fund, in the most pressing emergencies of the State.   Their pleasures were to be preferred to their preservation.   Every reader of Demosthenes knows that, even when Philip was disclosing his projects of ambition by a train of measures obviously calculated for the subjugation of all Greece, it was impossible to adopt any effective scheme of defence, because of this truly Sybaritical enactment.

Under the head of salaries or compensation for public services in time of peace, the most important were the wages of the general assembly, the Senate of 500, and the Dicasts or judges. The pay of the last, although trifling, amounted to a great deal at the end of the year, on account of the multitude of judges and the immense litigiousness of the people.   Besides their own lawsuits, too, they tried those of their allies, and we are not to wonder, therefore, at the result which is thus—somewhat strongly— stated by our author.

"Nearly the third part of the citizens sat as judges every day : hence that passion for judging necessarily arose, which Aristophanes describes in the Wasps, and the citizens were thus not only made averse to every profitable and useful employment, but were rendered sophistical and litigious ; and the whole town became full of pettifoggers and chicaners, who were without any real knowledge of law or justice, and on that account only the more rash and thoughtless   According to the expression of the comic poet, they sat, like sheep, muffled up in their cloaks and with their judicial staff, for three oboli a day, thinking indeed that they managed the affairs of the State, while they were themselves the tools of the party leaders." p. 304.

We would remark, in this connection, that, although we are any thing but admirers of the Athenian system of judicature, and have no doubt that great injustice and uncertainty in the tenure of property and the transactions of mankind were the fruits of these popular decisions upon points of law, yet such an order of things was not without its compensation. It was a school in which the public mind was trained, and (better still) restrained. The Dicasts were selected from the multitude, whose eyes were upon them. Their responsibility, and, what is of more moment, their own sense of it, were very much enhanced by that circumstance alone. There is something, too, in the very function of judicature, so important, so solemn, so elevated, that has an effect even upon the basest and most depraved of the species. There are men, who would vote for a bill of attainder, in a legislative assembly, in times of popular excitement, against an individual, whom they would not, sitting as judges, find guilty of the alleged crime. Bad as the Athenian people were in the Ecclesia, they were, we incline to think, somewhat better in the trial of public causes. They were there made to feel the obligations of *duty*—to find that some restraints had been, or ought to be, imposed even upon their own divine prerogatives—to have some little consideration for the rights of others—and to perceive—too faintly, too transiently, to be sure, but still occasionally to perceive—to get a glimpse of—the sublime and everlasting truth, that the difference between liberty and despotism is precisely that between *law* and *will*—between the law which never changes—which neither loves, nor hates, nor fears—impartial as the justice it executes, unerring as the reason which guides it—and the wayward, passionate and perverse caprices of miserable mortals. The discipline in their tribunals, we admit, was none of the best, but still it was better than none—especially in an age when all instruction was communicated *orally*, and there was no reading public at all. It deserves to be added, by the way, that it is in this point of view that we deem with such high reverence of our system of Jury-Trial. It is an admirable scheme of discipline. It is the true school of republican liberty. A single prætor, a high justiciary, might, perhaps, dispose of cases—even of fact merely—as correctly in the long run—but, we verily believe, our political institutions, well poised as they are, would perish with such an innovation.

The wages of the popular assembly*—at first an obolus, afterwards three oboli a day—were a comparatively recent invention—that is to say, more recent than the administration of Pericles, though before the Ecclesiazusæ of Aristophanes, as appears from the ridicule thrown upon it by that great political

[* On an average 5000 attended. Thucyd. l. viii. 72.]

satirist. The other items of public expenditure need not be much dwelt upon. We were rather struck with M. Boeckh's estimate of the number of paupers, or pensioners, on account of their poverty alone, which he thinks amounted to 500*—at least, after the losses of property and the general distress, public and private, occasioned by the Peloponnesian war. As for the gold crowns, and other rewards of merit or success, it is sufficient to remark, of so inconsiderable an item of expense, that they were far more rarely bestowed, when the number of those who deserved them was greater, than in a later and a degenerate age. They who restored the democracy after the Anarchy, who brought the people up out of the house of bondage, received chaplets of leaves as a recompense for their virtue, while Demetrius Phalereus saw 360 statues erected in his honour, within not quite as many days.†

If we sum up all the expenses stated by M. Boeckh, it will be found that they did not amount, at the lowest estimate, to less than 400 talents a year, but making allowance for occasions of extraordinary profusion, 1000 talents, he thinks, might have been easily consumed, in time of peace. It is impossible to determine the real value of the precious metals, that is to say, their value in relation to the necessaries of life, at so distant a period, with any sort of certainty. But it may be safely stated, as in the work before us, at only a third of their present value—an estimate undoubtedly too low. Even at that rate, however, it must be admitted, that a standing annual expenditure of a thousand talents a year, for a population of 500,000, three-fourths of whom were slaves, was very great, in an age when all the resources of industry and commerce were so very inferior to what they now are. But this does not include that source of ruinous prodigality—war: and Athens, as we have remarked, was perpetually at war. It is true that, the *matériel* and munitions of an army were far less costly to the State, than they are in our times, and the whole system of warfare, as we have seen, was more simple and less onerous than the modern. Add to this that, until the administration of Pericles, the troops received no pay, citizen soldiers would (many of them, at least) provide their own arms and accoutrements, and that, by the trierarchy, the rich were compelled to bear the greater part of the expense of equipping the fleet. After making every allowance of the sort, however, a warlike and ambitious commonwealth, at the head of a confederacy of commercial cities, the rival of Sparta, the representative and champion of democratic power

[* The number of parochial poor, at Brussels, this winter, '32–'33—is stated at no less than 30,000! This year, 1834, it is reduced to 29,000!]

† They were demolished still more speedily. See the melancholy and instructive sequel in Diog. Laert. lib. v. Menander, the comic poet, came very near being condemned, because he had been the friend of Demetrius! Alas! "how near the Capitol is the Tarpeian Rock!"

against Dorian oligarchy, the refuge of the feeble and the oppressed, with a form of society and with habits of profusion, such as we have described, must often have been straitened for money, in an age of which the industry and credit were any thing but flourishing. Thus, the single item of pay for the troops, in the Sicilian expedition, amounted (annually) to 3600 talents, a sum equal to the whole revenue of the State in its best condition, and greatly exceeding its average amount.

We now proceed to consider the subject of the third and fourth books—the revenues, ordinary and extraordinary—of the Athenian Commonwealth.

Direct taxes, and, of all others, a poll tax,* were regarded by the people with great aversion. Besides, that the mode of levying such taxes is, even in its mildest forms, in some degree inquisitorial and vexatious, they thought it not agreeable to the genius of a free government thus openly to exact, by virtue of a prerogative, from the very nature of the case, despotic and arbitrary—the money of its subjects.

> "With bare-faced power to sweep it from their *purse*,
> And make its *will* avouch it."

They felt that taxation, in this form at least, is confiscation—and our author seems even to doubt whether, before the urgent exigencies of the Peloponnesian war demanded it, such an expedient had ever been resorted to by the Athenians. We do not think the authority relied on bears him out to the whole extent of this position,† but at any rate, it cannot be denied that impositions of the sort had been, before that period, very light and merely occasional, and that, at all times, a people, impatient of control, even where it was most salutary, and rather accustomed to look to government for their own sustenance than to think of contributing to its support, were disposed to countenance every other scheme of finance preferably to this. But, disguise it as you will, taxation is still confiscation, which nothing but the necessities of the State can excuse—and duties on consumption—although recommended by the double merit of being less offensive in their form, and adjusting themselves with greater ease and precision to the capacity to pay them—are obviously not the less unjust (if they exceed the proper limits) on that account. It argues excessive apathy or thoughtlessness in a people to acquiesce in such an abuse, while they resist another which differs

[* L'impôt par tête est plus naturel a la servitude; l'impôt sur les marchandises est plus naturel a la liberté, parcequ'il se rapporte d'une manière moins directe à la personne. Esprit des Lois xiii. c. 14.]

† He cites Thucydides III. 19. A German writer (Tittman) has some good remarks upon this passage, and quotes on the other hand, Pollux VIII. 108. Hesychius in v. ναύκλαρος, Ammonius in v. ναύκραροι, Thom. Magister in v. ναύκληροι and cf. Thucyd. l. i. 141.

from it precisely as robbery does from stealing privily from the person—both of them made capital felonies by our law, the one because of its outrageous and alarming character, the other on account of the facility of perpetrating it and the difficulty of detection. The Athenians, it is true, did not fall into this error through their horror of direct taxes, for their custom-duties amounted only to 2 per cent. *ad valorem*, indiscriminately levied upon imports and exports, and even when they came to exchange the tributes paid by their allies for an impost of the same kind—oppressive as their general policy in regard to these dependencies was—they thought one of 5 per cent. an adequate compensation for a most important branch of their revenue.* But their repugnance to direct impositions, led to other and greater abuses. It led to this very oppression of their allies—to the misapplication of funds, contributed by all Greece for the common defence, to local, thriftless, wanton and corrupt expenditures—to a train of measures that made Athens the scourge, instead of the shield and glory of the democratical confederation—and thus—in spite of her great vigour and resources, in spite of her immense services at Marathon, at Salamis, and Artemisium,† and her unrivalled and conceded superiority in whatever adorns civilized life—to her being crushed, even in her proudest estate, beneath the universal odium which her arbitrary measures most justly entailed upon her. It led to the same kind of tyranny at home—to schemes by which the few were compelled to bear almost the whole burthen of the State, while the many lived, or rather rioted, upon its bounty—to acts of confiscation and plunder, infinitely worse, as far as they went, than the worst taxation in its regular forms, and utterly unworthy of a free people.

All the *ordinary* revenues of Athens are reduced by M. Boeckh to the four following classes: 1. Duties ($τέλη$), arising partly from the public domains including the mines—partly from the customs and excise, and some taxes upon industry and persons, which extended only to aliens and slaves. 2. Fines and forfeitures ($τιμήματα$), together with justice fees and the proceeds of confiscated property ($δημιόπρατα$). 3. Tributes of the allied or subject States ($φοροι$) and the regular Liturgies‡ ($λειτουργίαι ἐγκύκλιοι$). It is a remark generally applicable to these various branches of revenue, with the exception of the *fines*, (and, we may add, the war-taxes, hereafter to be noticed,) that the State, in order to save itself trouble and expense, devolved the collection of them upon publicans or farmers-general. This wretch-

[* Thycyd. vii. c.—They thought it an advantageous exchange.]
[† She was undoubtedly the saviour of Greece, says Herodotus, l. vii. 139.]
‡ Public contributions, in the nature of personal services, exacted of the rich, which will be explained in the sequel.

ed system—pregnant with fraud and oppression—ruinous to the citizen without benefiting the public—greatly aggravated the evils of an imperfect scheme of finance. The very name of publican became a bye-word of reproach. In the Roman Commonwealth these people played an important part, as one would naturally conjecture from the extent of the empire and its immense resources. Cicero always speaks of them with profound respect as an *order*—as almost a separate *estate* of the realm. Yet we have his evidence—in a letter to his brother, written for the particular edification of Quintus, during his administration in Asia—to shew that, unless their rapacity were curbed by the authority of the pro-consul, there was no excess to which it would not go in the provinces. Indeed, their conduct had been intolerable even in Italy—so much so, indeed, that all customs had been abolished, in order to get rid of the extortioners, who farmed them of the State. Yet, bad as the Roman publicans were, Cicero does not think the Greeks of Asia Minor ought to be alarmed at their *name*—because the Greeks had always been accustomed to a system, the same in principle, and administered with fully as much severity and oppressiveness.* When the branches or items of revenue to be let out in this way were of too much magnitude to be taken by one man, several or many entered into a species of partnership, or joint-stock company for that purpose. The practices of these bodies were, as usual, still worse than those of individual farmers. They were mere conspiracies, at once, against the exchequer and the people. There was a perfect understanding among them to *jockey* the public in the auctions at which the revenues were let out, and they seldom failed to accomplish their double purpose of paying the government as little as possible, for the power to wring as much as possible out of the tax payers.

The mines were the most important part of the public domains. The State was sole proprietor of them, but they were always worked by private persons, to whom they were granted on a sort of perpetual lease or fee-farm, assignable, like any other kind of property, by the lessee and his heirs. Besides the price given for this lease in the first instance, the tenant paid, as a yearly rent, the twenty-fourth part of the net produce. The most considerable of the mines were those of silver on Mount Laurium, which extended from shore to shore, over a space of seven English miles. Their productiveness gradually decreased, from the time of Themistocles, when it appears to have been some 30 or 40 talents a year, to that of Strabo, when the working of them was quite discontinued on account of their exhaustion. They were let out generally by shares to companies, and the number

* Ad Quint. l. I. 1. He speaks of their "Societies" with all the respect due to bodies of great influence in the commonwealth. Yet the truth leaks out.

of possessors was considerable. They had, as tenants, or usu-
fructuary holders of the property of the State, some privileges—
such, for instance, as exemption from the liturgies and their consequence, the *antidosis*. Their interests, together with those of
the public, were protected by a special code—the law of the
mines—and a peculiar procedure was adopted to give them
speedy justice, as in the courts of the Stannaries in Cornwall.
As to mines out of Attica, it does not appear that the Athenians
claimed the property of any of them, by right of conquest or
otherwise, except the gold mines of the Thasians in Thrace, of
which the most productive were those of Scapte Hyle, on the
continent—a place made still more memorable, as the residence
of Thucydides during his long exile, and by the composition of
his immortal history. That great writer, it may be added, became by marriage possessed of a large proprietary interest in
some of the gold mines of Thrace—it is not certain which.

We have already spoken of a duty of two per cent. paid on
imports and exports. There are no means of ascertaining satisfactorily what the whole annual amount of it was. Mr. Boeckh
conjectures that it was from 30 to 36 talents—which shows the
gross value of the exports and imports to have been short of 2000
talents. It is to be regretted that we have no data that can be
safely depended on in relation to so interesting a point. In
addition to the customs, our author ventures an opinion that a
small port-duty (ἐλλίμενιον) was exacted of all vessels for the use
of the harbours. This, too, is a matter of mere conjecture; nor
is it quite clear what was the nature of the duties levied upon all
sales in the market. From the importance, however, attached
to the tax, it seems fair to conclude, that it was an excise. Under this head must, also, be classed the 5 per cent. imposed upon
the allies in lieu of their former contributions, and a toll of 10
per cent. extorted after the 92¾ Olympiad on all cargoes going
into or coming out of the Pontus. This last source of revenue,
however, which was probably not inconsiderable, was cut off,
with so many others, by the fatal defeat at Ægospotamos; and,
though re-established by Thrasybulus about the ninety-seventh
Olympiad, was soon abolished for the second time.

Of the other items of revenue that fall under the first head
it will not be necessary to take very particular notice, with the
exception of the μετοίκιον or protection money of resident aliens.
This was a tax of 12 drachmas a head upon every foreigner
domiciled in Attica. The jealous spirit of their laws treated
persons so situated as of an inferior caste. They were compelled to put themselves under the care of a guardian or patron (προςάτης)—they had no *persona standi in judicio*, and were
in short, in a state of perpetual pupilage and incapacity. The
imposition thus levied upon them, was exacted with the most

unmerciful rigour, as we may learn from the noted example of Xenocrates, a disciple of Plato and his second successor in the Academy, who, distinguished as he was in philosophical pursuits and by morals of the most unimpeachable purity, was sold as a slave for a default in this particular.* Yet to the consequences of this barbarous law, 10,000 foreigners, on an average, were willing to expose themselves every day—such were the irresistible fascinations of Athens! It is sufficient barely to mention the taxes upon fortune-tellers, jugglers, and other the like impostors—the πορνικὸν τέλος which sullied the codes of the Roman emperors even after the conversion of Constantine, and exists at this day, in some States, (calling themselves civilized) on the other side of the ocean—and a duty upon slaves scarcely distinguishable in the few traces that remain of it.

The justice-fees—the second of the four heads of revenue mentioned above—are treated by Mr. Boeckh at very considerable length, and with a great display of exact and extensive knowledge. He distinguishes carefully between the various denominations under which they fall—the Prytaneia, the Parastasis, the Epobelia, and the Paracatabole. But this nice and technical knowledge can only be acquired by a diligent perusal of all that our author has written—and we will merely add that the proceeds of the two first descriptions of fees were appropriated to the payment of the Dicasts; and that, owing to the excessive litigation that prevailed at Athens, they went far to accomplish that object.

We come now to those financial expedients, which were most fearful instruments of corruption in the hands of the demagogues, and led necessarily to such tyrannical abuses of power, as all men are, under certain circumstances, unhappily prone to, but none more than the impetuous, petulant and reckless populace of Athens—fines and forfeitures.† The former, which, in the age of Solon (owing, in some degree, perhaps, to the scarcity of the precious metals), had been very low, became afterwards quite as exorbitant. The following examples are cited, with the double view of shewing to what a pitch they were carried and how justly (in respect of the persons at least) they sometimes happened to be inflicted.

"These fines were necessarily made a productive branch of the public revenue by the injustice of the demagogues, by party hatred, and the liti-

---

* Diog. Laert. lib. iv. Demetrius Phalereus bought and emancipated him.

[Immo *Lycurgus* Orator, qui publicani caput baculo imminuit, sed et eum in vincula, suâ auctoritate conjecit. Plutarch in Lycurg., 552, B. Photius Cod. 268. Plutarch et in vita Flaminii. cap. XII. Scrib. Brux. 1833.]

† We refer the reader on this whole subject of the practices of the Demagogues and the corruption of the people to Aristotle, Polit. lib. v. c. 5. "A demagogue has need of a needy populace." cf. Isocrates περί Εἰρηνῆς.

gious disposition which prevailed. The popular leaders, seldom guided by purely moral principles, raised themselves by flattering the people, and by the lavish administration and distribution of the public money. The majority of them however so little forgot their own gain, when they had reached their high station, that they omitted no means of enriching themselves, and the people on the other hand rejoiced in condemning and overthrowing them. What great demagogue was there who did not meet with an unhappy destiny? Was not this the fate of Miltiades, Themistocles, Aristides, Timotheus, and Demosthenes? And fortunate was he who escaped with the payment of a heavy fine, while others suffered the penalty of death, or were condemned to forfeiture of property, or to exile. Thrasybulus, son of the restorer of the freedom of Athens (who himself, if he had not died, whould have been capitally condemned), paid a fine of 10 talents, probably an action for malversation in an embassy (γραφὴ παραπρεσβείας). Callias, the Torchbearer, concluded a most advantageous and honourable peace with the king of Persia, according to which no army was to approach the cost within a day's march of cavalry, and no armed Persian vessel was to appear in the Grecian seas; yet, although he obtained much celebrity by these negociations, as Plutarch relates in the life of Cimon, he was condemned to a fine of 50 talents, when he rendered an account of his official conduct, for having taken bribes. And how large was the number of those who were codemned to severe punishments for treason or bribery. Cleon was compelled to pay five talents, probably not, as the Scholaist of Aristophanes supposes, for having injured the Knights, but for having taken bribes from the allies, in order to procure a mitigation of their tributes; and, to omit the fine of 50 minas, which Aristides is stated (probably without truth) to have paid for having received bribes, Timotheus was condemned upon the same grounds to a fine of 100 talents by an indictment for treason (γραφὴ προδοσίασ), a sum greater than ever had been paid until that occasion: nine parts out of ten were however remitted to his son Conon, and the tenth he was forced to expend upon the repair of the walls for which Athens was indebted to his grandfather. Demosthenes was sentenced to a fine of 50 talents by an action for bribery (γραφὴ δωροδοκίας), and also thrown into prison; the latter punishment having doubtless been imposed in addition by the court (προστίμημα). According to the strict law he should have paid ten times the amount of the sum received; five times the amount is however the only fine mentioned, and even this he was unable to pay: nor can we determine how this fine was calculated, as the statements of the sums received are so contradictory, that Dinarchus speaks of 20 talents in gold, and refers to the Areopagus for authority, with whom Plutarch agrees, who relates that he received 20 talents in a royal golden goblet; whereas others speak of 30 talents, and even of so small a sum as 1000 darics. Demosthenes remained in debt 30 talents of his fine, which upon his recal were remitted to him for the building of an altar. Miltiades was accused of treason, and condemned to pay 50 talents, not for a compensation, as Nepos ignorantly asserts, but according to the usual form of assessing the offence. The fine was paid by his son. Before this occasion, Miltiades had also been sentenced to a fine of 30 talents. Cimon himself narrowly escaped being condemned to death for a supposed intent to overthrow the existing government, which penalty was commuted for a fine of 50 talents. The illustrious Pericles was vehemently accused, after the second invasion of Attica by the Lacedæmonians, the people being dissatisfied with his method of carrying on the war, and particularly with the surrender of their own country, by which many individuals suffered such severe losses, and the Athenians were not contented, as Thucydides says, until they had sentenced him to a fine. The highest sum stated was, according to Plutarch, 50 talents, the lowest 15; the former was probably the assessment of the accuser, the latter of the court. Fines of a less amount did however occur in important cases, as e. g. a fine of only 10 talents in an indictment for treason." vol. li. pp. 114–118.

They who incurred these fines became immediately public debtors, and two incidents to that condition were *atimia* (degradation or loss of civil *status**) and imprisonment. But this was not all, for, if payment were not made in nine months, the debt was doubled, and the property of the debtor sequestered until the State were satisfied. This was harsh and summary enough—but, unfortunately, there were many other cases in which confiscation, together with infamy, slavery, exile, or death, awaited, justly or unjustly, the victims of popular vengeance. A regular account of such forfeitures was rendered to the people at the first assembly of every Prytaneia—so much a matter of daily occurrence were they—and manifest as was the tendency of such strong temptations to seduce the cupidity of a rabble of judges†, deeply interested in increasing the eleemosynary fund of the State, yet nothing is more certain than that such detestable decrees were one of the most ordinary sources of revenue in Greece. The following passage shows what ruinous waste, what havoc and dilapidation, were the consequence of such things, with, comparatively speaking, scarcely any benefit, even in a pecuniary point of view, to the commonwealth, by whose authority they were perpetrated, and whose name they dishonored.

"Notwithstanding the frequency of confiscation of property, the State appears to have derived little essential benefit from it; as we see that the plunder of the church-property has for the most part been of little advantage to modern States. Considerable sums were squandered in this manner, such as the property of Diphilus, which amounted to 160 talents; in many cases a part of the property was received by the accuser, and, in most, as appears from the above-quoted examples, the third part. In certain cases the person who informed against the public debtors received three parts of the confiscated possessions; this regulation appears however to have been confined to concealed property, which was discovered by the informer. A tithe of the property of persons condemned for treason, or for having endeavored to subvert the democracy, and probably also of all or of most other escheats, belonging of right to Minerva of the Parthenon. Many kinds of property were received by the temples without any deduction, so that nothing passed into public coffers: and how great must have been the loss occasioned by fraud or by sale of property under its value. "You know," says a person in Lysias threatened with confiscation of property, "that part of my property will be plundered by these persons (his adversaries,) and that what has considerable value will be sold at a low price: the community, he remarks, derives less profit from the forfei-

* Cf. Thucyd. lib. v. cap. 34.

[† Aristoph. Eq. 1359, et seq. Lysias, Κατὰ Επικρατ. ἁ—Isæus, περὶ του φιλοκτημονοσ κληρου. ιλ.— Immo locus communis planè.]

ture, than if the proprietors retained the property, and performed the services annexed to it by law. Again, the offender frequently concealed his property under a fictitious name, or relations and friends claimed it from the State, and, finally, the accused sought to excite pity, by speaking of orphans, heiresses, age, poverty, maintenance of the mother, &c.; and it is a beautiful and praiseworthy feature in the character of the Athenians, that this appeal was seldom made in vain, but part of the property was commonly transferred to the wife or the children. Upon the whole, the receipts actually obtained were in general far less than was expected, as is shown by Lysias' speech for the property of Aristophanes. If there was any suspicion of concealment, this again furnished material for fresh accusations. Thus when Ergocles the friend of Thrasybulus was deprived of his property by confiscation, for having embezzled thirty talents of the public money, and the value of that found in his possession was inconsiderable, his treasurer Epicrates was brought before the court, suspicions being entertained that the property lay concealed in his house." vol. ii. pp. 130–132.

But the most important source of revenue, beyond comparison, were the tributes of the allies (φόροι). This fund was the common treasury of a confederation, of which Athens was only the head, enjoying a certain precedence, and entrusted with the appointment of the Helenotamiæ, or treasurers and administrators of the contribution. At the first institution of it, in the 77. 3 Olympiad, this fund amounted to 460 talents a year. It was deposited in the temple of Delos, where also the allies convened, for the purpose of directing the appropriation of it to its legitimate object, the common defence against the Barbarians. In process of time, however, that object was wholly lost sight of. The Athenians gradually extended their influence and encroachments—a contribution in money and ships was substituted for personal service from such of the allies as were bound to perform it—the payment of the tribute was exacted as a duty, while the correlative privilege of voting in the assembly was denied them—and, when the treasury was at length removed from Delos to Athens, the league had obviously degenerated into a *societas leonina*—and the allies were no longer allies, but vassals and tributaries. Still there was some colour—some shadow of apology or palliation for this abuse. The head of the confederacy professed, at least, to protect its members, and this fund, though not under the control of those who contributed it, might be supposed to be appropriated to its original objects. Another step remained to be taken to complete the injustice, and it was taken. The taxes paid for the great purposes of the confederation were wholly and avowedly diverted from them. Pericles was the author of this innovation. "He taught the Athenian people," says the book, "that they were not accountable to the allies for these contributions, as the Athenians waged war in their defence against the Barbarians, while their States did not provide a horse, a ship, or a soldier; that it was their duty to apply their money to objects which would both promote their interest and enhance their celebrity, and that, by devoting their resources to the erection of works of art, they would maintain every hand in employment, and, at the same time, most splendidly adorn their city." Bad as this policy was, however, both with regard to the allies whom it injured, and, perhaps, the people of Athens, whom it had a tendency to debauch, still the amount of the tribute money was not much increased, for Pericles, about the 80th Olympiad, collected only 600 talents annually. But within less than 40 years it was swelled up to 1200 and even 1300 talents—an exaction so intolerable to the confederates, that many of them abandoned their homes in despair, and emigrated to Magna Græcia. It was not long after this, that the tributes were commuted, as we have seen, for a duty of 5 per cent. on imports and exports, which was, in its turn, abolished by the defeat at Ægospotamos.

After stating that some of the allied States were not bound to pay tribute to the Athenians, M. Boeckh goes on to remark—

"The nature of our inquiry limits us to the censideration of the perpetual allies, who may be divided into independent (αὐτόνομοι), and subject (ἠπήκοοι). In order then first to point out the chief distinction between the two conditions, the former class retained possession of unlimited jurisdiction, whereas the subject allies were compelled to try all their disputes in the courts of Athens. The nature of this compulsion has not however been as yet satisfactorily ascertained. I should in the first place remark that Casaubon, by the misconception of a passage in Athenæus, imagined that the Athenian Nesiarchs (although in fact no officers of this name ever existed) originally decided the law-suits of the Islanders, and that, at a subsequent period when these offices were abolished, all litigations were carried on at Athens. It is however more probable that, when the jurisdiction was taken away from the allied States, it was immediately made compulsory upon them to refer all disputes to the Athenian courts. The model of this regulation, by which Athens obtained the most extensive influence and an almost absolute dominion over the allies, was probably found in other Grecian States which had subject confederates, such as Thebes, Elis, and Argos. But, on account of the remoteness of many countries, it is impossible that every trifle could have been brought before the courts in Athens; we must therefore suppose that each subject State had an inferior jurisdiction of its own, and that its supreme jurisdiction alone belonged to Athens. Can it indeed be supposed that persons would have travelled from Rhodes or Byzantium to Athens for the sake of a lawsuit for 50 or 100 drachmas? In private suits a sum of money was probably fixed, above which, the inferior court of the allies had no jurisdiction: while cases relating to higher sums were referred to Athens; hence the amount of the prytaneia, which were only paid in private causes, was by this interdiction of justice augmented in favour of the Athenians. The public and penal causes were, however, of far greater importance to the Greeks from their being habituated to a free government. There can be no doubt, that cases of this description were, to a great extent, decided at Athens, and the definite statements which are extant refer to law-suits of this nature. Thus Isocrates speaks of sentences of death passed against the allies: the law-suit of Hegemon the Thasian, in the age of Alcibiades, was evidently a public suit; and the oration of Antiphon concerning the murder of Herodes, is a defence of a Mytilenean, who was proceeded against by a criminal prosecution subsequently to the revolt of his state, in consequence of which defection it was made subject, and planted with Cleruchi. From the latter orator we learn that no subject State has the right of condemning an accused person without the consent of the Athenians, but that it had the power of setting the investigation on foot (an arrangement which was indispensably necessary,) and the Athenian court only gave judgment. For more determinate accounts on this point, I have in vain sought. The independent allies must also have had the power of deciding for themselves with regard to war and peace, and at least a formal share in all decrees, although the preponderance of Athens deprived the latter right of its force: while the subject States were, according to the legal conditions, governed by the will of the Athenians. Both had their own public officers; for that this was the case, with the subject States, is proved by the Delian Archons who occur in the 100th Olympiad, at a time when Delos was so far in the power of Athens, that the latter State was in possession of the temple, which was managed by its own Amphictyons. , Nevertheless we find that Athens sometimes appointed Archons or governors of its own in the States of the subject allies. These officers may be compared with the Harmosts of the Spartans.

* * * * * * * * *

"Both classes of the allied States had unquestionably the unrestricted administration of their home affairs, and the power of passing decrees. The subject States were necessarily in this point limited to a narrow circle; it is however wholly inconceivable that every decree which they passed required a ratification from Athens or the Athenian authorities. The obligation to pay a tribute was held originally not to be incompatible with independence, nor indeed in later times was it absolutely identical with dependence or subjection; but the independent allies of the Athenians were commonly exempted from tribute, and were only bound to provide ships and their crews (οὐχ ὑποτελεῖσ φόρου, ναῦς δὲ παρέχοντες: ναυσὶ καὶ οὐ φόρῳ ὑπήκοοι; νεῶν παροχῇ αὐτόνομοι;) the subject allies however paid a tribute (ὑποτελεῖς, φόρου ὑποτελεῖς); although it should be remembered that the subject allies were sometimes, in spite of the tributes, compelled to serve in the fleet or by land. Independence, together with an obligation to pay a tribute to Athens, and without any alliance with the Athenians, was granted in the peace of Nicias, in Olymp. 89. 3., to the cities of Argilus, Stageirus, Acanthus, Scolus, Olynthus, and Spartolus, and the Athenians were only empowered to induce them to an alliance upon their own voluntary agreement. This qualified dependence, which was also extended to some other cities, was a perfect model of the original form of the Athenian confederacy." vol. ii. pp. 140–147.

The empire of Athens extended, with some few exceptions, over all the islands, from Byzantium to Cythera, in one direction, and Rhodes and Carpathus, in another, including Eubœa. To these we must add the coast of Caria, the Dorians bordering upon Caria, Ionia, the Hellespont, and the Grecian territory in Thrace. Within these limits were comprehended some of the most renowned cities of antiquity—Miletus, Halicarnassus, Cuidos, Ephesus, Colophon, Teos, Priene, Erythræ, Smyrna, and the rest of the Ionian towns. Besides these her dominion in-

cluded Antandros, Abydos, Lampsacus, Cyzicus, Chalcedon, Byzantium, Selymbria, Perialthus, Sestos, and the Thracian Chersonesus—the whole southern coast of Thrace, the coast of Mace-
donia, including the important cities of Amphipolis, Olynthus,
Acanthus, Stageirus, Potidæa, and others.   Athens thus sat "a
sea-Cybele," enthroned amidst her thousand cities,* and exercising an absolute sway over the isles of the Gentiles.   She owed
this supremacy to the policy of Themistocles, (a consummate
statesman,) who made her the first naval power of Greece, and
to the comparative aversion of Lacedæmon from external in ·
terests and ambitious purposes.   After the expulsion of the Mede,
the Spartans† were at the head of United Greece, but they volun-
tarily withdrew from a post as troublesome as it was honorable.
Their great maritime competitor grasped with avidity the sceptre which thus passed away from them—for nearly half a century she dictated laws to a nominal confederacy—and it was, at
length, to depress a too formidable rival and to overthrow a common oppressor, that all Greece conspired, with Lacedæmon at
its head, to wage, *ad internecionem*, the Peloponnesian war.

This war eventuated in the downfall of the Athenian power.
It was restored, however, by Thrasybulus and Conon—but, by
the peace of Antalcidas, (Olymp. 9S. 2) this aspiring city was
again shorn of her beams and reduced to her original estate, the
islands of Scyros, Lemnos, and Imbros alone.   Yet a few years
afterwards, Olymp. 100. 3,) the moderation, which she had learned from adversity, bringing back to her the friends whom her
insolence had once disgusted, she made the most of a happy turn
in affairs, and the victories of Chabrias, Iphicrates, and Timotheus, especially the last, restored her to all her former influence
and dominion.   The new confederacy, which was formed after
the Olymp. 100. 4, was a more equal one than the first.   The
different States, which had been admitted as parties to it, retained
all their independence.   A congress (σύνέδριον) met at Athens, in
which that city presided, but each member of the league had an
equal voice.   To conciliate the minds of her allies, the *cleruchiæ*
(of which we shall presently speak) were abolished, and although
the tributes were again introduced, they were disguised under the
less odious appellation of *contributions*.   But this moderation
soon ceased to characterize her policy.   The tributes were again
arbitrarily imposed and rigorously exacted, and the allies, as M.
Boeckh thinks, once more subjected to the jurisdiction of her
courts.   The confederate States became discontented, and the
Social war, which ended in Olymp. 106. 1, resulted in the inde-

* Aristoph. Vesp. 506.
[† They were afraid, too, with their habitual αξενια—αμιξια—of contamination—as in the case of Pausanias—See on the whole subject Thucyd. lib. l. c.
95.]

pendence of as many of them as revolted. This contest had so
much shattered the finances of the State, that when Demosthenes,
soon after the close of it, began to urge the Athenians to vigorous measures against Philip, none but the weakest islands still
adhered to them, and the whole amount of the contributions was
45 talents, which his able administration of their affairs gradually
increased to 500.*

We shall proceed briefly to notice two other institutions of
great importance in the public economy of Athens, and often alluded to in the course of these remarks, viz. the *Cleruchiæ* and
the *Liturgies*.

The right of civilized nations to appropriate to themselves,
with force and arms, the lands occupied by barbarians, seems to
have been recognized in all ages, and is consecrated as a fundamental principle in the jurisprudence of a new world.† But,
when Greek met Greek, the conflict was felt to involve the
rights and interests of more than *one* party, and the degradation
of the Penestæ in Thessaly, and of the Messenians and the
Helots in the Peloponnesus, to a condition worse, (if possible)
than that of the Catawbas and the Cherokees, must be admitted to have been rather a high handed measure. The policy
was kept up in later times, and nothing is more common in the
history of Athens than the expulsion of a whole people *en masse*,
or the entire confiscation of their lands.‡ It was a great resource for the demagogues, ever ready to purchase popularity at
the expense of others; and what reasonable objection could any
true Athenian have to the dividing—by a lottery too, in which
every one might have his chance—the lands of foreigners, occasionally, even enemies of the State, among his brother patriots?
We must not be surprised, therefore, to learn that this sort
of philanthropy flourished amazingly in so congenial a soil.
Bdelycleo, in the Wasps of Aristophanes, after declaiming against
the niggardliness of the demagogues, who might, if they would,
out of the spoils of a thousand cities, supply their fellow-citizens with all manner of dainties, instead of keeping them,
as they did, on miserably short commons, adds that, whenever these same demagogues got alarmed at the just discontents of a stinted people, they threw a sop to them by promising a division of Eubœa; or fifty pecks of corn a piece.§

[* Cf. Plutarch Lycurgi (orat.) vita. χιλια διακοσια ταλ. προσοδου τη πολει
κατεστησε προτερον εξηκοντα προσιοντων—Lycurgus scilicet.]

† See Johnson and McIntosh, 10. Wheat. What would an Indian jurist say
to this *jus gentium*?

‡ See the case of the Mytilenians, Thucyd. lib. iii. c. 50; and the still more
shocking case of the Delians, Id. lib. v. c. 1.; and, worst of all, that of the Melians,
ibid. c. 116.

§ Verse 715. The whole play is deeply instructive upon the subject of Athenian
character and customs.

How sharp-set the commonality of Athens were in regard to these land-lotteries appears, as M. Boeckh observes, from the joke of the same poet in another of his comedies. When Strepsiades, in the Clouds, sees the figure of geometry in the school of the sophists, and is told its name—he inquires what is the use of it. To measure the earth is the reply, which the honest citizen takes, with great *naïveté* of course, to mean the land distributed by lottery (χληρουχιχη). This institution, oppressive as it manifestly must have been to the allies, answered two good ends—besides "blessing" the capacious "maw" of Demus. It was, in the first place, a means of keeping a conquered country in subjection, and extending, more and more, the influence of the Athenian commonwealth. The other effects was still more beneficial. It was a means of drawing off—

> "All the unsettled humours of the land,
> Rash, inconsiderate, fiery voluntaries."

These, indeed, we take to have been the two great objects of the colonial policy of antiquity. Macchiavelli adverts to the former, in speaking of the Roman colonies, and, to a country aiming at conquest, it is difficult to overrate the importance of such frontier posts. But, with a view to order and good government at home, the latter advantage was of the greatest moment. How much has been done and how much more will yet be done, for the stability of our institutions, and the prevention of the crime and misery incident to a crowded and impoverished population, by the field which the Western forests offer to bold, enterprising and determined spirits?

The liturgies or public services (*corvées*)* were a sort of extraordinary taxation by which certain expenditures, which ought to have been provided for out of the common treasury, were made to fall only upon people of considerable estate. They were divided into two kinds, the ordinary and the extraordinary. Of the former the most important were the Choregia, the Gymnasiarchy and the Hestiasis†—of the latter, the Trierarchy. No man was compelled to perform them unless his fortune were about three talents. The appointment was made by the several tribes, which shared in whatever credit was gained by the magnificence of their representatives. Great emulation was thus excited among the performers, and a prodigality, not the less ruin-

*Λειτουργίαι quisa λητουργίαι from λήιτον—λειτον publicum and ἔργον.

† That is to say, the providing, furnishing and maintaining the choruses in the plays and other festivals—the superintendence of the sacred games—and the feasting of the tribes.

[‡ How great a merit it was to have performed the liturgies well appears from all the Orations of Isæus, especially περὶ του Απολλοδωρου χληρου η., which is a good illustration of the whole text. *E contra*, Socrates, in his fearful picture

ous for being voluntary, was too often the fruit of it‡. To prevent their becoming unnecessarily oppressive, there were some rules and restrictions—for instance, that no one should be called on to perform for two years in succession, or more than one liturgy at a time, that orphans should be altogether exempt from them, and that, if a person required to undertake them, could shew that another ought to be appointed in his stead, he might propose an exchange of fortunes with that other, in case he declined the liturgy.

The *extraordinary* revenues of the Athenian commonwealth which forms the subject of the fourth book, were a direct tax, and the extraordinary liturgy or trierarchy.

Before he enters upon the discussion of these modes of taxation, the author thinks it necessary to inquire into the gross amount of the national wealth and the *valuation* of Attica. No part of the whole work strikes us as more able than this. He undertakes to refute the account of this matter which Polybius gives in the second book of his history,* and he appears to us to have succeeded completely, not only in accomplishing that purpose, but in throwing a broad and clear light over the whole subject of Athenian taxation and assessments. The result of the examination is thus summed up.

"In short, however, Polybius states the valuation (τίμημα) of Attica, with perfect correctness at 5750 talents; but it is the valuation, not the value, of the whole property: he only knew how much the valuation of the whole property amounted to ; but, not being aware of the principles upon which it had been obtained, he erroneously supposed that it was the value of the whole property. For the valuation taken during the Archonship of Nausinicus was, as will be shewn, of a certain and fixed portion of the property, which was considered as being properly subject to taxation. This portion varied in the different classes ; in the first class a fifth part was taxable, in the inferior classes a smaller part: very inconsiderable properties were doubtless not admitted into the valuation of all. Consequently the national wealth was far more than five times the valuation, and exclusively of the public property, which was tax-free, may be estimated at thirty or forty thousand talents ; the annual incomes obtained from this amount of capital were at the least double what an equal sum would produce at the present time, and consequently every tax was at the most only half as large as it appears ; or rather even smaller still, for the possessor of a moderate property of five or six talents could hardly have consumed the returns from it upon his maintenance, without very expensive habits." vol. ii. p. 256.

But there is too much both of novelty and of interest in the subject, to admit of its being treated of very concisely, and our author pursues it through many pages with so much ability

of the slavery of the rich at Athens. *Xenoph. Econ. I.* says, you are loaded with *liturgies*, &c., of which, if you don't acquit yourselves well, the Athenians punish you just as if you had embezzled their money.]
    * C. 62–63, the Domesday Book of Attica.

and such a profusion of curious and recondite learning, that we shall furnish our readers with several other extracts of considerable length*—a step which we are the more inclined to take, because this valuable work has not (so far as we know) been reprinted in this country, and is not at all in general circulation here.

The following passage will serve as an introduction to what is to follow.

"The regulations with regard to the Athenian taxes before the time of Solon cannot be accurately ascertained. I consider it as certain that, before the changes introduced by this lawgiver, *all* the four tribes had not a share in the governing power; the Hopletes were the ruling aristocracy; under them were the Cultivators (Τελέοντες), the Goatherds (Αἰγικόρεις), and the Manual Labourers ('Αργάδεις); the Hopletes being the supreme and dominant class, the Cultivators paid them the sixth part of the produce, the same portion which in India the king formerly received; and these latter were, like the Penestæ or the Clients, bondmen or Thetes in the original sense, without any property in land, which belonged solely to the Hopletes. The latter bore arms when they served in war, and took their attendants into the field like the Thessalian Knights; for the maintenance of the State in time of peace little or nothing was necessary, and their wars were too inconsiderable to require an artificial structure of finance. The temples and priests were supported from the sacred estates, tithes, and sacrifices; and the administrators of justice were remunerated by gifts or fees (γέρα) upon each separate decision. The constitution of Solon first, as it appears, wholly abolished bondage, which must not however be confounded with slavery: the laws gave to all freemen, that is, to all the four tribes, a share in the government, apportioning their rights however according to the valuation (τίμημα, *census*); by which means the form of government was brought near a democracy, without actually being one. For Solon, according to the manner in which he instituted the Areopagus, placed a half-aristocratical counterpoise in the opposite scale; and also by only allowing the fourth class the right of voting in the assembly, and a share in the jurisdiction, but not permitting them to fill any office of government, he gave an influence to the upper and wealthier classes, by means of which the constitution was made to resemble a Timocracy, or an Oligarchy founded upon property. However without wishing to develope the whole system of Solon's institution of classes, we shall inquire into its nature in reference to the valuation and the public services.

"Solon made four classes (τιμήματα, τέλη), a number afterwards adopted by Plato in his works on laws; the methods according to which they fixed them were however very different. The first class was the Pentacosiomedimni; that is to say, those who received 500 measures either dry or liquid, from their lands, medimni of dry, and metretæ of liquid measure. For the second class he took those who received 300 measures, and could afford to keep a horse, viz. a war-horse ('ίππος πολεμιστήριοσ), to which was added another for a servant, and they must also necessarily have required a yoke of animals: this class was called Knights (ἱππῆς, ἱππάδα τελοῦντεσ). The third class are the Zeugitæ (ζεμγἶται), and their valuation is called the valuation of the Zeugitæ (ζευγίσιον τελεῖν); by which however is not to be understood a particular tax upon cattle used in ploughing, as might be supposed from the account given by Pollux. Their name is derived from keeping a yoke (ζεῦγος), whether of common mules, or of working-horses or oxen. Their income is stated in general at 200 measures of dry and liquid measure. The last class is the Thetes, whose valuation was less than that of the Zeugitæ. "The Pentacosiomedimni," says Pollux, "expended upon the public weal (ἀνήλισκον ἐς τὸ δημόσιον) one talent, the second 30 minas, the third 10 minas, and the Thetes nothing." vol. ii. pp. 258–261.

The question arises upon this statement of Pollux, which, M. Boeckh remarks, modern writers have repeated with great complacency, as shewing the *amount of taxes* paid by the several classes to the State, without being aware of the absurdity involved in that construction. One thing strikes us immediately, which is that, upon such a supposition, the revenue of the State must have been very large indeed, whereas it never amounted at any time to more than 2000 talents at the outside. Another obvious inference would be that the direct taxes imposed by it were enormously high. The contrary, however, was certainly the fact. In ten years Demosthenes paid two per cent. of his whole property, while the same property, well managed, brought in, for the same space of time, 100 per cent.* The conclusion is that the statement of Pollux must either be rejected altogether or be taken as containing a hitherto unexplained truth. This latter inference is Mr. Boeckh's and he appears to us to have solved, in a satisfactory manner, a very intricate problem, not at all understood by his predecessors.

"A tax according to the valuation can therefore be only supposed to have occurred upon extremely rare occasions under the institution of classes by Solon. The imposition of taxes was only a subordinate consideration; the chief objects were the obligation to military services, the Liturgies, and the apportioning of the rights of government. But, in order to comprehend how the scale was arranged in each case as it occurred, we must premise an observation upon the meaning of the word *valuation*, τίμημα). Custom has comprehended under this term a collection of very different ideas. Every estimate of the value of any article is so called; the estimate of property, the assessment of a fine, the estimate of a tax; in short, every thing that is valued. But a part of the property, which serves to regulate the apportioning of taxes, might be, with equal propriety, called by that name. Solon gave to each of the classes, except the Thetes, a fixed valuation, or Timema, and even the classes themselves are so called (τέτταρα τιμήματα) in Plato and in most other writers who mention them. This valuation, which we will call *the taxable capital*, is not absolutely identical with the estimate of property, and is very different from the tax. The grammarians had not formed any idea of Timema as taxable capital, for they sometimes confound it with the estimate of property; while Pollux considered it as the tax, and thus fell into a most important error. No rational explanation can be given of Solon's institution of classes, as far as it regards the direct taxation, but by embracing this view of the question. When so considered however we recognize his wisdom. Solon estimated the value of the medimnus at a drachma. Now if he had wished to ascertain the landed property of each class from the produce, his only way

* Vol. ii., pp. 293—294.

would have been to consider the number of medimni, or their equivalent in liquid measure, as the produce accruing from the land, taking however as his standard only the net proceeds, which were received as rent. We must therefore consider these 500, 300, 150 measures as net profits obtained from what an estate yielded as rent: a course which was the more natural, as many estates particularly those of the wealthy, were let by their masters to Thetes or to bond-slaves, as we are expressly informed with regard to the Thetes. That the rent was computed in kind, and not in money, is what might have been naturally expected. This practice indeed frequently occurs, even in later times ; nor would any other method have been possible at that period, on account of the small quantity of money in circulation. The next question to be considered is at what per-centage of the value of the property did Solon fix this net produce ? We are informed that rents were low in ancient times ; so late as in the speeches of Isæus we read of an estate which was let at eight per cent. We have therefore good reason for assuming that Solon, whose intention it must have been to encourage low rents, took the net proceeds as the twelfth part of the value of the land, or $8\frac{1}{3}$ per ct., and according to that scale fixed the property of a Pentacosiomedimnus at a talent, that is, at twelve times his income. According to the same calculation, the landed property of a Knight amounted to 3600 drachmas, of a Zeugites to 1800. The principle of this arrangement is perfectly correct; for the smaller the amount of the incomes, the less in proportion must the State take from an equally large part of the income of a citizen ; as every man must first provide maintenance for himself and his family, and the poor are oppressed to a greater degree than the rich, if they are taxed in the same proportion, and according to the same rate. Now this principle, so well adapted to the philanthropic lawgiver, may have been put in operation by Solon in two manners; either by the inferior class returning a smaller part of their property than the superior, for example, the first $\frac{1}{2}$ per cent. the second $\frac{1}{4}$ per cent, the third $\frac{1}{8}$ per cent ; or by the taxable capital being so rated, that in the lower classes only part of the property was considered as taxable. The first method renders the arrangement difficult and complicated ; the other is far more intelligible: the government knows the sum total of the taxable capital, and the amount of its own necessities, and it can be seen at once what part of the taxable capital must be demanded. This regulation appears to have been invariably followed at Athens, after it had been once taught by Solon. The Pentacosiomedimnus was, according to the regulation of his class, entered in the register with his whole productive landed property, the Knight with five-sixths, the Zeugites with five ninths of it ; but all paid the same part of the taxable capital when a duty was imposed. Supposing that the whole valuation, or the sum of all the taxable capitals, amounted to 3000 talents, and that the State was in need of 60 talents, a fiftieth must have been raised, and the division was in that case made as the following table shews :

Classes.	Incomes.	Landed estates.	Taxable capital.	Tax of a 50th.
Pentacos.	500 drachmas	6000 drachmas	6000 drachmas	120 drachmas
Knights	300 drachmas	3600 drachmas	3000 drachmas	60 drachmas
Zeugitæ	150 drachmas	1800 drachmas	1000 drachmas	20 drachmas

A more beautiful division is scarcely conceivable. It should be observed

however that it is possible, or even probable, that there existed some difference in the amount of taxes in the same class.* We may suppose that,
adhering still to the standard of property, they imposed the tax in such a
manner that in each class the taxable capital was fixed according to the
same proportion; as is shewn by the following table:

Classes.	Incomes.	Landed pro-perty.	Of which was taxable.	Taxable Capitals.	Tax of a 50th.
Pentacosio-medimni	1000 dr.	12000 dr.	The whole	12000 dr.	240 dr.
	750 dr.	9000 dr.	The whole	9000 dr.	180 dr.
	500 dr.	6000 dr.	The whole	6000 dr.	120 dr.
Knights	450 dr.	5400 dr.	Five-sixths	4500 dr.	90 dr.
	400 dr.	4800 dr.	Five-sixths	4000 dr.	80 dr.
	300 dr.	3600 dr.	Five-sixths	3000 dr.	60 dr.
Zeugitæ	250 dr.	3000 dr.	Five-ninths	1663¾ dr.	33⅓ dr.
	200 dr.	2400 dr.	Five-ninths	1333⅓ dr.	26⅔ dr.
	150 dr.	1800 dr.	Five-ninths	1000 dr.	20 dr.†

The principle of this classification, although very much questioned in our days, (which have seen some strange paradoxical
notions broached upon other points connected with this subject,)
has received the sanction of the most enlightened political economists of modern times. Adam Smith thought it "not very
unreasonable that the rich should contribute to the public expense, not only in proportion to their income, but something
more than in that proportion," and for this reason he approves of
a tax upon house-rents, because it would, in general, fall heav-
iest upon the rich.‡ And M. Say has expressed himself still
more decidedly to the same effect. Adverting to this opinion of
the great father of his science, he declares that "he has no hesitation in going farther and saying, that taxation cannot be equitable, unless its ratio be progressive."§ This valuation of Solon
seems to have been abolished during or about the time of the
Archonship of Euclid, (Olymp. 94.2. nearly 50 Olympiads after
it was established), but another was made twenty-five years,
when Nausinicus filled that office. The historical evidence of
the existence and the nature of this valuation is excessively
scanty, but, by a patient examination of scattered texts, M. Boeckh
comes to the following conclusion:

"From the simple explanation it is evident that, in the valuation taken
in the Archonship of Nausinicus, the principle of Solon's valuation was
followed in three points, viz. in the registration of the property itself
(οὐσία), the taxable part of it, or the valuation (τίμημα), and, lastly, the tax fixed

[* Montesquieu Esprit des lois, l. 13. c. 7.]
† In the above extract, it is obvious to observe, M. Boeckh confounds *rent* with
the whole produce of the land.
‡ Wealth of Nations, b. v. c. ii part ii. art. I. § 3.
§ Pol. Econ. lib. 3, c. 8, sect. 1, 2.

according to the valuation ($\varepsilon i \sigma \varphi o \varrho \dot{\alpha}$ in the limited sense). The estimate of the property was obtained by a valuation of all moveables and immoveables; the valuation, or the taxable capital, was only a certain part of this general census, and, in the highest classes, to which Timotheus and Demosthenes belonged, was the fifth part; in the others however it was a smaller portion; for Demosthenes expressly says that only those who had the highest valuations were rated at 500 drachmas for each 25 minas. If, for example, we reckon four classes, the valuation of the second may perhaps have been one-sixth of the property, of the third one-eighth, and of the fourth one-tenth, in order that the poor might be taxed in a fair proportion. It should be also observed that those persons in the same class whose property was different did not contribute an equally high valuation, but only the same part of their property; in the first class it was five for every 25 minas; thus the possessor of 15 talents contributed three, of 25 contributed five, of 50 contributed 10; for the reason that the estimate of the whole property of Demosthenes amounted to three talents was that for 25 minas five was in his class the rate of the taxable capital. But of the taxable capital each person paid the same part whenever any tax was imposed; and how large a part was to be taken could be easily determined, as the sum total of all the valuations was known, which in the Archonship of Nausinicus amounted to 5750 talents. In order to make this clear let us assume, for the sake of example, four classes, and in the second one-sixth, in the third one-eighth, in the fourth one-tenth, as the portion on which the tax was imposed: farther, as the least property from which taxes were paid, 25 minas; so that the latter is the lowest estimate of property in the last class: as the lowest estimate in the third class two talents, in the second class six, in the first twelve: which are arbitrary assumptions, except that, as we shall remark below, 25 minas were probably taken as the lowest property which was subject to taxation. If then a twentieth was to be raised, the tax would have fallen in the manner shewn by the following table:

Classes.	Property.	Of which was taxable.	Taxable capital.	Property tax of $\frac{1}{20}$
First of 12 talents and over.	500 talents	One fifth	100 talents	5 talents
	100 talents	One fifth	20 talents	1 talent
	50 talents	One fifth	10 talents	30 minas
	15 talents	One fifth	3 talents	9 minas
	12 talents	One fifth	2 tal. 24 min.	720 drachmas
Second of 6 talents and over, under 12 talents.	11 talents	One sixth	1 tal. 50 min.	550 drachmas
	10 talents	One sixth	1 tal. 40 min.	500 drachmas
	8 talents	One sixth	1 tal. 20 min.	400 drachmas
	7 talents	One sixth	1 tal. 10 min.	350 drachmas
	6 talents	One sixth	1 talent	300 drachmas
Third of 2 talents and over, under 6 talents.	5 talents	One eighth	37½ minas	187½ drachmas
	4 talents	One eighth	30 minas	150 drachmas
	3 talents	One eighth	22½ minas	112½ drachmas
	2¼ talents	One eighth	18¾ minas	93¾ drachmas
	2 talents	One eighth	15 minas	75 drachmas
Fourth of 25 minas and over, under 2 talents	1½ talents	One tenth	900 drachmas	45 drachmas
	1 talent	One tenth	600 drachmas	30 drachmas
	45 minas	One tenth	450 drachmas	22½ drachmas
	30 minas	One tenth	300 drachmas	15 drachmas
	15 minas	One tenth	250 drachmas	12½ drachmas *

* Vol. ii., pp. 288–290.

Of the *Symmoriæ*—classes or companies into which the citizens were divided for the purpose of paying the property-tax,
and of which Demosthenes declares that they had ceased at
that period (the delivery of the second Olynthiac) to be of any
use as a financial arrangement, having been turned—as such
things are apt to be—into a mere engine of factious politics—
the author has not been able to give an entirely satisfactory account. He cries out lustily for help to the editor of the oration
against Leptines (Wolf). Yet his own contribution to the clearing up of this difficult question is by no means inconsiderable.
We shall content ourselves, however, with barely citing the passage of Ulpian, the Scholiast of Demosthenes, ("the ignorant" is
his epithet with M. Boeckh,) which contains the fullest account
of them that has been left by any ancient writer.

" 'Each of the ten tribes," says he, "was obliged to specify 120 of its
own members who were the most wealthy. These 120 then divided themselves into two parts, so that there were sixty whose property was very
large, and the other sixty less rich. They did this in order that if a war
should suddenly break out, and the less wealthy should not happen to
have any money at their disposal, those who were more rich might advance the taxes for them, and be afterwards repaid at the convenience of
the others. This body of sixty was called a Symmoria." In the second
part, which is the work of a different hand, it is stated, that, "since each
of the ten tribes specified 120, the whole number of Liturgi (as they are
here called) was 1200: that they were distributed into two divisions, each
of 600 persons or ten Symmoriæ; that these two great divisions were
again subdivided into two smaller, each of which was composed of 300
persons or five Symmoriæ. One of these bodies of 300 was made up of
the most wealthy, who paid the taxes either before the others or for them
(προεισήφερον τῶν ἄλλων), the other 300 being in all things subject to them."
vol. ii. p. 299.

The object of the *Trierarchy*—the last subject we shall remark upon—was to provide for the *equipment* and *management* of the ships of war. The *equipment* and *management*
merely—for the State furnished the vessel itself, as well as the
pay and provision for the crew.* This explains a passage in
the oration of Æschines against Ctesiphon, which is a stumb-
ling block in the way of all beginners. Speaking of the "ac-
countability"—to use a cant word of our own politicians—of
public agents, he mentions that it extended even to the Trierarchs, though their business was to advance their own money
for the service of the commonwealth. Besides what he received
for the purposes above-mentioned, it was his duty to procure the
crew, which often required him to pay large sums in the shape
of bounties, and his office, to command the ship and accompany
it, either in person or by deputy, wherever it went.

It must strike every one as a very singular institution in a

* We refer for a pregnant illustration of this, as well as some other points discussed in this Article, to the 31st ch. of the 6th book of Thucydides.

maritime State, like Athens, engaged in incessant wars, her superiority in which was mainly due to her naval power, and having many dependencies, similarly situated, to defend, or to overawe, or to punish by means of her fleets, to leave the equipment of her ships in private hands, instead of making, what was the first of public interests, the first also of public concerns. It is vain to speak, as our author does, of the benefits arising out of the emulation excited among the Trierarchs, by the honors and distinctions awarded to the most zealous or liberal of them. A commonwealth must not reckon upon extraordinary impulses. A system of politics, calculated upon an enduring enthusiasm, can lead to nothing but imbecility and disgrace. It is taking the exception instead of the rule for its foundation—it is opposing the sure, constant, unchangeable tendencies of nature, and only destroying the more certainly and more hopelessly the very power it is compelled to exert in so wild an enterprize. Accordingly we find that, however it may have answered in the earlier ages of the republic, the Trierarchy was the cause of great embarrassments, when all the energies and resources of the State were called for to resist the ambitious encroachments of Philip.

It was, however, one of the most ancient institutions of Athens, and many methods, both of coercion and encouragement, had been adopted to make its efficiency adequate to the exigencies of war, carried on as war was wont to be among the Greeks. Officers were specially charged with the duty of seeing the fleets equipped in due time—the zeal, activity, or magnificence of the Trierarchs was rewarded with an appropriate crown—they who performed this liturgy were exempted from all others—the terms of service was limited to one year, and an interval of two more must have elapsed before a repetition of it could be required of the same person. If any one appointed to undertake this burthen thought that some other individual in the State—not legally exempted—was better able to bear it, he had his remedy in the *Antidosis*, or Exchange of fortunes, and, after the 3d year of the 105th Olmpiad, *Symmoriæ* were resorted to from necessity in this Liturgy, as they had been before in the property tax.

We subjoin an extract with a view of illustrating that singular institution, the *Antidosis*—one of the most odious and intolerable, it appears to us, that has ever been submitted to by a free people.

"Solon was the author of this regulation, which, though obviously subject to many difficulties, was neither unjust nor absurd, and it provided a ready means of redress against arbitrary oppression. To assist every man in obtaining his right, and to afford protection to the poor, were the predominant objects of the legislation of Solon, which he pursued without paying any regard to the inconveniences which might arise from the means employed in attaining them. The Exchange most frequently occured in the case of the Trierarchy, and not uncommonly in that of the Choregia; it existed however in the other Liturgies, and could also be had recourse to as a relief from the property-tax, if, for exanple, any one complained that his means were not greater than those of some other person who was rated to a lower class, or, as was frequently the case, that persons could prove themselves unfairly included in the class of the three hundred. This proceeding was allowed every year to the persons nominated for the Liturgies by the regular authorities, which in the case of the Trierarchy and property-taxes were the generals, to the great delay of military affairs. The offerer immediately laid a sequestration upon the property of his opponent, and sealed up his house, if he refused to accept the Liturgy; the house was however free to the first party. The next step was that both the parties undertook upon oath to give an account of their property, and were bound within the space of three days to deliver in an inventory (ὑπόφανσις) to each other. Then the cause was decided by the court. If the verdict was unfavourable to the party who made the offer, the proposed exchange did not take place; and it was in this manner that Isocrates gained his cause by means of his son Aphareus, against Megacleides, who had demanded to exchange property with him. If however the decision was in favour of the offerer, the opponent was free either to accept the exchange, or to perform the Liturgy. On that account Isocrates undertook the third of the three Trierarchies performed by himself and his son, when Lysimachus had claimed to exchange with him; and it is to this the oration concerning the Exchange refers, a speech of great length, but barren of information. Lastly, the party, to whom the offer was made, could not bring the cause into court, after the seal had been once imposed; but he was then obliged to take the Liturgy; as was the case with Demosthenes." vol. ii. pp. 368–370.

We close this paper with the following account of the iron money of Sparta.

"The employment of the base kinds of money derives its origin either from fraud, a scarcity of the precious metals, or from the notion that the precious metals are a source of corruption, and that therefore their home-circulation must be prohibited. From this latter cause, Plato in his second State imagines, according to the Doric model, a money circulating in the country, and devoid of value abroad (νόμισμα, ἐπιχώριον), deriving its, currency from the countenance of the State; and, together with this another coinage, not in circulation, but kept in the public coffers, of universal currency (Κοινὸν Ἑλληνικὸν νόμισμα), for the use of persons travelling in foreign parts, and the carrying on of war. This is not mere theory, but was actually put into practice in Sparta. Even in the time of the Trojan war, the precious metals were well known in the Peloponnese, and the Achaic Spartan Menelaus is particularly mentioned to have possessed both gold and silver; but the former remained scarce for a long time; whereas silver in the Grecian, as well as in all other nations, must have been the most general medium of exchange, as there were few places in which it could not be procured; in the more early times, however, it was not coined, but circulated in bars of a certain weight. But the Dorians, a people inhabiting a mountainous district, and carrying on no trade, were doubtless scantily supplied with the precious metals; and since it was a national principle, which existed both by usage and institution, and was afterwards confirmed by what is called the legislation of Lycurgus, to prevent as much as possible all intercourse with other tribes, they strictly prohibited, at a time long previous to the coining of money, the use of silver and gold as a medium of exchange, and thus effectually prevented their introduction into the country. If this regulation had not been made in early times, the interdiction of silver and gold could not have been ascribed to Lycurgus; no modern institution would have been attributed to so ancient a name. The Spartans therefore were driven to the use of some other metal as the common medium of exchange, and iron being abundantly obtained in the country, they made use of bars of that metal (ὀβελοὶ ὀβελίσκοι,) which was stamped with some mark in the iron furnaces of Laconia; while in the other countries bars of copper or silver were current; whence the obolus or *spit*, and the drachma or *handful* received their names. When afterwards Pheidon abolished the use of metallic bars and introduced coined money, the Spartans also began to stamp their iron in large, rude pieces; for which purpose they either used, as the author of the Eryxias asserts, lumps of this metal, which were useless for other purposes, such perhaps as are now used for making cannon balls, or, according to other accounts, they softened the best iron, so as to render it unfit for working, by cooling it when hot in vinegar. But, when Sparta began to aim at foreign dominion, it had need of a coinage that should be current abroad, for which purpose it imposed tributes upon the inhabitants of the islands, and demanded a contribution of a tenth from all the Greeks; a large quantity of the precious metals were also brought into the country by Lysander; and, as we learn from the first Alcibiades of Plato, the wealthy possessed much gold and silver, for when once imported it was never suffered to leave the country. But at this very time the prohibition to all of the private use of the precious metals was re-enacted, and the possession of gold or silver made a capital crime, the government remaining by law the exclusive possessor, as in the ideal State of Plato: a sufficient proof that this was an extremely ancient custom of the Spartans; although it again fell into disuse in the times which immediately succeeded, it being found impossible to maintain so unnatural a prohibition after the advantages of gold had been once made known to the people. In this instance therefore the iron-money was founded upon ancient usage and moral views." vol. ii. pp. 385–387.

Such was the Public Economy of Athens—a system, in many respects, rude and inartificial, in many, oppressive and vexatious, in all, widely different from any thing we see in our happy forms of government—and such, upon the whole, as no American citizen could bear to live under. Yet Athens, like the little democracies* of Italy in the 12th and 13th centuries, for some time flourished, even amid the storms that so often shook and desolated her. The spirit of republican *equality*, bold, energetic, vivifying, aspiring, acting upon minds constituted as no others seem ever to have been, before or since, produced many illustrious examples of the heroic in conduct—many more of the sublime in thought and sentiment. Herodotus, who saw her in her palmy state, and recorded her most glorious past, ascribes all her fortunes to this *equality*,† and, in a much later age, she is mentioned as a singular instance of a democracy that had risen to

[* Cf. the pointed remarks of Bettinelli, v. 1, p. 183, et seq.]
† Lib. v. cc. 77, 78.

grandeur and power.*   Before the well balanced constitution of
Solon was subverted by the demagogues of a later age, she had
made such progress that she could live through a long period of
misrule and adversity, not only without any apparent decay, but
even, in some respects, with seemingly increased splendor, and
the elegant compliment of Isocrates was well earned, that she
had made the Greek name a designation, not of a *race* of men,
but of a particular state of civilization, so that *they* were Greeks,
whom not a common origin, but her refined discipline identified as one people.

* Strabo, lib. iv., c. 35, § 3.

D'AGUESSEAU.

1. Memoir of the Life of Henry Francis D'Aguesseau, Chancellor of France; and of his Ordonnances for consolidating and amending certain portions of the French Law: And an historical and literary account of the Roman and Canon Law. By Charles Butler, Esq. Barrister at Law. Fourth Edition. *London. Murray.* 1830.

2. Œuvres complétes du Chancelier D'Aguesseau nouvelle édition, augmentée, de pièces échappées aux premiers éditeurs et d'un discours préliminaire. Par M. Pardessus, Professeur à la faculté de droit de Paris. (16 tom. 8vo.) *Paris.* 1819.

In the little volume placed at the head of this article, Mr. Butler has surpassed himself. Notorious as he is for a garrulous smattering in all things knowable, we did not think it possible he should put forth such a scandalous piece of book-making, on such a subject as the life of D'Aguesseau. We sent for his work with hopes which have been most cruelly disappointed. We have long thought a complete view of the services, the talents, the learning, and the character of the illustrious subject of this Memoir, a desideratum in English legal literature. It struck us, too, that Mr. Butler was as well qualified for such a task as any English lawyer of whom we have recently heard, except the late Sir Samuel Romilly. But what are we to think of a miserable little compilation of some seventy or eighty pages octavo, with as much margin as text, recording of one, who, for sixty years together, filled by far the largest space in the eyes of the French nation of any legal character since the Chancellor De l'Hospital, and who, for full half that period, was the *very* successor of that great man in the dignity, the duties, and we may add, the glory of the highest station in the judicature of France, very little more than might be learnt from his epitaph? We will venture to assert that a more satisfactory account—and beyond all comparison more satisfactory—of D'Aguesseau is to be found in the notes to Thomas' Eloge, alone, than in this work of Mr. Butler. But if it is strange that the author should publish such a thing as this, what shall we say of the people that encourage him? It appears that this book has actually passed through four editions. Nor is this to be ascribed to the value of the "historical and literary account of the Roman and Canon

Law," that accompanies the "Memoir." Qui Bavium non odit, amet tua carmina Mavi. A reading public which can patronize one of these enterprises is quite worthy of the other: and we confess that, taken together, the success of them gives us a very unfavorable notion of that part of the English reading public that is interested in the science and literature of law. Or shall we rather infer that so impatient is its curiosity about such things, that, rather than have nothing at all said about them, they are willing to look favorably even upon the drivellings of Mr. Butler?

We are afraid that this last suggestion is altogether improbable. Some five and twenty years ago, when Mr. Evans published his translation of Pothier on Obligations, it is evident that even he had but just made the acquaintance of D'Aguesseau. The readers of that valuable work know that it is enriched by a dissertation on mistakes of law, from the pen of D'Aguesseau, and by two of his *plaidoyers*, when Avocat-Général. The translator himself professes to have come to his knowledge of those admirable productions but a short time before the publication of his own book, and he is so enraptured at his discovery, that nothing prevented his imparting to the public a much larger share in his new acquisitions but the painful conviction that the public had not the least desire to partake of them. The truth is that, if a man were called upon to name the sort of intellectual pursuit which was most at variance with all elegance of taste, all literary acquirement, all comprehensive and profound philosophy, all liberal and enlarged views of science and of society, in short, with all that made D'Aguesseau—what he was—the most accomplished of advocates, of jurists and of magistrates, as well as of scholars and gentlemen—he would without any hesitation name the Common Law of England, as it has been generally studied by the practitioners of Westminster Hall. In a passage from Hotman, quoted by Mr. Butler elsewhere,* Polydore Virgil is represented as having pronounced the jurisprudence of that country a mingled or chaotic mass of foolishness and captious subtlety, and Erasmus breathes a sigh over the fate of Sir Thomas Moore, constrained by circumstances to devote his elegant mind to the study of a body of laws, than which nothing, in the opinion of the Dutch scholar, could be more *illiterate*.† We have more than once, in the course of our labors, had occasion to make a similar remark, which we shall have now a fair opportunity more fully to develope and illustrate. We would not be understood to detract from the unquestionable and

---

* Pref. to Coke—Littleton.—We remarked, in a former number, a ludicrous blunder of Mr. Butler, in translating the words of Hotman—a blunder unaccountable in a man of his education—or of any education.

† Quibus nihil illiteratius.

transcendant merits of the common law, whether it be considered in reference to its rules of property, its system of legal logic,* or the maxims of justice, of morality, and of sound policy which it is studious to inculcate and enforce. Above all, we do not mean to dispute its justly conceded pre-eminence, as a scheme of liberty—a scheme of practical liberty—better, by far, than any other people, either of ancient or of modern times, have ever enjoyed. Our objection goes to form rather than substance, to the manner of teaching rather than to the things taught. With the exception of some men, who would be exceptions to any rule—such as Bacon and Mansfield—the lights of Westminster Hall have been mere practical lawyers, with abundance of knowledge, and exact knowledge, but without one spark of philosophy. Take Lord Coke and Lord Eldon, for example—the two men, perhaps, of the greatest amount of legal acquirement, that have ever adorned the bench in England—whose very *dicta* are oracles, and who never touch upon a subject, however incidentally, without pouring out upon it a flood of curious learning. For all practical purposes these great judges deserve the consideration they enjoy, yet it would be difficult to name two men who fall so miserably short of that elegant and finished model upon which the distinguished civilians seem to have formed themselves. If any of our readers doubt this, we recommend to their dispassionate perusal the writings of Domat, of Pothier, and, above all, of the Chancellor D'Aguesseau.

The appearance of Lord Mansfield, as Chief-Justice of the King's Bench, was an era of signal improvement. That great judge was not a better magistrate than Lord Hardwicke. Perhaps, if, in the administration of the laws, preference is to be awarded to either of them, it is due to the latter, in whose person Wisdom herself, as Mr. Fox observed of him, seemed to deliver the responses of the Law. But his great rival had to work upon materials less tractable than the subjects of Chancery jurisdiction. He had to contend with more inflexible technical forms—and the yet more inflexible prejudices of technical men. This latter difficulty may be easily imagined from the disposition manifested by Lord Kenyon, on all occasions, to overrule or qualify decisions which, however agreeable to a refined equity, and even to sound principles of law, that narrow minded man, wherever there happened to be no case in point, naturally enough regarded as so many dangerous innovations. But the reputation of Lord Mansfield has increased with the progress of time—as the conclusions of enlightened reason must ever be confirmed by the voice of experience. He is admitted to have been, in some sort, the founder of a new school of jurisprudence—not that he invented any thing (which would have been rather a sinister

* Generally speaking, that is.

glory in a judge or jurist) but that he introduced a new *me-thod*—that he pointed out connections where none had been be-fore observed, and simplified the science by comprehensive ge-neralizations—in a word, that he did much to perfect the har-mony and concordance of the law, and to shew that its seeming-ly arbitrary rules generally coincide with the dictates of right reason. Yet, great as Lord Mansfield's pre-eminence among English lawyers confessedly is, he is indebted for it, in no small degree, to the writings of the civilians. They were his masters and his model. In every branch of commercial law, they fur-nished him not only with ascertained principles, but even with express precepts and established precedents—and Mr. Evans* has shown, by a very curious collation of the text of the civili-ans, that, even in laying down the rules which govern the action for money had and received, he adopted not only their doctrines but their very words.

The great advantage—unquestionable, we think—of the man-ner in which subjects are treated of by the Roman lawyers and those who have succeeded them in modern times, is implied in what we have said of Lord Mansfield. It consists in looking upon jurisprudence as a science, and an ethical science, of which the principles—however modified, occasionally, and controlled by the policy of society—are to be found in the conclusions of right reason and the unalterable feelings of human nature. Of law, they justly conceived, with Cicero,† that it is the recorded morality of a nation—a rule of social duty, no less than of civil conduct—of which the great object is not only security in the possession and certainty in the transmitting of property, but the consecration, if we may so express it, of good faith, of integrity, of loyalty—the impressing upon men's minds, by enforcing in all their commerce with each other, the sanctity of obligations— the setting the seal of the public will and understanding, the unanimous assent of a whole society, and that society a great people, upon the principles of a refined equity and an enlarged benevolence, reduced to practice in the daily concerns of life, with the precision, the consistency and the uniformity of an ex-act science. The great lawyers of antiquity, in the golden age of the Roman law especially, were great philosophers as well. Their disquisitions, their dicta, their very definitions, all smack of the schools. In the progress of the Roman law this spirit made itself more and more apparent. At first there were many arbitrary rules in it, and from these were sometimes deduced, by an over-refined and captious logic, conclusions more subtle than sound, which gave to that jurisprudence the same technical and artificial air that strikes us in the writings of the bulk of our

---

* Translation of Pothier, vol. ii. p. 379.
† De Legib. de Republica.

common lawyers. By degrees, these rules were modified by the Edict of the Prætor, evaded by the interpretations of the jurisconsults, and formally abolished by the Emperors. It is not necessary to read further than the Institutes and the Antiquities of Heineccius to perceive how many salutary changes were introduced, one by one, by the Cæsars, and, at length, in a whole body, by Justinian, of which the object was to substitute rational for arbitrary legislation, and to give to the law a simplicity, at once elegant in theory and convenient in practice— the *simplicitas legibus amica*, as Tribonian happily enough expresses it. The civilians, as we remarked on a former occasion,* distinguished carefully between the *jus civile*, or positive law of a single people, and the *jus gentium*, the law of nature, universally recognized by the nations. Their scheme of improvement was to make the former part of their jurisprudence approximate, as nearly as might be, to the latter—to make them coincide, if possible, by merging the one in the other—and, in this scheme, they succeeded far beyond all other examples. The proof of this is equally obvious and decisive. Their labours have almost superseded those of modern legislators and jurists. Their great collection—though arranged in a manner altogether unworthy of the wisdom it has preserved and perpetuated—was brought to light in a semi-barbarous age. It was hailed with joy and gratitude, as a revelation of the holiest mysteries of justice—the understandings of men, comparatively unenlightened as they were, at once assented to the reason, while their hearts felt the morality of its precepts—and, in the schools of philosophy and literature, all over Europe, the most learned professors of their day, were employed to explain and disseminate its principles, which it was thought scarcely possible to improve. The strength of the evidence, in favour of this system of laws, increased with the severity of the tests to which it was subjected. In the progress of society, its relations become every day more complex and extensive, and rules adapted to the various exigencies of human affairs were wanted. The barbarous customs, local and general—the comparatively few, and very imperfect ordinances of the Kings—tended rather to confound than to inform and to guide those who were to execute justice, in matters of contract, between man and man. Yet the deficiences of domestic legislation—which would have been so embarrassing under other circumstances—were scarcely felt when the Corpus Juris Civilis was to be found in every library. Those volumes presented to the rising commonwealths of Europe a body of jurisprudence, not local, temporary and occasional, but so purged of what is merely arbitrary and technical, as to be almost equally well adapted to all times and nations—a

* So. Review—No, 3, Art. iii.

collection of written reason, as it has been well called, ratified by the experience of centuries, and approaching so nearly, in its dispositions, to the ideal perfection of universal law, as to have left but little to be done by succeeding ages, in the way of any substantial addition or improvement in the most important departments of jurisprudence. This is the brief account of the introduction of the Civil Law into every enlightened forum on the continent of Europe, and of the profound respect with which it is regarded even by those who do not acknowledge its authority.

If the excellence of that system of jurisprudence—as it stood in the third century, its Augustan age, and has been transmitted to us with some modifications in the Justinian collection—is so conspicuous, the manner in which it has been cultivated and administered in modern times has contributed to maintain it in all its perfection. We shall have occasion to dwell more upon the constitution of the continental courts, in the sequel, but it may as well be remarked here that they who have adorned the tribunals and the law chairs, in the Universities of France, have resembled, in their habits and thoughts, such men as Lord Coke and Lord Eldon, almost as little, as the Corpus Juris resembles the Grand Coutumier. The prominent men of Westminster Hall, we have said, have been, generally speaking, mere men of business. Some of them who have attained to the highest reputation, Saunders for instance, made their way to eminence by skill in the merest technicalities of the science, helped, perhaps, by low arts in the practice. It was a saying in Edinburgh that no barrister who had inherited £2000, had ever done much in the Parliament house. The remark is more strictly applicable to Westminster Hall. Necessity—not fame—"is the spur that the clear spirit doth raise, to spurn delights and live laborious days" in the Inns-of-Courts, and their results have been just what might be expected from the causes and the inspiration. What conception could an illiterate, narrow-minded, plodding, *pragmatic*, like Lord Kenyon, have formed of such a judicial mind as D'Aguesseau's or l'Hospital's?* How utterly impossible were

---

* By way of specimen of the studies, no less elegant than profound, of the great civilians, we extract the following passage from the *Dialogue des Avocats du Parlement de Paris* of Loisel, which contains some sportive Latin verses of this celebrated man.

"L'autre conte est que Bariot s'étant depuis fait conseiller, était si amoureux de procez, qu'il prenait plaisire à faire attacher ses sacs par ordre en l'une de ses chambres, lesquels il allait souvent visiter et compter avec autant de contentement que fait un laboureur ses troupeaux de moutons ; ce que feu M. le chancelier de l'Hospital prist plaisir de representer par ces vers.

　　　　Nam memini quemdam plenum gravitatis et annis,
　　　　Burgundà de gente senem, cui mille ligatis
　　　　Inclusæ saccis pendebant ordine lites:
　　　　Has omnes animi causà semel omnibus horis

it for any man of that age, or, we may add, of any subsequent age, trained for success in the English Courts, to have produced such a work as Grotius' de Jure Belli et Pacis ? The materials of that noble monument of genius, learning and taste, were supplied by the same education which fitted its author to shine in professional and political life in his own country and times, but no man encumbered with such superfluous accomplishments could have risen into notice, much less to renown, as a lawyer in England. If Murray's wit and Blackstone's comparatively moderate acquirements were obstacles to *their* preferment, we ought not to wonder that the schools of the common law have never produced a Hugo Grotius. Now promotion of all sorts, in England, has almost uniformly awaited those only who have succeeded at the bar—and they only have succeeded who have thought of little else but promotion. A great special pleader has been in more request even than an eloquent advocate, and both were very much preferred before a profound and philosophical jurist. They ordered things differently in France—as we shall see.

There is certainly a broad and permanent distinction between practical and speculative talent, that must be, more or less, perceived and acknowledged every where. It is remarked, in a valuable old monument of French legal literature,* that professors of colleges, however learned and able, seldom succeeded even in the Parliament of Paris. So we have it, upon the same venerable authority, that neither Bodin nor Dumoulin —immense as was their learning—was distinguished at the bar. But it is impossible to compare the *plaidoyers* of the most celebrated French advocates with the arguments of counsel in the reports of English cases, without seeing that the skill required in these latter must be acquired by a very different sort of training from that which formed the wisdom and elegance of D'Aguesseau. The necessity—unknown in a civil law court—of narrowing down a controversy to a single issue for the purpose of jury-trial, and the character of this sort of trial itself, have, no doubt, their share in producing this effect. But the excessive subtlety and technical rigour of the pleadings, and the forms both of practice and conveyancing, have done still more. Add

Ille recensebat, minimumque putabat ad assem,
Quid tandem lucri numero speraret ab illo:
Ut pastor, cui mille boves in montibus errant,
Quem ferat ex vitulis fructum, quem lacte reportet
Presso vel liquido, quem denique matribus ipsis
Subducit tacitus: nummo nec fallitur uno.

J'ay voulu, says M. Pasquier in the Dialogue referred to, apprendre ces vers par cœur, car ils le meritent bien ; et veux que vous scachiez que c'est de luy qu'il doivent être entendus."

* The Dialogue des Avocats just referred to in a note, edited with some other pieces by M. Dupin, Paris, 1818, vol. i. p. 323.

to this the endless intricacies of the law of estates—the oppro-
brium of a philosophic age—and the pedantic bigotry with
which the *practitioners,* who have found their way to the English bench, have followed precedents, however, at variance
with principle, and excluded the lights of foreign law, even
when most clear and satisfactory. If such a man as Lord Mansfield had lived in the time of Lord Coke, the jurisprudence of
England, without being, in any of its essential provisions, very
materially altered, whould have assumed a different external form
and air. As it is, the shape impressed upon it in the times of
school divinity is still clearly perceivable, and it is difficult to
read the Abbé de Mably's criticism upon Dumoulin and Loyseau, without applying it, in some measure, to the author of the
Commentary upon Littleton and his scholars and successors.*

But if the civilians, as a body of professed jurists, are to be
preferred, in respect of the philosophy of law, to the great men
of Westminster Hall, D'Aguesseau is, in this and some other
respects, entitled to the highest place even among the civilians.
Not that in the mere science of jurisprudence he has excelled
them all. It would be manifestly extravagant to say so. France
(to confine ourselves to her) has illustrious names to boast of in
this, as in every other department of thought and knowledge.
She has her l'Hospitals and her Lamoignons, her Domats and
her Pothiers, her Cujas', and her Brissons, her Cochins and her
Patrus. Of these great men some adorned the bar and the
bench with whatever, in the character of the judge and the
advocate, can invest the judgment-seat of an enlightened people

---

* En lisant Dumoulin et Loyseau, qu'on appelle par habitude les lumières du
barreau, on a quelque peine à concevoir comment ils conservent leur ancienne
réputation; elle devrait être un peu déchue, depuis qu'on met de la dialectique
dans les ouvrages, qu'on raisonne sur des idées et non pas sur des mots, qu'on
commence à connaitre le droit naturel, &c. He goes on to say "Dumoulin, trés
supérieur à Loyseau était un trés grand génie, c'était le plus grand homme de
son siècle; mais il en avait plusieurs défauts, s'il renaissait dans le notre, il
rougirait de ses erreurs et nous éclairerait." Observat: sur l'histoire de France.
lib. iv. c. 3. in note. We quote these words by way of illustration merely—not
as assenting to the justness of the strictures they contain. Of Dumoulin we
know only what we have gathered from other writers—especially from Pothier,
who frequently cites and discusses his opinions. The Abbé de Mably, though
an able and learned man, was not a lawyer; and so is not to be regarded as a
good authority on such subjects. D'Aguesseau pronounces Dumoulin "l'auteur
le plus analytique qui ait écrit sur la jurisprudence." And M. Camus, speaking'
of the commentators on the Coutume de Paris, says, "Dumoulin le premier
d'entr'eux, est au droit Français ce que Cujas est au droit Romain." Lettres
sur l'etude du Droit Français; lett. 4e. After declaring his Treatise on fiefs and
rents to be an inexhaustible mine, in which all the principles of French law are
contained, he proceeds to add: "On a reproché á Dumoulin qu'il est prolix;
que ses périodes sont interminables, ses distinction et ses limitations sans fin, &c.
Ces reproches, le dernier surtout, annoncent des gens qui se sont contentés
d'ouvrir Dumoulin." It is worth while to observe that Dumoulin was a great
master of the Logic of the schools. It was his habit, says M. Camus, to discuss
the *pour* and *contre* of every proposition—de mettre ce principe *en thèse*—and to
decide, generally, according to the reasonings which he placed last.

with authority and dignity and commanding influence. Others filled the chairs of her universities with eminent usefulness in their own generation, and published works in which the leading minds of all nations have sought and found the helps of profound research and exact and comprehensive speculation. His mind and his heart were equally and perfectly well disciplined. He had received the sort of education which metaphysicians have mentioned as the best practical fruit of mental philosophy. All the powers and capacities of his intellectual and moral being seem to have been cultivated with a view to its highest perfection. His was that harmony of character, the music of the well attuned soul, in which the Platonists in their dreams of that perfection make it to consist. Truth and beauty—eternal truth, the unblemished form of ideal beauty which can neither vary nor fade away—were never revealed in greater purity and loveliness to the vision of any man. In those admirable discourses—the *mercuriales*—of which we shall presently say more — D'Aguesseau has embodied, so to speak, his conceptions of excellence, and not the mere naked conceptions, as a metaphysician might have done, but glowing with life, radiant with glory, clothed in such shapes and hues as genius is sure to bestow upon the objects of its "desiring phantasy." His works are justly pronounced, by his last editor, one of the best courses of lectures on rhetoric and morals, that is any where to be found.* Throughout the whole range of his inquiries—involving all the subjects that are most interesting to man as a social and responsible being—religion, ethics, jurisprudence, political justice and political economy, literature, metaphysics—the same enlarged views, the same refined criticism, the same sound judgment are every where displayed, in a style, which we cannot better characterise than by saying that it is in every respect worthy of the age of Racine and Boileau and Bossuet and Fenelon.

Henry Francis D'Aguesseau was born, at Limoges, on the 16th of November, 1668. St. Simon says "his grand-father was a *maître des comptes*, and it is just as well to go no farther back."† This *maître des comptes*, however, succeeded in marrying his children into noble families, and in transmitting to the subject of these remarks, through his son Henry D'Aguesseau, an inheritance of virtue and honour, far better than the puerile distinctions of rank which were so precious in the eyes of St. Simon, and which the present century has seen altogether exploded in France. Henry D'Aguesseau, father of the Chancellor, filled many important public offices with distinguished use-

* M. Pardessus. Discours Preliminaire. p. 23, et seq.

† Œuvres de St. Simon, v. ix. p. 1. Yet Thomas (Eloge Note I.) says, Du côte de son père, il descendait d'une ancienne famille qui a possédé des terres en Saintonge et dan l'isle d'Oleron, &c.

fulness and reputation. While intendant successively of Guienne, Limousin and Languedoc, a paternal administration endeared him to the provinces which it made flourishing and
prosperous.   It were sufficient for his fame that he contributed
very much to the accomplishment of that great work, the canal
of Languedoc, and that, amid the scenes of persecution and civil
strife that preceded and followed the revocation of the edict of
Nantes, he had wisdom, philanthropy and courage enough, to
preach and even to practise toleration.   In all the relations of
life, he displayed the same unblemished and stern virtues ; and
it is difficult to conceive a more perfect character than his illustrious son has drawn of him, in an elaborate discourse—one of
his finest compositions—written in exile, for the double purpose
of strengthening his own resolutions by the contemplation of
such an example, and of recommending it, in the most impressive and affecting manner, to the imitation of his children. "You
will see in the following sketch"—it is thus that he speaks of
this second Agricola—"a character always consistent with itself,
and uniformly sustained from early youth to an extreme old
age—a mind, comprehensive, fertile, luminous, as winning by
its natural graces as it was admirable for its great elevation, so
gifted as to be able to dispense with the help of labor, and yet so
laborious that it seemed unconscious of its happy gifts—a heart
full of sensibility, noble, generous, always occupied with the interests of other people, and never with its own, devoting itself to
all mankind with a charity that knew no bounds but those which
limit the wants of humanity—a man, simple and sincere, an
enemy to all ostentation, humble even to excess, if it were possible for man to be too humble, respectable for his wisdom, venerable for his sanctity—in a word, a man adorned with every virtue, and whom during the course of a long life, no word or deed
ever escaped which was not inspired by reason and consecrated
by religion."   The character of a father is not always important
in a biography of his son, but the whole education of D'Aguesseau, in the proper sense of that most comprehensive word, was
received under the eyes, the direction and the influence of this
exemplary and wise man.   In this respect he enjoyed the same
advantage which the younger Pitt derived from the personal instructions of Chatham, and we must not wonder that we find him,
like that great man, at the early age of twenty-two, taking a decided lead, among the sagest counsellors of France, in the Parliament of Paris, and pronouncing, from the parquet, discourses
which are perfect models of their kind.   It was at that age that
D'Aguesseau was appointed, at the request of his father, to the
place of third Avocat-Général in that court.

Properly to appreciate the merit of any man, it is indispensable that we consider the condition of the art or profession to

which he belongs at the period of his first essays in it. It is with this view that we quote the following passage from a discourse of M. Pardessus, prefixed to his edition of the works of D'Aguesseau.

"Au moment où D'Aguesseau fût revêtu de la place d'Avocat-Général au Parlement de Paris, le barreau Français ne jetait point l'éclat dont il brilla peu de temps après.

"L'éloquence de la Chaire, qu'un savant distingué trouvait, au commencement du dix-septième siècle, si basse, qu'on n'en pouvait rien dire, était arrivé sous Louis XIV. au plus haut degré qu' elle peut atteindre ; tandisque celle du barreau, qui avait commencé la premiere à sortir de la barbarie, était restée dans l'enfance et ne consistait que dans l'enflure l'accumulation de citations de tout espèce, l'emploi sans discernement de toutes ces figures de rhétorique, dont la comédie des Plaideurs offre un tableau piquant.

"Si Patru, qu'on ne saurait soupçonner d'être arrivé par le credit des gens de cour, ou la bassesse des sollicitations, à siéger dans l'académie, auprés de Bossuet et de Fénélon, dut cette honneur à sa grande supériorité sur les autres avocats, quelle idée faut il que nous ayons de l'éloquence du barreau à cette époque.

On ne saurait cependant, comme l'ont fait quelques écrivains, s'en prendre à l'imperfection des études et au défaut d'instruction véritable.

"Lamoignon et Domat, s'élevant dans leurs écrits jusqu' à l'origine et à la raison des lois, avaient substitué la simplicié du style et la sagesse de la méthode à la stérile abondance et à la savante obscurité de leurs dévanciers.

*   *   *   *   *   *   *   *

"Il est donc plus simple de reconnaître que le même âge qui produit les hommes supérieurs dans un genre, en est quelquefois avare un autre. Les deux plus célèbres avocats du siècle de Louis XIV, Lemaître et Patru, méritaient sans doute, par rapport à leurs contemporains, le rang qu'ils occupaient.

"Ils l'émportaient certainement sur leurs émules pour la science d'appliquer les lois, d'établir et de disposer les preuves ; ils ne manquaient même de force dans les raisonnements, ni quelquefois de chaleur ou de pathétique dans le style ; mais ils ne connaissaient pas ce bon gout qui fait vivre les productions de l'esprit ; ou s'ils l'ont connu, ils n'ont pas eu la force de quitter la route commune, et de secouer le joug des préjugés." *Discours Préliminaire* xviii.

Although this account of the state in which D'Aguesseau found the eloquence of the French bar is probably somewhat exaggerated, we may safely affirm that much was to be done in order to raise it to the standard of ideal excellence in the art.*

"Un jeune homme de vingt-deux ans devoit faire une révolution complète. Elevé par un père qui connaissait le prix d'une éducation solide, admis, dès sa plus tendre jeunesse, dans la societé de Racine et de Boileau, D'Aguesseau n'avait négligé aucune des études qui peuvent former l'orateur.

___

* We say exaggerated, because Voltaire, a judge above all exception, ascribes to Patru the high honour of having been one of the earliest models of elegance and purity in French, and having thus contributed much to improve the taste of the nation.—Siècle de Louis XIV.

"Nourri de tout ce que la poésie offre de plus riche et de plus brillant, l'histoire de plus solide et de plus instructif, les mathématiques de plus exact et de plus profond, la philosophie de plus grave et de plus élevé, l'éloquence de plus sublime et de plus gracieux, il fixa, par ses premiers essais, les regards et l'admiration. Le public fut étonné et comme transporté par des discours qui réunissaient aux charmes de l'imagination, aux richesses de la science, à la noble simplicité du style, la force et l'autorité de la raison ; et jamais prédiction ne fut plus vraie et mieux accomplie, que celle du fameux Denis Talon : *Je voudrais finir comme ce jeune homme commence !*

"Chaque année multipliait ses succès et developpait en lui les traits auxquels on reconnait l'orateur jurisconsulte. Ce titre si rare lui fut déféré de son vivant : il en était d'autant plus digne qu'il n'en fut point ébloui, et l'on pouvait dire de lui comme de Caton, que *moins qu'il cherchait la gloire, plus elle le suivait.*

"Sa juste admiration pour les grands modèles l'avait amené à se former un style qui réunît les beautés particulieres à chacun d'eux. On trouve, dans ses harangues, la séverité et l'énergie de Démosthène, le nombre et l'harmonie de Cicéron, la hauteur de pensées de Bossuet, et la douceur persuasive de Fénélon.

"Cequ'il a écrit sur la nécessité de se former par l'étude des grands écrivains, ne doit pas, moins que son example, encourager les jeunes athlétes du barreau à puiser dans ces sources de beautés immortelles. En voyant un homme qui né avec un génie véritable, s'honorait de suivre les exemples et les leçons des maîtres de l'art, ils se convaincront que l'esprit ne suffit point ; qu'il faut apprendre pour bien penser ; savoir, pour bien dire ; qu'il n'y a qu'une imprudente témerité à prétendre s'ouvrir une route nouvelle, et que c'est en marchant sur les traces des anciens qu'on parvient à les égaler." *Ibid.* xx. xxi.

From the time that D'Aguesseau entered upon the office of Avocat-Général until his death—a period of sixty years—he was engaged in the highest judicial functions. Of this period for somewhat less than ten years he continued in that office— for somewhat more than sixteen he was Procureur-Général— during the remainder—including the time passed in exile, for he was twice *disgraced*—he was Chancellor of France. It is impossible to form a just estimate of some of the most important productions of his genius, without comprehending precisely the nature of these different offices and the duties which were incident to them. It is, again, not very easy to explain the functions of the Avocat and Procureur-Général, without looking into the constitution of the Parliaments (as they were called) especially that of Paris. With this view, we give place to the following passage from Mr. Butler's Memoir.

"Speaking generally, in England, the judges of the royal courts are chosen from the barristers : all England would stand aghast at a different appointment. In France, no avocat or barrister was raised to the seat of a judge in a royal court. The wisdom of this arrangement is maintained by many respectable writers on the continent. To us, and, as we believe, to every Englishman, it must appear preposterous in the extreme. Still we are not to suppose that the French judges were unlearned, because they were not taken from the bar. They always went regularly through previous courses of civil and canon law, and studied systematically the written and unwritten laws of their country. On these they afterwards underwent a solemn and serious examination; if they were found deficient they were either remanded for a further examination, or were absolutely rejected. The first volume of the quarto edition of the works of the Chancellor D'Aguesseau contains a 'Discourse" addressed by him to his son 'on the Study of the Laws.' It shews the extensive reading and just views of the Chancellor; but so little of this Discourse is applicable to the study of the law of England, that, although we are thoroughly sensible of its value, we shall make no further comment on it in this place.

"The close of the *fifteenth* century is described by the French writers as the golden age of the French magistracy. It is every where said that the knowledge, which the members of it possessed of the law, was at once extensive and profound, and that they were equally conversant in its theory and its practice; that they respected their profession, and were aware of the importance of a proper discharge of their duties; and that, while their undeviating attention and gravity convinced the lowest class of subjects that justice would be fully and impartially administered to them, they equally intimated to persons in the highest classes of society that, in the scales of justice, rank was of no account.

"At six o'clock in the morning, both winter and summer, the magistrates took their seats in court. At ten o'clock, the beadle entered the court and announced the hour; they then went to dine. After dinner, they returned to their seats; at six o'clock, the business of the courts was closed, the rest of the day was devoted to their families: literary pursuits were their only relaxation. 'To feel,' says the *Abbé Gédoyn*, in one of his entertaining memoirs, 'that magistrates were, in those days, more addicted, than they are in our times, to professional and literary studies, it is sufficient to compare the state of Paris at that time with its present state. At the time we speak of, the police of Paris was very bad; the city was ill built, and had not half either of the houses or the inhabitants which it now contains. The streets were ill laid out, excessively dirty, never lighted, and therefore, after dusk, unsafe. The only public spectacles were vulgar farces, after which the populace ran with avidity, but which all decent persons avoided. Their meals were frugal; there was nothing in them to attract company; the fortunes of individuals were small, and parsimony was the only means of increasing them. A coach of any kind was hardly seen; persons of high rank walked on foot, in galoches or small boots, which, when they paid a visit of ceremony, they left in the ante-chamber, and resumed when they quitted it. The magistrates rode on mules when they went to courts of justice, or returned from them. It followed that when a magistrate, after the sittings of the court, returned to his family, he had little temptation to stir again from home. His library was necessarily his sole resource: his books his only company. Speaking generally, he had studied hard at college, and had acquired there a taste for literature, which never forsook him. To this austere and retired life, we owe the Chancellor de l'Hospital, the President de Thou, Pasquier, Loisel, the Pithous, and many other ornaments of the magistracy. These days are passed; and they are passed because the dissipation of Paris is extreme. Is a young man of family now destined for the law? Before he attains his sixteenth year, a charge is obtained for him, and he sports a chariot. With such facilities of going and coming, what a wish must there be to be in every place where pleasure calls! Consider only the time given, even by persons of decent habits of life, to music and the opera! What a subtraction it is from that portion of time which the magistrates of old gave to professional study and literature.' " pp. 22–26.

If there is one thing in human institutions which would be pronounced *a priori* more absurd than all others—if there is any thing which the common law of the Anglo-Saxon race may be said, without a figure, to abhor—it is the venality of judicial office.   Yet strange to say, in the opinion of some able writers, this monstrous anomaly produced in France effects the very reverse of what would have been anticipated in all sound speculation.   That country, "so fertile of great men, in the sixteenth and seventeenth centuries," says Hallam,* "might better spare, perhaps, from her annals, any class and description of them than her lawyers."   This is an indisputable truth, and the paradox we have noticed, strange as it should appear, would not be stranger than many others, by which history teaches how hazardous and unsatisfactory all speculative reasoning in politics must forever be.   We are aware that other wise men have reprobated and witty men ridiculed (as it was at once natural and easy to do) this feature of French judicature.   Voltaire, in his history of the Parliament of Paris†—after stating that it was the Chancellor du Prat, in the reign of Francis I., who, in order to raise money to resist the Swiss, excited against France by Leo X., offered for sale at public auction twenty offices of Counsellors (Judges)—goes on to show the evil consequences of the innovation.   He cites the instance of Genti, a treacherous clerk of Samblançay, Superintendent of Finances, who, to escape punishment for a piece of villainy in procuring the condemnation of his master, bought the office of Counsellor and afterwards became a President—but, persisting in his iniquities, was, at last, degraded and condemned to the gallows by the parliament itself. And, speaking of the *paulette*—a tax upon the income of judicial offices invented by one Paulet—he declares it to be perhaps the only stain upon the administration of Sully.‡   We have still higher authority than Voltaire's.   It is D'Aguesseau's.   In his "General Views as to a Reform in the Law," he pronounces the sale of offices "the source of almost all the disorders that creep into the administraiton of justice."§   Yet a candid inquiry into its history will result in the conviction (to borrow once more the language of Mr. Hallam) that "the name of the Parliament of Paris must ever be respectable.   It exhibited, on various occasions, virtues from which human esteem is as inseparable as

---

* Mid. Ages, v. i. 163.   † p. 70.

‡ Ibid 215.   "All those who had obtained judicial offices paid, every year, the 60th part of their official income, in consideration of which their places were secured to their heirs, who could keep them or sell them to others, as they might assign a leasehold tenement."

This tax, he adds, was frequently altered afterwards—yet the disgrace of venality—la honte d'acheter le droit de vendre la justice—continued to his day.

§ Œuvres, tom. xiii. p. 224.   See also the preface to the Dialogue des Avocats, written by Claude Jolly, grandson of Loisel, the author.

the shadow from the substance; a severe adherence to principle, an unaccommodating sincerity, individual disinterestedness,
and consistency." Although merely a judicial body, it exercised a sort of legislative power by refusing to register the
edicts of the monarch. It was at one time the only organ, and
at all times a most effective auxiliary, of public opinion. It
resisted even Louis XI., when he would have sacrificed the liberties of the Gallican Church by repealing the Pragmatic Sanction of his father—it resisted the abominations of the Regency,
when Law defrauded and ruined France, as well as the ridiculous pretensions of Cardinal Fleuri with the Bull Unigenitus—
and, at a period of far deeper and mightier agitation, it gave
the first decisive impulse to the Revolution of '89, by demand-
ing a call of the States-General. We have seen, in an extract
just made from the work of Mr. Butler, that the close of the fifteenth (quære *sixteenth*) century is described by French writers
as the golden age of the magistracy. D'Aguesseau, in his Mercuriales, is perpetually dwelling upon the degeneracy of the
bench in his times; and Voltaire, in a work already referred to,*
represents the Parliament of Paris, in the reign of Louis XV., as
a set of young men, who found consolation in their disgrace by
condemning a cat to death in imitation of the sentence passed
upon a dog in Racine's Plaideurs. Yet we have the unimpeachable testimony of Mr. Butler himself—from personal intercourse
and knowledge—in favour of the magistracy of France, such as
it was at the close of the last century.

"With the magistracy of France in the last century, and their general
habits, the writer of these pages was well acquainted. All were eminently
decent, and a large proportion of them was edifying. Most were literary,
or lovers of the arts. They collected men of learning or science round
them. There were societies, amusements, and other scenes of gaiety,
which a respectable portion of the other classes thought open to them, but
from which the magistrates of France and their families thought their character excluded them. All the magistrates were loyal, but sincerely attached to the ancient constitution of their country. They were very
attentive to the duties of their profession: they lived in their families;
their relaxations were always suited to their character. Such were the
Lamoignons, the D'Aguesseau's, the Pothiers, the Montesquieus, the Mal-
lesherbes, the des Brossesses, the Seguiers, the Joly-de-Fleurys. It may
be truly said that the world has not produced a more learned, enlightened,
or honourable order of men than the French Magistracy." pp. 27, 28.

Montesquieu—many of our readers will doubtless be surprised
to hear it—is an advocate for this sale of judicial offices. His
observations are extremely judicious, and as they have a strong
bearing upon the subject before us, we scruple not to make use
of them. "The sale of offices," says he,† "cannot exist in despotic States; as it is essential to despotism, that every officer

* Hist. du Parlem. 286.   † Esprit des Lois. lib. v. c. 19.

should be liable to be, at any time, appointed or displaced at the mere will of the prince. It is proper in monarchies, since it makes the study of the law a kind of qualification, which otherwise the party would not be at the pains of acquiring, to enable him to hold a family dignity. It gives an early direction to duty, and tends to confer permanence on an order of great public use in the State. It is a just observation of Suidas that, by the sale of offices, the Emperor Anastasius converted the empire into an aristocracy; Plato could not endure it. He declares it to be the same thing as if persons on ship-board should chose a pilot for money. But Plato is *speaking of a republic of which the basis is virtue: we are speaking of a monarchy.* There, if the sale of offices were not allowed by law, the greediness and avarice of the courtiers would, in spite of the law, make them saleable. As the sales of them are now regulated by our laws, the chance of having them properly filled is greater than if the nomination to them depended upon the mere will of the courtiers. Finally, such a way of advancing one's self by wealth both inspires and, sustains industry; and, in a monarchy, every thing that excites noble families to industry ought to be encouraged." We are inclined, after all, to subscribe to the justness of these remarks, as applied to the condition of the French people under the old régime. Montesquieu admits that such a system would not suit with the republican form of government— no more than jury-trial (which is not without its defects and anomalies) would suit with the condition of a servile or unenlightened nation. The truth is that all abstract rules are wholly unsafe in such things, and an institution, excellent in one country, as being in harmony with the national character, might be absolutely intolerable in another. If *honour* was ever the principle of monarchical government, it was surely in France, and a seat in the Parliament was sought from precisely the same motives as a commission in the army, as a place of dignity and distinction. Add to all this the important fact that it was a place attended with scarcely any other advantages but dignity and distinction. Salary, perquisites and *épices* (compliments made them by the parties) included, the official incomes of the judges did not equal the interest of the price paid for their offices, so that they not only administered justice gratuitously, but even, in some degree, at their own expense.

The Parliament of Paris, thus constituted, bore, we should think, some resemblance to the *Selecti Judices* of Rome. Such a court, without admitting of the animated popular eloquence addressed to juries in England and America, was evidently a less severe and pedantic body, than a bench of judges administering the common law according to our ideas. There was more room for topics of persuasion—for the copiousness of philosophical discourse and the beauties of finished composition—in short, for the arts and embellishments of rhetoric, but a rhetoric sobered and chastened by the gravity of the subjects and occasions, and restrained by the rules of a well ascertained science. An English reader of D'Aguesseau should bear this in mind. His style, which is the perfection of language, considered in reference to time, place and auditory, might otherwise appear somewhat florid and ostentatious.

Another observation, growing out of the composition of the Parliament, has a bearing upon the duties of the Avocat and Procureur Général—in the regular discharge of which, a large proportion of D'Aguesseau's works was composed. These great law-officers, besides representing the King in government-causes, as the Attorney and Solicitor General do in England, stood towards the Parliament in the relation of advisers and instructors. This was more especially the case with the Avocat-Général. It was his business to *sum up* the arguments on both sides of a question, and, after putting them in the most favourable lights for the respective parties, and weighing them with a scrupulous criticism, to recommend to the adoption of the Court, the conclusion which seemed most agreeable to the law and the evidence. His function was, therefore, strictly judicial. His responsibility was even greater than that of the judges whom he advised. He stood alone—he was selected for his learning and ability, not advanced by accident for money—he was required to give not merely an opinion, but reasons for it, and those reasons had to be stated and enforced in a public discussion. Such an officer was not unfrequently wanted in a body constituted like the Parliament of Paris, in which, as we have seen, many inexperienced, however well educated, young men had places by inheritance or purchase. The discourses called Mercuriales—of which eighteen delivered by D'Aguesseau are published in M. Pardessus' edition of his works—are a further and a still more remarkable illustration of this connection between the King's law-officers and the tribunals of justice. These discourses were delivered either by the Procureur Général or one of his substitutes, the Avocats-Généraux, at the opening of the *terms*. The institution seems to have been an ancient and solemn one. It appears to have owed its origin to an ordonnance of Charles VIII., in the year 1493.* The object of it was the establishment of a regular censorship, to prevent or reform the abuses that might, otherwise, have crept into the courts. The discourses delivered on these occasions were neither more nor

* Œuv. de D'Aguesseau, t. 9, p. 441. Mémoire sur l'affaire de M. le Président de * * * * * *. His words are, "Mais à l'égard de la première [ordonnance], elle n'établit que la règle de tenir les Mercuriales tous les mois dans les parlemens, pour la réformation des mœurs et de la discipline des officiers qui les composent.

less than lectures read to the Parliaments, on various points of official character and duty, by the King's Counsel.* The subjects of which D'Aguesseau treats in his are the independence of the advocate—the love of the profession—the dignity of the. magistrate, his manners, his justice, his firmness, his authority, &c.—discipline, patriotism, prejudice, talent and knowledge, greatness of soul, the employment of time. We shall submit to our readers, hereafter, some specimens of these beautiful compositions, in which the author, in his often repeated picture of a perfect magistrate, has only painted his own likeness.

The effects produced upon the mind of D'Aguesseau, by the exescise, during ten years, and those the first ten years of manhood, of such a function as we have just described, could not fail to be very sensible. The habits of thought and the style of speaking, which it was apt to superinduce, may be easily inferred from the following remarks of M. Pardessus. We shall presently advert to another account of the same matter by M. de St. Simon.

"Les conclusions du ministère public diffèrent essentiellement des plaidoyers que les avocats prononcent dans l'intérêt de leurs clients.

"Le plaidoyer admet tout ce qui peut émouvoir, intéresser en faveur d'une partie ; il n'interdit pas même, pourvu qu'on se renferme dans de justes bornes, l'emploi de traits vigoureux, pour dévoiler et dénoncer à l'indignation des magistrats la mauvaise foi, l'injustice d'un adversaire ; ou d'une ironie qui livre au ridicule des prétensions exaggerées ou absurdes.

"Impassible et sévère comme la loi dont il est l'organe, grave comme la puissance qu'il représente, l'Avocat Général doit fixer les véritables circonstances de la cause, si souvent dénaturées et tronquées dans les débats des parties ; mettre sous les yeux des juges l'analyse des moyens respectifs réduits à ce qui appartient à la contestation ; critiquer ou réfuter les principes faux ou hazardés: rechercher et établir les véritables, proposer enfin les motifs qui lui paraissent les plus propres à déterminer le jugement.

"L'ordre et la clarté, sous le premier de ces rapports ; l'exactitude et l'impartialité sous le second ; la science du droit et la force du raisonnement sous le troisième, sont le mérite propre de ses conclusions.

"La nature des causes dans lesquels il doit être entendu, le titre de sa mission, annonce qu'ils a moins à s'occuper des intérêts particuliers, que des intérêts de la société dont le Roi qu'il représente est le conservateur nécessaire. Il ne doit pas être moins énergique et moins fidèle au but de son institution dans les procès des plus obscurs citoyens ou dans ceux qui semblent offrir le moins d'intéret pécunaire, que dans ces causes où la fortune et le rang des parties la réputation des avocats, la singularité et quelquefois, hélas, le scandale des faits, attirent la foule aux audiences qu'on nomme *solennelles.*

*   *   *   *   *   *   *   *

"Aussi, les vrais jurisconsultes recherchent-ils tonjours avec empressement les recueils qui contiennent les conclusions des officiers chargés du ministère public.

* Œuv. de D'Aguesseau, t. 1, p. 59. Deuxième Mercuriale. La censure publique.

"S'il eût été possible de rassembler toutes celles de D'Aguesseau cette collection serait d'un prix inestimable.   *   *   *   *
"L'extrème facilité que lui donnait l'habitude des affaires, la science du droit, qui lui faisait trouver sur-le-champ, avec la solution convenable, les motifs qui devaient la justifier, lui procurèrent l'avantage de parler souvent sans avoir rédigé ses conclusions par écrit; et ce qui fut pour lui un titre de gloire est pour nous un nouveau sujet de regrets." &c. *Disc. Prelim.* xxv.

The office of Procureur-Général, (of whom the Avocat-Général was properly speaking only a deputy) though higher in point of dignity, was not so favorable to the display of D'Aguesseau's great talents as a public speaker. But, if in that capacity he did not address the Parliament so frequently *vivâ voce*, his connection with it was not less intimate or influential. If we may judge from what we read of that tribunal in the "Dialogue of the Advocates," the Procureur-Général, held it almost in a state of pupilage.* The written opinions or arguments, called *requêtes*, presented to the court by D'Aguesseau while he filled that office, give one an exalted idea of his knowledge of that part of the law which came more especially within the sphere of his duties. All causes relating to the patrimony of the crown were the particular province of the Procureur-Général. This made it necessary that he should be profoundly versed in the feudal jurisprudence of France, and that jurisprudence, owing to the multiplicity and importance of fiefs, was more intricate and complicated there, than in any other European kingdom. Ably to represent the King, as lord paramount of all these perplexed tenures, his law-officer was required to be a perfect master of the history and antiquities of the realm—including the thousand little conditions and qualifications, local or otherwise, which had been imposed upon estates in their various deviations from the original simplicity of the feud. Of the other duties of the Procureur-Général, it will be sufficient, for the present, to notice one. He was expected to furnish the King's ministers with *Mémoirs* on projected changes in the law. In the exercise of this high function, the wisdom of the legislator, no less than the science of the jurist, was called for—and the general views of D'Aguesseau, in regard to legal reform, were worthy of his genius and philosophy.

Whoever considers the state of the law in France, at that time, will readily conceive "that nothing was more rare, than

* Speaking of the conduct of M. Noël Brulart, in the office of Procureur-Général, (conference 3e) Pasequier, says, "Il l'exerça avec une telle integrité prud' hommie et authorité, et a rendu sa mémoire si recommandable, qu'elle a servi et servira d'exemple et de patron à tous ses successeurs Procureurs Generaux : particuliérement en ceque venant de bon matin au Palais, il allait par les chambres voir si chacun faisait son devoir; et s'il trouvoit aucuns de Messieurs hors d'icelles causans ou allans de chambre en chambre, ils les regardoient de tel œil, que sa seule countenance et gravité les faisoit retirer et contenir en leur devoir."

to find a man of whom it might be said, that he was master of the whole body of French jurisprudence."* France was, in truth, so far as jurisdiction went, a mere confederacy of independent states. Many of the provinces, when they submitted to the crown, had expressly stipulated for the maintenance of their established laws and privileges. None of the courts was, properly speaking, supreme—that is to say, exercised an absolute control over the rest either by way of appeal, prohibition or otherwise. Although the Parliament of Paris was the most distinguished among them—although it had been for a long time the only royal tribunal, and there were still some cases in which its authority extended throughout the whole kingdom—yet its decrees (arrêts) could not be executed, within the jurisdiction of the other Parliaments, without a special edict or writ of *"pareatis"* from the monarch.† These courts had gradually acquired some share of legislative power by the part they were allowed to act in the formal promulgation of the laws. The King's mouth, like Jack Cade's, was the sovereign legislature, yet it was thought necessary (as it certainly was right and expedient) to have his edicts solemnly registered by the Parliaments. When these bodies thought a new law improper, they naturally expressed their dissatisfaction—at first they would register and then remonstrate—at length they remonstrated before they would register—and the whole power of the crown was sometimes necessary to subdue their contumacy. One obvious consequence of this singular institution was to aggravate the Babylonish confusion of laws under which France labored. The great distinction between the provinces, north and south of the Loire, *into pays de droit écrit*, and *pays de droit coutumier*, turning upon the prevalence of the Roman law on the one side, and the Teutonic customs on the other, and corresponding in some measure to the old national diversity between the *langue d'oc* and the *langue d'oil*—was lost in endless subordinate differences. "The ordinances," says M. Camus, "as well as the arrêts are scattered over a multitude of volumes; each province has its particular custom, sometimes diametrically opposite to that of a neighbouring province, and the same variety exists to a certain degree in the ordinances. Such or such an edict, registered at Paris, may not have been so at Toulouse or Rouen, and consequently will not be law there ; or, else, it may have been registered but with modifications which restrain its provi-

* D'Aguesseau, Œuv. tom. xiii. p. 200. Mémoire fait en 1715, sur la réformation de la justice.

† D'Aguesseau, tom. ix. p. 295. In the same Mémoir, (the title of which is Sur les contrastes passés en pays étrangers,) the author says, "Il serait bien plus avantageux aux étrangers et au royaume même, de décider la question par une déclaration genérale que de la juger par un arrêt particulier, qui n'aurait d'autorité tout au plus que dans le ressort du Parlement." p. 300.

sions."* The result of all this conflict of legislation and judicature may be strongly summed up in the words of D'Aguesseau himself : "that amid so great a variety of customs [and courts] the merits of the question were virtually disposed of, by the judgment which determined the competence of the tribunal."†

While he was yet Procureur-Général, D'Aguesseau wrote, for the benefit of his eldest son, a plan of studies proper to form the mind of the future magistrate. These instructions embrace the whole circle of learning sacred and profane, and contrast, in every point of view excèpt their elegance, not more strikingly than honourably, with the frivolous letters of Chesterfield, written for a similar purpose, some years after. That part of them, which more immediately refers to the accomplishments and discipline necessary to prepare the young aspirant for the place of King's advocate, reveals the immense extent of knowledge put in requisition by its functions, and brought to the exercise of them by the experienced writer himself. Besides the whole body of the French law—ordinances, arrêts, customs general and local, practice and procedure—which we have already seen was a labyrinth of darkness, difficulty and confusion—it was indispensable that the officer in question should be thoroughly versed in the civil and canon law. In all these systems of jurisprudence, again, he was to be master of the public no less than of the private law. Thus, the relation in which the Gallican church, with its vaunted liberties, stood to the Pontifical throne, was a most interesting subject and ever fruitful of learned and profound discussion. So it was, as we have seen, with the public law of the kingdom itself—embracing an infinite variety of feudal tenures and services, all mediately or immediately connecting those who held or owed them, with the King, as sovereign or lord paramount. That D'Aguesseau was as familiarly conversant with every branch of this multifarious learning, as any single man—especially if he mingle in the affairs, and above all, the political affairs of the world—can be expected to make himself, no one will doubt who will be at the pains of reading his voluminous works. Of these works the greater part are merely occasional ; his *plaidoyers* and official correspondence alone filling many volumes. Yet even these may challenge a comparison, as to every sort of doctrine, with the most elaborate productions of speculative jurists. His unfinished treatise (unfinished in every sense of the word) on errors of law is an admirable piece of legal criticism. It is written (most of it) in Latin. The main object of it is to refute an opinion of Cujas, founded upon the texts, by a comparison of other texts and reasonings on the analogies. But he goes into the philosophy of the matter, and shews that the doctrine of that

*Lettres sur l'étude du Droit Français. †Préambule de l'ordonnance de 1731.

first of civilians comes into conflict with several positions, every one of which is an admitted and fundamental principle.

In reading the works of D'Aguesseau we find much that is obsolete. All the customary law of France—described by him as consisting in usage and precedent, rather than in immutable principles and conclusions deduced immediately from the rules of natural justice—has been obliterated forever by the Five Codes. It is no longer expected of any one but an antiquary, that he should read many volumes—rich with the spoils of time—which were once useful to advocates and judges—such as the Capitularies, the Establishment of St. Louis, the Assizes of Jerusalem, the anciennes Coutumes de Beauvoisis by Philip de Beaumanoir, the Somme Rurale of Bouteiller, the Decisions of Jean Desmarés, and even Bracton and Littleton, the latter edited by M. Houard, as a repository of the old Norman law. The chasm is a terrible one, and it is appalling to reflect how much of the knowledge of a lawyer, whose studies have been principally confined to matters of positive legislation and local custom, may be swept away by a single repealing cause. But there is enough both of natural equity and immutable truth in the sixteen volumes before us, to make them an invaluable accession to the library of every student aspiring to the reputation of an accomplished jurist. We are firmly persuaded that jurisprudence is destined to attain, in this country, to a much higher degree of perfection, both in theory and practice, than is compatible with the situation of things and the character of the profession in England; but, long before the dawn of philosophic light, which we believe to be opening upon us, shall have brightened into perfect day, the name of D'Aguesseau, with the kindred names of Domat and Pothier—his contemporaries, his friends and even his *protégés*—will be as familiar to us as those of Mansfield and Hale.

In 1717, upon the death of the Chancellor Voisin, the Duke of Orleans, then regent, immediately presented the seals to D'Aguesseau, at that time in his forty-ninth year. In this connection we will venture to quote a well known passage from Thomas' *Eloge*—a specimen of eloquence not much to our taste, tho' not a great deal worse than the panegyrics of Pliny and Procopius, and commended to our approbation by the academic crown with which it was honored.

"Porté tout-à-coup dans une place qu'il n'attendait pas, ne désirait pas, mais dont il sent toute la grandeur, le nouveau Chancelier contemple, avec un effroi mêlé de respect, le nombre et l'étendue de ses devoirs. En effet, qu' est-ce qu 'un Chancelier? C'est un homme qui est dépositaire de la partie la plus importante et la plus-sacrée de l'autorité du prince, qui doit veiller sur tout l'empire de la justice, entretenir la vigueur des loix qui tendent toujours à s'affaiblir, ranimer les lois utiles, que les temps ou les passions des hommes ont anéanties, en créer de nouvelles, lorsque la corruption augmentée, ou de nouveaux besoins découverts exigent de nouveaux remèdes; les faire exécuter, ce qui est plus difficile encore que de les créer; observer d'un œil attentif les maux qui, dans l'ordre politique, se mêlent toujours au bien; corriger ceux qui peuvent l'être; souffrir ceux qui tiennent à la constitution de l'état, mais en les souffrant, les resserrer dans les bornes de la nécessité; connaître et maintenir les droits de tous les tribunaux; distribuer toutes les charges à des citoyens dignes de servir l'état; juger ceux qui jugent les hommes; savoir ce qu'il faut pardonner et punir dans les magistrats dont la nature est d'être faibles, et le devoir de ne pas l'être; présider à tous les conseils où se discute le sort des peuples balancer la clémence du prince et l'interêt de la justice; êtres auprès du souverain le protecteur et non le calomniateur de la nation. Tel est le fardeau immense que porte D'Aguesseau."

In short—to condense all this rhetoric into two expressive old French phrases—as Chancellor of France, D'Aguesseau was now become "the mouth of the Prince," and "the first man in the kingdom."

His conduct in this exalted and responsible station was every way worthy of the reputation which he had acquired in that of Procureur-Général, and that is saying every thing.* This is, so far as we know, the unanimous testimony of the French writers, with the exception of St. Simon. But (to borrow the language of M. Pardessus), after pronouncing him the most eloquent, the most learned, the most upright, and the wisest magistrate of the age, we should have to add to our encomium still rarer traits, if we would do justice to D'Aguesseau. With the science of the lawyer he combined the enlarged views, "the prophetic eye" of the legislator, and with all the qualities that adorn the ermine, he possessed the spirit of self-sacrifice, which exalts them into heroic virtue. He inculcated the necessity, and, so far as it was practicable at that time, set the example of reform in the law, with the double purpose of making it more perfect in itself and uniform throughout France. A great number of edicts, worthy of the legislation which produced the Ordonnance de la Marine were issued from the throne at his instance, correcting abuses both in principle and practice. That his reforms were not complete and radical—that he did not project such a code as has been since completed, under the auspices of Bonaparte—must be ascribed to the situation of France. Such a scheme, however desirable and even necessary, amidst the conflict of law and jurisdiction already described, would have been quite chimerical at any period anterior to the sitting of the Constituent Assembly.

But the point of view in which D'Aguesseau appears to the greatest advantage—the occasion on which he displayed the glory and perfection of the judicial character—was in resisting the Regent and his sybaritical and unprincipled court, in

* With regard to D'Aguesseau's conduct as Procureur-Général, especially in the administration of the criminal law and the relief of the poor, see the 7th note to Thomas' Eloge.

measures conceived in the very wantonness and, if we may so
express it, drunkenness of despotic power, and fraught with infamy and ruin. The story of Law and the Mississippi scheme
is too well known to be repeated here. D'Aguesseau had the
firmness to do all that he could to open the eyes of the prince
and the people to the terrible consequences—the wide spread
bankruptcy, the sudden revolutions in fortune, the fraud, the
immorality, the desolation and despair—which would be inevitably produced by that disastrous project. He was ordered into exile. He obeyed without a murmur, but, in the repose of his
rural solitude and the leisure which banishment afforded him, he
composed, for the instruction of his fellow citizens, two papers
upon the engrossing subject of the day, worthy, even now, of the
profound attention of the philosopher, statesman, and jurist.
The compositions we allude to are the *Considérations sur les
Monnoies*, and the *Mémoire sur le commerce des actions de la
compagnie des Indes.* The latter strikes us as the more masterly performance of the two, though both are admirable and
contain, as M. Pardessus justly remarks, principles of political
economy truly extraordinary in an age when the very name of
that science was unknown in France. We do not think that
this discussion of the morality of stock-jobbing will suffer by a
comparison with any work involving the principles of moral
obligation or natural law, that any age has produced. Nor are
the views of the policy of society, in regard to currency, credit,
&c., less just and profound. It is inconceivable to us how Voltaire, with these evidences of statesman-like wisdom and ability
before his eyes, could speak of D'Aguesseau as "un homme
élevé dans les formes du palais, très instruit dans la jurisprudence, mais moins versé dans la connoissance de l'interieur, difficile et incertain dans les affaires.*" The *mémoire sur le commerce des actions* is rather better than any political product of
"the manufacture of Ferney."

Amidst the consternation occasioned by the failure of the Mississippi scheme, D'Argenson, who had succeeded to the place of
D'Aguesseau with the title of Vice-Chancellor, was compelled
to retire in disgrace, and the latter, in obedience to the universal
voice of the public, was recalled and restored to power. Voltaire censures him for consenting to resume the seals while Law
was still at the head of the Finances. His language is as
follows :—

"Lass (Law) lui porta la lettre de son rappel, et D'Aguesseau l'accepta
d'une main dont il ne devait rien recevoir. Il était indigne de lui et de sa
place de rentrer dans le conseil quand Lass gouvernait toujours les finances. Il parut sacrifier encore plus sa gloire en se prêtant à de nouveaux
arrangemens chimériques que le Parlement refusa, et en souffrant patiem-

* Hist. du Parlement, p. 276.

ment l'exil du Parlement, qui fut envoyé à Pontoise. Jamais tout le Parlement n'avait été exilé depuis son établissement."*

It is not unimportant to remark, as to the banishment of the Parliament, that, according to the testimony of Voltaire himself, their opposition to the Bull *Unigenitus* had at least as much to do with that catastrophe, as their hostility to Law's system. The registry of the obnoxious Bull was a favorite project of the Secretary of State, Dubois, who was countenanced by the Regent himself. D'Aguesseau, it seems, made no objection to it, and this, too, Voltaire, as was very natural from his vehement hatred to every thing connected with the Church of Rome, denounces, in the Chancellor, as an abandonment of all his principles, and an act of disgraceful subserviency to Dubois. We are no advocates of the Bull *Unigenitus*, but, having read D'Aguesseau's *Réquisitoire*, while he was yet Avocat-Général,† for the registering of another Bull—that which condemned Fenelon's book of the "Maxims of the Saints"—we can see nothing inconsistent with the analogy of his conduct and character, still less any thing evincing a want of principle, and, least of all, a base subserviency to the insolent upstart at the head of the department of State, in his barely acquiescing in the sentence passed upon the Parliament, whose course he probably disapproved, and whose fate he certainly could not have averted. The charge of obsequiousness or timidity in regard to Dubois appears to us totally unfounded. We want no other testimony to this point than that of Voltaire himself. He mentions that, in 1722, when the Duke of Orleans allowed Dubois, then Cardinal and Prime Minister, to take precedence of the Princes of the blood, the Chancellor resolutely resisted the indignity, and, rather than abandon his pretensions, consented to be disgraced a second time, and to retire to his solitude at Fresne. The words of the historian are as follows:—

"Le jour que Dubois vint prendre séance, le Duc de Noailles, les maréchaux de Villeroi et de Villars, sortirent, le Chancelier D'Aguesseau s'absenta. Le Chancelier et le duc de Noailles tinrent ferme. D'Aguesseau soutint mieux les prérogatives de sa place contre Dubois qu'il n'en avait maintenu la dignité lorsqu'il revint à Paris à la suite de l'Ecossais Lass. Le resultat fut qu'on l'envoya une seconde fois à sa terre de Fresne."

And there, Voltaire adds, he was, for several years, utterly forgotten by the public. That a fallen minister should be forgotten by the public is no very marvellous phenomenon at any time, but it should not be forgotten by our readers that the public of that day in France was not exactly the same that it is now. It is not by any means so remarkable that a Court and a City dissolved in pleasures and governed by *calembours* and

* Hist. du Parl. p. 286.　　† Œuv. tom. 1e. p. 258. This was in 1699.

vaudevilles, should nôt always think of a venerable lawyer
whose mode of life was a silent reproof upon their own, as
that they were sure to think of him in times of emergency and
trouble.   As for the Chancellor's returning to Paris *à la suite
de l'écossais Lass,* it may be good pleasantry, but we can see
nothing very humiliating in the situation, and still less any
thing very censurable in his conduct.   Such a return looked
much more like a triumph than a disgrace.   It was sending
Varro to beg pardon of Fabius.   Law, who had been the occasion, and probably the author of D'Aguesseau's *disgrace,* (the
French for a *fall from power,*) was despatched, in the name of
the Regent, the Ministry, the Court, the whole people, to make
the *amende honorable,* and to beseech him, or command him
(if the phrase be preferred) to return to his post and save a sinking State.   What was it the part of a virtuous man to do—of
a true patriot, not listening to the whispers of a morbid self-love,
but consulting his sense of duty ?   Had he any option of all ?
Hale consented to administer the law under Cromwell, and Milton wrote a sonnet in his praise ; and citing these examples, we
think we may safely affirm that we vouch the two men of all
time in whom the dignity of human nature suffered least from
the perils and temptations of misfortune.   The truth is, that by
far the most difficult problem that can be proposed to a good
man is, how far he is bound to submit to those who abuse or
have usurped the government, in order to serve his country—or
to abandon and even to embarrass the service of the country, in
order to defeat and to overthrow her domestic tyrants.   It is a
question not to be reduced to any general rules; and which it is
far more desirable to discuss in the conduct of others, than to
have to decide for ourselves in our own.

Let us hear what the lively writer in question says of the
Chancellor.

"D'Aguesseau, de taille médiocre, était gros avec un visage fort plein et

agréable jusqu' à ses dernières disgraces, et toujours avec une physiono-
mie sage et spirituelle, ayant un œil plus petit que l'autre.

"Il n'a jamais eu voix délibérative avant d'être Chancelier: on se piquait
au Parlement de ne pas suivre ses conclusions par une jalousie de l'éclat
de sa réputation dont il n'a joui qu' à sa mort, cette jalousie l'ayant emporté
sur l'estime intérieure qu'on était obligé d'avoir pour lui: il avait beaucoup d'esprit, d'application, de pénétration, de savoir en tous genres, de
gravité de magistrature, d'équité, de piété, d'innocence de mœurs qui firent
le fond de son caractère; on peut dire même que c'était un bel esprit et un
homme incorruptible; avec cela il fut doux, bon, humain, d'un accès facile
et agréable, et dans le particulier, avec de la gaieté et de la plaisanterie
salée, mais sans blesser personne; extrêmement sobre, poli, sans orgeuil et
noble sans la moindre avarice, naturellement paresseux, dont il lui était
resté de la lenteur.

"Qui ne croirait qu'un magistrat, orné de tant de vertus et de talens,
dont la mémoire,* la vaste lecture, l'éloquence à parler et à écrire, la jus-
tesse jusque dans les moindres expressions des conversations les plus communes, avec des grâces, de la facilité, n'eût été le plus grand Chancelier
qu'on eût vu depuis plusieurs siècles ?"†

Every body would think so of course. We do not remember
to have read a more flattering panegyric compressed within the
same number of lines. The laboured and pompous eulogy of
Thomas has not done half so much to exalt the character of a
man whom it was his ambition to praise, as this rapid and careless sketch from the hand of a professed and rather censorious
critic. We must submit the other side of the picture to our
readers, but we think they will agree with us that the qualifications are neither weighty nor well founded enough, seriously to
diminish the lustre of the whole character.

"Il est vrai qu'il aurait été un premier président sublime; et il ne l'est
pas moins que devenu chancelier, il fit regretter jusques aux d'Aligre et
Boucherat; ce paradoxe est difficile à comprendre: il se voit pourtant à
l'œil depuis trente ans qu'il est chancelier, et avec tant d'évidence que je
pourrais m'en tenir là; un fait si étrange mérite d'être développé."

It certainly does. Let us hear and examine the account which
the author gives of "so strange a fact." The first charge we
have already adverted to—it is that the Chancellor, contrary to
the duty of his station, always sided with the Parliament against
the crown.

* His memory was extraordinary. One of the notes (22) to Thomas' Eloge is
as follows: "La lecture des autres poetes fut, selon son expression, *une passion
de sa jeunesse.* Un jour il lisait un poèt grec avec M. Boivin, si connu par sa
vaste érudition: *Hâtons nous,* dit-il, *si nous allions mourir avant d'avoir achevé!*
Il avait une mémoire prodigieuse; il lui suffisait, pour retenir, d'avoir lu, une
seule fois avec application. Il n'avait point appris autrement les poètes grecs,
dont il récitait souvent des vers et des morceaux entiers. A l'âge de quatre
vingt-un ans, un homme de lettres, ayant cité peu exactement devant lui une
épigramme de Martial, il lui en récita les propres termes, en avouant qu'il n'avait
point vu cet auteur depuis l'âge de douze ans. Il répétait quelquefois ce qu'il
avait seulement entendu lire. Boileau lui ayant un jour récité une de ces pièces
qu'il venait de composer, M. D'Aguesseau lui dit tranquillement qu'il la connaissait et sur le champ la lui répéta toute entière."

† Œuvres de St. Simon, tom. 9e. p. 3.

"La longue et unique nourriture qu'il avait prise dans le sein du parlement l'avait pétri de ses maximes et prétensions, jusqu' à le regarder avec plus d'amour, de respect et de considération que les Anglais n'en ont pour leur parlement ; et je ne dirai pas trop, quand j'avancerai qu'il ne regardait pas autrement tout-ce-qui émanait de cette compagnie, qu'un fidèle, bien instruit de sa religion, regarde les décisions des conciles œcuméniques.

"De cette sorte de culte naissait *trois extrêmes défauts* qui se montraient trés-fréquemment. *Le premier qu'il était toujours pour le parlement,* quoi qu'il pût entreprendre contre l'autorité royale, ou d'ailleurs audelà de la sienne ; tandis que son office, qui le rendait le supérieure et le modérateur des parlemens et de la bouche du Roi à leur égard, l'obligeait à le contenir quand il passait ses bornes, surtout quand il attentait à l'autorité du Roi ; alors son équité et ses lumières lui montraient bien l'égarement du parlement ; mais de la réprimer, était plus fort que lui.

"La mollesse secondée de cette sorte de culte dont il l'honorait, était peinée et affligée de le voir en faute ; mais de laisser voir qu'il y fût tombé, c'était un crime à ses yeux dont il gémissait de voir souillés les autres et dont il ne pouvait se souiller lui-même.

"Il mettait donc tous ses talens à pallier, couvrir, excuser, donner des interprétations captieuses, à éblouir sur les fautes du parlement, à négocier avec lui d'une part et avec le Régent de l'autre ; à profiter de sa timidité, de sa facilité, de sa légéreté pour tout émousser, tout énerver en lui ; en sorte qu'au lieu d'avoir dans le magistrat un ferm soutien de l'autorité du Roi, et un vrai juge des justices, on en tirait à peine quelque bégaiment forcé, qui affaiblîssait encore le peu à quoi il avait pu à peine se résoudre, et qui donnait courage, force et hauteur au parlement ; et si quelquefois il s'est expliqué avec lui en d'autres termes, ce n'était toujours qu' après un long combat, et toujours bien plus facilement qu'il n'était convenu de faire."

So saith M. de St. Simon, Duc et Pair de France. Now it does appear to us that this first censure is almost the only compliment which could have been added to the comprehensive panegyric that precedes it. The standing reproach against the continental lawyers was a servile spirit, a repugnance, not to say hostility, to all institutions favourable to public liberty which they confounded with license and anarchy. Their maxims were those of the imperial law. In the Byzantine court, and even earlier, the image of oriental despotism had been impressed upon a system of jurisprudence, of which one of the great founders was the stern Labeo—a republican uncorrupted by the arts, unsubdued by the power of Augustus—and the will of the Prince was recognized as the only true source of legislation. In this school were educated the lawyers whom the kings of Europe employed gradually to undermine the power of the feudal barons. The privileges of these lords were denounced as usurpations upon the prerogatives of Cæsar. The whole system of tenures—which, bad as it was, contained the germs of a wild liberty—was their abomination. The Civil and Canon Law furnished them with artillery for its destruction, and it was plied unsparingly and with tremendous effect. The French lawyers of the fourteenth and fifteenth centuries frequently give their King the title of emperor and treat disobedience to him as sacrilege.*

In this important particular our common lawyers boast a glorious superiority over the civilians. The feudal lords in England had never been strong enough to do more than *check* the monarch, and it was one of their confederacies for this purpose, that resulted in the compromise or treaty, so well known and so worthy to be known, by the title of *Magna Charta.* The primitive spirit of Teutonic liberty was confirmed by this fundamental compact, and it was kept sacred, by the stubborn bigotry which wholly excluded the Civil, and very much restrained the Canon Law in that fortunate island. Through all subsequent times, the lawyers of England have been the stoutest champions of her liberties. Their defence of them has been, perhaps, somewhat deformed by the technicality of the profession,† but it has been conducted, on the other hand, with all its practical ability, its shrewd skill, its adherence to the forms of popular trial, its zeal for "common right" and the good old customs of the realm; and even its religious, and, it may be, superstitious veneration for established precedent, has contributed not a little, at once, to fortify their conquests against the throne, and to save them from the opposite and not less formidable perils of a mere revolutionary levity.

It is in the highest degree honourable to D'Aguesseau, that he should have incurred the censure of such a man as St. Simon, for such a cause as the love of liberty. It is the privilege of great men, and of them only, to be above their age, above their profession, above the powers of the world. That this eminent civilian wished to limit the prerogative—that the minister resisted the caprices of his prince—that a Chancellor of France, in the court of the Regent, dared to expose the fraudulent stock-jobbing of Law, and to rebuke the upstart insolence of Dubois—is his best title to the admiration of men. It is a proof that the grandeur of his soul was equal to his eloquence and learning, and elevates the good citizen into a hero. The most sublime of functions, beyond all comparison, is that of a judge, when the oppressed fly for refuge to the law, against "the brute and boisterous force of violent men." To look power—whether of one or of many—in the face—to despise the *vultus instantis tyranni*, and what is in some instances, a thousand times worse—the *civium ardor prava jubentium*—to declare what the law is, to execute what the law prescribes, in times of trouble, when tyrants would abuse its powers, and clothe their

---

* Mably, iv. c. 2. note 10, and Hallam, ubi. sup. 160. The same thing was observed under Frederick Barbarossa in the contests of the twelfth century.

† Witness the discussions about the word "abdicate," at the time of the Revolution.

unhallowed purposes in its venerable forms—is to achieve a greater victory than was ever won upon a field of blood, and to do the state more service than by the conquest of cities and provinces. But wo to the nation whose oracles "philippize"—whose judges take counsel of the rulers of the people—whose magistrates, would pervert, for the love or the fear of man, the unchangeable ordinances of the law! The conduct of Lord Coke in the case of the Commendams was worthy of him who drew the Petition of Right, and his answer to James that when the occasion occurred, he should do what would become a judge, deserves a place among the grandest sayings of the heroes of the earth.

The second defect with which D'Aguesseau is charged by St. Simon, was an overweening tenderness and respect for gentlemen of the robe, whose condemnation, it seems, he could never be brought to pronounce without the fullest evidence to convict them, and that, even though complaints were made against them by the first men of the land! We should think this partiality—or rather *prevention*—even if it did exist, quite a pardonable foible; but from the manner in which the accusation is preferred there is room to suspect that the whole head and front of the offending was that D'Aguesseau was not so convenient an instrument in the hands of the courtiers, as they could have wished.

"Un second *inconvénient* qu'on trouvait dans le personnel de D'Aguesseau était l'extension de ce culte particulier du parlement à tout ce qui portait robe, qui devait, selon lui, imposer le respect. Quoiqu' il fût, on ne pouvait s'en plaindre qu' avec la derniere circonspection; les plaintes n'étaient pas écoutées sans de longues preuves juridiquement ordonnées; avec cela même elles étaint rejetées avec grand dommage pour le plaignant, si grand qu'il fût, si elles n'étaient appuyées de la derniere evidence."

According to our ideas of criminal law, the language of this sentence, not only conveys no censure upon a judge, but the very definition and formulary of his duty.

The third charge, made by St. Simon, is a superstitious attachment to mere forms, and a scepticism and irresolution extremely inconvenient in affairs, which destroyed the usefulness of the Chancellor at the council-board.

"Le Chancelier fit en deux ou trois occasions la tentative d'alléguer les formes au conseil des dépêches: quoique vivant bien avec lui, le l'interrompis autant de fois et je combattis sa tentative: à chaque fois elle demeura inutile, avec un grand regret de sa part qu'il montra franchement.

"Le long usage du parquet avait gâté l'esprit à D'Aguesseau; l'état du parquet est de ramasser, examiner, peser, comparer les raisons de deux et différentes parties; car il y en a souvent plusieurs au même procès; et d'établir cette espèce de bilan avec toutes les grâces et les fleurs d'éloquence; sans que les juges sachent de quel côté l'avocat-général sera avant qu'il ait commencé à conclure.

"Quoique le procureur-général, qui ne donne ses conclusions que par écrit, ne soit pas exposé au même étalage; il est obligé au même examen, au même bilan avant de conclure et cette continuelle habitude, pendant vingt-quatre ans, dans un esprit *scrupuleux en équité et en formes*, fécond en vues, savant en droit, en arrêts, l'avait formé à une incertitude, qui lui faisait tout prolonger à l'infini.

"Il en souffrit le premier c'etait un accouchement pour lui que de se déterminer. S'il était pressé par un conseil de régence ou autre il flottait, errant sans se décider, jusqu'au moment d'opiner, étant de la meilleure foi du monde, tantôt d'une opinion, tantôt d'une autre, et il opinait à son tour comme il lui venait dans cet instant.

"Je l'ai dit du duc de Chevreuse, et le répéte du chancelier : il coupait un cheveu en quatre, aussi étaient ils fort amis. La vieille duchesse d'Estrées, Vaubrun, qui pétillait d'esprit, et son amie, fut pressée de lui parler pour quelqu'un ; elle s'en défendit par la connaissance qu'elle avait de ce terrain raboteux ; *mais, madame,* dit le client *il est votre ami intime :* cela est vrai dit-elle ; mais c'est *un ami travesti en ennemi.*"

This last trait—we must remark by the way—and indeed the whole portrait of St. Simon, shews conclusively the incorruptible virtue, the unapproachable independence and elevation of D'Aguesseau, in the discharge of his official duty.

St. Simon goes on to account for these defects of character.

"Ces défauts venaient de trop de lumières, de vues, et de trop d'habitude au parquet : d'ailleurs il était homme savant, aimait les langues savantes, la physique. les mathématiques, et la metaphysique. A huis clos il faisait chez lui des exercises sur les sciences, avec ses enfans et avec des savans obscurs, et ils y passaient un temps infini, qui désespérait ceux qui avaient affaire à lui.

"C'était pour les sciences que D'Aguesseau était né ; il eût été, il est vrai, encore excellent premier président : mais à quoi il eût été plus propre, c'est d'être à la tête de la litérature, des academies, de l'observatoire, du collège royal et de la librairie ; il eût eu affaire à des savans comme lui et non avec le monde qu'il ne connut jamais, et dont, à la politesse près, il n'avait aucun usage.

* * * * * * * *

"Voilà un long article ; mais je l'ai cru d'autant plus curieux, qu'il fait mieux connaître comment un homme, de tant de droiture, de talens est de réputation, est peu à peu parvenu á rendre sa droiture équivoque, ses talens, pires qu' inutiles, à perdre sa réputation et à devenir le jouet de la fortune."

The reader must observe that these strictures of St. Simon refer not to the judicial, but to the political conduct of D'Aguesseau. He admits, as we have seen, his admirable abilities as a lawyer and his qualifications for the presidency of a court of justice. But, as Chancellor of France, he was one of the most important members of the Council of State ; he was the official adviser of the monarch in the exercise of his legislative and executive functions ; the strength of will, the rapid sagacity, the adventurous spirit which leads on to fortune in the business of life, and especially public life, were almost as necessary to that high officer, as vast legal attainments and a comprehensive and enlightened understanding. Now, it was in these qualities—inferior in dignity and splendor, perhaps, but most effective in the

world—that D'Aguesseau is charged with having been found
wanting.   His was not the scepticism of Lord Eldon—mere speculative scepticism: he was not at a loss what to *think* in a matter
of science, but what to *do* in the affairs of life.   What St. Simon
says of him happens to have been said of two other great men,
filling the same exalted office, and resembling D'Aguesseau, unfortunately, much more in intellectual abilities than in moral
character.   Mr. Pitt characterized Lord Thurlow in the Privy-
Council, as proposing nothing, opposing every thing, and acquiescing in any thing, and Thomson sings of Bacon thus :

"———————— Him for the studious shade,
Kind nature formed deep, comprehensive, clear,
Exact and elegant, in one rich soul,
Plato, the Stagirite and Tully joined."

There is possibly some truth in what St. Simon says of
D'Aguesseau in this particular, and much reason in his way of
accounting for it.   But we are satisfied that he has greatly exaggerated the defect, however justly he may have described its
effects in the long run, upon the fortunes of the Chancellor.
The French are a vivacious people—the court was reckless and
unprincipled even as a court, and it was an age distinguished
above all others by frivolous pursuits, and the affectation of a
sparkling, superficial cleverness, which passed for philosophy and
wit.   At such a period, it is not at all to be wondered at that
D'Aguesseau—with his "rigor, and advice, with scrupulous head,
and strict age and sour severity," was voted a bore as soon as the
panic about Law's paper-money was fully passed away, and the
bonne compagnie restored to its wonted complacency and com-
posure.

The saying of Chancellor Oxenstiern, which is in every
body's mouth, is true as far as it goes, but it does not go far
enough.   He ought to have told his son that he would see, not
only with how little wisdom the world *is* governed, but with
how little it must, in the nature of things, ever continue to be
governed—another excellent reason for thinking, as we do, that
the best policy of government is to do nothing.   Figaro was not
very much in the wrong when he affirmed that it had cost him
more science and calculation to earn a bare subsistence than had
been expended in the administration of the whole Spanish empire for the last hundred years,* and his description of politics,
as a profession, though a caricature, was *then* and is still—
though not in the same degree—a likeness.†

* Nôces de Figaro, Act. v. sc. 3.
† Feindre d'ignorer ce qu'on sait, de savoir tout ce qu'on ignore; d'entendre ce
qu'on ne comprend pas, de ne point voir ce qu'on entend ; surtout de pouvoir au
delà de ses forces; avoir quelquefois pour grand secret, de cacher qu'il n'y en a
point; s'enfermer pour tailler des plumes et paraitre profond, quand on n'est

The truth of the matter really is that there must be more or less of empiricism in the policy and the views even of the most philosophic statesman. We may talk of politics as a science, if we please, and there are doubtless some great leading principles which it is possible to ascertain and profitable to study. But, after all, the springs and causes which operate in human events are so mysterious, so multifarious, so modified by the slightest circumstances, the most subtile and shadowy influences, that nothing is more unsafe than a political theory. The test of accurate knowledge in matters of inductive science, is to be able to predict the effects of any given cause. In the collision of bodies, the mechanical philosopher can demonstrate all that is to ensue from the composition and the resolution of forces—a chemist, in his synthetical experiments, would be laughed at if he produced heat instead of cold, or lighted up a fire when he promised water—and there is not a half-witted astronomer in the pay of an almanac maker, but can calculate eclipses and the other phenomena of the sun, moon and stars for the current year.* But a politician should avoid prophecy as much as possible. Hume exemplified this in the instance of Harrington, who thought he had found out the secret of all government in the arrangements of property, and, on the strength of his discovery, ventured to affirm most confidently that monarchy could never be re-established in England. The words were scarcely written before the prediction was falsified by the restoration.

The knowledge of this truth—a consciousness of the fallibility and imperfection of human reason in matters of such immense public concernment--ought to impress even upon the most unthinking a deep sense of responsibility and an unaffected self-distrust. But it does so happen that the finest minds, the minds best disciplined and practised in the investigation of truth, are most alive to this feeling--and that

"Fools rush in where angels fear to tread."

There is another line (of the same poet, we believe,) which condenses all that can be said on the subject.

"Too rash for thought, for action too refined."

This verse is a volume. It points out, with great precision, the distinction between the sublime genius which is fitted to excel in speculative philosophy, and the coarser and more common

comme on dit, que vide et creux ; jouer bien ou mal un personnage ; répandre des espions et pensionner des traitres, &c., voilà toute la politique ou je meurs. *Ibid.* Act. iii. sc. 5.

* The changes of the weather, alas! defy his calculations—and *meteorology* is like politics. There is a laughable instance of a political prediction falsified in Moore's Life of Byron. Somebody had made a book about the Swedish constitution, which met with the same fate as Harrington's in the text.

ability that leads to success in life, and fully explains how it happens that, as Voltaire expresses it, *c'est par le caractère et non par l'esprit, qu'on fait fortune.* We have no doubt that Dr. Channing is quite right in his estimate of the class of mind displayed by conquerors and usurpers. Nothing is so much overrated by an astonished world as an ability to do mischief in this way. Great revolutions in society are often brought about by very slender means. The supremacy of such an insignificant creature—such "a man-killing-idiot"—as Robespierre—the triumph of the Mountain-party over the talents, eloquence and patriotism of the Girondists*—is a memorable lesson on that subject. But the Reign of Terror was as wonderful as the conquests of Alexander or Napoleon—indeed, it would, we rather think, strike a philosophic inquirer into the history of the species, as the more signal achievement and the more unaccountable phenomenon of the two. Yet that was brought about—and maintained—and overthrown—with just as little science and calculation as Figaro ascribes to the government of Spain. Cunning and confidence—the latter especially—these comparatively vulgar, and considered, *per se*, somewhat vicious qualities, explain the success of the first steps, and the first steps lead on to all the rest.

Qui sibi fidit dux regit examen.

While just men doubt, while wise men deliberate, bold and reckless men decide and do. They lead because they go on—they are believed because they affirm—they intimidate because they boast and threaten—and they are obeyed because they dare to command. M. Camus, who had excellent experience of the means of controlling the public will, has, in a work we have already referred to, a sentence which we cannot refrain from quoting. "J'ai bien des fois entendu l'amour-propre donner d'autres leçons; dire qu'on maîtrissait les volontés, qu'un homme habile conduisait les autres où bon lui semblait : j'ai vu en effet, qu'avec de l'addresse on se formait un parti ; qu'avec des crimes on rendait ce parti dominant ; qu'avec de la terreur on étouffait les plaintes; qu'avec de l'effronterie on obtenait des acclamations; mais j'ai vu aussi qu' á la longue tout s'usait, addresse, crimes, terreur, effronterie; et qu'alors on périssait misérablement, étouffé de remords et chargé de l'indignation publique." This is the picture of usurpation every where. It succeeds more by the qualities it has not, than by those it has—by want of the foresight which reveals the hazards of an enterprise, by want of sen-

---

[*Be it remembered, however, that these gentlemen got up the storm of the 10th Août, which led of course to the doings of September. Louvel à Max. Robespierre, &c., p. 20. Recherches sur les Girondins, p. 58. Shall ye sow the wind and not reap the whirlwind ?]

sibility to the evils that may result from it, by want of scruple as to the means necessary to accomplish it. Add to these negative endowments some address in winning men, and a great deal of good luck, which passes for sagacity, and a nation is at the foot of the adventurer and a diadem upon his brow. The 9th Thermidor, and the 18th Brumaire, and every other day (or nine out of ten of them) in the calendar of revolution and ambition, are accounted for in the same way. Demosthenes inculcates upon the Athenians that fortune does much, yea, every thing in the affairs of men, and Warburton records a saying of Cromwell, which is very much in point here, viz: "that a man never riseth so high as when he doth not know whither he goeth." Cromwell was authority on that point.

D'Aguesseau himself furnishes us with a fine illustration of our views. He is writing, in the "Discourse on the Life and Death of M. D'Aguesseau," of the cautious scepticism of his father.

"J'ai connu des esprits vifs et ardens qui regardaient cette attention surprenante de mon père, comme une espèce de défaut; ils l'accusaient de pêcher par le désir même de la perfection, et de tomber par là dans une lenteur qui faisait trop attendre les fruits de ses travaux. D'autres attribuaient cette lenteur apparente à la perplexité d'un esprit indécis, qui par un excés de lumières ou de scrupule, hesitait longtemps avant que se déterminer, et rendait sa marche trop longue, pour vouloir la rendre trop assurée. Ainsi parlaient quelquefois *des ministres d'un génie plus prompt que solide, qui ne trouvaient pas que mon père les servît toujours au gré de leur impatience.*

"A la vérité, il ne se livrait pas volontiers à cette vivacité vraiment française, qui avait fait de si grands progrés en son absence; et au lieu que ces nouveaux ministres mesuraient souvent le mérite de l'ouvrage par la diligence de l'ouvrier, il était encore dans la vieille erreur, si c'en est une qu'on travaille toujours assez vîte, lorsque l'on travaille assez bien. Il aimait à passer par le doute pour arriver plus surement à la décision; mais ce n'était pas un doute oisif qui vient de l'embarras ou de l'obscurité de son esprit, c'était au contraire, un doute agissant, un doute d'examen, de recherches, de méditations, qui le conduisait à une plenitude de lumières, et à une sureté presqu' infaillible de jugement. Si elle était quelquefois différée, on y gagnait même du côté du temps. Les projets des autres paraissaient finis plutôt que les siens; mais il ne l'étaient pás, il fallait y revenir plusieurs fois, y changer, y suppléer, en retrancher, et, souvent par des difficultés qu'ils n'auraient pas prévues, recommencer l'ouvrage dans le temps qu'on le croyait fini. Ceux de mon père lui coûtaient plus de peine, mais ils n'en coûtaient qu' à lui: ils étaient si bien digérés et si solidement construits, qu'on eût dit qu'il travaillait pour l'éternité, et lorsque l'on comparait le temps qu'il fallait perdre à redresser les vues des autres, avec celui que mon père employait utilement à porter d'abord les siennes à la perfection, on trouvait que sa lenteur avait été beaucoup plus diligente que leur promptitude, et l'on était forcé de reconnaître avec lui, que le seul moyen de finir promptement un ouvrage, c'est de le bien finir."

It is evident from the style of the censure, as well as the character of the critic, that St. Simon's objection to D'Aguesseau's want of decision, proceeds in no small degree from the levity and impatience of a courtier—especially of that age and nation. Perfectly reckless about consequences himself, he made no allowance for the scruples of a conscientious, or the doubts of a wise man. At the council-board of the Regency where such persons as Law and Dubois sat,

> ———————————— in a ring
> Of mimic-courtiers and their merry king—

the chancellor was altogether out of place. That he should be perplexed by the tortuous policy of a gang of political libertines—that he should be embarrassed by a perpetual conflict between the right and the expedient, and should be often at a loss to determine how far his duty as a subject and a minister (under a despotism) called upon him for the sacrifice of his private feelings and opinions—especially in matters of no very great moment—is not at all to be wondered at. But we have the express testimony of St. Simon himself that the conduct of D'Aguesseau was innocent and his virtue incorruptible—and the course which he pursued, in relation to by far the most important political measure of the times, gives no shadow of countenance to the imputation attempted to be fixed upon him.* His resistance to the Mississippi-scheme was, as we have seen, prompt, decided, and uncompromising, and we venture to affirm that there was not to be found in all France at that time, a single individual but himself, who could have justified his hostility to that wild project, by such triumphant and unanswerable reasonings as those contained in the pieces we have already noticed. Yet we think it very possible thát St. Simon's criticism (and Voltaire says something of the same kind) may be, to a certain extent, just, as it certainly is plausible. The habit of discussing most questions *pour et contre* for nearly thirty years—the delicacy of a most scrupulous conscience—the very fertility of his mind and the forecast that presented to it all possible consequences of "coming events," together with the uncertainty inherent in the nature of political subjects—were well calculated to produce such an effect. Still it is, no doubt, an imperfection in character, and so far as he was justly chargeable with it to any serious degree, D'Aguesseau must yield the palm to the only other Chancellor of France who fills the same space in the eyes of the world, the deservedly celebrated de l'Hospital. The conduct of this great man, as a minister of the crown in the most trying and tempestuous times, was as admirable, as his scholarship, his knowledge of the law and his general abilities and wisdom. One thing, at least, is most certain, that D'Aguesseau's influence over the minds of men in his lifetime was not by any means

---

* Cf. Thomas' Eloge, Note 10, for another instance of his self-devotion.

equal to l'Hospital's in an age when the subtlety of Italian politics, the insolent ambition of the Guises, a *League* that overshadowed the throne,* and the infernal spirit of civil war and
religious persecution conspired to make France a scene of horrors only to be paralleled by her own recent history.

As to D'Aguesseau's alleged scrupulousness about mere forms,
this is another consequence, and no very unusual one, of professional habits. But here, too, a medium must be observed.
To sacrifice the substance of things to punctilios of this kind, to
be at a loss in affairs where reason and principles alone must be
our guide, and to be forever endeavoring to reduce the business
of life within the formulary of a notary's office, is the worst sort
of pedantry and totally unfits a man for public administration of
any sort. But to despise all forms, as it is plain M. de St. Simon
does, is the very spirit of despotism. Forms are, to be sure, inconvenient things to men in power—they create delay, they favor defence, they protect liberty. The administration of the law
in England errs by the excessive complication in procedure and
practice—but it is a great deal more to our taste than the summary mode of executing the will of a Cadi, with which the subjects of the Grand Seignor are blessed, [or of a *tribunal révolu-
tionaire* disposing of a *fournée* of *suspects*].

We would willingly give a more particular account of the writings of D'Aguesseau—but the length to which these remarks
have already run out, admonish us to bring them, as speedily as
possible, to a close. We cannot consent to do so, however, without briefly adverting to some of his works, not hitherto mentioned, and making a few extracts from others, by way of specimens. The *Méditations, Métaphysiques* and the *Essai d'une
Institution au Droit Public*, show how profoundly and systematically he had reflected upon the principles of universal law.
The subject of the former is the origin of our ideas of justice
and injustice. Originally intended only as an answer to the inquiries of a friend, the speculation grew under his hands, to the
size of a thick octavo volume. It is a masterly disquisition, and
gives color to St. Simon's opinion that D'Aguesseau would have
shone most in academic pursuits. The other dissertation is of
the same cast. It treats of the duties of life—the duties, for instance, which man owes to himself, body and soul included—in
a manner that strongly reminded us of the Stoical philosophers.
A question discussed in it, is—whether the rules which an enlightened reason prescribes or rather reveals, touching our duties
to God, to others and to ourselves, can be considered as *laws*, in

* One of de l'Hospital's wisest and boldest measures was the abolition of the
confréries or fraternities by which the Cardinal de Lorraine was contriving to supersede the constituted authorities of France, and subject her to the control of the
League—to wit, that of his own haughty house.

the proper sense of that word.   The author thinks that they may, and endeavors to shew that these natural laws are enforced by appropriate and adequate sanctions—by the fear of an omniscient and almighty law-giver, by the terrors of conscience, by respect for the opinions and apprehension from the hostility of mankind, by the consequences to which a course of conduct, as a series of moral or rather physical causes, necessarily leads, &c.   Another remarkable composition is his *Réflexions divverses sur Jésus Christ.*   This is an unfinished work.   It presents, however, the outlines of a learned and exact inquiry into the evidences of Christianity, and an exposition of its true spirit and character.

We proceed to submit some specimens of the style of D'Aguesseau.   We spoke just now of one of his speculations which strongly suggested to us those of the Portico.   A part of the following extract is quite Platonic, as the reader will perceive. It is taken from the fourth Mercuriale, delivered in the year 1700. The subject is the "dignity of the magistrate."

"Nous savons qu'l y a une dignité qui ne dépend point de nous parce qu'elle est en quelque manière hors de nous-mêmes.   Attachée dans le jugement du peuple à la puissance extérieure du magistrat, avec elle on la voit croître, avec elle on la voit diminuer, le hasard nous la donne, et le hasard nous l'enlève.   Comme elle ne s'accorde pas toujours au mérite, on peut l'acquérir sans mérite, on peut la perdre sans honte : et reprocher au magistrat de ne pas conserver cette espèce de dignité, ce serait souvent lui reprocher l'injustice du sort et le crime de la fortune.

"Mais il est une autre dignité qui survit à la première, qui ne connaît ni la loi des temps, ni celle des conjonctures, qui loin d'être attachée en esclave au char de la fortune, triomphe de la fortune même.   Elle est tellement propre, tellement inhérente à la personne du magistrat, que comme lui seul peut se la donner, lui seul aussi peut la perdre.   Jamais il ne la doit à son bonheur, jamais son malheur ne la lui ravit.   Plus respectable souvent dans les temps de disgrâce que dans les jours de prospérité, elle consacre la mauvaise fortune ; elle sort plus lumineuse du sein de l'obscurité dans laquelle on s'efforce de l'ensevelir : et jamais elle ne paraît plus sainte et plus vénérable, que lorsque le magistrat dépouillé de tous les ornements étrangers, renfermé en lui même, et recueillant toutes ses forces, ne brille que de sa lumière, et jouit de sa seule vertu.

"Vivre convenablement à son état, ne point sortir du caractère honorable dont la justice a revêtu la personne du magistrat, conserver les anciennes mœurs, respecter les examples de ses pères, et adorer, si l'on peut parler ainsi, jusqu'aux vestiges de leurs pas ; ne chercher à se distinguer des autres hommes, former son intérieur sur les conseils de la sagesse, et son extérieur sur les règles de la bienséance ; faire marcher devant soi la pudeur et la modestie ; respecter le jugement des hommes, et se respecter encore plus soi même ; *enfin mettre une telle convenance et une proportion si juste entre toutes les parties de sa vie, qu'elle ne soit que comme un concert de vertu et de dignité, et comme une heureuse harmonie dans laquelle on ne remarque jamais le moindre dissonnance, et dont les tons, quoique différens, tendent tous à l'unité ;* voilà la route qui dans tous les temps nous sera ouverte pour arriver à la veritable dignité.   On est joujours assez élevé quand on l'est autant que son état.   Les fonctions de la magistrature peuvent diminuer, mais la solide grandeur du vertueux magistrat ne diminuera jamais."

The manner in which the study of languages contributes to the formation of a correct taste, and a standard of universal or ideal beauty is well explained in a passage of the third "Instruction" to his son.

"Telle est la condition des ouvrages humains, parceque telle est aussi la condition des hommes, on n'y trouve aucun bien pur et sans mélange ; mais le bon esprit consiste à connaître le mauvais, pour l'éviter, et à profiter du bon pour l'imiter ; et au lieu de dire ceque Justin dit des Scythes, *plus in illis proficit vitiorum ignoratio quàm cognatio virtutis* je dirais volontiers, par rapport à ces auteurs, *non minus proficit exploratio vitiorum quàm cognitio virtutum.* C'est ce qui forme véritablement le goût : c'est ce qui épure la critique. Je trouve d'ailleurs, dans cette étude, des défauts de nation, et, pour ainsi dire, de climat, où un degré de soleil de plus change le style, aussi bien que l'accent et la déclamation ; quelque chose qui étend l'esprit, qui le met en état de comparer les meilleures productions de chaque pays, *qui le conduit ainsi et l'élève jusqu' à la connaissance de ce vrai, et de ce beau universel* qui a une proportion si juste et une si parfaite harmonie avec la nature de notre esprit, qu'il produit toujours sûrement son effet, et qu'il frappe tous les hommes, malgré la différence de leur nation, de leurs mœurs, de leurs préjugés ; en sorte que, pour se servir encore des termes de Platon, on pourrait le regarder comme l'idée primitive et originale, comme l'archétype de tout ce qui plaît dans les ouvrages d'esprit ; et, c'est à mon sens, une des plus grandes utilités que l'on puisse tirer de la connaissance de plusieurs langues." Tom. 15e. p. 98.

D'Aguesseau was educated in the school of Boileau and Racine. His taste was pure and classical ; his mind was deeply imbued with the love of the beautiful, and he aimed, in his compositions, at perfect excellence, and in his studies, at profound erudition. This is, in short, the character of an Augustan age, such as that of Louis XIV. But when genius has had its day, that of *esprit* succeeds—a sort of brilliant, lively, second-rate order of mind—and the master-pieces of eloquence and art with all solid learning and exact science, disappear, to make way for things better adapted to a frivolous and fastidious age. This was the case, at least, in France, during the eighteenth century, and D'Aguesseau admirably characterizes the new school in several passages of the Mercuriales, of which the following is one.

"Semblable à ces arbres dont la stérile beauté a chassé des jardins l'utile ornement des arbres fertiles ; cette agréable délicatesse, cette heureuse légèreté d'un génie vif et naturel, qui est devenue l'unique ornement de nôtre âge, en a banni la force et la solidité d'un génie profond et laborieux : et le bon esprit n'a point eu de plus dangereux, ni de plus mortel ennemi, que ce qu'on l'honore dans le monde du nom trompeur de bel esprit. *Des causes de la décadence de l'éloquence.* (*Discours* III.)

"Que cette conduite est éloignée de celle de ces grands hommes, dont le nom fameux semble être devenu le nom de l'éloquence même !

"Ils savaient que le meilleur esprit a besoin d'être formé par un travail persévérant et par une culture assidue ; que les grands talens deviennent aisément de grands défauts, lorsqu'ils sont livrés et abandonnés à eux-mêmes ; et que tout ce que le ciel a fait naître de plus excellent, dégénere bientôt, si l'éducation, comme une seconde mère, ne conserve l'ouvrage que la nature lui confie aussitôt qu'elle la produit."

The following beautiful panegyric on the Civil Law illustrates the subject of our opening remarks.

"Ces règles, il est vrai, ont presque tous leur fondement dans le droit naturel; mais qui pourrait remonter par le seul effort d'une sublime spéculation, jusqu' à l'origine de tant de ruisseaux qui sont à présent si éloignés de leurs source? Qui pourrait en descendre comme par degrés, et suivre pas à pas les divisions presque infinies de toutes les branches qui en derivent, pour devenir en quelque manière, l'inventeur et comme le créateur de la jurisprudence?

"De semblables efforts s'élévent au-dessus des bornes ordinaires de l'humanité. Mais heureusement d'autres hommes les ont fait pour nous: un seul livre que la science ouvre d'abord au magistrat, lui dévéloppe sans peine les premiers principes, et les dernières conséquences du droit naturel.

"Ouvrage de ce peuple que le ciel semblait avoir formé pour commander aux hommes, tout y respire encore cette hauteur de sagesse, cette profondeur de bon sens, et pour tout dire en un mot, cet esprit de législation qui a été le caractère propre et singulier des maîtres du monde. Comme si les grandes destinées de Rome n'étaient pas encore accompliées, elle règne dans toute la terre par sa raison, après avoir cessé d'y régner par son autorité. On dirait en effet que la justice n'a pleinement dévoilé ses mystères qu' aux jurisconsultes romains. Législateurs encore plus que jurisconsultes, de simples particuliers dans l'obscurité de la vie privée, on mérité par la supériorité de leurs lumières, de donner des lois à toute la posterité. Lois aussi étendues que durables, toutes les nations les interrogent encore à présent, et chacune en reçoit des réponses d'une eternelle vérité. C'est peu pour eux d'avoir interprété la loi des douze tables et l'èdit du préteur, ils sont les plus sûrs interprètes de nos lois mêmes: ils prêtent, pour ainsi dire, leur esprits à nos usages, leur raison à nos coutumes; et par les principes qu'ils nous donnent, ils nous servent de guide, lors même que nous marchons dans une route qui leur était inconnue. (XIII. Mercuriale.)"

There is a Mercuriale (the fifteenth) on the *firmness* required in the judicial function which we would, if we had space enough, transcribe at full length. But we must close this paper with the single observation, that as the defects imputed to the character of D'Aguesseau proceeded from an excess of knowledge and reflection, so his style has no fault except its faultlessness. Le défaut de vôtre discours, (said his father to him on some occasion) est d'être trop beau: il serait moins beau si vous le retouchiez encore.

[THE END.]